Fourth Workshop on Scholarly Document Processing (SDP 2024)

Bangkok, Thailand
16 August 2024

ISBN: 979-8-3313-0154-5

Printed from e-media with permission by:

Curran Associates, Inc.
57 Morehouse Lane
Red Hook, NY 12571

Some format issues inherent in the e-media version may also appear in this print version.

Association for Computational Linguistics
209 N. Eighth Street
Stroudsburg, Pennsylvania 18360

Phone: 1-570-476-8006
Fax: 1-570-476-0860

acl@aclweb.org

Additional copies of this publication are available from:

Curran Associates, Inc.
57 Morehouse Lane
Red Hook, NY 12571 USA
Phone: 845-758-0400
Fax: 845-758-2633
Email: curran@proceedings.com
Web: www.proceedings.com

SDP 2024

The Fourth Workshop on Scholarly Document Processing

Proceedings of the Workshop

August 16, 2024

The SDP organizers gratefully acknowledge the support from the following sponsors.

Best Paper Award

AI2

Best Paper Award (DAGPap shared task)

ELSEVIER

Message from the SDP 2024 Organizing Committee

Welcome to the Fourth Workshop on Scholarly Document Processing (SDP) at ACL 2024.
As the body of scholarly literature grows, automated methods in NLP, text mining, information retrieval, document understanding etc. are needed to address issues of information overload, disinformation, reproducibility, and more. Though progress has been made, there are significant unique challenges to processing scholarly text that require dedicated attention. The goal of the Scholarly Document Processing series of workshops is to provide a venue for addressing these challenges, as well as a platform for tasks and resources supporting the processing of scientific documents. Our long-term objective is to establish scholarly and scientific texts as an essential domain for NLP research, to supplement current efforts on web text and news articles.
This workshop builds on the success of prior workshops: the SDP workshop held at COLING in 2022, NAACL in 2021 and EMNLP in 2020, and the SciNLP workshop held at AKBC 2020 and AKBC 2021. As in previous years, we have sought to bring together researchers and practitioners from various backgrounds focusing on different aspects of scholarly document processing. We believe that the interdisciplinary nature of the ACL venues greatly assists in encouraging submissions from a diverse set of fields.

Organizing Committee

Program Chairs

Tirthankar Ghosal, Oak Ridge National Laboratory, USA
Amanpreet Singh, Allen Institute for AI, USA
Anita de Waard, Elsevier, Netherlands
Philipp Mayr, GESIS - Leibniz Institute for the Social Sciences, Germany
Aakanksha Naik, Allen Institute for AI, USA
Orion Weller, Johns Hopkins University, USA
Yoonjoo Lee, KAIST, Korea
Shannon Shen, Massachussets Institute of Technology, USA
Yanxia Qin, National University of Singapore, Singapore

Steering Committee members

Arman Cohan, Yale University, USA
Dayne Freitag, SRI International, USA
Tom Hope, Hebrew University of Jerusalem, Israel
Petr Knoth, Open University, UK
Kyle Lo, Allen Institute for AI, USA
Lucy Lu Wang, University of Washington, USA

Program Committee

Reviewers

Anurag Acharya, Daniel Acuna, Akiko Aizawa, Hamed Alhoori, Nikita Andreev, Tamjid Azad, Hosein Azarbonyad, Ibrahim Al Azher

Faiza Belbachir, Ioana Buhnila

Yupeng Cao, Soham Chitnis, Arman Cohan

Abdelhalim Hafedh Dahou, Sourish Dasgupta, Sourish Dasgupta, Anita De Waard, Jay DeYoung, Danilo Dessi, Yixi Ding, Doug Downey, James Dunham, Nicolau Duran-Silva

Alexander Fabbri, Dayne Freitag

Tirthankar Ghosal, John Michael Giorgi, German Gritsai, Nianlong Gu

Allan Hanbury, Tianyong Hao, Drahomira Herrmannova, Tosho Hirasawa, Tom Hope, Sameera Horawalavithana

Daisuke Ikeda

Xiaoliang Jiang

Lars Benedikt Kaesberg, Yavuz Selim Kartal, Yury Kashnitsky, Roman Kern, Halil Kilicoglu, Petr Knoth, Buse Sibel Korkmaz, Sandeep Kumar, Wojciech Kusa

Xiangci Li, Kyle Lo, Xinyuan Lu

Biswadip Mandal, Yoshitomo Matsubara, Philipp Mayr, Zoran Medić, Vladislav Mikhailov, Shufan Ming, Miftahul Jannat Mokarrama, Dana Moukheiber

Aakanksha Naik, Kazuya Nishimura

Wolfgang Otto, Yagmur Ozturk

Yanxia Qin

Abhinav Ramesh Kashyap, Julio C. Rangel, Tohida Rehman, Allen G Roush, Terry Ruas

Angelo Salatino, Debarshi Kumar Sanyal, Sebastian Schellhammer, Tim Schopf, Pierre Senellart, Kiran Sharma, Zejiang Shen, Alexander Shirnin, Amanpreet Singh, Neil R. Smalheiser, Nina Smirnova, Markus Stocker, Wojtek Sylwestrzak

Sotaro Takeshita, Naaman Tan, Hiroki Teranishi, Autumn Toney, Tornike Tsereteli

Sharmila Upadhyaya, Ashok Urlana

Boris Veytsman

Jan Philip Wahle, Lucy Lu Wang, Taro Watanabe, Orion Weller

Peter Zhang, Shiyuan Zhang, Jun Zhuang, Brian Douglas Zimmerman, Wuhe Zou

Keynote Talk
How to InterText? Elevating NLP to the cross-document level

Iryna Gurevych
Technical University Darmstadt and head of the UKP Lab

Abstract: While modern language models do a great job at finding documents, extracting information from them and generating naturally sounding language, the progress in helping humans read, connect, and make sense of interrelated long texts has been very much limited. Funded by the European Research Council, the InterText project brings natural language processing (NLP) forward by developing a general framework for modeling and analyzing fine-grained relationships between texts – intertextual relationships. This crucial milestone for AI would allow tracing the origin and evolution of texts and ideas and enable a new generation of AI applications for text work and critical reading. Using the scientific domain as a prototypical model of collaborative knowledge construction anchored in text, this talk will provide an overview of UKP Lab's past and ongoing research demonstrating our intertextual approach to NLP in the scientific domain. Specifically, we will highlight two lines of our work. The first one is related to task design, practical applications and intricacies of data collection in the peer-review domain. The second one is about scientific text generation targeting (i) citation text and (ii) attitude and theme-guided rebuttals. To conclude, we will briefly describe our ongoing efforts towardsfine-grained linking of multiple documents, temporal analysis of scientific datasets and research novelty modeling.

Bio: Iryna Gurevych is a German computer scientist. She is Professor at the Department of Computer Science of the Technical University of Darmstadt and Director of Ubiquitous Knowledge Processing Lab. She has a strong background in information extraction, semantic text processing, machine learning and innovative applications of NLP to social sciences and humanities.Iryna Gurevych has published over 300 publications in international conferences and journals and is member of programme and conference committees of more than 50 high-level conferences and workshops (ACL, EACL, NAACL, etc.). She is the holder of several awards, including the Lichtenberg-Professorship Career Award und the Emmy-Noether Career Award (both in 2007). In 2021 she received the first LOEWE-professorship of the LOEWE programme. She has been selected as a ACL Fellow 2020 for her outstanding work in natural language processing and machine learning and is the Vice-president-elect of the ACL since 2021.

Keynote Talk
AI Plays Medicinal Chemist

Heng Ji
University of Illinois at Urbana-Champaign

Abstract: There exist approximately 166 billion small molecules, with 970 million deemed druglike. Despite this vast pool, only 89 tyrosine kinase inhibitors are currently approved across global healthcare systems. This scarcity underscores the urgent need for innovative approaches, calling upon the NLP community to contribute significantly to medicine. However, the challenges are manifold. Existing large language models (LLMs) alone are insufficient due to their tendency to generate erroneous claims confidently (hallucinate). Moreover, traditional knowledge bases do not adequately address the issue; none of the 89 kinase inhibitors are documented in popular human-constructed databases. This gap persists because chemistry language diverges significantly from natural language, demanding specialized domain knowledge, multimodal information integration, and long context understanding. Using drug discovery as a case study, I will present our approaches to tackle these challenges and turn an AI agent into a Medicinal Chemist. I will share preliminary results from animal testing conducted on drug variants proposed by AI algorithms. Furthermore, I advocate for a paradigm shift towards 'slow science', emphasizing the integration of feedback loops from molecule synthesis and animal testing. This new paradigm aims to evaluate AI techniques in scientific contexts, moving beyond chasing precision/recall scores at leaderboards which are prevalent in the current computer science community.

Bio: Heng Ji is a professor at Computer Science Department of University of Illinois at Urbana-Champaign. She received her B.A. and M. A. in Computational Linguistics from Tsinghua University, and her M.S. and Ph.D. in Computer Science from New York University. Her research interests focus on Natural Language Processing, especially on Information Extraction and Knowledge Base Population. She is selected as Young Scientist and a member of the Global Future Council on the Future of Computing by the World Economic Forum in 2016 and 2017. The awards she received include AI's 10 to Watch Award by IEEE Intelligent Systems in 2013, NSF CAREER award in 2009, PACLIC2012 Best paper runner-up, 'Best of ICDM2013' paper award, Best of SDM2013 paper award, ACL2018 Best Demo paper nomination, Google Research Award in 2009 and 2014, IBM Watson Faculty Award in 2012 and 2014 and Bosch Research Award in 2014-2018. She has coordinated the NIST TAC Knowledge Base Population task since 2010. She is the associate editor for IEEE/ACM Transaction on Audio, Speech, and Language Processing. She has served as the Program Committee Co-Chair of NAACL-HLT2018, NLP-NABD2018, NLPCC2015, CSCKG2016 and CCL2019, and senior area chair for many conferences. She has led several multi-institute research efforts including DARPA DEFT Tinker Bell team of seven universities and DARPA KAIROS RESIN team of six universities. She is the task leader of the U.S. ARL projects on information fusion and knowledge networks construction between 2009-2019. She is invited by the Secretary of the Air Force and AFRL to join Air Force Data Analytics Expert Panel to inform the Air Force Strategy 2030.

Keynote Talk

Chasing high-precision NLP at discount prices: Lessons for accelerating science

Doug Downey
Northwestern University and Allen Institute for AI, USA

Abstract: Natural language processing (NLP) has made major strides in recent years, due to the increasing capabilities of large language models. However, using NLP to power real applications is still challenging: the best models are expensive to apply at scale and are still prone to errors. I'll describe recent lessons we've learned on the Semantic Scholar team as we've built and deployed applications using NLP aimed at accelerating science, including PDF content extraction, automatically-constructed topic pages for science, and complex question answering. While recent NLP breakthroughs do enable exciting new experiences, fully delivering on the potential of this technology will require solving multiple open research problems.

Bio: Doug is a Research Director at AI2. He is currently on leave from Northwestern University, where he is an Associate Professor of Computer Science. His research focuses on information extraction, natural language processing, and machine learning. Outside of work, he enjoys spending time with family, exploring the outdoors, and watching movies.

Keynote Talk

Large language models as research assistants: workflows and challenges

Anna Rogers
University of Copenhagen

Abstract: Research practices in our and other fields are being actively reshaped by the new tools based on large language models. For every step in the traditional research pipeline, from experimentation to writing, commercial 'solutions' are already actively marketed. This talk will discuss to what extent the marketing is realistic, how the research practices seem to be changing, and how all this interacts with considerations of publication ethics and security.

Bio: Anna Rogers is an assistant professor in the Center for Social Data Science at the University of Copenhagen. She is currently also a visiting researcher with the RIKEN Center for Computational Science (Japan). Her main research area is Natural Language Processing, in particular model analysis and evaluation of natural language understanding systems.

Table of Contents

Program

Friday, August 16, 2024

08:30 - 17:30 *For the final SDP2024 Program Schedule, see the workshop website: https://sdproc.org/2024/.*

Overview of the Fourth Workshop on Scholarly Document Processing

Tirthankar Ghosal[a] **Amanpreet Singh**[b] **Anita de Waard**[c] **Philipp Mayr**[d]
Aakanksha Naik[b] **Orion Weller**[e] **Yoonjoo Lee**[f] **Shannon Shen**[g] **Yanxia Qin**[h]

Abstract

The workshop on Scholarly Document Processing (SDP) started in 2020 to accelerate research, inform policy and educate the public on natural language processing for scientific text. The fourth iteration of the workshop, SDP24 was held at the 62nd Annual Meeting of the Association for Computational Linguistics (ACL24) as a hybrid event. The SDP workshop saw a great increase in interest, with 57 submissions, of which 28 were accepted. The program consisted of a research track, four invited talks and two shared tasks: 1) DAGPap24: Detecting automatically generated scientific papers and 2) Context24: Multimodal Evidence and Grounding Context Identification for Scientific Claims. The program was geared towards NLP, information extraction, information retrieval, and data mining for scholarly documents, with an emphasis on identifying and providing solutions to open challenges.

1 Workshop description

Scholarly literature is the chief means by which scientists and academics document and communicate their results and is therefore critical to the advancement of knowledge and improvement of human well-being.

At the same time, this literature poses challenges to NLP uncommon in other genres, such as specialized language and high background knowledge requirements, long documents and strong structural conventions, multi-modal presentation, citation relationships among documents, an emphasis on rational argumentation, and the frequent availability of detailed metadata. These challenges necessitate the development of NLP methods and resources optimized for this domain. The Scholarly Document Processing (SDP) workshop provides a venue for discussing these challenges, bringing together stakeholders from different communities including computational linguistics, machine learning, text mining, information retrieval, digital libraries, scientometrics and others, to develop methods, tasks, and resources in support of these goals.

In addition to the shared tasks (see Section 4), SDP invited research submissions on a diversity of topics ranging from technical challenges posed by scholarly texts to novel applications facilitating scholarly work.

The first **Scholarly Document Processing** (SDP) workshop was co-located online with the EMNLP 2020 conference (Chandrasekaran et al., 2020), and provided a dedicated venue for those working on SDP to submit and discuss their research. Following this succes and the clear appetite for venues to foster discussions around scholarly NLP, SDP 2021 co-located with NAACL (Beltagy et al., 2021), and SDP 2022 with COLING (Cohan et al., 2022) again aimed to connect researchers and practitioners from different communities working with scientific literature and data and created a premier meeting point to facilitate discussions on open problems in SDP.

2 Program

The SDP 2024 workshop consisted of four keynote talks, a research track and a shared task track. SDP 2024 received 57 submissions, of which 28 were accepted (49% acceptance rate).

[a]Oak Ridge National Laboratory, USA
[b]Allen Institute for AI, USA
[c]Elsevier, Netherlands
[d]GESIS — Leibniz Institute for the Social Sciences, Germany
[e]Johns Hopkins University, USA
[f]Korea Advanced Institute of Science & Technology, South Korea
[g]Massachussets Institute of Technology, USA
[h]National University of Singapore, Singapore

Proceedings of the Fourth Workshop on Scholarly Document Processing (SDP 2024), pages 1–6
August 16, 2024 ©2024 Association for Computational Linguistics

Since the workshop will be hybrid, there will be both in-person and virtual presentations at the conference venue and online. Topics of the presentations run the gamut, and include representation learning of scientific documents (including tables and images), citation text as well as paper text generation, peer review processing, scientific document summarization, AI-generated text detection, scientific intuition and reasoning, scientific papers to proposals, entity recognition and author disambiguation, scientific claim verification, and many more. As expected, we see a sharp increase in papers that employ large language models for downstream SDP tasks. The full program with links to papers, videos and posters is available at https://sdproc.org/2024/program.html.

3 Keynotes

This year we had four keynote lectures from researchers who are prominent in Natural Language Processing for scholarly documents:

- **Doug Downey**, Associate Professor at Northwestern University and Research Director at Allen Institute for AI, USA.
- **Iryna Gurevych**, Professor at Technical University Darmstadt and head of the UKP Lab, Germany.
- **Anna Rogers**, Assistant Professor, University of Copenhagen, Denmark.
- **Heng Ji**, Professor, University of Illinois at Urbana-Champaign, USA.

Speaker Iryna Gurevych

Title "How to InterText? Elevating NLP to the cross-document level"

Abstract While modern language models do a great job at finding documents, extracting information from them and generating naturally sounding language, the progress in helping humans read, connect, and make sense of interrelated long texts has been very much limited. Funded by the European Research Council, the InterText project brings natural language processing (NLP) forward by developing a general framework for modeling and analyzing fine-grained relationships between texts – intertextual relationships. This crucial milestone for AI would allow tracing the origin and evolution of texts and ideas and enable a new generation of AI applications for text work and critical reading. Using the scientific domain as a prototypical model of collaborative knowledge construction anchored in text, this talk will provide an overview of UKP Lab's past and ongoing research demonstrating our intertextual approach to NLP in the scientific domain. Specifically, we will highlight two lines of our work. The first one is related to task design, practical applications and intricacies of data collection in the peer-review domain. The second one is about scientific text generation targeting (i) citation text and (ii) attitude and theme-guided rebuttals. To conclude, we will briefly describe our ongoing efforts towardsfine-grained linking of multiple documents, temporal analysis of scientific datasets and research novelty modeling.

Speaker Heng Ji

Title "AI Plays Medicinal Chemist"

Abstract There exist approximately 166 billion small molecules, with 970 million deemed drug-like. Despite this vast pool, only 89 tyrosine kinase inhibitors are currently approved across global healthcare systems. This scarcity underscores the urgent need for innovative approaches, calling upon the NLP community to contribute significantly to medicine. However, the challenges are manifold. Existing large language models (LLMs) alone are insufficient due to their tendency to generate erroneous claims confidently (hallucinate). Moreover, traditional knowledge bases do not adequately address the issue; none of the 89 kinase inhibitors are documented in popular human-constructed databases. This gap persists because chemistry language diverges significantly from natural language, demanding specialized domain knowledge, multimodal information integration, and long context understanding. Using drug discovery as a case study, I will present our approaches to tackle these challenges and turn an AI agent into a Medicinal Chemist. I will share preliminary results from animal testing conducted on drug variants proposed by AI algorithms. Furthermore, I advocate for a paradigm shift towards 'slow science', emphasizing the integration of feedback loops from molecule synthesis and animal testing. This new paradigm aims to evaluate AI techniques in scientific contexts, moving beyond chasing precision/recall scores at leaderboards which are prevalent in the current computer science community.

Speaker Doug Downey

Title "Chasing high-precision NLP at discount prices: Lessons for accelerating science"

Abstract Natural language processing (NLP) has made major strides in recent years, due to the increasing capabilities of large language models. However, using NLP to power real applications is still challenging: the best models are expensive to apply at scale and are still prone to errors. I'll describe recent lessons we've learned on the Semantic Scholar team as we've built and deployed applications using NLP aimed at accelerating science, including PDF content extraction, automatically-constructed topic pages for science, and complex question answering. While recent NLP breakthroughs do enable exciting new experiences, fully delivering on the potential of this technology will require solving multiple open research problems.

Speaker Anna Rogers

Title "Large language models as research assistants: workflows and challenges"

Abstract Research practices in our and other fields are being actively reshaped by the new tools based on large language models. For every step in the traditional research pipeline, from experimentation to writing, commercial 'solutions' are already actively marketed. This talk will discuss to what extent the marketing is realistic, how the research practices seem to be changing, and how all this interacts with considerations of publication ethics and security.

4 Shared Task Track

SDP 2024 hosted two shared tasks. Both shared tasks had their own organizing committees consisting of several members of the SDP 2024 organizers and/or other collaborators. Detailed overview papers of the shared tasks are referred to and followed in the proceedings.

4.1 Detecting automatically generated scientific papers (DAGPap24)

Organizers: Savvas Chamezopoulos, Drahomira Herrmannova, Anita de Waard, Domenic Rosati, Yury Kashnitsky

A big problem with the ubiquity of Generative AI is that it has now become very easy to generate fake scientific papers. This can erode public trust in science and attack the foundations of science: are we standing on the shoulders of robots? The Detecting Automatically Generated Papers (DAGPap) competition aims to encourage the development of robust, reliable AI-generated scientific text detection systems, utilizing a diverse dataset and varied machine learning models in a number of scientific domains.

Building on the DagPap22 Competition Kashnitsky et al. (2022), this year's dataset consisted of 30,000 scientific articles sourced from ScienceDirect [1] that were processed to integrate various alteration methods within the human-written content. 28 teams participated in the task, with a total of 457 submissions. Out of these, 19 teams managed to beat the SciBERT baseline on the development set, and 12 teams managed to beat the SciBERT baseline on the test set. Four top teams exceeded an F1-score of 99%. For more details on the challenge, please see the DAGPap24 overview paper, elsewhere in this proceedings.

4.2 Multimodal Evidence and Grounding Context Identification for Scientific Claims (Context24)

Organizers: Joel Chan, Matt Akamatsu, and Aakanksha Naik

Interpreting scientific claims in the context of empirical findings is a valuable practice, yet extremely time-consuming for researchers. Such interpretation requires identifying key results (e.g., figures, tables, etc.) that provide supporting evidence from research papers, and contextualizing these results with associated methodological details (e.g., measures, sample, etc.). In this shared task, we released datasets to encourage the development of models for automatic identification of key results and additional grounding context, given a scientific claim. Context24 consisted of two tracks: (i) evidence identification, and (ii) grounding context identification. For track 1, we released a training dataset of 474 claims with key figure/table annotations, and manually extracted figures, tables and captions for all papers to avoid PDF parsing issues. For track 2, given the challenging annotation process, we released a limited training set of 42 claims to encourage exploration of zero-shot or few-shot methods. We also released full-texts for all associated papers

[1]https://www.sciencedirect.com/

parsed using PaperMage (Lo et al., 2023), and full-texts for $\sim$17,000 additional related papers (i.e., papers cited by/citing the original set) to encourage investigation of data augmentation and weak supervision-based approaches. Finally we released test sets consisting of 111 and 109 instances for tracks 1 and 2 respectively. For track 1, we received submissions from seven teams, while only two participated in track 2 possibly due to the low-resource nature of the task. We observed modest to strong performance improvements in both tracks as measured by automated evaluation metrics indicating that models find this task tractable but still have room to improve further. System reports from top three participating teams as well as an overview paper summarizing future directions (Chan et al., 2024) are included in the workshop proceedings.

5 Workshop Overview and Outlook

The organizers were gratified by both the size and breadth of the response to the fourth edition of SDP. The subjects of accepted papers ranged from end uses of the scholarly literature to challenges associated with automated understanding to adaptations of recent successes of LLMs in the broader field of NLP. It is apparent that automated processing of the scholarly literature is a problem that meets with substantial interest. And it seems likely that we are observing the beginnings of a research community with a narrow enough focus to make rapid progress, but a broad enough set of concerns to offer ample opportunities for cross-pollination.

To a first approximation, we regard SDP as a confluence of three communities: NLP, information retrieval, and scientometrics. Given our colocation with ACL, it is perhaps not surprising that the majority of our submissions emphasized NLP. As we consider future iterations of the workshop, we are discussing ways to increase its subject diversity. With SDP 2024 we have begun to present a more varied set of shared tasks, each highlighting challenges unique to the automated processing of the scholarly literature. As we proceed with planning and advertising, a key objective will be to elicit high-quality submissions from researchers interested in the uses and meta-linguistic aspects of scholarly communication.

6 Conclusion

The scholarly literature has long served as a rich source of interesting and challenging problems for computer science, and there is substantial prior work in information retrieval, scientometrics, data mining, and computational linguistics, but many important challenges remain. In many respects, our efforts to faithfully capture the semantics of scholarly communication through automated means are still in their infancy. At the same time, recent events regarding misinterpretation of scholarly information accentuate the importance of better approaches to the automated processing of scholarly literature.

By drawing attention to these problems and offering a forum for interested scientists from a range of disciplines to collaborate, we hope that this and future instances of SDP encourage the application of recent advances in relevant fields to this problem area, identify new use cases or improve our understanding of existing ones, and ultimately foster solutions that improve the practice of scholarship and serve society.

7 Program Committee

1. Abdelhalim Hafedh DAHOU, Universität Ulm
2. Abhinav Ramesh Kashyap, National University of Singapore
3. Akiko Aizawa, NII, Tokyo Institute of Technology
4. Alexander Fabbri, SalesForce.com
5. Alexander Shirnin, Higher School of Economics
6. Allan Hanbury, Complexity Science Hub and Technische Universität Wien
7. Allen G Roush, Oracle
8. Angelo Salatino, KMI - Open University
9. Anurag Acharya, Pacific Northwest National Laboratory
10. Arman Cohan, Yale University and Allen Institute for Artificial Intelligence
11. Ashok Urlana, Tata Consultancy Services Limited, India
12. Autumn Toney, Georgetown University
13. Biswadip Mandal, University of Texas at Dallas
14. Boris Veytsman, Chan Zuckerberg Initiative and George Mason University
15. Brian Douglas Zimmerman, University of Waterloo
16. Buse Sibel Korkmaz, Imperial College London
17. Daisuke Ikeda, Kyushu University and Kyushu

University

18. Dana Moukheiber, Massachusetts Institute of Technology
19. Daniel Acuna, Computer Science Department, University of Colorado at Boulder
20. Danilo Dessi, GESIS
21. Dayne Freitag, SRI International
22. Debarshi Kumar Sanyal, Indian Association for the Cultivation of Science
23. Doug Downey, Allen Institute for Artificial Intelligence and Northwestern University
24. Drahomira Herrmannova, Elsevier
25. Faiza BELBACHIR, Institut polytechnique des sciences avancees
26. German Gritsai, Université Grenoble Alpes
27. Halil Kilicoglu, University of Illinois at Urbana-Champaign
28. Hamed Alhoori, Northern Illinois University
29. Hiroki Teranishi, Nara Institute of Science and Technology, Japan and RIKEN
30. Hosein Azarbonyad, Elsevier
31. Ibrahim Al Azher, Northern Illinois University
32. Ioana Buhnila, Université de Lorraine
33. James Dunham, Georgetown University
34. Jan Philip Wahle, University of Göttingen, Germany
35. Jay DeYoung, Northeastern University
36. John Michael Giorgi, Toronto University
37. Julio C. Rangel, RIKEN
38. Jun Zhuang, Boise State University and Indiana University Purdue University Indianapolis
39. Kazuya Nishimura, Kyushu University
40. Kiran Sharma, BML Munjal University
41. Kyle Lo, Allen Institute for Artificial Intelligence
42. Lars Benedikt Kaesberg,
43. Lucy Lu Wang, University of Washington and Allen Institute for Artificial Intelligence
44. Markus Stocker, TIB Leibniz Information Centre for Science and Technology
45. Miftahul Jannat Mokarrama, Northern Illinois University
46. Naaman Tan, National University of Singapore
47. Neil R. Smalheiser, University of Illinois at Chicago
48. Nianlong Gu, University of Zurich
49. Nicolau Duran-Silva, Universitat Pompeu Fabra
50. Nikita Andreev, Yandex
51. Nina Smirnova, GESIS – Leibniz Institute for the Social Sciences
52. Peter Zhang, University of California, Berkeley
53. Petr Knoth, Open University
54. Pierre Senellart, Ecole Normale Supérieure
55. Roman Kern, Know Center GmbH and Technische Universität Graz
56. Sameera Horawalavithana, Pacific Northwest National Laboratory
57. Sandeep Kumar, Indian Institute of Technology, Patna
58. Sebastian Schellhammer, GESIS Leibniz Institute for the Social Sciences
59. Sharmila upadhyaya, Gesis leibniz Institute
60. Shiyuan Zhang, University of Illinois at Urbana-Champaign
61. Shufan Ming, University of Illinois at Urbana-Champaign
62. Soham Chitnis, Birla Institute of Technology and Science Pilani
63. Sotaro Takeshita, Universität Mannheim
64. Sourish Dasgupta, Dhirubhai Ambani Institute of Information & Communication Technology
65. Tamjid Azad, Northern Illinois University
66. Taro Watanabe, Nara Institute of Science and Technology, Japan
67. Terry Ruas, Georg-August Universität Göttingen
68. Tianyong Hao, South China Normal University
69. Tim Schopf, Technische Universität München
70. Tohida Rehman, Jadavpur University
71. Tom Hope, Allen Institute for Artificial Intelligence and Hebrew University, Hebrew University of Jerusalem
72. Tornike Tsereteli, Universität Mannheim
73. Tosho Hirasawa, Omron Sinic X
74. Vladislav Mikhailov, University of Oslo
75. Wojciech Kusa, Allegro
76. Wojtek Sylwestrzak, University of Warsaw
77. Wolfgang Otto, GESIS
78. Xiangci Li, Google
79. Xiaoliang Jiang, University of Illinois at Urbana-Champaign
80. Xinyuan Lu, national university of singaore, National University of Singapore
81. Yagmur Ozturk, Université Grenoble Alpes
82. Yavuz Selim Kartal, Gesis
83. Yixi Ding, National University of Singapore
84. Yoshitomo Matsubara, Spiffy AI
85. Yupeng Cao, Stevens Institute of Technology
86. Yury Kashnitsky, Google
87. Zoran Medić, UniZg-FER, University of Zagreb

88. Wuhe Zou, Netease Group

Acknowledgements

We organizers wish to thank all those who contributed to this workshop series: The researchers who contributed papers, the many reviewers who generously offered their time and expertise, and the participants of the workshop.

Philipp Mayr received funding via the OUTCITE project (Backes et al., 2024) at GESIS Cologne and University Stuttgart (Funder: Deutsche Forschungsgemeinschaft; Grant: MA 3964/8-2).

References

Tobias Backes, Anastasiia Iurshina, Muhammad Ahsan Shahid, and Philipp Mayr. 2024. Comparing Free Reference Extraction Pipelines. *International Journal on Digital Libraries.*

Iz Beltagy, Arman Cohan, Guy Feigenblat, Dayne Freitag, Tirthankar Ghosal, Keith Hall, Drahomira Herrmannova, Petr Knoth, Kyle Lo, Philipp Mayr, Robert Patton, Michal Shmueli-Scheuer, Anita de Waard, Kuansan Wang, and Lucy Lu Wang. 2021. Overview of the second workshop on scholarly document processing. In *Proceedings of the Second Workshop on Scholarly Document Processing*, pages 159–165, Online. Association for Computational Linguistics.

Chu Sern Joel Chan, Aakanksha Naik, Matt Akamatsu, Hanna Bekele, Erin Bransom, Ian Campbell, and Jenna Sparks. 2024. Overview of the context24 shared task on contextualizing scientific claims. In *The 4th Workshop on Scholarly Document Processing @ ACL 2024.*

Muthu Kumar Chandrasekaran, Guy Feigenblat, Dayne Freitag, Tirthankar Ghosal, Eduard Hovy, Philipp Mayr, Michal Shmueli-Scheuer, and Anita de Waard. 2020. Overview of the First Workshop on Scholarly Document Processing (SDP). In *Proceedings of the First Workshop on Scholarly Document Processing*, pages 1–6, Online. Association for Computational Linguistics.

Arman Cohan, Guy Feigenblat, Dayne Freitag, Tirthankar Ghosal, Drahomira Herrmannova, Petr Knoth, Kyle Lo, Philipp Mayr, Michal Shmueli-Scheuer, Anita de Waard, and Lucy Lu Wang. 2022. Overview of the third workshop on scholarly document processing. In *Proceedings of the Third Workshop on Scholarly Document Processing*, pages 1–6, Gyeongju, Republic of Korea. Association for Computational Linguistics.

Yury Kashnitsky, Drahomira Herrmannova, Anita de Waard, Georgios Tsatsaronis, Catriona Fennell, and Cyril Labbé. 2022. Overview of the DAGPap22 shared task on detecting automatically generated scientific papers. In *Proceedings of the Third Workshop on Scholarly Document Processing*, Gyeongju, Republic of Korea. Association for Computational Linguistics.

Kyle Lo, Zejiang Shen, Benjamin Newman, Joseph Chang, Russell Authur, Erin Bransom, Stefan Candra, Yoganand Chandrasekhar, Regan Huff, Bailey Kuehl, Amanpreet Singh, Chris Wilhelm, Angele Zamarron, Marti A. Hearst, Daniel Weld, Doug Downey, and Luca Soldaini. 2023. PaperMage: A unified toolkit for processing, representing, and manipulating visually-rich scientific documents. In *Proceedings of the 2023 Conference on Empirical Methods in Natural Language Processing: System Demonstrations*, pages 495–507, Singapore. Association for Computational Linguistics.

Overview of the DagPap24 Shared Task on Detecting Automatically Generated Scientific Papers

Savvas Chamezopoulos[1] **Drahomira Herrmannova**[1] **Anita de Waard**[1]
Domenic Rosati[2] **Yury Kashnitsky**[1]
Elsevier, USA[1] Dalhousie University, Canada [2]
{s.chamezopoulos, d.herrmannova, a.dewaard}@elsevier.com,

Abstract

This paper provides an overview of the 2024 ACL Scholarly Document Processing workshop shared task on the detection of automatically generated scientific papers. Unlike our previous task, which focused on the binary classification of whether scientific passages were machine-generated or not, one likely use case for text generation technology in scientific writing is to intersperse human-written text with passages of machine-generated text. We frame the detection problem as a multi-class span classification task: given an expert of text, label token spans in the text as human-written or machine-generated We shared a dataset containing excerpts from human-written papers as well as artificially generated content collected by Elsevier publishing and editorial teams. As a test set, the participants were provided with a corpus of openly accessible human-written as well as generated papers from the same scientific domains of documents. The shared task saw 457 submissions across 28 participating teams and resulted in three published technical reports. We discuss our findings from the shared task in this overview paper.

1 Introduction

A big problem with the ubiquity of Generative AI is that it has now become very easy to generate fake scientific papers. This can erode public trust in science and attack the foundations of science: are we standing on the shoulders of robots? One notorious example is how Rafael Luque massively used chatGPT to "polish" papers that were later found[1] in authorship for sale advertisements. According to a recent study (Gray, 2024), chatGPT "contamination" is seen in at least 60,000 published papers (slightly over 1% of all articles). For the publishing year 2023, it is found that several specific words like "commendable", "intricate" or "meticulously" show a distinctive and disproportionate increase in their prevalence, which might be an indication of LLM assistance in writing.

The Detecting Automatically Generated Papers (DAGPap[2]) competition aims to encourage the development of robust, reliable AI-generated scientific text detection systems, utilizing a diverse dataset and varied machine learning models in a number of scientific domains.

Building on the DagPap22 competition Kashnitsky et al. (2022), this year's dataset consisted of 30,000 scientific articles sourced from ScienceDirect[3] that were processed to integrate various alteration methods within the human-written content.

As for the previous challenge, the 2024 DagPap challenge is a collaboration between a publisher (Elsevier) and the research community to attempt a resolution through technical means.

2 Related work

Since the DagPap22 competition, there have been several more efforts on addressing the same problem.

SemEval 2024 hosted a task[4] on multi-generator, multi-domain, and multilingual black-box machine-generated text detection (Wang et al., 2024) (to appear at NAACL 2024). The Shared Task offered 4 subtasks (monolingual and multilingual text classification, multi-way classification and human-machine text boundary detection) and attracted a couple hundred teams. The organizers found that all classification tasks turned out to be

[1] https://tinyurl.com/rafaelluque

[2] https://sdproc.org/2024/sharedtasks.html#dagpap

[3] https://www.sciencedirect.com/

[4] https://github.com/mbzuai-nlp/SemEval2024-task8

Proceedings of the Fourth Workshop on Scholarly Document Processing (SDP 2024), pages 7–11
August 16, 2024 ©2024 Association for Computational Linguistics

relatively easy to solve, with many teams beating baselines. The boundary detection problem, however, turned out to be harder to solve.

CLIN33 hosted a similar Shared Task (Fivez et al., 2024) aimed at automatic detection of AI-generated texts in English and Dutch, spanning multiple genres: medium-length news articles, tweets from the social media platform X (previously known as Twitter), product reviews, short-form poetry, and journal columns. Thus, the task focused on a cross-domain multilingual binary classification setup that included entirely new held-out test genres. The results were close to perfect for some genres (e.g., news and reviews) yet unsatisfactory for others (e.g., poetry).

Kaggle, a popular platform for machine learning competitions, also hosted a similar contest[5] "LLM - Detect AI-Generated Text" (King et al., 2023). The competition attracted over 5,000 participants from 4,300 teams and over 110,000 submissions. Although Kaggle is well-known for establishing state-of-the-art in applied machine learning (e.g., the usage of DeBERTa (He et al., 2021) for most NLP tasks), the focus of many competitors of the mentioned contest were on reverse-engineering the prompts used to generate the test set. This may limit the generalizability and applicability of these findings to real-world scenarios.

Some more similar competitions include AuTexTification (Automated Text Identification) (Sarvazyan et al., 2023) and MLMAC (Merkhofer et al., 2023) (Machine Learning Model Attribution Challenge). Interestingly, MLMAC organizers note that the most successful approaches were manual, as participants observed similarities between model outputs and developed attribution heuristics based on public documentation of the base models.

Some notable leaderboards for human- vs. machine-text detection and author attribution are:

- TuringBench (Uchendu et al., 2021), which consists of 20 labels (19 AI text-generators and human) and includes 200K articles, created by prompting AI text-generators with titles of 10K news articles from sources like CNN;
- MULTITuDE (Macko et al., 2023) is a large-scale multi-lingual benchmark comprising 74,000 texts generated by 8 LLMs in 11 languages. Here, authors conclude that detectors struggle with generalizing to the unseen languages, texts from different domains, writing styles, and unknown language models, decoding strategies, or obfuscation efforts. Notably, some commercially available detectors fail at this benchmark. In accordance with Kaggle experience, DeBERTA-v3 is the best base for machine learning types of detectors;
- RAID (Dugan et al., 2024) is probably the largest benchmark at the time of writing: in includes over 6 million generations spanning 11 models, 8 domains, 11 adversarial attacks and 4 decoding strategies. Using RAID, the authors evaluate the out-of-domain and adversarial robustness of 8 open- and 4 closed-source detectors and find that current detectors are easily fooled by adversarial attacks, variations in sampling strategies, repetition penalties, and unseen generative models.

[5] `https://www.kaggle.com/competitions/llm-detect-ai-generated-text`

While most of the competitions and leaderboards address the problem of full-text classification into different classes (human/machine or several LLMs as origins; and only SemEval subtask 3 is an exception); for DAGPap24, we focus on a token-level text classification, for a scenario when human writing is interspersed with passages of machine-generated text.

3 Corpus creation

The dataset comprised 30,000 scientific articles sourced from ScienceDirect[6]. These articles' full texts were processed to integrate various alteration methods within the human-written content. For each alteration, the text segment contained between 2,500 to 4,000 characters. Approximately 25% of the entire text was modified using one of the following techniques:

1. **Synonym Replacement using NLTK** (Bird et al., 2009): Approximately 75% of the eligible words were substituted with random choices from their respective synonyms. An eligible word is defined as a non-stop word that has at least one synonym other than itself.

[6] `https://www.sciencedirect.com/`

Column name	Data
index	0
text	Across the world...
annotations	[[0, 3779, human], [3780, 7601, chat_gpt], ...
tokens	[Across, the, world, ...
token_label_ids	[0, 0, 0, 0, 0, 0, 0, 0, 0, 0, 0, ...

Table 1: Example data row

2. **Text Summarization with T5-Small** (Raffel et al., 2020): The T5-small model, implemented through HuggingFace (Wolf et al., 2020), was utilized for text summarization. The summarized text ranges between 80% to 120% of the original text length.

3. **Paraphrasing using ChatGPT** [7]: The ChatGPT 3.5 Turbo model (accessed via the API) was employed for text paraphrasing, refining the original text into alternative expressions.

Before applying any alterations, the texts were segmented into individual sentences. This segmentation was crucial to maintain proper readability and to better simulate scenarios where machine learning and AI are utilized as writing assistants. A significant aspect of this dataset creation is the incorporation of randomness. Both the text chunks where alterations would be made and the selection of the alteration method were determined at pseudo-random intervals. After processing, the text was tokenized into whole words. These tokens, along with their respective annotation spans, constitute the label columns. An example row of the final dataset can be found in Table 1.

4 Competition setup

4.1 Metric and data split

The metric chosen in the competition is Macro F1 score. For each full text, the macro F1 score is calculated and the final score is the average across all scores.

The final data was divided into train, development (dev), and test sets, resulting in 5000 training records 5000 dev records, and 20000 test records for the competition[8].

[7]https://chatgpt.com/

[8]https://www.codabench.org/competitions/2431/#/pages-tab

4.2 Baselines

As organizers, we provided 3 baselines:

- A fine-tuned DistilBERT (Sanh et al., 2019) with an **84%** test set average macro F1 score
- A fine-tuned SciBERT (Beltagy et al., 2019) with an **87%** test set average macro F1 score
- An indicative all-zeros prediction with a **36%** test set average macro F1 score

All instructions and baseline code were made public to the participants via CodaBench [9]. The competition was comprised of two phases: the development and the testing phase. During the development phase, both the training and dev sets were made available to the competitors. Of course, the label columns were not available in the dev set. They could freely measure the performance of their systems on the dev set by providing a set of predictions to be measured against the correct labels in a pre-configured online platform. During the testing phase, the test set (excluding labels) was shared with the competitors, and they could post up to two prediction files to test their models.

4.3 Awards

Elsevier sponsored monetary prizes for a total of USD $5000 to the three top ranking teams. For more details, see the competition website[10].

5 Results

28 teams participated in the task this year, with a total of 457 submissions. Out of these, 19 teams managed to beat the SciBERT baseline on the development set, and 12 teams managed to beat the SciBERT baseline on the test set. The performance of the top 4 teams was particularly impressive, all exceeding an F1-score of 99% on the test set.

3 papers got accepted at the Scholarly Document Processing workshop dedicated to the shared task (Gritsai et al., 2024; Andreev et al., 2024; Zhao et al., 2024).

In (Zhao et al., 2024), they address the challenge by using two tokenization methods, fine-tuning various language models, introducing an Anomalous Label Smoothing (ALS) method and

[9]https://github.com/ChamezopoulosSavvas/DAGPap24

[10]https://www.codabench.org/competitions/2431/#/pages-tab

employing a majority voting method for ensembling model predictions. ALS is similar to a Conditional Random Fields (CRF) in filtering out unreasonable labels. It ensures that the distribution of predicted labels aligns with that of the training set. The team finished at the 2nd place on the final leaderboard with 0.9948 and 0.9944 F1 scores during the development and testing phases respectively. We are interested to see how similar techniques can be applied to the problem in general, when test data distribution does not always match the training data distribution.

The authors of (Andreev et al., 2024) achieved an F1 score of 89.83 during the competition (landing at the 6th place on the leaderboard) and 99.46 afterward by fixing a tokenization issue. Their solution was also to ensemble several models, here they ensembled several DeBERTa models with varying the number of layers frozen, and input token lengths.

Finally, (Gritsai et al., 2024) provided a multitask setting where one linear layer was trained for the binary prediction task (human- or machine-written), and the other was multi-class. They used the binary classifier to guide whether they used the multi-class classifier.

6 Discussion

During the previous iteration of the DAGPap challenge (Kashnitsky et al., 2022), the participants were able to achieve $>$ 99% F1 scores. Our hypothesis was that one of the reasons for this could be that the techniques used for generating "fake" examples tended to generate content that often included specific patterns. For example, the model used for summarization tended to open with phrases like "This paper is focused on ..." or "In this paper, the authors ...". To alleviate this issue, for this round of the competition, we leveraged more robust techniques for generating the competition corpus, specifically, gpt-3.5-turbo models, T5-Small, and NLTK synonym replacement. The task was also reformulated from sequence classification in the previous round to token classification in this round.

Despite these changes, some participants were still able to achieve over 99% F1 scores. We believe this demonstrates the difficulty in creating representative training corpora for the detection of machine-generated scientific content – in the experience of our teams at Elsevier and as reported in (Rosati, 2022; Macko et al., 2023; Dugan et al., 2024), detection of machine-generated scientific content is still a challenging task despite these encouraging results. However, we believe that the DAGPap24 shared task did offer a step forward to explore this challenging problem, and we hope to work together with the community on resolving this pernicious issue.

For future work, we plan to design a competition that focuses on real-world scenarios where human-written and machine-generated scientific texts are mixed. We also plan to investigate the robustness of detection systems against adversarial attacks in the scientific domain, where the generated text is intentionally modified to evade detection.

Acknowledgements

The work is partially supported by the European Research Council (ERC) grant agreement no. 951393.

References

Nikita Andreev, Alexander Shirnin, Vladislav Mikhailov, and Ekaterina Artemova. 2024. Papilusion at DAGPap24: Paper or illusion? detecting AI-generated scientific papers. In *The 4th Workshop on Scholarly Document Processing @ ACL 2024*.

Iz Beltagy, Kyle Lo, and Arman Cohan. 2019. SciBERT: A pretrained language model for scientific text. In *Proceedings of the 2019 Conference on Empirical Methods in Natural Language Processing and the 9th International Joint Conference on Natural Language Processing (EMNLP-IJCNLP)*, pages 3615–3620, Hong Kong, China. Association for Computational Linguistics.

Steven Bird, Ewan Klein, and Edward Loper. 2009. *Natural language processing with Python: analyzing text with the natural language toolkit.* " O'Reilly Media, Inc.".

Liam Dugan, Alyssa Hwang, Filip Trhlik, Josh Magnus Ludan, Andrew Zhu, Hainiu Xu, Daphne Ippolito, and Chris Callison-Burch. 2024. Raid: A shared benchmark for robust evaluation of machine-generated text detectors.

Pieter Fivez, Walter Daelemans, Tim Van de Cruys, Yury Kashnitsky, Savvas Chamezopoulos, Hadi Mohammadi, Anastasia Giachanou, Ayoub Bagheri, Wessel Poelman, Juraj Vladika, Esther Ploeger, Johannes Bjerva, Florian Matthes, and Hans van Halteren. 2024. The clin33 shared task on the detection of text generated by large language models. *Computational Linguistics in the Netherlands Journal*, 13:233–259.

Andrew Gray. 2024. Chatgpt "contamination": estimating the prevalence of llms in the scholarly literature.

German Gritsai, Ildar Khabutdinov, and Andrey Grabovoy. 2024. Multi-head span-based detector for AI-generated fragments in scientific papers. In *The 4th Workshop on Scholarly Document Processing @ ACL 2024*.

Pengcheng He, Xiaodong Liu, Jianfeng Gao, and Weizhu Chen. 2021. Deberta: Decoding-enhanced bert with disentangled attention. In *International Conference on Learning Representations*.

Yury Kashnitsky, Drahomira Herrmannova, Anita de Waard, George Tsatsaronis, Catriona Catriona Fennell, and Cyril Labbe. 2022. Overview of the DAGPap22 shared task on detecting automatically generated scientific papers. In *Proceedings of the Third Workshop on Scholarly Document Processing*, pages 210–213, Gyeongju, Republic of Korea. Association for Computational Linguistics.

Jules King, Perpetual Baffour, Scott Crossley, Ryan Holbrook, and Maggie Demkin. 2023. Llm - detect ai generated text.

Dominik Macko, Robert Moro, Adaku Uchendu, Jason Lucas, Michiharu Yamashita, Matúš Pikuliak, Ivan Srba, Thai Le, Dongwon Lee, Jakub Simko, and Maria Bielikova. 2023. MULTITuDE: Large-scale multilingual machine-generated text detection benchmark. In *Proceedings of the 2023 Conference on Empirical Methods in Natural Language Processing*, pages 9960–9987, Singapore. Association for Computational Linguistics.

Elizabeth Merkhofer, Deepesh Chaudhari, Hyrum S. Anderson, Keith Manville, Lily Wong, and João Gante. 2023. Machine learning model attribution challenge.

Colin Raffel, Noam Shazeer, Adam Roberts, Katherine Lee, Sharan Narang, Michael Matena, Yanqi Zhou, Wei Li, and Peter J. Liu. 2020. Exploring the limits of transfer learning with a unified text-to-text transformer. *Journal of Machine Learning Research*, 21(140):1–67.

Domenic Rosati. 2022. SynSciPass: detecting appropriate uses of scientific text generation. In *Proceedings of the Third Workshop on Scholarly Document Processing*, pages 214–222, Gyeongju, Republic of Korea. Association for Computational Linguistics.

Victor Sanh, Lysandre Debut, Julien Chaumond, and Thomas Wolf. 2019. Distilbert, a distilled version of bert: smaller, faster, cheaper and lighter.

Areg Mikael Sarvazyan, José Ángel González, Marc Franco-Salvador, Francisco Rangel, Berta Chulvi, and Paolo Rosso. 2023. Overview of autextification at iberlef 2023: Detection and attribution of machine-generated text in multiple domains.

Adaku Uchendu, Zeyu Ma, Thai Le, Rui Zhang, and Dongwon Lee. 2021. Turingbench: A benchmark environment for turing test in the age of neural text generation. In *Proceedings of the Findings of the 2021 Empirical Methods in Natural Language Processing (EMNLP)*, Punta Cana, Dominican Republic.

Yuxia Wang, Jonibek Mansurov, Petar Ivanov, Jinyan Su, Artem Shelmanov, Akim Tsvigun, Osama Mohammed Afzal, Tarek Mahmoud, Giovanni Puccetti, Thomas Arnold, Chenxi Whitehouse, Alham Fikri Aji, Nizar Habash, Iryna Gurevych, and Preslav Nakov. 2024. Semeval-2024 task 8: Multidomain, multimodel and multilingual machine-generated text detection.

Thomas Wolf, Lysandre Debut, Victor Sanh, Julien Chaumond, Clement Delangue, Anthony Moi, Pierric Cistac, Tim Rault, Rémi Louf, Morgan Funtowicz, Joe Davison, Sam Shleifer, Patrick von Platen, Clara Ma, Yacine Jernite, Julien Plu, Canwen Xu, Teven Le Scao, Sylvain Gugger, Mariama Drame, Quentin Lhoest, and Alexander M. Rush. 2020. Huggingface's transformers: State-of-the-art natural language processing.

Yuan Zhao, Junruo Gao, Junlin Wang, Gang Luo, and Liang Tang. 2024. Utilizing an ensemble model with anomalous label smoothing to detect generated scientific papers. In *The 4th Workshop on Scholarly Document Processing @ ACL 2024*.

Overview of the Context24 Shared Task on Contextualizing Scientific Claims

Joel Chan[◇*] **Aakanksha Naik**[♣] **Matthew Akamatsu**[♡] **Hanna Bekele**[♡]
Erin Bransom[♣] **Ian Campbell**[♡] **Jenna Sparks**[♣]
[◇] University of Maryland
[♣] Allen Institute for AI
[♡] University of Washington

Abstract

To appropriately interpret and use scientific claims for sensemaking and decision-making, it is critical to contextualize them, not just with textual evidence that the claim was in fact asserted, but also with key supporting empirical evidence, such as a figure that describes a key result, and methodological details, such as the methods of data collection. Retrieving this contextual information when encountering claims in isolation, away from their source papers, is difficult and time-consuming for humans. Scholarly document processing models could help to contextualize scientific claims, but there is a lack of datasets designed for this task. Thus, we contribute a dataset of 585 scientific claims with gold annotations for supporting figures and tables, and gold text snippets of methodological details, that ground the key results behind each claim and run the Context24 shared task to encourage model development for this task. This report describes details of our dataset construction process, summarizes results from the shared task conducted at the 4th Workshop on Scholarly Document Processing (SDP), and discusses future research directions in this space. To support further research, we also publicly release the dataset on HuggingFace.

1 Introduction

People read and use scientific claims both within the scientific process (e.g., in literature reviews, problem formulation, making sense of conflicting data) and outside of science (e.g., evidence-informed deliberation). To appropriately interpret, appraise, and ultimately use claims for sensemaking and decision-making, it is critical to *contextualize* claims with key supporting empirical evidence (e.g., figures presenting key results) and methodological details (e.g., measures, sample).

The goal of contextualizing claims with *empirical* evidence differs slightly from other evidence identification tasks, in that it is aimed at retrieving very targeted (down to the sub-figure) multimodal evidence (i.e., figures or tables grounding a scientific claim), rather than simply a set of text snippets, as is common in claim verification tasks and datasets (Vladika and Matthes, 2023).

This distinction between empirical — vs. general textual — evidence for a claim is crucial for sensemaking and decision-making: knowing that a scientific claim has been asserted in a paper is significantly different from knowing that a scientific claim is associated with empirical evidence (or not) that can be further assessed. Without a clear distinction between these forms of evidence, downstream sensemaking and synthesis may be compromised by the spread of "ghost claims" that lack empirical evidence but are asserted as if they do have evidential weight. In a striking illustration of this, (Harzing, 1995) found that a widely circulated claim about high failure rates for expatriates who are sent abroad to work was based on misquotations from three articles, only one of which contained solid empirical evidence that was in fact contrary to the focal claim. Therefore, despite the increased difficulty, linking claims to empirical evidence is crucial for the scientific process.

However, scientific claims are often encountered and used in settings far removed from the source materials and data, such as in brief citation statements in research papers, or conversations in discussion threads or on social media. In such cases, retrieving needed contextual information in the moment can be difficult and time-consuming for humans. Scholarly document processing models trained for scientific claim verification and fact checking (Vladika and Matthes, 2023), figure captioning (Hsu et al., 2021), and data extraction for systematic reviews (Schmidt et al., 2023) could potentially assist with the task of contextualizing

[*]Corresponding author: joelchan@umd.edu

Proceedings of the Fourth Workshop on Scholarly Document Processing (SDP 2024), pages 12–21
August 16, 2024 ©2024 Association for Computational Linguistics

scientific claims in these settings. However, the community currently lacks datasets specifically formulated for this task.

We bridge this gap by contributing a dataset of 585 scientific claims actually in use in lab notes and discussions for synthesis and research planning, across the domains of biology, computer science, and the social sciences. For each claim, the dataset includes gold annotations for figures/tables that ground the key empirical evidence for the claim (Track 1); for a subset of these claims, the dataset also includes gold examples of text snippets that describe the key methodological details that ground each claim (Track 2). As part of the 4th Workshop on Scholarly Document Processing (SDP) at ACL 2024, we ran a shared task with this dataset, with official submissions from a total of 6 teams for Track 1, and 2 teams for Track 2. In this report, we describe the details of the dataset construction, summarize the results from the shared task, and discuss implications and future research directions in this space. To support further research on this task, our full dataset (including gold test data) is available on HuggingFace [1].

2 Related Work

The task of contextualizing scientific claims can be formulated similarly to tasks like claim verification and fact checking. Additionally, modeling techniques used for this task have parallels in work on figure captioning and data extraction from scientific literature.

2.1 Claim Verification

Claim verification is typically formulated as the task of predicting support/refute relationships between claims and snippets of source texts, such as research abstracts (Vladika and Matthes, 2023). There are several datasets for scientific claim verification, but most widely used ones like SciFact (Wadden et al., 2020), SciFact-Open (Wadden et al., 2022), COVID-Fact (Saakyan et al., 2021), and HealthVER (Sarrouti et al., 2021) focus on pairing claims with textual evidence.

There are, however, a few more specific datasets that focus on verifying scientific claims against figures or tables. For instance, MuLMS-Img (Tarsi et al., 2024) includes 78 queries (and their corresponding figures) over materials science figures, sourced from domain experts, while SCITAB (Lu et al., 2023) includes 1.2k expert-annotated claims associated with *tables* from a corpus of computer science papers. Our work extends these datasets in terms of size (7x more queries than MulMS-Img), and breadth of scientific domains included (social sciences, HCI, and cell biology vs. materials science or computer science specifically).

2.2 Scientific Figure Captioning

There is a substantial body of work on figure captioning and alt-text generation, supported by many figure captioning datasets, such as SciCap (Hsu et al., 2021), SciOL (Tarsi et al., 2024), MedICaT (Subramanian et al., 2020), PMC-OA (Lin et al., 2023), and Multimodal ArXiv (Li et al., 2024).

The task of generating text describing a figure can be viewed as the inverse of the task of retrieving a figure that matches a scientific claim, thus these datasets and models built using them can be leveraged to build better techniques for our task. Some dataset, such as MedICaT (Subramanian et al., 2020) and PMC-OA (Lin et al., 2023), focus not just on overall figure captioning, but also sub-figure and sub-caption alignment. Thus, to the extent that these figures describe empirical evidence, subsets from these datasets can be as additional weak supervision for our task. However, figure captioning datasets at present do not focus solely on empirical evidence subsets, which can be hard to filter. Another complication to using these datasets directly for our task is that the quality and descriptiveness of figure captions in scientific texts can vary widely (Chintalapati et al., 2022).

2.3 Data Extraction from Scientific Literature

The subtask of retrieving methodological details relevant to a claim is analogous to the task of data extraction in systematic reviews, which has a long history in biomedical informatics and NLP (Schmidt et al., 2023). There are, however, limited public datasets for this task. EBM-NLP (Nye et al., 2018) is the primary public dataset available for use: it consists of 5k medical abstracts annotated with ***Population***, ***Intervention*** (collapsed with ***Comparator***), and ***Outcome*** elements from the PICO framework (Richardson et al., 1995), which is widely used to structure systematic reviews in evidence-based medicine, often focusing specifically on randomized controlled trials (RCTs). PubMed PICO (Jin and Szolovits, 2018) is a much larger dataset with 24k RCT abstracts, but PIO

[1] `https://huggingface.co/datasets/joelchan/contextualizing-scientific-claims`

annotations are automatically assigned based on structured abstract section headings. There are also smaller, disease-specific datasets with PICO annotations (Hu et al., 2023), though these are not publicly available, and datasets with more fine-grained experimental findings annotated (Naik et al., 2024). Beyond medical abstracts, some datasets focus on information extraction and question answering over other scientific domains like computer science (Jain et al., 2020; Dasigi et al., 2021).

We extend this body of work by focusing on scientific claims from a wider range of scientific domains, and with a more specific focus on extracting methodological details.

3 Shared Task Tracks

3.1 Track 1: Evidence Identification

Task formulation. Given a scientific claim c, and a set of figures ($F = \{f_1, ..., f_n\}$) and tables ($T = \{t_1, ..., t_n\}$) from the paper that contains the claim, models must produce a ranking of all items in $F \cup T$, based on whether they provide supporting evidence for the claim c. Therefore, this task can be modeled as an image-text retrieval task. Figure 1 shows an example supporting figure for a claim in our dataset.

Evaluation. We use standard retrieval metrics to assess model performance — normalized discounted cumulative gain (nDCG) at 5 and 10. An issue that complicates relevance computation in our case is that many figures are compound figures, with one or more sub-figures providing supporting evidence for a claim in place of the entire figure. This was especially true for biology-related claims in our dataset (see Table 2). For instance, in Figure 1, the claim is supported by sub-figure (C) but a model might produce a ranking like Figure 1, Figure 1(C). In this case, the top-ranked prediction is a parent of the gold figure, and could be considered partially correct. We tackle this by assigning a partial relevance score of 0.5 to the top-ranked figures/tables that were parent or sub-figures of a gold figure/table.

3.2 Track 2: Grounding Context Identification

Task formulation. Given a scientific claim c, and the full-text of the research paper that contains the claim, models must return a set of text snippets $S = \{s_1, ..., s_n\}$ that describe key methodological details for the experiments that provide empirical evidence supporting the claim. Therefore, this task can be modeled as query-based extractive summarization.

Evaluation. We use automated summarization evaluation metrics to assess model performance — ROUGE (Lin, 2004) and BERTScore (Zhang et al., 2020). Specifically, predicted text snippets are mapped to their best-match gold snippets based on highest ROUGE/BERT scores, which are then averaged to produce the final score.

4 Dataset Collection and Preprocessing

Our dataset curation process consists of three stages: (i) claim construction, (ii) collecting annotations for evidence and grounding context identification, and (iii) sourcing supplementary data (e.g., extracted figures/tables, paper full-texts, etc.) to ease model development for participants.

4.1 Claim Construction

The claims used in this shared task were created in the course of naturalistic synthesis work across a range of real-world research contexts listed below:

- `akamatsulab`: Literature review and research planning in a cell biology lab.
- `megacoglab`: Literature review and research planning in a human-computer interaction lab.
- `BIOL403`: Synthesis activities in a microbiology seminar.
- `social-media`: Focused interdisciplinary systematic review of effects of social media on polarization.

A total of 585 claims were created across all contexts, split into sets of 474 and 111 claims, sourced from 229 and 46 unique research papers, for training and testing respectively. The mean number of figures and tables in each paper was approximately 6 and 2, though with a considerable range (up to 24 and 18 figures per paper in train and test, and 19 and 14 tables in train and test).

4.2 Annotation Process

Track 1. The annotation process for track 1 requires identifying key figures and tables that provide supporting evidence for a claim. These figures and tables were captured as screenshots from paper PDFs, alongside figure/table numbers, using a note-taking tool called Roam Research.[2] Because all claims were created in the course of ongoing

[2] `https://roamresearch.com/`

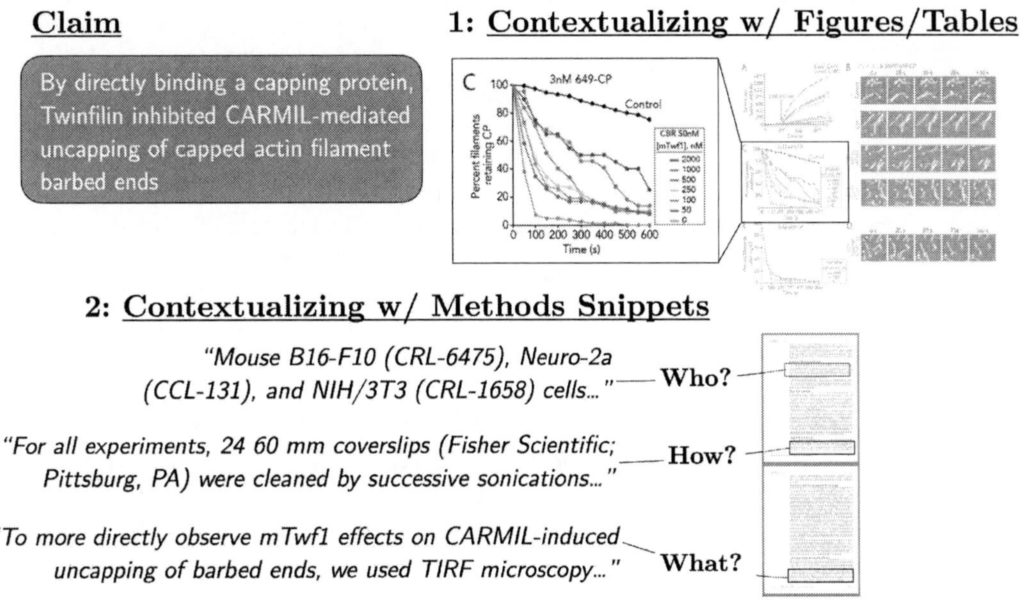

Figure 1: Example claim with figures/tables (Track 1) and methods snippets (Track 2) that contextualize the empirical evidence behind the claim. Relevant figures are often subsets of compound figures, and methods snippets are often distributed throughout source texts.

Dataset	Domain(s)	Train	Test
akamatsulab	Cell biology	213	51
BIOL403	Cell biology	60	
social-media	Social sciences (political science, economics, HCI)	78	
megacoglab	Various (HCI, psychology, economics, public health)	123	60
Total		**474**	**111**

Table 1: Number and source of scientific claims for training and test splits in Track 1.

Dataset	Figure	Table	Subfigure
Training split			
akamatsulab	205	4	165
BIOL403	60	0	49
social-media	57	26	2
megacoglab	51	89	5
Test split			
akamastulab	51	0	50
megacoglab	37	41	2

Table 2: Number of claims contextualized by figures, tables, and/or subfigures, by dataset.

synthesis work, all screenshots and labels were captured by researchers with relevant domain knowledge. To further ensure accuracy, the first and third authors, who are PIs of each research group (Chan for social-media and megacoglab; Akamatsu for akamatsulab and BIOL403) either personally captured the relevant screenshots and labels, or verified screenshots and labels captured by students or research assistants. Notes from Roam were exported to markdown and figure/table labels were parsed out using a Python script. The first author again manually verified each figure label for accuracy. These labels were collected for all 474 training claims and 111 test claims. The breakdown of the number of claims in training and test splits for track 1 across various research contexts is shown in Table 1. Also, the breakdown of type of context (figure, table, and/or subfigure) is shown in Table 2). Note that subfigures are very common n the biology-focused subset of the data, while tables as context are more common in the social-science/HCI subset o the data.

Track 2. The annotation process for track 2 requires identifying all methodological details for experiments that support a claim. Since our claims covered a range of disciplines and methodologies, including experimental studies, biological compu-

Dataset	Domain(s)	Dev	Test
akamatsulab	Cell biology	28	49
megacoglab	Various (HCI, psychology, economics, public health)	14	60
Total		**42**	**109**

Table 3: Number and source of scientific claims for dev and test splits in Track 2.

tational simulations, observational studies, and so on, we conceptualized a generalized schema for defining three aspects of methodological context that are needed to interpret and appraise the empirical evidence for a claim (see Figure 1 for examples from our data):

- **What** observable measures/data were collected
- **How** (with what methods, analyses, etc.) from
- **Who(m)** (which participants, what dataset, what population, etc.)

This annotation schema was primarily shaped by the expressed information needs of the researchers who wrote and use the claims in this dataset, and informed in part by other schemas for synthesis, such as the PICO framework for medical systematic reviews (Richardson et al., 1995), which also focus on the who (population), how (intervention and comparator), and what (outcome). While this schema enabled us to reliably identify all methodological details researchers needed across the range of disciplines and methodologies in our data, in practice it was often difficult to cleanly distinguish between some of the schema categories. For instance, in observational studies, data collection and preparation details could either be classified as *what* data were used in analysis or *how* data was obtained; this separation between data collection and analysis is somewhat cleaner in experimental studies, where there are substantially more details on procedure, materials, and design. Thus, we did not include snippet categorization into who/how/what, and only assessed model performance on snippet identification. However, we described our annotation schema to participants to clarify task requirements and provide additional motivation for modeling approaches.

All methodological details were captured as text quotes from PDFs copied into the Roam Research note-taking tool. As with figure/table snippets, the first and third authors either personally captured relevant text quotes, or verified quotes captured by students or research assistants. Due to the high labor cost of obtaining text quotes for track 2, which requires exhaustive annotation over paper full-texts, we did not annotate the entire training set of claims. Instead, we collected and released annotations for a small development set of 42 claims (out of 474), and posed this as a few-shot task. For testing, we collected annotations for 109 claims. The research context breakdown of development and test splits for track 2 are shown in Table 3.

4.3 Supplementary Data Sourcing

Extracting figures, tables and captions. Track 1, which focuses on ranking all figures and tables from a paper based on whether they provide supporting evidence for a claim, requires models to accurately extract figures and tables from paper PDFs. Our preliminary exploration showed that even state-of-the-art toolkits such as PaperMage (Lo et al., 2023) perform poorly on figure and table extraction, particularly for cell biology ($\sim$20% accuracy). This motivated us to get all figures, tables and captions manually extracted from paper PDFs and release them as supplementary data.

For this annotation process, all paper PDFs were rasterized and uploaded to the Label Studio data labeling platform. [3] Annotators then labeled all figures, tables and captions by drawing bounding boxes, annotating figures at the smallest sub-figure level. We recruited three annotators with experience in reading and writing scientific text from Upwork.[4] All annotators were trained to do the task on a small pilot set of PDFs annotated by two authors, and paid \$20-\$24 an hour. Bounding box coordinates collected via this process were used then to crop out figures, tables and captions. Sub-figures were concatenated into a compound figure since the entire figure might be labeled as supporting evidence in some instances. For example, if a Figure 1 had subfigures 1A, 1B, and 1C, we provided a compound Figure 1 besides Figure 1A, Figure 1B and Figure 1C as candidates for ranking. Lastly, we also ran optical character recognition (OCR) using the Nougat library (Blecher et al., 2023) on caption images and released caption texts.

Extracting full-texts. Track 2 requires participants to extract methodological details from paper full-texts. To make participation easier, we released

[3] https://labelstud.io/

[4] https://www.upwork.com/

parsed full-texts for all PDFs extracted using PaperMage (Lo et al., 2023). Because we could not guarantee the accuracy of section labels, the full-text parses did not have section information.

Silver data generation. Since track 2 has limited training data, we release additional unlabeled text resources to encourage exploration of weak supervision-style approaches. Specifically, we also provided full text parses for 17,007 papers from 1-2 hop in-bound and out-bound citations of the original papers present in our training data.

The training, development, and blind test data (without gold annotation) for both tracks are available on HuggingFace[5].

5 Official Results

The training data for this shared task was released on Github, alongside evaluation scripts, on April 11, 2024. The test phase was released as an open competition on Eval.Ai[6] on May 31, 2024. Participants were allowed to upload a maximum of five submissions per day during the seven-day testing phase. We received official submissions from a total of 6 teams for track 1, and 2 teams for track 2. The official results from the leaderboard, as well as the performance of some baseline systems, are shown in Tables 4 and 5 for tracks 1 and 2, respectively.

Team	nDCG@5	nDCG@10
CSIRO-LT	**0.73**	**1.06**
OSX	0.64	0.69
UW24	0.26	0.30
larch24	0.25	0.29
KISTI	0.17	0.22
SLTD	0.14	0.14
Baselines		
CC-Sim	0.28	0.36
CC-Sim (Sci)	0.29	0.36
CC-LLM-Rank	0.33	0.36
LLaVA	0.20	0.29
GPT-4o	0.64	0.68

Table 4: Official results for Track 1. For each team, we report the performance of the highest-scoring run submitted to the leaderboard

5.1 Track 1

Baseline systems. For track 1, we report the performance of the following baselines:

- **CC-Sim:** Ranking figures/tables in decreasing order of cosine similarity between the claim and figure/table caption texts embedded using MPNet (Song et al., 2020). We use the all-mpnet-base-v2 version from Sentence Transformers (Reimers and Gurevych, 2019).[7]
- **CC-Sim (Sci):** Same as above, except claim and caption texts are embedded using SPECTER (Cohan et al., 2020).
- **CC-LLM-Rank:** Prompting an LLM to rank figures/tables in decreasing order of support given a claim and figure/table caption texts. We use GPT-4-Turbo.
- **LLaVA:** Prompting a multimodal LLM to produce relevance scores given a claim and figure/table pair, which are then used for ranking. We use the llava-1.5-7b-hf version from Huggingface.
- **GPT-4o:** Same as above, except using GPT-4o.

Participant submissions. Though six teams participated, we only received reports from the top three teams: CSIRO-LT, OSX, and UW24. Interestingly, all three adopted different approaches to the task. Team OSX opted for the most straightforward approach of prompting multimodal LLMs, but explored sophisticated prompting strategies such as chain-of-thought prompting, multiple retries, etc., which significantly boosted their performance. Team UW24 focused on data augmentation and leveraged datasets for related tasks like scientific image captioning to train a better scientific image-text similarity model, but this technique was less successful. Lastly, CSIRO-LT had the most complicated system design consisting of an ensemble of retrieval approaches, which differed in retrieval strategy used (BM25, embeddings, etc.) and how text *documents* representing figures/tables are constructed (LLM-based descriptions, captions, etc.). Consistent with the findings of other teams, they also observed that their text-based systems outperformed all approaches that tried to train an image-text similarity model.

The top-performing team (CSIRO-LT) achieved nDCG@5 = 0.73 and nDCG@10 = 1.06. Note that

[5]https://huggingface.co/datasets/joelchan/contextualizing-scientific-claims

[6]https://eval.ai/web/challenges/challenge-page/2306/overview

[7]https://sbert.net/docs/sentence_transformer/pretrained_models.html

Team	BERTScore	ROUGE-1	ROUGE-2	ROUGE-L
CSIRO-LT	**0.87**	**0.35**	**0.18**	**0.27**
OSX	0.86	0.32	0.17	0.26
Baselines				
GPT-4	0.70	0.28	0.16	0.22
Mixtral-8x22B	0.80	0.29	0.14	0.23

Table 5: Official results for Track 2. For each team, we report the performance of the highest-scoring run submitted to the leaderboard

our partial relevance score modification can sometimes lead to nDCG scores > 1 if both the correct sub-figures as well as parent figures are present in the top ranked predictions. With the exception of the top two teams, all others had worse results than our weakest baseline, indicating the difficulty of this task. On the other hand, GPT-4o achieves very strong performance with our simple zero-shot baseline prompting strategy, almost matching the performance of the team ranked second, indicating that closed LLMs are now improving the tractability of this task.

5.2 Track 2

Baseline systems. For track 2, we report the performance of the following baselines:

- **GPT-4:** Prompting an LLM to return all relevant quotes about methodological details given a claim and the paper full-text. We use GPT-4-Turbo.
- **Mixtral-8x22B:** Same as above with an open LLM, we use Mixtral-8x22B-Instruct-v0.1 owing to its large context length which can ingest full-texts.

Participant submissions. Only CSIRO-LT and OSX participated in track 2, with OSX continuing to rely on prompting LLMs. CSIRO-LT again leveraged retrieval approaches, additionally exploring rule-based and LLM-based postprocessing of retrieved snippets to further push performance.

For track 2, both participating teams had very close scores, improving moderately over our baselines. We note here that the BERTScores were in general substantially higher than the ROUGE scores. Interestingly, we observed that Mixtral achieved slightly better performance than GPT-4 indicating that this task is tractable for SOTA open LLMs too (unlike track 1 where LLaVA significantly underperformed GPT-4o).

6 Discussion and Future Directions

Overall, our baseline experiments and participant submissions for both shared task tracks demonstrate that the problem of contextualizing scientific claims is still challenging but starting to become tractable. For instance, baseline performance was quite low, but two teams were able to substantially outperform these baselines while still leaving some room for improvement. Our experiences constructing the dataset, and reflections on participants' technical reports, also suggest fruitful future directions.

Better image-text similarity models. Contrastively trained image-text similarity models like CLIP could be beneficial for our task since they can adapt to other scientific domains with little training data (necessary for real-world use given high costs of collecting annotated data). However, a common theme across participants' reports was that using image-text similarity models did not perform well compared to relying entirely on text or prompting multimodal LLMs. Exploring why models like CLIP do not work well on our task and how to improve them could lead to stronger models for our task, as well as advancements in image-text representation learning. One potential direction may be to explore augmentation of figures with textual mentions (Yang et al., 2023).

PDF pre-processing. An ideal system for contextualizing scientific claims would be able to operate end-to-end from research paper PDFs. However, state-of-the-art PDF preprocessing toolkits (e.g., PaperMage (Lo et al., 2023)) were not able to extract figures/tables with sufficient accuracy, particularly for some domains like biology papers; thus, to make this shared task tractable, we provided manually extracted figures/tables/captions to participants. This suggests that further work is needed to improve PDF preprocessing tasks such as structured content extraction (Shen et al., 2022; Lo et al., 2023), or converting PDFs to more accessible HTML (Wang et al., 2021), which could enable development of better end-to-end contextualization methods, especially across scientific domains.

Evaluation metrics for context identification. Finally, from an evaluation perspective, we suggest that better evaluation metrics may be needed for assessing the extraction of methodological details as context for claims. Similar to other summarization tasks, in our setting, methodological details can be presented at multiple points in a paper, and models might choose different snippet(s) expressing the same information. Our choice of BERTScore as a complement to ROUGE partially mitigated this issue: however, this approach may overestimate performance since it relies on overall text similarity rather than assessing whether all relevant facts are retrieved. Thus, better automated evaluation for this subtask is still an open problem. Future work could explore adapting factuality-style evaluations, such as extracting atomic facts from gold snippets and measuring whether they are covered/supported by model-retrieved snippets (Min et al., 2023) or explore model-based evaluation using LLMs as judges (Bubeck et al., 2023).

7 Conclusion

In this paper, we described a new dataset and results from a shared task for contextualizing scientific claims with empirical evidence and methodological details. Our dataset consists of 585 scientific claims with gold annotations for figures and tables, and gold text snippets of methodological details, that ground the key results behind each claim. Experiments with text embedding and (multimodal) LLM-based baselines demonstrate the challenging nature of the task. Performance gains over these baselines from official submissions to the Shared Task for this dataset at SDP 2024 show the tractability of the task, and reveal promising directions for future work, such as improving image-text similarity models, PDF-processing, and automated evaluation metrics for context identification.

Acknowledgements

The authors would like to thank William Ammon, Anthea Weng, and Nessma Hassan for their help with figure, table and caption annotation, Kyle Lo and Joseph Chee Chang for their assistance with PaperMage and Gunjan Chhablani for supporting our Eval.Ai platform setup during the testing phase.

References

Lukas Blecher, Guillem Cucurull, Thomas Scialom, and Robert Stojnic. 2023. Nougat: Neural Optical Understanding for Academic Documents. *arXiv preprint*. ArXiv:2308.13418 [cs].

Sébastien Bubeck, Varun Chandrasekaran, Ronen Eldan, Johannes Gehrke, Eric Horvitz, Ece Kamar, Peter Lee, Yin Tat Lee, Yuanzhi Li, Scott Lundberg, et al. 2023. Sparks of artificial general intelligence: Early experiments with gpt-4. *arXiv preprint arXiv:2303.12712*.

Sanjana Shivani Chintalapati, Jonathan Bragg, and Lucy Lu Wang. 2022. A Dataset of Alt Texts from HCI Publications: Analyses and Uses Towards Producing More Descriptive Alt Texts of Data Visualizations in Scientific Papers. In *Proceedings of the 24th International ACM SIGACCESS Conference on Computers and Accessibility*, ASSETS '22, pages 1–12, New York, NY, USA. Association for Computing Machinery.

Arman Cohan, Sergey Feldman, Iz Beltagy, Doug Downey, and Daniel Weld. 2020. SPECTER: Document-level representation learning using citation-informed transformers. In *Proceedings of the 58th Annual Meeting of the Association for Computational Linguistics*, pages 2270–2282, Online. Association for Computational Linguistics.

Pradeep Dasigi, Kyle Lo, Iz Beltagy, Arman Cohan, Noah A. Smith, and Matt Gardner. 2021. A Dataset of Information-Seeking Questions and Answers Anchored in Research Papers. In *Proceedings of the 2021 Conference of the North American Chapter of the Association for Computational Linguistics: Human Language Technologies*, pages 4599–4610, Online. Association for Computational Linguistics. 00002.

Anne-Wil K. Harzing. 1995. The persistent myth of high expatriate failure rates. *The International Journal of Human Resource Management*, 6(2):457–474. Publisher: Routledge _eprint: https://doi.org/10.1080/09585199500000028.

Ting-Yao Hsu, C Lee Giles, and Ting-Hao Huang. 2021. SciCap: Generating Captions for Scientific Figures. In *Findings of the Association for Computational Linguistics: EMNLP 2021*, pages 3258–3264, Punta Cana, Dominican Republic. Association for Computational Linguistics.

Yan Hu, Vipina K Keloth, Kalpana Raja, Yong Chen, and Hua Xu. 2023. Towards precise PICO extraction from abstracts of randomized controlled trials using a section-specific learning approach. *Bioinformatics*, 39(9):btad542.

Sarthak Jain, Madeleine van Zuylen, Hannaneh Hajishirzi, and Iz Beltagy. 2020. SciREX: A challenge dataset for document-level information extraction. In *Proceedings of the 58th Annual Meeting of the Association for Computational Linguistics*, pages 7506–7516, Online. Association for Computational Linguistics.

Di Jin and Peter Szolovits. 2018. PICO Element Detection in Medical Text via Long Short-Term Memory Neural Networks. In *Proceedings of the BioNLP 2018 workshop*, pages 67–75, Melbourne, Australia. Association for Computational Linguistics.

Lei Li, Yuqi Wang, Runxin Xu, Peiyi Wang, Xiachong Feng, Lingpeng Kong, and Qi Liu. 2024. Multimodal ArXiv: A Dataset for Improving Scientific Comprehension of Large Vision-Language Models. *arXiv preprint*. ArXiv:2403.00231 [cs].

Chin-Yew Lin. 2004. ROUGE: A package for automatic evaluation of summaries. In *Text Summarization Branches Out*, pages 74–81, Barcelona, Spain. Association for Computational Linguistics.

Weixiong Lin, Ziheng Zhao, Xiaoman Zhang, Chaoyi Wu, Ya Zhang, Yanfeng Wang, and Weidi Xie. 2023. PMC-CLIP: Contrastive Language-Image Pre-training using Biomedical Documents. *arXiv preprint*. ArXiv:2303.07240 [cs] version: 1.

Kyle Lo, Zejiang Shen, Benjamin Newman, Joseph Chang, Russell Authur, Erin Bransom, Stefan Candra, Yoganand Chandrasekhar, Regan Huff, Bailey Kuehl, Amanpreet Singh, Chris Wilhelm, Angele Zamarron, Marti A. Hearst, Daniel Weld, Doug Downey, and Luca Soldaini. 2023. PaperMage: A Unified Toolkit for Processing, Representing, and Manipulating Visually-Rich Scientific Documents. In *Proceedings of the 2023 Conference on Empirical Methods in Natural Language Processing: System Demonstrations*, pages 495–507, Singapore. Association for Computational Linguistics.

Xinyuan Lu, Liangming Pan, Qian Liu, Preslav Nakov, and Min-Yen Kan. 2023. SCITAB: A Challenging Benchmark for Compositional Reasoning and Claim Verification on Scientific Tables. In *Proceedings of the 2023 Conference on Empirical Methods in Natural Language Processing*, pages 7787–7813, Singapore. Association for Computational Linguistics.

Sewon Min, Kalpesh Krishna, Xinxi Lyu, Mike Lewis, Wen-tau Yih, Pang Koh, Mohit Iyyer, Luke Zettlemoyer, and Hannaneh Hajishirzi. 2023. FActScore: Fine-grained atomic evaluation of factual precision in long form text generation. In *Proceedings of the 2023 Conference on Empirical Methods in Natural Language Processing*, pages 12076–12100, Singapore. Association for Computational Linguistics.

Aakanksha Naik, Bailey Kuehl, Erin Bransom, Doug Downey, and Tom Hope. 2024. CARE: Extracting experimental findings from clinical literature. In *Findings of the Association for Computational Linguistics: NAACL 2024*, pages 4580–4596, Mexico City, Mexico. Association for Computational Linguistics.

Benjamin Nye, Junyi Jessy Li, Roma Patel, Yinfei Yang, Iain Marshall, Ani Nenkova, and Byron Wallace. 2018. A Corpus with Multi-Level Annotations of Patients, Interventions and Outcomes to Support Language Processing for Medical Literature. In *Proceedings of the 56th Annual Meeting of the Association for Computational Linguistics (Volume 1: Long Papers)*, pages 197–207, Melbourne, Australia. Association for Computational Linguistics.

Nils Reimers and Iryna Gurevych. 2019. Sentence-bert: Sentence embeddings using siamese bert-networks. In *Proceedings of the 2019 Conference on Empirical Methods in Natural Language Processing*. Association for Computational Linguistics.

W Scott Richardson, Mark C Wilson, Jim Nishikawa, and Robert S Hayward. 1995. The well-built clinical question: a key to evidence-based decisions. *ACP journal club*, 123(3):A12–3.

Arkadiy Saakyan, Tuhin Chakrabarty, and Smaranda Muresan. 2021. COVID-Fact: Fact Extraction and Verification of Real-World Claims on COVID-19 Pandemic. In *Proceedings of the 59th Annual Meeting of the Association for Computational Linguistics and the 11th International Joint Conference on Natural Language Processing (Volume 1: Long Papers)*, pages 2116–2129, Online. Association for Computational Linguistics. 00015.

Mourad Sarrouti, Asma Ben Abacha, Yassine Mrabet, and Dina Demner-Fushman. 2021. Evidence-based Fact-Checking of Health-related Claims. In *Findings of the Association for Computational Linguistics: EMNLP 2021*, pages 3499–3512, Punta Cana, Dominican Republic. Association for Computational Linguistics.

Lena Schmidt, Ailbhe N. Finnerty Mutlu, Rebecca Elmore, Babatunde K. Olorisade, James Thomas, and Julian P. T. Higgins. 2023. Data extraction methods for systematic review (semi)automation: Update of a living systematic review. *F1000Research*, 10:401.

Zejiang Shen, Kyle Lo, Lucy Lu Wang, Bailey Kuehl, Daniel S. Weld, and Doug Downey. 2022. VILA: Improving Structured Content Extraction from Scientific PDFs Using Visual Layout Groups. *Transactions of the Association for Computational Linguistics*, 10:376–392.

Kaitao Song, Xu Tan, Tao Qin, Jianfeng Lu, and Tie-Yan Liu. 2020. Mpnet: Masked and permuted pre-training for language understanding. *Advances in neural information processing systems*, 33:16857–16867.

Sanjay Subramanian, Lucy Lu Wang, Ben Bogin, Sachin Mehta, Madeleine van Zuylen, Sravanthi Parasa, Sameer Singh, Matt Gardner, and Hannaneh Hajishirzi. 2020. MedICaT: A Dataset of Medical

Images, Captions, and Textual References. In *Findings of the Association for Computational Linguistics: EMNLP 2020*, pages 2112–2120, Online. Association for Computational Linguistics.

Tim Tarsi, Heike Adel, Jan Hendrik Metzen, Dan Zhang, Matteo Finco, and Annemarie Friedrich. 2024. SciOL and MuLMS-Img: Introducing A Large-Scale Multimodal Scientific Dataset and Models for Image-Text Tasks in the Scientific Domain. In *2024 IEEE/CVF Winter Conference on Applications of Computer Vision (WACV)*, pages 4548–4559, Waikoloa, HI, USA. IEEE.

Juraj Vladika and Florian Matthes. 2023. Scientific Fact-Checking: A Survey of Resources and Approaches. In *Findings of the Association for Computational Linguistics: ACL 2023*, pages 6215–6230, Toronto, Canada. Association for Computational Linguistics.

David Wadden, Shanchuan Lin, Kyle Lo, Lucy Lu Wang, Madeleine van Zuylen, Arman Cohan, and Hannaneh Hajishirzi. 2020. Fact or Fiction: Verifying Scientific Claims. In *Proceedings of the 2020 Conference on Empirical Methods in Natural Language Processing (EMNLP)*, pages 7534–7550, Online. Association for Computational Linguistics. 00092.

David Wadden, Kyle Lo, Bailey Kuehl, Arman Cohan, Iz Beltagy, Lucy Lu Wang, and Hannaneh Hajishirzi. 2022. SciFact-Open: Towards open-domain scientific claim verification. In *Findings of the Association for Computational Linguistics: EMNLP 2022*, pages 4719–4734, Abu Dhabi, United Arab Emirates. Association for Computational Linguistics.

Lucy Lu Wang, Isabel Cachola, Jonathan Bragg, Evie Yu-Yen Cheng, Chelsea Haupt, Matt Latzke, Bailey Kuehl, Madeleine N van Zuylen, Linda Wagner, and Daniel Weld. 2021. Scia11y: Converting scientific papers to accessible html. In *Proceedings of the 23rd International ACM SIGACCESS Conference on Computers and Accessibility*, pages 1–4.

Zhishen Yang, Raj Dabre, Hideki Tanaka, and Naoaki Okazaki. 2023. SciCap+: A Knowledge Augmented Dataset to Study the Challenges of Scientific Figure Captioning. *arXiv preprint*. ArXiv:2306.03491 [cs].

Tianyi Zhang, Varsha Kishore, Felix Wu, Kilian Q Weinberger, and Yoav Artzi. 2020. Bertscore: Evaluating text generation with bert. In *International Conference on Learning Representations*.

Controllable Citation Sentence Generation with Language Models

Nianlong Gu
Linguistic Research Infrastructure,
University of Zurich
nianlong.gu@uzh.ch

Richard H.R. Hahnloser
Institute of Neuroinformatics,
University of Zurich and ETH Zurich
rich@ini.ethz.ch

Abstract

Citation generation aims to generate a citation sentence that refers to a chosen paper in the context of a manuscript. However, a rigid citation generation process is at odds with an author's desire to control specific attributes, such as 1) the citation intent, e.g., either introducing background information or comparing results, and 2) keywords that should appear in the citation text. To provide these degrees of controllability during citation generation, we propose to integrate the manuscript context, the context of the referenced paper, and the desired control attributes into a structured template and use it to fine-tune a language model (LM) via next-token prediction. We then utilize Proximal Policy Optimization to directly optimize the LM in favor of a high score of our proposed controllability metric. The proposed workflow harmoniously combines citation attribute suggestion and conditional citation generation into one LM, allowing for better user control. [1]

1 Introduction

A common practice in scientific writing is to cite and discuss relevant papers that support an argument, provide background information, or compare results (Penders, 2018). Recent studies aim to facilitate this citation process by using neural networks to generate a citation sentence based on the context of the manuscript and the paper to be cited. These efforts focused primarily on developing a sequence-to-sequence pipeline that works in a fully automated, uncontrolled manner, leaving little room for users to control the generation process. We believe control is desirable because authors often have a clear motivation before writing a citation sentence. For example, they may have a specific *intent* to cite, such as comparing results or presenting background information, or they may have *keywords* in mind to appear in the citation sentence. When the generated citation does not match an author's motivation, the author may wish to change the generation by specifying certain attributes, such as citation intent or keywords.

This study aims to develop a citation generation model that is controllable, such that users can alter the citation intent or topic by explicitly providing the citation intent and keywords. Our proposed method involves the following two phases:

Supervised fine-tuning. We design a structured prompt template that systematically and consecutively incorporates contextual information, citation attributes (intent and keywords), and the citation sentence into a sequence of tokens, and fine-tune an LM via next-token prediction. Through supervised fine-tuning, the LM learns to generate citation sentences not only based on the manuscript/cited paper's context but also conditioned on the citation attributes, thus allowing flexible control of generation by altering the citation attributes (Keskar et al., 2019).

Controllability enhancement via reinforcement learning. We propose measuring the controllability of a citation generation system from multiple aspects with the following metrics: i. Intent Alignment Score (IAS), which measures whether the intent of the generated citation sentence matches the given control intent; ii. Keyword Recall (KR), which measures the recall of the control keywords in the generated citation; iii. Fluency Score (FS); and iv. ROUGE-F1 (Lin, 2004) score of the generated sentence compared with the groud-truth citation. These controllability evaluation metrics provide a further opportunity to guide the training of our system by using them to estimate a reward function for Proximal Policy Optimization (PPO) (Schulman et al., 2017). This allows us to explore the effect of using feedback from our chosen metrics to improve our system's controllability.

Our contributions are summarized as follows:

- We present a novel strategy that unifies cita-

[1] Our code and data are available at https://github.com/nianlonggu/LMCiteGen

Proceedings of the Fourth Workshop on Scholarly Document Processing (SDP 2024), pages 22–37
August 16, 2024 ©2024 Association for Computational Linguistics

tion attributes and citation sentence generation within one language model, thereby enabling user control of the citation generation process.

- We evaluate the control exerted by the various attributes, employing a multi-metric system that includes an intent matching score, keyword recall, ROUGE score, and a referenceless fluency score, and we use these controllability metrics as a reward for Proximal Policy Optimization (PPO) to effectively improve the controllability of our model following its initial supervised training.

- We curate a comprehensive dataset, parsing both contextual text and citation attributes, to offer a valuable resource for future controllable citation generation research.

2 Related Work

Previous work in citation generation, including Xing et al. (2020); Ge et al. (2021); Wang et al. (2022), approached the task as a sequence-to-sequence translation problem, utilizing recurrent networks and knowledge graph enhancements. Nikiforovskaya et al. (2020) proposed a BERT-based extractive summarizer (Liu, 2019) that produces a paper review by extracting one sentence from each of the related papers. Chen and Zhuge (2019) proposed automatically generating a related work section by extracting information on how papers in the reference list have been cited in previous articles. Xing et al. (2020) developed an RNN-based pointer generator network that can copy words from the manuscript and the abstract of the cited paper based on cross-attention. Ge et al. (2021) further extended this work by enhancing citation generation using information from the citation graph. Despite their advances, these approaches do not fully address the complexities of citation sentence generation. Our research highlights the importance of user-specified attributes and illustrates the limitations of large language models in reliably inferring key attributes such as topic keywords. We propose that this semantic gap necessitates a shift towards models that take explicit user control into account in citation generation.

Recent research Jung et al. (2022); Wu et al. (2021); Yu et al. (2022) has also explored controlled citation generation, though the focus is often limited to controlling a single attribute like citation intent. Our work extends this concept to a broader range of attributes, introducing methods to suggest potential attributes and balance the automation and controllability of citation generation. We further differentiate our research by conducting extensive experiments with cutting-edge language models and investigating the augmentation of controllability via reinforcement learning, contributing to a more comprehensive understanding of controlled citation generation. In addition, we go beyond prompt-based approaches (Yang et al., 2022) by investigating enhancing the controllability of our citation generation system with reinforcement learning.

3 Method

We first describe our supervised method for fine-tuning an LM, and then we describe how we measure the control of the generated sentence by the attributes. Finally, we introduce strategies for enhancing controllability through reinforcement learning. Our method is illustrated in Figure 1.

3.1 LM Supervised Fine-tuning

We fine-tune a language model (LM) to generate a citation sentence $\mathcal{S}$ given the context $\mathcal{C}$ and citation (control) attributes $\mathcal{A}$. The context, denoted as $\mathcal{C}$, consists of information from three distinct sources: 1) the local manuscript context, including up to N_s sentences from the same section (we use $N_s = 5$) that precede the citation sentence to be generated; 2) the manuscript's title and abstract, serving as the global context; and 3) the title and abstract of the paper to be cited, providing an external context.

The citation attributes denoted $\mathcal{A}$, include the combined citation intent and keywords. Following the framework proposed in Cohan et al. (2019), we define three categories of citation intents: 1) *background*: The citation offers context or background information about a pertinent problem, concept, method, or topic. 2) *method*: The citation refers to a specific method, tool, approach, or dataset in the cited paper. 3) *result*: The citation contrasts or compares the results or findings of the manuscript with those in the referenced paper. In terms of keywords, we define keyword attributes as one or two noun phrases extracted from the target citation sentence that bears semantic similarity to the context of either the manuscript or the cited paper.

The training objective is to optimize the LM to maximize the log-likelihood of generating both the citation attributes $\mathcal{A}$ and the citation sentence $\mathcal{S}$

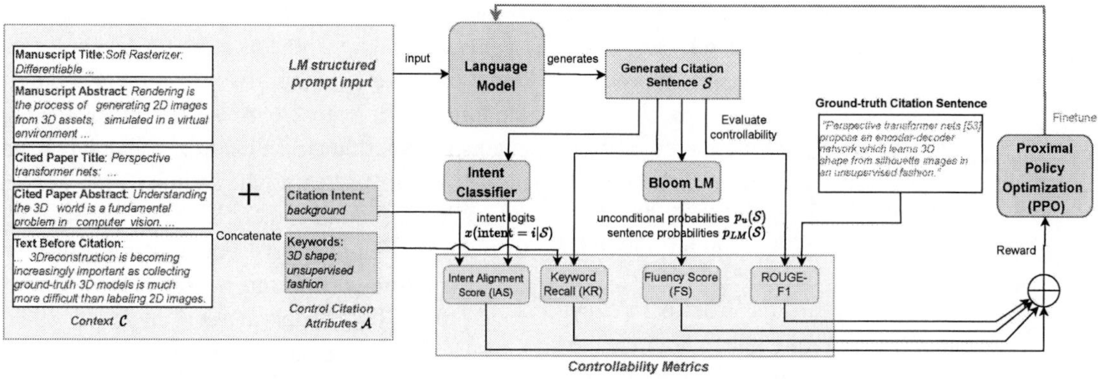

Figure 1: A schematic representation of the workflow for generating citation sentences using a Language Model, with subsequent controllability evaluation, and optimization using Proximal Policy Optimization (PPO) with the summed controllability metrics as a reward.

given the context $\mathcal{C}$. Let a_i and s_i be the tokens in $\mathcal{A}$ and $\mathcal{S}$, with total tokens $|A|$ and $|S|$ respectively, the training objective can be expressed as:

$$
\begin{aligned}
\hat{\theta} &= \arg\max_{\theta} \log p(\mathcal{S}, \mathcal{A}|\mathcal{C}) \\
&= \arg\max_{\theta} [\log p(\mathcal{A}|\mathcal{C}) + \log p(\mathcal{S}|\mathcal{A}, \mathcal{C})] \\
&= \arg\max_{\theta} \Bigg[\sum_{i=1}^{|\mathcal{A}|} \log p(a_i|a_1 \dots a_{i-1}, \mathcal{C}) + \\
&\qquad \sum_{i=1}^{|\mathcal{S}|} \log p(s_i|s_1 \dots s_{i-1}, \mathcal{A}, \mathcal{C}) \Bigg]
\end{aligned} \tag{1}
$$

Such an objective allows us to fine-tune a single LM for two purposes: 1) inferring citation attributes $\mathcal{A}$ given the context $\mathcal{C}$, and 2) crafting citation sentences $\mathcal{S}$ based on the context $\mathcal{C}$ and control attributes $\mathcal{A}$. This dual-purpose training strategy enables the fine-tuned LM to switch dynamically between controlled and uncontrolled modes: In the **controlled mode**, the LM assimilates the context and the user-specified control attributes to generate the citation sentence. In the **uncontrolled mode**, the LM initiates by automatically inferring possible citation attributes based solely on the context, and uses these inferred attributes to guide itself when generating the citation sentence. This flexibility also allows us to compare the performance of our citation generation model between uncontrolled and controlled modes in a fair manner, since we can compare the performance on the same model just with different working modes.

Structured Input Template for Supervised Fine-tuning. We design an input template to help the LM differentiate between input sources. The template arranges different input components into a unique prompt, including the cited paper's global context, the manuscript's local and global contexts, and the citation attributes, as in Raffel et al. (2020); Keskar et al. (2019); Taori et al. (2023). The final input text is structured as follows:

```
###Manuscript Title: XXX XXX
###Manuscript Abstract: XXX XXX
###Cited Paper Title: XXX XXX
###Cited Paper Abstract: XXX XXX
###Text Before Citation:
        XXX XXX (manuscript local context)
###Citation Intent: XXX (one word from
'background', 'method' and 'result')
###Keywords: XXX; XXX (keywords relevant to
the citation, separated by '; ')
###Citation: XXX XXX (target citation sentence)
```

For decoder-only LMs like GPT-NEO (Black et al., 2021), the fine-tuning phase uses the generated prompt as input for next-token prediction, masking context-related tokens (from "`###Manuscript Title: XXX`" to "`###Text Before Citation: XXX`") to confine prediction loss within citation attributes $\mathcal{A}$ and citation sentence $\mathcal{S}$, as per Equation (1). In the inference stage, the LM is fed with the template up to "`###Citation Intent:`", "`###Keywords:`", and "`###Citation:`" when the task is to decode the citation intent, keywords, and the citation sentence, respectively. In contrast, for encoder-decoder LMs like BART (Lewis et al., 2020), context-related tokens are the encoder input during both fine-tuning and inference. During fine-tuning, the LM learns to decode tokens within $\mathcal{A}$ and $\mathcal{S}$. At inference, the decoder generates citation attributes and sentences based on the provided prompt.

3.2 Controllability Evaluation Metrics

We deem good controllability by control attributes can be reflected in the following aspects:

1. The generated citation sentence matches the given intent. For example, given a control intent "background", the model will generate a sentence that introduces the background of the cited paper.
2. The generated citation sentence contains the given control keywords.
3. The generated sentence is fluent so that the control keywords are embedded into the sentence in a logically coherent way.
4. The generated sentence is content-wise related to the cited paper and fits well with the context of the manuscript.

Along this vein, apart from the human evaluation (Section 6.4), we propose the following four automatic metrics, each corresponding to one aspect:

1. **Intent Alignment Score (IAS)** evaluates the alignment between the generated citation sentence and the specified citation intent. Suppose the control intent is i (one of three possible intents: '*background*', '*method*', and '*result*') and LM generates a citation sentence $\mathcal{S}$, we use SciBERT (Beltagy et al., 2019) to process the citation sentence (preceded by a "[CLS]" token) and compute the last hidden state of "[CLS]", which we input to the intent scoring head, a fully connected two-layer network to yields the intent logits $x(\text{intent} = i|\mathcal{S})$ for three possible intents. The intent alignment score IAS($\mathcal{S}$) is given by the probability of the intent i by applying softmax to the logits:

$$\text{IAS}(\mathcal{S}) = \frac{\exp\left(x(\text{intent} = i|\mathcal{S})\right)}{\sum_{k \in \text{all intents}} \exp\left(x(\text{intent} = k|\mathcal{S})\right)} \tag{2}$$

The intent scorer is trained using the SciCite dataset (Cohan et al., 2019) containing human-annotated intents. Details on training and evaluating are further described in Appendix A.

2. **Keyword Recall (KR)** is a metric that assesses the presence of provided keywords in the generated citation sentence. A higher value signifies that the generated sentence includes the given keywords, indicating good control over keyword incorporation. Given a generated citation sentence $\mathcal{S}$, the keyword recall KR($\mathcal{S}$) is calculated using ROUGE-L recall to compare the keyword attribute (or a concatenated string of multiple keywords, if applicable) with $\mathcal{S}$.

3. **Fluency Score (FS)** evaluates the fluency of the generated citation sentence $\mathcal{S}$. In addition to keyword recall, the fluency metric ensures that the citation generator incorporates the keyword attributes naturally and logically without compromising fluency. Drawing inspiration from Kann et al. (2018), we employ SLOR, a language model-based fluency metric, and we normalize this score using a sigmoid function. FS($\mathcal{S}$) is calculated as follows:

$$\begin{aligned} \text{FS}(\mathcal{S}) &= \frac{1}{1 + e^{-(\text{SLOR}(\mathcal{S}) - \eta)}} \\ \text{SLOR}(\mathcal{S}) &= \frac{1}{|\mathcal{S}|}(\log(p_{LM}(\mathcal{S})) - \log(p_u(\mathcal{S}))) \end{aligned} \tag{3}$$

In this equation, $|\mathcal{S}|$ denotes the number of tokens in sentence $\mathcal{S}$, $p_{LM}(\mathcal{S})$ represents the probability of generating the sentence with a pre-trained language model, and $p_u(\mathcal{S})$ is the product of the unconditional probabilities of all tokens in the sentence. The unconditional probability of a token refers to the probability of that token being generated as the first token in a sentence. As SLOR($\mathcal{S}$) does not naturally range between [0,1], we apply an offset η and a sigmoid function to normalize the score. The offset η is introduced to the SLOR scores before sigmoid normalization, allowing greater distinguishability between fluency scores for fluent and less fluent sentences. We set the offset η to 4 based on empirical observations. We utilize the 560m-Bloom (Scao et al., 2023) language model to calculate the SLOR because its expansive vocabulary of 250k tokens helps to avoid over-segmenting words into subtokens.

4. **ROUGE-F1** measures the textual alignment between the generated citation sentence and the ground truth. A high score is desired, as it implies that the produced sentence is informative and contextually fitting. We used ROUGE-1,2,L F1 scores also to validate the effectiveness of citation attributes in controlling generation.

3.3 Controllability Enhancement via PPO

To enhance the controllability of our citation generator, we opted for Proximal Policy Optimization (PPO) (Schulman et al., 2017; Ramamurthy et al., 2023) due to its capability to use controllability metrics (IAS, KR, FS, ROUGE) as rewards, facilitating a direct optimization of the LM. While cross-entropy loss during supervised fine-tuning does provide some controllability, it does not consistently ensure that specific controllability criteria are satisfied. To illustrate, consider the ground-truth sentence centered on keywords "**L1; sparse parameters**": "*L1 regularization leads to sparse parameters after training.*" Two possible generated sentences are:

A. "*L1 optimization leads to dense parameters after training.*" and

B. "*We show that L1 regularization results in sparse parameters in the model's learned weights.*"

Despite sentence A seemingly being favored by cross-entropy loss, it misinterprets the keyword "sparse" and thus alters the sentence's meaning completely. Conversely, sentence B aptly captures the essence, emphasizing keyword recall. This underscores the limitation of relying solely on cross-entropy for optimal controllability. PPO's adaptability, allowing for controllability metrics as rewards, ensures the language model's outputs are both accurate and controllable, offering a more nuanced and flexible optimization strategy than other prevalent methods like adjusting beam search or 'bag of words' techniques (Pascual et al., 2020; Dathathri et al., 2020).

We used the parameters of the supervised fine-tuned model to initialize the LM. During the PPO training process, given the context and citation attributes used as input, the LM generated a batch of citation sentences, which we refer to as "episodes". These episodes were evaluated using the reward:

$$R = \frac{1}{4}\Big(\text{IAS}(\mathcal{S}) + \text{KR}(\mathcal{S}) + \text{FS}(\mathcal{S}) + \text{RS}(\mathcal{S})\Big), \quad (4)$$

where $\text{RS}(\mathcal{S})$ is the sum of ROUGE-1/2/L F1 scores, allowing its magnitude to be comparable with the other metrics. Importance sampling was used during the optimization step, with mini-batches of episodes sampled along with their associated rewards, to estimate the expected return under the new policy using data collected with the old policy, aiming to minimize divergence from the previous policy while improving the expected return. We implemented the PPO training using the Transformer Reinforcement Learning (TRL) framework (von Werra et al., 2020).

Information	Training	Validation	Test
# samples	233,616	1,299	1,080
# citing papers	120,425	1,175	1,005
# cited papers	69,664	998	846

Table 1: The statistics of our dataset.

4 Dataset

From a subset of arXiv computer science papers, we extracted triplets consisting of the citing paper (treated as the manuscript), the citation sentence within it, and the corresponding cited paper. The necessary components for the input context, including the local and global contexts of the manuscript, as well as the global context of the cited paper, were then extracted from these triplets.

Regarding the citation attributes, we used the SciBERT-based intent scorer, as outlined in Section 3.2, to predict the most probable citation intent for each citation sentence. To obtain the keywords attribute, we extracted noun phrases from each citation sentence and ranked them based on the cosine similarity between the keyword's Sentence-BERT (version "all-mpnet-base-v2", Apache License 2.0) (Reimers and Gurevych, 2019) embeddings and the embeddings of both the manuscript and the cited paper. This approach allowed us to retrieve up to two keywords per citation sentence.

To create the training, validation, and test sets, we used a chronological split. All the citing papers used in the training set were published before March 1st, 2023, while those in the validation and test sets were published after this date. This strategy prevents any unfair advantage for the tested language models (Section 5) by ensuring they have not previously encountered the same papers and their associated citation sentences in the validation and test sets during pretraining. The statistics of our dataset are shown in Table 1.

5 Experiment

We experimented with the encoder-decoder model BART (Lewis et al., 2020) and decoder-only models including GPT-Neo (Black et al., 2021), Galactica (Taylor et al., 2022), and LLaMa (Touvron et al., 2023), which varied in size from 125M to 7B parameters. All models were pretrained with corpora before March 1st, 2023. During supervised fine-tuning, the smaller models (125M to 1.3B parameters) were fine-tuned in float16 precision with a learning rate of 1e-5. For larger models like Galactica-6.7B and LLaMa-7B, we utilized INT4 low-precision quantization (Dettmers et al., 2023) and Low-Rank Adaptation (LoRA) (Hu et al., 2021) to reduce the GPU memory footprint. We set the LoRA parameters with the rank $r = 16$ and the scaling factor $\alpha = 32$. For these larger models, we used a higher learning rate of 1e-4, in line with the guidance from Taori et al. (2023); von Werra et al. (2020). All models were optimized with the AdamW optimizer, using default betas (0.9, 0.999), weight decay 0.05, and cosine learning rate decay. Models were fine-tuned for 5k steps with a batch size of 128 with a maximum token length of 1024. We selected the best model checkpoint based on the validation set loss every 1k steps.

To enhance controllability, we subjected Galactica and LLaMa to additional fine-tuning using Proximal Policy Optimization (PPO), as described in Section 3.3. During this process, the language models generated batches of citation sentences (termed 'episodes') for subsequent mini-batch-wise backpropagation. We set the learning rate to 1.41e-5 for all PPO fine-tuning. The PPO-finetuned models are named Galactica-125M-PPO, Galactica-6.7B-PPO, and LLaMa-7B-PPO, respectively (Table 3). More PPO hyperparameter details and hardware requirements are described in Appendix B.

In addition to fine-tuning models, we leveraged GPT-3.5-turbo-0301[2], the backbone of ChatGPT, through prompt engineering. The aim was to compare our fine-tuned models' performance against a large language model with carefully crafted prompts. We designed specific prompts (detailed in Appendix C) for the ChatGPT API to generate citation sentences. We conducted this in controlled (providing context and citation attributes) and uncontrolled (providing only context) modes.

6 Results and Discussion

We aimed to investigate several key questions: 1) whether and to what extent controllability offers advantages in citation generation, 2) whether PPO helps to improve controllability, and 3) how the model size and the nature of pretraining tasks influence overall performance. In addition, we conducted a human evaluation to compare the controllability of our fine-tuned citation generator against GPT-3.5. This evaluation provided insights beyond the automatic metrics discussed in Section 3.2.

[2]https://platform.openai.com/docs/models/overview

Model	Intent precision	Keyword ROUGE-1 (%)		
		precision	recall	F1
BART-base-140M	0.6083	22.05	16.70	17.62
BART-large-400M	<u>0.6454</u>	24.92	18.47	19.68
GPT-Neo-125M	0.5861	21.10	16.36	17.13
GPT-Neo-1.3B	0.6352	28.00	23.18	23.58
Galactica-125M	0.6204	26.15	21.86	22.11
Galactica-1.3B	**0.6602**	**29.89**	**25.53**	**25.86**
Galactica-6.7B	0.6380	<u>29.49</u>	<u>24.78</u>	<u>25.10</u>
LLaMa-7B	0.6352	28.13	22.78	23.40

Table 2: Performance of LMs on citation attribute inference given context. We present ROUGE-1 metrics for keyword predictions in relation to the ground-truth keywords of the target citation sentence, alongside the precision of intent prediction, represented as the proportion of correctly inferred intents in the test set. The top scores are bolded, and the next best are underlined.

6.1 Controllability Is Necessary

We assessed LMs in three modes: 1) uncontrolled mode, where the LMs utilize only the given context to infer citation attributes, and then use the inferred attributes to guide themselves when generating citation sentences; 2) intent-controlled mode, where we provide the gold citation intent to control generation while the keywords are still model-inferred; and 3) intent- and keywords-controlled mode, where the LMs are given all relevant input: context, citation intent, and keywords, from which the LMs generate citation sentences taking into account all available information.

Given only the context as input (same as the setting in Xing et al. (2020); Ge et al. (2021)), we observed limited success of LMs in matching inferred attributes with ground-truth attributes extracted from the target citation sentence (Table 2). Even the best-performing model, Galactica-1.3B, achieves an intent prediction precision of just 0.66 and a keyword ROUGE-1 F1 of only 0.26. Consequently, misinterpreted citation attributes can lead to off-topic generated citation sentences, as reflected by low ROUGE scores achieved by all LMs in the uncontrolled mode (refer to Table 3).

Intriguingly, a marked improvement in ROUGE scores was already observed when LMs generated citations merely with gold citation intent in the intent-controlled mode (Table 3). Even though the citation intent is not an explicit part of the citation sentence, its presence guides LMs to generate sentences that are more aligned with the tar-

Model	Uncontrolled generation			Intent-controlled generation			Intent- and keywords-controlled generation					
	R1	R2	RL	R1	R2	RL	R1	R2	RL	IAS	KR	FS
BART-base-140M	25.49	4.26	18.28	26.05	4.52	18.71	31.63	8.79	22.74	0.6789	0.6444	0.7156
BART-large-400M	27.39	5.67	19.85	27.90	6.00	20.17	32.33	9.12	23.20	0.6521	0.5877	0.7510
GPT-Neo-125M	23.54	3.67	17.58	23.62	3.69	17.59	30.48	9.44	22.83	0.6252	0.6793	0.7996
GPT-Neo-1.3B	28.48	6.12	20.78	29.04	6.39	21.28	36.26	13.48	26.81	0.7018	0.7936	0.7595
Galactica-125M	28.03	5.77	20.23	28.70	6.27	20.96	35.67	13.07	26.50	0.7037	0.7914	0.7540
Galactica-1.3B	30.07	7.34	22.06	30.66	7.62	22.64	38.06	15.21	28.50	0.6925	0.8299	0.7399
Galactica-6.7B	**30.61**	**7.97**	**22.59**	30.89	8.03	**22.87**	38.29	15.58	28.70	0.6734	0.8150	0.7468
LLaMa-7B	30.19	7.28	22.13	30.49	7.46	22.32	37.71	14.80	28.30	0.6688	0.8380	0.7584
Galactica-125M-PPO	–	–	–	28.81	6.12	20.97	36.49	13.55	27.09	**0.7273**	0.8313	0.7651
Galactica-6.7B-PPO	–	–	–	**31.00**	**8.16**	22.85	**38.49**	**15.81**	**28.98**	0.6740	0.8334	0.7519
LLaMa-7B-PPO	–	–	–	30.64	7.64	22.51	37.72	14.83	28.31	0.6769	**0.8430**	0.7591
GPT-3.5-turbo	23.04	3.88	14.93	23.92	3.61	15.66	29.10	8.11	18.97	0.5716	0.8420	**0.8493**

Table 3: Performance comparison of various language models (LMs) in citation generation across three operational modes: uncontrolled, intent-controlled, and intent- and keywords-controlled. The table lists ROUGE F1 scores (R1, R2, RL) in percentages, as well as Intent Alignment Score (IAS), Keyword Recall (KR), and Fluency Score (FS), with higher scores indicating superior performance. IAS, KR, and FS definitions are provided in Section 3.2.

get citations, as evidenced by enhanced ROUGE scores. This enhancement is further amplified when ground-truth keywords are provided along with the citation intent, with some models witnessing a doubling in ROUGE-2 F1 scores.

Case Study. We further demonstrated the effectiveness of controllability with a case study in Table 4. In the uncontrolled mode, the generated citation sentence was a background sentence and semantically mismatched with the gold citation. By just providing the citation intent "result", the generated sentence presented the results accurately that matched well with the gold citation. Finally, introducing the control keyword "policy iteration-based algorithms" further contributed to accurately including the keyword in the generated citation sentence, yielding the highest ROUGE-L F1. Our results underscore the importance of citation attribute controllability in citation generation.

6.2 PPO Enhances LM Controllability

We compared the LMs' performance in the intent-controlled and intent- and keywords-controlled modes before and after PPO. We excluded the uncontrolled mode from this comparison, as we assume that post-PPO, the LMs consistently operate in a controlled mode where citation attributes are given. Comparing Galactica-125M-PPO with Galactica-125M, Galactica-6.7B-PPO with Galactica-6.7B, and LLaMa-7B-PPO with LLaMa-7B, we observed a consistent and marked improvement in the IAS, KR, FS, and ROUGE F1 scores, especially for the Galactica-6.7B-PPO model, which achieved clear improvement in all metrics and the best performance in terms of ROUGE-F1. This result underscores the efficacy of PPO in directing the language model to adhere to the specifications of the provided attributes more effectively. Consequently, the generated citations better align with the specified intent, more comprehensively incorporate attribute keywords, and exhibit improved fluency, suggesting the effectiveness of PPO in enhancing the controllability of the LM citation generator.

6.3 Model Size and Pretraining Matter

A noticeable trend of improved performance accompanies the increase in language model (LM) size, underlining the role of model scale in citation generation tasks. Additionally, notable variations in performance exist among LMs of identical sizes. Galactica consistently outperforms its counterparts, while GPT-Neo tends to underperform. Despite both models being based on the Transformer's decoder, the performance disparity can be ascribed to their distinct pretraining datasets: GPT-Neo is pretrained on a diverse corpus with only a minor portion of scientific literature, whereas Galactica's pretraining is on a large corpus of scientific texts. This result indicates that the specificity of pretraining data can significantly enhance citation generation performance, underlining the critical influence of pretraining corpora on performance.

cited title: Reinforcement Learning: A Survey **cited abstract:** This paper surveys the field of reinforcement learning from a computer-science perspective. It is written to be accessible to researchers familiar with machine learning. Both the historical basis of the field and a broad ... **text before citation:** ... the agent is trained against multiple environments simultaneously and gains shared experience, leading to faster convergence and improved performance. Besides, NNDP approach is value iteration–based RL algorithm, whereas our approach is policy iteration–based RL algorithm. ***»generate a citation sentence HERE«***
Ground truth citation sentence: In general, the policy iteration-based algorithms converge faster than value iteration-based algorithms #REFR, which is another reason for the superior performance of our approach. Our experimental results further support our arguments.
Generated citation sentences of different modes: **Mode**: Uncontrolled, **Intent**: N/A, **Keywords**: N/A, **ROUGE-L F1**: 24.14 Value iteration-based RL algorithm learns the value function of each state, whereas policy iteration-based RL algorithm learns the policy of each state #REFR. **Mode**: Intent-controlled, **Intent**: result, **Keywords**: N/A, **ROUGE-L F1**: 34.62 It has been shown that policy iteration-based RL algorithm converges faster than value iteration-based RL algorithm #REFR. **Mode**: Intent- and keywords-controlled, **Intent**: result, **Keywords**: policy iteration-based algorithms, **ROUGE-L F1**: 50.00 Policy iteration-based algorithms are known to converge faster than value iteration-based algorithms #REFR.

Table 4: A case study shows that citation sentences generated by Galactica-6.7B-PPO are guided by the citation intent and the keywords.

Metric	User Preference (%)		
	GPT-3.5-turbo	Neutral	Galactica-6.7B-PPO
Intent Alignment	17.1	57.1	**25.7**
Keyword Recall	15.2	67.6	**17.1**
Fluency	**34.3**	50.5	15.2
Similarity to GT	24.8	30.5	**44.8**

Table 5: Percentage distribution of user preferences for citation sentences generated by GPT-3.5-turbo and Galactica-6.7B-PPO across four criteria. "Neutral" indicates an equal preference for both sentences. Values in bold denote the model with a higher preference.

6.4 Human Evaluation

Intriguing disparities emerge in our comparative analysis of GPT-3.5-turbo and the fine-tuned LM Galactica-6.7B-PPO (Table 3). Despite the second-best KR score and the best FS, GPT-3.5-turbo's performance falls short in ROUGE-F1 and IAS metrics. Such a disparity in automatic controllability metrics poses challenges in comparing the performance and controllability between models. To this end, a deeper understanding of these discrepancies was sought through a user study involving a subset of 105 examples randomly sampled from the test set. For each example, two citation sentences were presented - one generated by Galactica-6.7B-PPO, the other by GPT-3.5-turbo with the structured prompt (Appendix C), and the presentation order was randomized to avoid bias. Four voluntary participants (PhD candidates with NLP research background, which matches well with the domain of our test dataset) were asked to express their preference using a four-criterion scale (intent alignment, keyword recall, fluency, and similarity to the ground truth), mirroring our automatic metrics (IAS, KR, FS, and ROUGE). A "no preference" option was also provided (Figure 4) in case participants have equal preference for both sentences.

The results from the user study (Table 5) aligned with our automatic evaluations (Table 3). GPT-3.5-turbo-generated sentences, while preferred for fluency, often diverged significantly from the ground-truth citation sentences. This suggests that GPT-3.5-turbo struggles to generate contextually accurate citation sentences using our prompt template despite its prompting capabilities. Thus, high-capacity models like GPT-3.5-turbo may require further prompt refinement or few-shot tuning to enhance citation generation performance.

7 Conclusion

In this study, we introduced a controllable citation generation framework that leverages language models, highlighting the importance of user-specified attributes in the generation process. We emphasized the necessity for attribute control, underlining the complexities of citation generation, and explored the potential of enhancing controllability through Proximal Policy Optimization (PPO). Our experiments affirmed that large language models pretrained on scientific corpora are essential for citation generation, with the fine-tuned model showing advantages over GPT-3.5-turbo in both automatic metrics and human evaluations.

Acknowledgements

We acknowledge support from the Swiss National Science Foundation (grant 31003A_182638) and the NCCR Evolving Language, Swiss National Science Foundation Agreement No. 51NF40_180888. We also thank the anonymous reviewers for their useful comments.

References

Iz Beltagy, Kyle Lo, and Arman Cohan. 2019. SciBERT: A pretrained language model for scientific text. In *Proceedings of the 2019 Conference on Empirical Methods in Natural Language Processing and the 9th International Joint Conference on Natural Language Processing (EMNLP-IJCNLP)*, pages 3615–3620, Hong Kong, China. Association for Computational Linguistics.

Sid Black, Leo Gao, Phil Wang, Connor Leahy, and Stella Biderman. 2021. GPT-Neo: Large Scale Autoregressive Language Modeling with Mesh-Tensorflow. If you use this software, please cite it using these metadata.

Jingqiang Chen and Hai Zhuge. 2019. Automatic generation of related work through summarizing citations. *Concurrency and Computation: Practice and Experience*, 31(3):e4261. Number: 3 _eprint: https://onlinelibrary.wiley.com/doi/pdf/10.1002/cpe.4261.

Arman Cohan, Waleed Ammar, Madeleine van Zuylen, and Field Cady. 2019. Structural scaffolds for citation intent classification in scientific publications. In *Proceedings of the 2019 Conference of the North American Chapter of the Association for Computational Linguistics: Human Language Technologies, Volume 1 (Long and Short Papers)*, pages 3586–3596, Minneapolis, Minnesota. Association for Computational Linguistics.

Sumanth Dathathri, Andrea Madotto, Janice Lan, Jane Hung, Eric Frank, Piero Molino, Jason Yosinski, and Rosanne Liu. 2020. Plug and Play Language Models: A Simple Approach to Controlled Text Generation. *arXiv:1912.02164 [cs]*. ArXiv: 1912.02164.

Tim Dettmers, Artidoro Pagnoni, Ari Holtzman, and Luke Zettlemoyer. 2023. Qlora: Efficient finetuning of quantized llms.

Yubin Ge, Ly Dinh, Xiaofeng Liu, Jinsong Su, Ziyao Lu, Ante Wang, and Jana Diesner. 2021. BACO: A Background Knowledge- and Content-Based Framework for Citing Sentence Generation. In *Proceedings of the 59th Annual Meeting of the Association for Computational Linguistics and the 11th International Joint Conference on Natural Language Processing (Volume 1: Long Papers)*, pages 1466–1478, Online. Association for Computational Linguistics.

Edward J. Hu, Yelong Shen, Phillip Wallis, Zeyuan Allen-Zhu, Yuanzhi Li, Shean Wang, Lu Wang, and Weizhu Chen. 2021. Lora: Low-rank adaptation of large language models.

Shing-Yun Jung, Ting-Han Lin, Chia-Hung Liao, Shyan-Ming Yuan, and Chuen-Tsai Sun. 2022. Intent-controllable citation text generation. *Mathematics*, 10(10):1763.

David Jurgens, Srijan Kumar, Raine Hoover, Dan McFarland, and Dan Jurafsky. 2018. Measuring the evolution of a scientific field through citation frames. *Transactions of the Association for Computational Linguistics*, 6:391–406.

Katharina Kann, Sascha Rothe, and Katja Filippova. 2018. Sentence-level fluency evaluation: References help, but can be spared! In *Proceedings of the 22nd Conference on Computational Natural Language Learning*, pages 313–323, Brussels, Belgium. Association for Computational Linguistics.

Nitish Shirish Keskar, Bryan McCann, Lav R. Varshney, Caiming Xiong, and Richard Socher. 2019. Ctrl: A conditional transformer language model for controllable generation.

Mike Lewis, Yinhan Liu, Naman Goyal, Marjan Ghazvininejad, Abdelrahman Mohamed, Omer Levy, Veselin Stoyanov, and Luke Zettlemoyer. 2020. BART: Denoising sequence-to-sequence pre-training for natural language generation, translation, and comprehension. In *Proceedings of the 58th Annual Meeting of the Association for Computational Linguistics*, pages 7871–7880, Online. Association for Computational Linguistics.

Chin-Yew Lin. 2004. ROUGE: A package for automatic evaluation of summaries. In *Text Summarization Branches Out*, pages 74–81, Barcelona, Spain. Association for Computational Linguistics.

Yang Liu. 2019. Fine-tune bert for extractive summarization. *ArXiv*.

Anna Nikiforovskaya, Nikolai Kapralov, Anna Vlasova, Oleg Shpynov, and Aleksei Shpilman. 2020. Automatic generation of reviews of scientific papers. In *2020 19th IEEE International Conference on Machine Learning and Applications (ICMLA)*, pages 314–319.

Damian Pascual, Beni Egressy, Florian Bolli, and Roger Wattenhofer. 2020. Directed beam search: Plug-and-play lexically constrained language generation. *CoRR*, abs/2012.15416.

Bart Penders. 2018. Ten simple rules for responsible referencing. *PLOS Computational Biology*, 14(4):e1006036.

Colin Raffel, Noam Shazeer, Adam Roberts, Katherine Lee, Sharan Narang, Michael Matena, Yanqi Zhou, Wei Li, and Peter J. Liu. 2020. Exploring the limits of transfer learning with a unified text-to-text transformer. *Journal of Machine Learning Research*, 21(140):1–67.

Rajkumar Ramamurthy, Prithviraj Ammanabrolu, Kianté Brantley, Jack Hessel, Rafet Sifa, Christian Bauckhage, Hannaneh Hajishirzi, and Yejin Choi. 2023. Is reinforcement learning (not) for natural language processing: Benchmarks, baselines, and building blocks for natural language policy optimization.

Nils Reimers and Iryna Gurevych. 2019. Sentence-bert: Sentence embeddings using siamese bert-networks. In *Proceedings of the 2019 Conference on Empirical Methods in Natural Language Processing*. Association for Computational Linguistics.

BigScience Workshop: Teven Le Scao, Angela Fan, and et al. 2023. Bloom: A 176b-parameter open-access multilingual language model.

John Schulman, Filip Wolski, Prafulla Dhariwal, Alec Radford, and Oleg Klimov. 2017. Proximal policy optimization algorithms.

Rohan Taori, Ishaan Gulrajani, Tianyi Zhang, Yann Dubois, Xuechen Li, Carlos Guestrin, Percy Liang, and Tatsunori B. Hashimoto. 2023. Stanford alpaca: An instruction-following llama model. `https://github.com/tatsu-lab/stanford_alpaca`.

Ross Taylor, Marcin Kardas, Guillem Cucurull, Thomas Scialom, Anthony Hartshorn, Elvis Saravia, Andrew Poulton, Viktor Kerkez, and Robert Stojnic. 2022. Galactica: A large language model for science.

Hugo Touvron, Thibaut Lavril, Gautier Izacard, Xavier Martinet, Marie-Anne Lachaux, Timothée Lacroix, Baptiste Rozière, Naman Goyal, Eric Hambro, Faisal Azhar, Aurelien Rodriguez, Armand Joulin, Edouard Grave, and Guillaume Lample. 2023. Llama: Open and efficient foundation language models.

Leandro von Werra, Younes Belkada, Lewis Tunstall, Edward Beeching, Tristan Thrush, and Nathan Lambert. 2020. Trl: Transformer reinforcement learning. `https://github.com/lvwerra/trl`.

Yifan Wang, Yiping Song, Shuai Li, Chaoran Cheng, Wei Ju, Ming Zhang, and Sheng Wang. 2022. Disencite: Graph-based disentangled representation learning for context-specific citation generation. *Proceedings of the AAAI Conference on Artificial Intelligence*, 36(10):11449–11458.

Jia-Yan Wu, Alexander Te-Wei Shieh, Shih-Ju Hsu, and Yun-Nung Chen. 2021. Towards generating citation sentences for multiple references with intent control.

Xinyu Xing, Xiaosheng Fan, and Xiaojun Wan. 2020. Automatic Generation of Citation Texts in Scholarly Papers: A Pilot Study. In *Proceedings of the 58th Annual Meeting of the Association for Computational Linguistics*, pages 6181–6190, Online. Association for Computational Linguistics.

Intent Category (# samples)	Background (1,014)	Method (613)	Result (260)	Average (Macro)
Jurgens et al. (2018)	84.7	74.7	78.2	79.2
Cohan et al. (2019)	87.8	84.9	79.5	84.0
SciBERT+scaffolds (Ours)	**89.1**	**87.1**	**84.0**	**86.7**

Table 6: The F1 scores on three citation intent categories and the average (macro) F1, tested on the SciCite dataset created by Cohan et al. (2019).

Kexin Yang, Dayiheng Liu, Wenqiang Lei, Baosong Yang, Mingfeng Xue, Boxing Chen, and Jun Xie. 2022. Tailor: A prompt-based approach to attribute-based controlled text generation.

Mengxia Yu, Wenhao Yu, Lingbo Tong, and Meng Jiang. 2022. Scientific comparative argument generation.

A Training and Evaluation of SciBERT-based Intent Scorer

To train the SciBERT-based intent scorer, we employ a multitask training strategy (Cohan et al., 2019) with the main task being citation intent classification, which aims to minimize the cross-entropy loss:

$$\mathcal{L} = -\log \frac{\exp\left(x_{\text{intent}}(i_{\text{true}})\right)}{\sum_{i \in \text{all intents}} \exp\left(x_{\text{intent}}(i)\right)} \tag{5}$$

Additionally, we incorporate two auxiliary classification tasks (scaffolds) (Cohan et al., 2019) to enhance the main task's performance: 1) classifying the title of the section (from 5 normalized section titles: Introduction, Related Work, Method, Experiments, Conclusion) in which the cited sentence appears, and 2) determining the citation worthiness of the sentence. We utilize a separate functional head, a two-layer fully connected network for each auxiliary task, with the SciBERT-encoded "CLS" hidden states as input. The training loss is a weighted sum of the three cross-entropy losses (Equation (5)), with weights of 1.0 for the main task, and 0.05 and 0.01 for the first and second auxiliary tasks, respectively. The accuracy of the intent scorer is shown in Table 6.

B Hardware Requirements and PPO Training Hyperparameters

We used 4x NVIDIA A100 80 GPUs for training and a single NVIDIA RTX A6000 for inference. During PPO training, we adjusted the batch and mini-batch sizes according to the model size and architecture. Specifically, we used (256, 16) for Galactica-125M, (256, 4) for Galactica-6.7B, and

(32, 2) for LLaMa-7B, and we ran the PPO steps until no further improvement in reward.

C Prompt Templates for Querying GPT-3.5-turbo API

The prompt templates utilized to query the GPT-3.5-turbo (version 0301) API are presented in this section. As illustrated in Listing 1, the template for uncontrolled citation generation creates a citation sentence solely based on the context. In contrast, Listing 2 demonstrates the template for the controlled citation generation mode, where citation attributes are included alongside the context to guide the generation process. Before sending the query message to the API, we need to provide the actual content of the parameters that are listed at the beginning of the templates, such as the cited paper's title and abstract, the manuscript's title and abstract, and the local context (the text before the target citation sentence in the manuscript), and specify the citation intent and keywords in the controlled generation mode. During the API call to GPT-3.5-turbo, we configured the maximum token limit to 2k and set the generation temperature at 0.1.

D Influence of Beam Size on Citation Generation Performance

During the citation generation process with Language Models (LMs), we conducted experiments with multiple beam sizes: 1, 2, 4, and 8. The performance metrics derived from the validation set suggest that the use of a beam size of 1 yields the most consistent results. Interestingly, larger beam sizes do not enhance the performance, but negatively influence the ROUGE scores (Table 7). These results could hint that larger beam sizes introduce a broader diversity in the generated text, which may affect its precision. For instance, it could impact the accurate generation of specific topic keywords and affect the control over the generation process. In a scenario where a keyword citation attribute is provided, LMs operating with a larger beam size may opt to generate a citation sentence encompassing synonyms of the keywords rather than the keyword itself, which could consequently lead to a decrease in ROUGE scores. As a result, in our experiments, we defaulted to a beam size of 1. We will delve deeper into this phenomenon in future research.

E Citation Generation Examples

We showcase instances (Figure 2 and 3) of citation sentences produced by Galactica-6.7B-PPO in three modes: 1) Uncontrolled, 2) Intent-Controlled, and 3) Intent- and Keywords-Controlled. Notably, Figure 2 is the complete example of the case study in Table 4. With the provision of accurate citation intent alone, the language model citation generator can align well with the stated intent, thereby enhancing ROUGE F1 scores. The addition of keyword attributes further boosts these scores.

F Web Interface for Human Evaluation

We have designed a web interface using Streamlit[3] to assess the citation sentences produced by Galactica-6.7B-PPO and GPT-3.5-turbo. As shown in Figure 4, this user-friendly platform enables participants to peruse context details, citation attributes, the original citation, and the model-generated sentences with ease. Upon rating the generated sentences based on the four provided criteria, participants can submit their evaluation by clicking on the "Submit" button, thereby preserving the data. A "Skip" button is also available, allowing participants to bypass any examples that fall outside their area of expertise and proceed to the next one.

[3] https://streamlit.io/

```
cited_paper_title = "****Cited paper's title****"
cited_paper_abstract = "****Cited paper's abstract****"
manuscript_title = "****Manuscript's title****"
manuscript_abstract = "****Manuscript's abstract****"
manuscript_local_text_before_citation = "****The sentences before the target
    citation sentence in the manuscript (local context)****"

messages = [
    {
        "role": "system",
        "content": "You are a scientific writing assistant. Your task is to infer
    the citation intent and relevant keywords based on the provided context, and
    generate a citation sentence for a given manuscript. The citation sentence
    should seamlessly follow the local context, reflect the inferred citation intent
    , and incorporate the inferred keywords."
    },
    {
        "role": "user",
        "content": f"""
The authors need to cite the reference paper:

Title: {cited_paper_title}
Abstract: {cited_paper_abstract}

, in the manuscript with the global context:

Title: {manuscript_title}
Abstract: {manuscript_abstract}

, immediately following the provided local context:

{manuscript_local_text_before_citation}

Your task:
Please generate a citation sentence that cites the reference paper and seamlessly
    follows the local context. The citation sentence should implicitly reflect one
    of the following citation intents and incorporate relevant keywords:

1) Background: The citation provides background information or additional context
    about a relevant problem, concept, approach, or topic.
2) Method: The citation refers to the use of a specific method, tool, approach, or
    dataset from the reference paper.
3) Result: The citation compares or contrasts the results or findings of the
    manuscript with those in the reference paper.

Requirements:
1. Insert the citation marker "#REFR" at the position in the sentence where the
    reference paper should be cited.
2. Put the citation marker "#REFR" correctly in the generated citation sentence. The
     citation marker should replace the entire in-text citation (e.g., authors and
    year of publication), should not be enclosed in any brackets, and should be
    placed within the sentence before the ending punctuation.

Please return only the generated citation sentence.
            """
    },
]
```

Listing 1: The presented template was employed for querying the GPT-3.5-turbo (version 0301) API instructing it to generate a citation sentence given the context which comprises the title and abstract of the cited paper the title and abstract of the manuscript and the local context (sentences before the target citation in the manuscript). The generation was executed in an uncontrolled mode without the control of explicit citation attributes.

```
cited_paper_title = "****Cited paper's title****"
cited_paper_abstract = "****Cited paper's abstract****"
manuscript_title = "****Manuscript's title****"
manuscript_abstract = "****Manuscript's abstract****"
manuscript_local_text_before_citation = "****The sentences before the target
    citation sentence in the manuscript (local context)****"
citation_intent = "****Specified citation intent****"
keywords = "****Specified keywords****"

messages = [
    {
        "role": "system",
        "content": "You are a scientific writing assistant. Your task is to generate
     citation sentences for a given manuscript, following detailed instructions.
    These instructions involve taking into account the context, desired citation
    intent, specific keywords in your responses."
    },
    {
        "role": "user",
        "content": f"""
The authors need to cite the reference paper:

    Title: {cited_paper_title}
    Abstract: {cited_paper_abstract}

, in the manuscript with the global context:

    Title: {manuscript_title}
    Abstract: {manuscript_abstract}

, immediately following the provided local context:

    {manuscript_local_text_before_citation}

Your task:
Please generate one citation sentence that cites the reference paper, seamlessly
    follows the local context, reflects the specified citation intent, and
    incorporates the specified keywords.

Requirements:
1. The generated citation sentence should reflect the citation intent: {
    citation_intent}. Citation intents include:
    1) background: The citation provides background information or additional
    context about a relevant problem, concept, approach, or topic.
    2) method: The citation refers to the use of a specific method, tool, approach,
    or dataset from the reference paper.
    3) result: The citation compares or contrasts the results or findings of the
    manuscript with those in the reference paper.
2. The generated citation sentence should contain the specified keywords: {keywords
    }. All the provided keywords should be used. If no keywords are specified,
    please infer one or two keywords by yourself and generate the citation sentence
    based on them.
3. Insert the citation marker "#REFR" at the position in the sentence where the
    reference paper should be cited.
4. Put the citation marker "#REFR" correctly in the generated citation sentence. The
     citation marker should replace the entire in-text citation (e.g., authors and
    year of publication), should not be enclosed in any brackets, and should be
    placed within the sentence before the ending punctuation.

Please return only the generated citation sentence.
        """
    },
]
```

Listing 2: The presented template was employed for querying the GPT-3.5-turbo (version 0301) API instructing it to generate a citation sentence given the context which comprises the title and abstract of the cited paper the title and abstract of the manuscript and the local context (sentences before the target citation in the manuscript). The generation was also controlled by the specified citation attributes including citation intent and keywords.

Cited Paper:

Title: Reinforcement Learning: A Survey

Abstract: This paper surveys the field of reinforcement learning from a computer-science perspective. It is written to be accessible to researchers familiar with machine learning. Both the historical basis of the field and a broad selection of current work are summarized. Reinforcement learning is the problem faced by an agent that learns behavior through trial-and-error interactions with a dynamic environment. The work described here has a resemblance to work in psychology, but differs considerably in the details and in the use of the word ``reinforcement.'' The paper discusses central issues of reinforcement learning, including trading off exploration and exploitation, establishing the foundations of the field via Markov decision theory, learning from delayed reinforcement, constructing empirical models to accelerate learning, making use of generalization and hierarchy, and coping with hidden state. It concludes with a survey of some implemented systems and an assessment of the practical utility of current methods for reinforcement learning.

Manuscript:

Title: Evolving Reinforcement Learning Environment To Minimize Learner'S Achievable Reward: An Application On Hardening Active Directory Systems

Abstract: We study a Stackelberg game between one attacker and one defender in a configurable environment. The defender picks a specific environment configuration. The attacker observes the configuration and attacks via Reinforcement Learning (RL trained against the observed environment). The defender's goal is to find the environment with minimum achievable reward for the attacker. We apply Evolutionary Diversity Optimization (EDO) to generate diverse population of environments for training. Environments with clearly high rewards are killed off and replaced by new offsprings to avoid wasting training time. Diversity not only improves training quality but also fits well with our RL scenario: RL agents tend to improve gradually, so a slightly worse environment earlier on may become better later. We demonstrate the effectiveness of our approach by focusing on a specific application, Active Directory (AD). AD is the default security management system for Windows domain networks. AD environment describes an attack graph, where nodes represent computers/accounts/etc., and edges represent accesses. The attacker aims to find the best attack path to reach the highest-privilege node. The defender can change the graph by removing a limited number of edges (revoke accesses). Our approach generates better defensive plans than the existing approach and scales better.

Text Before Citation: NNDP attacker's policy #OTHEREFR trains the model against one defensive plan at a time, due to which it forgets the previous plan. This way, it keeps learning and forgetting the plans. However, we train our RL based attacker's policy against multiple defensive plans at a time, due to which it learns shared experience and performs better. For RL agent, diverse environment configurations are only different in the "opening games", whereas the "end games" or "mid games" are likely to be similar across different environments. The similarity in later stages can be utilized in parallel training, where the agent is trained against multiple environments simultaneously and gains shared experience, leading to faster convergence and improved performance. Besides, NNDP approach is value iteration-based RL algorithm, whereas our approach is policy iteration-based RL algorithm.

Ground-truth Citation Sentence:

In general, the policy iteration-based algorithms converge faster than value iteration-based algorithms #REFR , which is another reason for the superior performance of our approach. Our experimental results further support our arguments.

Generated Citation Sentences:

Uncontrolled Mode:

Citation Intent: N/A

Keywords: N/A

Generation: Value iteration-based RL algorithm learns the value function of each state, whereas policy iteration-based RL algorithm learns the policy of each state #REFR.

ROUGE F1: R1: 34.48 R2: 17.86 RL: 24.14

Intent-controlled Mode:

Citation Intent: result

Keywords: N/A

Generation: It has been shown that policy iteration-based RL algorithm converges faster than value iteration-based RL algorithm #REFR.

ROUGE F1: R1: 34.62 R2: 24.00 RL: 34.62

Intent- and keywords-controlled Mode:

Citation Intent: result

Keywords: policy iteration-based algorithms

Generation: Policy iteration-based algorithms are known to converge faster than value iteration-based algorithms #REFR.

ROUGE F1: R1: 50.00 R2: 43.48 RL: 50.00

Figure 2: Example citation sentences generated by Galactica-6.7B-PPO under the uncontrolled mode, the intent-controlled mode, and the intent- and keywords-controlled mode.

Model	Uncontrolled generation			Intent-controlled generation			Intent- and keywords-controlled generation					
	R1	R2	RL	R1	R2	RL	R1	R2	RL	IAS	KR	FS
Galactica-125M-beam1	27.93	6.00	20.39	28.67	6.41	21.09	35.85	13.44	26.88	0.7128	0.7667	0.7539
Galactica-125M-beam2	27.26	5.80	19.61	28.00	6.26	20.24	36.00	13.81	26.68	0.6946	0.7865	0.7526
Galactica-125M-beam4	27.15	6.01	19.50	27.69	6.29	19.98	35.44	13.59	26.13	0.6872	0.7656	0.7466
Galactica-125M-beam8	26.47	6.03	18.87	26.91	6.38	19.44	34.99	13.67	25.91	0.6724	0.7400	0.7425

Table 7: Performance of the supervised fine-tuned Galactica-125M model on the validation set, utilizing various beam sizes for inference.

```
Cited Paper:
    Title:    Optimal Scheduling For Discounted Age Penalty Minimization In Multi-Loop Networked Control
    Abstract: Age-of-information (AoI) is a metric quantifying information freshness at the receiver. Since AoI
combines packet generation frequency, packet loss, and delay into a single metric, it has received a lot of rese
arch attention as an interface between communication network and application. In this work, we apply AoI to the
problem of wireless scheduling for multi-loop networked control systems (NCS), i.e., feedback control loops clos
ed over a shared wireless network. We model the scheduling problem as a Markov decision process (MDP) with AoI a
s its observable states and derive a relation of control system error and AoI. We further derive a stationary sc
heduling policy to minimize control error over an infinite horizon. We show that our scheduler outperforms the s
tate-of-the-art scheduling policies for NCS. To the best of our knowledge, this is the first work proposing an A
oI-based wireless scheduling policy that minimizes the control error over an infinite horizon for multi-loop NC
S.

Manuscript:
    Title:    Large Population Games On Constrained Unreliable Networks
    Abstract: This paper studies an N-agent cost-coupled game where the agents are connected via an unreliable
capacity constrained network. Each agent receives state information over that network which loses packets with p
robability p. A Base station (BS) actively schedules agent communications over the network by minimizing a weigh
ted Age of Information (WAoI) based cost function under a capacity limit C < N on the number of transmission att
empts at each instant. Under a standard information structure, we show that the problem can be decoupled into a
scheduling problem for the BS and a game problem for the N agents. Since the scheduling problem is an NP hard co
mbinatorics problem, we propose an approximately optimal solution which approaches the optimal solution as N →
∞. In the process, we also provide some insights on the case without channel erasure. Next, to solve the large p
opulation game problem, we use the mean-field game framework to compute an approximate decentralized Nash equili
brium. Finally, we validate the theoretical results using a numerical example.
    Text Before Citation: Further, we improve upon the convergence guarantees in #OTHEREFR for the case where t
he network is erasure free by proposing a novel scheduling policy. Finally, we employ this policy to construct a
n approximate Nash solution for the finite-agent consensus problem. In literature, the early works #OTHEREFR , #
OTHEREFR have dealt with an optimal control problem with unreliable communication, albeit, for a single agent sy
stem and an unconstrained network under the TCP and the UDP communication protocols. The work #OTHEREFR extends
the setting to multi-agent games; however, the considered network is unconstrained. In order to measure timeline
ss in communication networks, age of information (AoI) has been introduced as a potential metric.

Ground-truth Citation Sentence:
    In the context of networked feedback systems, the AoI-based policies have been proposed for solving resource
allocation and enduser uncertainty reduction problems as in #REFR .

Generated Citation Sentences:
Uncontrolled Mode:
    Citation Intent: N/A
    Keywords: N/A
    Generation: The work #REFR studies a wireless scheduling problem for multi-loop networked control systems (N
CS), i.e., feedback control loops closed over a shared wireless network.
    ROUGE F1: R1: 23.08 R2: 0.00 RL: 11.54

Intent-controlled Mode:
    Citation Intent: method
    Keywords: N/A
    Generation: The authors in #REFR have used AoI to solve a wireless scheduling problem for multi-loop network
ed control systems.
    ROUGE F1: R1: 35.56 R2: 4.65 RL: 13.33

Intent- and keywords-controlled Mode:
    Citation Intent: method
    Keywords: networked feedback systems
    Generation: The work #REFR proposes an optimal scheduling policy for a multi-loop networked feedback systems
based on AoI.
    ROUGE F1: R1: 36.36 R2: 9.52 RL: 22.73
```

Figure 3: Example citation sentences generated by Galactica-6.7B-PPO.

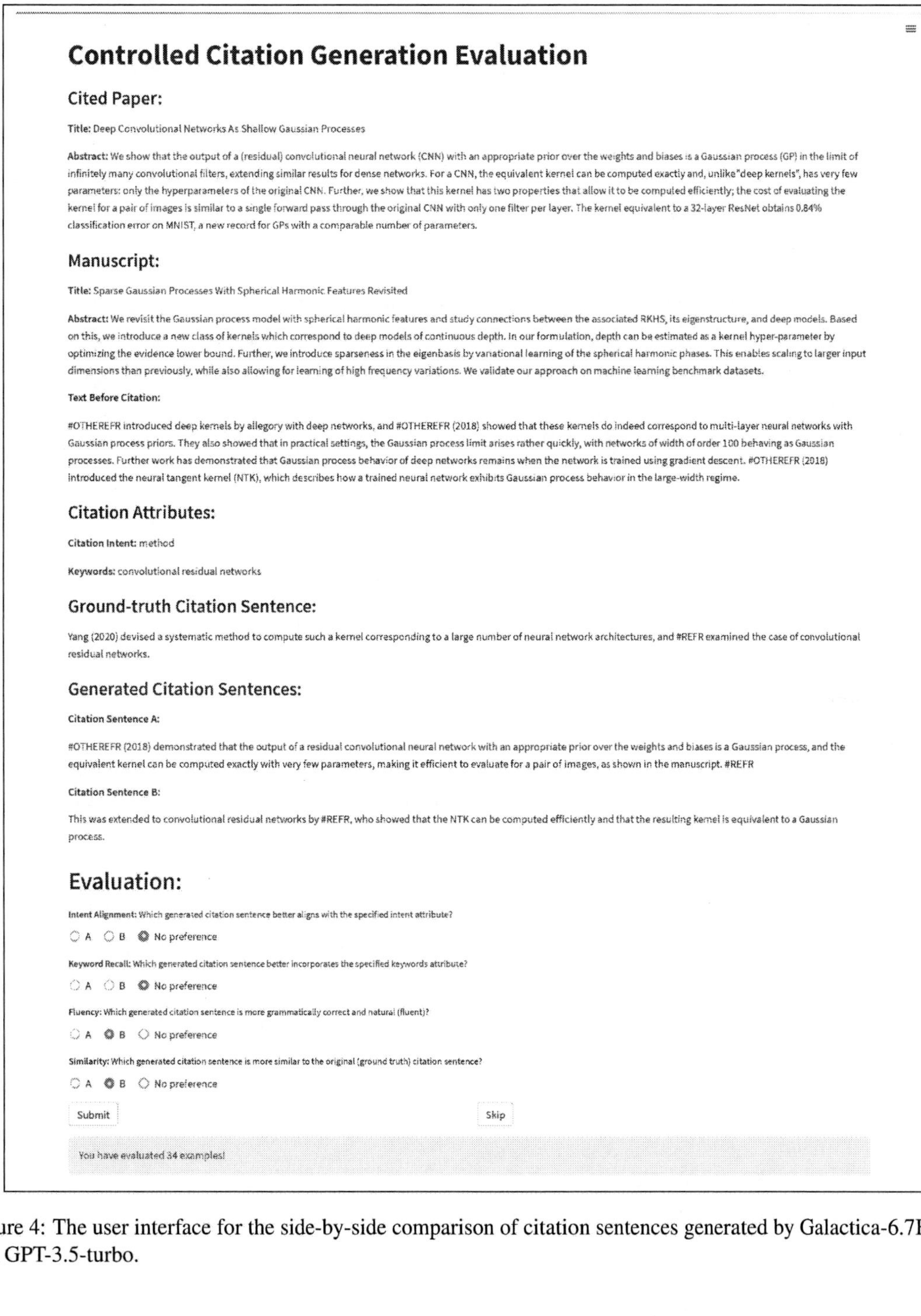

Figure 4: The user interface for the side-by-side comparison of citation sentences generated by Galactica-6.7B-PPO and GPT-3.5-turbo.

Toward Structured Related Work Generation with Novelty Statements

Kazuya Nishimura[1], **Kuniaki Saito**[2], **Tosho Hirasawa**[2], **Yoshitaka Ushiku**[2]
[1] National Cancer Center Japan
[2]OMRON SINIC X Corp.

Abstract

To help readers understand the novelty and the research context, an excellent related work section is structured (*i.e.,* the section consists of multiple paragraphs organized by several research topics) and includes descriptions of novelty. However, previous studies viewed related work generation as just multi-document summarization, and the structure and novelty statements are ignored. In this paper, we redefine the related work generation task as structured related work generation with novelty statement (**STRoGeNS**), and we propose datasets and automatic evaluation metrics for structure and novelty for STRoGeNS. On our structured related work generation with novelty statement, we investigate the state-of-the-art language models and deliver insights about the effects of pre-training and input context. In addition, we confirm the validity of the proposed automatic evaluation metrics with human evaluation. [1]

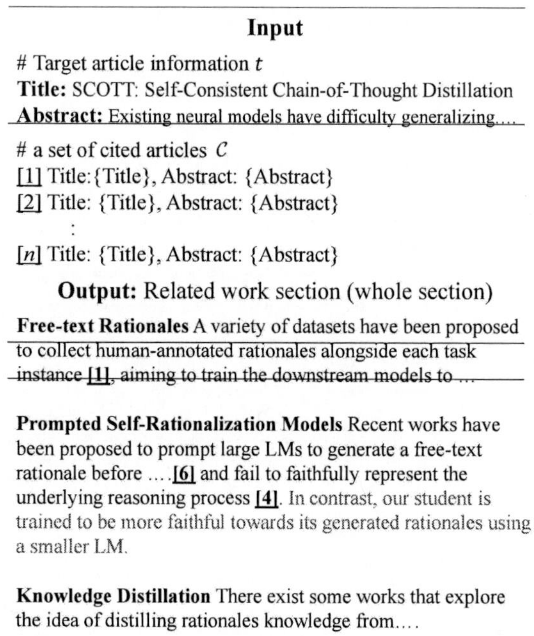

Figure 1: Overview of STRoGeNS. Given target article t and a set of cited articles C, our task aims to output a related work section with multiple paragraphs determined based on research topics with citations. The number of the cited article is used as an identifier (*i.e.,* [#i]) in the target text. Red text indicates a novelty statement.

1 Introduction

A related work section of a scientific article plays an important role in helping readers understand the context of the research field and the novelty of their work (Hoang and Kan, 2010). The well-written related work is properly structured (*i.e.,* make paragraphs with topics determined from the relations between current work and previous works) and clearly described novelty. To write such a related work section, authors must categorize a number of articles into several topics, summarize them, and highlight the novelty compared to them, which requires a deep and broad understanding of the research field, and is, of course, a very time-consuming process.

Given the difficulty, the automatic related work generation has been proposed (Hoang and Kan, 2010; Hu and Wan, 2014). However, existing studies viewed the related work generation as multi-document summarization and do not sufficiently consider the structure of the related work (i.e., whether paragraphs are organized based on research topics reflected by the target research field) and whether it states the novelty of the current work. For example, current abstractive related work studies aim to generate a single paragraph (Lu et al., 2020; Chen et al., 2021, 2022) or citation sentence of related work (Mao et al., 2022), and the outputs of them assume a single research topic and do not require structuring. While Liu et al. (2022) aimed to generate structured summarization, the target is a literature review constructed not with research topics but with components of the document such as background and method, and the objective is not always to highlight novelty.

[1]We will release our dataset and scripts upon publication.

Proceedings of the Fourth Workshop on Scholarly Document Processing (SDP 2024), pages 38–57
August 16, 2024 ©2024 Association for Computational Linguistics

In this paper, we redefine related work generation not just as summarization but as a STructured Related Work Generation with Novelty Statement (**STRoGeNS**) and propose dataset and evaluation metrics. Here, we define a structured related work as a section in which each paragraph is organized by research topics, and the articles related to the topic of the paragraph are cited and summarized in the paragraph.

Our contributions to generate STRoGeNS are as follows.

- We propose a novel related work generation task, namely structured related work generation with novelty statement (**STRoGeNS**), that aims to generate a related work section with multiple paragraphs organized by research topics and descriptions of novelty statements.
- We propose large-scale datasets and automatic evaluation metrics for structured related work generation with novelty statement. The datasets focus on the trade-off of quantity and quality, and the evaluation metrics are designed to evaluate structure and novelty.
- We evaluate state-of-the-art summarization models on our STRoGeNS task and find two challenges: the text generation beyond summarization and the capability of utilizing long contexts.

2 Related work

Extractive related work generation. The prototype of automated related work section generation has been proposed by Hoang and Kan (2010). They viewed the task as a topic-biased summarization and proposed an extraction method by selecting sentences based on given topics. Inheriting this setting, several extractive summarization methods have been proposed by Hu and Wan (2014); Chen and Zhuge (2019); Wang et al. (2020b, 2018); Deng et al. (2021).

Abstractive related work generation. The first trial of abstractive related work generation is citation sentence generation (AbuRa'ed et al., 2020; Xing et al., 2020), and afterward, a paragraph of related work has also attracted attention (Lu et al., 2020; Chen et al., 2021, 2022). For example, Chen et al. (2022) has proposed target-aware related work generation to generate target-centric related work. Liu et al. (2023a) has improved quality and readability with the causality invention module. There are discussions about the task of the related work generation. Shi et al. (2023) has proposed a task that combines reference retrieval and related work generation. Funkquist et al. (2023) unified previous datasets and defined related work generation as cited generation task.

However, these studies viewed related work generation as a summarization task and did not focus on the structure and novelty of related work. Unlike previous studies, we aim to generate structured related work with novelty statements.

Automatic evaluation. Several n-gram-based evaluations have been proposed to measure the overlap of the gold standard and generated text, such as BLEU (Papineni et al., 2002), ROUGE (Lin, 2004). To reflect the context of a sentence, embedding-based evaluations, which measure the similarity of the embedding vectors extracted from the text by the NLG model, have been proposed, such as (Yuan et al., 2022; Zhao et al., 2019). Recently, evaluations using a large language model (LLM) have been proposed (Liu et al., 2023b; Fu et al., 2023). Unlike n-gram and embedding-based evaluation, this evaluation reflects the evaluation criteria by prompts and allows for evaluation across various criteria, such as coherence, consistency, and fluency. This paper verified unexplored novelty evaluation with the LLM-based evaluation.

Task-specific evaluation. Since the generation aims differ depending on the target task, evaluation metrics are studied for each downstream task. For example, Durmus et al. (2020); Wang et al. (2020a) focused on consistency of summary, Ye et al. (2021); Ghazarian et al. (2022) focused on the coherence of the dialogue response generation, and Funkquist et al. (2023); Gao et al. (2023); Rashkin et al. (2021) focused on citations of generated text. However, the evaluation of related works has not been considered. To the best of my knowledge, this is the first trial to evaluate the novelty and structure of related work.

3 Structured Related work generation with Novelty statements (STRoGeNS)

We propose a new challenge, namely STructured Related Work Generation with Novelty Statement (**STRoGeNS**), for related work generation. STRoGeNS is motivated by two mandatory properties

Dataset	Pairs	Words (input)	Words (Output)	Input Doc (Num)	#Para.
Multi-XScience (Lu et al., 2020)	40,528	778.1	116.4	4.4	1
S2ORC (Chen et al., 2021)	136,655	1067.4	148.7	5.0	1
Delve (Chen et al., 2021)	78,927	622.6	228.6	3.7	1
TAS2 (Chen et al., 2022)	117,700	1036.0	134.8	4.8	1
TAD (Chen et al., 2022)	218,255	1071.4	162.3	5.2	1
BigSurvey-MDS (Liu et al., 2022)	4,478	11,893.1	1,051.7	76.3	1
SciReviewGen (Kasanishi et al., 2023)	10,130	11,734.4	7,193.8	68.1	1
STRoGeNS-arXiv22	85,853	3,046.2	514.3	16.6	4.22
STRoGeNS-conf22	15,079	3,669.1	508.5	20.4	4.27
STRoGeNS-conf23	4,762	4,836.6	504.6	25.7	4.04

Table 1: Statistics and feature of relevant datasets.

(structure and novelty statement) of related work for improving readers' understanding and writers' inspiration.

3.1 Task definition

Our STRoGeNS is defined as follows: Given target article information $\mathbf{t}$ and a set of n cited articles $\mathcal{C} = \{\mathbf{c}_i\}_i^n$, the model generates related work section R of the target article, which R consists of m paragraphs $\mathbf{p}_1, ..., \mathbf{p}_m$ [2]. When the $\mathbf{c}_i$ is cited in $\mathbf{p}_i$, [#i] is used as identifier. Figure 1 shows the example of the input and output of our task.

Unlike previous abstractive related work generation task (Liu et al., 2022; Funkquist et al., 2023), which outputs a single paragraph of related work as a summary, our task outputs a related work section with structure and novelty statements in addition to a summary.

3.2 Dataset

Construction. Collecting samples with high-quality structure and accurate novelty statements is necessary to generate our target. On the other hand, a sufficient number of articles is required to understand a wide range of research fields. We address this trade-off between quality and quantity by creating a quantity-oriented dataset (**STRoGeNS-arXiv22**) and a quality-oriented dataset (**STRoGeNS-conf22**). Additionally, we create a dataset for test (**STRoGeNS-conf23**).

STRoGeNS-arXiv22: To generate a quantity-oriented dataset, we collect articles that include related works from 1,882,082 articles of unarXiv 2022 (Saier et al., 2023), a large-scale dataset of arXiv[3]. With fully structured text and citations of unarXiv 2022[4], we extract titles, abstracts, sections with associated or previous work tags, and titles of cited articles. Since the abstracts of cited articles are not contained in unarXiv 2022, we retrieve the abstract using Semantic Scholar API (Ammar et al., 2018). As a result, 130,585 related works with citation information are collected. Then, samples with only one paragraph ($m = 1$) or more than eight paragraphs ($m > 8$) or less than five cited articles ($n < 5$) were excluded. Finally, we collected 85,853 articles. Here, all citation identifiers are replaced with [#i]. Although this dataset is ensured in quantity, it may contain many low-quality structured sections and inaccurate novelty statements because it contains articles that have not been peer-reviewed.

To generate a quality-oriented dataset, we generate two datasets for training and test from top-tier peer-reviewed proceedings. First, we collected PDFs of conference proceedings from conference proceedings websites. Then, the PDFs are converted to structured markdown-styled text with Neural Optical Understanding for Academic Documents (NOUGAT) (Blecher et al., 2023), which is a transformer-based optical character recognition model. The title of the cited article is obtained by matching the identifiers in references with the identifiers in the paragraph based on the citation identifier such as [#i] or Author, et al., where regular expression operations are used to extract the citation identifiers. Similar to STRoGeNS-arXiv22,

[2]While our dataset includes paper IDs that allow access to the full text, we only use titles and abstracts for inputs ($\mathbf{t}$ and $\mathbf{c}_i$) in terms of input length and ease of data collection.

[3]We could not use S2ROC dataset (Lo et al., 2020), a large-scale annotated scientific dataset, as it was poorly structured and difficult to retrieve paragraphs accurately.

[4]unarXiv 2022 parsed the LaTeXsource file and has JSON-styled text with paragraphs, sections, and citation links.

Category	#article
Computer Science	73.8 %
Physics	1.67 %
Mathematics	6.19 %
Statistics	13.7 %
Quantitative Biology	0.41 %
Quantitative Finance	0.14 %
Electrical Engineering and Systems Science	3.93 %
Economics	0.12 %

Table 2: Distribution of category in STRoGeNS-arXiv22.

Conferences	#article
ACL	7.61 %
EMNLP	12.1 %
NAACL	4.61 %
CVPR	35.9 %
ECCV	9.00 %
ICCV	13.7 %
ICLR	9.62 %
ICML	7.58 %

Table 3: Distribution of conferences in STRoGeNS-conf22.

Conferences	#article
ACL	11.9%
CVPR	37.5%
ICCV	37.2%
ICML	13.4%

Table 4: Distribution of conferences in STRoGeNS-conf23.

Dataset	r_{SE}	r_{PE}	r_{SR}
STRoGeNS-arXiv22	18.8%	-	81.2%
STRoGeNS-conf22	12.8%	9.27%	77.9%
STRoGeNS-conf23	11.4%	6.90%	81.7%

Table 5: Quality analysis of datasets (%). SE, PE, and SR indicate the rate of retrieval errors of Semantic Scholar, parse errors by the Nougat, and successfully obtained citations.

cleaning is performed based on the number of paragraphs and the number of citations articles, and the abstracts are parsed by Semantic scholar API.

STRoGeNS-conf22. This dataset focuses on the quality of articles and is used for training. We collected 28,211 PDFs from CVPR, ECCV, ICCV, ACL, EMNLP, NAACL, ICML, and ICLR published before 2022. Finally, we collected 15,079 structured related work sections from the PDFs using the above steps.

STRoGeNS-conf23. We use the article published after 2023 for the test. We collected 7,248 PDFs from four conferences: ACL, CVPR, ICCV, and ICML, and 5,578 related works were collected by above steps. Since some articles may have been uploaded to arXiv before being accepted at the conferences, we remove samples by manually checking the title to avoid data leakage. First, fuzzy matching is performed between the titles of STRoGeNS-arXiv22 and STRoGeNS-conf23, and articles with a match score over 90 are collected. Then, we manually checked the 534 collected articles and removed 409 articles. Finally, 4,762 structured related work sections are corrected by parsing PDFs.

Statistics. Table 1 shows statistics of our datasets and related previous datasets. Unlike previous datasets for single-paragraph generation, our dataset averages about four paragraphs. Although our datasets aim to generate an entire related work section, they are comparable in size to S2ORC and TAS2.

Table 2 shows the distribution of the category of samples in STRoGeNS-arXiv22. Since related work is often described in computer science articles, 73.8 % of articles are in computer science. Table 3, and 4 show distribution of conference in STRoGeNS-conf22 and STRoGeNS-conf23. Due to the explosive increase in the number of papers on computer vision, the proportion of CVPR, ICCV, and ECCV documents is large. Although we use the proposed datasets without considering the category in this trial, the proposed dataset has tags of category and conference, so it can also be used for studies that take the category into account.

Quality. Our dataset contains two retrieval errors of citation information: a retrieval error caused by Semantic Scholar API (SE) and a parse error of NOUGAT (PE). Table 5 shows the rate of SE, PE, and the successful retrieval SR. Our datasets successfully retrieved about 80% of the abstract of citations on average.

3.3 Automatic Evaluation

We evaluate the generated text of models from three viewpoints: **Summarization** whether the generated contains meaningful information, **Structure** whether the citations within the paragraphs are accurately grouped, and **Novelty statement** whether the generated section contains a novelty statement.

Summarization. We use a ROUGE (Lin, 2004), widely used as an automatic evaluation metric in summarization. The metrics measure the n-gram overlap between a generated text and a gold standard. We use ROUGE-1.5.5 implementation of (Lin, 2004) with "-n 2" option, and input is whole sections of the gold standard and generated text.

Structure. Paragraphs of well-structured related works should cite articles according to the topics determined from the target research field. In our test data, most related work sections are expected to follow the above requirements because they are collected from peer-reviewed top-tier proceedings. Therefore, we design structure metrics based on whether the citation trends in the paragraph are similar to the citation trends in the gold standard section.

We propose four metrics: (1) F1, (2) ARI, (3) ARI' and (4) $\mathrm{MAE_p}$.

The F1 measures the citation similarity among most similar paragraphs of the gold standard and generated text. F1-based metrics are defined as follows:

$$\mathrm{F1} = \frac{1}{m}\sum_{i=1}^{m}\max_{j}\mathrm{F1}(f(\mathbf{p}_i), f(\hat{\mathbf{p}}_j)), \tag{1}$$

where f is a function that extracts a citation identifier, p_i is i-th paragraph in the gold standard, $\hat{p}_j$ is j-th paragraph in the generated section, and F1 is F1-score calculation. Since the metric is calculated between the most similar paragraphs, the paragraphs with low similarity are ignored, and the entire paragraphs cannot be measured.

We propose a metric that introduced the Adjusted Rand Index (ARI) (Steinley, 2004; Hubert and Arabie, 1985), a clustering metric to evaluate citation trends of low-similarity paragraphs. As shown in Figure 2, citation trends could be evaluated with a clustering evaluation manner by treating the paragraphs of the original and generated section as clusters. By applying clustering, changes in the number of paragraphs can be treated in the same way as changes in the number of clusters, and thus, citation trends for the whole section can be evaluated. We calculate the Adjusted Rand Index (ARI) with assigned cluster IDs of the gold standard and generated section.

As shown in Figure 2, citations may be used in multiple paragraphs, unlike clustering. Then, some articles will not have corresponding IDs, as shown in the unmatched citation (UC) in Figure 2. To address this problem, we modify the Adjusted Rand Index to account for unmatched pairs (UC) caused by multi-paragraphs. RI is formulated as $\mathrm{RI} = \frac{\#\mathrm{TPair}}{\#\mathrm{Pair}}$, where $\#$Pair and $\#$TPair are the total

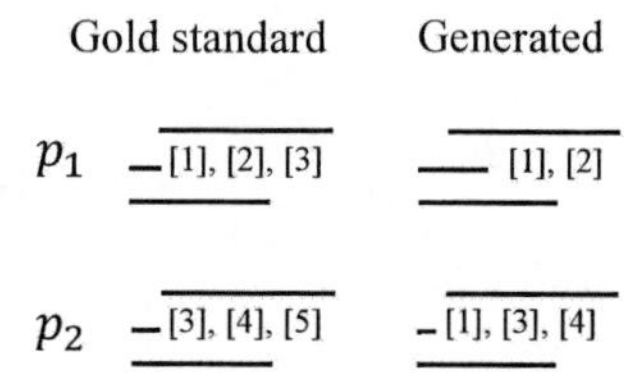

Ref. ID	Cluster ID Gol.	Cluster ID Gen.
[1]	1	1
[2]	1	1
[3]	1	UC
[1]	UC	2
[3]	2	2
[4]	2	2
[5]	2	MC

Figure 2: Example of structure evaluation with ARI. The gold standard and generated related work sections have two paragraphs with citations. Then, cluster ID is assigned for each reference, as shown in the right table. UC and MC indicate an unmatched citation and a missed citation, respectively.

number of pairs and the number of pairs that have correct relation. We add the number of unmatched samples ($\#$UC) to the denominator of RI. Then, modified RI' are formulate as follows:

$$\mathrm{RI}' = \frac{\#\mathrm{TPair}}{\#\mathrm{Pair} + \#\mathrm{UC}}. \tag{2}$$

Adjusted Rand Index is calculated with modified RI' as follows: $\mathrm{ARI}' = \frac{\mathrm{RI}' - \mathrm{ExpectedRI}}{\max(\mathrm{RI}) - \mathrm{ExpectedRI}}$. This metric is calculated like regular ARI when there are no unmatched citations, and the score decreases with unmatched citations.

In addition, we calculate the mean absolute error with the number of paragraphs in reference and generated (MAE_p).

Finally, we use four metrics F1, ARI, ARI', MAE_p for structure evaluation.

Novelty statement. To evaluate whether the generated text contains a novelty statement, we used the prompt-based evaluation method using LLM (Liu et al., 2023b). It has been reported that when used for evaluation, LLM correlates better with human evaluation than traditional automated evaluation metrics in terms of consistency, conciseness, and grammar. However, whether it is a valid index for novelty evaluation has not been explored.

We follow G-Eval (Liu et al., 2023b), which combines chain-of-thoughts (CoT) and a form-filling paradigm for LLM-based evaluation. G-Eval consists of two steps: evaluation step generation and score prediction. First, we manually write an initial prompt $\mathbf{a}_{\mathrm{init}}$ with a task instruction and evaluation criteria. Then, GPT generates evaluation steps. Next, we create a prompt a with task instruction and evaluation criteria, evaluation steps, and related work section to judge, and output format (the prompt is shown in appendix B.). Finally, the Novelty score $s_n \in \{0, 1\}$ is obtained from GPT prediction $s_n = \mathbf{GPT}(\mathbf{a})$.

The model is trained to use all cited articles in this setting. However, sometimes generated text misses cite all articles, as shown in [5] in Figure 2. Since the above metrics ignore such missing citations, we also evaluate the rate of missing citation r_{MC}.

4 Experiments

4.1 Experimental setting

Model. We evaluated the performance of various extractive and abstractive summarization models on our dataset:

TextRank (Mihalcea and Tarau, 2004) and LexRank (Erkan and Radev, 2004): graph-based unsupervised extractive summarization methods using the page rank technique and centrality scoring, respectively.

GPT3.5 and GPT4 (Brown et al., 2020): A largea language model released by Openai. We used the latest GPT-3.5 Turbo model (`gpt-3.5-turbo-1106`) and GPT4 (`gpt-4-0613`) for generation.

BART (Lewis et al., 2019): A famous encoder and decoder transformer pre-trained with autoregressive and denoising tasks.

PEGASUS (Zhang et al., 2020): A encoder and decoder transformer pre-trained for summarization with Gap Sentences Generation and Masked Language Model.

LED (Beltagy et al., 2020): A Longformer-Encoder-Decoder (LED) is an encoder and decoder transformer that introduces local and global attention instead of self-attention to utilize long context.

Llama2-7B (Touvron et al., 2023): An open-source large language model developed by Meta. The model has a 4096 context length with seven billion parameters and is trained in an autoregressive manner.

In this comparison, we fine-tuned abstractive models first pre-trained model with STRoGeNS-arxiv22 for 20 epochs and then fine-tuned with STRoGeNS-conf22 for 20 epochs.

Implementation. The models were trained using the AdamW optimizer with a learning rate of $3e-5$. The learning rate was adjusted using a linear scheduler with warm-up. For other parameters, we used the default parameter of huggingface implementation. All the models are trained on NVIDIA A100 80GB with batch size $= 64$. To match the max token length of the abstractive models, we truncated each abstract of the cited articles.

The implementation details for each model are as follows. We added a "/n" token to the PEGASUS tokenizer to generate paragraphs. LED is fine-tuned with 8,192 token length. For Llama2-7B, we used LoRA (Hu et al., 2021) with $r = 64$, $\alpha = 32$, dropout $= 0.1$ parameters.

4.2 Results

Evaluation with summarization and structure metrics. Table 6 compares the model in terms of summarization and structure metrics comparisons. The (+digit or -digit) indicates the increase or decrease in the performance from only fine-tuned with STRoGeNS-conf22 to this condition. Table 7 shows the performance of each model fine-tuned on STRoGeNS-conf22 (C) or STRoGeNS-arxiv22 (A) in terms of R-1, F1, and r_{MC} (full results are shown in Appendix D). Overall, BART achieved the best performance in terms of both metrics. We summarize the points of the results below.

Evaluation with novelty metrics. Table 8 shows the average novelty score for each method. Due to budget constraints, we verified the novelty score with GPT4 (`gpt-4-0613`) on 100 randomly sampled test samples. The generated texts of each model were input to the GPT with our prompts, and novelty scores were estimated. It shows that the text generated by BART contains a larger number of novelty statements than that of other models. 0.91 is a good trend since about 10% of original articles do not contain novelty statements. LED and Llama2 can handle long contexts, but the proportion of novelty statements decreases. This suggests that our task requires a novelty-centered model rather than simply using long inputs.

Pre-training for summarization does not contribute to improving performance. The performance of PEGASUS is significantly inferior to BART on both metrics. The main difference between PEGASUS and BART lies in their pre-training approaches; PEGASUS specializes in summarization tasks, whereas BART is designed for general generation tasks. Therefore, the characteristics of our task differ from simple summarization tasks, suggesting that it involves difficulty in summarization, citations, and structure ability.

Method	Summarization			Structure				Other
	R-1 ↑	R-2 ↑	R-L ↑	F1 ↑	ARI ↑	ARI' ↑	MAE_p ↓	r_{MC} ↓
TextRank	31.6	7.5	24.7	-	-	-	-	-
LexRank	31.5	8.19	21.6	-	-	-	-	-
GPT3.5	38.2	7.7	28.5	69.0	39.6	33.9	2.12	56.7%
GPT4*	41.4	7.8	29.8	66.7	32.1	29.8	1.73	41.2 %
BART	**47.4** (+4.9)	**13.1** (+1.3)	**32.7** (+1.7)	69.1 (+6.6)	**55.1** (+15.5)	**54.0** (+15.6)	2.03 (+0.07)	5.42% (-0.38)
PEGASUS	25.4 (+7.3)	6.2 (+1.2)	19.1 (+5.6	48.8 (+17.6)	11.3 (-0.8)	11.0 (+5.4)	4.04 (+0.68)	21.2% (+9.0)
LED	44.0 (+2.5)	11.8 (+0.5)	29.2 (+0.7)	59.5 (+3.4)	35.2(+9.1)	33.7 (+9.1)	2.18(-0.1)	**5.0 %** (-0.4)
Llama2-7B	42.7 (+0.1)	9.0(+0.1)	29.4(+0.2)	**69.8**(-0.2)	48.7(+0.4)	47.3 (+0.4)	**1.66** ±0	15.9% (-0.9)

Table 6: Comparisons on each model in terms of summarization and structure. The methods above the dashed line are unsupervised methods, and below the supervised methods. (+digit or -digit) indicates the increase or decrease in the performance from only fine-tuned with STRoGeNS-conf22 to this condition. Text colors red and blue indicate positive and negative effects, respectively. *: Due to budget constraints, we generated related work with GPT4 using only 1500 samples; thus, the results are for reference purposes.

Models accepting long context fail to utilize the rich context of cited articles. Surprisingly, the performances of LED and Llama2 are inferior to BART. Since we truncated the abstract of cited articles for max token length, BART can only use the first few sentences, and LED can use all sentences (The example of input text is shown in Appendix C). Although LED and Llama2 can use a rich context of the research field, models failed to utilize the context to improve performance. Since LED achieved great performance on other long text summarization (Liu et al., 2022, 2023a), our task requires understanding the relationships between articles from a long text, and it seems that the ability to process long scientific papers, which are different from traditional tasks, is insufficient.

5 Discussion

5.1 Model analysis

Quality vs. Quantity. As shown in Table 7, pre-training under STRoGeNS-arxiv22 is more effective than STRoGeNS-conf22 on models with short input token lengths (BART and PEGASUS). On the other hand, the performance under condition STRoGeNS-arxiv22 is inferior to condition STRoGeNS-conf22 on long input token length models (LED and Llama2). When using long context, the variation of inputs increases, and it becomes more difficult to process long input by understanding the meaning than short input lengths. Then, the long context model could not leverage the benefit of arxiv22 which has large variations and low-quality articles. The result suggests that to train models with longer input lengths, the dataset's quality becomes more crucial than for those with shorter inputs.

Method	D	R-1 ↑	F1 ↑	r_{MC} ↓
BART	C	42.5	62.5	5.8%
	A	**46.1**	66.4	2.8%
PEGASUS	C	18.1	31.2	12.0%
	A	17.7	40.2	6.0%
LED	C	41.5	56.1	**5.4 %**
	A	40.9	12.3	95.0%
Llama2-7B	C	42.6	**70.0**	16.8%
	A	37.6	9.0	95.2%

Table 7: Comparisons on each dataset. C: fine-tuning with STRoGeNS-conf22, A: fine-tuning with STRoGeNS-arxiv22.

Validity of novelty statements. As shown in Table 8, the generated section of BART contained the highest number of novelty statements compared to other models. However, since the input of BART is truncated (see Appendix C), it may not deeply understand the research field. In this study, we assessed whether the generated section contains novelty statements, but evaluating the validity of these statements is necessary for future work.

The potential of large language models. While GPT3.5 contains many missed citations, it achieves comparable performance with fine-trained Llama2 on structure metrics. Llama2 achieved the best performance in terms of structure when the fine-tuned models on STRoGeNS-conf22 (Table 7). These results suggest that under conditions of a small amount of training data, LLM exhibits superior structuring capabilities compared to other models.

Method	Novelty score
GPT3.5	0.17
BART	**0.91**
LED	0.53
Llama2	0.56

Table 8: Average novelty score of each model for 100 samples. The score is estimated by GPT in a G-EVAL manner.

Method	r	ρ	τ
F1	47.2	56.4	31.9
ARI	33.4	31.5	20.8
ARI'	38.3	35.7	24.9
MAE_p	-41.6	-45.8	-32.3

Table 9: Correlation between human evaluation with structure metrics. r, ρ, τ indicate Pearson's, Spearman's, and Kendall's correlation, respectively.

On the other hand, despite Llama2 having a wider range of academic knowledge than other models, the total performance is inferior to BART (Table 6). The reason is that the Llama2 does not fully leverage the benefits of quantity-oriented STRoGeNS-arxiv22. Therefore, we should explore methods that can utilize the advantages of both large models and datasets.

The concern with the language model is the number of missing citations. GPT, which is attracting attention for its generation of citations (Gao et al., 2023), fails citations for over 50 % of the articles on zero-shot settings on zero-shot condition. Even using GPT4, the rate of missed citations is still high. The rate of missed citation of fine-tuned Llama2 is 15%, and it is larger than BART.

5.2 Meta-evaluation

We conducted human evaluations to run meta-evaluation of structure and novelty metrics.

Structure metrics. We evaluated the structure of the generated section by Llama2 for 25 randomly selected samples from STRoGeNS-conf2023. Four annotators have manually inspected the structure score by comparing the generated section with the gold standard based on the following five criteria: (1) All topics of the paragraph do not match, (2) most topics of the paragraph do not match, (3) the topics of almost half do not match, (4) the few topics in the section do not match, (5) all topics in the section match.

Table 9 shows a correlation between human evaluation with our proposed metrics (F1, ARI, ARI', and MAE_p) in terms of Pearson's (r), Spearman's (ρ), and Kendall's (τ). The Fleiss' kappa (Warrens, 2010) among annotators is 0.156 and shows slight agreements. F1, ARI, and ARI' show a positive correlation, and MAE_p show a negative correlation with human evaluations. ARI', the extended version of ARI, shows a higher correlation than ARI, and it demonstrates the effectiveness of the proposed extension. The lower MAE_p, which is a difference in the number of paragraphs, is better, but it does not reflect the meaning within the paragraphs. In this human evaluation, a single score is given to one related work; hence, reflecting on each paragraph's quality is difficult. While ARI' focuses on each paragraph, F1 focuses only on the highest similarity paragraphs. Therefore, F1 seems to show a higher correlation. While not reflected in human evaluation, we argue that the quality of each paragraph is also important, and it is desirable to use both ARI' and F1.

Novelty metrics. We randomly selected 100 samples from the STRoGeNS-conf23 dataset and annotated them with sentence-level spans of novelty statements, finding 90 samples have novelty statements. Additionally, we synthesize the samples lack of novelty statements by removing annotated novelty statements from 90 samples. Then, we asked GPT4 (gpt-4-0613) used in our novelty metrics to determine whether each of the 190 samples contains novelty statements or not. As a result of evaluating 190 samples of novelty statements using GPT, the accuracy was 92%. This result supports that GPT is capable to judge the presence of novelty statements in related work, and consequently the validity of the novelty metrics used in our task.

6 Conclusion

In this paper, we redefined automatic related work generation as STructured Related Work Generation with Novelty Statement (**STRoGeNS**). For STRoGeNS, we proposed datasets focusing on the trade-off of quality and quantity and automatic evaluation metrics for structure and novelty. Using the quantity-oriented and quality-oriented datasets, we evaluated the performance of state-of-the-art models and showed that the task is not solved by simple summarization ability, and the ability to handle input length is required. In addition, we conducted human evaluation and demonstrated the effectiveness of the proposed automated evaluation metrics.

Limitations

Our dataset for STRoGeNS is mainly covered English and the computer science category. It contains Mathematics and Mathematics, but the test data only covers conferences of computer science. We should extend to the cross-domain and cross-lingual for the future.

We evaluated structure on the assumption that the citations of generated text are somewhat correct. However, as discussed in the discussion of citation evaluation (Funkquist et al., 2023), some citations do not take their meaning into account. Ideally, we should have factual consistency of citation. To carry this point, we should build a model that can evaluate the factual consistency of scientific articles using citation text datasets such as (Mao et al., 2022; Li et al., 2022).

In this paper, related work sections were just generated using an off-the-shelf language model. As in the early research (Hoang and Kan, 2010; Hu and Wan, 2014), when considering the entire section, a method that focuses on the topics handled within the section is required. We should consider using topic relationships between paragraphs rather than just generating entire sections with LLM.

Ethics Statement

Our datasets consist of articles from the scientific field, and we do not foresee a negative societal impact. As with text generation, the model tuned with our dataset may have risk to output factually inconsistent and biased texts.

Acknowledgements

This work is supported by JST Moonshot R&D Program Grant Number JPMJMS2236. We used the computational resources of AI Bridging Cloud Infrastructure (ABCI) provided by National Institute of Advanced Industrial Science and Technology (AIST).

References

Ahmed Ghassan Tawfiq AbuRa'ed, Horacio Saggion, Alexander V. Shvets, and Àlex Bravo. 2020. Automatic related work section generation: Experiments in scientific document abstracting. *Scientometrics*, 125:3159 – 3185.

Waleed Ammar, Dirk Groeneveld, Chandra Bhagavatula, Iz Beltagy, Miles Crawford, Doug Downey, Jason Dunkelberger, Ahmed Elgohary, Sergey Feldman, Vu Ha, Rodney Kinney, Sebastian Kohlmeier, Kyle Lo, Tyler Murray, Hsu-Han Ooi, Matthew Peters, Joanna Power, Sam Skjonsberg, Lucy Lu Wang, Chris Wilhelm, Zheng Yuan, Madeleine van Zuylen, and Oren Etzioni. 2018. Construction of the literature graph in semantic scholar. In *North American Chapter of the Association for Computational Linguistics: Human Language Technologies (NAACL-HLT)*, pages 84–91.

Iz Beltagy, Matthew E. Peters, and Arman Cohan. 2020. Longformer: The long-document transformer. *ArXiv*, abs/2004.05150.

Lukas Blecher, Guillem Cucurull, Thomas Scialom, and Robert Stojnic. 2023. Nougat: Neural optical understanding for academic documents. *ArXiv*, abs/2308.13418.

Tom Brown, Benjamin Mann, Nick Ryder, Melanie Subbiah, Jared D Kaplan, Prafulla Dhariwal, Arvind Neelakantan, Pranav Shyam, Girish Sastry, Amanda Askell, et al. 2020. Language models are few-shot learners. In *Advances in Neural Information Processing Systems (NeurIPS)*, pages 1877–1901.

Jingqiang Chen and Hai Zhuge. 2019. Automatic generation of related work through summarizing citations. *Concurrency and Computation: Practice and Experience*.

Xiuying Chen, Hind Alamro, Li Mingzhe, Shen Gao, Rui Yan, Xin Gao, and Xiangliang Zhang. 2022. Target-aware abstractive related work generation with contrastive learning. *Proceedings of the 45th International ACM SIGIR Conference on Research and Development in Information Retrieval*.

Xiuying Chen, Hind Alamro, Li Mingzhe, Shen Gao, Xiangliang Zhang, Dongyan Zhao, and Rui Yan. 2021. Capturing relations between scientific papers: An abstractive model for related work section generation. In *Association for Computational Linguistics (ACL)*.

Zekun Deng, Zixin Zeng, Weiye Gu, Jiawen Ji, and Bolin Hua. 2021. Automatic related work section generation by sentence extraction and reordering. In *Workshop on AI + Informetrics (AII)*.

Esin Durmus, He He, and Mona Diab. 2020. FEQA: A question answering evaluation framework for faithfulness assessment in abstractive summarization. In *Association for Computational Linguistics (ACL)*.

Günes Erkan and Dragomir R Radev. 2004. LexRank: Graph-based lexical centrality as salience in text summarization. *Journal of artificial intelligence research*, 22:457–479.

Jinlan Fu, See-Kiong Ng, Zhengbao Jiang, and Pengfei Liu. 2023. GPTScore: Evaluate as you desire. *ArXiv*, abs/2302.04166.

Martin Funkquist, Ilia Kuznetsov, Yufang Hou, and Iryna Gurevych. 2023. CiteBench: A benchmark for scientific citation text generation. In *Empirical Methods in Natural Language Processing (EMNLP)*.

Tianyu Gao, Howard Yen, Jiatong Yu, and Danqi Chen. 2023. Enabling large language models to generate text with citations. In *Empirical Methods in Natural Language Processing (EMNLP)*.

Sarik Ghazarian, Nuan Wen, Aram Galstyan, and Nanyun Peng. 2022. DEAM: Dialogue coherence evaluation using AMR-based semantic manipulations. In *Association for Computational Linguistics*.

Cong Duy Vu Hoang and Min-Yen Kan. 2010. Towards automated related work summarization. In *International Conference on Computational Linguistics (Coling)*.

J. Edward Hu, Yelong Shen, Phillip Wallis, Zeyuan Allen-Zhu, Yuanzhi Li, Shean Wang, and Weizhu Chen. 2021. LoRA: Low-rank adaptation of large language models. *ArXiv*, abs/2106.09685.

Yue Hu and Xiaojun Wan. 2014. Automatic generation of related work sections in scientific papers: An optimization approach. In *Empirical Methods in Natural Language Processing (EMNLP)*.

Lawrence J. Hubert and Phipps Arabie. 1985. Comparing partitions. *Journal of Classification*, 2:193–218.

Tetsu Kasanishi, Masaru Isonuma, Junichiro Mori, and Ichiro Sakata. 2023. SciReviewGen: A large-scale dataset for automatic literature review generation. In *Findings of Association for Computational Linguistics: ACL 2023*.

Mike Lewis, Yinhan Liu, Naman Goyal, Marjan Ghazvininejad, Abdel rahman Mohamed, Omer Levy, Veselin Stoyanov, and Luke Zettlemoyer. 2019. BART: Denoising sequence-to-sequence pre-training for natural language generation, translation, and comprehension. In *Association for Computational Linguistics (ACL)*.

Xiangci Li, Biswadip Mandal, and Jessica Ouyang. 2022. CORWA: A citation-oriented related work annotation dataset. In *North American Chapter of the Association for Computational Linguistics: Human Language Technologies (NAACL-HLT)*.

Chin-Yew Lin. 2004. ROUGE: A package for automatic evaluation of summaries. In *Association for Computational Linguistics (ACL)*.

Jiachang Liu, Qi Zhang, Chongyang Shi, Usman Naseem, Shoujin Wang, Liang Hu, and Ivor Tsang. 2023a. Causal intervention for abstractive related work generation. In *Findings of the Association for Computational Linguistics: EMNLP 2023*.

Shuaiqi Liu, Jiannong Cao, Ruosong Yang, and Zhiyuan Wen. 2022. Generating a structured summary of numerous academic papers: Dataset and method. In *International Joint Conference on Artificial Intelligence (IJCAI)*.

Yang Liu, Dan Iter, Yichong Xu, Shuohang Wang, Ruochen Xu, and Chenguang Zhu. 2023b. G-eval: NLG evaluation using gpt-4 with better human alignment. In *Empirical Methods in Natural Language Processing (EMNLP)*.

Kyle Lo, Lucy Lu Wang, Mark Neumann, Rodney Kinney, and Daniel Weld. 2020. S2ORC: The semantic scholar open research corpus. In *Association for Computational Linguistics (ACL)*.

Yao Lu, Yue Dong, and Laurent Charlin. 2020. Multi-XScience: A large-scale dataset for extreme multi-document summarization of scientific articles. In *Empirical Methods in Natural Language Processing (EMNLP)*.

Yuning Mao, Ming Zhong, and Jiawei Han. 2022. CiteSum: Citation text-guided scientific extreme summarization and domain adaptation with limited supervision. In *Empirical Methods in Natural Language Processing (EMNLP)*.

Rada Mihalcea and Paul Tarau. 2004. TextRank: Bringing order into text. In *Empirical Methods in Natural Language Processing (EMNLP)*.

Kishore Papineni, Salim Roukos, Todd Ward, and Wei-Jing Zhu. 2002. Bleu: a method for automatic evaluation of machine translation. In *Association for Computational Linguistics (ACL)*.

Hannah Rashkin, Vitaly Nikolaev, Matthew Lamm, Michael Collins, Dipanjan Das, Slav Petrov, Gaurav Singh Tomar, Iulia Turc, and D. Reitter. 2021. Measuring attribution in natural language generation models. *Computational Linguistics*, 49:777–840.

Tarek Saier, Johan Krause, and Michael Färber. 2023. unarXive 2022: All arXiv Publications Pre-Processed for NLP, Including Structured Full-Text and Citation Network. In *Joint Conference on Digital Libraries (JCDL)*.

Zhengliang Shi, Shen Gao, Zhen Zhang, Xiuying Chen, Zhumin Chen, Pengjie Ren, and Zhaochun Ren. 2023. Towards a unified framework for reference retrieval and related work generation. In *Findings of the Association for Computational Linguistics: EMNLP 2023*.

Douglas L. Steinley. 2004. Properties of the hubert-arabie adjusted rand index. *Psychological methods*, 9 3:386–96.

Hugo Touvron, Louis Martin, Kevin R. Stone, Peter Albert, Amjad Almahairi, Yasmine Babaei, Nikolay Bashlykov, Soumya Batra, Prajjwal Bhargava, Shruti Bhosale, Daniel M. Bikel, Lukas Blecher, Cristian Cantón Ferrer, Moya Chen, Guillem Cucurull, David Esiobu, Jude Fernandes, Jeremy Fu, Wenyin Fu, Brian Fuller, Cynthia Gao, Vedanuj Goswami, Naman Goyal, Anthony S. Hartshorn, Saghar Hosseini, Rui Hou, Hakan Inan, Marcin Kardas, Viktor Kerkez, Madian Khabsa, Isabel M. Kloumann, A. V. Korenev, Punit Singh Koura, Marie-Anne Lachaux,

Thibaut Lavril, Jenya Lee, Diana Liskovich, Yinghai Lu, Yuning Mao, Xavier Martinet, Todor Mihaylov, Pushkar Mishra, Igor Molybog, Yixin Nie, Andrew Poulton, Jeremy Reizenstein, Rashi Rungta, Kalyan Saladi, Alan Schelten, Ruan Silva, Eric Michael Smith, R. Subramanian, Xia Tan, Binh Tang, Ross Taylor, Adina Williams, Jian Xiang Kuan, Puxin Xu, Zhengxu Yan, Iliyan Zarov, Yuchen Zhang, Angela Fan, Melanie Kambadur, Sharan Narang, Aurelien Rodriguez, Robert Stojnic, Sergey Edunov, and Thomas Scialom. 2023. Llama 2: Open foundation and fine-tuned chat models. *ArXiv*, abs/2307.09288.

Alex Wang, Kyunghyun Cho, and Mike Lewis. 2020a. Asking and answering questions to evaluate the factual consistency of summaries. In *Association for Computational Linguistics (ACL)*.

Pancheng Wang, Shasha Li, Haifang Zhou, Jintao Tang, and Ting Wang. 2020b. ToC-RWG: Explore the combination of topic model and citation information for automatic related work generation. *IEEE Access*, 8:13043–13055.

Yongzhen Wang, Xiaozhong Liu, and Zheng Gao. 2018. Neural related work summarization with a joint context-driven attention mechanism. In *Empirical Methods in Natural Language Processing (EMNLP)*.

Matthijs J Warrens. 2010. Inequalities between multi-rater kappas. *Advances in data analysis and classification*, 4:271–286.

Xinyu Xing, Xiaosheng Fan, and Xiaojun Wan. 2020. Automatic generation of citation texts in scholarly papers: A pilot study. In *Association for Computational Linguistics (ACL)*.

Zheng Ye, Liucun Lu, Lishan Huang, Liang Lin, and Xiaodan Liang. 2021. Towards quantifiable dialogue coherence evaluation. In *Association for Computational Linguistics and International Joint Conference on Natural Language Processing (ACL-IJCNLP)*.

Weizhe Yuan, Graham Neubig, and Pengfei Liu. 2022. BARTScore: Evaluating generated text as text generation. In *Advances in Neural Information Processing Systems (NeurIPS)*.

Jingqing Zhang, Yao Zhao, Mohammad Saleh, and Peter J. Liu. 2020. PEGASUS: Pre-training with extracted gap-sentences for abstractive summarization. In *International Conference on Machine Learning (ICML)*.

Wei Zhao, Maxime Peyrard, Fei Liu, Yang Gao, Christian M. Meyer, and Steffen Eger. 2019. MoverScore: Text generation evaluating with contextualized embeddings and earth mover distance. In *Empirical Methods in Natural Language Processing and International Joint Conference on Natural Language Processing (EMNLP-IJCNLP)*.

You will be given one related work and title and abstract written for a computer science paper. Your task is to rate the related work on several metrics.

target paper info
Title, abst.
...
references
[1] {title}, {abst}
...
[N] {title}, {abst}

Output format
Output format:
Output is related work section that consists of 3~8 paragraphs with novelty statement. Ensure that there is a line break between each paragraph. When citing references, use the format '[reference number]' for citations. Enclose related work contents with <>.

Figure 3: Prompt for related work generation with GPT.

A Novel n-gram of dataset.

To measure how abstracted the dataset is, we report the proportion of novel n-grams in the target-related work section. Table 12 shows the n-grams for each dataset. Our dataset trends are similar to Bigsurvey and SciReviewGen, which aims to generate a literature review.

B Prompts for GPT

Figure 3 shows the prompt for GPT to generate related work.

Figure 4 shows our prompt for novelty evaluation. First, Evaluation steps s are generated by GPT. Then, we obtain the novelty score by inputting the whole prompt.

Table 11 shows the performance of Llama2-7B at each conference. Although our dataset contains a lot of computer vision articles, we can not confirm any major differences in performance.

C Example of input for each model

The default maximum token lengths of BART, Llama2, and LED are 1,024, 4,096, and 16,384. The average token length of our dataset is about 6,000. Therefore, we set the length for LED to 8,192 We set the maximum output token length of Llama2 as 640, so the input length of Llama2 is 3456.

Task introduction **i**
You will be given one related work, title, and abstract written for a computer science paper. Your task is to rate the related work on the following metric. Please make sure you read and understand these instructions carefully. Please keep this document open while reviewing, and refer to it as needed.

Evaluation criteria **e**
Evaluation Criteria:
Novelty statement (0 or 1) - whether related work contains novelty statement.

Evaluation steps **s** (GPT generated)
1. Read the Related Work Section Thoroughly: Begin by reading the entire related work section carefully. This will give you a complete understanding of the context and how the authors have positioned their work in relation to existing research.
2. Identify the Novelty Statement: Look specifically for a statement or a set of statements where the authors articulate what is new or different about their work compared to the existing literature. This can often be found towards the end of the related work section, but it might also be interspersed throughout the section.
3. Evaluate the Novelty Statement:
Presence (0 or 1): Determine if there is a clear statement of novelty. If such a statement exists, score it as '1'. If there is no explicit or implicit statement that outlines what makes the paper's contribution new or unique, score it as '0'.

Sample to judge **d**
Related work: {Related work}

Output format **f**
Output format:

Output only rate with JSON format.

Novelty statement: {}

Figure 4: Prompt for novelty evaluation.

Figure 5, 6, and 7 shows example of input length of each model. BART input only contains a few sentences of abstract for each cited article, Llama2 contains about 80% of abstract, and LED contains almost all abstract, on average.

D Result of fine-tuning on each dataset

Table 10 shows the full performance of each model on fine-tuned with WREWD-arxiv22 for 20 epochs (A) and WREWD-conf22 for 20 epochs (C). For BART and PEGASUS with a maximum token length of 1,024, the summarization and structure performance is better than the conditions using the STRoGeNS-conf22 dataset. On the other hand, LED and Llama2, which can use longer contexts, perform worse than conditions using the STRoGeNS-conf22 dataset.

E Examples of generated results of BART and Llama2

Figure 8 and 9 shows examples of input and output. Both BART and LLAMA results have paragraphs organized by research topics and contain a novelty statement.

BART (1024 token)

Target paper:
Title: Curvature-Aware Training for Coordinate Networks
Abstract: Coordinate networks are widely used in computer vision due to their ability to represent signals as compressed, continuous entities. However, training these networks with first-order optimizers can be slow, hindering their use in real-time applications. Recent works have opted for shallow voxel-based representations to achieve faster training, but this sacrifices memory efficiency. This work proposes a solution that leverages second-order optimization methods to significantly reduce training times for coordinate networks while maintaining their compressibility. Experiments demonstrate the effectiveness of this approach on various signal modalities, such as audio, images, videos, shape and neural radiance fields (NeRF).

[1] CoIL: Coordinate-based Internal Learning for Imaging Inverse Problems, Abstract: We propose Coordinate-based Internal Learning (CoIL) as a new deep-
[2] Implicit Neural Representations with Periodic Activation Functions, Abstract: Implicitly defined, continuous, differentiable signal representations parameterized by neural networks have emerged as a
[3] Learning Implicit Fields for Generative Shape Modeling, Abstract: We advocate the use of implicit fields for learning generative models of shapes and introduce an implicit field decoder
[4] Local Deep Implicit Functions for 3D Shape, Abstract: The goal of this project is to learn a 3D shape representation that enables accurate surface reconstruction, compact storage,
[5] The Implicit Bias of Minima Stability: A View from Function Space, Abstract: The loss terrains of over-parameterized neural networks have multiple global min
[6] DeepSDF: Learning Continuous Signed Distance Functions for Shape Representation, Abstract: Computer graphics, 3D computer vision and robotics communities have produced multiple approaches to representing 3D
[7] Nerfies: Deformable Neural Radiance Fields, Abstract: We present the first method capable of photorealistically reconstructing deformable scenes using photos/videos captured
[8] D-NeRF: Neural Radiance Fields for Dynamic Scenes, Abstract: Neural rendering techniques combining machine learning with geometric reasoning have arisen as one of the most promising approaches for
[9] DeRF: Decomposed Radiance Fields, Abstract: With the advent of Neural Radiance Fields (NeRF), neural networks can now render novel views of a 3
[10] PIFu: Pixel-Aligned Implicit Function for High-Resolution Clothed Human Digitization, Abstract: We introduce Pixel-aligned Implicit Function
[11] NeRF-: Neural Radiance Fields Without Known Camera Parameters, Abstract: Considering the problem of novel view synthesis (NVS) from only a set of 2D images
[12] pixelNeRF: Neural Radiance Fields from One or Few Images, Abstract: We propose pixelNeRF, a learning framework that predicts a continuous neural scene representation conditioned on
[13] NICE-SLAM: Neural Implicit Scalable Encoding for SLAM, Abstract: Neural implicit representations have recently shown encouraging results in various domains, including promising progress
[14] Factor Fields: A Unified Framework for Neural Fields and Beyond, Abstract: We present Factor Fields, a novel framework for modeling and representing signals. Factor Fields decomposes a signal
[15] Optimizing Neural Networks with Kronecker-factored Approximate Curvature, Abstract: We propose an efficient method for approximating natural gradient descent in neural networks
[16] Adaptive, Limited-Memory BFGS Algorithms for Unconstrained Optimization, Abstract: The limited-memory BFGS method (L-BFGS)
[17] Stochastic L-BFGS: Improved Convergence Rates and Practical Acceleration Strategies, Abstract: We revisit the stochastic limited-memory Broyden–F
[18] A Linearly-Convergent Stochastic L-BFGS Algorithm, Abstract: We propose a new stochastic L-BFGS algorithm and prove a
[19] Shampoo: Preconditioned Stochastic Tensor Optimization, Abstract: Preconditioned gradient methods are among the most general and powerful tools in optimization. However,
[20] Efficient Full-Matrix Adaptive Regularization, Abstract: Adaptive regularization methods pre-multiply a descent direction by a preconditioning matrix. Due

Figure 5: Example of truncated input text for BART.

LLAMA2 (4096 – 640=3456)

Input: Target paper:
Title: Curvature-Aware Training for Coordinate Networks
Abstract: Coordinate networks are widely used in computer vision due to their ability to represent signals as compressed, continuous entities. However, training these networks with first-order optimizers can be slow, hindering their use in real-time applications. Recent works have opted for shallow voxel-based representations to achieve faster training, but this sacrifices memory efficiency. This work proposes a solution that leverages second-order optimization methods to significantly reduce training times for coordinate networks while maintaining their compressibility. Experiments demonstrate the effectiveness of this approach on various signal modalities, such as audio, images, videos, shape and neural radiance fields (NeRF).

[1] CoIL: Coordinate-based Internal Learning for Imaging Inverse Problems, Abstract: We propose Coordinate-based Internal Learning (CoIL) as a new deep-learning (DL) methodology for the continuous representation of measurements. Unlike traditional DL methods that learn a mapping from the measurements to the desired image, CoIL trains a multilayer perceptron (MLP) to encode the complete measurement field by mapping the coordinates of the measurements to their responses. CoIL is a self-supervised method that requires no training examples besides the measurements of the test object itself. Once the MLP is trained, CoIL generates new measurements that can be used within a majority of image reconstruction methods. We validate CoIL on sparse
[2] Implicit Neural Representations with Periodic Activation Functions, Abstract: Implicitly defined, continuous, differentiable signal representations parameterized by neural networks have emerged as a powerful paradigm, offering many possible benefits over conventional representations. However, current network architectures for such implicit neural representations are incapable of modeling signals with fine detail, and fail to represent a signal's spatial and temporal derivatives, despite the fact that these are essential to many physical signals defined implicitly as the solution to partial differential equations. We propose to leverage periodic activation functions for implicit neural representations and demonstrate that these networks, dubbed sinusoidal representation networks or Sirens, are ideally suited for representing complex natural signals and their derivatives. We analyze Sir
[3] Learning Implicit Fields for Generative Shape Modeling, Abstract: We advocate the use of implicit fields for learning generative models of shapes and introduce an implicit field decoder, called IM-NET, for shape generation, aimed at improving the visual quality of the generated shapes. An implicit field assigns a value to each point in 3D space, so that a shape can be extracted as an iso-surface. IM-NET is trained to perform this assignment by means of a binary classifier. Specifically, it takes a point coordinate, along with a feature vector encoding a shape, and outputs a value which indicates whether the point is outside the shape or not. By replacing conventional decoders by our implicit decoder for representation
[4] Local Deep Implicit Functions for 3D Shape, Abstract: The goal of this project is to learn a 3D shape representation that enables accurate surface reconstruction, compact storage, efficient computation, consistency for similar shapes, generalization across diverse shape categories, and inference from depth camera observations. Towards this end, we introduce Local Deep Implicit Functions (LDIF), a 3D shape representation that decomposes space into a structured set of learned implicit functions. We provide networks that infer the space decomposition and local deep implicit functions from a 3D mesh or posed depth image. During experiments, we find that it provides
...
[20] Efficient Full-Matrix Adaptive Regularization, Abstract: Adaptive regularization methods pre-multiply a descent direction by a preconditioning matrix. Due to the large number of parameters of machine learning problems, full-matrix preconditioning methods are prohibitively expensive. We show how to modify full-matrix adaptive regularization in order to make it practical and effective. We also provide a novel theoretical analysis for adaptive regularization in non-convex optimization settings. The core of our algorithm, termed GGT, consists of the efficient computation of the inverse square root of a low-rank matrix. Our preliminary experiments show improved iteration-wise convergence rates across synthetic tasks and standard deep learning benchmarks, and that
Related work:

Figure 6: Example of truncated input text for Llama2.

LED (8192 token)

Target paper:
Title: Curvature-Aware Training for Coordinate Networks
Abstract: Coordinate networks are widely used in computer vision due to their ability to represent signals as compressed, continuous entities. However, training these networks with first-order optimizers can be slow, hindering their use in real-time applications. Recent works have opted for shallow voxel-based representations to achieve faster training, but this sacrifices memory efficiency. This work proposes a solution that leverages second-order optimization methods to significantly reduce training times for coordinate networks while maintaining their compressibility. Experiments demonstrate the effectiveness of this approach on various signal modalities, such as audio, images, videos, shape and neural radiance fields (NeRF).

[1] CoIL: Coordinate-based Internal Learning for Imaging Inverse Problems, Abstract: We propose Coordinate-based Internal Learning (CoIL) as a new deep-learning (DL) methodology for the continuous representation of measurements. Unlike traditional DL methods that learn a mapping from the measurements to the desired image, CoIL trains a multilayer perceptron (MLP) to encode the complete measurement field by mapping the coordinates of the measurements to their responses. CoIL is a self-supervised method that requires no training examples besides the measurements of the test object itself. Once the MLP is trained, CoIL generates new measurements that can be used within a majority of image reconstruction methods. We validate CoIL on sparse-view computed tomography using several widely-used reconstruction methods, including purely model-based methods and those based on DL. Our results demonstrate the ability of CoIL to consistently improve the performance of all the considered methods by providing high-fidelity measurement fields.
[2] Implicit Neural Representations with Periodic Activation Functions, Abstract: Implicitly defined, continuous, differentiable signal representations parameterized by neural networks have emerged as a powerful paradigm, offering many possible benefits over conventional representations. However, current network architectures for such implicit neural representations are incapable of modeling signals with fine detail, and fail to represent a signal's spatial and temporal derivatives, despite the fact that these are essential to many physical signals defined implicitly as the solution to partial differential equations. We propose to leverage periodic activation functions for implicit neural representations and demonstrate that these networks, dubbed sinusoidal representation networks or Sirens, are ideally suited for representing complex natural signals and their derivatives. We analyze Siren activation statistics to propose a principled initialization scheme and demonstrate the representation of images, wavefields, video, sound, and their derivatives. Further, we show how Sirens can be leveraged to solve challenging boundary value problems, such as particular Eikonal equations (yielding signed distance functions), the Poisson equation, and the Helmholtz and wave equations. Lastly, we combine Sirens with hypernetworks to learn priors over the space of Siren functions.
[3] Learning Implicit Fields for Generative Shape Modeling, Abstract: We advocate the use of implicit fields for learning generative models of shapes and introduce an implicit field decoder, called IM-NET, for shape generation, aimed at improving the visual quality of the generated shapes. An implicit field assigns a value to each point in 3D space, so that a shape can be extracted as an iso-surface. IM-NET is trained to perform this assignment by means of a binary classifier. Specifically, it takes a point coordinate, along with a feature vector encoding a shape, and outputs a value which indicates whether the point is outside the shape or not. By replacing conventional decoders by our implicit decoder for representation learning (via IM-AE) and shape generation (via IM-GAN), we demonstrate superior results for tasks such as generative shape modeling, interpolation, and single-view 3D reconstruction, particularly in terms of visual quality. Code and supplementary material are available at https://github.com/czq142857/implicit-decoder.
...
[20] Efficient Full-Matrix Adaptive Regularization, Abstract: Adaptive regularization methods pre-multiply a descent direction by a preconditioning matrix. Due to the large number of parameters of machine learning problems, full-matrix preconditioning methods are prohibitively expensive. We show how to modify full-matrix adaptive regularization in order to make it practical and effective. We also provide a novel theoretical analysis for adaptive regularization in ...

Figure 7: Example of truncated input text of LED.

Method	Dataset	Summarization			Structure				Other
		R-1	R-2	R-L	F1	ARI	ARI'	MAE_p	r_{MC}
BART	A	0.461	0.131	0.327	0.664	0.499	0.482	1.811	2.79 %
	C	0.425	0.118	0.310	0.625	0.396	0.384	1.963	5.8%
PEGASUS	A	0.177	0.053	0.140	0.402	0.071	0.044	3.486	5.99%
	C	0.181	0.050	0.135	0.312	0.121	0.057	3.364	12.0%
LED	A	0.409	0.098	0.281	0.123	0.113	0.113	2.145	95.0%
	C	0.415	0.113	0.285	0.561	0.261	0.246	2.275	5.4 %
Llama2-7B	A	0.376	0.075	0.268	0.090	0.090	0.090	1.623	95.21%
	C	0.426	0.089	0.292	**0.700**	0.483	0.469	1.668	16.8%

Table 10: Fine-tuning result with STRoGeNS-arxiv22 and STRoGeNS-conf22. A: indicates STRoGeNS-arxiv22, C: indicates STRoGeNS-conf22

Conferences	Summarization			Structure				Other
	R-1	R-2	R-L	F1	ARI	ARI'	MAE_p	r_{MC}
ACL	0.412	0.073	0.277	0.722	0.484	0.464	1.354	12.38 %
CVPR	0.430	0.093	0.296	0.698	0.490	0.478	1.718	17.05 %
ICCV	0.430	0.094	0.297	0.694	0.482	0.469	1.709	17.69 %
ICML	0.413	0.075	0.279	0.707	0.465	0.443	1.673	17.64 %

Table 11: Performance of Llama2 on each conference.

Method	unigrams	bigrams	trigrams	4-grams
S2ROC	27.1 %	73.8 %	91.7 %	98.2 %
Delve	29.4 %	78.1 %	93.5 %	98.3 %
TAS2	26.9%	77.5%	93.6%	97.5%
TAD	27.0 %	77.5 %	93.8 %	97.5 %
Bigsurvey	16.3 %	62.1 %	88.0 %	95.7 %
SciReviewGen	14.9 %	59.3 %	85.7 %	94.0 %
STRoGeNS-arxiv22	17.4 %	62.0 %	86.2 %	95.4 %
STRoGeNS-conf22	16.0%	59.5%	84.6%	93.9%
STRoGeNS-conf23	14.3%	57.1%	84.3%	94.4%

Table 12: Novel n-grams of target sentence.

Input

Target paper:
Title: Space Engage: Collaborative Space Supervision for Contrastive-based Semi-Supervised Semantic Segmentation **Abstract:** Semi-Supervised Semantic Segmentation (S4) aims to train a segmentation model with limited labeled images and a substantial volume of unlabeled images. To improve the robustness of representations, powerful methods introduce a pixel-wise contrastive learning approach in latent space (i.e., representation space) that aggregates the representations to their prototypes in a fully supervised manner. However, previous contrastive-based S4 methods merely rely on the supervision from the model's output (logits) in logit space during unlabeled training. In contrast, we utilize the outputs in both logit space and representation space to obtain supervision in a collaborative way. The supervision from two spaces plays two roles: 1) reduces the risk of over-fitting to incorrect semantic information in logits with the help of representations; 2) enhances the knowledge exchange between the two spaces. Furthermore, unlike previous approaches, we use the similarity between representations and prototypes as a new indicator to tilt training those under-performing representations and achieve a more efficient contrastive learning process. Results on two public benchmarks demonstrate the competitive performance of our method compared with state-of-the-art methods.

[1] Adversarial Learning for Semi-supervised Semantic Segmentation, Abstract: We propose a method for semi-supervised semantic segmentation using an adversarial network. While most existing discriminators are trained to classify input images as real or fake on the image level, we design a discriminator in a fully convolutional manner to differentiate the predicted probability maps from the ground truth segmentation distribution with the consideration of the spatial resolution. We show that the proposed discriminator can be used to improve semantic segmentation accuracy by coupling the adversarial loss with the standard cross entropy loss of the proposed model. In addition, the fully convolutional discriminator enables semi-supervised learning through discovering the trustworthy regions in predicted results of unlabeled images, thereby providing additional supervisory signals. In contrast to existing methods that utilize weakly-labeled images, our method leverages unlabeled images to enhance the segmentation model. Experimental results on the PASCAL VOC 2012 and Cityscapes datasets demonstrate the effectiveness of the proposed algorithm.

...

'[25] A Simple Framework for Contrastive Learning of Visual Representations, Abstract: This paper presents SimCLR: a simple framework for contrastive learning of visual representations. We simplify recently proposed contrastive self-supervised learning algorithms without requiring specialized architectures or a ... accuracy, which is a 7% relative improvement over previous state-of-the-art, matching the performance of a supervised ResNet-50. When fine-tuned on only 1%

Gold standard

The aim of S4 is to train a segmentation model with the semi-supervised setting (_i.e._, a few labeled images and a large number of unlabeled images) to classify each pixel in an entire image. The critical issue of S4 is how to leverage unlabeled images to train the model. Some methods [1][2][3][4] based on GANs [5], adversarial training [6], and consistency regularization paradigm [7][8][9][10]. Meanwhile, self-training [11][12][13][14][15] is also a striking paradigm, which always generates pseudo-labels from model and retrains the model with the combined supervision of human annotations and pseudo-labels. One essential issue of self-training is the accuracy of pseudo-labels. Some methods [16][17][18][19] try to polish pseudo-labels and provide reliable guidance. Some methods [20][21][22][23] focus on the class-imbalance problems in the dataset and try to alleviate the negative effect from class-biased pseudo-labels generated by the model pre-trained on imbalanced labeled images. We build our framework based on the self-training and additionally explore semantic information among different images.

Pixel-wise contrastive learning explores semantic relations not only in the individual image but also among different images. Different from instance-wise contrastive learning [24][25][26], pixel-wise contrastive learning [27][28][29][30] project each pixel to the representation in representation space with the cooperation of encoder and representation head. Representations are then aggregated in their prototypes and are separated from each other in different classes. In semi-supervised settings, most methods [31][32][33][34] use pseudo-labels based on logits to provide semantic information contrastive learning process during training on unlabeled images. Meanwhile, the confidence of logit is used as an indicator to involve the contrastive learning process, _e.g._, [32] uses the hard representations whose corresponding logit confidence is lower than a threshold to contrast for effective training. As opposed to the above methods, we use collaborative space supervision for contrastive learning on unlabeled images and use a new indicator to involve the contrastive learning progress.

Prototype-based learning has been widely studied in few-shot learning [35][36][37] and unsupervised domain adaption [38][39][40][41][42]. Recently, it is restudied in semantic segmentation as known as a non-parametric prototype-based classifier [43]. Concretely, the classes in the dataset are presented by a set of non-learnable prototypes, and the dense semantic predictions are thus achieved by assigning the output features to its most similar prototype. Under semi-supervised settings, some methods maintain the consistency between predictions from a linear predictor and a prototype-based predictor. The two predictors are followed by the encoder and project the features to logit space and representation space, respectively. In this work, we combine the semantic information in the logit and representation spaces to provide supervision in a collaborative way during semi-supervised learning.

LLAMA2-7B

Semi-Supervised Semantic Segmentation. Semi-supervised semantic segmentation (S4) aims to leverage abundant unlabeled data to improve the segmentation performance of limited labeled images [1][2][3][4][5][6]. The basic workflow of S4 models is first to predict the probabilities for the unlabeled images (assigning pseudo labels) and then train the model with these pseudo labels and real labeled images [7][8][9][10][11]. Although robust models trained with S4 have achieved outstanding performance, it still struggles in real-world applications due to the insufficient supervision from the labeled data [12][13][14][15][16][17][18]. In recent years, self-training (ST) based methods have emerged as a popular approach and has achieved significant improvements in segmentation accuracy and temporal stability compared with other traditional S4 methods [13][12][19][20][21][22][23].

However, previous self-training methods mainly rely on the fully-supervised model outputs in logits space to improve the robustness of feature representations. In contrast, contrastive learning has been widely used in unsupervised visual representation learning to disentangle visual features by utilizing strong supervision [24][25][26][27]. Recently, contrastive learning has been introduced to semi-supervised learning to improve the representations of images and their associated pseudo labels [28][29][30][31][32].

Most of these contrastive-based methods introduce the pseudo labels to form an augmented input dataset to supplement the limited labeled data and train the segmentation model with this augmented dataset. An Augmented Learning-based Pixel-wise Contrastive Framework (ALP) introduces a contrastive loss and a representation loss to improve the robustness of feature representation, but it is designed to work with a fully-supervised image labeling scheme in the segmentation pipeline (i.e., images are labelled before training). Also, the inputs used in ALP are obtained with the ground truth labels. S4[33] simply selects highly confident pixels as pseudo labels and updates the model with the augmented dataset, thus does not have similar supervision as ALP. In contrast, C3-SS [14] trains a segmentation model with pseudo labels in logit space and the ground-truth labels in representation space. The features extracted from the logit-space segmentation model are fed into a contrastive loss to enhance their robustness. We also use the features in logit space to produce a contrastive loss, but unlike previous contrastive-based S4 methods, we propose to enhance the similarity between the representations and prototypes with an extra representation-to-prototype contrastive loss. Furthermore, unlike C3-SS which only uses the network outputs in

BART

Semi-Supervised Semantic Segmentation (SSL) aims to learn a segmentation model with limited labeled data and a substantial volume of unlabeled data. Adversarial-based methods [1][2][3][4] utilize GANs [5] to generate pseudo-labels for unlabelled data. VAT [6] and CCT [7] use adversarial training to encourage the predictions to be consistent with the ground truth. UCC [8] and CPS [9] use uncertainty estimation to enhance pseudo-label generation. Transformer-CNN Cohort [10] introduces a self-training framework that combines a teacher model and a student model. Self-training methods [11][12][13][14][15][16][17][18][19][20][21][22][23] are also widely used in S4. FixMatch [18] combines self-supervised learning and consistency regularization. ST++ [19] improves FixMatch by applying multi-level perturbations. CReST [21] uses class-rebalancing to improve the quality of pseudo labels.

Contrastive-based Learning [24][25][26] has achieved great success in unsupervised visual representation learning. Recently, contrastive learning has also been introduced to SSL. C3-SemiSeg [14] uses a contrastive loss in the pixel-level. Pixel-wise contrastive methods [27][28][29][30][31][32][33][34] also show promising results. PiPa [29] and PiPaV2 [27] perform pixel-wise and feature-level contrastive losses. PCC [30] and PCC-v2 [31] use a consistency loss between global and local features. UCT [33] uses unreliable predictions from the teacher model to supervise the student model, which is similar to Mean-Teacher [12].

Prototype-based learning [35][36][37][38][39][40][41][42] has been applied to many tasks, such as few-shot learning and domain adaptation. PCL [34] is the first work to use prototypes to boost the performance of SSL. However, PCL only uses the supervision from the output in logit space. In contrast, we utilize the outputs in both logit and representation spaces to supervize each other.

proposes a contrast-based method to learn discriminative features for image classification. SimCLR [25] proposes a simple framework that performs instance discrimination in the latent space. Inspired by these works, we propose a pixel-wised contrastive method for S4, which differs from previous works in two aspects. First, we use the similarity between representations and prototypes as a new indicator to tilt training those under-performing representations. Second, we enhance the knowledge transfer between the two spaces by introducing a collaborative learning strategy.

introduces a contrast loss to learn transferable features in a fully supervised manner. [43] extends this idea to S4 and proposes a dual-path self-distillation method to improve

Figure 8: Example of generated related work section 1. Both BART and Llama2-7B results are organized research topics with multiple paragraphs and contain novelty statements. Red text indicate sentence of novelty statement.

Input

Target paper:
Title: Don't Generate, Discriminate: A Proposal for Grounding Language Models to Real-World Environments
Abstract: A key missing capacity of current language models (LMs) is grounding to real-world environments. Most existing work for grounded language understanding uses LMs to directly generate plans that can be executed in the environment to achieve the desired effects. It thereby casts the burden of ensuring grammaticality, faithfulness, and controllability all on the LMs. We propose Pangu, a generic framework for grounded language understanding that capitalizes on the discriminative ability of LMs instead of their generative ability. Pangu consists of a symbolic agent and a neural LM working in a concerted fashion: The agent explores the environment to incrementally construct valid plans, and the LM evaluates the plausibility of the candidate plans to guide the search process. A case study on the challenging problem of knowledge base question answering (KBQA), which features a massive environment, demonstrates the remarkable effectiveness and flexibility of Pangu: A BERT-base LM is sufficient for setting a new record on standard KBQA datasets, and larger LMs further bring substantial gains. Pangu also enables, for the first time, effective few-shot in-context learning for KBQA with large LMs such as Codex.1Footnote 1: The Pangu library: OSU-NLP-Group/Pangu.

[1] A Comprehensive Exploration on WikiSQL with Table-Aware Word Contextualization, Abstract: We present SQLova, the first Natural-language-to-SQL (NL2SQL) model to achieve human performance in WikiSQL dataset. We revisit and discuss diverse popular methods in NL2SQL literature, take a full advantage of BERT {Devlin et al., 2018) through an effective table contextualization method, and coherently combine them, outperforming the previous state of the art by 8.2% and 2.5% in logical form and execution accuracy, respectively. We particularly note that BERT with a seq2seq decoder leads to a poor performance in the task, indicating the importance of a careful design when using such large pretrained models. We also provide a comprehensive analysis on the dataset and our model, which can be helpful for designing future NL2SQL datsets and models. We especially show that our model's performance is near the upper bound in WikiSQL, where we observe that a large portion of the evaluation errors are due to wrong annotations, and our model is already exceeding human performance by 1.3% in execution accuracy.

...

[23] SmBoP: Semi-autoregressive Bottom-up Semantic Parsing, Abstract: The de-facto standard decoding method for semantic parsing in recent years has been to autoregressively decode the abstract syntax tree of the target program using a top-down depth-first traversal. In this work, we propose an alternative approach: a Semi-autoregressive Bottom-up Parser (SmBoP) that constructs at decoding step t the top-K sub-trees of height ≤ t. Our parser enjoys several benefits compared to top-down ... semantically-vacuous partial trees. We apply SmBoP on Spider, a challenging zero-shot semantic parsing benchmark, and show that SmBoP leads to a 2.2x speed-up in decoding time and a ~5x speed-up in training time, compared to a semantic parser that uses autoregressive decoding. SmBoP obtains 71.1 denotation accuracy on Spider, establishing a new state-of-the-art, and 69.5 exact match, comparable to the 69.6 exact match of the autoregressive RAT-SQL+Grappa.

Gold standard

The Seq2Seq framework ([5]; [4]) has been the _de facto_ choice for grounded language understanding, where the LM directly generates a plan given an input utterance. However, the lack of grounding during pretraining makes generating valid plans from LMs challenging. Recent studies endeavor to alleviate this issue via _input augmentation_ or _constrained decoding_. For input augmentation, the environment (or some relevant portion of it) is fed to the LM's encoder together with the utterance ([1]; [6]; [7]). Such methods rely on the LM to understand the interplay between the language requests and the environment and correctly factor that into plan generation. They therefore require substantial training data to learn and also provide no guarantee for grammaticality or faithfulness. In contrast, constrained decoding methods regulate the decoder's behavior to guarantee grammaticality ([8]; [3]) or even faithfulness ([9]; [2]). However, such uses still cast the burden of generating valid plans on the LM itself; controlling the generation process of an LM can be difficult and specific to each planning language and/or environment. In our proposal, the LM is only used to discriminate valid plans proposed by an agent through a controllable search process. More detailed comparison is presented in SS5.3.

Large language models (LLMs) (; [17]) have demonstrated strong few-shot learning capabilities in various tasks, from writing programs to query structured and unstructured data ([16]; [13]; [10]), interacting with online websites ([11]; [14]), to generating procedural plans and guiding embodied agents in virtual environments ([15]; [18]; [12];). Most existing work still capitalizes on the generative ability of LLMs. A common strategy to encourage an LLM to produce valid plans is to directly _describe_ the environment in the LLM's context (_i.e._, input augmentation), which is difficult for complex environments like KBs. A concurrent work of ours () asks the LLM to directly generate a proxy plan from the input question without the environment description, which is then used to retrieve a valid plan from a set of candidate plans. However, this design is tailored specifically to the KB query language and is limited to generating plans with at most two hops due to the combinatorial explosion in their candidate enumeration. In contrast, Pangu shields the LLM from the complexity of the environment and lets the LLM focus on evaluating the plausibility of candidate plans proposed by an agent. One interesting related work is [18], where an LLM is used to score atomic action (skill) proposals, which are guaranteed to conform to affordance constraints, from an embodied agent. Pangu shares a similar spirit of using LMs for discrimination, but we support more complex plans through a search process in the environment guided by an LM.

Our instantiation of Pangu on KBQA is closely connected to bottom-up semantic parsing, particularly SmBoP ([23]), a text-to-SQL model that iteratively constructs a complex plan from a set of subplans. Pangu similarly constructs a complex plan incrementally from smaller subplans, but it makes the following main departures. First, SmBoP requires all ingredients (_i.e._, column headers, table names, and DB values) at the beginning of parsing. This assumption does not generally hold for more complex or partially observable environments, where ingredients need to be discovered through search. In our method, only topic entities are needed as the initial plan, which can be readily obtained using an entity linker ([21]). Second, our scoring function is based on a straightforward application of LMs, while SmBoP uses a more intricate architecture with extra parameters. Also related is an array of earlier KBQA methods that adopt an enumerate-and-rank approach ([20]; [19]; [22]). Because they try to enumerate all candidate plans up front, the maximum plan complexity is bound to be small. Our adaptive search process allows for flexible construction of more complex plans.

LLAMA2-7B

Language Understanding with Language Models. Large pre-trained language models (LMs) have emerged as powerful tools for a variety of tasks in natural language processing ([5]; [4]). In the past years, great efforts have been devoted to understanding the knowledge encoded in LMs ([6]; ; [1]), bridging LMs and traditional program synthesis methods ([16]; ; [12]; [15]), and transferring LMs to different tasks, such as text-to-SQL () and text-to-text (; ; [7]; [13]; [9]; [14]; [11]; [3]; [8]; [2]; [10]; [17]; [18]).

Knowledge Base Question Answering. Recent research on KBQA aims to ground LMs on knowledge bases to enhance the reasoning and comprehension abilities ([22]; [23]; [20]; ; [21]; [2]). Specifically, several works train general-purpose LMs on a large amount of KBQA data to improve the reasoning ability ([22]; [23]), and others use a hyper-parameter-tuning strategy to deal with the out-of-distribution (OOD) KBQA problem ([24]; [19];). Differently, the proposed Pangu directly implements grounding.

BART

Knowledge Base Question Answering. Knowledge base question answering (KBQA) is a long-standing problem in natural language processing (NLP) [19]; ; [3]; [1]; [7]; [2]; [6]. Most existing work on KBQA is based on the Seq2Seq framework [5]; [4], which encodes the question and the knowledge base into a joint embedding space, and then decodes the answer to the question using a decoder that takes the embedding as input.

Grounded Language Understanding. Recently, there has been a surge of interest in grounding language models to symbolic languages, such as code [17]; [10]; [9]; [8], HTML [11]; [14], and SQL [13]; ; ; [6]; ;. Most of the existing work for grounded language understanding uses LMs to directly generate plans that can be executed in the environment to achieve the desired effects. This casts the burden of ensuring grammaticality, faithfulness, and controllability all on the LMs. In contrast, Pangu leverages the discriminative ability of LMs instead of their generative ability, and thus enables, for the first time, grounding to real-world environments. Our work is also related to [15]; [12]; [18]; [16], which also use LMs for task planning. However, unlike Pangu, these methods do not explicitly consider the plausibility of the generated plans, and hence cannot guarantee the correctness of the plans. In addition, they do not scale well to large LMs, which are required for our applications.

Semantic Parsing. Semantic parsing is the task of converting natural language questions into executable programs, which can then be executed by a symbolic agent to obtain the answer [20]; [23]; [21]; [22]. In particular, [20] propose a staged query graph generation (SQG) framework, which first generates a query graph from the question, and subsequently uses it to answer the question. [21] propose an end-to-end entity linking framework that first generates an entity linking graph and then links the entities in the graph to the answer. [23] propose to use a semi-progressive bottom-up semantic parsing framework to first generate a set of candidate answers and then select the best answer from the top-k answers. In this work, we propose to leverage a discriminator to guide the search process of the symbolic agent, so that the generated programs can be more likely to be valid.

propose a framework for symbolic question answering, which is similar to our work in spirit, but differs in several important ways. First, they only consider the question as input, and do not consider the context in which the question is expressed. Second, their framework only considers the question in the context of a single question, while our framework considers the context from multiple questions. Third, their work only focuses on SQL, whereas our work focuses on the more challenging task of knowledge graph question answering. Fourth, our framework can scale to larger LMs and

Figure 9: Example of generated related work section 2. BART tends to contain novelty statements.

F Datasheets for datasets

Motivation

For what purpose was the dataset created? Was there a specific task in mind? Was there a specific gap that needed to be filled? Please provide a description.

The dataset was created to enable research to generate structured related work with novelty statement: given target article information and cited articles information, generate related work section with paragraph whether paragraphs are written based topics determined from the relations between current work and previous work and novelty statement.

Who created this dataset (e.g., which team, research group) and on behalf of which entity (e.g., company, institution, organization)?

OMRON SINIC X Corp.

Who funded the creation of the dataset? If there is an associated grant, please provide the name of the grantor and the grant name and number.

See acknowledgement.

Composition

What do the instances that comprise the dataset represent (e.g., documents, photos, people, countries)? Are there multiple types of instances (e.g., movies, users, and ratings; people and interactions between them; nodes and edges)? Please provide a description.

The instances are related work sections extracted from scientific articles, together with the title and abstract of the target article and cited paper information (*i.e.,* title, abstract).

How many instances are there in total (of each type, if appropriate)?

See Table 1, 2, 3, 4.

Does the dataset contain all possible instances or is it a sample (not necessarily random) of instances from a larger set? If the dataset is a sample, then what is the larger set? Is the sample representative of the larger set (e.g., geographic coverage)? If so, please describe how this representativeness was validated/verified. If it is not representative of the larger set, please describe why not (e.g., to cover a more diverse range of instances, because instances were withheld or unavailable).

Our dataset relies on open-source top conference proceedings. Therefore, we can collect more instances by parsing the proceedings.

What data does each instance consist of? "Raw" data (e.g., unprocessed text or images) or features? In either case, please provide a description.

Each instance consists of the text associated with the articles. We only used articles that could correctly extract the title, abstract, related work, and the list of cited articles and removed articles with a related work paragraph of 1 and 8 or more paragraphs or fewer than five cited articles. All citation identifiers such as Author and year are replaced [#i].

Is there a label or target associated with each instance? If so, please provide a description.

Randomly sampled 100 samples were annotated for novelty statement sentences for novelty evaluation.

Is any information missing from individual instances? If so, please provide a description, explaining why this information is missing (e.g., because it was unavailable). This does not include intentionally removed information, but might include, e.g., redacted text.

As shown in Table 5, some samples missing abstract of cited article information cause retrieval errors of semantic scholar API. In the conference datasets, some title of cited articles are missing due to parse errors of NOUGAT.

Are relationships between individual instances made explicit (e.g., users' movie ratings, social network links)? If so, please describe how these relationships are made explicit.

None explicitly. Some instances are cited in other instances.

Are there recommended data splits (e.g., training, development/validation, testing)? If so, please provide a description of these splits, explaining the rationale behind them.

We recommended using STRoGeNS-arXiv22, STRoGeNS-conf22 as training and STRoGeNS-arXiv23 as test to avoid data leak. The dataset is separated by published years of articles and the split setting reflects the actual usage of related work generation.

Are there any errors, sources of noise, or redundancies in the dataset? If so, please provide a description.

The datasets collected from the top conferences may contain parse errors of NOUGAT.

Is the dataset self-contained, or does it link to or otherwise rely on external resources (e.g., websites, tweets, other datasets)? If it links to or relies on external resources, a) are there guarantees that they will exist, and remain constant, over time; b) are there official archival versions of the complete dataset (i.e., including the external resources as they existed at the time the dataset was created); c) are there any restrictions (e.g., licenses, fees) associated with any of the external resources that might apply to a future user? Please provide descriptions of all external resources and any restrictions associated with them, as well as links or other access points, as appropriate.

STRoGeNS-arxiv2022 contains OpenAlex links for each citation and license link.

Does the dataset identify any subpopulations (e.g., by age, gender)? If so, please describe how these subpopulations are identified and provide a description of their respective distributions within the dataset.

See Table 2, 3, and 4.

Collection Process

How was the data associated with each instance acquired? Was the data directly observable (e.g., raw text, movie ratings), reported by subjects (e.g., survey responses), or indirectly inferred/derived from other data (e.g., part-of-speech tags, model-based guesses for age or language)? If data was reported by subjects or indirectly inferred/derived from other data, was the data validated/verified? If so, please describe how.

The data is observable as raw text.

What mechanisms or procedures were used to collect the data (e.g., hardware apparatus or sensor, manual human curation, software program, software API)? How were these mechanisms or procedures validated?

To collect the conference PDFs, we used Beautiful Soup and parsed by NOUGAT. Then, abstracts of citations are collected by Semantic Scholar API.

Who was involved in the data collection process (e.g., students, crowdworkers, contractors) and how were they compensated (e.g., how much were crowdworkers paid)?

Two researchers collected the dataset.

Over what timeframe was the data collected? Does this timeframe match the creation timeframe of the data associated with the instances (e.g., recent crawl of old news articles)? If not, please describe the timeframe in which the data associated with the instances was created.

Conference datasets are collected from conference proceedings from 2017 to 2023. unarXiv2022 is a collected articles uploader until 2022.

Preprocessing/cleaning/labeling

Was any preprocessing/cleaning/labeling of the data done (e.g., discretization or bucketing, tokenization, part-of-speech tagging, SIFT feature extraction, removal of instances, processing of missing values)? If so, please provide a description. If not, you may skip the remainder of the questions in this section.

The samples that had one paragraph, more than eight paragraphs, and less than five citations were removed. Regarding conference datasets, we only use related work sections that collected the title, the abstract, the related work section, and the references of the target paper.

Was the "raw" data saved in addition to the preprocessed/cleaned/labeled data (e.g., to support unanticipated future uses)? If so, please provide a link or other access point to the "raw" data.

Yes.

Distribution

Will the dataset be distributed to third parties outside of the entity (e.g., company, institution, organization) on behalf of which the dataset was created? If so, please provide a description.

STRoGeNS-arXiv22 is constructed based on each license of arXiv papers. Therefore, please follow the license of arXiv paper.

How will the dataset be distributed (e.g., tarball on website, API, GitHub) Does the dataset have a digital object identifier (DOI)?

We will publish processing codes to Github and dataset by the website as long as the license allows.

When will the dataset be distributed?

The paper is accepted.

Will the dataset be distributed under a copyright or other intellectual property (IP) license, and/or under applicable terms of use (ToU)? If so, please describe this license and/or ToU, and provide a link or other access point to, or otherwise reproduce, any relevant licensing terms or ToU, as well as any fees associated with these restrictions.

ACL, EMNLP, NAACL, and ICLR are follows licensed under the Creative Commons Attribution-NonCommercial-ShareAlike 3.0 International License. CVPR, ICCV, ECCV, ICML, and arXiv follow all rights therein are retained by authors or by other copyright holders.

Understanding Survey Paper Taxonomy about Large Language Models via Graph Representation Learning

Jun Zhuang
Department of Computer Science
Boise State University
junzhuang@boisestate.edu

Casey Kennington
Department of Computer Science
Boise State University
caseykennington@boisestate.edu

Abstract

As new research on Large Language Models (LLMs) continues, it is difficult to keep up with new research and models. To help researchers synthesize the new research many have written survey papers, but even those have become numerous. In this paper, we develop a method to automatically assign survey papers to a taxonomy. We collect the metadata of 144 LLM survey papers and explore three paradigms to classify papers within the taxonomy. Our work indicates that leveraging graph structure information on co-category graphs can significantly outperform the language models in two paradigms; pre-trained language models' fine-tuning and zero-shot/few-shot classifications using LLMs. We find that our model surpasses an average human recognition level and that fine-tuning LLMs using weak labels generated by a smaller model, such as the GCN in this study, can be more effective than using ground-truth labels, revealing the potential of weak-to-strong generalization in the taxonomy classification task.

1 Introduction

Collective attention in Natural Language Processing (NLP)—and the wider public—has turned to Large Language Models (LLMs) (Lyu et al., 2022; Xie et al., 2023; Jin et al., 2024). It has become so difficult to keep up with the proliferation of new models that many researchers have written survey papers to help synthesize research progress. Survey papers are often crucial for newcomers to gain an in-depth understanding of the research evolution. However, volumes of survey papers have become unruly for researchers—especially newcomers—to sift through. As illustrated in Figure 1, the number of survey papers has been increasing significantly. This leads to our research question: Is it possible to automatically reduce the barriers for newcomers in a way that can keep up with the constant influx of new information? This question underscores one of the challenges in scholarly document processing (Chandrasekaran et al., 2020).

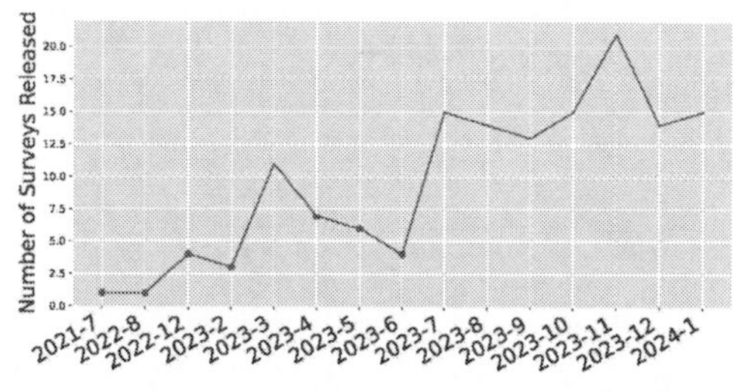

Figure 1: Trends of survey papers about large language models since 2021. Numbers reflect the year and month (e.g., 2023-3 is March 2023).

In this work, we address the above question by developing a method that can automatically assign survey papers to a taxonomy. Such a taxonomy will help researchers see new trends in the field and focus on specific survey papers that are relevant to their research. Classifying papers into a taxonomy may seem an ordinary task, but it is actually quite challenging for the following reasons:

1. Our dataset contains 144 papers. While this number for the survey papers is uncommonly large, the number of instances in the dataset is still relatively small.
2. We propose a new taxonomy for the collected survey papers, where the distribution of each category is not uniform, which leads to a substantial class imbalance issue.
3. Authors usually use similar terminologies to describe LLMs in the title and abstract. Such textual similarity introduces significant difficulties in taxonomy classifications.

To answer our research questions, we investigate three types of attributed graphs: text graphs, co-author graphs, and co-category graphs. Extensive experiments indicate that leveraging graph structure information of co-category graphs can help better classify the survey papers to the corresponding categories in the proposed taxonomy.

Proceedings of the Fourth Workshop on Scholarly Document Processing (SDP 2024), pages 58–69
August 16, 2024 ©2024 Association for Computational Linguistics

Moreover, we validate that graph representation learning (GRL) can outperform language models in two paradigms, fine-tuning pre-trained language models and zero-shot/few-shot classifications using LLMs. Inspired by a recent study, which indicates that leveraging weak labels, which are generated by smaller (weaker) models, may help enhance the performance of larger (stronger) models (Burns et al., 2023), we further examine whether using weak labels, which are generated by GNNs in this study, in the fine-tuning paradigm can help the pre-trained language models. The experiments demonstrate that fine-tuning using weak labels can exceed that using ground-truth labels. For the latter paradigm, we use the results of human recognition as the baseline. The analysis demonstrates that GRL achieves higher accuracy and F1 scores, and even surpasses the average human recognition level by a substantial margin. Overall, our primary contributions can be summarized as follows:

- We collected and analyzed 144 survey papers about LLMs and their metadata.[1]
- We propose a new taxonomy for categorizing the survey papers, which will be helpful for the research community, particularly newcomers and multidisciplinary research teams.
- Extensive experiments demonstrate that graph representation learning on co-category graph structure can effectively classify the papers and substantially outperform the language models and average human recognition level on a relatively small and class-imbalanced dataset with high textual similarity.
- Our results also reveal the potential of fine-tuning pre-trained models using weak labels.

2 Related Work

Taxonomy Classification Conventional taxonomy classification is a subset of Automatic Taxonomy Generation (ATG), which aims to generate or augment taxonomy for processing scholarly documents (Krishnapuram and Kummamuru, 2003; Smirnova and Mayr, 2023; Lo et al., 2023; Kinney et al., 2023; Lee et al., 2024). The main challenge in ATG is to cluster the unlabeled topics into different hierarchical structures. Thus, most existing methods in ATG are clustering-based methods. Zamir and Etzioni (1998) design a mechanism, Grouper, that dynamically groups and labels the search results. Vaithyanathan and Dom (1999) propose a model to generate hierarchical clusters. Lawrie et al. (2001) discover the relationship among words to generate concept hierarchies. Within these methods, a subset, called co-clustering, clusters keywords and documents simultaneously (Frigui and Nasraoui, 2002; Kummamuru et al., 2003). Different from ATG, we classify survey papers into corresponding categories in the proposed taxonomy on small and class-imbalanced datasets with highly similar terminologies.

Graph Representation Learning Graph representation learning (GRL) is a powerful approach for learning the representation in graph-structure data (Zhou et al., 2020), whereas most recent works achieve this goal using Graph Neural Networks (GNNs) (Defferrard et al., 2016; Veličković et al., 2018; Xu et al., 2018; Liu et al., 2022, 2021). Bruna et al. (2013) first introduce a significant advancement in convolution operations applied to graph data using both spatial method and spectral methods. To improve efficiency, Kipf and Welling (2016) simplify graph convolutions to a first-order polynomial while yielding superior performance in semi-supervised learning. Hamilton et al. (2017) propose an inductive-learning approach that aggregates node features from corresponding fixed-size local neighbors. Regarding ATG via GNNs, several works attempt to generate or expand taxonomies using new proposed graph models (Shen et al., 2020; Xu et al., 2022). Compared to model-based approaches, we first improve the performance of taxonomy classification from data-driven perspectives.

3 Methodology

In this section, we first introduce the procedure of data collection and then explore the metadata. We further explain the process of constructing three types of attributed graphs and how we learn graph representation via graph neural networks.

3.1 Data Collection and Exploration

We scraped the metadata of survey papers about LLMs from arXiv and further manually supplemented the metadata from Google Scholar and the ACL anthology. The papers range from July 2021 to January 2024. Given these survey papers, we designed a taxonomy and assigned each paper to a corresponding category within the taxonomy. Our motivation is that a reasonable taxonomy can provide a clear hierarchy of concepts for readers to bet-

[1]We release our datasets and source code at https://github.com/junzhuang-code/TaxonomyClassification

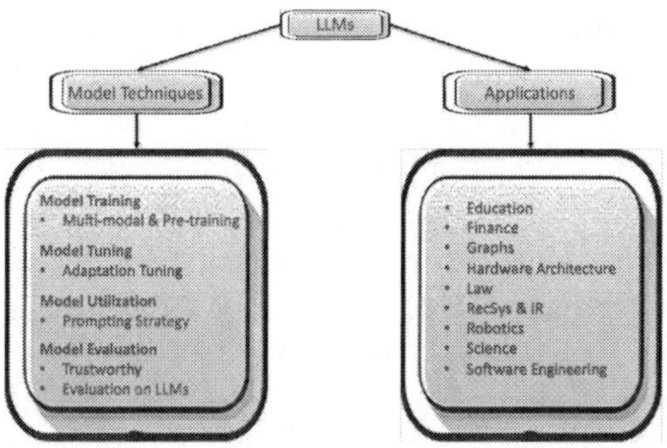

Figure 2: The mind map of survey papers about large language models. Besides "Comprehensive" and "Others" that are not included in the mind map, we highlight fourteen categories in our proposed taxonomy. The total number of categories for the 144 papers is sixteen.

ter understand the relationship among a large number of survey papers. Though survey papers can be taxonomized differently, we noticed two broad categories: *applications* and *model techniques*. The *applications* category further sub-divides into specific domains of focus (e.g., education or science), whereas *model techniques* further sub-divides into ways of effecting models (e.g., fine-tuning).

We visualize our proposed taxonomy and highlight fourteen classes, i.e., the leaf nodes, in Figure 2. The total classes in the labels are sixteen, including *comprehensive* and *others* (not shown in the figure). To better understand the distribution of the classes, we present the class distribution in Figure 3. The distribution indicates that the class is extremely imbalanced, introducing a challenge to the taxonomy classification task.

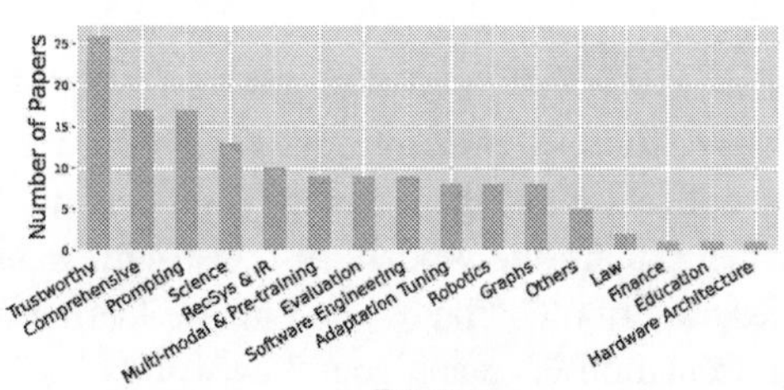

Figure 3: Distribution of classes in the taxonomy.

After visualizing the proposed taxonomy, we further explain the motivation for proposing a new taxonomy instead of using the arXiv categories. In Figure 4, we present the distribution of survey papers across different arXiv categories. Top-2 frequent categories are `cs.CL` (Computation and Language), and `cs.AI` (Artificial Intelligence), which means that most authors choose these two categories for their works. However, these choices cannot help readers to better distinguish the survey papers. For example, papers related to model techniques are indistinguishable in arXiv categories. Thus, designing a new taxonomy is an essential step in this study.

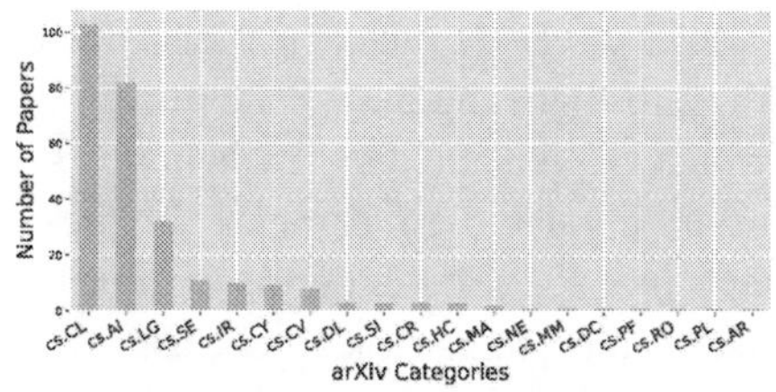

Figure 4: Distribution of survey papers that we found across different arXiv categories.

We also present the word frequency in Figure 5 to show which words have been frequently used in abstracts. These distributions suggest that the abstracts of these papers contain many similar terms, which increases the difficulty of text classification.

Attributes	Descriptions
Taxonomy	Proposed taxonomy
Title	Paper title
Authors	Lists of author's name
Release Date	First released date
Links	Links of papers
Paper ID	The arXiv paper ID
Categories	The arXiv category
Summary	Abstract of papers

Table 1: Data attributes and descriptions.

Overall, we present the data description of their attributes in Table 1. After designing the taxonomy and building the dataset, we explain how we classify documents into the taxonomy categories in the following section.

3.2 Building Attributed Graphs

The goal of building the graphs is to utilize the graph structure information to classify the taxonomy. Before building the graphs, We first define the attributed graphs as follows:

Definition 1 *An attributed graph $\mathcal{G}$ is a topological structure that represents the relationships among vertices associated with attributes. $\mathcal{G}$ consists of a set of vertices $\mathcal{V} = \{v_1, v_2, ..., v_N\}$ and edges $\mathcal{E} \subseteq \mathcal{V} \times \mathcal{V}$, where N is the number of vertices in $\mathcal{G}$.*

Given the Definition 1, we further define the matrix representation of an attributed graph as follows:

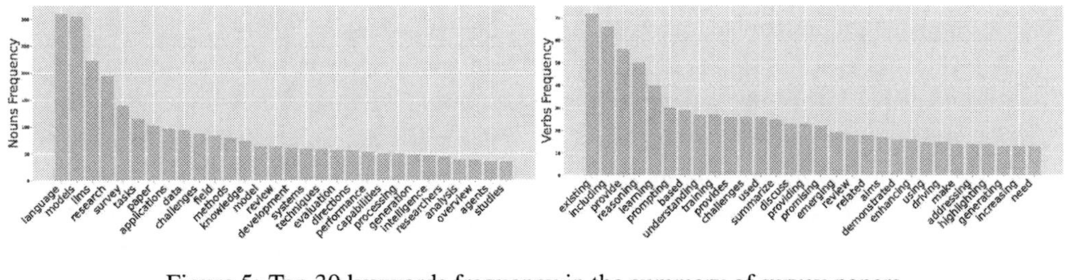

Figure 5: Top 30 keywords frequency in the summary of survey papers.

Definition 2 *Given an attributed graph $\mathcal{G}(\mathcal{V}, \mathcal{E})$, the topological relationship among vertices can be represented by a symmetric adjacency matrix $\mathbf{A} \in \mathbb{R}^{N \times N}$. Each vertex contains an attribute vector, a.k.a., a feature vector. All feature vectors constitute a feature matrix $\mathbf{X} \in \mathbb{R}^{N \times d}$, where d is the number of features for each vertex. Thus, the matrix representation of an attributed graph can be formulated as $\mathcal{G}(\mathbf{A}, \mathbf{X})$.*

Based on the above definitions, we build the graph by creating the term frequency-inverse document frequency (TF-IDF) feature matrices for both title and summary (i.e., abstract) columns, where the term frequency denotes the word frequency in the document, and inverse document frequency denotes the log-scaled inverse fraction of the number of documents containing the word. TF-IDF matrix is commonly used for text classification tasks because it helps capture the distinctive words that can indicate specific classes (Yao et al., 2019). After establishing the TF-IDF matrices, we apply one-hot encoding on the arXiv's categories and then combine three matrices along the feature dimension to build the feature matrix $\mathbf{X}$.

To leverage the topological information among vertices, we proceed to construct the graph structures to connect the attribute vectors. In this study, we are interested in three types of graphs: text graph, co-author graph, and co-category graph. We explain each type as follows.

Text Graph We follow the same settings as TextGCN (Yao et al., 2019) to build the text graph. Specifically, the edges of the text graph are built based on word occurrence (paper-word edges) in the paper's text data, including both title and summary, and word co-occurrence (word-word edges) in the whole text corpus. To obtain the global word co-occurrence information, we slide a fixed-size window on all papers' text data. Moreover, we calculate the edge weight between a paper vertex and a word vertex using the TF-IDF value of the word in the paper and calculate the edge weight between two-word vertices using point-wise mutual information (PMI), a popular metric to measure the associations between two words. Note that in the text graph, we don't use the above feature matrix because only paper vertices contain attribute vectors. To retain consistency, we set all values in the feature matrix as one. For the same reason, only the paper vertices are assigned labels, whereas all word vertices are labeled as a new class, which is not touched during the training or testing phase.

Co-author Graph In the co-author graph, we introduce an edge connecting two vertices (papers) if they share at least one common author.

Co-category Graph In the co-category graph, an edge is added between two vertices with at least one common arXiv category. In the co-authorship and co-category graphs, each vertex is assigned one class (taxonomy) as the label. Note that in this study all edges are undirected.

3.3 Taxonomy Classification via Graph Representation Learning

Given the well-built attributed graphs $\mathcal{G}(\mathbf{A}, \mathbf{X})$, we aim to investigate whether graph representation learning (GRL) using graph neural networks (GNNs) can help classify survey papers into the taxonomy. Before feeding the matrix representation, $\mathbf{A}$ and $\mathbf{X}$, of the attributed graphs $\mathcal{G}$ into GNNs, we first preprocess the adjacency matrix $\mathbf{A}$ as follows:

$$\hat{\mathbf{A}} = \tilde{\mathbf{D}}^{-\frac{1}{2}} \tilde{\mathbf{A}} \tilde{\mathbf{D}}^{-\frac{1}{2}}, \qquad (1)$$

where $\tilde{\mathbf{A}} = \mathbf{A} + I_N$, $\tilde{\mathbf{D}} = \mathbf{D} + I_N$. I_N is an identity matrix. $\mathbf{D}_{i,i} = \sum_j \mathbf{A}_{i,j}$ is a diagonal degree matrix.

After preprocessing, we utilize GNNs to learn graph representation. The layer-wise message-passing mechanism of GNNs can be generally formulated as follows:

$$f_{\mathbf{W}^{(l)}}\left(\hat{\mathbf{A}}, \mathbf{H}^{(l)}\right) = \sigma\left(\hat{\mathbf{A}} \mathbf{H}^{(l)} \mathbf{W}^{(l)}\right), \qquad (2)$$

where $\mathbf{H}^{(l)}$ is a node hidden representation in the l-th layer. The dimension of $\mathbf{H}^{(l)}$ in the input layer, middle layer, and output layer is the number of features d, hidden units h, and classes K, respectively. $\mathbf{H}^{(0)} = \mathbf{X}$. $\mathbf{W}^{(l)}$ is the weight matrix in the l-th layer. σ denotes a non-linear activation function, such as ReLU.

In general node classification tasks, GNNs are trained with ground-truth labels $\mathbf{Y} \in \mathbb{R}^{N\times 1}$. In this study, we assign ground-truth labels based on our proposed taxonomy. To simplify the problem, each paper is assigned one primary category as the label, even if the paper sometimes may belong to more than one category. During training, we optimize GNNs with cross-entropy.

In brief, we address the Taxonomy Classification problem via GRL approaches in this study and formally state the problem as follows:

Problem 1 *After building an attributed graph $\mathcal{G}(\hat{\mathbf{A}}, \mathbf{X})$ and the ground-truth labels $\mathbf{Y}$ based on the survey metadata, we train a graph neural network (*GNN*) on the train data and evaluate the taxonomy classification performance on the test data. Our goal is to design a method to better understand (classify) the taxonomy of the survey papers.*

4 Experiment

In this section, we evaluate the graph representation learning (GRL)'s effectiveness compared with two paradigms using language models.

Subsets	Graphs	$\lvert\mathcal{V}\rvert$	$\lvert\mathcal{E}\rvert$	$\lvert F\rvert$	$\lvert C\rvert$
$Data_{Nov23}$	Text	737	94,943	737	16
	Co-author	112	204	3,065	15
	Co-category	112	4,908	3,065	15
$Data_{Jan24}$	Text	951	137,709	951	17
	Co-author	144	332	3,542	16
	Co-category	144	8,140	3,542	16
$Data_{subset}$	Text	905	128,575	905	12
	Co-author	134	302	3,394	11
	Co-category	134	6,964	3,394	11

Table 2: Statistics of graph datasets. $\lvert\mathcal{V}\rvert$, $\lvert\mathcal{E}\rvert$, $\lvert F\rvert$, and $\lvert C\rvert$ denote the number of nodes, edges, features, and classes, respectively.

Experimental Settings To examine the generalization of our method on various graph structures, we investigate three types of attributed graphs: text graphs, co-author graphs, and co-category graphs, and compare the classification performance of GRL with that of fine-tuning pre-trained language models across three subsets of our data. Both $Data_{Nov23}$ and $Data_{Jan24}$ contain survey papers collected at the end of corresponding months (November 2023 and January 2024). $Data_{Jan24}$ includes a new category, *Hardware Architecture*. We further construct the third subset $Data_{subset}$ by removing some proposed categories with fewer instances in $Data_{Jan24}$; these categories are *Law*, *Finance*, *Education*, *Hardware Architecture*, and *Others*. The motivation for constructing three subsets is to validate the generalization of our method across different subsets since the classification performance may significantly change on small datasets. Also, new categories may emerge at any period because research on LLMs is developing rapidly, and so are related survey papers. For example, a new category, *Hardware Architecture*, emerges in $Data_{Jan24}$. The change of categories may affect the performance as well. Therefore, we investigate our method on three subsets that contain different categories. The statistics of our dataset and corresponding attributed graphs are presented in Table 2. Recall that the text graph consists of paper vertices and word vertices, and thus contains one additional class because all word vertices are labeled as a new class, which is not touched during the training or testing phase.

To evaluate our model, we split the train, validation, and test data as 60%, 20%, and 20%. Due to the potential for random splits to result in an easier task for our model, we ran the experiments five times using random seed IDs from 0 to 4 and reported the mean values with corresponding standard deviations, mean (std). We evaluate the classification performance by accuracy and weighted f1 score. Accuracy is a common metric on classification tasks, whereas the weighted f1 score provides a balanced measure of the class-imbalanced dataset.

4.1 Leveraging Graph Structure Information for Taxonomy Classification

We investigate whether leveraging the graph structure information can help better classify the papers to their corresponding categories in the proposed taxonomy. In this experiment, we construct the attributed graphs based on the text data (including the title and summary) and the relationship of the co-authorship and co-category. To examine the generalization of GRL, we employ GCN (Kipf and Welling, 2016) as a backbone GNN on various graph structures across three subsets. According to Table 3, GNNs fail to learn graph representation on

	$Data_{Nov23}$		$Data_{Jan24}$		$Data_{subset}$	
	Accuracy	Weighted-F1	Accuracy	Weighted-F1	Accuracy	Weighted-F1
Text	20.91 (5.45)	14.20 (4.41)	17.86 (7.14)	16.31 (4.49)	23.08 (4.87)	18.82 (1.50)
Co-author	33.04 (8.06)	33.06 (8.69)	20.00 (8.56)	19.24 (8.79)	29.63 (7.03)	29.24 (6.02)
Co-category (All)	63.48 (18.36)	62.82 (16.96)	75.17 (5.52)	74.60 (4.81)	**79.26 (6.87)**	**77.88 (7.52)**
Co-category (Rm cs.CL)	70.43 (9.28)	68.46 (9.63)	67.59 (15.36)	65.81 (17.03)	76.30 (12.31)	73.83 (14.53)
Co-category (Rm cs.AI)	**73.91 (18.03)**	**72.41 (18.28)**	**75.86 (8.99)**	**75.79 (9.62)**	77.04 (3.63)	74.15 (4.11)
Co-category (Rm cs.CL, cs.AI)	26.09 (10.65)	20.19 (10.56)	37.93 (8.45)	35.97 (7.92)	49.63 (7.63)	47.32 (7.59)
Co-category (Rm cs.IR)	63.48 (18.36)	62.82 (16.96)	75.17 (5.52)	74.60 (4.81)	79.26 (6.87)	77.88 (7.52)
Co-category (Rm cs.RO)	63.48 (18.36)	62.82 (16.96)	75.17 (5.52)	74.60 (4.81)	79.26 (6.87)	77.88 (7.52)
Co-category (Rm cs.SE)	65.22 (11.00)	63.21 (10.37)	74.48 (8.33)	75.10 (6.77)	82.96 (6.02)	82.93 (6.22)
Co-category (Rm cs.IR, cs.RO)	63.48 (18.36)	62.82 (16.96)	75.17 (5.52)	74.60 (4.81)	79.26 (6.87)	77.88 (7.52)
Co-category (Rm cs.IR, cs.SE)	65.22 (11.00)	63.21 (10.37)	74.48 (8.33)	75.10 (6.77)	82.96 (6.02)	82.93 (6.22)
Co-category (Rm cs.RO, cs.SE)	65.22 (11.00)	63.21 (10.37)	74.48 (8.33)	75.10 (6.77)	82.96 (6.02)	82.93 (6.22)
Co-category (Rm cs.IR, cs.RO, cs.SE)	65.22 (11.00)	63.21 (10.37)	74.48 (8.33)	75.10 (6.77)	82.96 (6.02)	82.93 (6.22)

Table 3: Evaluation of graph representation learning on three types of attributed graphs across three subsets of our data. We also conducted ablation studies on the graph structure of co-category graphs by removing (denoted by Rm) some arXiv categories. We ran the experiments five times and presented the mean (std).

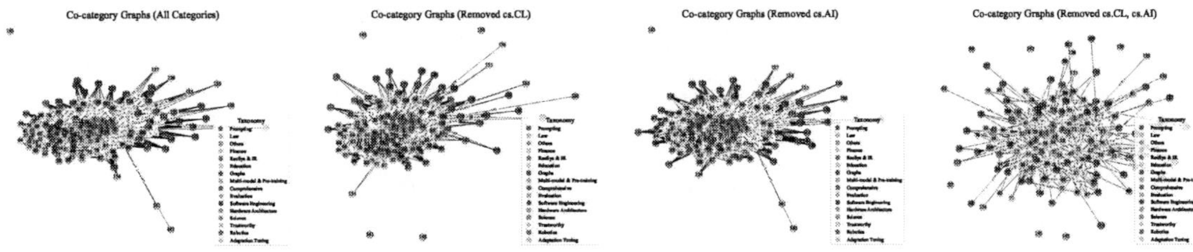

Figure 6: Visualization of four graph structures on co-category graphs by removing the categories.

both the text graph and the co-author graph. For the text graph, we argue that the degradation may be caused by excessively similar words in the summary of survey papers. When constructing the text graph, these word vertices connect with many paper vertices, resulting in the paper vertices being less distinguishable. For the co-author graph, we conjecture that it is challenging to categorize papers solely based on the sparse co-authorship in this dataset. Furthermore, we observe that some co-authorships come from a common mentor in the same lab whereas two first authors work on the survey papers in two distinct categories. These reasons weaken the effectiveness of using graph structure information. GNNs, in contrast, are very reliable (evaluated by both accuracy and weighted F1 score) in most co-category graphs.

Ablation Analysis We further examine the graph structures of co-category graphs by conducting ablation studies. First, according to Figure 4, most papers are assigned as `cs.CL` and `cs.AI` in the arXiv categories. Thus, we study how the categories, `cs.CL` and `cs.AI`, affect the performance by muting these two categories in a combinatorial manner. In Table 3, we observe that GNNs can maintain a comparable performance after removing either `cs.CL` or `cs.AI`. However, the performance dramatically drops after removing both categories. This is possible since most node connections are significantly sparsified after these two categories are removed. Even though both `cs.CL` and `cs.AI` do not directly map to the existing classes, either one can connect the nodes and further strengthen the message-passing in GNNs, allowing GNNs to learn better node representations.

We visualize co-category graphs in $Data_{Jan24}$ in Figure 6. The visualization indicates that most nodes are clustered well even if we remove the category either `cs.CL` or `cs.AI`. However, after removing these two categories simultaneously, we observe that node classifications gradually become disordered and several nodes are then isolated. This visualization illustrates the effectiveness of GRL.

We further visualize GCNs' hidden representation on the above co-category graphs in $Data_{Jan24}$ in Figure 7. The figures show that the nodes are well-classified in the hidden space even if either the category `cs.CL` or `cs.AI` is removed. However, the distribution of nodes tends to become chaotic when both of these two categories are removed simultaneously, shown in Table 3.

For completeness, we conducted another abla-

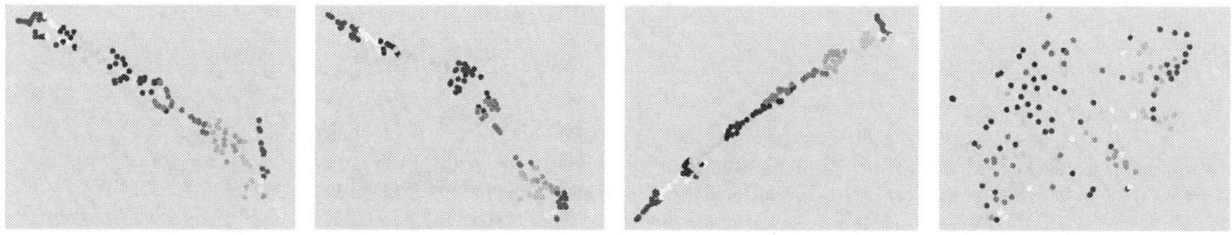

(a) All Categories (b) Removed cs.CL (c) Removed cs.AI (d) Removed cs.CL, cs.AI

Figure 7: Visualization of GCNs' hidden representation on co-category graphs in $Data_{Jan24}$ via t-SNE. Each dot represents one node and is labeled with one color.

	$Data_{Nov23}$		$Data_{Jan24}$		$Data_{subset}$	
	Accuracy	Weighted-F1	Accuracy	Weighted-F1	Accuracy	Weighted-F1
BERT (Devlin et al., 2018)	30.43 (18.45)	25.70 (19.91)	43.45 (18.84)	41.50 (22.31)	58.74 (6.87)	57.51 (6.94)
RoBERTa (Liu et al., 2019)	41.74 (20.32)	39.17 (22.84)	35.86 (17.53)	27.23 (23.67)	25.93 (12.17)	17.02 (15.16)
DistilBERT (Sanh et al., 2019)	**57.39 (8.87)**	**55.59 (10.66)**	**53.10 (2.76)**	**52.07 (4.47)**	**59.26 (7.41)**	**58.15 (8.82)**
XLNet (Yang et al., 2019)	25.22 (16.82)	21.59 (20.54)	27.59 (14.30)	21.59 (15.39)	28.52 (9.37)	21.51 (9.65)
Electra (Clark et al., 2019)	23.04 (4.76)	19.06 (4.06)	44.83 (7.23)	42.01 (8.39)	20.01 (6.87)	12.03 (8.45)
Albert (Lan et al., 2019)	11.30 (8.06)	4.85 (7.21)	15.17 (4.68)	5.14 (2.87)	20.74 (9.83)	11.41 (11.15)
BART (Lewis et al., 2020)	51.30 (17.48)	50.30 (17.62)	51.72 (3.08)	50.62 (2.79)	58.25 (8.11)	57.68 (8.90)
DeBERTa (He et al., 2020)	24.78 (8.06)	19.61 (10.36)	26.21 (11.03)	20.92 (14.25)	25.93 (10.73)	24.30 (10.52)
Llama2 (Touvron et al., 2023)	14.48 (8.72)	4.77 (4.35)	19.22 (5.90)	6.03 (4.21)	23.45 (8.72)	12.59 (7.23)

Table 4: Evaluation of fine-tuning pre-trained language models on the text data across three subsets.

tion study to examine how the categories, cs.IR, cs.RO, and cs.SE, affect the classification performance as their names are similar to that of some classes in our proposed taxonomy (recall that our proposed taxonomy is not based on the arXiv categories). According to Table 3, the classification performances are well-maintained no matter which category is removed, whereas removing cs.SE does slightly change the results (highlighted by gray color). We argue that the results are reasonable since these removals only drop a small number of edges and don't break the topological relationships in the graph. Overall, these studies verify that leveraging the graph structure information in co-category graphs can positively contribute to the taxonomy classification.

4.2 Fine-tuning Pre-trained Language Models

After verifying the effectiveness of GRL, we continue to investigate whether GRL can transcend fine-tuning pre-trained language models on the text data across three subsets in the taxonomy classification task. To preprocess the text data, we follow the same setup as the cleaning process for text graphs. In this fine-tuning paradigm, we use various transformer-based (Vaswani et al., 2017) pre-trained language models as competing models, such as BERT (Devlin et al., 2018), which learns bidirectional representations and significantly enhances performance across a wide range of contextual understanding tasks. The results in Table 3 and Table 4 gave us an affirmative answer to the superiority of GRL. In Table 4, we further observe that medium-size language models, such as DistilBERT (Sanh et al., 2019), work better on smaller text data. However, the performance may dramatically drop when the model size is too small, such as Albert (Lan et al., 2019) or too large, such as Llama2 (Touvron et al., 2023). We conjecture that a smaller pre-trained model may be more sensitive to the domain shift issue (our dataset has distinct class distributions compared to that of the dataset used to pre-train the language models), whereas a large pre-trained model may suffer overfitting issues when it is fine-tuned on a smaller text data.

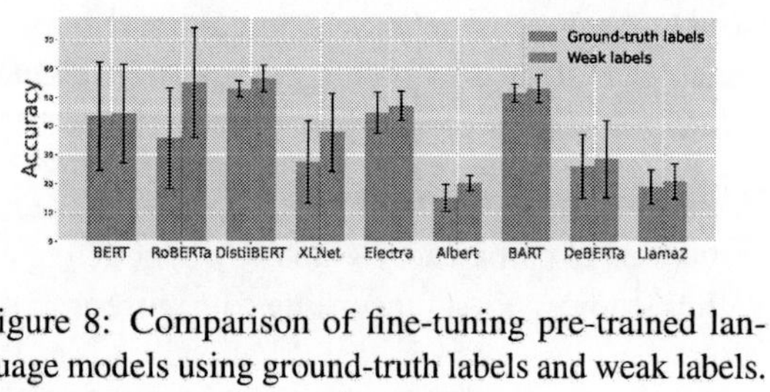

Figure 8: Comparison of fine-tuning pre-trained language models using ground-truth labels and weak labels. Whiskers denote standard deviation.

Fine-tuning with Weak Labels The above experiments confirmed that smaller ("weaker") GNNs can surpass larger ("stronger") language models in the taxonomy classification task. Recently, Burns et al. (2023). verified that training stronger models with pseudo labels, a.k.a. weak labels, generated by weaker models can enable the stronger models to achieve comparable performance as closely as those trained with ground-truth labels. In this experiment, we first generate weak labels by GCN on co-category graphs and then fine-tune pre-trained language models with weak labels. We present the results on $Data_{Jan24}$ in Figure 8 as an example. The results indicate that performance achieved through training with weak labels can surpass that of training with ground-truth labels. One possible reason is that training the model using noisy labels with a low noise ratio can be equivalent to a kind of regularization, improving the classification results (Zhuang and Al Hasan, 2022).[2]

This experiment demonstrates that leveraging weak labels generated by smaller models may effectively enhance the performance of larger models. This is one of the applications related to "weak-to-strong generalization" (Burns et al., 2023).

4.3 LLM Zero-shot/Few-shot Classification and Human Evaluation

	Accuracy	Weighted-F1
Human	58.73 (19.16)	59.50 (19.13)
Claude w.o. hints	11.61 (1.27)	12.66 (0.14)
Claude w. hints	10.27 (3.15)	12.81 (2.10)
GPT 3.5 w.o. hints	47.32 (3.25)	43.21 (4.33)
GPT 3.5 w. hints	**53.57 (2.81)**	**53.16 (3.13)**
GPT 4 w.o. hints	29.76 (7.22)	26.91 (9.66)
GPT 4 w. hints	33.04 (5.57)	27.78 (7.76)

Table 5: Evaluation of zero-shot and few-shot classification capabilities of large language models, Claude, GPT 3.5, and GPT 4. We compare these results with those from human recognition.

Major	CS	DS	Security	Math	Chemistry
#Students	9	4	2	2	1

Table 6: The number of students in each major. CS, DS, and Security denote the major in Computer Science, Data Science, and Cyber-security, respectively.

In this experiment, we evaluate zero-shot/few-shot classification capabilities of LLMs Claude (Bai et al., 2022), GPT 3.5 (Brown et al., 2020), and GPT 4 (Achiam et al., 2023), on the text data, which contains both title and summary, on $Data_{Nov23}$ as an example. We also compare the results with human participants. We recruited 18 students across five different majors in a graduate-level course. The number of students in each major is shown in Table 6. Each participant was given the titles and abstracts of survey papers and was asked to assign a category to each paper from our taxonomy. We present the mean value with the corresponding standard deviation in Table 5. For the LLMs, we ran the experiments five times. The standard deviation in human recognition is relatively large as some students do not have a strong technical background so they perform worse in this test. Among the LLMs, GPT 3.5 outperforms the other two models given that all models have not seen the data before (zero-shot). We further provide some hints to the models before classification (few-shot). For example, we release the keywords of the class "Trustworthy" to the models before classification. In this setting, both GPT 3.5 and GPT 4 can achieve higher accuracy and a weighted F1 score after obtaining some hints. In brief, GRL can outperform all three LLMs and human recognition, whereas these LLMs couldn't surmount human recognition, which reveals that LLMs still have much room to improve in taxonomy classification.

5 Conclusion

In this work, we aim to develop a method to automatically assign survey papers about Large Language Models (LLMs) to a taxonomy. To achieve this goal, we first collected the metadata of 144 LLM survey papers and proposed a new taxonomy for these papers. We further explored three paradigms to classify survey papers into the categories in the proposed taxonomy. After investigating three types of attributed graphs, we observed that leveraging graph structure information on co-category graphs can significantly help the taxonomy classification. Furthermore, our analysis validates that graph representation learning outperforms pre-trained language models' fine-tuning, zero-shot/few-shot classifications using LLMs, and even surpasses an average human recognition level. Last but not least, our experiments indicate that fine-tuning pre-trained language models using weak labels, which are generated by a weaker model, such as GCN, can be more effective than using ground-truth labels, revealing the potential for weak-to-strong generalization in the taxonomy classification task.

[2]Weak labels can be regarded as a kind of noisy label.

Limitations & Future Work Constructing a graph structure may encounter certain constraints. For instance, we build co-category graphs based on the arXiv categories. When papers come from distinct fields, such as biology, physics, and computer science, the graph structure may be very sparse, weakening the effectiveness of GRL.

In the future, our primary motivation extended from this study is to tailor GPT-based applications to assist readers in understanding survey papers more effectively. Also, we could consider different taxonomy designs, such as adopting the Computer Science Ontology or assigning multiple classes to an instance.

References

Josh Achiam, Steven Adler, Sandhini Agarwal, Lama Ahmad, Ilge Akkaya, Florencia Leoni Aleman, Diogo Almeida, Janko Altenschmidt, Sam Altman, Shyamal Anadkat, et al. 2023. Gpt-4 technical report. *arXiv preprint arXiv:2303.08774*.

Yuntao Bai, Saurav Kadavath, Sandipan Kundu, Amanda Askell, Jackson Kernion, Andy Jones, Anna Chen, Anna Goldie, Azalia Mirhoseini, Cameron McKinnon, et al. 2022. Constitutional ai: Harmlessness from ai feedback. *arXiv preprint arXiv:2212.08073*.

Tom Brown, Benjamin Mann, Nick Ryder, Melanie Subbiah, Jared D Kaplan, Prafulla Dhariwal, Arvind Neelakantan, Pranav Shyam, Girish Sastry, Amanda Askell, et al. 2020. Language models are few-shot learners. *Advances in neural information processing systems*, 33:1877–1901.

Joan Bruna, Wojciech Zaremba, Arthur Szlam, and Yann LeCun. 2013. Spectral networks and locally connected networks on graphs. *arXiv preprint arXiv:1312.6203*.

Collin Burns, Pavel Izmailov, Jan Hendrik Kirchner, Bowen Baker, Leo Gao, Leopold Aschenbrenner, Yining Chen, Adrien Ecoffet, Manas Joglekar, Jan Leike, et al. 2023. Weak-to-strong generalization: Eliciting strong capabilities with weak supervision. *arXiv preprint arXiv:2312.09390*.

Muthu Kumar Chandrasekaran, Guy Feigenblat, Dayne Freitag, Tirthankar Ghosal, Eduard Hovy, Philipp Mayr, Michal Shmueli-Scheuer, and Anita de Waard. 2020. Overview of the first workshop on scholarly document processing (sdp). In *Proceedings of the first workshop on scholarly document processing*, pages 1–6.

Kevin Clark, Minh-Thang Luong, Quoc V Le, and Christopher D Manning. 2019. Electra: Pre-training text encoders as discriminators rather than generators. In *International Conference on Learning Representations*.

Michaël Defferrard, Xavier Bresson, and Pierre Vandergheynst. 2016. Convolutional neural networks on graphs with fast localized spectral filtering. In *Advances in neural information processing systems*, pages 3844–3852.

Jacob Devlin, Ming-Wei Chang, Kenton Lee, and Kristina Toutanova. 2018. Bert: Pre-training of deep bidirectional transformers for language understanding. *arXiv preprint arXiv:1810.04805*.

Hichem Frigui and Olfa Nasraoui. 2002. Simultaneous categorization of text documents and identification of cluster-dependent keywords. In *2002 IEEE World Congress on Computational Intelligence. 2002 IEEE International Conference on Fuzzy Systems. FUZZ-IEEE'02. Proceedings (Cat. No. 02CH37291)*, volume 2, pages 1108–1113. IEEE.

Will Hamilton, Zhitao Ying, and Jure Leskovec. 2017. Inductive representation learning on large graphs. In *Advances in neural information processing systems*, pages 1024–1034.

Pengcheng He, Xiaodong Liu, Jianfeng Gao, and Weizhu Chen. 2020. Deberta: Decoding-enhanced bert with disentangled attention. *arXiv preprint arXiv:2006.03654*.

Can Jin, Hongwu Peng, Shiyu Zhao, Zhenting Wang, Wujiang Xu, Ligong Han, Jiahui Zhao, Kai Zhong, Sanguthevar Rajasekaran, and Dimitris N Metaxas. 2024. Apeer: Automatic prompt engineering enhances large language model reranking. *arXiv preprint arXiv:2406.14449*.

Rodney Kinney, Chloe Anastasiades, Russell Authur, Iz Beltagy, Jonathan Bragg, Alexandra Buraczynski, Isabel Cachola, Stefan Candra, Yoganand Chandrasekhar, Arman Cohan, et al. 2023. The semantic scholar open data platform. *arXiv preprint arXiv:2301.10140*.

Thomas N Kipf and Max Welling. 2016. Semi-supervised classification with graph convolutional networks. *arXiv preprint arXiv:1609.02907*.

Raghu Krishnapuram and Krishna Kummamuru. 2003. Automatic taxonomy generation: Issues and possibilities. In *International Fuzzy Systems Association World Congress*, pages 52–63. Springer.

Krishna Kummamuru, Ajay Dhawale, and Raghu Krishnapuram. 2003. Fuzzy co-clustering of documents and keywords. In *The 12th IEEE International Conference on Fuzzy Systems, 2003. FUZZ'03.*, volume 2, pages 772–777. IEEE.

Zhenzhong Lan, Mingda Chen, Sebastian Goodman, Kevin Gimpel, Piyush Sharma, and Radu Soricut. 2019. Albert: A lite bert for self-supervised learning of language representations. In *International Conference on Learning Representations*.

Dawn Lawrie, W Bruce Croft, and Arnold Rosenberg. 2001. Finding topic words for hierarchical summarization. In *Proceedings of the 24th annual international ACM SIGIR conference on Research and development in information retrieval*, pages 349–357.

Yoonjoo Lee, Hyeonsu B Kang, Matt Latzke, Juho Kim, Jonathan Bragg, Joseph Chee Chang, and Pao Siangliulue. 2024. Paperweaver: Enriching topical paper alerts by contextualizing recommended papers with user-collected papers. *arXiv preprint arXiv:2403.02939*.

Mike Lewis, Yinhan Liu, Naman Goyal, Marjan Ghazvininejad, Abdelrahman Mohamed, Omer Levy, Veselin Stoyanov, and Luke Zettlemoyer. 2020. Bart: Denoising sequence-to-sequence pre-training for natural language generation, translation, and comprehension. In *Proceedings of the 58th Annual Meeting of the Association for Computational Linguistics*, pages 7871–7880.

Lihui Liu, Boxin Du, Heng Ji, ChengXiang Zhai, and Hanghang Tong. 2021. Neural-answering logical queries on knowledge graphs. In *Proceedings of the 27th ACM SIGKDD conference on knowledge discovery & data mining*, pages 1087–1097.

Lihui Liu, Boxin Du, Jiejun Xu, Yinglong Xia, and Hanghang Tong. 2022. Joint knowledge graph completion and question answering. In *Proceedings of the 28th ACM SIGKDD Conference on Knowledge Discovery and Data Mining*, pages 1098–1108.

Yinhan Liu, Myle Ott, Naman Goyal, Jingfei Du, Mandar Joshi, Danqi Chen, Omer Levy, Mike Lewis, Luke Zettlemoyer, and Veselin Stoyanov. 2019. Roberta: A robustly optimized bert pretraining approach. *arXiv preprint arXiv:1907.11692*.

Kyle Lo, Joseph Chee Chang, Andrew Head, Jonathan Bragg, Amy X Zhang, Cassidy Trier, Chloe Anastasiades, Tal August, Russell Authur, Danielle Bragg, et al. 2023. The semantic reader project: Augmenting scholarly documents through ai-powered interactive reading interfaces. *arXiv preprint arXiv:2303.14334*.

Weimin Lyu, Songzhu Zheng, Tengfei Ma, and Chao Chen. 2022. A study of the attention abnormality in trojaned berts. *arXiv preprint arXiv:2205.08305*.

Victor Sanh, Lysandre Debut, Julien Chaumond, and Thomas Wolf. 2019. Distilbert, a distilled version of bert: smaller, faster, cheaper and lighter. *arXiv preprint arXiv:1910.01108*.

Jiaming Shen, Zhihong Shen, Chenyan Xiong, Chi Wang, Kuansan Wang, and Jiawei Han. 2020. Taxoexpan: Self-supervised taxonomy expansion with position-enhanced graph neural network. In *Proceedings of the web conference 2020*, pages 486–497.

Nina Smirnova and Philipp Mayr. 2023. Embedding models for supervised automatic extraction and classification of named entities in scientific acknowledgements. *Scientometrics*, pages 1–25.

Hugo Touvron, Louis Martin, Kevin Stone, Peter Albert, Amjad Almahairi, Yasmine Babaei, Nikolay Bashlykov, Soumya Batra, Prajjwal Bhargava, Shruti Bhosale, et al. 2023. Llama 2: Open foundation and fine-tuned chat models. *arXiv preprint arXiv:2307.09288*.

Shivakumar Vaithyanathan and Byron Dom. 1999. Model selection in unsupervised learning with applications to document clustering. In *ICML*.

Ashish Vaswani, Noam Shazeer, Niki Parmar, Jakob Uszkoreit, Llion Jones, Aidan N Gomez, Łukasz Kaiser, and Illia Polosukhin. 2017. Attention is all you need. *Advances in neural information processing systems*, 30.

Petar Veličković, Guillem Cucurull, Arantxa Casanova, Adriana Romero, Pietro Liò, and Yoshua Bengio. 2018. Graph attention networks. In *International Conference on Learning Representations*.

Tong Xie, Yuwei Wan, Wei Huang, Zhenyu Yin, Yixuan Liu, Shaozhou Wang, Qingyuan Linghu, Chunyu Kit, Clara Grazian, Wenjie Zhang, et al. 2023. Darwin series: Domain specific large language models for natural science. *arXiv preprint arXiv:2308.13565*.

Keyulu Xu, Weihua Hu, Jure Leskovec, and Stefanie Jegelka. 2018. How powerful are graph neural networks? *arXiv preprint arXiv:1810.00826*.

Lingjun Xu, Shiyin Zhang, Guojie Song, Junshan Wang, Tianshu Wu, and Guojun Liu. 2022. Taxonomy-enhanced graph neural networks. In *Proceedings of the 31st ACM International Conference on Information & Knowledge Management*, pages 2270–2279.

Zhilin Yang, Zihang Dai, Yiming Yang, Jaime Carbonell, Russ R Salakhutdinov, and Quoc V Le. 2019. Xlnet: Generalized autoregressive pretraining for language understanding. *Advances in Neural Information Processing Systems*, 32.

Liang Yao, Chengsheng Mao, and Yuan Luo. 2019. Graph convolutional networks for text classification. In *Proceedings of the AAAI conference on artificial intelligence*, volume 33, pages 7370–7377.

Oren Zamir and Oren Etzioni. 1998. Web document clustering: A feasibility demonstration. In *Proceedings of the 21st annual international ACM SIGIR conference on Research and development in information retrieval*, pages 46–54.

Jie Zhou, Ganqu Cui, Shengding Hu, Zhengyan Zhang, Cheng Yang, Zhiyuan Liu, Lifeng Wang, Changcheng Li, and Maosong Sun. 2020. Graph neural networks: A review of methods and applications. *AI open*, 1:57–81.

Jun Zhuang and Mohammad Al Hasan. 2022. Robust node classification on graphs: Jointly from bayesian label transition and topology-based label propagation. In *Proceedings of the 31st ACM International Conference on Information & Knowledge Management*, pages 2795–2805.

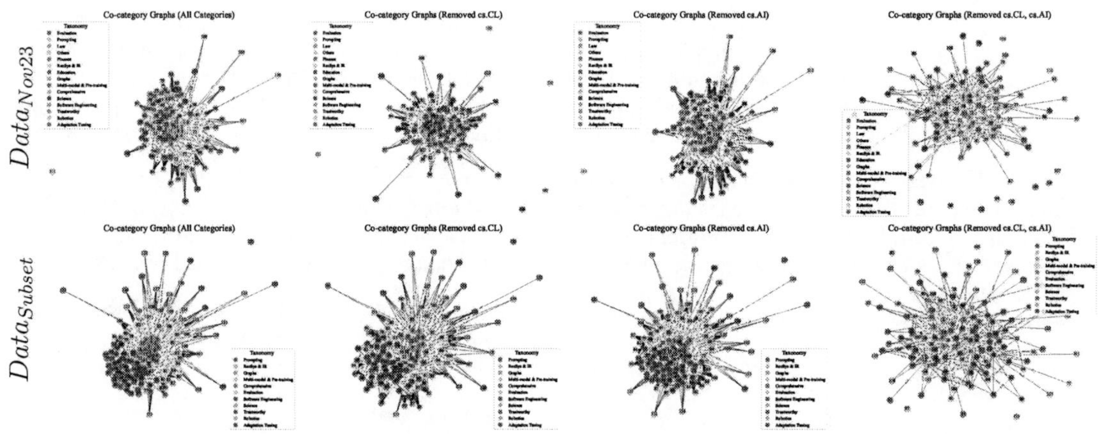

Figure 9: Additional visualization of co-category graphs (extended from Figure 6).

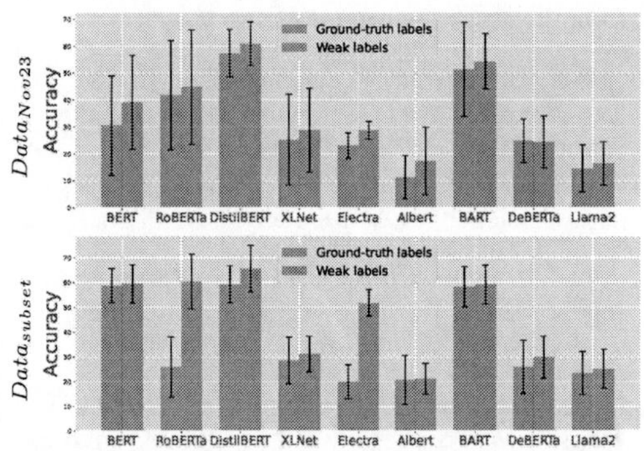

Figure 10: Additional comparison in the fine-tuning paradigm using weak labels (extended from Figure 8).

Language Models	Model Size
BERT (Devlin et al., 2018)	109.49M
RoBERTa (Liu et al., 2019)	124.66M
DistilBERT (Sanh et al., 2019)	66.97M
XLNet (Yang et al., 2019)	117.32M
Electra (Clark et al., 2019)	109.49M
Albert (Lan et al., 2019)	11.70M
BART (Lewis et al., 2020)	140.02M
DeBERTa (He et al., 2020)	139.20M
Llama2 (Touvron et al., 2023)	6.61B

Table 7: Model size of the pre-trained language models. For example, BERT has 109.49 million parameters.

A APPENDIX

In the appendix, we present the GNN and pre-trained language models' hyper-parameters and the hardware and software. We also include the additional comparison results about fine-tuning using weak labels and additional visualization of co-category graphs.

Hyper-parameters and Settings We employ a two-layer GCN (Kipf and Welling, 2016) with 200 hidden units and a ReLU activation function as the backbone GNN to examine the effectiveness of GRL. The GNN is trained by the Adam optimizer with a learning rate, 1×10^{-2} for both co-author graphs and co-category graphs and 2×10^{-2} for text graphs, and converged within 500 training epochs on all subsets. The dropout rate is 0.5.

We fine-tune the full pre-trained language models using the Adam optimizer with a 1×10^{-4} learning rate. We chose the batch size of 8 for the Llama2 and fixed the batch size of 16 for the rest of the models. We implement the pre-trained language models using HuggingFace packages (we choose the base version for all models without adding additional layers) and report the model size in Table 7. All models are tuned with 30 epochs. Note that, during the fine-tuning, we only save the checkpoints with better validation accuracy, i.e., some saved models were only fine-tuned for a small number of epochs.

Hardware and Software The experiment is conducted on a server with the following settings:

- Operating System: Ubuntu 22.04.3 LTS
- CPU: Intel Xeon w5-3433 @ 4.20 GHz
- GPU: NVIDIA RTX A6000 48GB
- Software: Python 3.11, PyTorch 2.1, HuggingFace 4.31, dgl 1.1.2+cu118.

Computational Budgets Based on the above computing infrastructure and settings, computational budgets in our experiments are described as follows. The experiment presented in Table 3 can be reproduced within one hour. The experiment displayed in Table 4 may take 93 hours to complete. Due to limited GPU memory, we implemented Llama2 using the CPU. This consumes around 90 hours in total. The experiment shown in Table 5 (excluding human recognition) can be finished in one hour.

Additional Visualization of Co-category Graphs Besides visualizing four graph structures in $Data_{Jan24}$ in Figure 6, we additionally present the visualization of four corresponding co-category graphs in both $Data_{Nov23}$ and $Data_{subset}$ in Figure 9. The visualization verifies the generalization of GRL across three subsets.

Additional Comparison of Fine-tuning Using Weak Labels Besides the results in Figure 8, we supplement the comparisons on both $Data_{Nov23}$ and $Data_{subset}$ in Figure 10. The comparisons across nice pre-trained language models further validate the effectiveness of fine-tuning using weak labels.

Ethical and Broader Impacts We confirm that we fulfill the author's responsibilities and address the potential ethical issues. In this work, we aim to help researchers quickly and better understand a new research field. Many researchers in academia or industry may potentially benefit from our work.

Statement of Data Privacy Our dataset contains the authors' names in each paper. This information is publicly available so the collection process doesn't infringe on personal privacy.

Disclaimer Regarding Human Subjects Results In Table 5, we include partial results with human subjects. We already obtained approval from the Institutional Review Board (IRB). The protocol number is IRB24-056. We recruited volunteers from a graduate-level course. Before the assessment, we have disclaimed the potential risk (our assessment has no potential risk) and got consent from participants.

Beyond Retrieval: Topic-based Alignment of Scientific Papers to Research Proposal

Rudra Nath Palit[†*] **Manasi Patwardhan**[†*] **Lovekesh Vig**[†] **Gautam Shroff**[†]

[†]TCS Research

{rudra.palit, manasi.patwardhan, lovekesh.vig, gautam.shroff}@tcs.com

Abstract

The inception of a research agenda typically commences with the creation of a comprehensive research proposal. The efficacy of the proposal often hinges on its ability to connect with the existing scientific literature that supports its ideas. To effectively assess the relevance of existing articles to a research proposal, it is imperative to categorize these articles into high-level thematic groups, referred to as topics, that align with the proposal. This paper introduces a novel task of aligning scientific articles, relevant to a proposal, with researcher-provided proposal topics. Additionally, we construct a dataset to serve as a benchmark for this task. We establish human and Large Language Model (LLM) baselines and propose a novel three-stage approach to address this challenge. We synthesize and use pseudo-labels that map proposal topics to text spans from cited articles to train Language Models (LMs) for two purposes: (i) as a retriever, to extract relevant text spans from cited articles for each topic, and (ii) as a classifier, to categorize the articles into the proposal topics. Our retriever-classifier pipeline, which employs very small open-source LMs fine-tuned with our constructed dataset, achieves results comparable to a vanilla paid LLM-based classifier, demonstrating its efficacy. However, a notable gap of 23.57 F1 score between our approach and the human baseline highlights the complexity of this task and emphasizes the need for further research.

1 Introduction

Researchers frequently draft research proposals to present new ideas, define research agendas and seek funding grants. An integral part of the proposal writing process is reviewing relevant literature and relating it to different aspects of the proposal. Several existing approaches designed for automatic retrieval of scientific articles can be applied to identify articles relevant to a proposal, with a detailed description (abstract) of the proposal serving as the query (Cohan et al., 2020b). However, there is often a further need to formulate high-level thematic categories (henceforth referred to as topics) relevant to the proposal and map retrieved relevant scientific articles to these categories for fine-grained contextualization. Such fine-grained mapping can further facilitate motivating the research problem, identifying its novelty, establishing baselines, synthesizing methods, and automatic literature review generation.

Given a set of reference article abstracts relevant to a proposal, Zhu et al. (2023); Martin-Boyle et al. (2024) auto-generates the thematic categories in a hierarchical form (termed as a catalogue) and organize references. However, the results demonstrate that the auto-generated catalogue does not match with the original-author-defined catalogue, leading to discrepancies in downstream literature review generation. This is due to inability of state-of-the-art LMs as well as subjectivity of the task. As opposed to this, we consider a more realistic setting, where we assume the availability of not only the reference papers retrieved to be relevant to a proposal; but also high-level topics provided by the researcher, for further literature categorization. With this assumption, we focus on the novel task of alignment of these reference papers, to one or more of these topics, offering a comprehensive understanding of its distinct contributions to the target proposal. This ensures a more personalized approach, aligning the cataloguing process closely with the researcher's unique perspective representing their understanding of the field.

Figure 1 illustrates an example, showcasing proposal topics, relevant reference papers and their mappings to the topics, with distinct text spans from the reference paper representing the relevant context (henceforth termed as the reference text

* Equal contribution

Proceedings of the Fourth Workshop on Scholarly Document Processing (SDP 2024), pages 70–83
August 16, 2024 ©2024 Association for Computational Linguistics

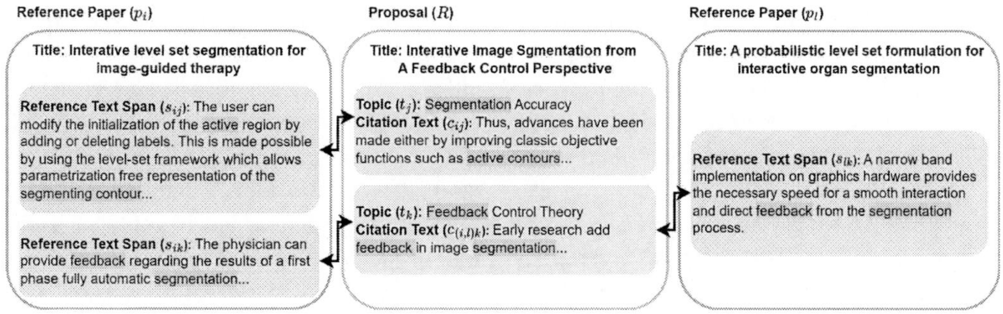

Figure 1: A sample from the dataset illustrating the many-to-many relationship between the proposal topics and reference papers. Reference Papers p_i and p_l are cited under Topic t_k, while Reference Paper p_i is cited by both Topics t_j and t_k with distinct reference text spans from the paper. The highlighted texts emphasize the similarities among the Topic, Citation Text, and Reference Text Spans.

span). Thus, a reference can be cited in more than one proposal topic with distinct context (reference text spans) (Li et al., 2023). Considering the token lengths of scientific articles, vanilla paid LLM-based approach for this task would be expensive. We consider the requirement of using smaller open-source LMs without compromising on the performance of LLMs. Hence, there is a need for a dataset to fine-tune domain-specific LMs for the task. As existing datasets for scientific document understanding (Clement et al., 2019; Lo et al., 2020; Saier et al., 2023; Kasanishi et al., 2023; Li et al., 2022) are not well-suited for this task, we extend the UnArXiv dataset (Saier et al., 2023), originally designed for literature review generation. We establish human and vanilla LLM baselines and define a novel three-stage approach for topic-based alignment of papers. Since ground truth labels for the reference text spans relevant to topics are not available, we augment the data by retrieving the reference text spans using the text around the article citation within the proposal topic (citation text), which is assumed to be available only for training. We use the synthesized pseudo pairs to train language models (LM) for retrieval of text spans from articles for a topic, and for classification of the retrieved articles to the topic. As opposed to all the prior approaches (Hoang and Kan, 2010; Hu and Wan, 2014; Chen and Zhuge, 2019; Wang et al., 2020; Pandey et al., 2022; Deng et al., 2021; Vajdecka et al., 2023), considering the realistic need of initial proposal writing stage, we neither assume the availability of citation text for the cited papers nor detailed description of the topics during inference. Our primary contributions are:

- We define the novel task of aligning reference articles relevant to a target proposal with user-defined proposal topics.
- We construct a dataset using a set of research papers as proposals, the subsection headings of the related work sections as the 'topics' and the papers cited under those sections as the reference papers relevant to those 'topics'.
- We establish human and LLM baselines and find that higher human F1 scores demonstrate task feasibility.
- We define a novel approach wherein we assume no citation text or detailed topic descriptions to retrieve reference text spans for a topic during inference. We devise a novel strategy using the citation text, available only for training, as a link between the topic and the reference text spans to create pseudo-labels for training a retriever and classifier pipeline.
- Our pipeline using much smaller LMs trained with pseudo-labels yields comparable performance to that of the LLM baseline, demonstrating the efficacy of the constructed dataset and the approach. In contrast, a significant gap (23.57 F1 score) exists between our approach and the human baseline indicating the need for more sophisticated solutions.

2 Related Work

2.1 Scientific Document Understanding

Literature Review Generation: Current approaches for automatic literature review generation either independently summarize articles (Hayashi et al., 2023; Urlana et al., 2022; Akkasi, 2022) or generate citation text (yan Wu et al., 2021; Jung et al., 2022; Wang et al., 2022) for each article without considering their inter-relations (Li et al., 2022; Li and Ouyang, 2024). These approaches often produce monolithic extractive (Hu and Wan, 2014; Wang et al., 2018) or abstractive (Chen et al., 2021, 2022; Kasanishi et al., 2023; Chen et al., 2021; Liu et al., 2023) reviews lacking any structure. Kasanishi et al. (2023); Martin-Boyle et al. (2024) introduce a method for generating reviews with well-structured subsections, grouping relevant articles by specific topics. However, they either assume the availability of the mapping of research articles to proposal topics or take human inputs for the same. Our task serves as an upstream task for comprehensive literature review generation and focuses on the automatic alignment of relevant articles to a set of proposal topics.

Citation Text Generation: Citation text generation crafts sentences that cite reference articles based on their abstracts, aiming to integrate them into a literature review. However, existing methods (yan Wu et al., 2021; Jung et al., 2022; Wang et al., 2022) assume precise knowledge of intents (background, methodology, etc), behind citing a paper which is largely unavailable in the early stages of proposal writing. Moreover, these approaches rely solely on the reference paper's abstracts, potentially lacking adequate information for appropriate mapping to an intent or topic. In contrast, our approach of extracting reference text spans from the reference paper ensures the availability of comprehensive information for alignment. Prior approaches to text span extraction from research papers use citation texts (Pandey et al., 2022; Zerva et al., 2020; Vajdecka et al., 2023) or queries (Li et al., 2023). In contrast, our approach considers the more practical setting at the proposal writing stage and retrieves text spans without relying on the availability of citation text or detailed queries assuming only the availability of high-level topics.

Citation Intent Detection: Citation intent detection (Lahiri et al., 2023; Roman et al., 2021; Berrebbi et al., 2022) presumes the presence of citation text to classify papers into predefined categories such as motivation, background, etc. However, during the proposal writing stage, citation text is unavailable. Moreover, the classification categories for potential reference papers differ for each target proposal. In contrast, our work introduces a new task of mapping potentially relevant papers to proposal-specific topics defined by users without assuming the availability of the citation text.

Scientific Paper Retrieval: Several approaches for retrieving scientific papers from a corpus rely either on abstracts and titles of a target paper (Singh et al., 2023; Cohan et al., 2020a), detailed textual queries (Sesagiri Raamkumar et al., 2017; Anand et al., 2017; Parisot and Zavrel, 2022; Medic and Šnajder, 2023), or relevant aspects such as the problem or methodology (Mysore et al., 2022; Ostendorff et al., 2022; Singh et al., 2023). These approaches employ strategies to generate suitable embeddings for queries and research papers, often focusing on pre-defined 'aspects' common across the target papers. In contrast, our work assumes the availability of research articles relevant to a proposal and perfoms a more fine-granular mapping of these articles to a set of user-defined topics.

2.2 Existing Datasets

We evaluate existing datasets for our task. The SciReviewGen (Kasanishi et al., 2023) dataset is designed for literature review generation, is derived from S2ORC (Lo et al., 2020) and consists of only survey papers with their contents extracted from their PDFs, resulting in highly erroneous extractions. CORWA (Li et al., 2022), derived from ArXiv (Clement et al., 2019), extracts information from the LaTeX version of ACL conference papers, ensuring relatively error-free extractions. However, while it employs a tagger to classify transitions in text-forming paragraphs, it falls short of extracting the associated chapter heading (topic in our context) for each text span. (Medic and Šnajder, 2023) utilize the CORWA dataset for scientific paper retrieval, under the assumption that the first transition text spans of extracted paragraphs indirectly refers to the topic. Our analysis, however, reveals that this assumption holds only for a smaller subset of the samples. UnArXiv dataset (Saier et al., 2023), derived from ArXiv papers, struggles to correctly identify in-text citations for these papers required to derive the mapping of topics to the corresponding reference papers. We extend the UnArXiv dataset and overcome this limitation with our own parser (details in Section 4).

3 Task Definition

Consider a research proposal with its title and abstract R and with a set of topics forming the catalogue denoted as $T_R = t_1, ..., t_K$. We assume a corpus of reference research papers $P_R = p_1, ..., p_n$ retrieved using R via existing retrieval methods

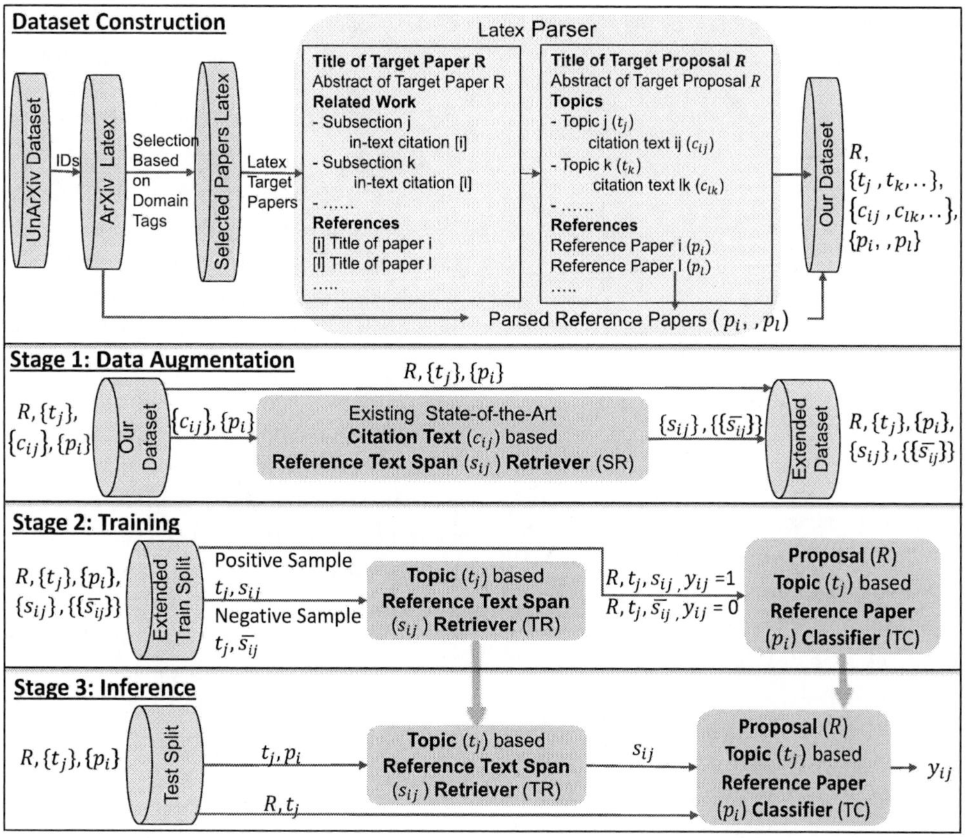

Figure 2: Stages of Proposal Topic based Reference Paper Alignment R: Proposal Title and Abstract, P_R: papers relevant to R, T_R: topics relevant to R, $p_i \in P_R$, $t_j, t_k \in T_R$, p_i, p_l are cited in t_j, t_k with citation text c_{ij}, c_{lk}, s_{ij}: reference text span from relevant paper p_i for topic t_j (Top-K chunks similar to query c_{ij}), $\{\overline{s_{ij}}\}$: text spans negatively sampled for topic t_j (Figure 3), y_{ij}, label set as 1 if paper p_i is aligned to topic t_j, otherwise 0.

such as Specter (Singh et al., 2023). The task aims to classify the mapping of each research paper $p_i \in P_R$ to each topic $t_j \in T_R$ using binary labels $y_{ij} \in 0, 1$. The dataset consists of positive tuples $< R, p_i, t_j, c_{ij} >$, where c_{ij} is the citation text citing the paper p_i under topic t_j and is only available during training. We define a process to augment the dataset with the reference text span s_{ij} by using the citation text c_{ij}. The reference text span refers to the contents of the referenced paper p_i, needed to determine whether p_i is relevant to the topic t_j. Again, we do not assume the availability of s_{ij} for training or inference in the dataset.

4 Dataset Construction

Figure 2 demonstrates the steps we have followed for the construction of our dataset. We utilize the papers in the UnArxiv dataset (Saier et al., 2023), with their titles and abstracts as target proposals R. We leverage the ArXiv tags of these papers to obtain their domains and focus on papers in AI and Computer Vision. This was to ensure high-quality annotations since the human annotator who facilitated the establishment of the baseline (Section 6.2) had expertise in these domains.

We use UnArxiv IDs to retrieve papers from ArXiv, obtain LaTeX sources, and employ a LaTeX parsing technique with Regex statements to extract in-text citations within our simulated proposal papers. Our parser identifies section headings from these target papers and extracts topics (t_j), from the subsection headings of the 'Related Work' or 'Literature Review' Sections. We selectively retain only those target proposals where multiple topics exist in the literature review. For each topic t_j thus identified, we further identify in-text citations for referenced papers $\{p_i\}$ and extract the corresponding citation texts $\{c_{ij}\}$. We then match the citation text with the corresponding entry in the references section of the paper to obtain the referenced paper title. We obtained the PDFs of the referenced papers from various sources like ArXiv, ACL, and

Semantic Scholar. The contents of the referenced papers are extracted using our PDF extractor.

Table 1: Dataset Statistics

Samples	Splits			Total
	Train	Validation	Test	
Target Proposals	1,934	241	242	2,417
Proposal Topics	5,680	720	723	7,123
Reference Papers	39,608	4,987	4,911	49,506
Avg. Topics / Proposal	2.94	2.99	2.99	2.95
Avg Papers / Topic	6.9	6.93	6.79	6.95
Topic-Paper Pairs	50,116	6,329	6,075	62,520

Thus, our final dataset consists of set-of research papers from selected domains from the UnArxiv dataset with each paper simulating a target proposal R. The dataset also includes the topics for each target proposal T_R and reference papers relevant to the target proposal P_R. Moreover, the ground truth labels of our task, in terms of alignments of reference papers to the topics are solicited from the in-text citations, explicitly specified by the authors of the target papers. For the training set, we assume the availability of the citation text c_{ij} for every pair t_j and p_i. Thus, a sample of the training data is depicted by the tuple $< R, p_i, t_j, c_{ij} >$. Whereas for the test set a sample is $< R, p_i, t_j >$. We split target proposals into train, validation, and test sets to prevent information leakage across splits. Dataset statistics are summarized in Table 1. The resulting corpus has target proposals pertaining to Artificial Intelligence (AI) (2.69 %), Machine Learning (ML) (15.56%), Computational Linguistics (CL) (7.28%), Computer Vision (CV) (73.23%) and a combination of CL and CV (1.24%). We make the dataset available at[1].

5 Approach

We break down our approach into three stages (Figure 2): (i) Augmenting the dataset with positive and negative reference text spans for a proposal topic, retrieved from papers relevant to the proposal, with the citation text as the query, using a state-of-the-art retriever model (SR) (ii) Training the Topic based reference text span Retriever (TR) and reference paper classifier (TC) using the augmented data (iii) Using TC to classify a reference paper for its relevance to a proposal topic in context of the proposal and the reference text span retrieved from the paper relevant to the topic using TR .

[1]https://github.com/NeuralNimbus/Beyond-Retrieval under license: GNU GPL v3

5.1 Stage 1: Data Augmentation

To train the retriever TR, we need positive and negative pairs of topics t_j and reference text spans s_{ij}. We do not have such pairs available in our training data. However, we do have the citation text c_{ij}, which we utilize as a 'link' to retrieve the reference text span s_{ij} from p_i, relevant to c_{ij} and consequently relevant to t_j. We assess the performance of existing retrieval models on equivalent tasks in the science domain, viz., (i) Retrieval of paragraphs from scientific documents given a question and (ii) Retrieval of a text span given the citation text. We identify a retriever model SR having the best zero-shot performance for both these tasks, making it generalizable for our task and dataset. Section 6.4, details the experiments performed to choose SR.

We chunk the reference paper p_i using a sliding-window approach choosing 7 sentences as a chunk with a stride of 3. The top-k chunks from the reference paper most relevant to the citation text c_{ij} retrieved using the best-performing retriever SR, serve as the retrieved reference text span $\hat{s_{ij}}$ of article p_i for the topic t_j. The similarity score between the citation text and a chunk of the reference paper is calculated on the lines of (Nogueira et al., 2020), by taking log softmax over 'True' and 'False' tokens to get the probability of 'True' token as the score and rank the chunks. The retrieved top-k chunks may or may not be contiguous, and we use a higher k value for good recall, avoiding information loss. The retrieved reference text span $\hat{s_{ij}}$ functions as a pseudo-positive pair for the topic t_j. We consider three distinct types of pseudo-negative reference text spans $\overline{s_{ij}}$ for topic t_j (Figure 3): (i) **Type 1**: The bottom-k chunks retrieved from p_i, with citation text c_{ij} of topic t_j as query, using SR serve as easy negatives for the topic t_j in proposal R. (ii) **Type 2**: Text spans (top-k chunks) retrieved from the reference paper p_l, **NOT** cited in topic t_j, but cited in t_k where $k \neq j$, with the citation text c_{lk} as query using SR, serve as easy negatives for the topic t_j in proposal R. (iii) **Type 3**: With each c_{ij} for topic t_j citing p_i as the query, we retrieve top-k chunks from reference articles p_l, **NOT** cited in topic t_j, but cited in t_k where $l \neq i$ and $k \neq j$ using SR. The top-k chunks demonstrating maximum similarity with one of the c_{ij} serve as hard negatives for the topic t_j in proposal R.

We augment our training dataset with these

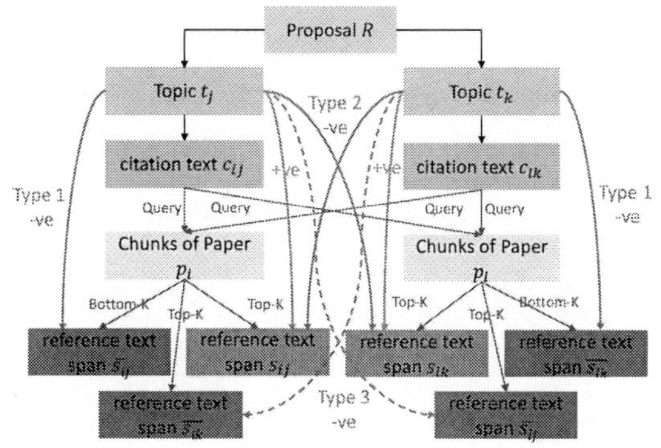

Figure 3: Negative sampling reference text spans for topics. Blue represents querying,Brown represents cross-querying,Green represents positive sample pairs, Red represents negative sample pairs

pseudo positive and negative reference text spans for each topic leading to the resultant dataset, where a sample is depicted by the tuple $< R, p_i, t_j, c_{ij}, \hat{s_{ij}}, \{\overline{s_{ij}}\} >$. The statistics of the augmented dataset are illustrated in Table 2.

Table 2: Augmented Dataset Statistics

Samples	Splits			Total
	Train	Test	Validation	
Positives	50,116	6,329	6,075	62,520
Easy Negatives	1,42,637	19,382	17,635	1,79,654
Hard Negatives	1,10,164	15,561	13,492	1,39,217
Total	3,02,917	41,272	37,202	3,81,391

5.2 Stage 2: Training

Topic based Reference Text Span Retriever (TR): We train TR, which is a Language Model (LM) using the positive and negative topic and reference text span pairs. Following the methodology discussed in (Nogueira et al., 2020), we try to maximize the probability $Pr(True|t_j, s_{ij})$ and $Pr(False|t_j, \overline{s_{ij}})$ using the cross-entropy loss. Due to the significantly higher number of negative samples compared to positives in the dataset, we include all positives but randomly sub-sample the negatives of each domain uniformly to maintain a balanced training dataset. Sampling is performed with replacement for every epoch to ensure that the model sees all negatives.

Proposal Topic based Reference Paper Classifier (TC): We train the TC using the augmented training dataset. We form samples $< R, t_j, \hat{s_{ij}} >$ with label $y_{ij} = 1$ and $< R, t_j, \overline{s_{ij}} >$ with label $y_{ij} = 0$. The model learns to classify if the paper p_i can be assigned to the topic t_j in the context of R and s_{ij}, with the supervision of the label y_{ij}. We try to maximize the probability $Pr(y = True|R, t_j, s_{ij})$ and $Pr(y = False|R, t_j, \overline{s_{ij}})$ using cross-entropy loss.

5.3 Stage 3: Inference

During inference, we feed the proposal title and abstract R and a topic t_j from the test set to TR along with chunks ch_q of a reference article p_i in the test set tagged as relevant to R. The model TR provides us with the a similarity score $sim_{jq} = TR(t_j, ch_q)$ for each ch_q. The score is calculated by applying a softmax on the logits of the 'True' and 'False' tokens and taking into consideration the probability $P(True|t_j, ch_q)$ (Nogueira et al., 2020). We rank ch_q for the given R and t_j based on sim_{jq} and use the top-k ranked ch_q of paper p_i as the retrieved reference text spans $\hat{s_{ij}}$ from paper $p_i j$, for topic t_j in R. We further feed $< R, t_j, \hat{s_{ij}} >$ to TC If probability $P(y = True|R, t_j, \hat{s_{ij}}) \geq 0.5$, then only we consider p_i to be aligned with t_j.

6 Experimentation and Results

6.1 Evaluation Metric

To assess the performance of SR on evidence and reference text span retrieval tasks (Section 6.4), we compute the evidence F1 score (Dasigi et al., 2021). For the evaluation of our pipeline (TR followed by TC), we utilize the binary ground truth labels depicting the alignment of each proposal topic and each reference paper relevant to that proposal and the labels predicted by TC in the context of retrieved reference text spans to compute the confusion matrix for the binary classification task. We choose the F1 score as the metric, given the label imbalance.

6.2 Baselines

To establish baselines we evaluate the 'Reference Paper Topic Classification' task with human and LLM-generated annotations. Our human annotator is a researcher with expertise in AI and allied fields. The details of the annotation interface are discussed in Appendix B. Considering the complexity, cognitive load and LLM cost for the task, the baselines are developed only on a smaller evaluation subset of the test set. We utilize GPT-3.5 Turbo[2] LLM. To ensure deterministic and reproducible results, we set the temperature to 0. The structure of the prompt is detailed in Appendix A. Acknowledging the limitation of over-representation of CV papers in the dataset (Section 4), we construct the evaluation subset by uniformly sampling random four proposals from each of the five domains from the test set and thus ensuring balanced domain representation. This results in selecting 20 proposals with 52 topics citing 362 reference papers, forming 378 positive topic-reference paper pairs.

We have the following baselines: (i) Random: We randomly assign Yes/No labels to the test samples, (ii) TR + Human: The human annotator is provided with information about the target proposal's title, abstract (R), topic t_j, reference paper title p_i, and the text span of the reference paper s_{ij}, retrieved using the topic t_j with our trained TR model. The task is to assess the relevance of the reference paper to the given topic, labelling it 1 if the reference paper is aligned to the topic; and 0 otherwise, (iii) LLM: For vanilla LLM baseline we provide the complete reference paper p_i to the LLM along with information about the target proposal's title, abstract (R), topic t_j as the part of the prompt (Appendix A) and ask the LLM to classify the reference paper's relevance to the topic in the context of the proposal. We truncate the tail of the paper if the token length of the paper exceeds the maximum token length of the LLM. This baseline does not take into consideration text span from the reference paper, which is relevant to the topic and hence can be treated as is topic-agnostic reference text span based method, (iv) TR + LLM: This is the same has TR + Human except the relevant information mentioned above is provided to LLM as opposed to the human annotator. In this case, the LLM performs the job of classification of reference paper alignment to topics in the context of the proposal and retrieved reference text spans from the paper, as opposed to the complete paper, which is the case in vanilla LLM. Note that, on similar lines to the LLM baseline we could have had only the Human baseline, where the human gets to read the complete reference paper to perform the classification task. However, due to the very high cognitive load of this task, we skip this baseline.

[2]https://platform.openai.com/docs/models/gpt-3-5-turbo

6.3 Models and Hyperparameter Setting

Topic-Based Reference Text Span Retriever (TR): We fine-tune a T5-base model(Raffel et al., 2019), consisting of 223M parameters with a batch size of 120, learning rate of 3×10^{-4} with the AdamW optimizer, on Nvidia A100 for 20 epochs taking 84 hours, evaluated every 500 steps on the validation split. The model with the best validation F1 is obtained after fine-tuning for 1000 steps.

Research Paper Topic Classifier (TC): We chose RoBERTa (Liu et al., 2019) and Flan-T5 (Chung et al., 2022) base consisting of 125M and 248M parameters respectively, for their robust reasoning capabilities, as TC. Both models are fine-tuned on a class-balanced dataset with the batch sizes 240 and 120, using the AdamW optimizer and learning rates 5×10^{-5} and 3×10^{-4}, respectively. Fine-tuning is performed for 50 epochs on an Nvidia A100 taking approximately 120 hours each. The models with the best validation F1 are obtained at 33 and 35 epochs for RoBERTa and Flan-T5, respectively.

6.4 Results

Table 3: Results on Evidence Retrieval Task on QASPER and Citation Text Span Retrieval Task on Cl-SciSumm. The numbers indicate F1 scores for top-k retrieved chunks where k=3

Models	Datasets	
	QASPER	Cl-SciSumm
CGSN* (Nie et al., 2022)	53.98	NA
CitRet* (Pandey et al., 2022)	NA	19.79
Specter 2 (Singh et al., 2023)	13.68	19.28
CoSentBert (Mysore et al., 2022)	17.28	15.08
MPNET (Song et al., 2020)	15.81	14.14
Mono T5 (Nogueira et al., 2020)	25.90	25.98

* State-of-the-Art supervised models

Citation Text based Reference Text Span Retrieval (SR): As discussed in Section 5.1, our dataset lacks ground truth reference text span labels s_{ij} from a reference paper p_i, which are relevant to a topic t_j. Given the availability of citation text c_{ij} belonging to a topic t_j for the train set, we perform experiments to identify a state-of-the-art model to retrieve the reference text spans s_{ij} for that topic. We evaluate existing retrieval models on the test sets of QASPER (Dasigi et al., 2021) for evidence retrieval and CLScisumm (Chandrasekaran et al., 2019) for reference text span retrieval. We assess the performance of models depicted in Table 3 in a zero-shot setting, to select the model most generalizable for our task and dataset. For the evidence retrieval task with QASPER, Specter 2 is used with the AdHoc Query Adapter for questions and the Proximity Adapter for paragraphs (Singh et al., 2022). For CLScisumm, Specter 2's AdHoc Query Adapter is employed to embed both the citation text and candidate citation text spans. Top-3 sentences are retrieved for each model, following the approach in (Pandey et al., 2022). We observe that Mono T5 achieves the highest F1 Score among pre-trained models for both datasets (Table 3). While not as good as the supervised state-of-the-art model CGSN (Nie et al., 2022) for QASPER, it surpasses the SOTA model CitRet (Pandey et al., 2022) in CL-SciSumm. Hence, we select Mono T5 as SR.

Table 4: F1 scores for the reference paper topic alignment task on the subset of test data (Section 6.2).

Annotation	Precision	Recall	F1 Score
Random	37.47	47.88	42.04
TR + Human	80.67	89.42	84.82
LLM [GPT-3.5 Turbo]	56.00	74.07	63.78
TR + LLM [GPT-3.5 Turbo]	57.77	72.75	64.40
TR+ TC [RoBERTa]*	52.27	65.60	61.16
TR+ TC [Flan-T5]*	56.17	72.22	63.19

* Our pipeline: models fine-tuned with our dataset. TR: T-5-Base Model fine-tuned with our dataset

Topic based Reference Text Span Retriever (TR) and Reference Paper Classifier (TC): Table 4 illustrates the evaluation of our inference pipeline discussed in section 5.3 on the subset of test data (Section 6.2). A high F1 score achieved by the human baseline establishes the task's feasibility. Higher F1 of our supervised models as compared to Random confirms task learnability. Higher F1 scores of TR + LLM as compared to LLM demonstrate the benefit of using our retrieval model. More importantly, comparable scores of our fine-tuned pipeline with very small (248M) LMs to that of pre-trained Large LM (175B), suggest the efficacy of utilizing our synthesized training data for task modelling. However, the noticeable difference in the human baseline concerning both the zero-shot LLM-based approach and our fine-tuned LM-based pipeline highlights the task's inherent difficulty, indicating a need for more sophisticated techniques. For a comprehensive evaluation, we evaluate the pipeline on our complete test set. RoBERTa and Flan-T5 yield F1 scores of 63.40% and 62.82%, respectively.

We conducted a detailed error analysis (Appendix C) of the errors made by the expert and identified author subjectivity, insufficient information in the retrieved reference text spans and lack of in-depth subject knowledge, as the challenges encountered by the expert. We further analyze the errors made by LLM and fine-tuned TC models for samples correctly classified by experts, detailed in Appendix C. The majority of errors are due to lexical overlap between topics and reference text spans with no semantic alignment causing False Positives or the models failing to perform complex reasoning required for the task.

7 Conclusion and Future Work

We have defined a novel task of mapping relevant scientific articles to research proposal topics as a precursor to the Literature Review Generation task for a new research proposal. We introduce a large-scale dataset for the task and establishment of competitive baselines by an expert and an LLM, underscoring task feasibility. We define a novel approach for the task and are the first ones to simulate the real-life scenario, at the early stage of proposal writing, of unavailability of citation text or detailed topic descriptions to retrieve topic-wise reference text spans from relevant articles. We came up with a novel strategy of using citation text (available for the training data) as a link between the topic and the text spans to create pseudo-labels for training a retriever. Our pipeline using much smaller open-source LMs trained with pseudo-labels yields comparable performance to that of the paid LLM baseline, demonstrating the efficacy of constructed data and designed pipeline. In contrast, a noticeable gap of 23.57 F1 score between our approach and the human baseline underscores the task's complexity, demanding more sophisticated solutions.

While organizing reference articles by topic, the hierarchy among these topics (catalogue), is crucial for a comprehensive understanding. However, we found it difficult to capture this hierarchy due to the PDF parsing challenges, treating every topic as a standalone entity. In future, with more sophisticated PDF parsing and semantic paragraph segmentation techniques, we plan to capture the topic hierarchy for task completeness.

References

Abbas Akkasi. 2022. Multi perspective scientific document summarization with graph attention networks (GATS). In *Proceedings of the Third Workshop on Scholarly Document Processing*, pages 268–272, Gyeongju, Republic of Korea. Association for Computational Linguistics.

Ankesh Anand, Tanmoy Chakraborty, and Amitava Das. 2017. Fairscholar: Balancing relevance and diversity for scientific paper recommendation. In *European Conference on Information Retrieval*.

Dan Berrebbi, Nicolas Huynh, and Oana Balalau. 2022. Graphcite: Citation intent classification in scientific publications via graph embeddings. In *Companion of The Web Conference 2022, Virtual Event / Lyon, France, April 25 - 29, 2022*, pages 779–783. ACM.

Muthu Kumar Chandrasekaran, Michihiro Yasunaga, Dragomir R. Radev, Dayne Freitag, and Min-Yen Kan. 2019. Overview and results: Cl-scisumm shared task 2019. In *BIRNDL@SIGIR*.

Jingqiang Chen and Hai Zhuge. 2019. Automatic generation of related work through summarizing citations. *Concurrency and Computation: Practice and Experience*, 31.

Xiuying Chen, Hind Alamro, Mingzhe Li, Shen Gao, Xiangliang Zhang, Dongyan Zhao, and Rui Yan. 2021. Capturing relations between scientific papers: An abstractive model for related work section generation. In *Proceedings of the 59th Annual Meeting of the Association for Computational Linguistics and the 11th International Joint Conference on Natural Language Processing (Volume 1: Long Papers)*, pages 6068–6077, Online. Association for Computational Linguistics.

Xiuying Chen, Hind Alamro, Li Mingzhe, Shen Gao, Rui Yan, Xin Gao, and Xiangliang Zhang. 2022. Target-aware abstractive related work generation with contrastive learning. *Proceedings of the 45th International ACM SIGIR Conference on Research and Development in Information Retrieval*.

Hyung Won Chung, Le Hou, S. Longpre, Barret Zoph, Yi Tay, William Fedus, Eric Li, Xuezhi Wang, Mostafa Dehghani, Siddhartha Brahma, Albert Webson, Shixiang Shane Gu, Zhuyun Dai, Mirac Suzgun, Xinyun Chen, Aakanksha Chowdhery, Dasha Valter, Sharan Narang, Gaurav Mishra, Adams Wei Yu, Vincent Zhao, Yanping Huang, Andrew M. Dai, Hongkun Yu, Slav Petrov, Ed Huai hsin Chi, Jeff Dean, Jacob Devlin, Adam Roberts, Denny Zhou, Quoc V. Le, and Jason Wei. 2022. Scaling instruction-finetuned language models. *ArXiv*, abs/2210.11416.

Colin B. Clement, Matthew Bierbaum, Kevin P. O'Keeffe, and Alexander A. Alemi. 2019. On the use of arxiv as a dataset. *ArXiv*, abs/1905.00075.

Arman Cohan, Sergey Feldman, Iz Beltagy, Doug Downey, and Daniel Weld. 2020a. SPECTER: Document-level representation learning using citation-informed transformers. In *Proceedings of the 58th Annual Meeting of the Association for Computational Linguistics*, pages 2270–2282, Online. Association for Computational Linguistics.

Arman Cohan, Sergey Feldman, Iz Beltagy, Doug Downey, and Daniel S. Weld. 2020b. Specter: Document-level representation learning using citation-informed transformers. *ArXiv*, abs/2004.07180.

Pradeep Dasigi, Kyle Lo, Iz Beltagy, Arman Cohan, Noah A. Smith, and Matt Gardner. 2021. A dataset of information-seeking questions and answers anchored in research papers. In *Proceedings of the 2021 Conference of the North American Chapter of the Association for Computational Linguistics: Human Language Technologies*, pages 4599–4610, Online. Association for Computational Linguistics.

Zekun Deng, Zixin Zeng, Weiye Gu, Jiawen Ji, and Bolin Hua. 2021. Automatic related work section generation by sentence extraction and reordering. In *AII@iConference*.

Hiroaki Hayashi, Wojciech Kryscinski, Bryan McCann, Nazneen Rajani, and Caiming Xiong. 2023. What's new? summarizing contributions in scientific literature. In *Proceedings of the 17th Conference of the European Chapter of the Association for Computational Linguistics*, pages 1019–1031, Dubrovnik, Croatia. Association for Computational Linguistics.

Cong Duy Vu Hoang and Min-Yen Kan. 2010. Towards automated related work summarization. In *Coling 2010: Posters*, pages 427–435, Beijing, China. Coling 2010 Organizing Committee.

Yue Hu and Xiaojun Wan. 2014. Automatic generation of related work sections in scientific papers: An optimization approach. In *Proceedings of the 2014 Conference on Empirical Methods in Natural Language Processing (EMNLP)*, pages 1624–1633, Doha, Qatar. Association for Computational Linguistics.

Shing-Yun Jung, Ting-Han Lin, Chia-Hung Liao, Shyan-Ming Yuan, and Chuen-Tsai Sun. 2022. Intent-controllable citation text generation. *Mathematics*, 10(10).

Tetsu Kasanishi, Masaru Isonuma, Junichiro Mori, and Ichiro Sakata. 2023. SciReviewGen: A large-scale dataset for automatic literature review generation. In *Findings of the Association for Computational Linguistics: ACL 2023*, pages 6695–6715, Toronto, Canada. Association for Computational Linguistics.

Avishek Lahiri, Debarshi Kumar Sanyal, and Imon Mukherjee. 2023. Citeprompt: Using prompts to identify citation intent in scientific papers. *2023 ACM/IEEE Joint Conference on Digital Libraries (JCDL)*, pages 51–55.

Xiangci Li, Yi-Hui Lee, and Jessica Ouyang. 2023. Cited text spans for citation text generation. *ArXiv*, abs/2309.06365.

Xiangci Li, Biswadip Mandal, and Jessica Ouyang. 2022. CORWA: A citation-oriented related work annotation dataset. In *Proceedings of the 2022 Conference of the North American Chapter of the Association for Computational Linguistics: Human Language Technologies*, pages 5426–5440, Seattle, United States. Association for Computational Linguistics.

Xiangci Li and Jessica Ouyang. 2024. Explaining relationships among research papers. *ArXiv*, abs/2402.13426.

Jiachang Liu, Qi Zhang, Chongyang Shi, Usman Naseem, Shoujin Wang, Liang Hu, and Ivor Tsang. 2023. Causal intervention for abstractive related work generation. In *Findings of the Association for Computational Linguistics: EMNLP 2023*, pages 2148–2159, Singapore. Association for Computational Linguistics.

Yinhan Liu, Myle Ott, Naman Goyal, Jingfei Du, Mandar Joshi, Danqi Chen, Omer Levy, Mike Lewis, Luke Zettlemoyer, and Veselin Stoyanov. 2019. Roberta: A robustly optimized bert pretraining approach. *ArXiv*, abs/1907.11692.

Kyle Lo, Lucy Lu Wang, Mark Neumann, Rodney Kinney, and Daniel Weld. 2020. S2ORC: The semantic scholar open research corpus. In *Proceedings of the 58th Annual Meeting of the Association for Computational Linguistics*, pages 4969–4983, Online. Association for Computational Linguistics.

Anna Martin-Boyle, Aahan Tyagi, Marti A Hearst, and Dongyeop Kang. 2024. Shallow synthesis of knowledge in gpt-generated texts: A case study in automatic related work composition. *arXiv preprint arXiv:2402.12255*.

Zoran Medic and Jan Šnajder. 2023. Paragraph-level citation recommendation based on topic sentences as queries. *ArXiv*, abs/2305.12190.

Sheshera Mysore, Arman Cohan, and Tom Hope. 2022. Multi-vector models with textual guidance for fine-grained scientific document similarity. In *Proceedings of the 2022 Conference of the North American Chapter of the Association for Computational Linguistics: Human Language Technologies*, pages 4453–4470, Seattle, United States. Association for Computational Linguistics.

Yuxiang Nie, Heyan Huang, Wei Wei, and Xian-Ling Mao. 2022. Capturing global structural information in long document question answering with compressive graph selector network. In *Proceedings of the 2022 Conference on Empirical Methods in Natural Language Processing*, pages 5036–5047, Abu Dhabi, United Arab Emirates. Association for Computational Linguistics.

Rodrigo Nogueira, Zhiying Jiang, Ronak Pradeep, and Jimmy Lin. 2020. Document ranking with a pretrained sequence-to-sequence model. In *Findings of the Association for Computational Linguistics: EMNLP 2020*, pages 708–718, Online. Association for Computational Linguistics.

Malte Ostendorff, Till Blume, Terry Ruas, Bela Gipp, and Georg Rehm. 2022. Specialized document embeddings for aspect-based similarity of research papers. *2022 ACM/IEEE Joint Conference on Digital Libraries (JCDL)*, pages 1–12.

Amit Pandey, Avani Gupta, and Vikram Pudi. 2022. CitRet: A hybrid model for cited text span retrieval. In *Proceedings of the 29th International Conference on Computational Linguistics*, pages 4528–4536, Gyeongju, Republic of Korea. International Committee on Computational Linguistics.

Mathias Parisot and Jakub Zavrel. 2022. Multi-objective representation learning for scientific document retrieval. In *Proceedings of the Third Workshop on Scholarly Document Processing*, pages 80–88, Gyeongju, Republic of Korea. Association for Computational Linguistics.

Colin Raffel, Noam M. Shazeer, Adam Roberts, Katherine Lee, Sharan Narang, Michael Matena, Yanqi Zhou, Wei Li, and Peter J. Liu. 2019. Exploring the limits of transfer learning with a unified text-to-text transformer. *J. Mach. Learn. Res.*, 21:140:1–140:67.

Muhammad Roman, Abdul Shahid, Shafiullah Khan, Anis Koubâa, and Lisu Yu. 2021. Citation intent classification using word embedding. *IEEE Access*, 9:9982–9995.

Tarek Saier, John T. Krause, and Michael Färber. 2023. unarxive 2022: All arxiv publications pre-processed for nlp, including structured full-text and citation network. *2023 ACM/IEEE Joint Conference on Digital Libraries (JCDL)*, pages 66–70.

Aravind Sesagiri Raamkumar, Schubert Foo, and Natalie Pang. 2017. Using author-specified keywords in building an initial reading list of research papers in scientific paper retrieval and recommender systems. *Information Processing & Management*, 53(3):577–594.

Amanpreet Singh, Mike D'Arcy, Arman Cohan, Doug Downey, and Sergey Feldman. 2022. Scirepeval: A multi-format benchmark for scientific document representations. In *Conference on Empirical Methods in Natural Language Processing*.

Amanpreet Singh, Mike D'Arcy, Arman Cohan, Doug Downey, and Sergey Feldman. 2023. SciRepEval: A multi-format benchmark for scientific document representations. In *Proceedings of the 2023 Conference on Empirical Methods in Natural Language Processing*, pages 5548–5566, Singapore. Association for Computational Linguistics.

Kaitao Song, Xu Tan, Tao Qin, Jianfeng Lu, and Tie-Yan Liu. 2020. Mpnet: Masked and permuted pre-training for language understanding. *ArXiv*, abs/2004.09297.

Ashok Urlana, Nirmal Surange, and Manish Shrivastava. 2022. LTRC @MuP 2022: Multi-perspective scientific document summarization using pre-trained generation models. In *Proceedings of the Third Workshop on Scholarly Document Processing*, pages 279–284, Gyeongju, Republic of Korea. Association for Computational Linguistics.

Peter Vajdecka, Elena Callegari, Desara Xhura, and Atli Ásmundsson. 2023. Predicting the presence of inline citations in academic text using binary classification. In *Proceedings of the 24th Nordic Conference on Computational Linguistics (NoDaLiDa)*, pages 717–722, Tórshavn, Faroe Islands. University of Tartu Library.

Pancheng Wang, Shasha Li, Haifang Zhou, Jintao Tang, and Ting Wang. 2020. Toc-rwg: Explore the combination of topic model and citation information for automatic related work generation. *IEEE Access*, 8:13043–13055.

Yifan Wang, Yiping Song, Shuai Li, Chaoran Cheng, Wei Ju, Ming Zhang, and Sheng Wang. 2022. Disencite: Graph-based disentangled representation learning for context-specific citation generation. In *AAAI Conference on Artificial Intelligence*.

Yongzhen Wang, Xiaozhong Liu, and Zheng Gao. 2018. Neural related work summarization with a joint context-driven attention mechanism. In *Proceedings of the 2018 Conference on Empirical Methods in Natural Language Processing*, pages 1776–1786, Brussels, Belgium. Association for Computational Linguistics.

Jia yan Wu, Alexander Te-Wei Shieh, Shih Ju Hsu, and Yun-Nung Chen. 2021. Towards generating citation sentences for multiple references with intent control. *ArXiv*, abs/2112.01332.

Chrysoula Zerva, Minh-Quoc Nghiem, Nhung T. H. Nguyen, and Sophia Ananiadou. 2020. Cited text span identification for scientific summarisation using pre-trained encoders. *Scientometrics*, 125:3109–3137.

Kun Zhu, Xiaocheng Feng, Xiachong Feng, Yingsheng Wu, and Bing Qin. 2023. Hierarchical catalogue generation for literature review: A benchmark. In *Findings of the Association for Computational Linguistics: EMNLP 2023*, pages 6790–6804, Singapore. Association for Computational Linguistics.

A Prompt Structure for LLM Annotation

As outlined in Section 6.2, we employ GPT-3.5 Turbo to set a benchmark on the Annotated split of the dataset. After experimenting with various prompts, we find that the prompt depicted in Listing 1 yields the best results.

Listing 1: Prompt Structure for TR + LLM baseline. For vanilla LLM we replace the Text Span of paper 'B' with the actual reference paper.

```
system_prompt = '''
You are a Research Paper Relevance
    Classifier. Given the 'Title' and '
    Abstract' of Paper `A' and a 'Topic'
     of Paper 'A', and a text span from
    Paper 'B' predict whether Paper 'B'
    is directly related to the topic of
    Paper 'A', in context of the 'Title'
     and 'Abstract' of Paper 'A'. Output
     the model's prediction as:"

Output: [1] (for 'yes') or [0] (for 'no
    ')'''

user_prompt = '''
Title of Paper 'A':
<Target Proposal Title>
Abstract of Paper 'A':
<Target Proposal Abstract>

Topic of Paper 'A':
<Topic>

Text Span of Paper 'B':
<Reference Paper Title>
<Citation Text Span>

Is the content of Paper 'B' directly
    related to the topic of Paper 'A' (<
    Topic>)?
'''
```

B Annotation Interface

We have developed an Annotation tool aimed at offering a user-friendly interface to engage the human expert for annotating samples. The Annotator tool provides information on the target proposal's title, topic, reference paper title, abstract and the retrieved citation text span of the reference paper, as illustrated in Figure 6 (b). Moreover, we mandate the expert to review the disclaimer prior to the annotation process, ensuring that they are well informed about the context and ethical guidelines associated with the samples they are annotating, as reflected in Figure 6 (a).

C Error Analysis

We perform error analysis for the task of reference paper to topic mapping (classification). We use the sub-sampled test set discussed in Section 6.2 for the analysis.

C.1 Human Baseline

We analyze the False Positive and Negative samples with the annotations provided by the human expert.

The primary objective is to gain a profound understanding of the challenges inherent in the task. The identified 121 erroneous annotations provided by human are categorized into the following groups:

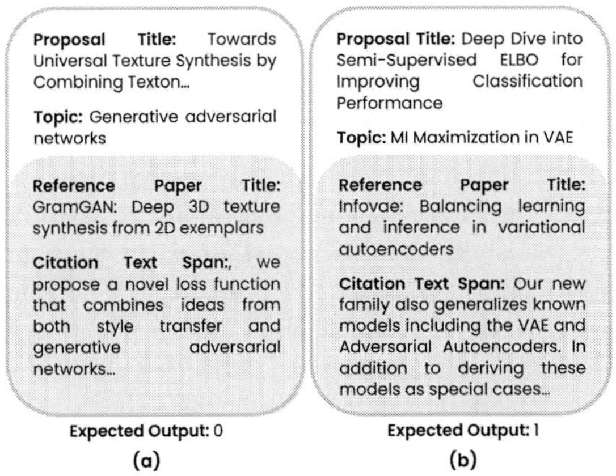

Figure 4: Samples illustrating Human errors due to (a) Subjectivity and (b) Insufficiency of information in the retrieved citation text span.

- **Subjectivity:** These errors, constituting 77.69% of total erroneous cases, stem from a misalignment between the thought processes of the author and the annotator. As shown in Figure 4 (a), the reference paper is not cited by the author under the given topic, however human annotator tends to map the reference paper to the topic due to the match between the semantics of the citation text span and the topic. In these instances, the annotator correctly deems the reference article relevant to the topic, while the author holds a contrasting view. This emphasizes the inherent subjectivity embedded in the task, where interpretations of relevance can diverge between individuals.

- **Insufficiency:** Errors in this category are 4.96% of total erroneous cases and are attributed to the insufficient information present in the retrieved citation text span. The experts face challenges in making well-informed decisions due to the lack of comprehensive details, impeding their ability to accurately assess the relevance of the reference article to the given topic. For example, as highlighted in Figure 4 (b), the citation text span does not carry enough information to let the author infer its mapping to the topic. We observe in some of these cases the citation text span may carry information semantically similar to the citation text and thus the topic, but the information is not sufficient to logically reason about the possible alignment of the reference paper to the topic. This problem can be addressed by having a better mechanism for citation text span retrieval given citation text, which would indirectly help us improve the results of topic based citation text span retrieval model to retrieve more relevant citation text spans. This can be improved by augmenting the pipeline with an entailment task following the retrieval, to evaluate which of the top-k retrieved citation text spans entails the citation text to accommodate the reasoning component. We leave this enhancement for future work.

- **Inadequacy:** Errors categorized under inadequacy, accounting for 7.44% of total erroneous cases, emerge due to the lack of subject matter knowledge of the expert annotator. This knowledge gap prevents her from accurately understanding the relevance of the reference article to the proposed topic.

- **True Errors:** This category, constitutes 9.92% of total erroneous cases, encompassing genuine mistakes made by human annotators. Despite concerted efforts to maintain accuracy, errors of this nature occur, underscoring the complexity and human cognitive load of the task.

The systematic categorization of these errors showcases the prevalence of subjectivity, arising from differences in the author's writing style and thought process which constitutes the majority of mis-classifications by human annotators.

C.2 LLM baseline and fine-tuned models against Human baseline

We analyze instances where human annotators correctly classified the samples that are misclassified by the LLM and fine-tuned models, as outlined in Table 5. We majorly categorize the error into two categories:

- **Requirement of complex reasoning:** These errors are due to the absence of direct alignment between the topics and the citation text span of the reference paper. It requires multi-hop complex reasoning for the mapping task. As demonstrated in Figure 5 (a), the reference paper is not directly relevant to the topic

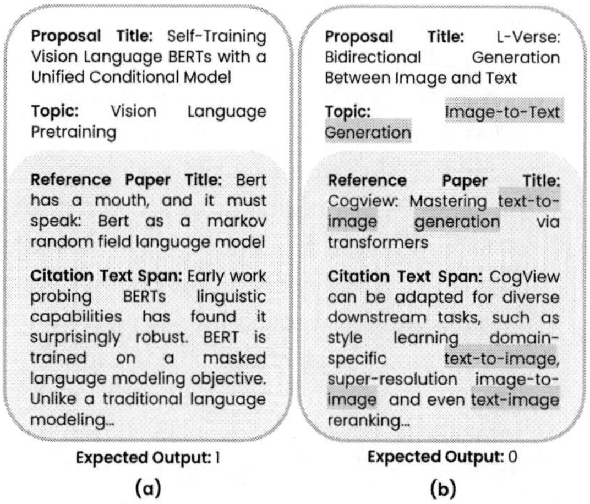

Figure 5: Samples correctly classified by humans but erroneously classified by LLM and fine-tuned models due to (a) Requirement of complex reasoning and (b) Misleading Lexical overlap between topic and retrieved citation text span but no semantic match

Table 5: Error Analysis of the Mis-classifications of LLM and fine-tuned models against Human baseline

Models	Samples	Complex Reasoning	Lexical Overlap
LLM [GPT-3.5 Turbo]	196	38.89%	61.11%
TC [RoBERTa]*	234	42.22%	57.78%
TC [Flan-T5]*	224	33.33%	66.67%

* models fine-tuned on our dataset.

'Vision Language Pretraining. However, the BERT model can be used as the text encoder for the vision language model. The fine-tuned models and LLM sometimes find it difficult to perform such complex reasoning to come up with the expected mapping.

- **Lexical:** Errors in this category stem from the presence or absence of identical words in the extracted citation text span when compared to those in the topic, leading to misclassification. A representative example of a lexical error is illustrated in Figure 5 (b), where there is lexical overlap between the topic name and citation text span, however, the semantics do not match.

The primary factor contributing to misclassifications of models is lexical similarity or dissimilarity between the topic and the retrieved citation text span. This highlights the model's challenge in comprehending contextual nuances, leading to misinterpretations.

D Limitations

Our pipeline is fine-tuned with our constructed dataset containing papers in the AI (majorly CV) domain. The results are demonstrated with a test set containing papers in the AI domain only, leading to comparable results with the zero-shot vanilla LLM baseline. Our pipeline may not perform well in cross-domain settings. However, our dataset construction technique can be easily applied to the scientific articles belonging to any domain, based on the availability of the articles. Extrapolating the current results demonstrated for the AI - CV domain, the retrieval-classifier pipeline fine-tuned with such domain-specific synthesized dataset should lead us to comparable results with the zero-shot vanilla LLM baseline, for any domain.

We create pseudo-topic-reference text span labels for the training data by considering the text under that topic (section) which is written to cite a reference article (citation text) as an explicit link to connect the topic and the reference article. It clearly carries the information of the relevance of the scientific article with regards to the proposal, in the context of the given topic. The citations to the same reference article but at other places in the proposal may not carry information on the relevance of the reference article in the context of the given topic to which the reference article is to be aligned. However, we are not completely denying the possibility of some other sections carrying information about the relevance of the reference article to the proposal in the context of the given topic. However as there is no explicit signal that we can exploit to derive this connection, we cannot consider that information while establishing the connection.

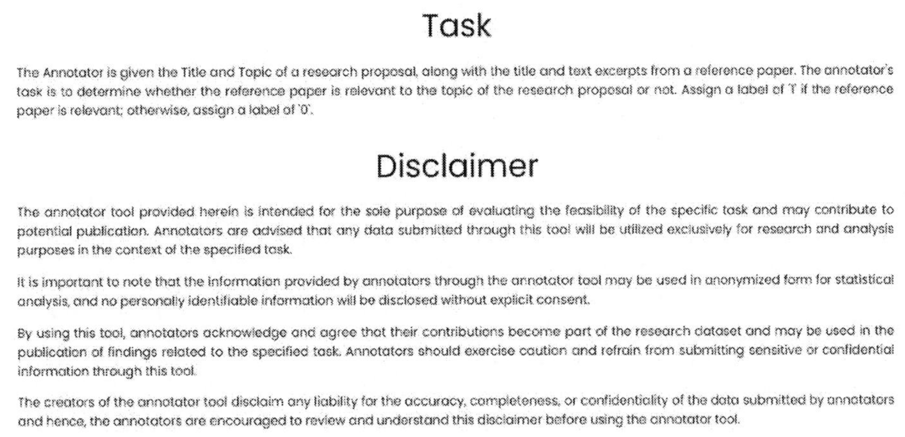

Task

The Annotator is given the Title and Topic of a research proposal, along with the title and text excerpts from a reference paper. The annotator's task is to determine whether the reference paper is relevant to the topic of the research proposal or not. Assign a label of '1' if the reference paper is relevant; otherwise, assign a label of '0'.

Disclaimer

The annotator tool provided herein is intended for the sole purpose of evaluating the feasibility of the specific task and may contribute to potential publication. Annotators are advised that any data submitted through this tool will be utilized exclusively for research and analysis purposes in the context of the specified task.

It is important to note that the information provided by annotators through the annotator tool may be used in anonymized form for statistical analysis, and no personally identifiable information will be disclosed without explicit consent.

By using this tool, annotators acknowledge and agree that their contributions become part of the research dataset and may be used in the publication of findings related to the specified task. Annotators should exercise caution and refrain from submitting sensitive or confidential information through this tool.

The creators of the annotator tool disclaim any liability for the accuracy, completeness, or confidentiality of the data submitted by annotators and hence, the annotators are encouraged to review and understand this disclaimer before using the annotator tool.

(a)

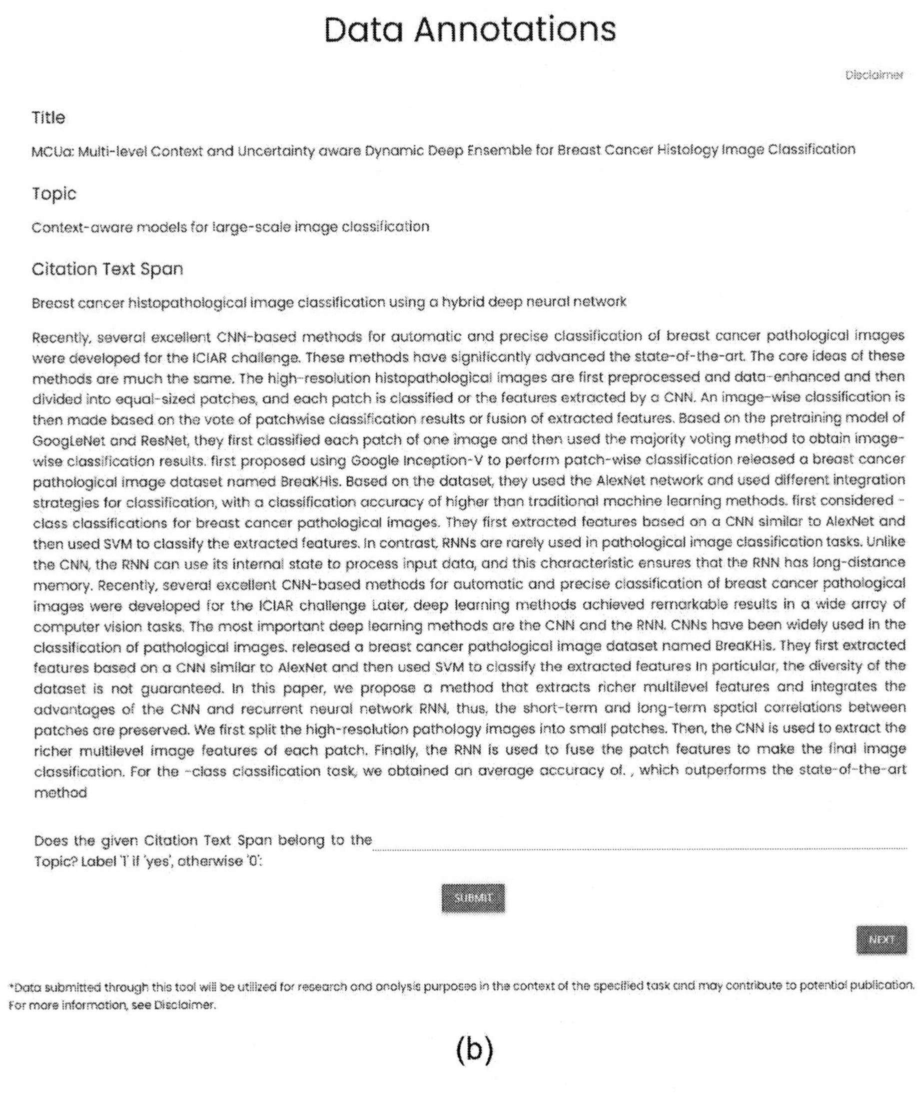

Data Annotations

Disclaimer

Title

MCUa: Multi-level Context and Uncertainty aware Dynamic Deep Ensemble for Breast Cancer Histology Image Classification

Topic

Context-aware models for large-scale image classification

Citation Text Span

Breast cancer histopathological image classification using a hybrid deep neural network

Recently, several excellent CNN-based methods for automatic and precise classification of breast cancer pathological images were developed for the ICIAR challenge. These methods have significantly advanced the state-of-the-art. The core ideas of these methods are much the same. The high-resolution histopathological images are first preprocessed and data-enhanced and then divided into equal-sized patches, and each patch is classified or the features extracted by a CNN. An image-wise classification is then made based on the vote of patchwise classification results or fusion of extracted features. Based on the pretraining model of GoogLeNet and ResNet, they first classified each patch of one image and then used the majority voting method to obtain image-wise classification results. first proposed using Google Inception-V to perform patch-wise classification released a breast cancer pathological image dataset named BreaKHis. Based on the dataset, they used the AlexNet network and used different integration strategies for classification, with a classification accuracy of higher than traditional machine learning methods. first considered -class classifications for breast cancer pathological images. They first extracted features based on a CNN similar to AlexNet and then used SVM to classify the extracted features. In contrast, RNNs are rarely used in pathological image classification tasks. Unlike the CNN, the RNN can use its internal state to process input data, and this characteristic ensures that the RNN has long-distance memory. Recently, several excellent CNN-based methods for automatic and precise classification of breast cancer pathological images were developed for the ICIAR challenge Later, deep learning methods achieved remarkable results in a wide array of computer vision tasks. The most important deep learning methods are the CNN and the RNN. CNNs have been widely used in the classification of pathological images. released a breast cancer pathological image dataset named BreaKHis. They first extracted features based on a CNN similar to AlexNet and then used SVM to classify the extracted features In particular, the diversity of the dataset is not guaranteed. In this paper, we propose a method that extracts richer multilevel features and integrates the advantages of the CNN and recurrent neural network RNN, thus, the short-term and long-term spatial correlations between patches are preserved. We first split the high-resolution pathology images into small patches. Then, the CNN is used to extract the richer multilevel image features of each patch. Finally, the RNN is used to fuse the patch features to make the final image classification. For the -class classification task, we obtained an average accuracy of. , which outperforms the state-of-the-art method

Does the given Citation Text Span belong to the Topic? Label '1' if 'yes', otherwise '0':

SUBMIT

NEXT

*Data submitted through this tool will be utilized for research and analysis purposes in the context of the specified task and may contribute to potential publication. For more information, see Disclaimer.

(b)

Figure 6: The Annotator Tool illustrating the (a) task description and disclaimer presented to the human expert before the annotation process and, (b) the annotation interface showcasing a sample from the dataset.

Evaluating the Effectiveness of Retrieval-Augmented Large Language Models in Scientific Document Reasoning

Sai Munikoti* **Anurag Acharya** **Sridevi Wagle** **Sameera Horawalavithana***

Pacific Northwest National Laboratory, Richland, WA, USA
firstname.lastname@pnnl.gov

Abstract

Despite the dramatic progress in Large Language Model (LLM) development, LLMs often provide seemingly plausible but not factual information, often referred to as hallucinations. Retrieval-augmented LLMs provide a non-parametric approach to solve these issues by retrieving relevant information from external data sources and augment the training process. These models help to trace evidence from an externally provided knowledge base allowing the model predictions to be better interpreted and verified. In this work, we critically evaluate these models in their ability to perform in scientific document reasoning tasks. To this end, we tuned multiple such model variants with science-focused instructions and evaluated them on a scientific document reasoning benchmark for the usefulness of the retrieved document passages. Our findings suggest that models justify predictions in science tasks with fabricated evidence and leveraging scientific corpus as pretraining data does not alleviate the risk of evidence fabrication.

1 Introduction

Large Language Models (LLMs) perform competitively in a majority of Natural Language Processing (NLP) tasks, but tend to hallucinate with seemingly plausible but misleading predictions (Mallen *et al.*, 2023; Jiang *et al.*, 2023) with no clear explanations or justifications for their predictions (Mialon *et al.*, 2023). Recently, retrieval-augmented LMs have helped address these issues by augmenting the LLMs with non-parametric memory by using neural retriever to extract relevant information from external knowledge resources like document corpora (Jiang *et al.*, 2023). Retrieving external knowledge helps models update with new knowledge, inject domain specific data, and memorize long-tail knowledge. These models are also relatively small in the number of parameters and require less training and inference costs (Borgeaud *et al.*, 2022).

While retrieval-augmented LMs (RALM) are shown to perform well on knowledge-intensive tasks (Izacard *et al.*, 2022), we have very limited understanding on their ability to perform on the science-focused downstream tasks. For example, we can provide scientific documents as external knowledge at test time, and test the ability of the model to perform on science question and answering (QA) task. In this setup, the model retrieves scientific documents relevant to the question, and then generates an answer based on the retrieved documents. Retrieved documents help the model predictions to be better interpreted and verified. At the same time, we can assess the trustworthiness of these models to understand whether they justify the model predictions with accurate and relevant evidence (Mallen *et al.*, 2023). Recognizing any failure modes is essential to ensuring the safe deployment, and avoiding potential risks or negative consequences of these models, specially across multiple scientific use cases and applications.

This work conducts an evaluation on RALMs to improve our understanding of these models to perform on science tasks. To this end, we used the ATLAS model architecture (Izacard *et al.*, 2022) as an instance of the retrieval-based language model family to drive our experiments. To adopt the models for science tasks, we provide a collection of scientific documents as external corpus during the pre-training, instruction tuning, and evaluation stages. We evaluate the model performance on SciRepEval (Singh *et al.*, 2022) benchmark to test whether model recognizes different scientific domains and disciplines from the given scientific documents. Our hypothesis is that these models will be able to retrieve relevant information from scientific documents, integrate knowledge from diverse scientific domains, and reason over complex scientific concepts. In particular, we evaluate the usefulness of

*These authors contributed equally to this work.

Proceedings of the Fourth Workshop on Scholarly Document Processing (SDP 2024), pages 84–89
August 16, 2024 ©2024 Association for Computational Linguistics

Table 1: Summary of different pretraining, instruction tuning and benchmark datasets used across T5 and ATLAS models. We report the performance of the standalone LLM i) T5 (pretrained with C4), retrieval-augmented LLMs, ii) ATLAS model (pretrained with CC and Wikipedia) and iii) ATLAS-Science model (pretrained with S2ORC) text datasets. We used the S2ORC dataset as the external retrieval corpus in the instruction tuning and evaluation stages to make a fair comparison.

Model	**Pretraining**		**Instruction Tuning**		**Evaluation**	
	Data	**Retrieval Corpus**	**Data**	**Retrieval Corpus**	**Data**	**Retrieval Corpus**
T5	C4	N/A	FOS	N/A	FOS	N/A
					MAG	
ATLAS	CC + Wiki	Wiki		S2ORC	FOS	S2ORC
					MAG	
ATLAS-Science	S2ORC	S2ORC			FOS	
					MAG	

retrieved passages in terms of their relevancy and diversity that support the model predictions.

2 Problem Formulation and Eval Setup

2.1 Problem Formulation

Previous research on Retrieval Augmented LLMs focused on solving three major research questions: i) what to retrieve (e.g., chunks, tokens), ii) how to retrieve (e.g., input, intermediary and output layers), and iii) when to retrieve (e.g., once every $n \geq 1$ tokens). A majority of proposed models such as REALM (Guu *et al.*, 2020), DPR (Karpukhin *et al.*, 2020), RAG (Lewis *et al.*, 2020), and ATLAS (Izacard *et al.*, 2022) retrieve text chunks and concatenate them in the input layer of the language model. For example, ATLAS combines autoregressive text generation with retrieval-based language model pre-training based on the encoder-decoder architecture and fine-tuned on open-domain QA.

In this work, we aim to improve our understanding on the development of retrieval-based LMs for evidence extraction. We focus on the following related research questions to drive our experiments.

(RQ1) How useful are the evidences generated from retrieval-augmented LLMs to justify model predictions in science tasks?

(RQ2) How do the retrieval-augmented LLMs behave when provided with the scientific knowledge as the external document store?

2.2 Evaluation Setup

In this section, we outline the datasets, models, benchmarks and metrics used in our experiments.

Scientific Text Datasets Retrieval Augmented LLMs provide ideal test bed for scientific applications since they can handle dynamic knowledge updates and different scientific domains and disciplines than what the models see during the pretraining. We focus on evaluating the Retrieval Augmented LLMs on their ability to understand scientific language and retrieve from multiple scientific knowledge sources. We preprocess the S2ORC (Lo *et al.*, 2019) dataset to create a collection of 354M text passages. Each passage has a maximum of 512 tokens, or 100 words that are concatenated with the corresponding title of the document the passage belongs to. We record 19 different scientific domains in the S2ORC collection.[1]

Models Our experiments are based on ATLAS (220M) (Izacard *et al.*, 2022) model architecture unless explicitly mentioned. ATLAS uses the Fusion-in-decoder architecture to fuse the retrieved text chunks with the input queries during the pretraining. In addition to the ATLAS model pretrained with common crawl (CC) and Wikipedia, we also train ATLAS-Science (220M) model from scratch with the S2ORC scientific text datasets. For a fair comparison with ATLAS, we initialize the ATLAS-Science model with the *T5-lm-adapt* (Raffel *et al.*, 2020) model and trained jointly with retrieval model, *Contriever* (Izacard *et al.*, 2021). Figure 1 shows the overview of different components used in the ATLAS-Science model. We provide the collection of scientific text passages as external retrieval corpus. First, we encode the scientific text passages (354M) with the *Contriever* model, and construct a document index in the FLAT (Izacard *et al.*, 2022) mode for faster retrieval. Second, we use the same passages for model pretraining and

[1] S2ORC dataset covers 19 scientific domains; Art, Philosophy, Political-Science, Sociology, Psychology, Geography, History, Business, Economics, Geology, Physics, Chemistry, Biology, Mathematics, Computer Science, Engineering, Environmental science, Material science, Medicine

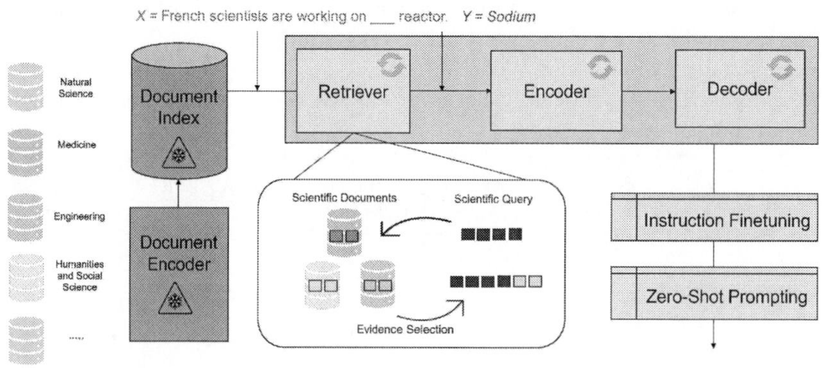

Figure 1: The main experimental setup of this research work, with all the major components displayed.

ensure that the passages used for pretraining are distinct from passages used to build the document index. Third, we train the retriever with the *query side finetuning* approach that originally introduced in the ATLAS model. This approach is very efficient in model training since it keeps the document encoder frozen while training the parameters corresponding to the query encoder (Figure 1). All the models are trained for the same number of tokens for a fair comparison.

Instruction Tuning We use the SciRepEval (Singh *et al.*, 2022) benchmark for training and evaluating the models for the scientific evidence extraction. SciRepEval provides 25 challenging tasks across four formats: classification, regression, ranking, and search. In this work, we focus on the classification tasks, *Fields of study (FoS)*[2] and *MAG* due to two main reasons. First, we need benchmark tasks that test the ability of the models to understand diverse scientific domains and disciplines. For example, FoS task tests the ability of the model to recognize which domain the given text passage belongs to. Second, we want to evaluate on specific instruction template to avoid any prompting bias. So we used the following instruction template:

```
"## Below is an input containing a title-abstract pair. Classify this input into one or more possible Field of Study categories. ### Possible Categories: [..] ### Input: ## Title: .. ## Response:"
```

[2]FoS tasks include instructions from following domains: Materials science, Economics, Chemistry, Medicine, Psychology, Geography, Geology, Political science, Engineering, Philosophy, Sociology, Physics, Computer science, Law, History, Biology, Agricultural and Food sciences, Environmental science, Business, Education, Art, Linguistics, Mathematics

Previous research (Izacard *et al.*, 2022) has shown that ATLAS model is able to learn knowledge intensive tasks with very few training examples (aka few shot learning). To allow the model to perform on the downstream tasks, we tune the model with scientific instructions. We design an instruction template to guide the model to generate the scientific domain that each passage belongs to. We tune the model with *Fields of study (FoS)* training data after converting them to instructions. This process resulted 541,218 training instructions that used to perform instruction tuning. For a fair comparison, we tune the T5 and ATLAS models with these instructions. In comparison to the T5 model, ATLAS models retrieve the top-k relevant passages from the S2ORC document store to augment the instruction tuning process. There are 68,147 and 3,751 test instructions in the FoS and MAG tasks, respectively. We use MAG instructions to test the out-of-distribution task performance. Table 1 summarizes the pretraining, instruction tuning and evaluation data used for the ATLAS and ATLAS-Science models.

Metrics We use the Exact Match (EM) and F1-Score to evaluate the task accuracy. EM metric evaluates the exact token overlap between the ground truth and generated answers. In addition, we design two metrics to evaluate the relevance and diversity of the extracted evidence: the *relevance* and *diversity* metrics. The relevance metric calculates the ratio of the domains present in Top-k evidences matching with the scientific domain corresponding to the query. The diversity metric calculates the ratio of the unique evidences in comparison to the total evidences. Both metrics are in the range of zero and one, with higher the metric scores, higher the quality in the generated evidences.

Table 2: Model ablation study to evaluate performance on in-distribution (SciDocs-FoS) and out-of-distribution (SciDocs-MAG) field of study instruction tuning datasets.

Model	In-distribution Performance				Out-of-distribution Performance			
	Accuracy		Evidence Generation		Accuracy		Evidence Generation	
	EM	F1	Relevance	Diversity	EM	F1	Relevance	Diversity
T5	83.33	0.87	N/A	N/A	57.90	0.72	N/A	N/A
ATLAS	84.42	0.92	0.06	5E-5	59.10	0.75	0.07	60E-5
ATLAS-Science	84.70	0.92	0.05	8E-5	57.80	0.73	0.05	100E-5

3 Measuring the Effectiveness of the Scientific Evidence Extraction

In this section, we address (RQ1) and (RQ2) by evaluating the usefulness of the evidence extracted from RALMs in performing science tasks. We test how retrieval-augmented LLMs behave when provided the scientific knowledge as external memory.

Retrieval-augmented LLMs justify model predictions in science tasks with fabricated evidence We evaluate the pretrained ATLAS model (Izacard *et al.*, 2022) on the benchmark tasks *Fields of study (FoS)* and *MAG*. Additionally, we tune ATLAS model with the *Fields of study (FoS)* instructions (as described in Section 2.2). We use the S2ORC document index to evaluate the instructions tuned ATLAS model in the zero-shot prompting stage. We report the performance of ATLAS model in Table 2. First, we observe that the accuracy of the ATLAS model is better than that of T5 in both the tasks, demonstrating the importance of retrieval augmentation. Second, we observe that although the ATLAS model has achieved a acceptable accuracy of 84.42% in *FOS* and 59.10% in *MAG*, the retrieved evidences are extremely poor in terms of relevance to the query topic. The model only achieves 0.06 relevance score suggesting that the passages returned by the model as evidences do not align with the domain of the query. For example, ATLAS model returns the passages in Geology, History and Chemistry as evidence for a Biology query as shown in Figure 2. The retrieved passages are not at all related to the corresponding query topics, rendering them useless. Finally, we also evaluate the faithfulness of the retrieved docs in terms of diversity score. This score is very low, suggesting that the evidences remain similar across all test queries. Our qualitative check suggests that the top-20 passages returned by the model for different queries are exactly same, while the generated answers are different and mostly accurate in comparison to the ground truth. These observations suggest that the ATLAS model fabricates the evidence to justify the model predictions.

Below is an input containing a title-abstract pair. Classify this input into one or more possible Field of Study categories. Possible Categories: ['..']

Input: Title: Integrate GWAS, eQTL, and mQTL Data to Identify Alzheimer's Disease-Related Genes. Abstract: It is estimated that the impact of related genes on the risk of Alzheimer's disease (AD) is nearly 70%. .. Among them, 93 SNPs and 2 genes are overlapped. Finally, we did 10 case studies to prove the effectiveness of our method.

Response: Biology

Evidence Traces:

Document 1: [Geology] Recent Morphologic Changes at Dog Keys Pass, Mississippi: Formation and Disappearance of Isle of Caprice: Approximately 70 years ago the Isle of Caprice, originally known as Dog Island, ..

Document 2: [History] The medieval world [SEP] His previous titles include "The Great Atlas of Discovery" (DK), "The Children\'s Concise History Encyclopedia" (World) and "Journey Through History"..

Document 3: [Chemistry] JV Task 117 - Impact of Lignite Properties on Powerspan's NOx Oxidation System. The system was commissioned on July 3, 2007, operated for 107 days, ..

Below is an input containing a title-abstract pair. Classify this input into one or more possible Field of Study categories. Possible Categories: ['..']

Input: Title: Two-dimensional arrays of superconducting and soft magnetic strips as dc magnetic metamaterials ## Abstract: We have theoretically investigated the magnetic response of two-dimensional (2D) arrays of superconducting and soft magnetic strips, which are regarded as models of dc magnetic metamaterials.

Response: Physics

Evidence Traces:

Document 1: [Environmental Science] Drying tests conducted on Three Mile Island fuel canisters containing simulated debris [SEP] If the canisters are not dried, but rather just dewatered, , ..

Document 2: [Medicine] Validation of memorial delirium assessment scale. [SEP] The MDAS had good internal consistency, with Cronbach alpha of .89 and Guttman split-half coefficient of 0.71,..

Document 3: [Engineering] The potential use of mimosa as fuel for power generation. [SEP] In 1998–99, Biomass Energy Services & Technology Pty Ltd, the Northern Territory Department of Infrastructure,..

Figure 2: Example generations of the ATLAS instruction tuned model in the SciRepEval-FoS (Singh *et al.*, 2022) task. We color the input query in gray, and the generated answer in red. We list three documents returned by the model as evidence to support the answer. We annotate each document by the corresponding scientific domain. For example, the model accurately generates the Biology domain that the passage belongs to, but justifies the answer with fabricated evidence as retrieved passages are in Geology, History and Chemistry.

Scientific knowledge provided as pretraining data does not alleviate the evidence fabrication To explore the impact of the pretraining data on downstream scientific tasks, we repeat the evaluation with the *ATLAS-Science* model (as described in Section 2.2). Note that the ATLAS-Science model is pretrained from scratch with S2ORC scientific text data provided as both pretraining and external document store. We evaluate the ATLAS-Science on two benchmark tasks. The results are tabulated in third row of Table 2. In comparison to ATLAS, the accuracy of ATLAS-Science model has a slight improvement in *FOS*, whereas it depreciates in *MAG*. Thus we see that scientific corpus does not help much in improving the performance of the model. More importantly, the relevance and diversity of the retrieved passages only slightly improves over ATLAS. This indicates that leveraging scientific corpus as pretraining data is not an effective approach to address the challenge of evidence fabrication.

4 Related Work

LLMs can be augmented with various external modules such as document corpus (Gao *et al.*, 2020), vector databases[3], etc. Typically, the augmentation is accomplished in two ways, namely sparse (such as Bag of words) and dense where Neural network is used to encode documents. Dense retrievers are widely used in present time mainly due to the good representation capability of neural networks. Recent works suggest that the retrieval-augmented LLMs has significant improvement over the standard LLMs across various tasks especially with respect to scale (Guu *et al.*, 2020; Lewis *et al.*, 2020). REALM and RAG are the initial efforts where they train the retriever and language model by representing documents as latent variable, and minimizing the language model objective (Guu *et al.*, 2020; Lewis *et al.*, 2020). REALM leverages masked-language modeling as an objective to pretrain the model in end to end fashion. However, it is computationally very expensive to train these models that requires to retrain the entire index with new knowledge. Guu *et al.* (2020) explored the concept of query-side finetuning that only refreshes the query encoder whereas document encoder remains frozen. Izacard et al. (Izacard & Grave, 2020; Izacard *et al.*, 2021) proposed various ways to improve the retrieval augmented models, including novel learning objectives to align retriever with the language model (Izacard *et al.*, 2021). Furthermore, RETRO (Borgeaud *et al.*, 2022) shows the benefits of scaling the retrieval memory to trillions of tokens. ATLAS (Izacard *et al.*, 2022) experiments with various design and training configurations for retrieval augmented models with a focus on few shot learning ability, while ATLANTIC (Munikoti *et al.*, 2024) shows an approach to utilize heterogeneous graph information to create a structure-aware RAG technique. Finally, Wagle *et al.* (2024) provides a word of caution, finding that while RAG-based language models tend to be more confident if fine-tuned on scientific documents, they also exhibit false confidence even for incorrect predictions.

[3]https://github.com/jerryjliu/llama_index

5 Conclusion

In this study, we explored the efficacy of retrieval augmented language models on science tasks. Our experiments were based on ATLAS model which is a state of the art retrieval augmented language model with few shot capability. We performed a systematic evaluation on the performance of different ATLAS model variants in two scientific document reasoning tasks. Our experiments on the pretrained ATLAS model reveal that the model demonstrates acceptable performance in science tasks but the evidences are fabricated. We also observe that pretraining the model with scientific corpus does not alleviate evidence fabrication. We plan to develop techniques to alleviate these issues in a future work.

Acknowledgements

This work was supported by the NNSA Office of Defense Nuclear Nonproliferation Research and Development, U.S. Department of Energy, and Pacific Northwest National Laboratory, which is operated by Battelle Memorial Institute for the U.S. Department of Energy under Contract DE-AC05–76RLO1830. This article has been cleared by PNNL for public release as PNNL-SA-189029.

References

Borgeaud, Sebastian, Mensch, Arthur, Hoffmann, Jordan, Cai, Trevor, Rutherford, Eliza, Millican, Katie, Van Den Driessche, George Bm, Lespiau, Jean-Baptiste, Damoc, Bogdan, Clark, Aidan, *et al.* 2022. Improving language models by retrieving from trillions of tokens. *Pages 2206–2240 of: International conference on machine learning*. PMLR.

Gao, Leo, Biderman, Stella, Black, Sid, Golding, Laurence, Hoppe, Travis, Foster, Charles, Phang, Jason, He, Horace, Thite, Anish, Nabeshima, Noa, *et al.* 2020. The pile: An 800gb dataset of diverse text for language modeling. *arXiv preprint arXiv:2101.00027*.

Guu, Kelvin, Lee, Kenton, Tung, Zora, Pasupat, Panupong, & Chang, Mingwei. 2020. Retrieval augmented language model pre-training. *Pages 3929–3938 of: International conference on machine learning*. PMLR.

Izacard, Gautier, & Grave, Edouard. 2020. Leveraging passage retrieval with generative models for open domain question answering. *arXiv preprint arXiv:2007.01282*.

Izacard, Gautier, Caron, Mathilde, Hosseini, Lucas, Riedel, Sebastian, Bojanowski, Piotr, Joulin, Armand, & Grave, Edouard. 2021. Unsupervised dense information retrieval with contrastive learning. *arXiv preprint arXiv:2112.09118*.

Izacard, Gautier, Lewis, Patrick, Lomeli, Maria, Hosseini, Lucas, Petroni, Fabio, Schick, Timo, Dwivedi-Yu, Jane, Joulin, Armand, Riedel, Sebastian, & Grave, Edouard. 2022. Few-shot learning with retrieval augmented language models. *arXiv preprint arXiv:2208.03299*.

Jiang, Zhengbao, Xu, Frank F, Gao, Luyu, Sun, Zhiqing, Liu, Qian, Dwivedi-Yu, Jane, Yang, Yiming, Callan, Jamie, & Neubig, Graham. 2023. Active retrieval augmented generation. *arXiv preprint arXiv:2305.06983*.

Karpukhin, Vladimir, Oğuz, Barlas, Min, Sewon, Lewis, Patrick, Wu, Ledell, Edunov, Sergey, Chen, Danqi, & Yih, Wen-tau. 2020. Dense passage retrieval for open-domain question answering. *arXiv preprint arXiv:2004.04906*.

Lewis, Patrick, Perez, Ethan, Piktus, Aleksandra, Petroni, Fabio, Karpukhin, Vladimir, Goyal, Naman, Küttler, Heinrich, Lewis, Mike, Yih, Wen-tau, Rocktäschel, Tim, *et al.* 2020. Retrieval-augmented generation for knowledge-intensive nlp tasks. *Advances in Neural Information Processing Systems*, **33**, 9459–9474.

Lo, Kyle, Wang, Lucy Lu, Neumann, Mark, Kinney, Rodney, & Weld, Dan S. 2019. S2ORC: The semantic scholar open research corpus. *arXiv preprint arXiv:1911.02782*.

Mallen, Alex, Asai, Akari, Zhong, Victor, Das, Rajarshi, Khashabi, Daniel, & Hajishirzi, Hannaneh. 2023. When not to trust language models: Investigating effectiveness of parametric and non-parametric memories. *Pages 9802–9822 of: Proceedings of the 61st Annual Meeting of the Association for Computational Linguistics (Volume 1: Long Papers)*.

Mialon, Grégoire, Dessì, Roberto, Lomeli, Maria, Nalmpantis, Christoforos, Pasunuru, Ram, Raileanu, Roberta, Rozière, Baptiste, Schick, Timo, Dwivedi-Yu, Jane, Celikyilmaz, Asli, *et al.* 2023. Augmented language models: a survey. *arXiv preprint arXiv:2302.07842*.

Munikoti, Sai, Acharya, Anurag, Wagle, Sridevi, & Horawalavithana, Sameera. 2024 (February). ATLANTIC: Structure-Aware Retrieval-Augmented Language Model for Interdisciplinary Science. *In: Proceedings of the Workshop on AI to Accelerate Science and Engineering (AI2ASE)*. Held in conjunction with the 38th AAAI Conference on Artificial Intelligence (AAAI 2024).

Raffel, Colin, Shazeer, Noam, Roberts, Adam, Lee, Katherine, Narang, Sharan, Matena, Michael, Zhou, Yanqi, Li, Wei, & Liu, Peter J. 2020. Exploring the limits of transfer learning with a unified text-to-text transformer. *The Journal of Machine Learning Research*, **21**(1), 5485–5551.

Singh, Amanpreet, D'Arcy, Mike, Cohan, Arman, Downey, Doug, & Feldman, Sergey. 2022. SciRepEval: A Multi-Format Benchmark for Scientific Document Representations. *arXiv preprint arXiv:2211.13308*.

Wagle, Sridevi, Munikoti, Sai, Acharya, Anurag, Smith, Sara, & Horawalavithana, Sameera. 2024 (February). Empirical evaluation of uncertainty quantification in retrieval-augmented language models for science. *In: Proceedings of the Workshop on Scientific Document Understanding (SDU)*. Held in conjunction with the 38th AAAI Conference on Artificial Intelligence (AAAI 2024).

Cited Text Spans for Scientific Citation Text Generation

Xiangci Li Yi-Hui Lee Jessica Ouyang
Department of Computer Science
University of Texas at Dallas
Richardson, TX 75080
lixiangci8@gmail.com,
{yi-hui.lee, Jessica.Ouyang}@UTDallas.edu

Abstract

An automatic citation generation system aims to concisely and accurately describe the relationship between two scientific articles. To do so, such a system must ground its outputs to the content of the cited paper to avoid non-factual hallucinations. Due to the length of scientific documents, existing abstractive approaches have conditioned only on cited paper *abstracts*. We demonstrate empirically that the abstract is not always the most appropriate input for citation generation and that models trained in this way learn to hallucinate. We propose to condition instead on the *cited text span* (CTS) as an alternative to the abstract. Because manual CTS annotation is extremely time- and labor-intensive, we experiment with distant labeling of candidate CTS sentences, achieving sufficiently strong performance to substitute for expensive human annotations in model training, and we propose a human-in-the-loop, keyword-based CTS retrieval approach that makes generating citation texts grounded in the full text of cited papers both promising and practical.

1 Introduction

An automatic citation generation system aims to concisely and accurately describe the relationship between two scientific articles, a citing paper and a cited paper. Due to the rigorous nature of academic research, even large language models (LLMs), such as the GPT family (Brown et al., 2020; OpenAI, 2023), still have to ground their outputs to the input cited papers to avoid non-factual hallucinations.

Given a set of papers to cite, prior extractive approaches (Hoang and Kan, 2010; Hu and Wan, 2014; Chen and Zhuge, 2019; Wang et al., 2019a; Deng et al., 2021) selected salient sentences from the full text of the cited papers. However, existing abstractive approaches (AbuRa'ed et al., 2020; Xing et al., 2020; Ge et al., 2021; Luu et al., 2021; Chen et al., 2021; Li et al., 2022) generate citation texts conditioned on only cited paper *abstracts*, since the full texts of the papers often exceed the length limit of fine-tuned Transformer-based models (Li and Ouyang, 2022). Li et al. (2022) show that, when human judges are asked to rate the *relevance* of human-written gold citations with respect to the cited paper abstract (i.e. the generation system input), the scores are significantly lower than those of system-generated citations. We hypothesize that this discrepancy is caused by the gold citations referring to content from the cited paper body sections, not just the abstract, and these body sections are not available to either the generation model or the human judges.

Intuitively, the *cited text span* (CTS), the specific span of the cited paper that the gold citation refers to, should be a better alternative to the abstract for grounding a citation. Unfortunately, CTS labels are difficult to obtain. Existing manually-annotated sentence-level CTS datasets (Jaidka et al., 2018, 2019; AbuRa'ed et al., 2020) suffer from two key issues: annotation is extremely labor-intensive, even for domain experts, so the datasets are small; and inter-annotator agreement is relatively low (Cohen's κ of 0.16~0.52). Further, automatic CTS retrieval systems trained on these datasets give low performance (F1$<$0.2) and also use the gold citation text as input, making them inapplicable in a citation generation setting. Given these obstacles, CTS-based citation text generation is under-explored.

In this work, we study scalable CTS retrieval for citation text generation without expensive manual annotations. Our main contributions are as follows:

- We argue that CTS retrieval is an important and under-explored subtask of citation text generation. We demonstrate that citation texts generated using CTS are significantly more accurate and faithful than those using the existing approach of cited paper abstracts.

Proceedings of the Fourth Workshop on Scholarly Document Processing (SDP 2024), pages 90–104
August 16, 2024 ©2024 Association for Computational Linguistics

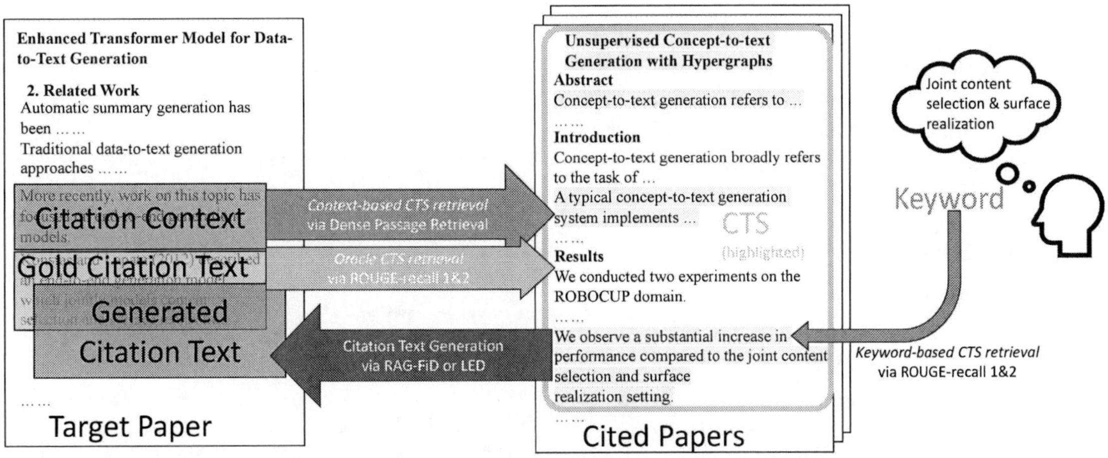

Figure 1: Overview of the proposed CTS-based citation generation approach. The *Context*, *Oracle*, and *Keyword* strategies are used to retrieve CTS from the cited paper (Konstas and Lapata (2012)) and generate a citation text for the target paper (Gong et al. (2019)). See Appendix Table 10 for details of the example.

- Because existing human-annotated CTS datasets are too small to train an effective CTS retrieval system, we show that distant CTS labeling achieves sufficiently good performance to substitute for expensive human annotations. Using this method, we create a large-scale, distantly-labeled CTS dataset.

- We argue that existing CTS retrieval systems are inappropriate for the citation generation task because they use the gold citation text as the retrieval query. Instead, we propose a simple, human-in-the-loop, keyword-based CTS retrieval method that makes generating citations grounded in the full text of the cited paper both promising and practical[1].

2 Background and Related Work

There are two main CTS datasets: Jaidka et al. (2018, 2019) proposed the CL-Scisumm shared task and manually annotated CTS, citation facets, and summaries for 364 citation texts that cite a set of 20 papers; AbuRa'ed et al. (2020) manually annotated sentence-level CTS for 20 related work sections. Unfortunately, both suffer from low inter-annotator agreement, and automatic CTS retrieval systems trained and evaluated on these datasets perform poorly (Jaidka et al., 2018, 2019; AbuRa'ed et al., 2020; Chandrasekaran et al., 2020).

Only a few studies have used CTS for scientific document summarization. ScisummNet (Yasunaga et al., 2019) leveraged a ROUGE-based CTS retrieval approach (Cao et al., 2015) to collect community-based evidence for summarizing a paper. Wang et al. (2019a) trained a feature-based ensemble model for CTS retrieval using ScisummNet and used the retrieved CTS for extractive related work generation. Syed et al. (2023) used BM25 and SciBERT (Beltagy et al., 2019) to retrieve CTS to provide more contexts for scientific paper summarization. However, all of these works used the target citation text as the query for CTS retrieval, which cannot be used in the citation generation setting that we tackle in this paper.

3 A Large-Scale CTS Dataset: Distant vs. Human Labeling

When authors cite a paper, they locate salient passages and compose a citation text grounded in these cited text spans (CTS). Unfortunately, such fine-grained CTS information is not recorded anywhere; even an author may not be able to precisely identify the CTS that they used. While prior CTS retrieval systems have trained on small, human-annotated CTS datasets (Jaidka et al., 2018, 2019; AbuRa'ed et al., 2020; Chandrasekaran et al., 2020), we argue that the relatively low inter-annotator agreement of these datasets suggests there can be multiple reasonable CTS for a given citation, just as there can be multiple valid extractive summaries of a document (see Section 3.3). Thus, distantly-labeled CTS is not necessarily of lower quality than human-annotated CTS, as long as the distant labels identify one of these multiple reasonable candidates. In this section, we use a simple distant approach, with the gold citation text as query,

[1] https://github.com/jacklxc/CTS4CitationTextGeneration

to automatically label plausible CTS candidates to create a large-scale CTS dataset without expensive and time-consuming human annotations. We demonstrate that our distantly-labeled CTS are of comparable quality to existing human-annotated datasets.

3.1 Approach

With the observation that high keyword overlap with the citation text is a crucial characteristic of CTS, we follow Cao et al. (2015); Yasunaga et al. (2019) in using gold citation texts as queries to rank the top-k sentences in the corresponding cited papers as CTS candidates. The similarity is measured by the average of the ROUGE-1 and -2 recall scores (Lin, 2004).[2] We use NLTK[3] to remove stop words for both the query and cited paper sentences. Compared to dense retrievers (Zhang* et al., 2020), ROUGE-based retrieval does not use GPUs, and thus computationally more efficient. Moreover, since there is no good fine-tuning dataset for CTS retrieval due to the small size of human-labeled datasets Jaidka et al. (2018, 2019), an unsupervised approach is preferable.

We use the human-labeled datasets of Jaidka et al. (2018, 2019) (CL-SciSumm) and AbuRa'ed et al. (2020) as test sets to evaluate our distantly-labeled CTS[4]. We take the union of all annotators' selected sentences as the human-labeled CTS.

3.2 Evaluation Metrics

Token overlap. We use ROUGE-recall to measure the coverage of the distantly-labeled tokens that support the gold citation text.

Faithfulness. We use QuestEval (Scialom et al., 2021) and ANLI (Nie et al., 2020) to compare the faithfulness of the gold citation text when grounded in human-labeled versus distantly-labeled CTS. For ANLI, we report the non-contradiction score (sum of *entailment* and *neutral*) given by a fine-tuned RoBERTa-large model (Liu et al., 2019).

3.3 Findings

Distant labeling has high coverage of human annotations. As Figure 2 shows, our top-40 retrieved CTS cover 80% and 95% of the human-labeled CTS in CL-SciSumm and AbuRa'ed, respectively. Further, as Figure 3 shows, the papers in these two datasets average 200 sentences long, so we can see that our automatic ranking concentrates the human-annotated CTS into roughly the top 20% (~40/200) of cited paper sentences.

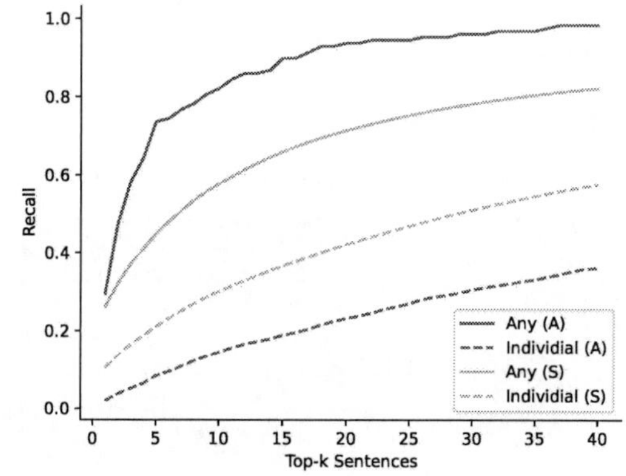

Figure 2: Performance of distantly-labeled CTS, measured by recall against human-labeled CTS. Solid lines ("Any"): each citation counts as one data point; a true positive is when at least one human-labeled sentence is distantly-labeled. Dotted lines ("Individual"): each human-labeled sentence is a separate data point. Green lines ("A"): AbuRa'ed. Yellow lines ("S"): CL-SciSumm.

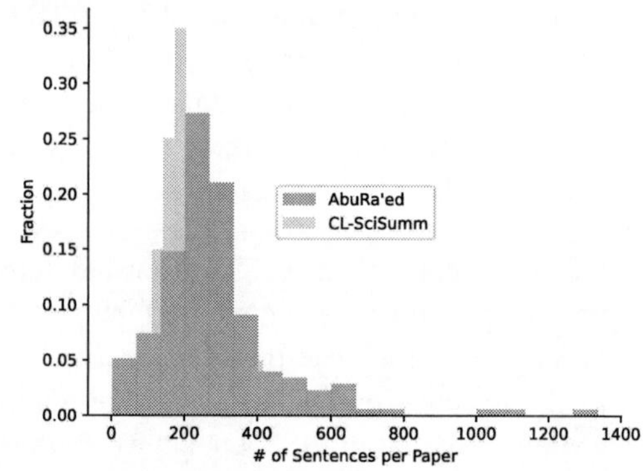

Figure 3: Distribution of the lengths of the cited papers by the number of sentences in CL-SciSumm and AbuRa'ed.

Distant labeling is more similar to the gold citation text. As Figure 4 and Table 1 show, although both human-labeled and distantly-labeled CTS are comparably faithful, distantly-labeled CTS has higher token overlap with the target citation text. This is unsurprising, given that using ROUGE as our similarity metric explicitly prioritizes token overlap, while human annotators may not do so. Evaluating human CTS in the intersection, rather than the union, of different annotators'

[2] We also experiment with BERTScore (Zhang* et al., 2020) as a dense retrieval approach, but the latter slightly underperforms ROUGE in all our experiments, including the comparison to human-labeled CTS (Figure 2).

[3] `https://www.nltk.org/index.html`

[4] We exclude 45 of AbuRa'ed et al. (2020)'s 239 cited papers due to an XML format error, but we do not expect this omission to affect the overall trend of our evaluation.

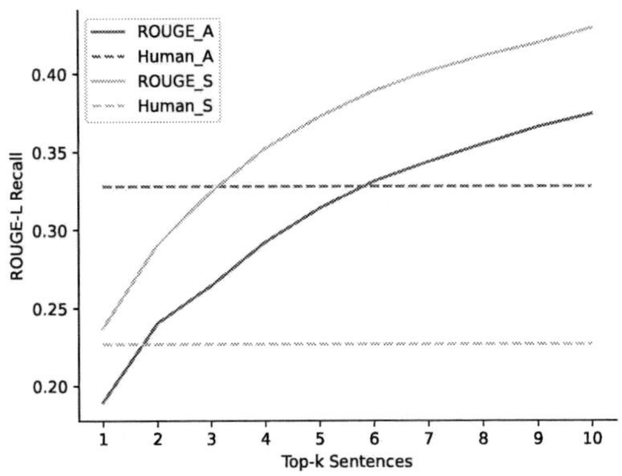

Figure 4: Overlap of the top-k distantly-labeled CTS (solid lines) & human-labeled CTS (dotted lines), measured by ROUGE-L recall against the gold citation text. Green lines ("A"): AbuRa'ed. Yellow lines ("S"): CL-SciSumm. The average length of human-labeled CTS is $|\overline{A}|$=16.8 and $|\overline{S}|$=2.5 sentences.

	Distantly-Labeled			*Human-Labeled*		
Config	**R-L**	**QEval**	**ANLI**	**R-L**	**QEval**	**ANLI**
AbuRa'ed	**0.376**	0.254	0.959	0.328	0.263	**1.000**
A-strict	-	-	-	0.224	**0.269**	0.992
SciSumm	**0.429**	0.259	**0.973**	0.225	0.258	0.922
S-strict	-	-	-	0.187	**0.275**	0.923

Table 1: Distant and human CTS labeling performance measured by ROUGE-L-recall, QuestEval, and ANLI against the gold citation text. "Strict" uses the intersection, rather than union, of human-labeled sentences by different annotators. $k = 10$ for distant-labeling.

labels (*strict*) has a noticeable impact on the token overlap, indicating that *individual annotators can select different, but all reasonable, CTS sentences.*

Distant labeling performs better on the downstream generation task. We also experiment with citation text generation using both distantly-labeled and human-labeled CTS, using the *LED-oracle* model described in Section 4. As Table 2 shows, distantly-labeled CTS performs comparably to human-labeled CTS for the AbuRa'ed dataset and outperforms human labels for CL-SciSumm, confirming that distant CTS labeling produces competitive performance on the downstream generation task. This experiment shows the upper bound of CTS performance using human and distant oracles, demonstrating that *it is not necessary to acquire expensive, human-labeled CTS for training a retriever for downstream citation text generation.*

4 Citation Text Generation Using CTS

In this section, we experiment with citation text generation conditioned on CTS, rather than the abstract-only approach used in prior work, and demonstrate that conditioning on CTS produces more accurate and faithful citations.

	Distantly-Labeled			*Human-Labeled*		
Config	**BLEU**	**METEOR**	**R-L**	**BLEU**	**METEOR**	**R-L**
AbuRa'ed	0.042	0.206	0.220	0.052	0.216	0.201
A-strict	-	-	-	**0.058**	**0.228**	**0.226**
SciSumm	**0.064**	**0.291**	**0.265**	0.061	0.252	0.242
S-strict	-	-	-	0.058	0.236	0.250

Table 2: Citation text generation performance measured by BLEU, METEOR and ROUGE-F1 against the gold citation. "Strict": intersection, rather than union, of human-labeled sentences.

4.1 Problem Formulation

Following Li et al. (2022), who note the information loss and leak issue of the citation *sentence* generation task, we aim to generate citation *spans* conditioned on (1) the citing paper context and (2) the full text of the cited paper(s) via retrieved CTS. We assume an auto-regressive generation setting, where citations are generated one at a time, in order of their appearance in the citing paper. Thus, we have access to up to two sentences before the target citation to use as context.

Data. We use the CORWA citation span[5] dataset Li et al. (2022), which is derived from the ACL partition of S2ORC (Lo et al., 2020). CORWA consists of a human-annotated *training* set and *test* set, as well as an automatically-labeled *distant* training set, with 1654, 1206, and 19784 "dominant"-type citation texts, respectively. We use only the dominant-type citations that are grounded to specific CTS, following Jaidka et al. (2018, 2019); AbuRa'ed et al. (2020), who filter out very short ("reference"-type) citations.

4.2 Approach

4.2.1 CTS Retrieval Strategies

Context-based retrieval. In this *fully automatic* approach, we retrieve CTS given only the target citation's context sentences. We apply the distant labeling approach described in Section 3 on the CORWA training set to create a large-scale CTS dataset and use this data to train a Dense Passage Retrieval (DPR; Karpukhin et al., 2020) model. We initialize both the query and candidate document encoders with Aspire (Mysore et al., 2022), a scientific sentence encoder fine-tuned on top of SciBERT (Beltagy et al., 2019). For training, we

[5]To avoid confusion between cited text *spans* and citation *spans*, we will refer to the generation targets as *citation texts*.

use the top-40 distantly-labeled CTS sentences as positive documents and the rest of the sentences in the cited papers as hard-negative documents.

Unsupervised oracle retrieval. The distant labeling method described in Section 3 uses the gold citation text as a query; while this approach cannot be used at test time when the target citation text is not known, we use it as an *Oracle* setting to explore the upper-bound of CTS-based citation text generation.

Human-in-the-loop keyword retrieval. There may be multiple reasonable citation texts given the same input context, depending on the interests of the reader. Therefore, we also experiment with a practical, human-in-the-loop scenario where a researcher already has a general idea of what they want to know about a particular cited paper, so they input some keywords as a query to guide CTS retrieval. To simulate this scenario, we apply a keyword extractor to the target citation texts and use the extracted keywords as simulated user-input keywords to retrieve CTS using unsupervised retrieval (*Keyword*). See Appendix Table 10 for an example.

To train the keyword extractor, we manually annotate a small set (673 instances) of citation keywords on top of the CORWA dataset. Each instance consists of a short, "reference"-type citation text with manually highlighted keywords[6]. We pre-train a T5-small model (Raffel et al., 2020) on the named-entity recognition labels of the SciREX training set (Jain et al., 2020) and further fine-tune it on manually annotated CORWA keywords as a sequence-to-sequence keyword extractor[7].

Table 3 shows the token overlap (ROUGE-L recall) between CTS retrieved using each of our three strategies and the target citation, as well as the faithfulness of the target citation grounded in the CTS; we compare against the cited paper abstract, which is used by existing citation generation systems instead of CTS. The token overlap of CTS is much higher than that of the abstract, as we expect, and more importantly, the faithfulness of the target citation grounded in CTS is higher than if it were grounded in the abstract, supporting our hypothesis

Setting	ROUGE-L	QuestEval	ANLI
Abstract	0.290	0.263	0.868
Context CTS	0.400	0.265	**0.964**
Oracle CTS	**0.533**	**0.271**	0.955
Keyword CTS	0.440	**0.271**	0.949

Table 3: Quality of citation generation input in terms of token coverage (ROUGE-recall) and faithfulness (QuestEval, ANLI) with respect to the target citation text.

	RAG-FiD			*LED*		
Setting	**BLEU**	**METEOR**	**R-L**	**BLEU**	**METEOR**	**R-L**
Abstract	0.214	0.397	0.194	0.142	0.380	0.189
Context	0.216	0.397	0.197	0.163	0.359	0.194
Oracle	**0.258**	**0.461**	**0.292**	**0.216**	**0.450**	**0.312**
Keyword	*0.239*	*0.437*	*0.262*	*0.182*	*0.404*	*0.270*

Table 4: Citation text generation performance measured by BLEU, METEOR and ROUGE-F1 against the gold citation. Citation marks are excluded in evaluation.

that the human-written target citations use information from the body sections of the cited papers. Thus, it is important to condition on CTS, not just the cited paper abstract, for citation generation.

4.2.2 Citation Text Generation Strategies

Retrieval-Augmented Generation. The Retrieval-Augmented Generation (RAG; Lewis et al., 2020b) bridges document retrieval and text generation by fine-tuning the query encoder and generator jointly. RAG uses DPR (Karpukhin et al., 2020) to retrieve k documents using the input query. We concatenate the target citation's context sentences and the retrieved CTS sentences[8] as the input to the citation text generator. We use Fusion-in-Decoder (FiD; Izacard and Grave, 2021) with BART-base (Lewis et al., 2020a) as the generator in our experiments.

Longformer-Encoder-Decoder. We also experiment with a simple Longformer-Encoder-Decoder (LED; Beltagy et al., 2020) model. We input the concatenation of the target citation context, the citation mark (eg. "Smith et al. (2024)"), and the retrieved CTS for each cited paper.

4.2.3 Experimental Settings

Training. We train on the large, automatically-labeled CORWA *distant* training set using cross-entropy loss and perform hyper-parameter tuning on the smaller, human-labeled *training* set; details and the hyper-parameter settings are reported in

[6]We use reference-type citations to train the keyword extractor only, not in any citation text generation experiments.

[7]Alternatively, any reasonable keyword extractor, such as recent LLMs, can also be used to simulate the user-input keywords.

[8]Unless explicitly specified, to balance performance and GPU memory usage, we retrieve the top $k = 10$ CTS in all experiments for the inference of citation text generation.

Setting	Fluency	Relevance	Coherence	Overall
Gold	4.71 (4.74)	4.04 (4.18)	**4.23 (4.41)**	3.87 **(4.16)**
Abstract	4.71 (4.72)	4.29 (4.26)	4.06 (3.96)	3.77 (3.63)
Context	4.80 (4.80)	**4.41 (4.31)**	4.00 (3.96)	**3.95** (3.85)
Oracle	4.80 (4.80)	4.18 (4.14)	4.07 (4.09)	3.86 (3.80)
Keyword	**4.84 (4.84)**	4.21 (4.16)	4.07 (4.07)	3.84 (3.76)

Table 5: Human evaluation with moderate inter-annotator agreement (avg. Kendall's $\tau = 0.239$). Scores in parentheses are from the second round after the gold citation texts are revealed to the judges.

	RAG-FiD		*LED*	
Setting	**R-L**	**ANLI**	**R-L**	**ANLI**
Abstract	0.556	0.745	0.591	0.744
Context	0.641	**0.959**	0.626	**0.954**
Oracle	**0.726**	0.940	**0.682**	0.950
Keyword	0.630	0.941	0.604	0.946

Table 6: Similarity and faithfulness of the generated citation texts with respect to their input setting, measured by ROUGE-recall and ANLI.

Appendix A. Each model takes about one day to train on one Nvidia Tesla V100S-32GB GPU.

Testing. For all experiments, we report performance on the human-labeled CORWA *test* set.

4.3 Human Evaluation

Following the setup used in prior works (Xing et al., 2020; Ge et al., 2021; Li et al., 2022), we recruit six NLP graduate students who are fluent in English as human evaluation judges. To increase their coverage of the test set, we split the judges into two groups of three and assign each group 25 instances sampled from the output of the RAG-FiD model. Each instance consists of a single target citation context and several candidate generations: one conditioned on the *Abstract* only and one for each of our three CTS retrieval strategies: *Context*, *Oracle*, and *Keyword*. The target citation context, cited paper abstracts, and retrieved CTS from all three strategies are also provided to the judges. Each generated citation is rated on a five-point Likert scale with respect to *Fluency*, *Relevance* (to the input; either abstract or CTS), *Coherence* (with respect to the context), and *Overall Quality*.

We perform two rounds of evaluation: first, the gold citation texts are mixed in with the candidate generations but are not identified to the judges; second, we reveal the gold citation texts and ask the judges to revise their ratings with this new information.

4.4 Results and Discussion

CTS-based generation outperforms abstract-only generation. Table 4 shows that the *Oracle* and *Keyword* CTS settings massively outperform the *Abstract* approach. Moreover, Table 5 shows that *Abstract* receives the lowest human *Overall* rating. In contrast with prior works in the abstract-only setting (AbuRa'ed et al., 2020; Xing et al., 2020; Ge et al., 2021; Luu et al., 2021; Chen et al., 2021; Li et al., 2022), all settings now score well on *Relevance* (higher than 4). Previously, even the gold citation text scored poorly on *Relevance* because the judges were only shown the abstract, which did not contain sufficient information to support the citation texts; our judges are shown the retrieved CTS sentences, which are a much better match for the citation texts.

CTS-based generation extracts more short phrases. The ROUGE-recall scores in Table 6 show that, compared to *Abstract*, CTS-based generations are more similar to their inputs, suggesting that models trained on CTS are more extractive. To investigate further, we use Grusky et al. (2018)'s *coverage* and *density* metrics. *Coverage* measures how much of the generated citation text is extracted from the input (abstract or CTS), while *density* measures the size of the extractions (e.g. individual unigrams versus entire sentences). Additionally, we calculate the compression ratio between the lengths of the inputs and the generated citation texts.

As Figure 5 shows, although the *Abstract* setting has the lowest compression ratio, it has a significantly lower *coverage* score than the CTS settings, confirming that the latter is more extractive. From this finding, along with the lower faithfulness scores in Table 6[9], we can infer that *Abstract* produces more non-factual hallucinations that distort the ideas of the cited paper. This finding supports our hypothesis that, in the abstract-only setting, *the citation generation input does not contain all of the information present in the target gold citation text, forcing the model to learn to hallucinate that missing information.*

Moreover, *Abstract* has a significantly higher *density* score, indicating longer copied sequences from the input, while the CTS-based settings extract and reorganize shorter phrases from the input. Since copying long text spans from other documents results in plagiarism in the citation generation setting, CTS-based generation is again preferable. Nonetheless, we stress that our CTS-

[9]We exclude QuestEval from this table due to an issue arising from the relative compression ratios of the different input settings.

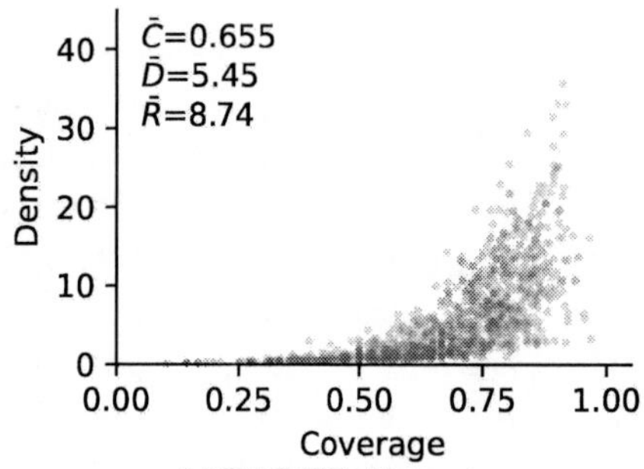

(a) RAG-FiD Abstract

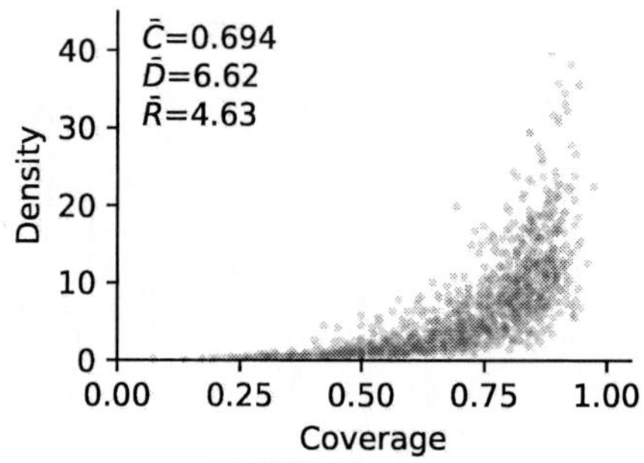

(b) LED Abstract

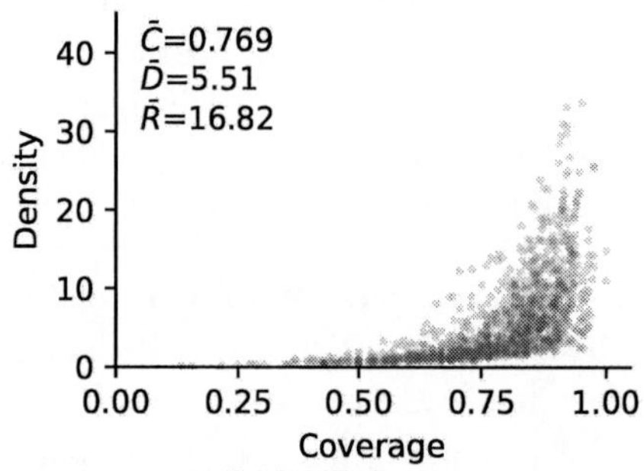

(c) RAG-FiD Context

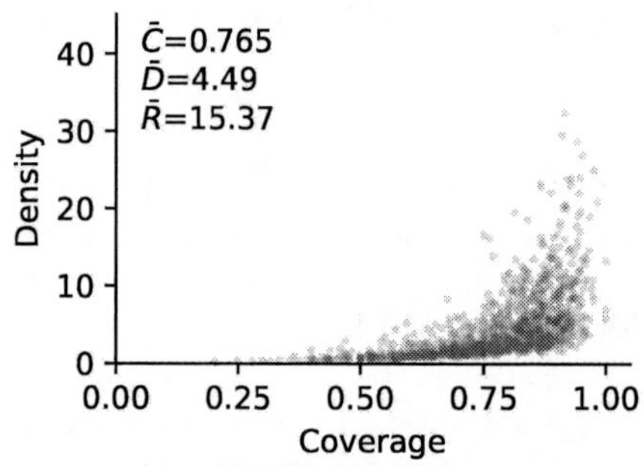

(d) LED Context

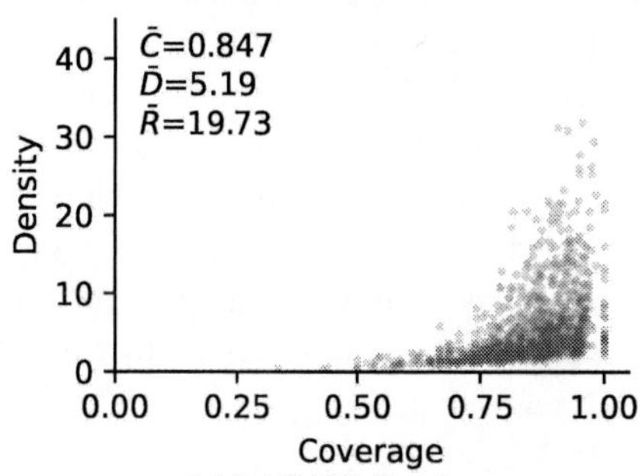

(e) RAG-FiD Oracle

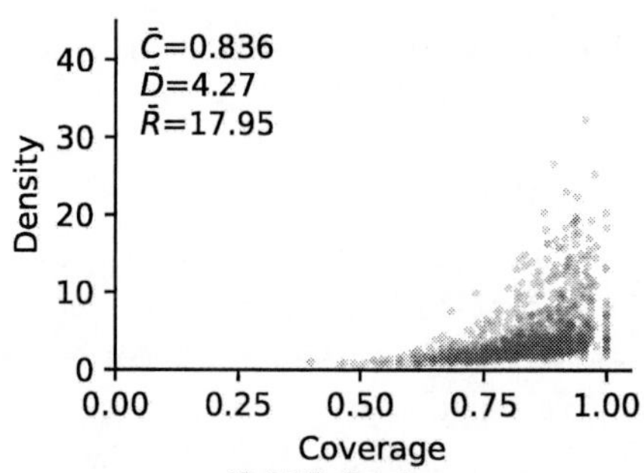

(f) LED Oracle

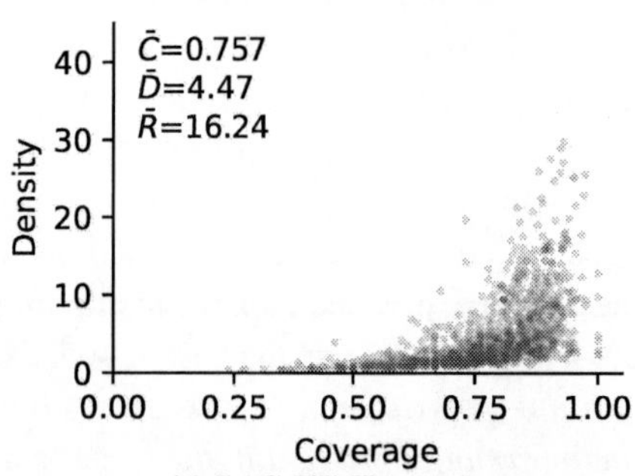

(g) RAG-FiD Keyword

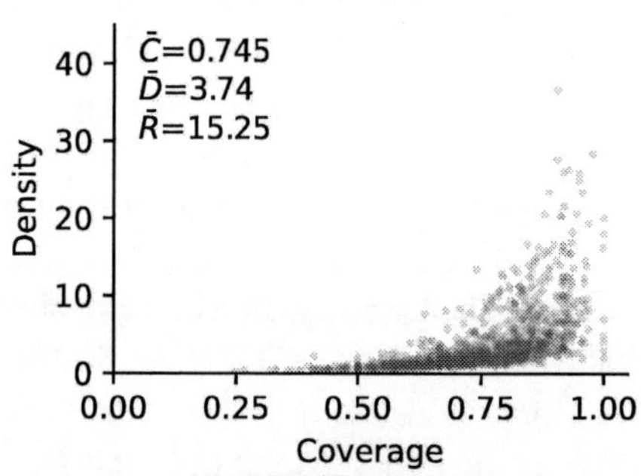

(h) LED Keyword

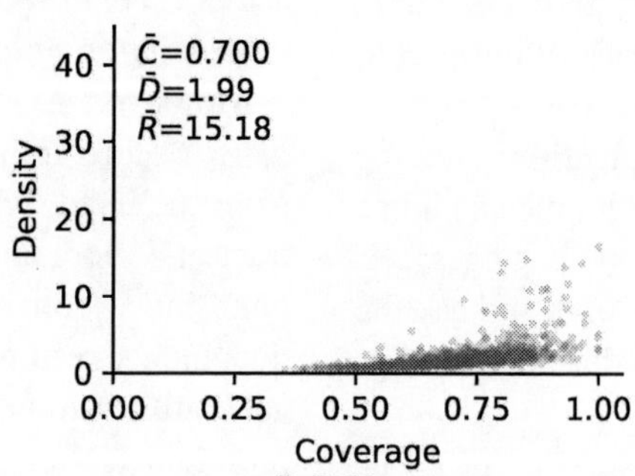

(i) Gold

Figure 5: Extractiveness of the generated citation texts, measured by *coverage* and *density* Grusky et al. (2018) against the generation input (abstract or CTS). The average coverage (C), density (D), and compression ratio (R) are shown for each generation setting. The "Gold" setting (Sub-figure 5i) is measured using Oracle CTS as the "input".

Section	Oracle	Keyword	Context
introduction	2155 (1)	1681 (1)	4140 (1)
related work	1217 (2)	634 (5)	401 (4)
model or architecture	903 (3)	1036 (2)	383 (5)
abstract	712 (4)	816 (3)	3667 (2)
experimental results	710 (5)	703 (4)	92 (8)
conclusion	508 (6)	589 (6)	316 (6)
approach	312 (7)	312 (8)	141 (7)
data	307 (8)	370 (7)	75 (9)
evaluation	210 (9)	215 (10)	38 (12)
discussion	88 (10)	75 (11)	15 (16)
title	73 (11)	262 (9)	921 (3)
background	67 (12)	74 (12)	54 (10)

Table 7: Counts (and ranks) of the most common section headers of retrieved CTS for the CORWA test set. Approximately 12,000 CTS are retrieved in total.

based generation approach is intended to increase accuracy and faithfulness and does not explicitly address the plagiarism issue; additional post-processing, such as a rewriting module, should be used to further reduce the risk of plagiarism.

Predicting CTS fully automatically is challenging. Although the fully automatic *Context* setting has strong input retrieval performance (Table 3), its performance on the downstream citation text generation task is mixed. It underperforms on automated metrics (Table 4), but human judges rate it slightly higher than *Oracle* and *Keyword* (Table 5). Table 7 shows that *Oracle* and *Keyword* tend to retrieve CTS from more specific sections, such as "Model or Architecture" or "Results" (Appendix Table 10), suggesting that the human judges may have felt that the generated citation texts contained too much unnecessary detail.

Fully automatic CTS retrieval given only the target citation context sentences is challenging because the citation context and the CTS candidates come from different papers (citing versus cited), and the semantic mismatch between them lowers the performance of the DPR module. In the example in Appendix Table 10, the citation context only mentions "end-to-end generation models", omitting the "content selection" and "surface realization" keywords that appear in the gold citation text, making CTS retrieval in *context* setting much harder than in *oracle* and *keyword*, which have explicit guidance with all important keywords from the gold citation text.

Interestingly, Table 5 shows that human evaluators cannot distinguish between gold and generated citation texts during the blind evaluation round. When the gold citation text is identified to the judges, they revise its scores higher, while lowering the scores of the generated candidates. This finding suggests that even humans need some guiding information to help them process citation texts. Thus, as Li et al. (2022) argue, the citation text generation task should be human-in-the-loop, leveraging a researcher's expertise to reduce both the search space size and cascading error propagation in the pipeline, and our *Keyword*-based CTS retrieval approach provides a practical workaround for the challenge of predicting CTS fully automatically.

5 Conclusion

In this work, we show that CTS-based citation text generation is more accurate and faithful than the abstract-based approaches used in prior work. We address the challenges that previously prevented CTS from being used effectively for citation text generation. Distant labeling, such as ROUGE-based labeling, achieves sufficiently strong performance to substitute for expensive manual CTS annotations, allowing us to build a dataset large enough to train a supervised CTS retriever. To avoid the pitfall of using the gold citation text as the retrieval query, which has been used in prior work but would not be possible in a real application, we propose a human-in-the-loop, keyword-based CTS retrieval approach that achieves strong performance in a practical and realistic setting. Finally, our experimental results show that, while retrieving CTS using only the citation context sentences is challenging and does not achieve the best performance using automated metrics, it is preferred by human judges and is a good direction for further investigation.

Limitations

Challenge of CTS retrieval. As discussed in Section 2, existing CTS retrieval approaches all use the gold citation text as the query. Our results also show that, while CTS retrieved using the gold citation text (or its keywords) yields strong generation performance, CTS retrieved with only the citation context sentences is not satisfactory. Therefore, we argue that citation text generation should be divided into two parts: support document retrieval and document-based citation text generation. Based on our results, we can achieve strong generation performance, but the automated retrieval part requires further investigation.

As a workaround solution without a strong,

context-based CTS retriever, we show that, when the user provides a few keywords to guide CTS retrieval, our models can perform quite well. This setting is practical under the human-in-the-loop configuration suggested by Li et al. (2022). However, we realize that this human-in-the-loop setting might be unfriendly to less-experienced researchers who are not sure what keyword to use. Future work may automatically predict the keywords of the gold citation text by performing paragraph- or document-level topic analysis using LLMs.

Choice of ROUGE-labeling approach & SOTA. We choose ROUGE-based labeling for CTS because it empirically shows the advantage of using even distantly labeled CTS for citation text generation, compared to using only cited paper abstracts. However, we do not claim that our RAG model using this retriever trained on these distant labels is SOTA. ROUGE-based labeling selects CTS with high lexical overlap with the target citation and may miss CTS that are semantically relevant but less lexically similar. In addition, there are many alternative ways to obtain better performance, such as using a more carefully crafted CTS retriever and training a larger generator with extensive hyper-parameter tuning. Instead, we simply claim that using CTS can improve citation text generation performance over using cited paper abstracts, and human labeling of CTS is not required because distantly labeled CTS is of comparable quality.

Quality Assurance of CTS. Due to the high cost of manually collecting or evaluating the quality of the retrieved CTS, we are not able to perform quality assurance of the distantly retrieved CTS on a large scale to avoid error-propagation to generated citation texts. Future work can incorporate a fact-checking module to further filter out CTS sentences that do not entail the citation text.

Ethics Statement

In this work, we focus on showing that retrieved CTS provides relevant support information to enable faithful citation text generation. Unsurprisingly, the trained CTS-based citation text generation models turn out to be more extractive (Section 4.4), directly copying parts of the input CTS to the output citation texts. This copying behavior has the potential to result in plagiarism if the output of our CTS-based citation text generator is directly without further modification. As we mention in Section 4.4, it may be necessary to apply a post-processing step, such as a rewriting module, to avoid plagiarism, which is out of the scope of this work and left for future investigation. We also point out that the existing, abstract-based approach to citation text generation extracts longer subsequences from its input, compared to our CTS-based approach, which extracts shorter subsequences and rearranges their order, so the plagiarism problem is not unique to CTS.

References

Ahmed AbuRa'ed, Horacio Saggion, and Luis Chiruzzo. 2020. A multi-level annotated corpus of scientific papers for scientific document summarization and cross-document relation discovery. In *Proceedings of the Twelfth Language Resources and Evaluation Conference*, pages 6672–6679, Marseille, France. European Language Resources Association.

Ahmed AbuRa'ed, Horacio Saggion, Alexander Shvets, and Àlex Bravo. 2020. Automatic related work section generation: experiments in scientific document abstracting. *Scientometrics*, 125:3159–3185.

Iz Beltagy, Kyle Lo, and Arman Cohan. 2019. SciBERT: A pretrained language model for scientific text. In *Proceedings of the 2019 Conference on Empirical Methods in Natural Language Processing and the 9th International Joint Conference on Natural Language Processing (EMNLP-IJCNLP)*, pages 3615–3620, Hong Kong, China. Association for Computational Linguistics.

Iz Beltagy, Matthew E Peters, and Arman Cohan. 2020. Longformer: The long-document transformer. *arXiv preprint arXiv:2004.05150*.

Tom Brown, Benjamin Mann, Nick Ryder, Melanie Subbiah, Jared D Kaplan, Prafulla Dhariwal, Arvind Neelakantan, Pranav Shyam, Girish Sastry, Amanda Askell, et al. 2020. Language models are few-shot learners. *Advances in neural information processing systems*, 33:1877–1901.

Ziqiang Cao, Furu Wei, Li Dong, Sujian Li, and Ming Zhou. 2015. Ranking with recursive neural networks and its application to multi-document summarization. In *Proceedings of the AAAI conference on artificial intelligence*, volume 29.

Muthu Kumar Chandrasekaran, Guy Feigenblat, Eduard Hovy, Abhilasha Ravichander, Michal Shmueli-Scheuer, and Anita de Waard. 2020. Overview and insights from the shared tasks at scholarly document processing 2020: Cl-scisumm, laysumm and longsumm. In *Proceedings of the first workshop on scholarly document processing*, pages 214–224.

Jingqiang Chen and Hai Zhuge. 2019. Automatic generation of related work through summarizing citations.

Concurrency and Computation: Practice and Experience, 31(3):e4261.

Xiuying Chen, Hind Alamro, Mingzhe Li, Shen Gao, Xiangliang Zhang, Dongyan Zhao, and Rui Yan. 2021. Capturing relations between scientific papers: An abstractive model for related work section generation. In *Proceedings of the 59th Annual Meeting of the Association for Computational Linguistics and the 11th International Joint Conference on Natural Language Processing (Volume 1: Long Papers)*, pages 6068–6077, Online. Association for Computational Linguistics.

Zekun Deng, Zixin Zeng, Weiye Gu, Jiawen Ji, and Bolin Hua. 2021. Automatic related work section generation by sentence extraction and reordering. In *AII@ iConference*, pages 101–110.

Jacob Devlin, Ming-Wei Chang, Kenton Lee, and Kristina Toutanova. 2019. BERT: Pre-training of deep bidirectional transformers for language understanding. In *Proceedings of the 2019 Conference of the North American Chapter of the Association for Computational Linguistics: Human Language Technologies, Volume 1 (Long and Short Papers)*, pages 4171–4186, Minneapolis, Minnesota. Association for Computational Linguistics.

Yubin Ge, Ly Dinh, Xiaofeng Liu, Jinsong Su, Ziyao Lu, Ante Wang, and Jana Diesner. 2021. BACO: A background knowledge- and content-based framework for citing sentence generation. In *Proceedings of the 59th Annual Meeting of the Association for Computational Linguistics and the 11th International Joint Conference on Natural Language Processing (Volume 1: Long Papers)*, pages 1466–1478, Online. Association for Computational Linguistics.

Li Gong, Josep Crego, and Jean Senellart. 2019. Enhanced transformer model for data-to-text generation. In *Proceedings of the 3rd Workshop on Neural Generation and Translation*, pages 148–156, Hong Kong. Association for Computational Linguistics.

Max Grusky, Mor Naaman, and Yoav Artzi. 2018. Newsroom: A dataset of 1.3 million summaries with diverse extractive strategies. In *Proceedings of the 2018 Conference of the North American Chapter of the Association for Computational Linguistics: Human Language Technologies, Volume 1 (Long Papers)*, pages 708–719, New Orleans, Louisiana. Association for Computational Linguistics.

Cong Duy Vu Hoang and Min-Yen Kan. 2010. Towards automated related work summarization. In *Coling 2010: Posters*, pages 427–435, Beijing, China. Coling 2010 Organizing Committee.

Yue Hu and Xiaojun Wan. 2014. Automatic generation of related work sections in scientific papers: An optimization approach. In *Proceedings of the 2014 Conference on Empirical Methods in Natural Language Processing (EMNLP)*, pages 1624–1633, Doha, Qatar. Association for Computational Linguistics.

Gautier Izacard and Edouard Grave. 2021. Leveraging passage retrieval with generative models for open domain question answering. In *Proceedings of the 16th Conference of the European Chapter of the Association for Computational Linguistics: Main Volume*, pages 874–880, Online. Association for Computational Linguistics.

Kokil Jaidka, Muthu Kumar Chandrasekaran, Sajal Rustagi, and Min-Yen Kan. 2018. Insights from cl-scisumm 2016: the faceted scientific document summarization shared task. *International Journal on Digital Libraries*, 19(2):163–171.

Kokil Jaidka, Michihiro Yasunaga, Muthu Kumar Chandrasekaran, Dragomir Radev, and Min-Yen Kan. 2019. The cl-scisumm shared task 2018: Results and key insights. *arXiv preprint arXiv:1909.00764*.

Sarthak Jain, Madeleine van Zuylen, Hannaneh Hajishirzi, and Iz Beltagy. 2020. SciREX: A challenge dataset for document-level information extraction. In *Proceedings of the 58th Annual Meeting of the Association for Computational Linguistics*, pages 7506–7516, Online. Association for Computational Linguistics.

Jeff Johnson, Matthijs Douze, and Hervé Jégou. 2019. Billion-scale similarity search with GPUs. *IEEE Transactions on Big Data*, 7(3):535–547.

Vladimir Karpukhin, Barlas Oguz, Sewon Min, Patrick Lewis, Ledell Wu, Sergey Edunov, Danqi Chen, and Wen-tau Yih. 2020. Dense passage retrieval for open-domain question answering. In *Proceedings of the 2020 Conference on Empirical Methods in Natural Language Processing (EMNLP)*, pages 6769–6781, Online. Association for Computational Linguistics.

Ioannis Konstas and Mirella Lapata. 2012. Unsupervised concept-to-text generation with hypergraphs. In *Proceedings of the 2012 Conference of the North American Chapter of the Association for Computational Linguistics: Human Language Technologies*, pages 752–761, Montréal, Canada. Association for Computational Linguistics.

Mike Lewis, Yinhan Liu, Naman Goyal, Marjan Ghazvininejad, Abdelrahman Mohamed, Omer Levy, Veselin Stoyanov, and Luke Zettlemoyer. 2020a. BART: Denoising sequence-to-sequence pre-training for natural language generation, translation, and comprehension. In *Proceedings of the 58th Annual Meeting of the Association for Computational Linguistics*, pages 7871–7880, Online. Association for Computational Linguistics.

Patrick Lewis, Ethan Perez, Aleksandra Piktus, Fabio Petroni, Vladimir Karpukhin, Naman Goyal, Heinrich Küttler, Mike Lewis, Wen-tau Yih, Tim Rocktäschel, et al. 2020b. Retrieval-augmented generation for knowledge-intensive nlp tasks. *Advances in Neural Information Processing Systems*, 33:9459–9474.

Xiangci Li, Biswadip Mandal, and Jessica Ouyang. 2022. CORWA: A citation-oriented related work annotation dataset. In *Proceedings of the 2022 Conference of the North American Chapter of the Association for Computational Linguistics: Human Language Technologies*, pages 5426–5440, Seattle, United States. Association for Computational Linguistics.

Xiangci Li and Jessica Ouyang. 2022. Automatic related work generation: A meta study. *arXiv preprint arXiv:2201.01880*.

Chin-Yew Lin. 2004. ROUGE: A package for automatic evaluation of summaries. In *Text Summarization Branches Out*, pages 74–81, Barcelona, Spain. Association for Computational Linguistics.

Yinhan Liu, Myle Ott, Naman Goyal, Jingfei Du, Mandar Joshi, Danqi Chen, Omer Levy, Mike Lewis, Luke Zettlemoyer, and Veselin Stoyanov. 2019. Roberta: A robustly optimized bert pretraining approach. *arXiv preprint arXiv:1907.11692*.

Kyle Lo, Lucy Lu Wang, Mark Neumann, Rodney Kinney, and Daniel Weld. 2020. S2ORC: The semantic scholar open research corpus. In *Proceedings of the 58th Annual Meeting of the Association for Computational Linguistics*, pages 4969–4983, Online. Association for Computational Linguistics.

Kelvin Luu, Xinyi Wu, Rik Koncel-Kedziorski, Kyle Lo, Isabel Cachola, and Noah A. Smith. 2021. Explaining relationships between scientific documents. In *Proceedings of the 59th Annual Meeting of the Association for Computational Linguistics and the 11th International Joint Conference on Natural Language Processing (Volume 1: Long Papers)*, pages 2130–2144, Online. Association for Computational Linguistics.

Sheshera Mysore, Arman Cohan, and Tom Hope. 2022. Multi-vector models with textual guidance for fine-grained scientific document similarity. In *Proceedings of the 2022 Conference of the North American Chapter of the Association for Computational Linguistics: Human Language Technologies*, pages 4453–4470, Seattle, United States. Association for Computational Linguistics.

Yixin Nie, Adina Williams, Emily Dinan, Mohit Bansal, Jason Weston, and Douwe Kiela. 2020. Adversarial NLI: A new benchmark for natural language understanding. In *Proceedings of the 58th Annual Meeting of the Association for Computational Linguistics*, pages 4885–4901, Online. Association for Computational Linguistics.

OpenAI. 2023. Gpt-4 technical report.

Colin Raffel, Noam Shazeer, Adam Roberts, Katherine Lee, Sharan Narang, Michael Matena, Yanqi Zhou, Wei Li, Peter J Liu, et al. 2020. Exploring the limits of transfer learning with a unified text-to-text transformer. *J. Mach. Learn. Res.*, 21(140):1–67.

Thomas Scialom, Paul-Alexis Dray, Sylvain Lamprier, Benjamin Piwowarski, Jacopo Staiano, Alex Wang, and Patrick Gallinari. 2021. QuestEval: Summarization asks for fact-based evaluation. In *Proceedings of the 2021 Conference on Empirical Methods in Natural Language Processing*, pages 6594–6604, Online and Punta Cana, Dominican Republic. Association for Computational Linguistics.

Kurt Shuster, Spencer Poff, Moya Chen, Douwe Kiela, and Jason Weston. 2021. Retrieval augmentation reduces hallucination in conversation. In *Findings of the Association for Computational Linguistics: EMNLP 2021*, pages 3784–3803, Punta Cana, Dominican Republic. Association for Computational Linguistics.

Swabha Swayamdipta, Sam Thomson, Kenton Lee, Luke Zettlemoyer, Chris Dyer, and Noah A. Smith. 2018. Syntactic scaffolds for semantic structures. In *Proceedings of the 2018 Conference on Empirical Methods in Natural Language Processing*, pages 3772–3782, Brussels, Belgium. Association for Computational Linguistics.

Shahbaz Syed, Ahmad Hakimi, Khalid Al-Khatib, and Martin Potthast. 2023. Citance-contextualized summarization of scientific papers. In *Findings of the Association for Computational Linguistics: EMNLP 2023*, pages 8551–8568, Singapore. Association for Computational Linguistics.

Pancheng Wang, Shasha Li, Haifang Zhou, Jintao Tang, and Ting Wang. 2019a. Toc-rwg: Explore the combination of topic model and citation information for automatic related work generation. *IEEE Access*, 8:13043–13055.

Yufei Wang, Mark Johnson, Stephen Wan, Yifang Sun, and Wei Wang. 2019b. How to best use syntax in semantic role labelling. In *Proceedings of the 57th Annual Meeting of the Association for Computational Linguistics*, pages 5338–5343, Florence, Italy. Association for Computational Linguistics.

Xinyu Xing, Xiaosheng Fan, and Xiaojun Wan. 2020. Automatic generation of citation texts in scholarly papers: A pilot study. In *Proceedings of the 58th Annual Meeting of the Association for Computational Linguistics*, pages 6181–6190, Online. Association for Computational Linguistics.

Michihiro Yasunaga, Jungo Kasai, Rui Zhang, Alexander R Fabbri, Irene Li, Dan Friedman, and Dragomir R Radev. 2019. Scisummnet: A large annotated corpus and content-impact models for scientific paper summarization with citation networks. In *Proceedings of the AAAI conference on artificial intelligence*, volume 33, pages 7386–7393.

Tianyi Zhang*, Varsha Kishore*, Felix Wu*, Kilian Q. Weinberger, and Yoav Artzi. 2020. Bertscore: Evaluating text generation with bert. In *International Conference on Learning Representations*.

Hyper-parameter	Search Range	Used
Learning rate	1e-5 ~ 5e-4	5e-5
RAG-FiD batch size	1 ~ 3	2
LED batch size	-	1
Epochs	2 ~ 10	5
RAG-FiD max sequence length	-	350
LED max sequence length	-	2048
Top k ROUGE-retrieval	1 ~ 20	10

Table 8: Hyper-parameter settings for CTS-based citation text generation.

A More Implementation Details

A.1 Opting Out of FAISS

The original RAG implementation was designed for Wikipedia-based dialogue response generation, where every Wikipedia article is a candidate for retrieval. Therefore, FAISS (Johnson et al., 2019) was used to speed up the search process. However, our search space is limited to cited paper sentences, and we need to retrieve CTS separately for each citation and its corresponding cited paper. Unfortunately, FAISS does not support partitioned search, so we replace FAISS with our simpler CTS retrieval strategies, as described in Section 4.2.1.

A.2 Freezing Query Encoder Weights

The RAG model retrieves candidate documents on the fly while jointly fine-tuning the pretrained DPR query encoder and the generator. In our preliminary experiments on retrieving CTS at the paragraph level, we did not find any significant improvement from fine-tuning the query encoder over simply freezing its weights. Further, due to the much larger candidate search space of the sentence-level CTS setting, the on-the-fly retrieval needed to update the query encoder becomes intractable. Therefore, in our citation text generation experiments, we retrieve and cache CTS sentences for all target citation/cited paper pairs in advance and do not fine-tune the query encoder.

A.3 Citation Text Generation Hyper-parameter Settings

Table 8 shows the tuned hyper-parameter settings for our CTS-based citation text generation experiments.

B More Related Work

B.1 Retrieval and Generation

Our proposed framework of retrieving useful information (CTS) to guide generation is partly inspired by work in knowledge-augmented, open-domain dialogue generation, where the combination of Dense Passage Retrieval (DPR; Karpukhin et al., 2020), Retrieval-Augmented Generation (RAG; Lewis et al., 2020b) and Fusion-in-Decoder (FiD; Izacard and Grave, 2021) has been shown to yield strong performance (Shuster et al., 2021).

DPR (Karpukhin et al., 2020) separately applies two BERT-like models (Devlin et al., 2019) as query and document encoders. The DPR model is trained with contrastive loss and uses maximum inner product search (MIPS) to retrieve the documents with the highest cosine similarity between the $[CLS]$ token representations of the query and the knowledge base documents.

Once informative documents have been retrieved, the RAG (Lewis et al., 2020b) paradigm can be applied using any sequence-to-sequence model. The conditional generation input is paired and encoded with each retrieved document in parallel, and the generation output is jointly decoded using all input/retrieved document pairs. RAG-sequence decodes the entire output sequence based on a fixed distribution over the retrieved documents, while RAG-token decodes each token using a different distribution over the retrieved documents. Finally, Shuster et al. (2021) proposed FiD (Izacard and Grave, 2021) as the decoder in the RAG framework by leverageing the attention mechanism to jointly decode from the retrieved document encodings.

	RAG-FiD			*LED*		
Setting	**R-L**	**QEval**	**ANLI**	**R-L**	**QEval**	**ANLI**
Abstract	0.556	**0.314**	0.745	0.591	**0.345**	0.744
Oracle	**0.726**	0.288	0.940	**0.682**	0.300	0.950
Keyword	0.630	0.297	0.941	0.604	0.304	0.946
Context	0.641	0.310	**0.959**	0.626	0.315	**0.954**

Table 9: Similarity and faithfulness of the generated citation texts with respect to their input setting, measured by ROUGE-recall, QuestEval, and ANLI.

C QuestEval and CTS-based Citation Text Generation

QuestEval (Scialom et al., 2021) is a question-answering-based faithfulness metric composed of a precision score, where questions are generated from the summary (citation text) and answered using the document (generation input), and a recall score, where questions are generated from the input and answered using the citation text. Table 9 shows the full faithfulness evaluation results for our citation text generation task, including QuestEval.

We find that QuestEval encounters some difficulty evaluating CTS-based citation texts because they are very short (Figure 5 shows that CTS-based citation texts have a much higher compression ratio than abstract-only citation texts); as a result, the QuestEval recall score is extremely low because many questions can be generated from the detailed information in the CTS, but the citation text is too short to contain all of the corresponding answers.

Table 11 shows an example of an *Oracle* CTS citation text that receives a low QuestEval score: Wang et al. (2019b) citing Swayamdipta et al. (2018). We can see that the retrieved CTS sentences include multiple entities and other detailed information that trigger QuestEval to generate many questions that the generated citation text cannot answer. However, a human reader can tell that the *Oracle* citation text is indeed factual; its claim about parse tree validity is supported by Swayamdipta et al. (2018)'s Introduction section: *"Since the scaffold task is not an end in itself, we relax the syntactic parsing problem to a collection of independent span-level predictions, with no constraint that they form a valid parse tree."*

We can also see that the *Abstract*-only citation text is longer and contains more entities than the *Oracle* citation text, while the *Abstract* input is much shorter and contains fewer entities than the *Oracle* input, so it does not suffer from the same low QuestEval recall score. We find many similar examples in our test set of longer *Abstract* citations being scored higher than shorter *Oracle* citations by QuestEval.

Citation context		
More recently, work on this topic has focused on end-to-end generation models.		
Citation texts		
Abstract	Konstas and Lapata (2012) proposed a joint model that jointly optimizes content selection and surface realization.	
Oracle	Konstas and Lapata (2012) present an end-to-end system that performs content selection and surface realization jointly.	
Keyword	Konstas and Lapata (2012) present an end-to-end generation model that performs content selection and surface realization jointly.	
Context	Konstas and Lapata (2012) proposed an unsupervised Concept-to-Text model that jointly optimizes content selection and surface realization. They represent their grammar compactly as a weighted hypergraph and perform decoding using a dynamic programming algorithm.	
Gold	Konstas and Lapata (2012) described an end-to-end generation model which jointly models content selection and surface realization.	
Cited text spans		
Section	*Sentence*	*Strategy*
Title	Unsupervised Concept-to-text Generation with Hypergraphs	c
Abstract	Concept-to-text generation refers to the task of automatically producing textual output from non-linguistic input.	ac
Abstract	We present a joint model that captures content selection ("what to say") and surface realization ("how to say") in an unsupervised domain-independent fashion.	aokc
Abstract	Rather than breaking up the generation process into a sequence of local decisions, we define a probabilistic context-free grammar that globally describes the inherent structure of the input (a corpus of database records and text describing some of them).	ac
Abstract	We represent our grammar compactly as a weighted hypergraph and recast generation as the task of finding the best derivation tree for a given input.	ac
Abstract	Experimental evaluation on several domains achieves competitive results with state-of-the-art systems that use domain specific constraints, explicit feature engineering or labeled data.	a
Introduction	A typical concept-to-text generation system implements a pipeline architecture consisting of three core stages, namely text planning (determining the content and structure of the target text), sentence planning (determining the structure and lexical content of individual sentences), and surface realization (rendering the specification chosen by the sentence planner into a surface string).	c
Introduction	Besides concentrating on isolated components, a few approaches have emerged that tackle concept-to-text generation end-to-end.	k
Introduction	Due to the complexity of the task, most models simplify the generation process, e.g., by creating output that consists of a few sentences, thus obviating the need for document planning, or by treating sentence planning and surface realization as one component.	c
Introduction	In this paper we describe an end-to-end generation model that performs content selection and surface realization jointly.	okc
Introduction	In order to ensure that our generation output is fluent, we intersect our grammar with a language model and perform decoding using a dynamic programming algorithm (Huang and Chiang, 2007).	c
Related Work	Our work is situated within the broader class of data-driven approaches to content selection and surface realization.	ok
Related Work	Given a corpus of database records and texts describing some of them, they learn a content selection model that simultaneously optimizes local label assignments and their pairwise relations.	c
Related Work	A few approaches have emerged more recently that combine content selection and surface realization.	o
Related Work	In contrast, Angeli et al. (2010) propose a unified content selection and surface realization model which also operates over the alignment output produced by Liang et al. (2009).	ok
Related Work	Similar to Angeli et al. (2010), we also present an end-to-end system that performs content selection and surface realization.	ok
Problem Formulation	Our goal then is to reduce the tasks of content selection and surface realization into a common probabilistic parsing problem.	ok
Results	We first assessed the performance of our generator (k-BEST) on joint content selection and surface realization and obtained a BLEU score of 24.88.	ok
Results	We observe a substantial increase in performance compared to the joint content selection and surface realization setting.	ok
Conclusions	We have presented an end-to-end generation system that performs both content selection and surface realization.	ok

Table 10: Citation text generation example: Gong et al. (2019) citing Konstas and Lapata (2012). The citation context is shown at the top, followed by the generated citation texts using the abstract and the three CTS strategies as inputs; the gold citation text is also shown. For each CTS sentence, "strategy" refers to the input setting(s) that included it: **a**bstract, **o**racle CTS, **k**eyword CTS, and **c**ontext CTS.

Citation context	
This information can be incorporated into an SRL system in several different ways.	
Citation text	
Abstract	Swayamdipta et al. (2018) introduced the Syntactic scaffold, an approach to incorporating syntactic information into semantic tasks. The scaffold is designed to avoid the expensive syntactic processing at runtime, only making use of a treebank during training, through a multitask objective, and achieves competitive performance on PropBank semantics, frame semantics, and coreference resolution.
Oracle	Swayamdipta et al. (2018) use syntactic information to predict spans, but it is not a guarantee that a span is a valid parse tree.
Cited text spans	
Abstract	We introduce the syntactic scaffold, an approach to incorporating syntactic information into semantic tasks. Syntactic scaffolds avoid expensive syntactic processing at runtime, only making use of a treebank during training, through a multitask objective. We improve over strong baselines on PropBank semantics, frame semantics, and coreference resolution, achieving competitive performance on all three tasks.
Oracle	Span Features: • width of the span in tokens (Das et al., 2014) • distance (in tokens) of the span from the target • position of the span with respect to the target (before, after, overlap) Each of these features is encoded as a one-hot embedding and then linearly transformed to yield a feature vector, a i: j . *Introduction: Since the scaffold task is not an end in itself, we relax the syntactic parsing problem to a collection of independent span-level predictions, with no constraint that they form a valid parse tree.* Latent variables.: The motivation behind joint learning of syntactic and semantic representations is that any one task is helpful in predicting the other (Lluís and Màrquez, 2008; Lluís et al., 2013; Henderson et al., 2013; Swayamdipta et al., 2016) . Semi-Markov CRF: In order to model the non-overlapping arguments of a given target, we use a semi-Markov conditional random field (semi-CRF; Sarawagi et al., 2004) . Coreference Resolution: Labels s 1 to s m indicate a coreference link between s and one of the m spans that precede it, and null indicates that s does not link to anything, either because it is not a mention or it is in a singleton cluster. Related Work: Using syntax as T 2 in a pipeline is perhaps the most common approach for semantic structure prediction (Toutanova et al., 2008; Yang and Mitchell, 2017; Wiseman et al., 2016) . Coreference Resolution: Since there is a complete overlap of input sentences between D sc and D pr as the coreference annotations are also from OntoNotes (Pradhan et al., 2012), we reuse the v for the scaffold task. Results: Tan et al. (2018) employ a similar approach but use feed-forward networks with selfattention. Results: Prior competitive coreference resolution systems (Wiseman et al., 2016; Clark and Manning, 2016b,a) all incorporate synctactic information in a pipeline, using features and rules for mention proposals from predicted syntax. Results: We follow the official evaluation from the SemEval shared task for frame-semantic parsing (Baker et al., 2007) .

Table 11: Citation text generation example, Wang et al. (2019b) citing Swayamdipta et al. (2018), showing the difference in compression ratio between the *Abstract* and *Oracle CTS* settings that results in unexpected QuestEval recall scores. The *Oracle* generation is supported by the *italicized* CTS sentence but still receives a low QuestEval score.

CiteAssist: A System for Automated Preprint Citation and BibTeX Generation

Lars Benedikt Kaesberg
Georg-August University / Göttingen
l.kaesberg@stud.uni-goettingen.de

Terry Ruas
Georg-August University / Göttingen
ruas@uni-goettingen.de

Jan Philip Wahle
Georg-August University / Göttingen
wahle@uni-goettingen.de

Bela Gipp
Georg-August University / Göttingen
gipp@uni-goettingen.de

Abstract

We present *CiteAssist*, a system to automate the generation of BibTeX entries for preprints, streamlining the process of bibliographic annotation. Our system extracts metadata, such as author names, titles, publication dates, and keywords, to create standardized annotations within the document. CiteAssist automatically attaches the BibTeX citation to the end of a PDF and links it on the first page of the document so other researchers gain immediate access to the correct citation of the article (see Figure 1). This method promotes platform flexibility by ensuring that annotations remain accessible regardless of the repository used to publish or access the preprint. The annotations remain available even if the preprint is viewed externally to CiteAssist. Additionally, the system adds relevant related papers based on extracted keywords to the preprint, providing researchers with additional publications besides those in related work for further reading. Researchers can enhance their preprints organization and reference management workflows through a free and publicly available web interface[1].

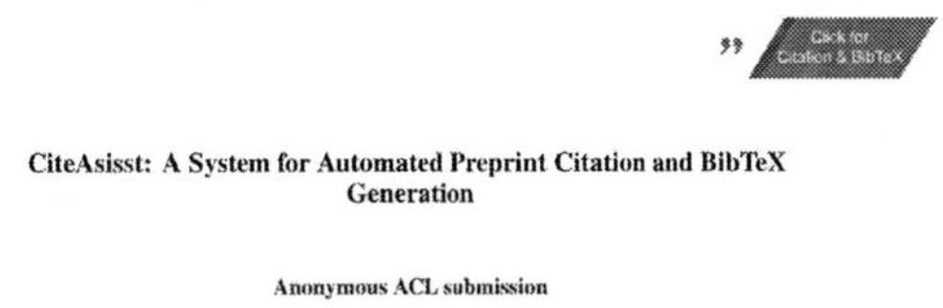

(a) The first preprint page with a generated annotation button.

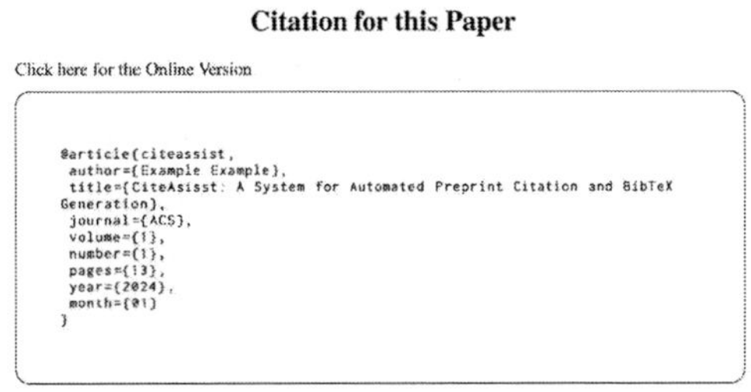

Citation for this Paper

Click here for the Online Version

```
@article{citeassist,
 author={Example Example},
 title={CiteAsisst: A System for Automated Preprint Citation and BibTeX
Generation},
 journal={ACS},
 volume={1},
 number={1},
 pages={13},
 year={2024},
 month={01}
}
```

(b) A generated citation box on the last page of the preprint.

Figure 1: Document enhanced with CiteAssist. A detailed version available in Appendix C).

1 Introduction

A common challenge in academic research is tracing citational information for preprints. Many researchers experience a low citational impact because their citational information is not accessible easily together with the preprint. This phenomenon is often evident on platforms like ResearchGate, where numerous articles are downloaded hundreds of times but receive only a few citations (Bollmann and Elliott, 2020). This discrepancy between reads and citations highlights a difference in how information is consumed and credited (a pattern also observed in contexts such as social media impressions versus likes) and specifically in citation analysis (Meho, 2006; Wahle et al., 2023, 2024).

An imbalance between reading and citing papers can have many reasons: researchers may judge a focal work as irrelevant to them, not exciting, not sound, or simply forgetting. Yet, a key reason is the accessibility of citational information (Bollmann and Elliott, 2020). If citation details are consistent and easily accessible, citations are generally higher (Ale Ebrahim et al., 2013; Bollmann and Elliott, 2020). Long review processes and publication timelines can slow scientific progress and hinder researchers from proposing state-of-the-art techniques. Thus, preprints are often used in modern scientific research. Public available preprints promote the rapid exchange of ideas and results before peer-reviewed publications are available, accelerating the spread of knowledge and driving scientific progress (Puebla et al., 2022). With the fast growth in the number of preprints, researchers are faced with an ever-growing sea of scientific information (Abdill and Blekhman, 2019a). The sheer volume of preprints make efficient retrieval challenging.

[1] https://preprint.larskaesberg.de

Proceedings of the Fourth Workshop on Scholarly Document Processing (SDP 2024), pages 105–119
August 16, 2024 ©2024 Association for Computational Linguistics

So far, there is no easy way to annotate preprints with citational information. While some repositories allow for archiving preprints (e.g., Zenodo, figshare, arXiv), the citation details of a paper are often only available through external infrastructure (e.g., publishers, scholarly search engines). To the best of our knowledge, no publicly available system provides the citation details of a paper within the PDF itself in simple format. Furthermore, we lack a common way to add recommended literature on related projects within preprints for further reading about a topic over the scope of related work sections. Those could be related ideas from other areas, books, or talks that complement a paper but are not directly discussed in related work.

We present CiteAssist, a system designed to simplify the creation and distribution of citation annotations by automatically generating and appending annotations to the preprint. This is achieved either by generating a new PDF with the annotation or by generating a LaTeX file that can be integrated directly into the source document. CiteAssist provides researchers with a convenient way to enhance their preprint by directly attaching citation information to it, improving the reference management workflow. These annotations capture metadata such as author names, publication details, and abstracts, enabling researchers to create bibliographic records for their preprints. The system also allows users to add custom metadata (e.g., keywords) to the BibTeX annotation. By automating this process, researchers can save time that would otherwise be spent on manual annotation. Our system is platform-independent as it incorporates all citation details within the paper. The annotation is attached to the preprint; thus, it can be published at any preprint repository. Unlike platform-specific solutions, our system accommodates various sources, making it accessible and useful to researchers in various fields. Figure 1 (a) shows the first page containing the button to the BibTex entry and (b) the generated annotation itself. In addition, CiteAssist suggests related papers at the end of an article to complement a traditional "related work" section. Related work sections focus on considering the proposed work and crediting previous ideas. However, they are bound to the researcher's awareness of these works, which may include *citation amnesia*, i.e., not citing good and relevant work (Singh et al., 2023; Wahle et al., 2024). CiteAssist mitigates this issue by suggesting additional literature on potentially forgotten or overlooked works. Researchers can manually add literature they wish to suggest to readers as additional resources.

2 Related Work

2.1 Preprint Platforms

Multiple platforms allow researchers to publish their preprints to repositories, e.g., arXiv, bioRxiv, ResearchGate, etc (Abdill and Blekhman, 2019b; Puebla et al., 2022). While these platforms support scholarly communication, they rely on external infrastructure that may not be accessible or familiar to all researchers. Some may prefer to upload their work to personal websites or may not know how to use LaTeX. Our system bridges these gaps, making preprint submission and formatting easier by providing a simplified interface that allows researchers to enter citation details directly into the paper.

2.2 Annotation Generation Tools

Annotation generation tools automatically extract metadata from scholarly articles and generate annotations. In this section, we discuss three relevant annotation generation tools relevant to CiteAssist, namely CERMINE (Tkaczyk et al., 2015), Neural ParsCit (Prasad et al., 2018), and Grobid (Lopez, 2008–2024).

CERMINE is a tool for extracting metadata from scholarly articles. It employs machine learning techniques like SVM, CRF, and clustering to parse PDF documents and extract structured information, including authors, titles, abstracts, and references (Tkaczyk et al., 2015). CERMINE can extract metadata from diverse scholarly articles, even with complex layouts and formatting. It generates structured XML output, creating annotations in various formats, such as BibTeX or CSL (Tkaczyk et al., 2015). Unlike CERMINE, which primarily extracts metadata for structured XML output, our system generates BibTeX annotations for scientific citation and proactively suggests related papers, increasing the visibility of preprints in the scientific literature. CiteAssist integrates related literature, which enhances the annotation process and the researcher's ability to explore related works. Additionally, while CERMINE outputs structured XML, our system directly attaches the generated BibTeX annotation to the paper, providing a more streamlined workflow for researchers.

Neural ParsCit focuses on extracting citation information from scientific articles. While its primary purpose is to parse and analyze citations, Neural ParsCit can also generate annotations using the extracted information. It identifies and extracts key metadata elements, including authors, titles, and publication venues. The tool focuses on citations, ensuring accurate extraction of citation-related metadata (e.g., identifying a citation string such as "Doe, J., Smith, A., & Johnson, K. (2020). Title of the article. 10(2), 123-134"). However, Neural ParsCit does not capture information like the publication date or journal (Tkaczyk et al., 2015). Therefore, additional processing or integration with other tools may be required to generate annotations for preprints (Prasad et al., 2018). In contrast, our tool provides a complete solution for BibTeX annotation generation and the integration of related papers. Unlike Neural ParsCit, CiteAssist leverages user input and keyword-based searches to generate BibTeX citations that are directly linked in the paper PDF and to include relevant literature.

Grobid provides an API for extracting metadata from papers, using both a small CRF model for quick results and a larger BidLSTM-CRF model for higher accuracy, though at greater computational cost (Lopez, 2008–2024). While it shares capabilities with CERMINE, like extracting titles, authors, and abstracts, Grobid does not capture journal information (Lopez, 2008–2024). Although Grobid's self-hostable API via Docker makes it an excellent component for CiteAssist to leverage for more advanced data extraction directly from the PDF text, it lacks the advanced PDF enhancement features that CiteAssist offers, such as direct annotation with BibTeX and the suggestion of related papers.

3 System Architecture

The system architecture of CiteAssist consists of a frontend, backend, and database. The frontend handles the user interaction and allows users to upload a PDF file, which is parsed by our method and in the backend with Grobid. We merge and display the results to the user for correction, if necessary. Furthermore, users can add related papers, either provided by the backend via keyword matching or with a provided DOI or arXiv id. The system generates a new PDF or LaTeX file with an attached BibTeX annotation and related papers. After user approval, these results are uploaded to the backend, where the PDF is stored locally and metadata forwarded to the database. We refer to Appendix A for a more detailed system architecture description.

4 Preprint Annotation Workflow

This section shows a practical example of how researchers can annotate preprints using CiteAssist. The workflow begins when a user uploads a preprint in PDF format to the CiteAssist homepage via a drag-and-drop interface or a file selection dialogue as seen in Figure 2. Users are then asked to review (Figure 3), edit potentially incorrect information, or add other relevant metadata (e.g., keywords). Users can select relevant suggested keywords and add new ones if desired. The system enhances the compatibility of these keywords through lemmatization. With refined keywords, the backend searches the database for related preprints and displays these on the frontend for user review and selection, as seen in Figure 5. CiteAssist compiles this information and generates a BibTeX annotation containing the edited metadata and selected related papers (Figure 11). The compiled annotation is attached at the end of the preprint. On the title page of the uploaded article, it adds a button that links to the annotation at the bottom, as shown in Figure 10. Users can download the final annotated PDF version or generate LaTeX files to include it directly in the source document. With user consent, the backend stores the annotated PDFs for future access. Users can view these files online, share them with colleagues, or download them again.

5 BibTeX Annotation Generation

We combine the `PDF-LIB` [2] library, Grobid, and our custom information extraction method to extract BibTeX annotation information. Our process can be divided into five steps:

1. **PDF Parsing:** The PDF file is parsed using the `PDF-LIB` library, which allows us to access the document's metadata (e.g., title, author, creation date) if available and saved in the PDF.

2. **Text Extraction:** Our custom function extracts the text content from the PDF file. This includes the text from the first page, which contains information such as the title, author, and more. The rest of the text is used for keyword extraction.

3. **Metadata Extraction:** We extract various metadata elements necessary for the BibTeX annotation. These elements include:

- **Article Type:** The publication category for the paper (e.g., proceedings, journal). Set to "article" as a default.

[2] `https://github.com/Hopding/pdf-lib`

- **Author:** Author name obtained from the PDF metadata or extracted from the text.
- **Title:** Title of the article from the first page's text. If unavailable, the PDF's title or the filename is used as a default.
- **Pages:** The total number of pages in the PDF document.
- **Date:** Publication date from the PDF metadata. If unavailable, the current date is used.

4. **Grobid:** Simultaneously, the frontend sends the PDF to the backend, which then forwards it to Grobid to extract relevant information, including the title, author, publication date, and keywords.

5. **Constructing the BibTeX Annotation:** We merge the information extracted from Grobid and our own. In cases where neither alternative provides the information, we resort to a fallback value that can be edited by the user. Next, we construct the BibTeX annotation following the required format from the extracted metadata. The annotation includes key-value pairs for elements such as author, title, journal, volume, pages, year, and DOI.

The combination of `PDF-LIBs` metadata extraction, Grobid, and our custom metadata extraction function allows us to generate BibTeX annotations for preprints shown in Figure 1b (a figure outlining the process can be found in Figure 9).

6 Integration of Related Papers

The integration of related papers is designed to augment the research experience by providing users with access to literature that, while not directly cited as related work, can indicate the reader to other possible related materials. We use keyword-based searches to retrieve a selection of papers that serve as complementary references, offering broader insights into the subject area without overlapping with the core related work already cited. This task involves the following functionalities:

- **Keyword Extraction:** The preprint's whole text is processed by our algorithm to extract the five most relevant keywords. This is done by removing stop words, applying lemmatization, and selecting based on frequency of occurrence. This functionality is currently only available for English texts. If the author has provided keywords, Grobid will also extract these.
- **User Input:** Users provide additional keywords or tags associated with the preprint being annotated. These keywords act as search criteria for finding related papers.
- **Search Query:** The system applies lemmatization to the provided keywords, converting them to their base forms for better matching. This improves the effectiveness of the query in retrieving related papers. The query returns the five most relevant papers, ranked by the number of matching keywords.
- **Selection and Integration:** Users can choose specific preprints from the provided suggestions to add to their annotation. They can also add new papers using either a DOI or arXiv ID. These selected papers are integrated into the annotation generation process.

Integrating related papers into the annotation enhances the paper by providing users access to related resources that contribute insights, broader the existing related work section and further context to their initial findings, and save researchers time and effort from authors and readers.

7 Final Considerations

In this work, we introduced CiteAssist, a system designed to streamline the creation and distribution of BibTeX annotations within preprints. CiteAssist standardizes the reference management process with the help of automatic generation and integration of annotations, either through a newly generated PDF or directly within a LaTeX source document. A button on the title page linking to the annotation improves the usability and accessibility of the citation information of the paper. Our system enhances the usability of preprints by embedding citation details and ensures that the annotations are readily accessible, regardless of the publication repository used. Additionally, CiteAssist offers suggestions for related papers, enriching the scope of resources available to researchers about a given publication. CiteAssist's development reflects the growing importance of digital tools in academic research. By allowing researchers to easily include their citational information into preprints, we see a direct impact on giving authors proper credit and to be cited correctly with the publication venue as opposed to the preprint server. Future enhancements could include recommending similar papers based on semantic similarity and providing a more comprehensive representation of the paper's content.

Limitations

Although CiteAssist has enhanced the preprint annotation process, it still has room for improvement. Implementing stopword removal for several languages during keyword extraction may improve the relevancy of the discovered keywords. Furthermore, integrating language models to extract keywords directly can take advantage of recent natural language processing advances (e.g., large context length (Ma et al., 2024)) to produce more accurate results. Incorporating large language models into CiteAssist can improve metadata extraction accuracy and cover a wider range of document layouts and formats, increasing the tool's overall efficiency. We plan to improve CiteAssist's UI and usability through user feedback sessions. By gathering insights directly from users, we will make iterative improvements to enhance the system's intuitiveness and functionality, ensuring it effectively meets researchers' needs.

References

Richard J Abdill and Ran Blekhman. 2019a. Meta-research: Tracking the popularity and outcomes of all biorxiv preprints. *eLife*, 8:e45133.

Richard J Abdill and Ran Blekhman. 2019b. Meta-research: Tracking the popularity and outcomes of all biorxiv preprints. *eLife*, 8:e45133.

Nader Ale Ebrahim, Hadi Salehi, Mohamed Embi, Farid Tanha, Hossein Gholizadeh, Seyed Mohammad Motahar, and Ali Ordi. 2013. Effective strategies for increasing citation frequency. *International Education Studies*, 6:93–99.

Marcel Bollmann and Desmond Elliott. 2020. On forgetting to cite older papers: An analysis of the ACL Anthology. In *Proceedings of the 58th Annual Meeting of the Association for Computational Linguistics*, pages 7819–7827, Online. Association for Computational Linguistics.

Patrice Lopez. 2008–2024. Grobid. `https://github.com/kermitt2/grobid`.

Xuezhe Ma, Xiaomeng Yang, Wenhan Xiong, Beidi Chen, Lili Yu, Hao Zhang, Jonathan May, Luke Zettlemoyer, Omer Levy, and Chunting Zhou. 2024. Megalodon: Efficient llm pretraining and inference with unlimited context length.

L. I. Meho. 2006. The rise and rise of citation analysis.

Jakob Nielsen. 1994. Enhancing the explanatory power of usability heuristics. In *Proceedings of the SIGCHI Conference on Human Factors in Computing Systems*, CHI '94, page 152–158, New York, NY, USA. Association for Computing Machinery.

Animesh Prasad, Manpreet Kaur, and Min-Yen Kan. 2018. Neural parscit: A deep learning based reference string parser. *International Journal on Digital Libraries*, 19:323–337.

Iratxe Puebla, Jessica Polka, and Oya Rieger. 2022. *Preprints: Their Evolving Role in Science Communication*. Against the Grain (Media), LLC.

Janvijay Singh, Mukund Rungta, Diyi Yang, and Saif Mohammad. 2023. Forgotten knowledge: Examining the citational amnesia in NLP. In *Proceedings of the 61st Annual Meeting of the Association for Computational Linguistics (Volume 1: Long Papers)*, pages 6192–6208, Toronto, Canada. Association for Computational Linguistics.

Dominika Tkaczyk, Pawel Szostek, Mateusz Fedoryszak, Piotr Jan Dendek, and Lukasz Bolikowski. 2015. Cermine: automatic extraction of structured metadata from scientific literature. *International Journal on Document Analysis and Recognition (IJDAR*, 18(4).

Jan Wahle, Terry Ruas, Mohamed Abdalla, Bela Gipp, and Saif Mohammad. 2023. We are Who We Cite: Bridges of Influence Between Natural Language Processing and Other Academic Fields. In *Proceedings of the 2023 Conference on Empirical Methods in Natural Language Processing*, pages 12896–12913. Association for Computational Linguistics.

Jan Philip Wahle, Terry Ruas, Mohamed Abdalla, Bela Gipp, and Saif M. Mohammad. 2024. Citation Amnesia: NLP and Other Academic Fields Are in a Citation Age Recession. volume abs/2402.12046.

A Detailed System Architecture

The system architecture of CiteAssist is designed to provide researchers with a responsive and user-friendly experience. It consists of a frontend, a backend, and a database, each component fulfilling specific functionalities to enable efficient and semi-automatic annotation generation.

A.1 Frontend and UI/UX Design

Our system's front end handles the user's interaction with the system. Researchers can upload their preprint in PDF format, and the system extracts metadata such as the preprint's title, author, year, and page numbers to generate the BibTeX annotation (see Figure 2). This process is done both in the frontend and in the back end with the help of Grobid, and then results are merged to achieve the most complete set of automatically extracted metadata. The data is displayed to the user, offering an overview of the preprint's details (see Figure 3). To guarantee accuracy, users can edit this extracted data as needed. Also, users can directly copy and paste a BibTeX they already have (for example from their venue) and the tool extracts the necessary metadata from that BibTeX. Once verified, the frontend sends the metadata, along with the user-specified keywords, to the backend.

Beyond metadata extraction, the frontend is responsible for generating the final PDF file. It receives related papers from the backend and integrates them with the BibTeX annotation into a new PDF document. The resulting PDF combines the preprint with the annotation and related literature. The system can also create a LaTeX file with the annotation that can be imported into the LaTeX source document. This makes it convenient to submit to source code-based repositories such as arXiv.

Design Principles: We dedicated our UI/UX design to user-centric principles. To support our design decisions, we looked at reputable UI/UX guidelines, such as those proposed by Nielsen (1994). Adopting these universally acknowledged design principles ensures our tool meets industry standards. We prioritized:

- **Simplicity:** We aimed for a clean and uncluttered interface, prioritizing simplicity to ensure ease of use. To achieve this, we employed a minimalist design approach, using a monochromatic color scheme and limiting the number of interactive elements visible at any one time. This approach reduces cognitive load and allows users to focus on task-relevant information.
- **Consistency:** We maintained consistent visual and interaction design throughout the tool to provide a cohesive user experience. We adopted a standard color palette and uniform typography across all pages. Navigation elements are consistently placed in the same locations across screens.
- **Intuitiveness:** We focused on creating an intuitive user interface, where users can easily understand the tool's functionalities without extensive instructions. Labels are descriptive and positioned adjacent to their respective controls, tooltips are provided for complex functions.
- **Responsive Design:** We adopted a responsive design approach, ensuring that the UI adapts seamlessly to different screen sizes and devices. We used a flexible grid layout to adjust the layout dynamically, providing an optimal viewing experience on tablets, phones, and desktops.

User Interface Components: The user interface components are designed to address user tasks through distinct components.

- **Upload Interface (Figure 2):** Users are presented with an interface to upload their preprint PDF files. The upload interface includes drag-and-drop functionality and instructions to guide users through the process.
- **Metadata Editing (Figure 3):** Users have the ability to edit the extracted metadata of the preprint, such as title, author, etc. A user-friendly form-based interface is employed, allowing users to make necessary modifications easily.
- **Keyword Input (Figure 3):** Users can input relevant keywords or tags associated with the preprint to search for related papers. The keyword input interface supports both manual entry and suggestions based on extracted keywords.
- **Related Papers Display (Figure 5):** The interface presents related papers retrieved based on the user's keywords. Users have the option to delete papers they consider irrelevant, or to add related papers with their Digital Object Identifier (DOI) or arXiv id.

User Experience Enhancements: We took steps to enhance user interaction with our system. This included:

- **Ease of Navigation:** The system provides seamless navigation between its different sections. To enhance ease of navigation, clear and intuitive navigation elements, such as a persistent top menu, have been implemented.
- **Feedback and Error Handling:** The tool provides error messages to guide users in case of incorrect inputs. Clear error messages, tooltips, and validation checks have been implemented to assist users in understanding and resolving issues effectively.
- **Visual Appeal:** The UI utilizes visually appealing design elements, such as appropriate color schemes, typography, and layout, to provide an engaging and aesthetically pleasing experience for users.

A.2 Backend

The backend component of our system searches for related preprints based on provided keywords. The primary role of the backend is to accept new preprint metadata from the frontend and store them in the database for future reference. It acts as a bridge, receiving the preprint information and passing it on to the database without directly processing the preprint content.

In addition, the backend supports querying the database of previously uploaded preprints for related works based on keywords provided by the user. When the frontend sends a request for related preprints, the backend performs the necessary database searches to identify relevant preprints.

The backend component of our tool also stores the actual PDF files of the preprints. This storage capability is crucial, as it allows for an easy retrieval of the original documents. When a user requests to view or download a specific preprint, the backend serves the corresponding PDF file back to the frontend.

A.3 Database

The database component of our system is responsible for storing and managing information about preprints. It serves as a central repository for preprint metadata, enabling efficient data storage and retrieval. The database stores information about each preprint, including its title, author, DOI, URL to the publication, year of publication, and keywords associated with it.

To ensure secure and reliable data storage, our system uses PostgreSQL as the database management system. PostgreSQL offers robust features such as data integrity, efficient indexing, and transaction support, making it well-suited for managing preprint information.

B CiteAssist Screenshots

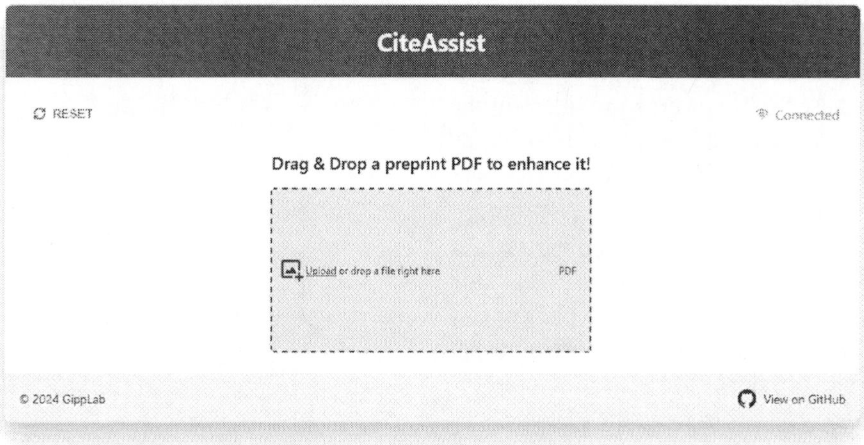

Figure 2: CiteAssist Homepage.

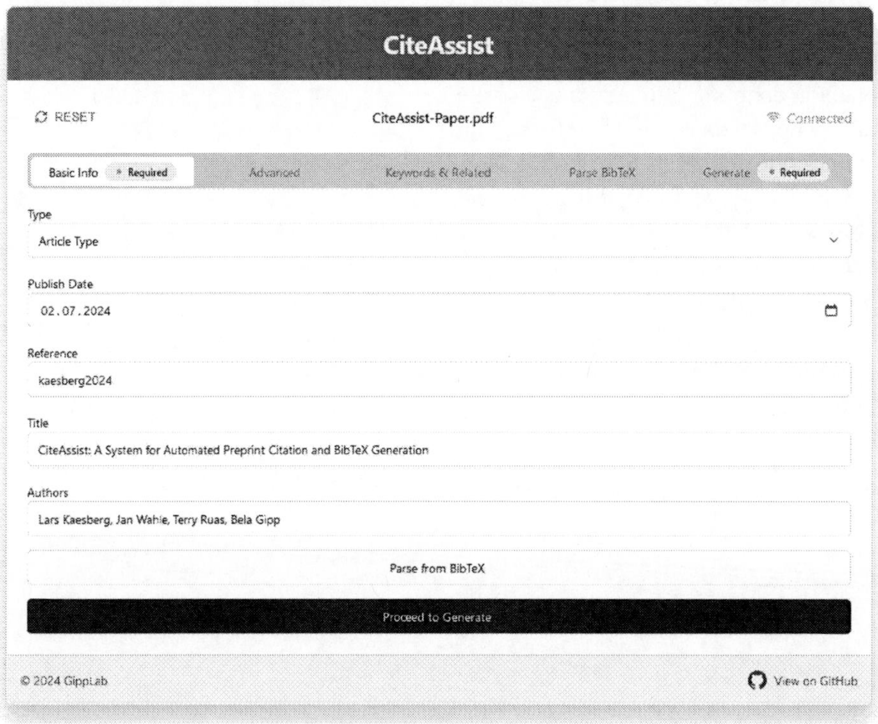

Figure 3: CiteAssist Edit Metadata Page.

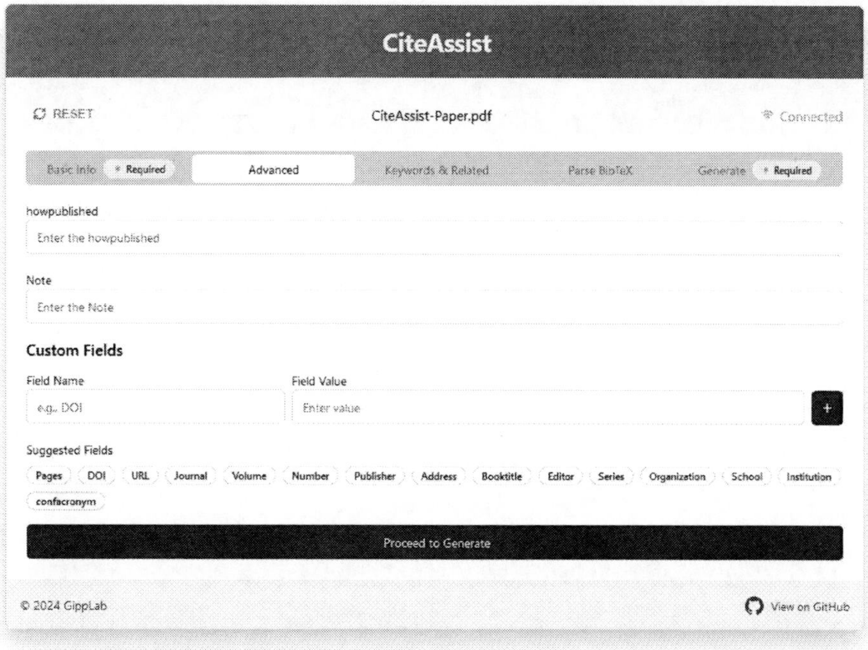

Figure 4: CiteAssist Advanced Edit Metadata Page.

Figure 5: CiteAssist Related Paper Page.

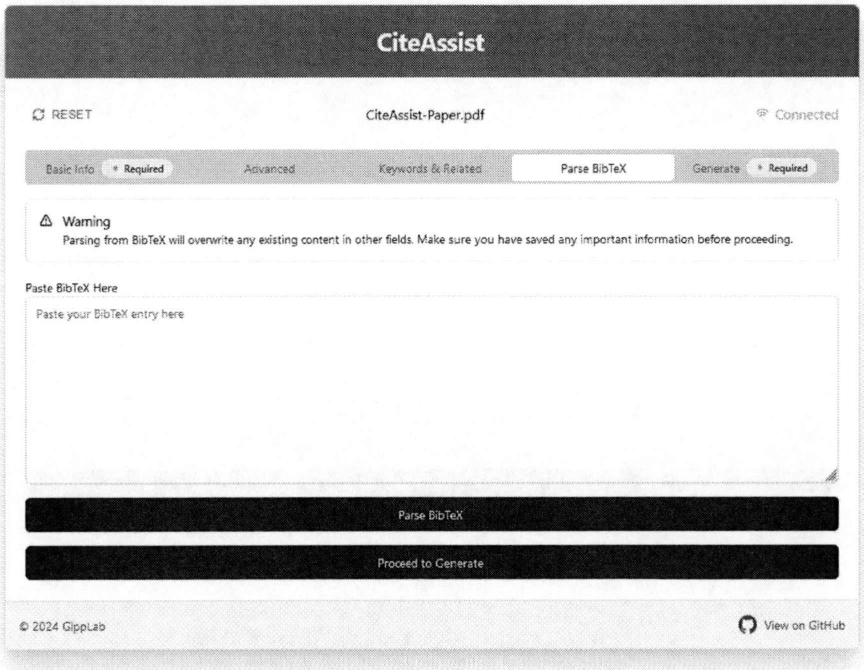

Figure 6: CiteAssist Parse BibTeX Page.

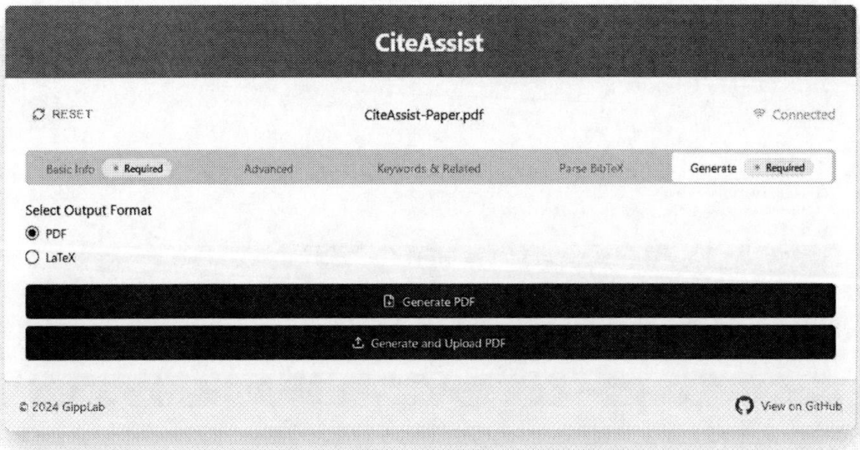

Figure 7: CiteAssist Generate Page.

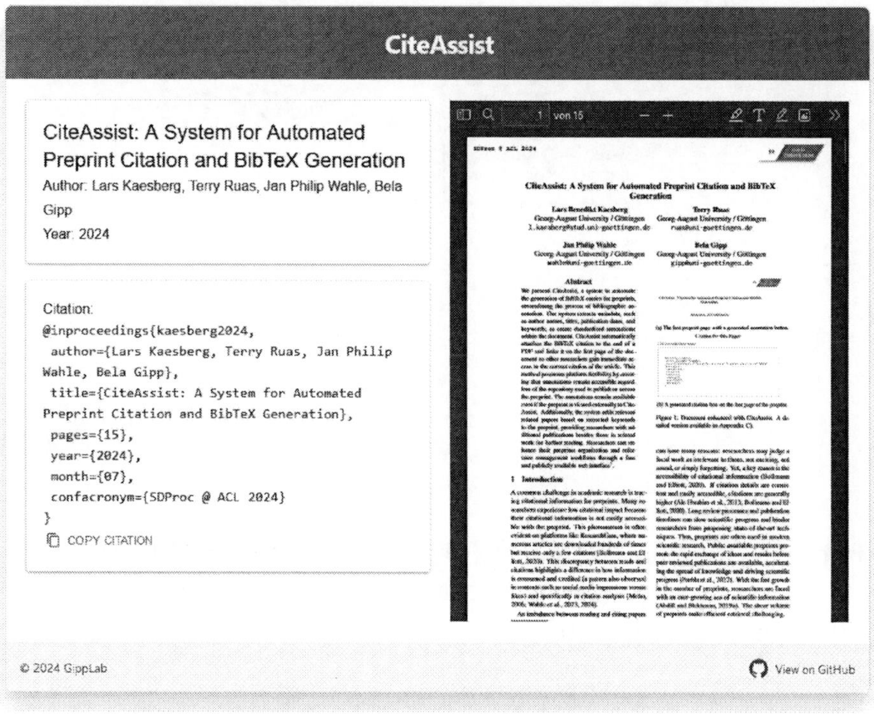

Figure 8: CiteAssist Preprint Webview.

C CiteAssist Enhanced Document

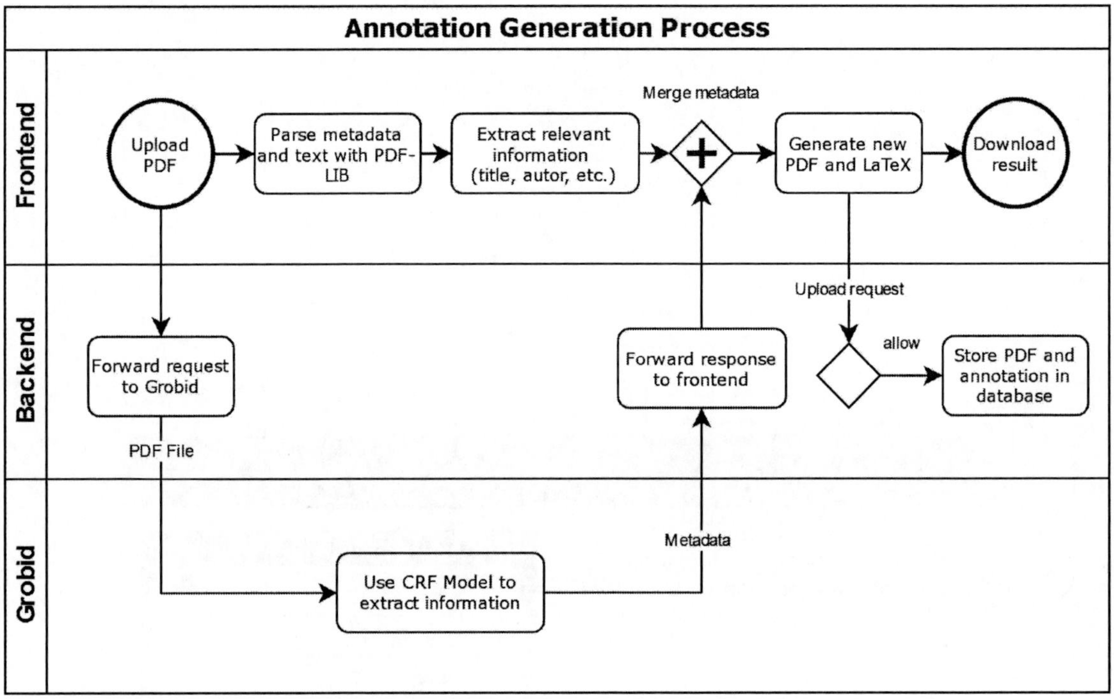

Figure 9: Generation process for a CiteAssist annotation.

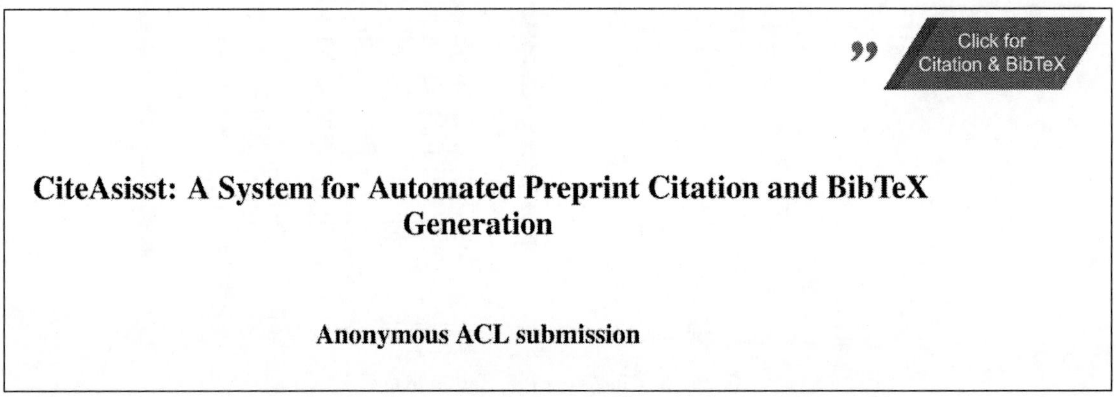

CiteAsisst: A System for Automated Preprint Citation and BibTeX Generation

Anonymous ACL submission

Figure 10: The first preprint page with a generated annotation button.

Citation for this Paper

Click here for the Online Version

```
@article{citeassist,
 author={Example Example},
 title={CiteAsisst: A System for Automated Preprint Citation and BibTeX
Generation},
 journal={ACS},
 volume={1},
 number={1},
 pages={13},
 year={2024},
 month={01}
}
```

Figure 11: A generated citation box on the last page of the preprint.

AI Usage Card for *Enhanced Preprint Generator*

CORRESPONDENCE(S)
Lars Benedikt Kaesberg

CONTACT(S)
l.kaesberg@stud.uni-goettingen.de

AFFILIATION(S)
Georg-August University Göttingen

PROJECT NAME
CiteAssist

KEY APPLICATION(S)
automate preprint generation

MODEL(S)
chat-gpt

DATE(S) USED
2023-06-07

VERSION(S)
3.5

IDEATION

GENERATING IDEAS, OUTLINES, AND WORKFLOWS
Not used

IMPROVING EXISTING IDEAS
Not used

FINDING GAPS OR COMPARE ASPECTS OF IDEAS
Not used

LITERATURE REVIEW
chat-gpt

FINDING LITERATURE
search for similar work/tools

FINDING EXAMPLES FROM KNOWN LITERATURE
Not used

ADDING ADDITIONAL LITERATURE FOR EXISTING STATEMENTS AND FACTS
Not used

COMPARING LITERATURE
Not used

METHODOLOGY

PROPOSING NEW SOLUTIONS TO PROBLEMS
Not used

FINDING ITERATIVE OPTIMIZATIONS
Not used

COMPARING RELATED SOLUTIONS
Not used

EXPERIMENTS

DESIGNING NEW EXPERIMENTS
Not used

EDITING EXISTING EXPERIMENTS
Not used

FINDING, COMPARING, AND AGGREGATING RESULTS
Not used

WRITING
chat-gpt

GENERATING NEW TEXT BASED ON INSTRUCTIONS
Not used

ASSISTING IN IMPROVING OWN CONTENT
rewrite own text to improve writing style

PARAPHRASING RELATED WORK
Not used

PUTTING OTHER WORKS IN PERSPECTIVE
Not used

PRESENTATION

GENERATING NEW ARTIFACTS
Not used

IMPROVING THE AESTHETICS OF ARTIFACTS
Not used

FINDING RELATIONS BETWEEN OWN OR RELATED ARTIFACTS
Not used

CODING	GENERATING NEW CODE BASED ON DESCRIPTIONS OR EXISTING CODE Not used	REFACTORING AND OPTIMIZING EXISTING CODE Not used
	COMPARING ASPECTS OF EXISTING CODE Not used	
DATA	SUGGESTING NEW SOURCES FOR DATA COLLECTION Not used	CLEANING, NORMALIZING, OR STANDARDIZING DATA Not used
	FINDING RELATIONS BETWEEN DATA AND COLLECTION METHODS Not used	
ETHICS	WHAT ARE THE IMPLICATIONS OF USING AI FOR THIS PROJECT? undefined	WHAT STEPS ARE WE TAKING TO MITIGATE ERRORS OF AI FOR THIS PROJECT? undefined
	WHAT STEPS ARE WE TAKING TO MINIMIZE THE CHANCE OF HARM OR INAPPROPRIATE USE OF AI FOR THIS PROJECT? undefined	THE CORRESPONDING AUTHORS VERIFY AND AGREE WITH THE MODIFICATIONS OR GENERATIONS OF THEIR USED AI-GENERATED CONTENT Yes

AI Usage Card v1.0 https://ai-cards.org PDF | BibTeX

An end-to-end entity recognition and disambiguation framework for identifying Author Affiliation from literature publications

Lianghong Lin, Wenxiu Xie, Zili Chen, Tianyong Hao
Lianghong Lin, School of Artificial Intelligence, South China Normal University, Guangzhou, China, linlianghong@m.scnu.edu.cn
Wenxiu Xie, Department of Computer Science, City University of Hong Kong, Hong Kong, China, wenxixie-c@my.cityu.edu.hk
Zili Chen, School of Professional Education and Executive Development, CPCE, The Hong Kong Polytechnic University, Hong Kong, China, spczili@speed-polyu.edu.hk
Tianyong Hao, School of Computer Science, South China Normal University, Guangzhou, China, haoty@m.scnu.edu.cn

Abstract

Author affiliation information plays a key role in bibliometric analyses and is essential for evaluating studies. However, as author affiliation information has not been standardized, which leads to difficulties such as synonym ambiguity and incomplete data during automated processing. To address the challenge, this paper proposes an end-to-end entity recognition and disambiguation framework for identifying author affiliation from literature publications. For entity disambiguation, an algorithm combining word embedding and spatial embedding is presented considering that author affiliation texts often contain rich geographic information. The disambiguation algorithm utilizes the semantic information and geographic information, which effectively enhances entity recognition and disambiguation effect. In addition, the proposed framework facilitates the effective utilization of the extensive literature in the PubMed database for comprehensive bibliometric analysis. The experimental results verify the robustness and effectiveness of the algorithm.

1 Introduction

Bibliometrics is becoming increasingly important in academia, revealing disciplinary trends and assessing the impact of research by analyzing literature data, and has become an important tool for promoting academic communication and research decision-making (Ninkov et al., 2022). In particular, assessing the contribution of research elements such as journals, countries/regions, institutions, and authors to a given field plays a key role in bibliometric analyses, helping to reveal the contribution and impact of scholarly research and guiding academic decision-making and resource allocation (Lim and Kumar, 2023). Such assessments provide an important basis for trends in disciplinary development, opportunities for collaboration and science policy development, and promote progress and innovation in academic research (Donthu et al., 2021).

The PubMed database plays a crucial role in providing rich, reliable, timely and standardized literature data for bibliometric analysis in the field of medicine in order to support quantitative analysis of quantitative features and patterns of medical research (Fiorini et al., 2018). It not only helps to improve the quality and efficiency of bibliometric analysis, but also promotes knowledge innovation and dissemination in the medical field (Lu, 2011; Kokol et al., 2021; Thompson et al., 2015). For datasets exported from PubMed databases, statistics on country/region or institution data often rely on author affiliation information existing in every publication. Author affiliation information in PubMed typically includes the name of the university, research institution, hospital, or company where the authors are affiliated, as well as possible department or laboratory names to indicate the institutional affiliation or organizational information of the authors. Additionally, author affiliation data includes information about the address of the institution, such as city, state or province, and country. There are problems of incomplete data and synonym ambiguity in the author affiliation

Proceedings of the Fourth Workshop on Scholarly Document Processing (SDP 2024), pages 120–129
August 16, 2024 ©2024 Association for Computational Linguistics

information. Specifically, the processing of textual affiliation data often encounter incomplete information (e.g., missing country)(Shao et al., 2020), inconsistent representation forms (e.g., University of Cambridge and Cambridge University)(Rimmert et al., 2017), and abbreviations (e.g., UCLA)(Huang et al., 2014), which may affect the results of subsequent analysis that assessed the contribution of the research elements to the field of study.

Author affiliation information disambiguation is essential because it concerns the use of entities such as institution, country, etc. in bibliometric analysis. The accuracy of bibliometric indicators provided by databases themselves is limited. Relying solely on these data for bibliometric analysis can lead to significant inaccuracies in the indicator values. As suggested by Donner et al. (2020), additional data cleaning is necessary to disambiguate affiliation data. While there are numerous studies on entity disambiguation, relatively few have explored author affiliation information, especially for PubMed databases. Moreover, existing research on author affiliation information is mainly confined to institutions mainly confined to institutional entities, ignoring the identification and disambiguation of Location entities (L'Hôte and Jeangirard, 2021). Furthermore, some disambiguation methods focus only on local features and ignore the semantic information embedded in the surrounding context, which may lead to inaccuracies and limitations in the results (Han and Zhao, 2009; D'Angelo et al., 2020).

Building upon this foundation, the paper presents an end-to-end framework designed for entity recognition and disambiguation within author affiliation text. Harnessing sophisticated entity recognition techniques, the framework meticulously extracts crucial details such as institutions, countries, and more from the textual data. To tackle entity ambiguity, an innovative disambiguation algorithm, amalgamating word embedding and spatial embedding, is introduced. This algorithm adeptly resolves ambiguities by capturing contextual semantic and geographic features. Specifically, word embedding endeavors to grasp the semantic relationships among entities, while spatial embedding enriches disambiguation prowess through geographical insights. By enhancing identification accuracy and robustness, this framework not only mitigates information redundancy and misidentification but also furnishes a more dependable groundwork for subsequent bibliometric analyses. Overall, the contributions of this work can be summarized as follows:

1) A novel framework for entity recognition and disambiguation is proposed to address inconsistencies and incompleteness in author affiliation texts.

2) A new disambiguation algorithm combining word embedding and spatial embedding is introduced by capturing contextual semantic and geographic features.

3) Experiment validation is conducted to demonstrate the superiority of the proposed algorithm over publicly available baseline models, showcasing its robustness and efficacy.

2 Related work

Entity disambiguation has been extensively studied in the past. Its methodological studies can be broadly categorized into three types: rule-based approaches, knowledge-based approaches, and combinations of these two approaches (Chandrasekaran and Mago, 2021). The rule-based approach relied mainly on manually crafted rules. These rules could be based on the name of the entity, contextual information, or other linguistic features, such as "IBM" commonly referring to the International Business Machines Corporation. However, these rules were often limited by their lack of generalization and scalability. With the emergence of large-scale corpora and structured knowledge bases, researchers began exploring how to fully leverage these rich resources to address entity disambiguation problems. Common knowledge bases include Wikipedia, DBpedia, and Yago (Sanyal et al., 2021). Knowledge-based approaches utilize the structured information and entity relationships within these knowledge bases, such as entity descriptions, hypernym relationships, and linking relationships, to enhance the accuracy and efficiency of entity disambiguation. Meanwhile, word embedding models such as Word2Vec, GloVe, and FastText were introduced and widely applied. These models map words to high-dimensional vector spaces and capture semantic relationships between words by learning distributed representations of words (Zwicklbauer et al., 2016). Pre-trained word embedding models can generate vector representations for entities and their contexts, encoding the semantic information of entities into positional relationships in continuous vector space. This approach enables the semantic information of entities to be more effectively utilized for entity disambiguation tasks, thereby improving the performance and effectiveness of entity disambiguation (Basile et al., 2024). In addition, methods such as tf-idf (Term Frequency-Inverse Document Frequency), LSI (Latent Semantic Indexing), and LDA (Latent Dirichlet Allocation) have also been introduced into entity disambiguation tasks to extract semantic information and contextual associations of entities in text (Bouarroudj et al., 2022).

The use of a single method no longer satisfies current research needs, prompting researchers to combine different methods to obtain richer semantic information and more accurate entity representations. Babelfy leverages large-scale multilingual knowledge graphs and word embedding models to achieve entity linking and disambiguation. It adopts a context-based approach by analyzing the contextual information surrounding entities in the text to determine their semantics. Specifically, Babelfy treats each word in the text as a potential entity mention and uses contextual information and semantic relationships in the knowledge graph to infer the most likely entity corresponding to each mention(Li et al., 2020). The WeLink model proposed by Bellatreche et al. achieves entity disambiguation by generating a list of entity candidates from knowledge graph DBpedia, and utilizing context similarity, entity coherence, relation exploitation, entity name distance, and syntactic features to compute scores and rank candidate entities (Nedelchev et al., 2020).

Some research focuses on social media datasets, such as tweets and news headlines, which often possess characteristics of brevity and noise. However, they also contain rich spatiotemporal metadata. Consequently, some researchers have begun exploring the utilization of spatiotemporal signals in the entity disambiguation process (Agarwal et al., 2018; Fetahu et al., 2021; Rafiei, 2016). Fang and Chang (2014) proposed a method for entity disambiguation of Weibo tweets by integrating spatiotemporal signals. Considering that the dataset used in this paper contains abundant spatial signals, we drew inspiration from their work and introduced spatial signals to enhance the results of semantic similarity calculation. In this process, we reference the method proposed by Srinivasan and Rafiei (2021) that utilizes containment relationships between locations. However, unlike them, they emphasize that location heavily depends on the locations mentioned in each document, while this paper directly considers all mentioned locations equally important.

3 The Proposed Framework

This paper proposes a new framework aimed at entity recognition and disambiguation of author affiliation data extracted from PubMed-exported datasets, which can provide a reliable basis for bibliometric analysis. As shown in Figure 1, the framework can be divided into two parts: text preprocessing and entity disambiguation. In general, text preprocessing can be summarized into two main steps. The first is to extract author affiliation information, and the second is to identify entities involved in the text, such as institution, country, and other bibliometric indicators. The purpose of text preprocessing is to prepare text data to ensure usability, providing efficient data processing for subsequent entity disambiguation tasks. Disambiguation is the most critical part of this framework, which addresses the issues of candidate generation and candidate ranking for ensuring that ambiguous entities are accurately disambiguated in order to determine the exact meaning and denotation.

3.1 Preprocessing

Although the dataset exported from PubMed contains a large amount of literature information, this paper mainly focuses on the processing of author affiliation data. Therefore, the author affiliation information is at first extracted using a rule-based approach. Then, standard tools are used to detect mention of named entity, where the named entity type is organization and location. The preprocessing process is important because it affects subsequent entity disambiguation tasks.

- Affiliation extraction

Author affiliation usually appears in the form of a specific identification, prefixed by "AD –", in datasets exported from PubMed databases. A rule-based approach is consequently used, specifically regular expressions to identify text paragraphs in the dataset that begin with "AD –" and to store these paragraphs. The "AD –" prefix is removed from the stored results to ensure the purity of the data. Such a process is intended to remove redundant information so that the data can be more efficiently prepared for subsequent analysis and research. Furthermore, an author may have multiple affiliations, with only the first one being taken as the author's affiliation address.

- Entity recognition

Named Entity Recognition (NER) is a natural language processing technique used to automatically identify and extract specific named entities from specified text, such as names of individuals, locations, and organizations (Naseer et al., 2021). Although the focus of this work is not on researching entity recognition methods, we are still committed to selecting NER tools suitable for this type of dataset. This is because the failure to recognize the corresponding entity can adversely impact subsequent processing results. In this study, the GliNER model is employed for the entity recognition task, selected for two main reasons. On one hand, previous studies have demonstrated the excellent performance of the GliNER model, particularly in zero-shot testing, where it outperforms ChatGPT and fine-tuned autoregressive language models. On the other hand, in the dataset used in this paper, a simple comparison with various NER toolkits including spaCy, NLTK, and Stanford NER reveals that the GliNER model exhibits superior performance (Loper and Bird, 2002; Schmitt et al., 2019).

The GLiNER model is a model for named entity recognition that utilizes a bidirectional Transformer structure. The framework of the GLiNER model is depicted in Figure 2. The input to the model is a uniform sequence containing the entity types represented in natural language and the input text to be processed for recognition.

While processing the input, the model computes the interactions between all the tokens through token representations, generating contextualized representations to better understand the relationships between tokens and the contextual information. Next, the Entity and Span Representation module encodes entity types and span embeddings into a unified latent space. In this process, the entity type is refined by a two-layer feedforward network, and the span is obtained by calculating the feedforward network results for the representations at the two locations. The computation of the span representation can be easily parallelized and an upper limit on the span length is set to maintain linear complexity. Finally, the Entity Type and Span Matching module calculates the matching score, which is used to assess whether the type and span correspond (Zaratiana et al., 2023).

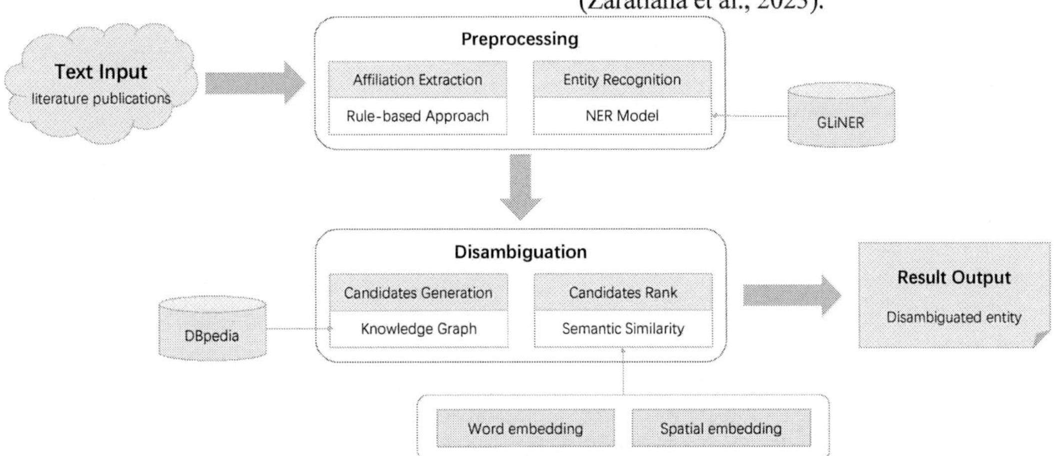

Figure 1: Overall framework of entity recognition and disambiguation.

Figure 2: The Architecture of GLiNER.

3.2 Disambiguation

- Candidates generation

DBpedia is a knowledge graph constructed based on Wikipedia content, covering a large number of entities and their related information, including attributes, relationships, abstracts, categories, and associations with other entities (Auer et al., 2017). By querying the DBpedia knowledge graph, one can obtain a list of candidate entities related to the mentioned entity. These entities have rich attribute descriptions and association information, which can provide important clues and support for subsequent entity ranking (Lehmann et al., 2015).

Candidate generation involves retrieving candidate entities related to entity mentions from the DBpedia knowledge graph, while retaining their characteristics, summaries, and other relevant information. To enhance matching accuracy and coverage, we not only directly obtain entities with names identical to the entity mentions from DBpedia, but also match entities related to the entity mentions, thereby expanding the matching scope of entities and making the query results more comprehensive. Additionally, entity types are utilized during candidate generation to limit the number of candidate words and to some extent eliminate ambiguity, thereby improving the quality of candidate word generation.

- Candidates Rank

Candidate ranking actually assigns a score to each candidate entity and ranks the generated candidate entities based on the score. The semantic similarity score is composed of context similarity and geographic similarity. The context similarity score of the candidate entity is obtained by comparing the semantic similarity between the context of the mentioned entity and each candidate entity. While geographic similarity is calculated by comparing the similarity between the geographic information contained in the input text and in the candidate entity abstracts.

1) Context similarity

Computing the similarity between entities and candidates using word embedding models is the most intuitive way to solve the ambiguity problem. Therefore, the similarity calculation between the entity context and the returned candidate entity summaries is performed using the word embedding model. At first, a pre-trained GloVe word embedding model is used, which maps words into a real vector space with hundreds of dimensions to capture semantic relationships between words. The selection of the GloVe model is based on its utilization of global co-occurrence information and its straightforward and efficient training methodology. The GloVe model learns word embeddings by minimizing the difference between the co-occurrence probabilities of words and their vector inner products (Pennington et al., 2014). For two words i and j , their co-occurrence probabilities can be represented by a co-occurrence matrix X . The element X_{ij} in this matrix represents the co-occurrence frequency of word i and word j. The optimization objective of the GloVe model is to minimize the loss function J in order to learn the best representation of the word vectors which allows the co-occurrence probabilities of the words to be well fitted.

$$J = \sum_{i,j=1}^{V} f(X_{ij})\left(w_i^T \cdot w_j + b_i + b_j - \log(X_{ij})\right)^2 \quad (1)$$

$f(X_{ij})$ is a weight coefficient introduced to regulate the effect of certain word pairs with too high co-occurrence frequency, w_i and w_j are the word vectors for words i and j, and b_i and b_j are bias terms used to regulate the position of the word vectors.

The text to be compared is converted into word embedding vectors, and then the overall representation vector of the text is obtained by simply averaging the vectors of all words in the text. Next, cosine similarity is used to calculate the similarity between the context vector V_e of the entity mention and the context vector V_c of the candidate entity.

$$Context_{similarity}(e,c) = \frac{V_e \cdot V_c}{\|V_e\| \cdot \|V_c\|} \quad (2)$$

2) Geographic similarity

The inheritance hypothesis refers to the assumption that the geographical location of a named entity can be inferred from the documents containing that entity (Kamalloo and Rafiei, 2018), such as news article headlines, tweet contents, etc. In other words, the frequency of occurrence of a certain location in the summary of a candidate entity can reflect the degree of association between the entity and that location. Using the NER tool to tag all locations l in the candidate summary d and obtain the corresponding frequency count $f(l,d)$. With these frequency counts, calculate the inheritance probability $P(l|d)$ of each location in the document. We assume that the geographical location with the highest frequency of occurrence l_c can represent the primary location of the candidate entities. It's worth noting that, unlike retrieving associated locations from the summary of candidate entities, entity mention l_e directly relies on the original input text. This is because affiliations often already contain relevant geographical location information.

$$P(l|d) = \frac{f(l,d)}{\sum_{l' \in d} f(l',d)} \quad (3)$$

The geographic names associated with entities and candidates are described as vectors and spatial similarity is calculated using cosine similarity.

$$Geographic_{similarity}(e,c) = \frac{V_{l_e} \cdot V_{l_c}}{\|V_{l_e}\| \cdot \|V_{l_c}\|} \quad (4)$$

During this process, for each mention of a possible location, a search is conducted in a geographic database to obtain a list of potential matches. Additionally, to address geographic ambiguity, the inclusion relationships between different mentions within the same text are utilized. Specifically, this involves mapping their names to corresponding geographic location names in a country-level hierarchical structure to specify the exact level of geographic entity and thus determine the name of the geographic entity. GeoNames is selected for the use of geodatabases. The GeoNames database is a global geographical information database that encompasses a wide range of geographical data, including place names, geographical features, and administrative divisions. This database contains geographic coordinates and related attribute information for millions of locations worldwide. Serving as a crucial data source, the GeoNames database provides fundamental support for the semantic information of geographical locations, effectively facilitating geographic relevance analysis and other related research endeavors (Grütter et al., 2017).

3) Objective function

Each mentioned entity e_i has multiple candidates, i.e., $|C(e_i)| \geq 2$, and for each candidate $c_{i,j} \in C(e_i)$, two different similarity scores need to be computed, namely, the similarity score between context-aware embeddings of the mentions and candidate embeddings, and the similarity score between spatial embeddings of the mentions and candidates. The overall disambiguation Score for each candidate is then obtained by combining the contextual similarity and spatial similarity and ranking the candidates according to the total score.

$$Score = \alpha \cdot Context_{similarity}(e_i, c_{i,j}) + \beta \cdot Geographic_{similarity}(e_i, c_{i,j}) \quad (5)$$

4 Experiments & results

4.1 Data

The data employed are author affiliations extracted from PubMed database. More specifically, the data is made up of strings containing information about organizations, regions, countries, etc. The annotation process is time-consuming as it usually requires manual annotation to recognize the raw data. In order to improve the efficiency of data labeling, a two-step strategy is used. Some entity names are first pre-labeled using a rule-based criterion that suggests target entity names, and then these suggested entity names are manually checked. The rule-based approach refers to the method of text processing based on predefined rules or patterns. Considering that the text structure and format of the dataset is relatively fixed, when pre-tagging the country entity data, it is straightforward to divide the text according to the specified punctuation and select the last part as the tagging target on the condition of ensuring that the last part is not an email message. While pre-tagging the data of institutional entities, texts containing terms such as "University", "Center", "College", "Institute", or "Foundation" are used as tagging targets, taking into account the common features and representative terms in the names of institutions. After the pre-tagging process, these suggested entity names are manually validated. The 9,000 records are annotated eventually. It is noteworthy that this study exclusively considers the highest organizational level of institutions, namely universities or research organizations. Specifically, all affiliations are simplified to their respective universities or primary research institutions, without further subdivision into colleges, departments, or divisions. This approach aids in data processing and analysis, enhancing data consistency and comparability.

The dataset is equally divided into three subsets S_1, S_2, and S_3, each of equal size, using K-fold cross validation (Bhagat and Bakariya, 2022). In each iteration, one of the subsets is used as the test set S_{test} and the concatenated set of the remaining parts is used as the training set S^L_{train}. To further analyze the effect of different sizes of training data on model performance, 1/3 of them are sampled from S^L_{train} as the medium-sized training set S^M_{train}, and then 1/20 of them are sampled from S^M_{train} as the smaller training set S^s_{train}. Three training sets with different sizes are obtained in the end: smaller S^s_{train}, medium S^M_{train}, and the initial size S^L_{train}. The inclusion relationship of these three training sets is $S^s_{train} \subset S^M_{train} \subset S^L_{train}$, i.e., S^s_{train} is a subset of S^M_{train}, which in turn is a subset of S^L_{train}.

4.2 The results

To assess the stability of the performance of model, we conducted a series of experiments covering training datasets of different scales, ranging from smaller-scale training data to the initial scale of training data. This design enables a comprehensive examination of the model's performance when faced with different data volumes, allowing for a more accurate evaluation of the performance and robustness of model. Table 1 intuitively demonstrates the performance of the model under different data volumes. Despite the differences in the scale of the training datasets, there is not much variation in the measured metrics of Precision, Recall, and F1-score on the test set. This indicates that our model exhibits a certain degree of stability and robustness when dealing with training data of different scales.

Table 1: the performance of proposed model on different size datasets

Data size	Precision	Recall	F1
Small-scale S^s_{train}	0.748	0.761	0.754
Medium-scale S^M_{train}	0.752	0.761	0.756
Large-scale S^L_{train}	0.745	0.771	0.758

Furthermore, to further evaluate the effectiveness of our algorithm, we conducted comparison experiments with other methods. From Table 2, it is evident that our algorithm demonstrates good performance, particularly in terms of accuracy. In fact, there is further potential for improvement in rule-based entity recognition and disambiguation, but this requires continuous observation of actual text samples and iterative adjustment and addition of rules based on identification results. This not only demands more time and effort but also rules may not comprehensively cover all cases, leading to less accurate or incomplete identification results in certain scenarios.

Table 2: compare with other models

Methodology	Precision	Recall	F1
Rule-based	0.582	0.708	0.639
WeLink	0.711	0.732	0.722
Our algorithm	0.745	0.771	0.758

To validate the importance of geographical information in semantic similarity calculation and to gain a deeper understanding of its impact on disambiguation results for different entity types, we conducted ablation experiments separately for location and organization entity types to explore the influence of geographical embeddings on disambiguation algorithm. The results are illustrated in Table 3. By incorporating geographical information, we can observe a significant improvement in disambiguation effectiveness for Location entity types. Specifically, the Precision metric increased by 0.288, Recall increased by 0.221, and the F1-score also relatively increased by 0.179. This is because utilizing containment relationships between geographical locations in the text can more effectively eliminate geographic ambiguity, thus enhancing the accuracy and overall performance of entity recognition. However, upon examining the analysis results, we found that when using the GeoNames database to process geographical names, especially when mapping them to the country level, the database cannot handle aliases of individual country names such as "UK", "The Netherlands". For instance, in the input text "Cancer Services, South Eastern Health & Social Care Trust, UK.", it fails to correctly identify the mentioned entity "UK" as "United Kingdom, and incorrectly maps it to "['Japan', 'Japan', 'Kazakhstan', 'Pakistan', 'Russia', 'Ukraine', 'United States']", which somewhat affects the ranking of candidates. Based on this, this study plans to solve the problem by creating a higher priority mapping table designed to store those country aliases that the GeoNames database cannot handle. As for entity type of Organization, their metric values also improved. Specifically, accuracy increased by 13.5%, recall increased by 3.8%, and F1-score increased by 8.1%. Although the improvement is not as significant as for Location types, it still contributes to enhancing entity disambiguation results. Particularly, when dealing with organizations with the same name, the introduction of geographical information can quickly identify the correct candidates. For example, it can effectively differentiate between the "University of California, Los Angeles" and "University of California, Santa Barbara". Additionally, it is noteworthy that compared to the recall values, the change in precision is more pronounced, indicating that the introduction of geographical information prioritizes improving the precision of entity disambiguation. Actually, some of the author affiliation information that is severely lacking in correct and necessary information does not lead to correct results. For example, "Department of Biology", but the proposed algorithm still significantly improves the precision and recall.

Table 3: proposed model with and without location embedding for different entity type

Entity Type	Methodology	Precision	Recall	F1
Location	Context	0.660	0.740	0.698
	Context + Geographic	0.948	0.961	0.955
Organization	Context	0.703	0.667	0.684
	Context + Geographic	0.838	0.705	0.765

5 Case study

Table 4: The top 10 institutions by count

Institution	Count
University of California	127
Stanford University	108
University of Texas	69
University of Washington	61
Massachusetts General Hospital	58
University of Pennsylvania	56
University of Oxford	54
Mayo Clinic	52
University of Michigan	44
University of Toronto	44

Table 5: The top 10 countries by count

Country	Count
United States	1843
China	1250
United Kingdom	489
India	413
Germany	344
Italy	333
Canada	324
France	265
Japan	263
Australia	259

In this paper, two case studies are defined to demonstrate the practical application of the proposed framework. In these case studies, we aim to identify the most productive organizations and countries on the topic of "artificial intelligence" in the PubMed database. We apply the proposed framework to extract author affiliation data and perform entity recognition and entity disambiguation. The 10 most productive institutions and countries are listed in Tables 4 and 5, respectively.

6 Conclusion

This paper proposes an end-to-end named entity disambiguation framework designed to achieve entity recognition and disambiguation for author affiliation texts, enabling direct application in bibliometric analysis. Particularly, a novel algorithm combining word embeddings and spatial embeddings is introduced for entity disambiguation. This work not only provides methodological references for handling homogeneous types of textual data but also facilitates the automation of dataset processing, entity recognition, and disambiguation, thereby minimizing post-processing steps. These advancements allow for direct application in bibliometric analysis, ultimately enhancing its efficiency. Certainly, the current focus of this paper is primarily on resolving named entity ambiguities at the entity type of LOC and ORG. In the future, we aim to extend this entity disambiguation algorithm to analyze other entity types, such as author name. Additionally, the Research Organization Registry (ROR) is a system for managing and recording information about various types of organizations or institutions, which can be utilized as a knowledge repository to further expand our research.

References

Agarwal, Prabal, et al. "diaNED: Time-aware named entity disambiguation for diachronic corpora." *Proceedings of the 56th Annual Meeting of the Association for Computational Linguistics (Volume 2: Short Papers).* 2018. https://doi.org/10.18653/v1/P18-2109

Auer, Sören, et al. "Dbpedia: A nucleus for a web of open data." *international semantic web conference*. Berlin, Heidelberg: Springer Berlin Heidelberg, 2007.https://doi.org/10.1007/978-3-540-76298-0_52

Basile, Alessandro, et al. "Disambiguation of company names via deep recurrent networks." *Expert Systems with Applications* 238 (2024): 122035. https://doi.org/10.1016/j.eswa.2023.122035

Bhagat, Meenu, and Brijesh Bakariya. "Implementation of logistic regression on diabetic dataset using train-test-split, k-fold and stratified k-fold approach." *National Academy Science Letters* 45.5 (2022): 401-404. https://doi.org/10.1007/s40009-022-01131-9

Bouarroudj, Wissem, Zizette Boufaida, and Ladjel Bellatreche. "Named entity disambiguation in short texts over knowledge graphs." *Knowledge and Information Systems* 64.2 (2022): 325-351. https://doi.org/10.1007/s10115-021-01642-9

Chandrasekaran, Dhivya, and Vijay Mago. "Evolution of semantic similarity—a survey." *ACM Computing Surveys (CSUR)* 54.2 (2021): 1-37. https://doi.org/10.1145/3440755

D'Angelo, Ciriaco Andrea, and Nees Jan Van Eck. "Collecting large-scale publication data at the level of individual researchers: A practical proposal for author name disambiguation." *Scientometrics* 123 (2020): 883-907. https://doi.org/10.1007/s11192-020-03410-y

Donner, Paul, Christine Rimmert, and Nees Jan van Eck. "Comparing institutional-level bibliometric research performance indicator values based on different affiliation disambiguation systems." *Quantitative Science Studies* 1.1 (2020): 150-170. https://doi.org/10.1162/qss_a_00013

Donthu, Naveen, et al. "How to conduct a bibliometric analysis: An overview and guidelines." *Journal of business research* 133 (2021): 285-296. https://doi.org/10.1016/j.jbusres.2021.04.070

Fang, Yuan, and Ming-Wei Chang. "Entity linking on microblogs with spatial and temporal signals." *Transactions of the Association for Computational Linguistics* 2 (2014): 259-272. https://aclanthology.org/Q14-1021

Fetahu, Besnik, et al. "Gazetteer enhanced named entity recognition for code-mixed web queries." *Proceedings of the 44th International ACM SIGIR Conference on Research and Development in Information Retrieval.* 2021. https://doi.org/10.1145/3404835.3463102

Fiorini, Nicolas, et al. "PubMed Labs: an experimental system for improving biomedical literature search." *Database* 2018 (2018): bay094. https://doi.org/10.1093/database/bay094

Grütter, Rolf, Ross S. Purves, and Lukas Wotruba. "Evaluating topological queries in linked data using DBpedia and GeoNames in Switzerland and Scotland." *Transactions in GIS* 21.1 (2017): 114-133. https://doi.org/10.1111/tgis.12196

Han, Xianpei, and Jun Zhao. "Named entity disambiguation by leveraging wikipedia semantic knowledge." *Proceedings of the 18th ACM conference on Information and knowledge management.* 2009. https://doi.org/10.1145/1645953.1645983

Huang, Shuiqing, et al. "Institution name disambiguation for research assessment." *Scientometrics* 99 (2014): 823-838. https://doi.org/10.1007/s11192-013-1214-2

Kamalloo, Ehsan, and Davood Rafiei. "A coherent unsupervised model for toponym resolution." *Proceedings of the 2018 world wide web conference.* 2018. https://doi.org/10.1145/3178876.3186027

Kokol, Peter, Helena Blažun Vošner, and Jernej Završnik. "Application of bibliometrics in medicine: a historical bibliometrics analysis." *Health Information & Libraries Journal* 38.2 (2021): 125-138. https://doi.org/10.1111/hir.12295

Lehmann, Jens, et al. "Dbpedia–a large-scale, multilingual knowledge base extracted from wikipedia." *Semantic web* 6.2 (2015): 167-195. DOI: 10.3233/SW-140134

L'Hôte, Anne, and Eric Jeangirard. "Using Elasticsearch for entity recognition in affiliation disambiguation." *arXiv preprint arXiv:2110.01958* (2021). DOI: 10.48550/arXiv.2110.01958

Li, Fei, et al. "An efficient approach for measuring semantic similarity combining WordNet and Wikipedia." *IEEE Access* 8 (2020): 184318-184338. DOI: 10.1109/ACCESS.2020.3025611.

Lim, Weng Marc, and Satish Kumar. "Guidelines for interpreting the results of bibliometric analysis: A sensemaking approach." *Global Business and Organizational Excellence* 43.2 (2024): 17-26. DOI: 10.1002/joe.22229

Loper, Edward, and Steven Bird. "Nltk: The natural language toolkit." *arXiv preprint cs/0205028* (2002). https://aclanthology.org/P04-3031

Lu, Zhiyong. "PubMed and beyond: a survey of web tools for searching biomedical literature." *Database* 2011 (2011): baq036. DOI: 10.1093/database/baq03

Naseer, Salman, et al. "Named Entity Recognition (NER) in NLP Techniques, Tools Accuracy and Performance." *Pakistan Journal of Multidisciplinary Research* 2.2 (2021): 293-308.

Nedelchev, Rostislav, et al. "End-to-end entity linking and disambiguation leveraging word and knowledge graph embeddings." *arXiv preprint arXiv:2002.11143* (2020). https://doi.org/10.48550/arXiv.2002.11143

Ninkov, Anton, Jason R. Frank, and Lauren A. Maggio. "Bibliometrics: methods for studying academic publishing." *Perspectives on medical education* 11.3 (2022): 173-176. DOI: 10.1007/S40037-021-00695-4

Pennington, Jeffrey, Richard Socher, and Christopher D. Manning. "Glove: Global vectors for word representation." *Proceedings of the 2014 conference on empirical methods in natural language processing (EMNLP)*. 2014. https://aclanthology.org/D14-1162

Rafiei, Jiangwei Yu, and Davood Rafiei. "Geotagging named entities in news and online documents." *Proceedings of the 25th ACM International on Conference on Information and Knowledge Management*. 2016. DOI: 0.1145/2983323.2983795

Rimmert, Christine, Holger Schwechheimer, and Matthias Winterhager. "Disambiguation of author addresses in bibliometric databases-technical report." (2017). https://pub.uni-bielefeld.de/record/2914944

Sanyal, Debarshi Kumar, Plaban Kumar Bhowmick, and Partha Pratim Das. "A review of author name disambiguation techniques for the PubMed bibliographic database." *Journal of Information Science* 47.2 (2021): 227-254. https://doi.org/10.1177/0165551519888605

Schmitt, Xavier, et al. "A replicable comparison study of NER software: StanfordNLP, NLTK, OpenNLP, SpaCy, Gate." *2019 sixth international conference on social networks analysis, management and security (SNAMS)*. IEEE, 2019. DOI: 10.1109/SNAMS.2019.8931850

Shao, Zhou, et al. "ELAD: An entity linking based affiliation disambiguation framework." *IEEE Access* 8 (2020): 70519-70526. DOI: 10.1109/ACCESS.2020.2986826

Srinivasan, Maithrreye, and Davood Rafiei. "Location-aware named entity disambiguation." *Proceedings of the 30th ACM International Conference on Information & Knowledge Management*. 2021. https://doi.org/10.1145/3459637.3482135

Thompson, Dennis F., and Cheri K. Walker. "A descriptive and historical review of bibliometrics with applications to medical sciences." *Pharmacotherapy: The Journal of Human Pharmacology and Drug Therapy* 35.6 (2015): 551-559. https://doi.org/10.1002/phar.1586

Zaratiana, Urchade, et al. "Gliner: Generalist model for named entity recognition using bidirectional transformer." *arXiv preprint arXiv:2311.08526* (2023). https://doi.org/10.48550/arXiv.2311.08526

Zwicklbauer, Stefan, Christin Seifert, and Michael Granitzer. "Robust and collective entity disambiguation through semantic embeddings." *Proceedings of the 39th International ACM SIGIR conference on Research and Development in Information Retrieval*. 2016. https://doi.org/10.1145/2911451.2911535

Utilizing an Ensemble Model with Anomalous Label Smoothing to Detect Generated Scientific Papers

Yuan Zhao[1] and **Junruo Gao**[1] and **Junlin Wang**[1] and **Gang Luo**[1,*] and **Liang Tang**[1]

[1]China Telecom Cloud Technology Co., Ltd

{zhaoyuan1,gaojr1,wangjl52,luog6,tangl33}@chinatelecom.cn

* Corresponding author

Abstract

Generative AI, as it becomes increasingly integrated into our lives, has brought convenience, though some concerns have arisen regarding its potential impact on the rigor and authenticity of scientific research. To encourage the development of robust and reliable automatically-generated scientific text detection systems, the "DAGPap24: Detecting Automatically Generated Scientific Papers" competition was held and shared the same task with the 4th Workshop on Scholarly Document Processing (SDP 2024) to be held at ACL 2024. In the DAGPap24 competition, participants were tasked with constructing a generative text detection model that could accurately distinguish between the human written fragment, the synonym replacement fragment, the ChatGPT rewrite fragment, and the generated summary fragment of a paper. In this competition, we first conducted a comprehensive analysis of the training set to build a generative paper detection model. Then we tried various language models, including SciBERT, ALBERT, DeBERTa, RoBERTa, etc. After that, we introduced an Anomalous Label Smoothing (ALS) method and a majority voting method to improve the final results. Finally, we achieved 0.9948 and 0.9944 F1 scores during the development and testing phases respectively, and we achieved second place in the competition.

1 Introduction

With the rapid development of NLP technology, especially with the emergence of ChatGPT[1], there is an increasing amount of text generated by non-human entities. However, machine-generated text may sometimes contain errors that are not easily discernible by humans, leading to a decline in the rigor and credibility of scientific papers. Current NLP generation technology has nearly reached parity with human writing, which poses the challenge of distinguishing them (Zhang et al., 2023). In response to this issue, Mitchell et al. (2023) propose a detection method that does not require training a classifier or collecting additional datasets. They argue that model-generated text is more sensitive to minor rewriting perturbations than human-written text. To further distinguish the sentences with various lengths, researchers in (Tian et al., 2023) propose a length-sensitive Multiscale positive-unlabeled Loss that can improve the ability of detection of BERT (Devlin et al., 2019) and RoBERTa (Liu et al., 2019). To further understand the achievements, this survey (Tang et al., 2024) provides an overview of existing techniques for detecting LLM-generated text.

In this paper, we mainly detail our work during the shared task DAGPap2024. We are tasked with detecting automatically generated papers. We can abstract this task into a token-level multi-classification problem. There are three challenges in this task. 1) Difficulty in efficiently bridging the gap between word-level tokenization and subword-level tokenization more rationally. The dataset provided in the competition is tokenized in word-level, while most of the existing language models using the subword-level tokenization method. If the two tokenized methods are not accurately mapped, it will not only lead to a waste of useful information but may also lead to misalignment of the prediction results and the test set. 2) Difficulty in ensuring that the distribution of the generated prediction results is consistent with the label distribution of the training set. We found that only relying on the model's predictions will lead to inconsistency in the distribution between the training set and test set. For example, there will be several other labels predicted in the middle of a continuous text. It leads to inconsistency in the distribution between training set and development set. 3) Difficulty in determining which model performs best on token-level classification tasks. Different models, each

[1]https://chatgpt.com/

Proceedings of the Fourth Workshop on Scholarly Document Processing (SDP 2024), pages 130–134
August 16, 2024 ©2024 Association for Computational Linguistics

with unique training parameters, yield varying predictions for this task, resulting in different label prediction outcomes for the same token. The selection of the final result directly impacts the F1 score. To overcome the aforementioned challenges and enhance our performance in the competition, we propose the following solutions:

- Based on our analysis, we adopted two ways to divide the data into sub-sentences. One is to divide the data into sub-sentences according to the token length of 240, and the other is to divide the tokenized data into sub-sentences with a max length of 500. These two tokenization ways can ensure that the prediction results can correspond back to the original text without the loss of information.

- Then, we fine-tuned DeBERTaV3$_{\text{large}}$(He et al., 2023), DeBERTaV2$_{\text{xxlarge}}$(He et al., 2021) and ALBERTV2$_{\text{xxlarge}}$(Lan et al., 2020) using token-level classification. We proposed an Anomalous Label Smoothing method (ALS) to guarantee the predicted results and the label distribution of the training set. Specifically, by scanning under different window lengths, we smooth out predicted anomalous labels, ensuring that there are no anomalous labels within the window.

- Finally, to take full advantage of different models, we used a majority voting method to ensemble the predictions of multiple models. By ensembling the results from the models, we attained F1 scores of 0.9948 and 0.9944 in the development and testing phases, respectively.

2 Task Overview

To enforce the reliability of scientific papers, we focus on detecting automatically generated scientific papers. We should distinguish human-written fragments, synonym-replaced fragments, ChatGPT-generated fragments, and summarized fragments, which can be abstracted as a token-level classification task. Fig. 1 provides a visualization of the fragments extracted from the training set.

2.1 Data

The original dataset is selected from scientific papers, consisting of 5,000 training samples, 5,000 development samples, and 20,000 test samples. Each

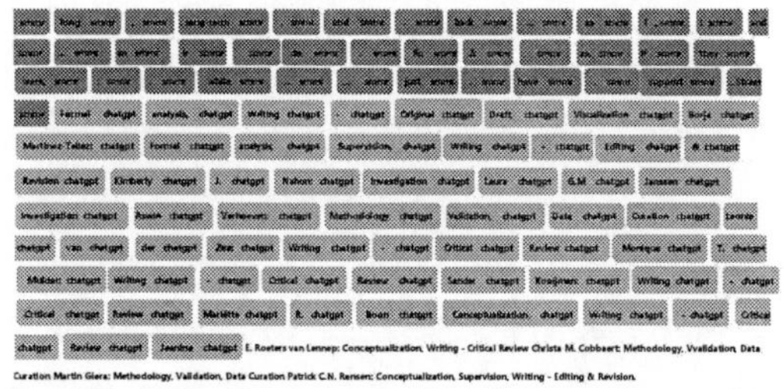

Figure 1: Visualization result of different types of fragments in a training sample.

sample may consist of fragments from the four categories mentioned above, appearing in different sequences and frequencies. The summarized fragments are obtained via a deep learning model, the synonym replacement fragments are obtained by substituting the original words with the synonyms from NLTK, and the ChatGPT fragments are obtained by rewriting the original fragments using ChatGPT. As Fig. 1 shows, the number of labels in this fragment is three. We statistically analyzed the number of the sequence of continuously labeled identical fragments and found that they were identically distributed in the training set, validation set and test set.

We processed the training set according to subword-level tokenization to avoid the loss of useful information (e.g., the information involved in the truncated sentences) and ensure the consistency of prediction results with the test set. We conducted a statistical analysis on the length of tokenized fragments for each category in the training set. The statistical results are shown in Table 1. The column "1%" denotes that, upon arranging all fragment lengths into ascending order, 1% of the fragments have lengths equal to or under the specified value. Columns like "50%" and "75%" are similarly conveyed in the same manner.

Category	0.5%	50%	75%	Mean
human	35.00	1204.00	2234.75	1640.87
synonym	29.00	587.00	672.50	612.20
ChatGPT	21.00	382.00	476.00	397.32
summary	22.84	359.00	413.00	381.25

Table 1: Statistics on the length of the fragments of each category in the training set.

3 Our Work

In this section, we will provide a detailed description of our work, which includes data analysis, data processing, models, and the anomalous label smoothing method. Our work is illustrated in the structural flowchart as shown in Fig. 2.

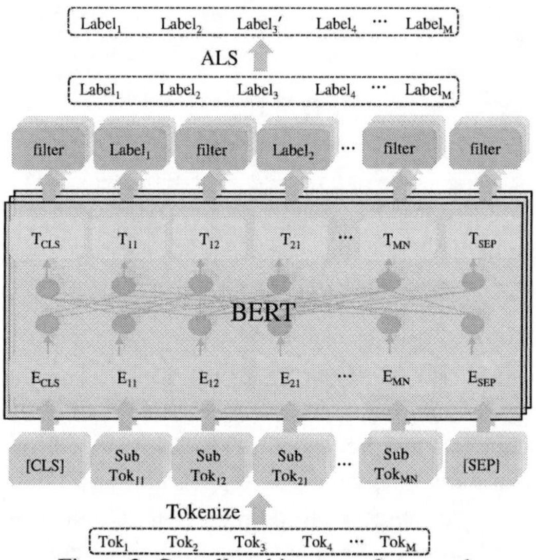

Figure 2: Overall architecture of our work.

3.1 Data Analysis and Data Processing

Initially, through analyzing the raw data, we discovered several key issues. The first was that sentences split according to the length of the word sequence may exceed the maximum length of the BERT sequence after word segmentation. This results in some training data being wasted since the information involved in the truncated sentences may be lost. It is difficult for the predicted label to correctly correspond to the test text. The second was that the 99.5% of continuous label lengths exceed 20.

During data pre-processing, we followed the method suggested by the given example and divided the raw train data into two parts, including the training set and the validation set. Based on the data analysis mentioned above, two data preprocessing methods were adopted. One method named TokV1 was to divide the sentences in the training set and Validation set into sub-sentences with a token list of length 240. The other one named TokV2 was to perform word tokenization before segmentation and then ensure that each sub-sentence after word tokenization was a tokenized text with a max of 500 tokens. This ensured that tokenized sentences would hardly exceed the maximum length of the pre-trained model, allowing the model to achieve the best training effect.

3.2 Models

For the token-level classification task, it is necessary to perceive the contextual relationships of the tokens. The models with a bidirectional attention mechanism might be a good choice, thus, we used models with an encoder structure, including DeBERTaV2$_{\text{xxlarge}}$, DeBERTaV3$_{\text{large}}$, and ALBERTV2$_{\text{xxlarge}}$ and conducted a series of experiments on these models. The details of these models are presented in Table 2.

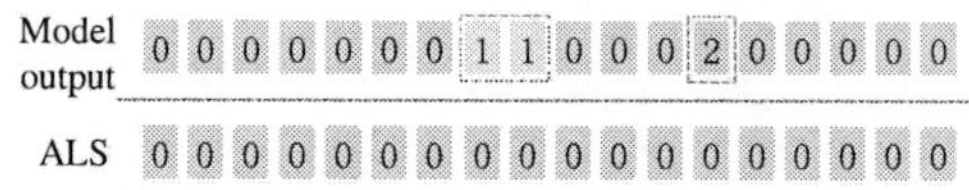

Figure 3: The process of Anomalous Label Smoothing to correct labels.

Model	Parameter	Hidden Size
SciBERT	110M	768
RoBERTa	355M	1024
ALBERTV2$_{\text{xxlarge}}$	223M	4096
DeBERTaV2$_{\text{xxlarge}}$	1.5B	1536
DeBERTaV3$_{\text{large}}$	304M	1024

Table 2: The configuration of the chosen models.

3.3 Anomalous Label Smoothing

We conducted data analysis on the models' outputs and discovered that within a sequence of continuously labeled identical data, there were discrete labels of other categories intermixed, which is different from our analysis results mentioned above. Thus, we designed a post-processing method named Anomalous Label Smoothing(ALS), which is similar to a Conditional Random Field (CRF) (Lafferty et al., 2001) in filtering out unreasonable labels. ALS method corrects label fragments smaller than the window size to the label of its left or right fragment by setting a window size and iterating through the prediction results. Initially select the label on the right, and for the rest, select the label of the fragment on the left. The size of the window is determined in specific experiments, based on the second key point from our previous data analysis. As shown in Fig. 3, through the ALS method, we have corrected the labels of other categories interspersed within a sequence of continuously identical labels.

Model	Score
SciBERT	0.8637
RoBERTa	0.8814
DeBERTaV3$_{\text{large}}$	0.8971
DeBERTaV2$_{\text{large}}$+TokV2	0.9892
ALBERTV2$_{\text{xxlarge}}$+TokV1+ALS$_{10,20}$	0.9885
DeBERTaV2$_{\text{xxlarge}}$+TokV1+ALS$_{10,20}$	0.9887
DeBERTaV3$_{\text{large}}$+TokV1+ALS$_{10,20}$	0.9844
ALBERTV2$_{\text{xxlarge}}$+TokV2+ALS$_{10,20,30}$	0.9897
DeBERTaV2$_{\text{xxlarge}}$+TokV2+ALS$_{10,20,30}$	0.9910
DeBERTaV3$_{\text{large}}$+TokV2+ALS$_{10,20,30}$	0.9919

Table 3: The F1 scores on the development set.

Ensembled	Base Model	Dev	Test
V1	DeBERTaV3$_{\text{large}}$ +TokV1+ALS$_{10,20}$ DeBERTaV2$_{\text{xxlarge}}$ +TokV1+ALS$_{10,20}$ ALBERTV2$_{\text{xxlarge}}$ +TokV1+ALS$_{10,20}$	0.9908	N/A
V2	EnsembledV1 DeBERTaV2$_{\text{large}}$ +TokV2 ALBERTV2$_{\text{xxlarge}}$ +TokV2+ALS$_{10,20,30}$ DeBERTaV2$_{\text{xxlarge}}$ +TokV2+ALS$_{10,20,30}$ DeBERTaV3$_{\text{large}}$ +TokV2+ALS$_{10,20,30}$	0.9948	0.9943
V2$_{\text{ALS}_5}$	EnsembledV1 DeBERTaV2$_{\text{large}}$ +TokV2 ALBERTV2$_{\text{xxlarge}}$ +TokV2+ALS$_{10,20,30}$ DeBERTaV2$_{\text{xxlarge}}$ +TokV2+ALS$_{10,20,30}$ DeBERTaV3$_{\text{large}}$ +TokV2+ALS$_{10,20,30}$	N/A	**0.9944**

Table 4: The F1 scores of the ensemble models.

3.4 Majority Voting

We performed majority voting on the prediction results from multiple models to enhance the robustness and accuracy of the overall outcome. We assume that the label corresponding to the token at position is $l_1, l_2 ... l_i ... l_n$, $l_i \in \mathbb{L} = \{0, 1, 2, 3\}$, where n represents the number of models. The frequency for each label is denoted as feq(l_i). Thus, the voting rule is as Eq. 1.

$$f(l) = \text{argmax}(\text{feq}(l_i)), i \in \mathbb{L} \tag{1}$$

At the same time, we observed that when determining the final labels through majority voting, if there is a disagreement among the opinions of each model participating in the vote, i.e., the frequency of any label is same, then the final result cannot be determined through voting. Therefore, based on Eq. 1, we optimized the voting rules. We selected the relatively better model output l_T to serve as a final result for such inconclusive situation, as depicted in Eq. 2.

$$g(l) = \begin{cases} l_T & \text{feq}(l_1) = \text{feq}(l_2) ... = \text{feq}(l_n) \\ f(l) & others \end{cases} \tag{2}$$

4 Experiments

During the modeling process, we tried different state-of-the-art models, including SciBERT, RoBERTa, DeBERTaV2$_{\text{xxlarge}}$, DeBERTaV3$_{\text{large}}$, ALBERTV2$_{\text{xxlarge}}$. ALS$_{10,20,30}$ was used to denote the length of Anomalous Label Smoothing, i.e., the smoothing windows were 10, 20, 30 respectively. We conducted numerous parameter tuning experiments and applied various training techniques, such as early stopping (Prechelt, 2002), n-fold validation (Raschka, 2018), and so on. The learning rate for DeBERTaV3$_{\text{large}}$, ALBERTV2$_{\text{xxlarge}}$, and DeBERTaV2$_{\text{xxlarge}}$ were set to 5e-5, 2e-5 and 5e-6 respectively. Due to space constraints, we list representative experimental results in Table 3.

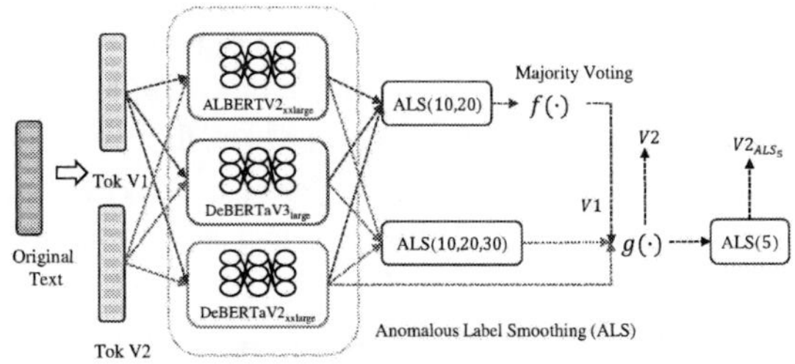

Figure 4: The process of our experiments.

Firstly, we finetuned some base models following the given settings, among which the DeBERTaV3$_{\text{large}}$ model performed best. The reason might be that the DeBERTaV3$_{\text{large}}$ model introduces the absolute word position embeddings, which can contribute to distinguishing between vocabulary usage in human language and machine-generated text. As analyzed in 3.1, differences in text tokenization methods, or inconsistencies of label distributions, would both decrease the F1 scores. Thus, we introduced two types of tokenization methods, which are named $TokV1$ and $TokV2$ to ensure that the length of tokenized input texts does not exceed the maximum length of the pre-trained model. Furthermore, we developed an Anomalous Label Smoothing method, referred to as ALS, to refine the predicted results, aiming to align the final results as closely as possible with the label distribution of the training set. We ultimately acquired several fine-tuned models base on DeBERTaV2$_{\text{large}}$, DeBERTaV2$_{\text{xxlarge}}$ and DeBERTaV3$_{\text{large}}$ models, all of which achieved F1 scores exceeding 0.98 on the development set. Finally, we employed model fusion to integrate the results of the models in Table 3. In that case, we can further improve the model's performance. Table 4 shows the results of the model fusion experiments.

5 Conclusion

In this paper, we mainly introduce the automatically generated papers detection and detail our solution for the DAGPap2024 competition. Firstly, based on the analysis of the data, we adopted two different tokenization ways to ensure that the predicted results can accurately correspond to the original text set. Then, we introduced an Anomalous Label Smoothing method to ensure that the distribution of predicted results is consistent with the label distribution of the training data set without the loss of information. Finally, we used model fusion to maximize the performance of different models. The above efforts ensured that we achieved a high F1 result in this competition, which was 0.9948 and 0.9944 on F1 score during the development and testing phases, and we achieved second place in the competition.

References

Jacob Devlin, Ming-Wei Chang, Kenton Lee, and Kristina Toutanova. 2019. BERT: pre-training of deep bidirectional transformers for language understanding. In *Proceedings of the 2019 Conference of the North American Chapter of the Association for Computational Linguistics: Human Language Technologies, NAACL-HLT 2019, Minneapolis, MN, USA, June 2-7, 2019, Volume 1 (Long and Short Papers)*, pages 4171–4186. Association for Computational Linguistics.

Pengcheng He, Jianfeng Gao, and Weizhu Chen. 2023. Debertav3: Improving deberta using electra-style pre-training with gradient-disentangled embedding sharing. In *The Eleventh International Conference on Learning Representations, ICLR 2023, Kigali, Rwanda, May 1-5, 2023*. OpenReview.net.

Pengcheng He, Xiaodong Liu, Jianfeng Gao, and Weizhu Chen. 2021. Deberta: decoding-enhanced bert with disentangled attention. In *9th International Conference on Learning Representations, ICLR 2021, Virtual Event, Austria, May 3-7, 2021*. OpenReview.net.

John D. Lafferty, Andrew McCallum, and Fernando C. N. Pereira. 2001. Conditional random fields: Probabilistic models for segmenting and labeling sequence data. In *Proceedings of the Eighteenth International Conference on Machine Learning (ICML 2001), Williams College, Williamstown, MA, USA, June 28 - July 1, 2001*, pages 282–289. Morgan Kaufmann.

Zhenzhong Lan, Mingda Chen, Sebastian Goodman, Kevin Gimpel, Piyush Sharma, and Radu Soricut. 2020. ALBERT: A lite BERT for self-supervised learning of language representations. In *8th International Conference on Learning Representations, ICLR 2020, Addis Ababa, Ethiopia, April 26-30, 2020*. OpenReview.net.

Yinhan Liu, Myle Ott, Naman Goyal, Jingfei Du, Mandar Joshi, Danqi Chen, Omer Levy, Mike Lewis, Luke Zettlemoyer, and Veselin Stoyanov. 2019. Roberta: A robustly optimized bert pretraining approach. *arXiv preprint arXiv:1907.11692*.

Eric Mitchell, Yoonho Lee, Alexander Khazatsky, Christopher D Manning, and Chelsea Finn. 2023. Detectgpt: Zero-shot machine-generated text detection using probability curvature. In *International Conference on Machine Learning*, pages 24950–24962. PMLR.

Lutz Prechelt. 2002. Early stopping-but when? In *Neural Networks: Tricks of the trade*, pages 55–69. Springer.

Sebastian Raschka. 2018. Model evaluation, model selection, and algorithm selection in machine learning. *arXiv preprint arXiv:1811.12808*.

Ruixiang Tang, Yu-Neng Chuang, and Xia Hu. 2024. The science of detecting llm-generated text. *Communications of the ACM*, 67(4):50–59.

Yuchuan Tian, Hanting Chen, Xutao Wang, Zheyuan Bai, Qinghua Zhang, Ruifeng Li, Chao Xu, and Yunhe Wang. 2023. Multiscale positive-unlabeled detection of ai-generated texts. *arXiv preprint arXiv:2305.18149*.

Zheng Zhang, Jie Gao, Ranjodh Singh Dhaliwal, and Toby Jia-Jun Li. 2023. Visar: A human-ai argumentative writing assistant with visual programming and rapid draft prototyping. In *Proceedings of the 36th Annual ACM Symposium on User Interface Software and Technology*, pages 1–30.

AffilGood: Building reliable institution name disambiguation tools to improve scientific literature analysis

Nicolau Duran-Silva[1,2], Pablo Accuosto[1], Piotr Przybyła[2,3], Horacio Saggion[2],
[1]SIRIS Lab, Research Division of SIRIS Academic, Barcelona, Spain,
[2]LaSTUS Lab, TALN Group, Universitat Pompeu Fabra, Barcelona, Spain,
[3]Institute of Computer Science, Polish Academy of Sciences, Warsaw, Poland

Abstract

The accurate attribution of scientific works to research organizations is hindered by the lack of openly available manually annotated data–in particular when multilingual and complex affiliation strings are considered. The AffilGood framework introduced in this paper addresses this gap. We identify three sub-tasks relevant for institution name disambiguation and make available annotated datasets and tools aimed at each of them, including i) a dataset annotated with affiliation spans in noisy automatically-extracted strings; ii) a dataset annotated with named entities for the identification of organizations and their locations; iii) seven datasets annotated with the Research Organization Registry (ROR) identifiers for the evaluation of entity-linking systems. In addition, we describe, evaluate and make available newly developed tools that use these datasets to provide solutions for each of the identified sub-tasks. Our results confirm the value of the developed resources and methods in addressing key challenges in institution name disambiguation.

1 Introduction

The availability and access to research outcomes are gradually becoming less of an issue in an open data and open science context (Fuster et al., 2020). This is due, in part, to the emergence and expansion of open scholarly knowledge graphs (Manghi et al., 2019; Priem et al., 2022; Kinney et al., 2023), open research information providers (Wilkinson, 2010; Hendricks et al., 2020), and the increasing trend of governments and public agencies to release their research and innovation (R&I) policy data (Fuster et al., 2023). However, effective metadata curation of large open databases remains a significant challenge. A persistent issue is how to uniquely identify institutions involved in research from unstructured affiliation strings in scientific publications, where organizations are mentioned in non-standard formats–even when authors are encouraged to use official institution name signatures when publishing (Purnell, 2022).[1]

The task of automatically identifying organizations in author-provided affiliation strings and linking them to unique identifiers from global registries–such as the Research Organization Registry (ROR)[2] or Wikidata–is known as *institution name disambiguation* or *affiliation normalization*. Linking scientific works to a regularly-updated human-curated registries of organizations is crucial for addressing organization changes over time, including institutional mergers and splits, as well as evolving naming conventions (Purnell, 2022). Accurate normalization of institutions is vital for research evaluation (Huang et al., 2014) and essential for analyzing scientific production trends, particularly within an open science context (L'Hôte and Jeangirard, 2021). Furthermore, research assessment may be affected by wrong attribution of publications to institutions (Purnell, 2022; Donner et al., 2020). To precisely attribute publications to institutions can be challenging due to the fact that organizations are frequently mentioned in diverse and unstructured manners, employing various patterns, languages,[3] and abbreviations. In addition, automatically extracted affiliation strings often include noise, irrelevant information, or typographical errors. Affiliations can also refer to different institutional levels, such as departments and collaborative institutions, adding complexity to the task. Illustrative examples of these challenges are presented in Table 1. Relevant examples of ambiguity are presented by Huang et al. (2014).

Despite several tools and methods having been proposed to tackle different subtasks, as described in

[1]In OpenAlex (Priem et al., 2022), for example, there are more than 8 million different raw affiliation strings in publications produced in 2023, with 72% of those not present in publications from the previous five years.

[2]ROR is a community-led registry of open persistent identifiers for research organizations available at `https://ror.org`

[3]From a sample of 50K affiliations from OpenAlex, we estimate that 23% of the strings are not in English.

Proceedings of the Fourth Workshop on Scholarly Document Processing (SDP 2024), pages 135–144
August 16, 2024

Challenge	Example
Non-English input	*Instytut Badań Literackich PAN, Zespół Badań nad Literaturą Zagłady*
Lack of punctuation	*IUM - INSEEC Research Center Strategy & Management Department International University of Monaco Monte-Carlo Monaco*
Overuse of acronyms	*IMSIA, ENSTA Paris, CNRS, CEA, Inst. Polytechnique de Paris, Palaiseau, France*
Diverse locations	*Deanery of Biomedical Sciences, University of Edinburgh, and TW2Informatics Ltd, Gothenburg, 42166, Sweden.*
Multiple organizations	*Virgen del Rocío University Hospital, Network Centre for Biomedical Research in Mental Health (CIBERSAM), Institute of Biomedicine of Seville (IBiS), University of Seville, First-episode Psychosis Research Network of Andalusia (Red PEPSur).*
Noisy content	*#N##TAB##TAB# California Institute of Technology#N##TAB# (S.W., C.H., J.H.T., M.F., M.G.L., D.E.H., T.E., L.K.)*
Irrelevant content	*emeritus professor of child and adolescent psychiatry at the Academic Medical Center in Amsterdam. Since his retirement (2009), he has been practicing the profession from behind the writing table.*
Missing information	*Faculty of Computer Science*

Table 1: Challenges in affiliation normalization.

Section 2, the problem of affiliation normalization is far from being solved, since most existing methods do not address most of the challenges presented in Table 1 and, there is no standard evaluation data available for the task (Donner et al., 2020; L'Hôte and Jeangirard, 2021).

Our contributions include: i) Providing training and evaluation datasets for affiliation span identification and named entity recognition (NER) subtasks, along with seven entity-linking validation datasets with varying difficulty levels (including multiple institutions, diverse formats, and several languages), and the disambiguated institutions with their ROR identifiers; ii) fine-tuning and evaluating new NER models based on RoBERTa and XLM-RoBERTa for identifying entities in affiliation strings (organizations and their locations); iii) using the entities predicted by our NER models as input for a two-step entity linking module that first retrieves candidate ROR identifiers via an information retrieval system, i.e. Elasticsearch, and then re-ranking them using a quantized generative model; iv) using our datasets to compare our modules' and the full pipeline's performance against existing methods; v) making datasets, code, and models available to the research community.[4] To our knowledge, this is the first effort to provide open, manually annotated data for institution name disambiguation in scientific papers and R&I projects.

2 Related work

Various approaches have been proposed to tackle the disambiguation of institution names, including knowledge- and rule-based approaches, name matching and search techniques, supervised learning, and clustering. Rule-based methods (Jonnalagadda and Topham, 2011; Donner et al., 2020) require great effort to develop and maintain rules and often depend on external sources such as thesauri containing organization names and variants. Although attempts have been made to automate the creation of rules (Shao et al., 2020) it is still challenging to extend rule-based methods to a global scale and to adapt them to growing and changing data. Clustering methods have been proposed in combination of rules to normalise and group name variants (Jonnalagadda and Topham, 2011; Cuxac et al., 2012). However, additional manual cleaning steps are often necessary to obtain reliable results.

L'Hôte and Jeangirard (2021) introduce *affiliation-matcher*, a tool aimed at linking affiliations to different registries of organizations, including ROR and Sirene,[5] using the Elasticsearch search engine[6] to match organization names and locations in affiliations and the destination registries. This approach, however, presents some limitations when information available in affiliation strings is noisy or with significant variations with respect to the data indexed in the registries. The *OpenAlex Institution Parsing*[7] tool also links affiliations strings to ROR institutions, and is the affiliation disambiguation system used in the OpenAlex database (Priem et al., 2022). The authors of this system model the normalization task as an extreme multi-label text classification problem: they propose to use two DistilBERT sequence classification models to predict ROR identifiers trained on synthetic affiliation strings obtained from the OpenAlex and based on different affiliation templates (including, for instance, organization names, aliases, acronyms, cities, regions, and countries). *AffRo*,[8] the affiliation matching algorithm used in OpenAIRE (Manghi et al., 2019), pre-processes affiliation strings in order to identify relevant segments in them and then employs cosine similarity for matching organization names with ROR entries, considering different similarity thresholds for universities and non-university organizations.

[4]Our code, models, and datasets are available at `https://github.com/sirisacademic/affilgood`

[5]Sirene is the "Système National d'identification et Du Répertoire Des Entreprises et de Leurs établissements" available at `https://www.sirene.fr/`

[6]`https://www.elastic.co`

[7]`https://github.com/ourresearch/openalex-institution-parsing`

[8]`https://github.com/openaire/affro`

S2AFF,[9] the affiliations linker module used in Semantic Scholar (Kinney et al., 2023) implements a three-steps method: a NER model first parses raw affiliation strings to extract main and child organizations as well as address components. The identified entities are used to retrieve a set of candidates from a ROR dump, which are then re-ranked by means of a parwise feature-based model, as described in 4.3.1. The main limitation of the S2AFF linker is that it has not been trained to deal with non-English affiliations. Chen et al. (2023) explore the use of a deep learning model to normalize organization names according to closed scholarly knowledge graphs: they classify parts of the affiliation strings as *institutional data* (first level and second level institutions) and *non-institutional data* (for address components) and then apply an institution matching and merging model that uses word embeddings and a set of manually formulated rules for data transformation and processing. The system also includes a relation extraction model to identify hierarchical institutional relationships.

3 Task definition and datasets

In line with previous work in this area (Kinney et al., 2023; Chen et al., 2023), we propose to approach affiliation normalization as a three-step pipeline that includes the following sub-tasks: (1) raw affiliation span identification (3.1), (2) named entity recognition (3.2), and (3) entity linking (3.3). We tackle the obstacle posed by the limited availability of annotated data for these tasks – in particular, for complex and/or multilingual cases – by compiling (creating/or curating and refining) new datasets with which to train and/or evaluate our modules individually, as well as the whole pipeline.

Addressing the unique identification of organizations in affiliation strings as three related subtasks has the additional advantage of allowing more flexibility, as each of the modules can be used independently in different downstream applications.[10]

3.1 Affiliation span identification

Raw affiliation span identification task is aimed at extracting and cleaning affiliation strings when there is noise and/or when there are multiple affiliation strings in the same signature. Typically, multiple institutions have been considered to be separated by semicolons. However, other punctuation marks, spaces or *and* connectors are frequently used to separate affiliations (see Fig 1).

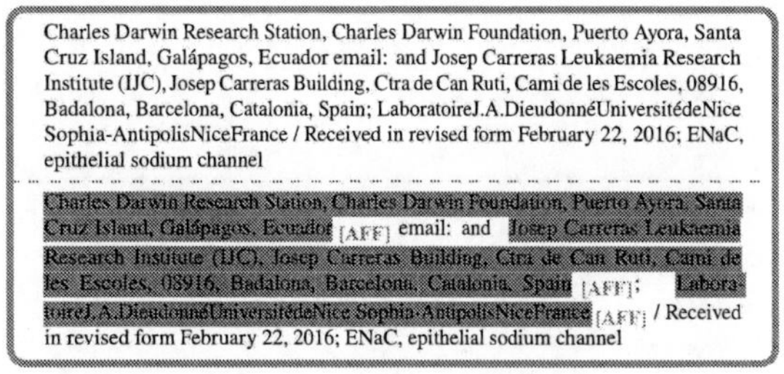

Figure 1: Example of affiliation span identification task from raw strings.

Dataset creation. We have annotated[11] a dataset containing 2,072 raw affiliation strings obtained from OpenAlex to identify spans containing relevant affiliation data within them. The annotated instances were selected by a stratified random sampling by country, focusing on ensuring diversity in affiliation languages and origins. Additional manually-chosen instances with noisy sequences were included in the annotated data so we could train our model to filter out non-affiliation strings. As shown in Fig. 1, it is frequent that affiliation data automatically extracted from PDF files contain texts that should have been discarded (e.g. email, acknowledgements or part of the contents of the publication). These data can introduce errors in the subsequent steps of the pipeline.[12]

3.2 Named entity recognition

Identifying named entities (organization names, cities, countries) in affiliation strings not only enables more effective linking with external organization registries, but it can also play an essential role in the geolocation of organizations and can also contribute to identify organizations and their position in an institutional hierarchy – especially for those not listed in external databases. Information automatically extracted by means of a NER model can also facilitate the construction of knowledge graphs, as suggested by Chen et al. (2023), and support the development of manually curated registries.

After analyzing hundreds of affiliations from multiple countries and languages, we defined seven en-

[9]`https://github.com/allenai/S2AFF`

[10]For instance, the entity linking module can be applied directly to the data sources from where the CORDIS and ETER datasets described in 3.3 are obtained, as they do not require the previous identification of named entities.

[11]For this task a single annotator was in charge of identifying the significant spans in raw strings.

[12]In the example, the string *ENaC* in Figure 1, for instance, could be wrongly assumed to correspond to the acronym of *École Nationale de l'Aviation Civile* in Toulouse, with ROR id `https://ror.org/022zdgq74`.

tity types: SUB-ORGANISATION, ORGANISATION, CITY, COUNTRY, ADDRESS, POSTAL-CODE, and REGION, detailed in Appendix A.

Charles Darwin Research Station, Charles Darwin Foundation, Puerto Ayora, Santa Cruz Island, Galápagos, Ecuador email:

Charles Darwin Research Station [SUB], Charles Darwin Foundation [ORG], Puerto Ayora , Santa Cruz Island [REGION], Galápagos [REGION], Ecuador [COUNTRY] email:

Josep Carreras Leukaemia Research Institute (IJC), Josep Carreras Building, Ctra de Can Ruti, Cami de les Escoles, 08916, Badalona, Barcelona, Catalonia, Spain.

Josep Carreras Leukaemia Research Institute (IJC) [ORG], Josep Carreras Building, Ctra de Can Ruti, Cami de les Escoles [ADDRESS], 08916 [POSTAL], Badalona , Barcelona [REGION], Catalonia [REGION], Spain [COUNTRY].

LaboratoireJ.A.DieudonnéUniversitédeNice Sophia-AntipolisNiceFrance

LaboratoireJ.A.Dieudonné [SUB] UniversitédeNice Sophia-Antipolis [ORG] Nice France [COUNTRY].

Figure 2: Example of entity recognition task.

Dataset creation. The NER dataset contains 5,266 raw affiliation strings obtained from OpenAlex (a superset of those used in 3.1). It includes multilingual samples from all available countries and geographies to ensure comprehensive coverage and diversity. To enable our model to recognize various affiliation string formats, the dataset includes a wide range of structures, different ways of grouping main and subsidiary institutions and various methods of separating organization names. We also included ill-formed affiliations and those containing errors resulting from automatic extraction from PDF files. Two annotators independently annotated different subsets of samples, as well as an overlapping sample of 100 strings, which we used to compute the inter-annotator agreement at token level, obtaining a macro-averaged $F_1 = 0.962$. Fig. 2 shows two examples of the output of the NER model, and Appendix B shows the frequency of each entity in the dataset.

3.3 Entity linking

As mentioned in 1, unambiguously linking organizations mentioned in affiliation strings and research projects is critical to enable accurate analysis of the scientific production of institutions and the collaboration between them. Fig. 3 shows four different examples of what we would expect the output of a system that links organization names to their ROR identifiers would be.

```
Charles Darwin Research Station -> None

Charles Darwin Foundation -> ror.org/01h9g5w38

Josep Carreras Leukaemia Research Institute (IJC) -> ror.org/00btzwk36

LaboratoireJ.A.Dieudonné -> ror.org/0274zdr66

UniversitédeNiceSophia-Antipolis -> ror.org/02k9vew78
```

Figure 3: Example of entity linking task.

Dataset creation. In the context of this work, seven evaluation datasets were developed and/or curated for linking raw affiliation strings to the ROR identifiers of institutions mentioned in them.[13] The datasets are designed to provide a rich coverage of examples with different levels of difficulties, including instances that present several of the challenges described in Table 1. Dataset sizes and sources are presented in Table 2.

Dataset	Source Type	Size	#Orgs/seq.
raw affiliation strings			
Multilingual Affiliations (MA)	Publications	322	0.93
French Affiliations (FA)	Publications	614	3.15
Non Related Multi-orgs (NRMO)	Publications	168	2.82
Mixed Affiliations (S2AFF*)	Publications	635	1.00
pre-segmented entities			
CORDIS	R&I project	3,329	0.83
ETER English (ETERe)	Statistical database	345	0.95
ETER Multilingual (ETERm)	Statistical database	417	0.91

Table 2: Statistics of each entity linking dataset from the raw affiliation strings (top) and pre-segmented entities (bottom). #Orgs/seq.: Avg. number of ROR ids per sequence.

We consider two groups of entity-linking datasets, described below: one group contains raw affiliation strings from scientific publications (MA, FA, NRMO, and S2AFF*), and the other one contains pre-segmented entities from research projects (CORDIS, ETERe, ETERm). The instances in the second group include separate columns for organization names, cities and countries (either country codes or names). The data for the pre-segmented datasets is obtained from UNICS (Gimenez et al., 2018). An example of each dataset is available in Appenix C. Having pre-identified instances allows us to independently evaluate the entity linking component isolating its performance from the errors that can be introduced in the NER module.

For the final pipeline integrating the NER and entity linking modules, we consider the seven datasets. For pre-segmented entities, we join them into a single string with each entity type separated by a colon, the most common format in affiliation strings. Both for the raw affiliation and the pre-segmented datasets, the instances include the manually assigned ROR identifiers with the format:

[13] We used, in all cases, the ROR version 41.

$org\_name_1\{ror\_id_1\}|...|org\_name_n\{ror\_id_n\}$

A strict criterion was applied when assigning gold-standard ROR identifiers: all organizations explicitly mentioned in the affiliation string were included in the list of gold labels, and only those. This means, for example, that assigning an institution the identifier of its parent organization is considered an error, as is an error assigning an institution the identifier of a child organization. Datasets are annotated according to ROR v.41.

Raw affiliation string datasets

- **Multilingual affiliations(MA)**: Manually curated version of a selection of raw affiliations obtained from OpenAlex with `langdetect`[14] for 20 languages[15].
- **French Affiliations (FA)**: Collection of complex French affiliations[16] selected from OpenAlex. Each affiliation was annotated by one annotator and checked/validated by another person.
- **Non-Related Multi-Organizations (NRMO)**: Manually curated version of a selection of raw affiliations obtained from OpenAlex, with non-related organizations in the same string.
- **Mixed Affiliations (S2AFF*)**: Our improved version of the dataset provided by S2AFF,[17] which contains a mix of affiliations from different countries. It was re-annotated according to ROR v.41 by two experts, fixing errors and allowing linking to multiple ROR entries, while the original does not.

Pre-segmented datasets

- **CORDIS**: Organizations involved in EU-funded R&I projects. ROR identifiers were assigned by two annotators. It includes several organizations that are not in ROR. For some organizations, it includes multiple-language versions of their names.
- **ETER English (ETERen)**: English version of organization names in the ETER education statistical registry.[18] ROR identifiers were assigned by two annotators.
- **ETER Multilingual (ETERm)**: Original version of organization names in ETER. ROR identifiers were assigned by two annotators.

4 Methods

As mentioned in 3 we divided the task of linking affiliation strings to ROR identifiers in three subtasks: *affiliation span identification*, *named-entity recognition*, and *entity linking*. In this section we describe the implementation of tools aimed at each of these tasks.

4.1 Adapting language models to raw affiliation strings

For the first two tasks, we fine-tuned two RoBERTa (Liu et al., 2019) and XLM-RoBERTa (Conneau et al., 2019) models for (predominantly) English and multilingual datasets, respectively. Gururangan et al. (2020) show that continuing pre-training language models on task-relevant unlabeled data might contribute to improve the performance of final fine-tuned task-specific models–in particular, in low-resource situations. Considering the fact that the affiliation strings' *grammar* has its own structure, which is different from the one that would be expected to be found in free natural language, we explore whether our affiliation span identification and NER models would benefit from being fine-tuned from models that have been *further pre-trained* on raw affiliation strings for the masked token prediction task.[19] Table 3 reports perplexity on 50k randomly held-out affiliation strings. In what follows, we refer to our adapted models as *AffilRoBERTa*[20] and *AffilXLM*.[21] Hyperparameters used for training are described in Appendix D.

Model	PPL_{base}	PPL_{adapt}
RoBERTa	1.972	1.106
XLM-RoBERTa	1.997	1.101

Table 3: We report masked language modeling loss as perplexity measure (PPL) on 50k randomly sampled held-out raw affiliation strings.

[14] `https://github.com/Mimino666/langdetect`

[15] Languages covered are: fr, de, es, pt, it, id, uk, ca, fa, ko, nl, pl, ro, sw, ru, zh-cn, ar, tr, sv, and ja.

[16] French affiliation strings in scientific papers often feature complex institutional names, including multiple department names, mixed research units, and associated universities, as well as specific terms and abbreviations (CNRS, INSERM, UMR, CHR), special characters, variable formatting, and language mixing.

[17] `https://github.com/allenai/S2AFF`

[18] `https://eter-project.com/`

[19] Further pre-trained on 10 million random raw affiliation strings from OpenAlex.

[20] Available at `https://huggingface.co/SIRIS-Lab/affilgood-AffilRoBERTa`

[21] Available at `https://huggingface.co/SIRIS-Lab/affilgood-AffilXLM`

4.2 Affiliation span and NER models

Both for span identification and entity recognition tasks, we fine-tuned the adapted and base models for token classification with the IOB annotation schema. We trained the models for 25 epochs, using 80% of the dataset for training, 10% for validation and 10% for testing. Hyperparameters used for training are described in Appendix D. The best performing epoch (considering macro-averaged F1 with *strict* matching criteria) was used to select the model.

4.3 Entity linking module

The entity linking module is aimed for associating identified organizations in affiliation strings (pre-identified or obtained from the NER step) with their corresponding ROR identifiers. In developing this module we consider the possibility of affiliation strings containing references to multiple ROR organizations as well as containing none (either because there are no organizations identified in the affiliation string or because the organizations are not included in ROR). Considering the list of entities previously obtained by means of the NER, in this module we first apply a set of heuristics to group named entities into single-organization affiliations.[22] Second, we determine the corresponding ROR identifier for each grouping (or *none* if no reliable match is found). For example, from the raw affiliation string: *Telethon Kids Institute, School of Physiotherapy and Exercise Science, Curtin University, Centre for Child Health, University of Western Australia, Perth, Australia*, we consider the following list of five potential affiliations:

- *Telethon Kids Institute, Perth, Australia*
- *School of Physiotherapy and Exercise Science, Curtin University, Perth, Australia*
- *Curtin University, Perth, Australia*
- *Centre for Child Health, University of Western Australia, Perth, Australia*
- *University of Western Australia, Perth, Australia*

We implement and evaluate three linking methods for each of the groupings obtained as described above: (i) S2AFF linker, (ii) Elasticsearch with no re-ranking, and (iii) Elasticsearch followed by a re-ranking step performed by means of a quantized generative model.

4.3.1 S2AFF linker

The entity linking component of the S2AFF package[23] involves two steps. First, a candidate-retrieval module extracts potential ROR identifiers from a ROR dump[24] by calculating n-gram and token Jaccard similarities between the affiliation string and ROR entries. This list of candidate ROR identifiers and their scores is then passed to a second module, which re-ranks the top N candidates using a trained LightGBM model. The top-ranked candidate from this step is considered the corresponding ROR id. A threshold of 0.20 is set as the minimum score for a reliable match.

4.3.2 Elasticsearch with no re-ranking

Entity linking is often modeled as an information retrieval task using full-text search engines like Apache Solr[25] and Elasticsearch,[26] leveraging their text matching and relevance ranking capabilities (L'Hôte and Jeangirard, 2021). We implemented an Elasticsearch-based entity linker by first indexing the ROR dump in Elasticsearch. During indexing, we enriched organization names and aliases from ROR with Wikidata[27] labels in English and local languages.[28]

The linking component uses queries that consider the organization's name (and its parent if it's a sub-organization) and location (city, region, and/or country). Multiple matching strategies are combined for organization names, including exact, fuzzy, and shingle-based matches. To discard unlikely matches, we set thresholds of 70 for Elasticsearch scores when linking a main organization and 200 for a sub-organization. The thresholds were determined by analyzing the distribution of Elasticsearch scores with a subset of 50 random instances.

4.3.3 Elasticsearch and generative model

As a third alternative for the entity linking component, we included a re-ranking step when the Elasticsearch scores of the top candidate and other retrieved ROR entries were similar. We assumed the top-ranked candidate to be correct if its score was at least three times that of the second candidate. Otherwise, we considered up to five candidates

[22]For instance, when a sub-organization is found, we group it with the first organization to its right, which is considered as the parent.

[23]See `https://github.com/allenai/S2AFF`.

[24]For our experiments we used the same ROR dump used in the other methods for a reliable comparison of the results.

[25]`https://solr.apache.org/`

[26]`https://www.elastic.co/`

[27]`https://www.wikidata.org`

[28]*E.g.*, for organizations in Spain, we indexed labels in Catalan, English, Euskera, Galego, and Spanish.

and used a generative model to determine the best match for the affiliation string.[29] For this, we used a quantized (4.16 GB) version[30] of Intel's Neural Chat model,[31] a fine-tuned version of the Mistral 7B model (Jiang et al., 2023).[32]

5 Results and discussion

In this section we report the results obtained by each of the three modules (span identification, NER, and entity linking) as well as the integration of the NER and entity linking components, and we compare them to baselines and other existing systems. We have not included the span identification task as part of the pipeline, because as our evaluation datasets contain few examples in which affiliation spans do not cover the whole raw affiliation string, we would obtain limited information to properly conduct an extrinsic evaluation of this modules' performance.

5.1 Raw affiliation span identification

Table 4 shows the results obtained for the affiliation span identification task with the base RoBERTa and XLM-RoBERTa models as well as with the adapted models AffilRoBERTa[33] and AffilXLM[34], obtained with the *further pre-training* strategy described in 4. We report the results obtained when considering both *exact* and *partial* matching criteria for the affiliation spans.[35]

Model	Exact F1	Partial F1
Semicolon split (baseline)	.793	.907
RoBERTa	.929	.981
XLM	.931	.978
AffilRoBERTa	**.938**	**.981**
AffilXLM	.927	.979

Table 4: *Exact* and *partial* F1 scores for raw affiliation span identification.

We observe that there is a gain–of .145 F1-points for the best-performing model with *exact* match–when predicting the affiliation spans by means of the fine-tuned models over the *naive* strategy used as baseline, while the adapted models obtained with the *further pre-training* strategy present a marginal gain with respect of the base models in the best validation epoch.

5.2 NER

Table 5 shows the performance of the NER model considering *strict* matching criteria.[36] We observe that there is a gain F1-points for the best-performing with adapted models. Adapted XLM-RoBERTa[37] achieves the best *strict* F1, and obtains the best result in four of the seven categories, however, adapted RoBERTa[38] also perform competitive results, specially in three of the categories. When we consider the evolution of the validation loss we observe that there is a considerable advantage of the adapted models in the initial fine-tuning epochs, but this distance is reduced in the final epochs. This indicates that the base models also learn to correctly identify the particular structure of the *affiliations' language* over time.

Category	RoBERTa	XLM	AffilRoBERTa	AffilXLM
ALL	.910	.915	.920	**.925**
ORG	.869	.886	.879	**.906**
SUB	.898	.890	**.911**	.892
CITY	.936	.941	.950	**.958**
COUNTRY	.971	.973	**.980**	.970
REGION	.870	.876	.874	**.882**
POSTAL	.975	.975	**.981**	.966
ADDRESS	.804	.811	.794	**.869**

Table 5: NER evaluation (*strict*). F1-score.

5.3 Entity Linking on pre-segmented datasets

Table 6 shows macro-averaged F1 scores obtained for the entity linking task evaluated on the pre-segmented datasets.

Method	CORDIS	ETERe	ETERm
$S2AFF_{Linker}$[39]	.837	.858	.834
Elasticsearch (top-ranked)	.825	.862	.861
Elasticsearch + qLLM	**.884**	**.914**	**.922**

Table 6: Entity linking results. F1 score.

Note that these metrics are not directly comparable to the ones reported for the full pipeline in Table 7 as the latter refers to example-based metrics in a multi-label context while in the results in Table 6 consider a single predicted identifier (or *none*).

[29]The prompt is included as supplementary material.
[30]neural-chat-7B-v3-2-GPTQ
[31]neural-chat-7b-v3-2
[32]Mistral-7B-v0.1
[33]Available at https://huggingface.co/SIRIS-Lab/affilgood-span
[34]Available at https://huggingface.co/SIRIS-Lab/affilgood-span-multilingual
[35]An *exact* match is considered when the boundaries match exactly, while *partial* matches require partial boundary match over the surface strings in the predicted and gold entities (Batista and Upson, 2020).

[36]A *strict* match is considered when both the boundaries and types of the entities match (Segura-Bedmar et al., 2013).
[37]Available at https://huggingface.co/SIRIS-Lab/affilgood-NER-multilingual
[38]Available at https://huggingface.co/SIRIS-Lab/affilgood-NER
[39]https://github.com/allenai/S2AFF
[40]https://github.com/ourresearch/openalex-institution-parsing
[41]https://github.com/allenai/S2AFF
[42]https://github.com/openaire/affro

	Raw affiliation strings				Pre-segmented		
Model	MA	FA	NRMO	S2AFF*	CORDIS	ETERe	ETERm
ElasticSearch	.545	.407	.470	.515	.751	.855	.847
OpenAlex[40]	.394	.118	.769	**.871**	.648	.859	.852
S2AFF[41]	.546	.367	.617	.785	.649	.668	.720
AffRo[42]	.452	.408	.558	.726	.641	.709	.617
AffilGoodNERm + $S2AFF_{Linker}$	.596	.685	.762	.841	.827	.887	.863
AffilGoodNER + $S2AFF_{Linker}$	.579	.685	.758	.850	.839	.895	.855
AffilGoodNERm + Elastic	.690	.587	.747	.640	.849	.887	.894
AffilGoodNER + Elastic	.649	.610	.755	.648	.855	.893	.881
AffilGoodNERm + Elastic+qLLM	**.710**	.721	**.774**	.790	.881	**.936**	**.916**
AffilGoodNER + Elastic+qLLM	.653	**.747**	.767	.799	**.891**	**.936**	.909

Table 7: Pipeline (NER+EL) results, evaluated by example-based F1-score. AffilGoodNERm correspond to the best-performing fine-tuned NER model with adapted XLM-RoBERTa, and AffilGoodNER, to the best with adapted English RoBERTa. Entities in pre-segmented datasets have concatenated with coma-separator. Disclaimer: we cannot guarantee that any of the baseline systems, such as OpenAlex or S2AFF, used samples from the original version of the S2AFF dataset for training, since it is open.

5.4 NER + Entity Linking pipelines

Table 7 shows example-based F1 scores for four openly available systems and our proposed NER + entity linking pipelines. This includes our two NER models for identifying organization names and locations, combined with the S2AFF entity linking module. Additionally, it includes our proposed system with an Elasticsearch candidate retrieval stage followed by a re-ranking step using a zero-shot quantized generative model, as described in 4.3.3. Appendix 5.3 shows macro-averaged F1 scores obtained for only the entity linking task evaluated on the pre-segmented datasets.

The obtained results show that the multilingual NER model AffilXLM-NER performs better on datasets containing affiliations in multiple languages (MA and ETERm). It can also be observed that the proposed two-step method based on Elasticsearch text matching coupled with a generative re-ranking stage consistently perform well across datasets, indicating their effectiveness in handling diverse affiliation strings and improving linking accuracy. This is particularly clear in the case of complex French affiliations (FA). It can also be observed that both the RoBERTa and XLM-based NER models fine-tuned with our NER dataset contribute to the performance of the whole pipeline. This is made evident when comparing the performance of the full S2AFF pipeline with the performance of the systems obtained when replacing the S2AFF NER with our models and keeping the S2AFF entity linker. The gain is more evident in the case of the difficult French examples, in which our NER models combined with the S2AFF linker obtain a percentage gain of 87% in terms of macro-averaged F1-score over the S2AFF full pipeline.

6 Conclusions

In this work, we have introduced the AffilGood institution name disambiguation framework, including two different datasets for information extraction from raw affiliation strings, and a collection of seven entity linking datasets connecting organizations mentioned in affiliation strings and/or research projects to ROR identifiers. We benchmark our entity linking datasets with openly available institution name disambiguation systems. Finally, we propose a flexible and multilingual multistep pipeline based on a named-entity recognition model and an entity linking module. The obtained results confirm the quality of the contributed datasets and the validity of the proposed systems to address some of the most difficult challenges in the institution name disambiguation task, including noisy and incomplete input data, affiliations in languages other than English and/or with mixed languages, and complex affiliations including diverse types of institutions – companies, universities, hospital, research centers – in different hierarchical levels. To facilitate reproducibility and promote future research in this area we make available all the data and systems developed in the context of this work.

Acknowledgements

Supported by the Industrial Doctorates Plan of the Department of Research and Universities of the Generalitat de Catalunya, by Departament de Recerca i Universitats de la Generalitat de Catalunya (ajuts SGR-Cat 2021), and by Maria de Maeztu Units of Excellence Programme CEX2021-001195-M, funded by MCIN/AEI /10.13039/501100011033. This work was co-funded by the EU HORIZON SciLake (Grant Agreement 101058573). The work of P. Przybyła is part of the ERINIA project, which has received funding from the European Union's Horizon Europe research and innovation programme under grant agreement No 101060930. Views and opinions expressed are however those of the author(s) only and do not necessarily reflect those of the funders. Neither the European Union nor the granting authority can be held responsible for them.

We thank Nees Jan van Eck and Martijn Visser from the Centre for Science and Technology Studies (CWTS) at Leiden University for providing relevant raw affiliation strings from OpenAlex for compiling the FA and NRMO entity linking evaluation datasets. We thank Justin Barrett from OurResearch for the help in executing the predictions of OpenAlex Institution Parser model, reported in Table 6.

References

David Batista and Matthew Antony Upson. 2020. nervaluate.

Yifei Chen, Xiaoying Li, Aihua Li, Y. Li, Xuemei Yang, Ziluo Lin, Shirui Yu, and Xiaoli Tang. 2023. A deep learning model for the normalization of institution names by multisource literature feature fusion: Algorithm development study. *JMIR Formative Research*, 7.

Alexis Conneau, Kartikay Khandelwal, Naman Goyal, Vishrav Chaudhary, Guillaume Wenzek, Francisco Guzmán, Edouard Grave, Myle Ott, Luke Zettlemoyer, and Veselin Stoyanov. 2019. Unsupervised cross-lingual representation learning at scale. *arXiv preprint arXiv:1911.02116*.

Pascal Cuxac, Jean-Charles Lamirel, and Valerie Bonvallot. 2012. Efficient supervised and semi-supervised approaches for affiliations disambiguation. *Scientometrics*, 97:47 – 58.

Paul Donner, Christine Rimmert, and Nees Jan van Eck. 2020. Comparing institutional-level bibliometric research performance indicator values based on different affiliation disambiguation systems. *Quantitative Science Studies*, 1(1):150–170.

Enric Fuster, Tatiana Fernández, Hermes Carretero, Nicolau Duran-Silva, Roger Guixé, Josep Pujol-Llatse, Bernardo Rondelli, Guillem Rull, Marta Cortijo, and Montserrat Romagosa. 2023. Towards building a monitoring platform for a challenge-oriented smart specialisation with ris3-mcat. *27th International Conference on Science, Technology and Innovation Indicators (STI 2023)*, abs/2401.10900.

Enric Fuster, Elisabetta Marinelli, Sabine Plaud, Arnau Quinquilla, and Francesco Massucci. 2020. Open data, open science & open innovation for smart specialisation monitoring. Technical report, Joint Research Centre (Seville site).

Xavi Gimenez, Alessandro Mosca, Fernando Roda, Bernardo Rondelli, and Guillem Rull. 2018. Unics: The open data platform for research and innovation? In *Proceedings of the Posters and Demos Track of the 14th International Conference on Semantic Systemsco-located with the 14th International Conference on Semantic Systems (SEMANTiCS 2018)*, volume 2198. CEUR-WS.

Suchin Gururangan, Ana Marasović, Swabha Swayamdipta, Kyle Lo, Iz Beltagy, Doug Downey, and Noah A. Smith. 2020. Don't stop pretraining: Adapt language models to domains and tasks.

Ginny Hendricks, Dominika Tkaczyk, Jennifer Lin, and Patricia Feeney. 2020. Crossref: The sustainable source of community-owned scholarly metadata. *Quantitative Science Studies*, 1(1):414–427.

Shuiqing Huang, Bo Yang, Sulan Yan, and Ronald Rousseau. 2014. Institution name disambiguation for research assessment. *Scientometrics*, 99:823–838.

Albert Q Jiang, Alexandre Sablayrolles, Arthur Mensch, Chris Bamford, Devendra Singh Chaplot, Diego de las Casas, Florian Bressand, Gianna Lengyel, Guillaume Lample, Lucile Saulnier, et al. 2023. Mistral 7b. *arXiv preprint arXiv:2310.06825*.

Siddhartha R. Jonnalagadda and Philip Topham. 2011. Nemo: Extraction and normalization of organization names from pubmed affiliation strings. *ArXiv*, abs/1107.5743.

Rodney Michael Kinney, Chloe Anastasiades, Russell Authur, Iz Beltagy, Jonathan Bragg, Alexandra Buraczynski, Isabel Cachola, Stefan Candra, Yoganand Chandrasekhar, Arman Cohan, Miles Crawford, Doug Downey, Jason Dunkelberger, Oren Etzioni, Rob Evans, Sergey Feldman, Joseph Gorney, David W. Graham, F.Q. Hu, Regan Huff, Daniel King, Sebastian Kohlmeier, Bailey Kuehl, Michael Langan, Daniel Lin, Haokun Liu, Kyle Lo, Jaron Lochner, Kelsey MacMillan, Tyler Murray, Christopher Newell, Smita R Rao, Shaurya Rohatgi, Paul Sayre, Zejiang Shen, Amanpreet Singh, Luca Soldaini, Shivashankar Subramanian, A. Tanaka, Alex D Wade, Linda M. Wagner, Lucy Lu Wang, Christopher Wilhelm, Caroline Wu, Jiangjiang Yang, Angele Zamarron, Madeleine van Zuylen, and Daniel S. Weld. 2023. The semantic scholar open data platform. *ArXiv*, abs/2301.10140.

Anne L'Hôte and Eric Jeangirard. 2021. Using elasticsearch for entity recognition in affiliation disambiguation.

Yinhan Liu, Myle Ott, Naman Goyal, Jingfei Du, Mandar Joshi, Danqi Chen, Omer Levy, Mike Lewis, Luke Zettlemoyer, and Veselin Stoyanov. 2019. Roberta: A robustly optimized bert pretraining approach. *arXiv preprint arXiv:1907.11692*.

Paolo Manghi, Alessia Bardi, Claudio Atzori, Miriam Baglioni, Natalia Manola, Jochen Schirrwagen, and

Pedro Príncipe. 2019. The openaire research graph data model.

Jason Priem, Heather A. Piwowar, and Richard Orr. 2022. Openalex: A fully-open index of scholarly works, authors, venues, institutions, and concepts. *ArXiv*, abs/2205.01833.

Philip J. Purnell. 2022. The prevalence and impact of university affiliation discrepancies between four bibliographic databases—scopus, web of science, dimensions, and microsoft academic. *Quantitative Science Studies*, 3(1):99–121.

Isabel Segura-Bedmar, Paloma Martínez, and María Herrero-Zazo. 2013. SemEval-2013 task 9 : Extraction of drug-drug interactions from biomedical texts (DDIExtraction 2013). In *Second Joint Conference on Lexical and Computational Semantics (*SEM), Volume 2: Proceedings of the Seventh International Workshop on Semantic Evaluation (SemEval 2013)*, pages 341–350, Atlanta, Georgia, USA. Association for Computational Linguistics.

Zhou Shao, Xiangying Cao, Sha Yuan, and Yongli Wang. 2020. Elad: An entity linking based affiliation disambiguation framework. *IEEE Access*, 8:70519–70526.

Max Wilkinson. 2010. Datacite: The international data citation initiative: Datasets programme.

A Annotation Guidelines

Annotation guidelines are available at `https://github.com/sirisacademic/affilgood`.

B NER dataset description

Table 8 shows number occurrences of each category in the whole dataset, included in the 5266 sequences.

Category	#Occurences
SUB	4,708
ORG	6,200
CITY	4,023
COUNTRY	4,157
REGION	1,024
POSTALCODE	1,424
ADDRESS	788
Total	2,2324

Table 8: Number of occurrences of named entities in our NER dataset.

C Examples of datasets

Table 9 shows a sequence of each of the seven entity linking datasets.

Dataset	Example
MA	*Fakultas Bisnis Universitas Kristen Duta Wacana#N#Jl. Dr. Wihidin Sudiro Husodo 5 - 25, Yogyakarta, 55224*
FA	*Inserm UMR 1011, Department of Cardiovascular Radiology, EGID (European Genomic Institute for Diabetes), université de Lille, Institut Cœur-Poumon, Institut Pasteur de Lille, CHU de Lille, FR3508, 59000 Lille, France*
NRMO	*EMBL Australia Node in Single Molecule Science, School of Medical Sciences, University of New South Wales, Sydney, Australia.*
S2AFF*	*Andrews Univ, Berrien Springs, MI;*
CORDIS	*ZENTRAL-UND LANDESBIBLIOTHEK BERLIN, BERLIN, DE*
ETERe	*University of Applied Sciences Schmalkalden*
ETERm	*Hochschule Schmmalkalden*

Table 9: Examples of sequences in each entity linking datasets.

D Experimental setup

We provide experiental detais of our baseline fine-tuning approaches. For all *futher-pretraining* and *fine-tuning*, we make use of the `huggingface` library. Training was run (using 1x NVIDIA A100 GPU) for all models with hyperparameter defined in Table 10 and Table 11.

Hyperparameter	Value
Learning Rate	2e-5
Learning Rate Decay	Linear
Weight Decay	0.01
Warmup Portion	0.06
Batch Size	128
Num. of steps	25k steps
Adam ϵ	1e-6
Adam β_1	0.9
Adam β_2	0.999

Table 10: Hyperparameters for adaptive pre-training to raw affiliation strings.

Hyperparameter	Value
Learning Rate	2e-5
Learning Rate Decay	Linear
Weight Decay	0.01
Batch Size	16
Max. Num. of Epochs	25

Table 11: Hyperparameters for fine-tuning NER.

Metadata Enhancement Using Large Language Models

Hyunju Song, Steven Bethard, Andrea K. Thomer
University of Arizona
{hyunjusong,bethard,athomer}@arizona.edu

Abstract

In the natural sciences, a common form of scholarly document is a *physical sample record*, which provides categorical and textual metadata for specimens collected and analyzed for scientific research. Physical sample archives like museums and repositories publish these records in data repositories to support reproducible science and enable the discovery of physical samples. However, the success of resource discovery in such interfaces depends on the completeness of the sample records. We investigate approaches for automatically completing the scientific metadata fields of sample records. We apply large language models in zero and few-shot settings and incorporate the hierarchical structure of the taxonomy. We show that a combination of record summarization, bottom-up taxonomy traversal, and few-shot prompting yield an F1 score as high as 0.928 on metadata completion in the Earth science domain.

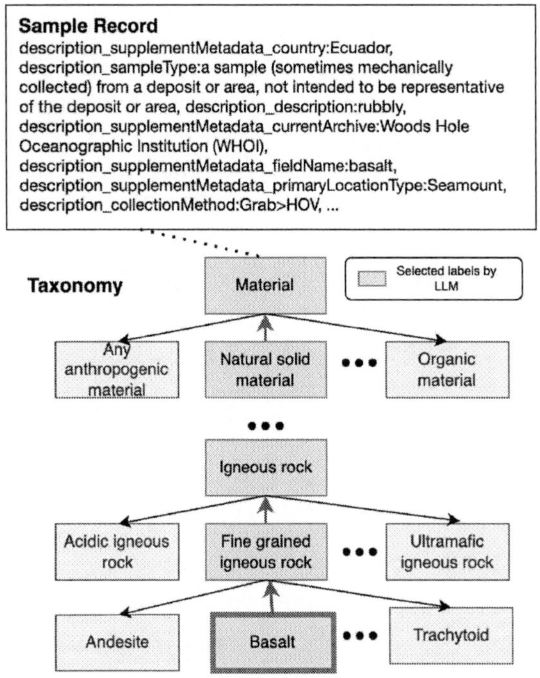

Figure 1: An illustration of our automatic metadata assignment workflow utilizing text classification with LLMs. The example record MATERIAL metadata field is predicted as result of tree traversal done on the taxonomy in a bottom-up manner.

1 Introduction

Not all scholarly documents are formal scientific articles. In the natural sciences (e.g. Earth science, biodiversity science, archaeology), a common form of scholarly document is a *physical sample record*. Also called *catalog records* or *specimen records*, sample records are documents written by scientists that describe samples (for instance, fossils, soil samples, sediment cores, etc.) collected and analyzed for scientific research. Since the 1980s, millions of dollars of grant funds have been dedicated to projects digitizing and sharing physical sample records through online data repositories (Nelson and Ellis, 2018; com, 2020). The specific contents of records varies by domain, but they typically contain metadata describing the type, material, and provenance of samples. Sample records are needed to find and reuse physical samples, and, when aggregated, can be treated as a scientific dataset in and of themselves. For instance, aggregated biodiversity sample records are frequently used for studies of global change biology (Heberling et al., 2021). Thus, the quality of these scholarly documents is crucial.

Sample record metadata may be incomplete for a variety of reasons, including data entry issues or schema mismatches when sample records are aggregated across different repositories. For example, among the sample records that describe the resources registered in the System for Earth Sample Registration (SESAR2) data repository[1] (Fig 2), 78% of the records, totaling 3,565,478

[1] https://www.geosamples.org/

Proceedings of the Fourth Workshop on Scholarly Document Processing (SDP 2024), pages 145–154
August 16, 2024 ©2024 Association for Computational Linguistics

records, exhibited missing values in the MATERIAL metadata field. Automatic metadata assignment has consequently emerged as a critical task in the processing of sample records and other metadata aggregations. For instance, some data repositories automatically assign geocoordinates and higher geographic classifications based on text-based locality descriptions using rules-based workflows (Chapman and Wieczorek, 2020). Other approaches to inferring missing categorical fields often represent metadata fields as vectors and utilized classifiers to fill in missing values from a controlled vocabulary (Han et al., 2003; Paynter, 2005).

Figure 2: An example of a physical sample record from SESAR2.

Often sample records contain many text fields that can be used to predict or infer missing values; thus, we approach automatic metadata assignment as a taxonomy-driven text classification problem. We propose a solution for metadata assignment based on large language models (LLMs) (fig. 1).

Our contributions are as follows:

- We compare zero and few-shot LLM formulations of the problem with competitive baselines like fine-tuning RoBERTa.
- We study different strategies to incorporate the taxonomy's hierarchy and show that a bottom-up approach is especially effective.
- We demonstrate that prompting LLMs to first summarize the sample record and then classify using the summary can sometimes outperform prompting LLMs to classify directly from the sample record.

Our evaluation focuses on sample records from the Earth science domain, though our approaches are general enough to be applied to many other domains. Our findings suggest that LLMs could provide a viable solution for digital libraries or aggregations facing missing metadata issues.

2 Related Work

Metadata Enhancement in Digital Libraries A common challenge in digital libraries or metadata aggregations is the "missing data" problem (Dushay and Hillmann, 2003). To tackle this issue, various automatic metadata assignment approaches including machine learning techniques have been employed. Paynter (2005); Tonkin and Muller (2008) used classification methods to automatically assign metadata values. Unlike these supervised learning methods, our approach employs LLMs with zero or few-shot samples to offer a more domain-agnostic solution.

LLMs for Text Classification With the advancement of larger-scale pre-trained language models trained on vast unlabeled corpora, approaches that utilize language models with instructions (zero-shot) and task-related examples directly in the prompt (few-shot) have been used. Prompting methods (Kojima et al., 2022; Wei et al., 2022) and domain-specific LLMs (Singhal et al., 2022; Taylor et al., 2022) have been investigated for text classification. Our work explores text classification with LLMs to assign metadata values.

Hierarchical Multi-Label Text Classification The task of assigning multiple hierarchically structured categories to a text is known as hierarchical multi-label text classification. Various methods have been explored to encode the hierarchical nature of the label space, including level-wise attention-based recurrent networks (Huang et al., 2019), graph convolutional networks (Xu et al., 2021), and LLMs with tree search strategies (Boyle et al., 2023). We also apply tree search strategies to LLMs, exploring both top-down and bottom-up approaches, which we find to be much more successful in our data.

3 Dataset

We are working with physical sample records from the Internet of Samples (iSamples) project, which aggregates physical sample metadata records from data repositories within the domains of Earth science, bioscience, and archaeology (Davies et al., 2021). To aggregate these records, iSamples developed a common metadata schema and controlled vocabularies for the MATERIAL and OBJECT TYPE fields of each sample record (Richard et al., 2024), to which each repository's records are crosswalked. This makes it possible to easily search across a diverse range of records within the iSamples interface. The MATERIAL and OBJECT TYPE fields are used as two primary facets in the search interface.

Here, we focus on records from SESAR2, which describe specimens from the Earth science domain, encompassing rocks, fossils, fluids, and other materials registered. A substantial portion of these records contains missing values in the MATERIAL field, which negatively impacts the discoverability within both iSamples and SESAR2. However, the records contain other metadata which can be used to infer the MATERIAL type.

To frame this as a text classification dataset, for each sample record, we construct the output from the metadata field to be predicted, and construct the input from all other available metadata fields. In section 4 we explore various ways of concatenating the many metadata fields into a single text for input, but in all cases, we include the following text in the text classification prompt:

```
You are a scientist. Your task is
to analyze the description of a material
sample and determine the kind of material
that constitutes it after <<<>>> into one
of the predefined material types:
{taxonomy}
You will only respond with the material
type. Do not include the word Material
type. Do not provide explanations or
notes.
###
<<<
Description: {text}
Material type:
>>>
```

where the *taxonomy* is a list of possible labels in the taxonomy to predict and the *text* is the input constructed from metadata fields. For the output, we use a multi-label formulation that includes all appropriate labels within the taxonomy. For example, if a sample should be labeled as BASALT, then it should also be labeled as ROCK since BASALT is a type of ROCK in the iSamples taxonomy (Figure 3). For evaluation on this multi-label dataset, we use the macro F1 score.

For our training and testing purposes, we utilized the 988,426 (22%) of records that contained the MATERIAL field value. Due to the dataset's highly imbalanced nature, we randomly selected and discarded sample records such that the maximum occurrence of a label could be 10,000, while ensuring that each label appeared at least 10 times in the entire dataset. As a result, the training dataset contained 294,420 records, the development dataset contained 63,090 records, and the test dataset contained 63,091 records. For the test dataset, we focused solely on labels that appeared at least 10 times and records that was annotated up to the leaf level to estimate performance of our experiments. The number of tokens in fields of these records is listed in Appendix A.

4 Experiments

We explore three LLMs for our multi-label text classification formulation of the metadata assignment problem: Llama-2-7B-chat-hf, Mistral-7B-Instruct, and Mistral-7B-OpenOrca. Using these models, we explore the following research questions:

1. How do different record-to-text conversions affect performance?

2. Is it useful to have an LLM summarize the record text?

3. Is top-down or bottom-up search better for incorporating the label hierarchy?

4. How much can few-shot prompting improve over zero-shot prompting?

To address each of these questions, we utilize the test dataset for evaluation purposes. Our findings indicate that the bottom-up search approach is the most effective for integrating the label hierarchy, and thus, we apply this method when conducting experiments for the first two questions. The following sections detail the experiments conducted to answer each of these research questions.

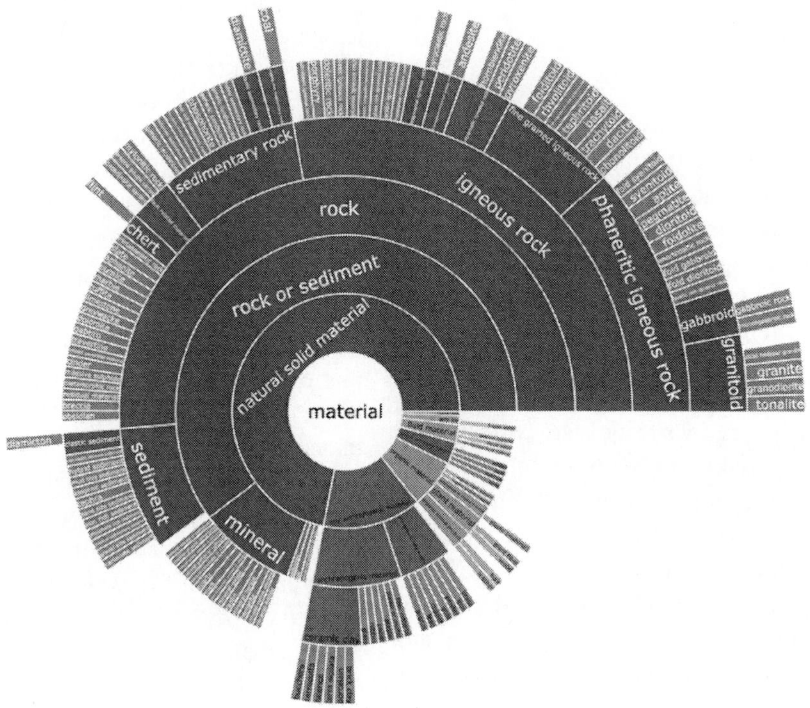

Figure 3: iSamples MATERIAL type taxonomy

Selected values	Input
Metadata field values	long cylindrical cores, Ship, Lamont-Doherty Core Repository at Columbia University (LDCR), ...
Metadata field name and value	description_sampleType is long cylindrical cores, description_supplementMetadata_platformType is Ship, description_supplementMetadata_currentArchive is Lamont-Doherty Core Repository at Columbia University (LDCR), ...
Metadata field description and value	The object type of sample is long cylindrical cores, The type of platform for the cruise is Ship, The name of institution, museum, or repository where the sample is currently stored is Lamont-Doherty Core Repository at Columbia University (LDCR), ...

Table 1: An example of different methods to generate the input for the language model.

4.1 How do different record-to-text conversions affect performance?

There are many possible ways to transform a sample record into an input for text classification. We compare the following approaches to create the input text, with examples of each shown in table 1.

Field value: We include only the values of the metadata fields.

Field name and value: For each metadata field, we include the field name, then the string " is ", then the field value.

Field description and value: The same as *Field name and value*, but instead of the field name, we include the description of the field name obtained from the SESAR collection website.

Table 2 shows the results of varying the text conversion strategy. We observe that using the metadata field description and value is the most effective across all three LLMs. This suggests that LLMs are more effective text classifiers when given a more verbose input that looks more like natural language text.

Model	Selected values	F1
Llama-7B-chat-hf	Field values	0.342
Llama-7B-chat-hf	Field name and value	0.365
Llama-7B-chat-hf	Field description and value	**0.370**
Mistral-7B-Instruct	Field values	0.377
Mistral-7B-Instruct	Field name and value	0.374
Mistral-7B-Instruct	Field description and value	**0.379**
Mistral-7B-OpenOrca	Field values	0.397
Mistral-7B-OpenOrca	Field name and value	**0.427**
Mistral-7B-OpenOrca	Field description and value	0.405

Table 2: Comparison of different methods to generate the text used as input for text classification applied to the Bottom-Up Tree Search with Zero-Shot Learning. Best performing method is in bold. Macro F1 is used for evaluation.

4.2 Is it useful to have an LLM summarize the record text?

We also explore an alternative approach to formulate the input to the LLM, by considering the LLM as a summarizer with noisy knowledge. In this approach, given the description and value of the metadata fields of the sample record, we instruct the LLM to generate a summary with a focus on the text portion relevant to the metadata field that is to be predicted. As the sample record may contain metadata fields with domain-specific terms, we also instruct the LLM to provide explanations for these metadata fields. The prompt that is used to generate the summary is as follows:

```
You are a scientist. User will give you a
description of a material sample it
sampled from the nature. You must generate
a summarized description of the sample.
Your task is to give a brief one sentence
summary of the given description, focusing
on the parts that are helpful in determining
the type of material that constitutes it.
###
<<<
Description: {text}
>>>
```

This summary is enriched with the explanation of metadata fields that is generated by the following prompt:

```
You are a scientist. User will give you
a term that indicates {metdata field
description}. You must generate a short
description of the term. Your task is to
give a brief one sentence description of
the given {metadata field} of the sample.
###
<<<
Term:{term}
>>>
```

Model	Model Input	F1
Llama-7B-chat-hf	Original description	0.370
Llama-7B-chat-hf	Summary + Explanation	0.428
Mistral-7B-Instruct	Original description	0.379
Mistral-7B-Instruct	Summary + Explanation	0.385
Mistral-7B-OpenOrca	Original description	0.405
Mistral-7B-OpenOrca	Summary + Explanation	0.439

Table 3: Result of Zero-Shot Classification with Summarize&Explain applied to the Bottom-up Tree Search. Macro F1 is used for evaluation.

This enriched summary is then used as the input to the LLM text classification prompt.

Table 3 shows the results of this experiment. We see that summarizing and explaining the sample record improves performance for all models, though it benefits Llama the most. This suggests that allowing the LLM to discard redundant or irrelevant metadata fields and provide an explanation of domain specific terms can make the text classification task easier for the LLM.

4.3 Is top-down or bottom-up search better for incorporating the label hierarchy?

We explored different approaches to utilizing the hierarchical label space:

Flat Disregard the hierarchy and treat the task as a flat multi-label classification problem. We include the entire label space in the prompt, expecting the model to return multiple labels for each physical sample record.

Top-Down Tree Search Follow the approach of Boyle et al. (2023), where predictions are made starting from the root of the hierarchy and recursively making new predictions over the children at each level of the hierarchical tree. The label space at each level is restricted to the children of the current node. The recursive process continues until the leaf level is reached.

Bottom-Up Tree Search Predictions are made starting from the leaf level, predict higher-level labels only if no valid prediction is found.

Table 4 shows the results of varying the strategy for handling hierarchical labels. We see that applying Bottom-Up Tree Search is effective across all LLMs. At the same time, Top-Down Tree Search

Model	Tree Search Strategy	F1
Majority Baseline	-	0.123
Llama-7B-chat-hf	Flat	0.154
Llama-7B-chat-hf	Top-Down Tree Search	0.114
Llama-7B-chat-hf	Bottom-Up Tree Search	0.370
Mistral-7B-Instruct	Flat	0.167
Mistral-7B-Instruct	Top-Down Tree Search	0.175
Mistral-7B-Instruct	Bottom-Up Tree Search	0.379
Mistral-7B-OpenOrca	Flat	0.241
Mistral-7B-OpenOrca	Top-Down Tree Search	0.238
Mistral-7B-OpenOrca	Bottom-Up Tree Search	0.405

Table 4: Result of Zero-Shot Classification with different Tree search strategies. Flat treats the task as a multi-label classification problem without considering label hierarchy. Macro F1 is used for evaluation.

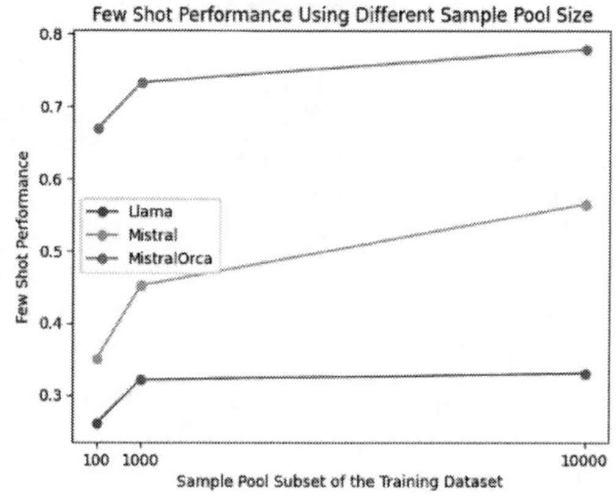

Figure 4: Sample Pool Size Impact for Few-Shot Learning with flat integration of hierarchy.

performs similarly to Flat, contradicting the previous results of Boyle et al. (2023), where using LLM-guided tree-search traversal in a top-down manner achieved state-of-the-art performance in the task of assigning diagnostic ICD codes. We suspect the failure of Top-Down Tree Search on our data is due to the terms in the top-level vocabulary, such as "any anthropogenic material" and "biogenic non-organic material", which can be difficult for the LLM to understand as they are low-frequency highly specialized terms that the LLM may not have large exposure to.

4.4 How much can few-shot prompting improve over zero-shot prompting?

We also conduct few-shot learning by including a sample of examples in the prompt to the model. We include the examples in the prompt as follows:

```
You are a scientist. Your task is
to analyze the description of a material
sample and determine the kind of material
that constitutes it after <<<>>> into one
of the predefined material types:
{taxonomy}
You will only respond with the material
type. Do not include the word Material
type. Do not provide explanations or
notes.
###
Here are some examples:
{examples}
###
<<<
Description: {text}
Material type:
>>>
```

For the selection of examples, we utilize a k-nearest neighbor (kNN) search methodology proposed by Khandelwal et al. (2019), wherein we select the k most similar examples from the training dataset for each test record. To determine the similarity between records, we represent the text of the record using a Sentence-BERT model which was trained to estimate the similarity of scientific publications (allenai-specter) (Cohan et al., 2020). The few-shot samples are ordered from least to most cosine similarity to the given test record according to the methodology proposed by Sun et al. (2023). Due to constraints on input context, Llama used 3-shot examples, while Mistral and Mistral-OpenOrca used 5-shot examples. The number of samples (k) was chosen as mentioned above, as we observed lower performance with larger k values.

Since the k examples are drawn from the training data, it is important to determine how large of a pool of training examples are needed for successful few-shot prompting. Figure 4 shows experiments with subsets of the training dataset, randomly selecting n = 100, 1000, and 10,000 records for each MATERIAL type. From the results, we see larger training dataset size enhances the performance as the probability of retrieving relevant in-context examples increases, which is consistent with prior research by Liu et al. (2021).

We compare few-shot prompting to both zero-shot prompting and the following baselines:

Most common label Predict the most common label, which is the ROCK label.

Multinomial Naive Bayes Applies a multinomial naive bayes classifier that represents the text metadata fields as TF-IDF vectors.

RoBERTa-Large-MNLI Applies a RoBERTa model that has been pre-trained on textual entailment data, is fine-tuned on the entire

Model	Model Input	Prompt	Hierarchy	F1
Most common label	-	-	Flat	0.123
Multinomial Naive Bayes	Field values	-	Flat	0.652
RoBERTA-Large-MNLI	Original description	-	Flat	0.721
kNN	Original description	-	[See text]	0.844
Llama-7B-chat-hf	Original description	Few-Shot	Flat	0.331
Llama-7B-chat-hf	Original description	Few-Shot	Bottom Up	0.504
Llama-7B-chat-hf	Summary + Explanation	Few-Shot	Bottom Up	0.501
Mistral-7B-Instruct	Original description	Few-Shot	Flat	0.565
Mistral-7B-Instruct	Original description	Few-Shot	Bottom Up	0.772
Mistral-7B-Instruct	Summary + Explanation	Few-Shot	Bottom Up	0.669
Mistral-7B-OpenOrca	Original description	Few-Shot	Flat	0.779
Mistral-7B-OpenOrca	Original description	Few-Shot	Bottom Up	0.880
Mistral-7B-OpenOrca	Summary + Explanation	Few-Shot	Bottom Up	**0.928**
Mistral-7B-OpenOrca (best zero-shot)	Summary + Explanation	Zero-Shot	Bottom Up	0.439

Table 5: Result of Few Shot Learning with Bottom-Up Tree Search and Summarize&Explain Approach with the entire training dataset used as sample pool. Best performing few-shot approach is in bold. Macro F1 is used for evaluation.

training data, and is used to classify text following Yin et al. (2019); Pàmies et al. (2023). Early stopping was used to prevent overfitting. Other hyperparameters used for fine-tuning are listed in Appendix B.

kNN Utilizing the same Sentence-BERT model employed in few-shot learning, we create embeddings representing each sample record, and label new sample records with the most common label from their 5-nearest neighbors. The most common label is determined by prioritizing the label that holds the deepest position within the taxonomy hierarchy and is most frequently observed among the neighboring labels.

Table 5 compares few-shot prompting to the best zero-shot prompting model and these baselines. The best few-shot setting is the same as the best zero-shot setting: Mistral-7B-OpenOrca, summarize and explain the input, and use the bottom up search strategy. But the best few-shot setting substantially outperforms the best zero-shot setting, 0.928 F1 to 0.439 F1. It also outperforms all the baselines, including those that are fine-tuned over the entire training data. The closest baseline is the k-nearest neighbors, achieving 0.844 F1, which indicates that selecting relevant training examples for few-shot prompting is driving a large part of the performance, but the knowledge embedded in the LLM provides extra power beyond those few-shot examples.

One difference that can be observed between the zero-shot and few-shot models is that the Summarize and Explain approach did not help Llama and hurt Mistral, while that approach benefited both models in the zero-shot setting (see table 3). This suggests that almost any summary helps without any training examples in the prompt, but as soon as the prompt contains relevant training examples, only the best summaries are helpful. A deeper analysis of the quality of summaries coming out of each model would help to confirm or deny this hypothesis.

5 Analysis

Given that sample records that were registered in the same institution often share similar characteristics, we investigate whether this introduces bias into our few-shot learning. Out of the 102 unique institutions in the test dataset, we filtered out the records of 50 institutions from the training dataset. We then used this dataset to create three models:

RoBERTA-Large-MNLI Applies the same approach as RoBERTA-Large-MNLI above, but fine-tuned on only the filtered training data.

kNN Applies the same approach as kNN above,

Model	Unseen	Seen	Both
RoBERTA-Large-MNLI	0.477	0.513	0.497
kNN	0.168	0.861	0.331
Mistral-7B-OpenOrca-Best	0.426	0.915	0.555
Mistral-7B-OpenOrca-Robust	0.491	0.878	0.620

Table 6: Different few shot approaches. Unseen stands for test records that come from institutions that have not been seen during training, and seen stands for test records that come from institutions that have been seen during training. Macro F1 is used for evaluation.

but neighbors are drawn only from the filtered training data.

Mistral-7B-OpenOrca-Best Applies the same approach as the best performing Mistral-7B-OpenOrca model but with few shot examples drawn only from the filtered training data.

Table 6 shows that all three models see a drop in performance when evaluated on institutions not present in the training data. The k-nearest neighbor model suffers the most severe drop, but the Mistral-7B-OpenOrca-Best also suffers a large drop, yielding 0.426 F1 on sample records from unseen institutions, lower than the 0.477 F1 of the RoBERTA model. These results suggest that few-shot learning will be substantially more effective when there exist sample records from the same institution in the training data that is used for example retrieval.

In an attempt to mitigate some of this bias, we conducted experiments by reducing the number of few-shot samples to k=3 and placing greater emphasis on the analysis of the given test record's description by adding the following to the prompt:

```
Answer what is the material type of the
sample by going through each sentence of
the given description and analyzing.
Choose from {taxonomy} the material type
that constitutes the given description.
```

This model, Mistral-7B-OpenOrca-Robust, was able to reduce the existing bias as we can see improvement in test records that originate from unseen institutions. We plan to further investigate to find a way to improve the robustness most effectively in future research.

6 Conclusion

Physical sample records, a form of scholarly document created by natural scientists, play a crucial role in ensuring the reproducibility and reusability of sample-based scientific knowledge; additionally, they are often used as scientific datasets in and of themselves. However, they are often incomplete, thereby impacting their usability and the usability of the data repositories that store them. In this research, we explore various methodologies aimed at leveraging recent developments in LLMs to address this issue.

To transform a sample record into an input suitable for text classification by LLMs, we find that maximizing verbosity by using descriptions of metadata field names and their corresponding values is beneficial. Additionally, we demonstrate that harnessing the LLM's inherent knowledge and summarization capabilities enhances the comprehensibility of inputs for text classification tasks.

Our results also reveal the effectiveness of integrating taxonomy hierarchies through bottom-up tree search, which we expect to be particularly beneficial for domain-specific taxonomies with which the LLM has limited exposure. Furthermore, incorporating few-shot examples into the prompt leads to substantial improvements. Notably, the best few-shot learning performance surpasses that of a fine-tuned RoBERTA textual entailment classifier, indicating a promising approach for embedding training data with minimal computational resources, applicable across diverse domains of sample records.

Overall, our experimental results suggest that LLMs hold potential as a solution for digital libraries and aggregations grappling with metadata quality issues, particularly in domain-specific cases. Our approach offers promise for addressing metadata quality challenges stemming from incomplete records across various domains.

7 Limitations

In this paper, our exploration was confined to a single data repository and taxonomy. To assess the applicability of the identified methods across different contexts and validate their effectiveness, further experimentation involving diverse data repositories is necessary.

Additionally, our study utilized a non-domain-specific LLM with a modest size of 7 billion parameters. Considering recent advancements in LLMs, leveraging larger-scale models or domain-specific models such as Galactica (Taylor et al., 2022), or using fine-tuned LLMs could lead to further improvements in performance.

8 Acknowledgements

This work was funded by NSF grant #2004562.

References

2020. *Biological Collections: Ensuring Critical Research and Education for the 21st Century*. National Academies Press, Washington, D.C.

Joseph S Boyle, Antanas Kascenas, Pat Lok, Maria Liakata, and Alison Q O'Neil. 2023. Automated clinical coding using off-the-shelf large language models. *arXiv preprint arXiv:2310.06552*.

Arthur Chapman and John Wieczorek. 2020. Georeferencing Best Practices. Publisher: [object Object].

Arman Cohan, Sergey Feldman, Iz Beltagy, Doug Downey, and Daniel S. Weld. 2020. SPECTER: Document-level Representation Learning using Citation-informed Transformers. In *ACL*.

Neil Davies, John Deck, Eric C Kansa, Sarah Whitcher Kansa, John Kunze, Christopher Meyer, Thomas Orrell, Sarah Ramdeen, Rebecca Snyder, Dave Vieglais, et al. 2021. Internet of samples (isamples): Toward an interdisciplinary cyberinfrastructure for material samples. *GigaScience*, 10(5):giab028.

Naomi Dushay and Diane I Hillmann. 2003. Analyzing metadata for effective use and re-use. In *International Conference On Dublin Core And Metadata Applications*, pages pp–161.

Hui Han, C Lee Giles, Eren Manavoglu, Hongyuan Zha, Zhenyue Zhang, and Edward A Fox. 2003. Automatic document metadata extraction using support vector machines. In *2003 Joint Conference on Digital Libraries, 2003. Proceedings.*, pages 37–48. IEEE.

J. Mason Heberling, Joseph T. Miller, Daniel Noesgaard, Scott B. Weingart, and Dmitry Schigel. 2021. Data integration enables global biodiversity synthesis. *Proceedings of the National Academy of Sciences*, 118(6). ISBN: 9782018093113 Publisher: National Academy of Sciences Section: Biological Sciences.

Wei Huang, Enhong Chen, Qi Liu, Yuying Chen, Zai Huang, Yang Liu, Zhou Zhao, Dan Zhang, and Shijin Wang. 2019. Hierarchical multi-label text classification: An attention-based recurrent network approach. In *Proceedings of the 28th ACM international conference on information and knowledge management*, pages 1051–1060.

Urvashi Khandelwal, Omer Levy, Dan Jurafsky, Luke Zettlemoyer, and Mike Lewis. 2019. Generalization through memorization: Nearest neighbor language models. *arXiv preprint arXiv:1911.00172*.

Takeshi Kojima, Shixiang Shane Gu, Machel Reid, Yutaka Matsuo, and Yusuke Iwasawa. 2022. Large language models are zero-shot reasoners. *Advances in neural information processing systems*, 35:22199–22213.

Jiachang Liu, Dinghan Shen, Yizhe Zhang, Bill Dolan, Lawrence Carin, and Weizhu Chen. 2021. What makes good in-context examples for gpt-3? *arXiv preprint arXiv:2101.06804*.

Gil Nelson and Shari Ellis. 2018. The history and impact of digitization and digital data mobilization on biodiversity research. *Philosophical Transactions of the Royal Society B: Biological Sciences*, 374(1763):20170391. Publisher: Royal Society.

Marc Pàmies, Joan Llop, Francesco Multari, Nicolau Duran-Silva, César Parra-Rojas, Aitor González-Agirre, Francesco Alessandro Massucci, and Marta Villegas. 2023. A weakly supervised textual entailment approach to zero-shot text classification. In *Proceedings of the 17th Conference of the European Chapter of the Association for Computational Linguistics*, pages 286–296.

Gordon W Paynter. 2005. Developing practical automatic metadata assignment and evaluation tools for internet resources. In *Proceedings of the 5th ACM/IEEE-CS joint conference on Digital libraries*, pages 291–300.

Stephen M Richard, David Vieglais, Andrea K Thomer, Hyunju Song, Neil Davies, John Deck, Quan Gan, Eric C Kansa, Sarah Kansa, John Kunze, Kerstin Lehnert, Danny Mandel, Christopher Meyer, Rebecca Snyder, Ramona L Walls, Yuxoan Zhou, and Hong Cui. 2024. A metadata schema for documenting material samples from multiple domains | www.semantic-web-journal.net.

Karan Singhal, Shekoofeh Azizi, Tao Tu, S Sara Mahdavi, Jason Wei, Hyung Won Chung, Nathan Scales, Ajay Tanwani, Heather Cole-Lewis, Stephen Pfohl, et al. 2022. Large language models encode clinical knowledge. *arXiv preprint arXiv:2212.13138*.

Xiaofei Sun, Xiaoya Li, Jiwei Li, Fei Wu, Shangwei Guo, Tianwei Zhang, and Guoyin Wang. 2023. Text classification via large language models. *arXiv preprint arXiv:2305.08377*.

Ross Taylor, Marcin Kardas, Guillem Cucurull, Thomas Scialom, Anthony Hartshorn, Elvis Saravia, Andrew Poulton, Viktor Kerkez, and Robert Stojnic. 2022. Galactica: A large language model for science. *arXiv preprint arXiv:2211.09085*.

Emma Tonkin and Henk L Muller. 2008. Semi automated metadata extraction for preprints archives. In *Proceedings of the 8th ACM/IEEE-CS joint conference on Digital libraries*, pages 157–166.

Jason Wei, Xuezhi Wang, Dale Schuurmans, Maarten Bosma, Fei Xia, Ed Chi, Quoc V Le, Denny Zhou, et al. 2022. Chain-of-thought prompting elicits reasoning in large language models. *Advances in neural information processing systems*, 35:24824–24837.

Linli Xu, Sijie Teng, Ruoyu Zhao, Junliang Guo, Chi Xiao, Deqiang Jiang, and Bo Ren. 2021. Hierarchical multi-label text classification with horizontal and vertical category correlations. In *Proceedings of the 2021 Conference on Empirical Methods in Natural Language Processing*, pages 2459–2468.

Wenpeng Yin, Jamaal Hay, and Dan Roth. 2019. Benchmarking zero-shot text classification: Datasets, evaluation and entailment approach. *arXiv preprint arXiv:1909.00161*.

A Average number of tokens in the dataset

Metadata field	Avg. # Token
supplementMetadata_province	1.26
sampleType	2.32
supplementMetadata_city	1.62
supplementMetadata_primaryLocationType	1.52
collectionMethodDescr	2.89
supplementMetadata_purpose	4.52
supplementMetadata_country	1.77
supplementMetadata_geologicalAge	1.49
supplementMetadata_geoUnit	2.82
supplementMetadata_primaryLocationType	1.52
supplementMetadata_locality	2.9
supplementMetadata_localityDescription	4.98
description	10.58
supplementMetadata_locationDescription	64.94
supplementMetadata_platformType	1.19
supplementMetadata_platformDescr	2.56
collectionMethodDescr	2.89
supplementMetadata_sampleComment	11.56
supplementMetadata_county	0.793
supplementMetadata_classificationComment	1.25
supplementMetadata_originalArchive	10.13
supplementMetadata_currentArchive	8.42
supplementMetadata_sampleComment	11.56
supplementMetadata_fieldName	2.55
supplementMetadata_cruiseFieldPrgrm	3.23
supplementMetadata_publicationUrl_description	8.38

Table 7: Average number of tokens of metadata fields in the dataset.

B Hyperparameters for finetuning

Hyperparameter	Value
Batch size	16, 32, 64
Learning rate	1e-5, 2e-5, 5e-05
Weight decay	0.01
Epochs	3

Table 8: Hyperparameters used for fine-tuning a RoBERTa-Large-MNLI. Grid search was used for choosing the optimal hyperparameter values.

MISTI: Metadata-Informed Scientific Text and Image Representation through Contrastive Learning

Pawin Taechoyotin
Department of Computer Science
University of Colorado Boulder

Daniel Acuna
Department of Computer Science
University of Colorado Boulder

{pawin.taechoyotin,daniel.acuna}@colorado.edu

Abstract

In scientific publications, automatic representations of figures and their captions can be used in NLP, computer vision, and information retrieval tasks. Contrastive learning has proven effective for creating such joint representations for natural scenes, but its application to scientific imagery and descriptions remains under-explored. Recent open-access publication datasets provide an opportunity to understand the effectiveness of this technique as well as evaluate the usefulness of additional metadata, which are available only in the scientific context. Here, we introduce MISTI, a novel model that uses contrastive learning to simultaneously learn the representation of figures, captions, and metadata, such as a paper's title, sections, and curated concepts from the PubMed Open Access Subset. We evaluate our model on multiple information retrieval tasks, showing substantial improvements over baseline models. Notably, incorporating metadata doubled retrieval performance, achieving a Recall@1 of 30% on a 70K-item caption retrieval task. We qualitatively explore how metadata can be used to strategically retrieve distinctive representations of the same concept but for different sections, such as introduction and results. Additionally, we show that our model seamlessly handles out-of-domain tasks related to image segmentation. We share our dataset and methods (https://github.com/Khempawin/scientific-image-caption-pair/tree/section-attr) and outline future research directions.

1 Introduction

The famous saying "a picture is worth a thousand words" takes on a new meaning in the context of scientific publications. Scientific articles are filled with textual descriptions paired with images, diagrams, and figures that are essential for understanding the results presented. Previous work on natural images, such as CLIP (Radford et al., 2021), has shown that contrastive learning can be used to jointly represent text and images. Relative to traditionally available natural image datasets, scientific images are unique in two ways. First, they have precise textual descriptions, known as captions, which provide additional context and information. Second, they have metadata, such as a paper's title, sections, and curated concepts, that enable us to contextualize an image. New open access repositories (e.g., Wang et al. (2020); Lin et al. (2023)) allow us to take advantage of these unique characteristics. In this article, we propose and evaluate a novel model that uses contrastive learning to jointly represent text and images in scientific publications enriched with such metadata information.

Scientific images are often accompanied by captions that provide additional context and information (Li et al., 2018). For example, a caption might describe the experimental setup, the results of an experiment, or the conclusions drawn from the results. Captions are essential for understanding the research presented in scientific articles, but they are sometimes overlooked in image retrieval tasks. Recent work has shown the potential of multimodal models (Yin et al., 2023), and their application to science is yet to be explored. In addition to captions, scientific images are often associated with metadata such as the paper's title, sections, and curated concepts. This metadata provides valuable information about the context in which the image appears and can be used to enhance the representation learned by the model. For example, the section of an article potentially provides information about the type of image (e.g., experimental setup, results, discussion) while the title can provide information about the general topic of the research. Although previous work has explored this line of research (Wei et al., 2023; Eslami et al., 2023), there is still much more to be done to fully leverage the range of metadata available in science.

Understanding the content of scientific diagrams and images and producing descriptions for them

Proceedings of the Fourth Workshop on Scholarly Document Processing (SDP 2024), pages 155–164
August 16, 2024 ©2024 Association for Computational Linguistics

are challenging tasks. For instance, a diagram might contain multiple components with a specific function or meaning. Captions provide additional context and information about the diagram but are often brief and may not fully explain its content. Conversely, writing captions for scientific diagrams is challenging, requiring concisely conveying complex information. These challenges become apparent during information retrieval, where we want to retrieve figures based on a textual description or vice versa. Building on the concepts of the CLIP model (Radford et al., 2021), we aim to build a vision text dual encoder model to facilitate scientific article generation. Similar to what happened to CLIP, the model can be used for other downstream tasks, such as image segmentation or zero-shot classification.

There are many image-caption datasets such as Flickr8k, Flickr30k (Wang et al., 2018), MSCOCO (Chen et al., 2015), RSICD (Lu et al., 2017), Medicat (Sanjay Subramanian and Hajishirzi, 2020) and other adaptations of image classification datasets namely CIFAR-10, and CIFAR-100 (Krizhevsky, 2009). These datasets are exceptional for their specific purposes, but the models do not generalize well into the scientific context. For instance, the captions and images in MSCOCO are mostly descriptions of everyday objects in everyday scenes. RSICD is a specialized dataset with captions of satellite images. Medicat is a specialized dataset with captions in the medical domain. On the other hand, captions in scientific articles are domain-specific for a particular field, with complex images representing diagrams, charts, or graphs. Apart from these datasets, there are image-caption scientific datasets with a diverse fields such as SciCap (Hsu et al., 2021), SciMMIR (Wu et al., 2024) and SCI-3000 (Darmanovic, 2022). Although these datasets are diverse but they lack the metadata associated with each image-caption pair which limits the context they belong to. Another aspect that is limited is the size of these datasets which will affect the representations learned.

To harness the richness found in images, we propose creating a new vision text dual encoder model to improve the performance of image retrieval tasks in scientific publications. We develop a dataset of scientific image captions based on open-access articles from PubMed Open Access Subset (National Library of Medicine, 2003). This dataset contains images and captions extracted from scientific articles and metadata such as a paper's title, sections, and curated concepts. We evaluate the usefulness of our model and dataset on various tasks. In sum, the contributions of our work are as follows:

- Develop a dataset of image captions derived from open-access scientific articles on PubMed.
- Implement a caption-enhancement technique to improve learned representations.
- Make the trained model and dataset publicly available to the scientific community.
- Present a variety of new tasks to assess the efficacy of contrastive learning within the scientific domain.

2 Related Work

2.1 Contrastive Representation Learning

Contrastive Learning is when we learn to tell apart objects by comparing the similarities between two or more similar objects and the differences between those objects and dissimilar ones. The goal is to make similar samples close in embedding space, and dissimilar samples far apart (Zimmermann et al., 2021). Recently, there has been a surge in the popularity of using such techniques to achieve better model performances (Yuan et al., 2022; Ciga et al., 2022; Wang et al., 2021). The performance improvements include the learning speed of the models, relevance in information retrieval or recommendation tasks, and reduced effort in dataset creation (Jaiswal et al., 2020). Even when we do not have access to supervised data, we can use contrastive learning effectively in a self-supervised setting (Falcon and Cho, 2020). In this paradigm, contrastive learning has thrived the most, especially in multi-modal tasks (Radford et al., 2021).

2.2 Dataset Enhancement in Deep Representation Learning

There are three key generalization factors for self-supervised contrastive learning (Huang et al., 2021): alignment of positive samples, divergence of class centers, and concentration of augmented data. The first key factor is related to the model's architecture, where the difference between the positive samples from the same class is minimized. The second key factor is related to the information behind the dataset: different classes should be significantly different; otherwise, we might encounter a "feature collapse," where the representations learned cannot distinguish between distinct classes. The third key factor is related to the density of positive samples, which adds more signal for the model to learn from. The work of (Wei et al., 2023) applied these principles to learn a joint representation of a text and an image. In their work, the captions were too generic and thus were enhanced with dictionary definitions. This approach used the exact architecture as proposed in (Radford et al., 2021). With such augmentation, there was a significant improvement in both zero-shot classification and zero-shot retrieval.

2.3 Scientific Article Metadata

Recent datasets have made available open access publications, including their full text and figures, such as the PubMed Open Access Subset (National Library of Medicine, 2003). Datasets of scientific publications can give us access to metadata in an easy-to-use format. For example, OpenAlex (Priem et al., 2022) contains indexes and metadata for a large number of articles spanning almost all human knowledge. These metadata include the publishing journals of each article, the fields associated with that journal, the concepts associated with each article, the authors associated with each article, and many more.

2.4 Scientific Vocabulary Embeddings

To process the text, we need to transform it into embeddings. The original CLIP model is based on RoBERTa. As demonstrated in MIREAD (Razdaibiedina and Brechalov, 2023), SciBERT (Beltagy et al., 2019), and SPECTER2 (Cohan et al., 2020), the vocabulary used to process text plays a great deal of importance in the performance of text encoding in the scientific domain. Therefore, other text encoders should be used for specific domains. These representations can be used as a starting point for the text encoding aspect of text-image contrastive learning methods.

3 Dataset and Methodology

This work focuses on enhancing the representation learning of scientific texts and images through metadata-informed embeddings. Our approach leverages scientific publications' unique vocabulary and metadata, such as concepts, keywords, and field-specific terminologies. To this end, we introduce a novel method that directly incorporates metadata into the training process of the contrastive learning models, and a specialized tokenizer to handle scientific metadata. This approach aims to improve the performance of embedding models on tasks such as zero-shot classification, information retrieval, and recommendation systems in the scientific domain.

This section will describe the model architecture of contrastive learning with a dual vision-text encoder, the information retrieval system, the process of building the dataset, the training parameters, and the evaluation metrics for information retrieval. The process includes extracting image-caption pairs from articles and metadata from OpenAlex.

3.1 A Scientific Image-Caption dataset

To build a new scientific image-caption dataset, we have analyzed over 4 million scientific articles from PubMed Open Access Subset (National Library of Medicine, 2003). A sample of a scientific article in XML format and the location of image-captions can be seen in figure 1A. This resulted in around 12 million image-caption pairs. Note that apart from the 12 million image-caption pairs, we have filtered out approximately 8 million image-caption pairs that were not found under a section in the articles. Among 12 million image-caption pairs, 9.78 million were used as the training dataset, 1.1 million as the validation set, and 1.1 million as the test set. One extra process was adding metadata from OpenAlex to each image caption based on the document's DOI. This led to an image-caption dataset that included the title of the related article, the related concept keywords, and the authors.

3.2 Model Architecture

The contrastive learning model architecture primarily consists of two components (Figure 1B). The first component, known as the text encoder, handles the tokenization and encoding of text into a 512-dimensional vector. A key subcomponent of the text encoder is the language embedding or vocabulary. To address this, we experiment with RoBERTa, MIREAD, SciBERT, and SPECTER2. RoBERTa is the only language embedding that was not trained on scientific text. The second component, the image encoder, is responsible for encoding images into a 512-dimensional vector. The model used for this component is the pre-trained Vision Transformer from CLIP (Radford et al., 2021), which takes 32 by 32 patches of the image and outputs a 512-dimensional vector. Training is performed by evaluating each batch separately. For each batch, all texts are encoded with the text encoder, and all images are encoded with the image encoder. We then maximize the cosine similarity between the paired encoded texts and images while minimizing the difference between non-paired images and texts. This process is illustrated in Figure 1B, where the green cells indicate the values to be maximized, and the white cells indicate the values to be minimized.

3.3 Information retrieval pipeline

The process of retrieving captions involves three steps. The first step is to encode all the reference captions, which we refer to as the dictionary. The second step is to encode the query image. The third step involves comparing the encoded query image with all the encoded captions. The outcome is a ranking of captions based on the similarity between the encoding of the query image and the captions. In information retrieval tasks, we typically define a parameter k, which specifies the number of samples to be returned. In this instance, we will use k equal to 1 to assess the model recall, formally known as Recall@1. We use Recall@1 due to each image having only 1 caption associated with it. Therefore, there is only 1 caption that is perfectly relevant for each image. Increasing k for Recall@5 or Recall@10 will only increase the evaluation score since there is a higher probability where the original caption will be in the top n rankings. On the other hand, there are other metrics that are commonly used such as ROUGE-n (Chin-Yew, 2004), BERTScore and BLEU. The reason we are not using such scores is that we are evaluating the representations not the output captions. Due to this, ROUGE-n which compares the matching n-gram between the original caption and the retrieved caption does not give us significant information regarding the representations learned. For BLEU, the score is used to evaluate the quality of the text compared to multiple reference captions. Since we only have 1 reference caption, it is essentially comparing only the retrieved caption to the single reference caption. This might result in the illusion that the retrieved caption is good in cases where both captions are similar in words but mean different things. Therefore, BLEU is not suitable in this case. For BERTScore, such metric is inherently used due to the ranking of captions based on the similarity between encodings.

3.4 Model training

The model was trained on a machine with 64 vCPUs and a NVIDIA A100. The vision encoder was a pre-trained Vision Transformer from OpenAI that takes in 32 by 32 patches of the image. As mentioned in Section 2.4, we systematically varied the language embedding model and the type of caption augmentation. This resulted in 16 variations, which comprise four language embedding models (MIREAD, ROBERTA, SCIBERT and SPECTER2) and four types of caption augmentations (no augmentation, augmenting with section, augmenting with section and metadata, and augmentation with operationalized metadata). Operationalized metadata means introducing special tokens representing these sections (see below). Since one training session spans 6 days, we created a subset of the full training data. This subset had a size of 700k image-caption pairs. These 16 models were trained on a batch size of 64 over 3 epochs with a learning rate of 0.00005 and a weight decay of 0.1.

Once the performance was measured, we selected the best validation variation to train on the rest of the training dataset. We increased the batch size to 192 and compared it to the equivalent model with textual metadata to demonstrate the effects of tokenizing the metadata.

3.5 Augmenting captions with additional metadata

We used three variations of augmentation on each caption: augmenting with sections, metadata, and metadata with separator tokens. The metadata comprises the article title, related concepts, and the location of the image caption within the article (i.e., section). The sections of the article are "Introduction," "Methods," "Results and Discussion," "Conclusion," and "Other." "Other" is used when the section title does not fit any known pattern.

Augmenting with section Enhancing the caption with the section is done by concatenating the section at the beginning of the caption. For example, a caption such as "western blot of protein nurturing" that appears in the "result and discussion" section will have an enhanced caption such as "result and discussion western blot of protein nurturing." The template is "<section> <caption>".

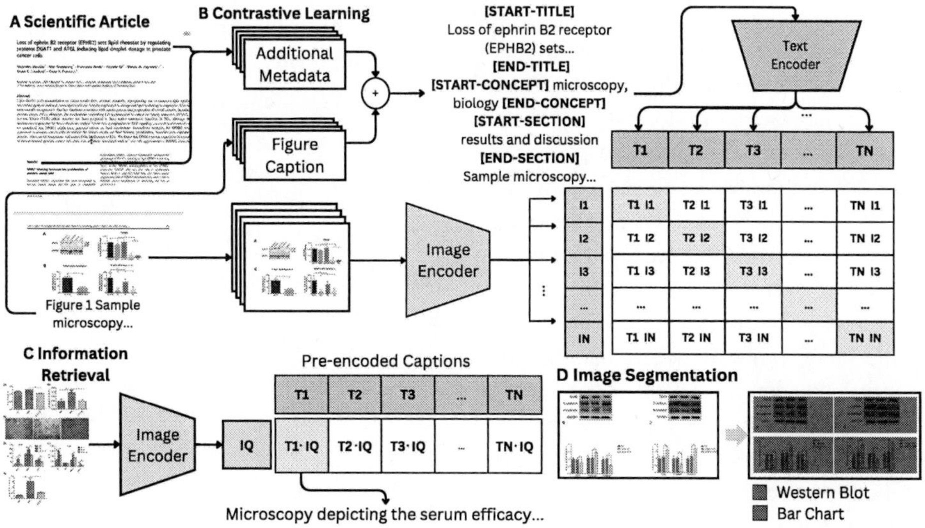

Figure 1: **A)** A sample scientific article and the XML representation depicting how images appear in scientific articles. **B)** A dual vision-text encoder architecture for contrastive learning between images and captions. It also illustrates how additional metadata are operationalized to enhance the captions during training. **C)** An illustration of text retrieval where each caption is pre-encoded with the text encoder. The query image is encoded and compared to each encoded caption. During retrieval, the image is encoded and compared to each encoded caption. **D)** A sample task such as image segmentation is performed by the learned representation. In this image, segments colored purple are classified as "Western Blot," and segments colored red are classified as "Bar Chart"

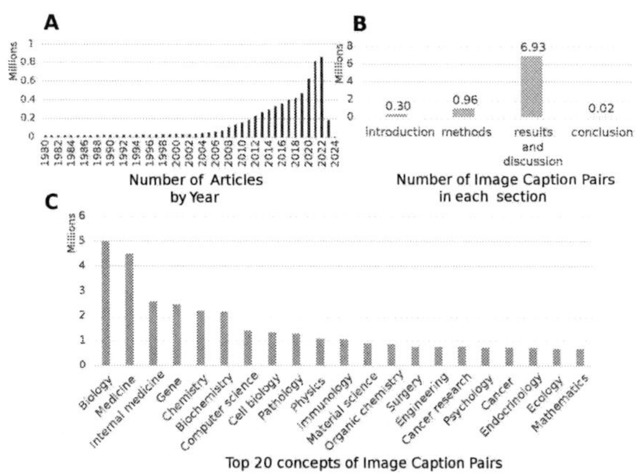

Figure 2: Statistics of scientific articles and training dataset. A) The extracted data was from 2.54 million articles. Most of the articles were published in the year 2016 to 2023. B) Distribution of the sections where each article's image captions are located. Most of the image-caption pairs were found in the result and discussion sections. C) Distribution of concepts related to each image-caption pair. Note that each image-caption pair might have more than one concept related to them.

Augmenting with section and metadata Enhancing the caption with metadata is similar to enhancing with only the section but includes more metadata about the caption which are the article title and the concepts of the article. For example, a caption as "structural integrity of ..." which appears in the "Methods" section in an article "Novel materials for..." with the related concepts as "Material Science, Tensile Strength" will have the enhanced caption as "Novel materials for... Material Science, Tensile Strength Methods structural integrity of ...". In this sense, the template we use is "<title> <concepts> <section> <caption>"

Augmenting with operationalized metadata To help the model distinguish text for each type of metadata and the caption, we enhanced the caption further by adding a special separating token for the title, concept, and section. The template we use is "[START-TITLE] <title> [END-TITLE] [START-CONCEPT] <concepts> [END-CONCEPT] [START-SECTION] <section> [END-SECTION] <caption>". We will call this type of augmentation as MISTI.

3.6 Relevance of Information Retrieval Sample

Information retrieval was used to evaluate the models. The query is an image, and the expected result is a caption. One key factor of information retrieval is defining the method of measuring relevance between the query and the retrieved sample. To address this, we used 3 metrics. The first metric is called *identity* metric, where the retrieved sample is only considered relevant if it matches the original caption paired with the query image. The second metric is called *section* metric, where the retrieved sample is only considered relevant if the section associated with the retrieved sample matches the section associated with the query image. The third metric is called *concept* metric, where we used the Jaccard Similarity index (Fletcher et al., 2018) to compute the overlap between the set of concepts associated with the retrieved caption and the set of concepts associated with the query image.

4 Results

4.1 Caption Retrieval

The performance of all models is shown in Table 1, where we illustrate the identity, section, and concept metric. We have included an average score across all three metrics to compare these models effectively. The baseline models had a Recall@1 of 0 on the identity metric. After fine-tuning the model on our scientific dataset, we see an increase in performance across all 3 metrics. The identity metric increased from 0 to around 0.06 with the original captions and captions augmented with sections. For the augmentation with Textual Meta and MIST, the score increased from 0 to around 0.05. Regarding the section metric, the scores increased to around 0.7 across all adaptations, and the concepts increased from 0.04 to 0.15. Overall, the RoBERTa adaptation saw the least improvement for the identity, section, and concept metric. Finally, the SPECTER2 MISTI + large batch performed the best with an average score of 0.4940. To summarize, all the baseline models performed sub-optimally. Fine-tuning the models on the scientific dataset improved the performance of the models. This indicates that the models have the potential to adapt to the dataset (Information in the dataset is not present in the pre-trained model). Lastly, all caption augmentations improved the performance of the model. However, each type of caption augmentations have different magnitudes of improvements on the models.

4.2 Qualitative Analysis of Information Retrieval

The results shown in Figure 3A and Figure 3B are for accurate and non-accurate retrieval, respectively. All the images associated with the retrieved caption are line charts that resemble the query image (Figure 3A). The images associated with the rank 0 and rank 1 caption resemble geographical plots, which align with the query image (Figure 3B). Conversely, images in rank 2 and 3 differ greatly from the query image, where rank 2 is a line chart and rank 3 is a stacked bar chart. To summarize, all the images for accurate retrieval are similar in nature but for non-accurate retrieval some retrieved results do not resemble the query image.

4.3 Retrieving images with different article sections

Figure 3C shows the images in different sections retrieval results. In such a task, we used the caption as "bar chart" and varied the section as "introduction," "method", "results and discussion", "conclusion", and "other". The results are the top 4 most similar images starting from rank 0, 1, 2, and 3. The "Other" section is used for section names that do not fit a standard keyword criterion. The results show that all section types, excluding "results and discussion," have matching rank 0 results but differ in the subsequent ranks. All retrieved images are bar charts, indicating that the retrieval results are qualitatively relevant to the queried caption.

4.4 Classification on Different parts of an image

Figure 4 shows a simple classification of image segments between the caption "bar charts" and "western blot". This task was done by encoding each textual category as a reference encodings. The image segments are then encoded and compared to each encoded textual category. The textual category that is the most similar to each encoded image segment is considered the output classification for those image segments. The result shows that image segments that resemble a "bar chart" are classified as a bar chart, and the image segments that resemble a "western blot" are classified as a western blot. Some segments are misclassified due to the segment being similar to both "bar chart" and "western blot." Additionally, some segments lack apparent

Model	Base + Adaptation	Recall@1			
		Identity	Section	Concepts	Average
Baseline	MIREAD	0.0000	0.5744	0.0465	0.2070
	(Radford et al., 2021) RoBERTa	0.0000	0.6175	0.0380	0.2185
	SciBERT	0.0000	0.2842	0.0423	0.1088
	SPECTER2	0.0001	0.4971	0.0428	0.1800
Text Model Finetuned Caption	MIREAD	0.0602	0.7157	0.1497	0.3085
	RoBERTa	0.0490	0.7091	0.1374	0.2985
	SciBERT	0.0595	0.7156	0.1484	0.3078
	SPECTER2	0.0595	0.7150	0.1485	0.3077
Caption + Section	MIREAD	0.0601	0.7220	0.1495	0.3105
	RoBERTa	0.0506	0.7197	0.1384	0.3029
	SciBERT	0.0609	0.7193	0.1499	0.3100
	SPECTER2	0.0603	0.7187	0.1501	0.3097
Caption + Section + Textual Meta	MIREAD	0.0549	0.7253	0.1497	0.3100
	RoBERTa	0.0366	0.7112	0.1333	0.2937
	SciBERT	0.0539	0.7193	0.1489	0.3074
	SPECTER2	0.0565	0.7231	0.1505	0.3100
	SPECTER2 + large batch	0.1717	0.7780	0.2826	0.4108
MISTI (Text Model Finetuned + Tokenized Meta)	MIREAD	0.0500	0.7163	0.1448	0.3037
	RoBERTa	0.0347	0.7128	0.1326	0.2934
	SciBERT	0.0518	0.7208	0.1462	0.3063
	SPECTER2	0.0527	0.7217	0.1485	0.3076
	SPECTER2 + large batch	**0.3000**	**0.7932**	**0.3889**	**0.4940**

Table 1: Table summarizes Recall@1 for caption retrieval across various models using a 70k-caption dictionary, evaluated on identity, section, and concepts metrics, alongside an overall average. Models are categorized into baseline (not finetuned), text model finetuned (subdivided into no augmentation, section augmentation, and section plus metadata augmentation), and text model finetuned with tokenized meta. The top performer, SPECTER2 large batch on text model finetuned with tokenized meta, is highlighted in bold.

features, such as the 4 segments at the bottom right corner.

5 Discussion

5.1 The effects of caption augmentation

Our analyses point out that the sub-optimal performance of the baseline model was due to the embedding of each sample being extremely close to each other. This closeness does not allow the model to distinguish between samples. This suggests that the representations of scientific contexts are even more densely packed, creating such bad performance. This trend of results applies to other tasks such as text to image retrieval where text to image and image to text retrieval performance are identical when varying the dictionary size. This aligns with how contrastive learning works in general (e.g., see Radford et al. (2021); Zimmermann et al. (2021); Yuan et al. (2022); Ciga et al. (2022); Wang et al. (2021)). Such a hypothesis is confirmed with the inclusion of the fine-tuned models, as performance increases due to the dispersion of samples. Moreover, augmenting the captions with Textual Metadata also increases the performance when compared to the baseline models. The degree of improvement is slightly lower than that of the model without the additional metadata on the identity metric, but the average performance is higher. In other words, the improvement on the section and concepts metric combined was higher than the delta of the identity metric. We understand that this is due to the additional metadata acting as a signal for the model to group samples with similar sections and concepts closer in the embedding space. This phenomenon correlates with adding dictionary definitions for vague captions as observed in (Wei et al., 2023). The metadata leads the model to create regions for each section/concept in the embedding space. Consequently, this leads to improvements in the performance of the section and concept metric. We tokenized the metadata with a special separator token to improve distinguishable abilities, increasing the model's performance. We see a substantial difference between 0.1717 for textual and 0.3 for tokenized metadata. The results of these new tokens led to the model capable of producing a substantial differentiation of samples, ultimately resulting in better representations, similar to what is described in (Huang et al., 2021). Thus, our caption augmentation task demonstrates how important it is to develop specialized scientific representations to tell samples apart.

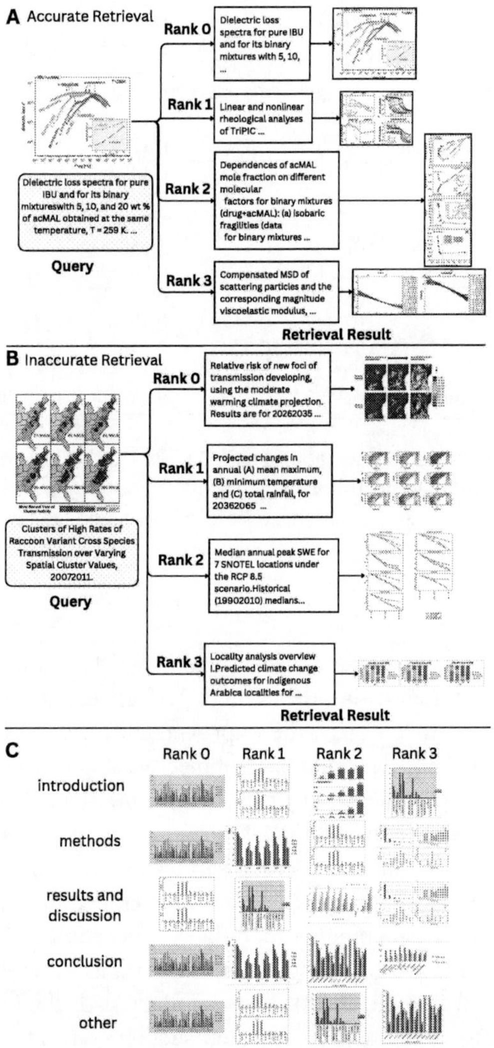

Figure 3: **Caption retrieval with corresponding images** A) Shows the top 4 captions that are retrieved when the top 1 caption retrieved is originally paired to the query image in the dataset. It also shows the original corresponding image pair for each retrieved caption. B) Shows the top 4 captions that are retrieved when the top 1 caption retrieved is not the originally paired to the query image in the dataset. It also shows the original corresponding image pair for each retrieved caption. C) Shows the retrieved image with different sections.

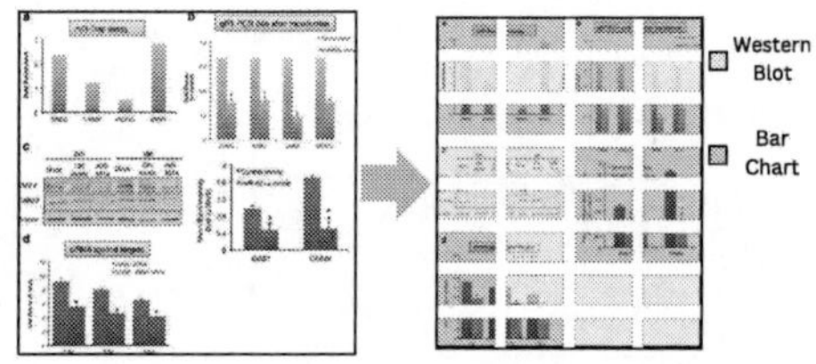

Figure 4: **Image Segment classification on "bar chart" and "western blot"**. The image on the left is the input image. The images on the right are segments of the image overlayed with colors to illustrate whether that segment is a "bar chart" or a "western blot". Green is for western blot and Red is for bar chart.

5.2 Qualitative Analysis of Information Retrieval

One hypothesis regarding the low performance on caption retrieval is that the model was retrieving results similar to the query but not the original pair (Wei et al., 2023). Based on the result in 4.2, accurate retrievals have similar images even though the images were never compared during training. This aligns with the findings of learning the image representation via text supervision (Radford et al., 2021). Simultaneously, we see the same behavior with non-accurate retrievals, but only the top 2 ranks are relevant. This implies that while quantitatively, we have a low recall, the retrieved information is still qualitatively relevant.

5.3 Retrieving Images with different article sections

According to the results in 4.3, the sections do affect the embedding, but the caption dominates in the end. This is interpreted from the result in rank 0 being the same but the subsequent ranks being different (Li et al., 2018). In other words, the results demonstrate how sections are essentially a style and can be applied to an image to adjust the visual details while conveying the original meaning of the caption. Similar results were studied for applying styles on images for fashion generative models (Baldrati et al., 2022; Sain et al., 2021).

5.4 Classification on image croppings

Classification of image segments to classes is one of the long-standing tasks for classification as seen in ResNet50 (Targ et al., 2016), VGG (Kaur and Gandhi, 2019) and Fast-R-CNN (Girshick, 2015).

These works performed well but were limited to fixed classes. Essentially, the final output layer of these models is a representation of the images compared to the predetermined classes. Therefore, it is understandable that our model can perform the classification tasks given the classes can be described in text form. Interestingly, our model performs on par with such dedicated models. However, prediction results can sometimes be incorrect when the similarity scores between the image and each possible class are extremely close to each other. This task showcases the potential of using our model on the downstream tasks in a zero-shot fashion.

5.5 Summary

In conclusion, our results show the important role of metadata augmentation in enhancing model performance in the scientific context. Our systematic incorporation of fine-tuning and specialized tokenization techniques shows that metadata improves contrastive learning substantially by helping the model distinguish between samples. The findings underline the potential of targeted data augmentation strategies in advancing the capabilities of NLP models, suggesting promising avenues for future research.

6 Conclusion

The goal of this project was to create representations of images and captions in scientific images based on the simultaneous learning of their relationship using contrastive learning. This representation can be applied to multiple tasks, such as improving the understanding of figures and textual descriptions of scientific concepts and helping generate better images and captions. Our zero-shot segmentation example demonstrates the numerous downstream tasks where our model can be applied. The substantial performance differences between the generic image-text models and our metadata-informed model show that more work is needed in the scientific domain. For future work, additional metadata such as authors, publication venues, and citations might be explored further to augment the data.

References

Alberto Baldrati, Marco Bertini, Tiberio Uricchio, and Alberto Del Bimbo. 2022. Conditioned image retrieval for fashion using contrastive learning and clip-based features. In *Proceedings of the 3rd ACM International Conference on Multimedia in Asia*, MMAsia '21, New York, NY, USA. Association for Computing Machinery.

Iz Beltagy, Kyle Lo, and Arman Cohan. 2019. SciBERT: A pretrained language model for scientific text. In *Proceedings of the 2019 Conference on Empirical Methods in Natural Language Processing and the 9th International Joint Conference on Natural Language Processing (EMNLP-IJCNLP)*, pages 3615–3620, Hong Kong, China. Association for Computational Linguistics.

Xinlei Chen, Hao Fang, Tsung-Yi Lin, Ramakrishna Vedantam, Saurabh Gupta, Piotr Dollar, and C. Lawrence Zitnick. 2015. Microsoft coco captions: Data collection and evaluation server.

Lin Chin-Yew. 2004. Rouge: A package for automatic evaluation of summaries. In *Proceedings of the Workshop on Text Summarization Branches Out, 2004.*

Ozan Ciga, Tony Xu, and Anne Louise Martel. 2022. Self supervised contrastive learning for digital histopathology. *Machine Learning with Applications*, 7:100198.

Arman Cohan, Sergey Feldman, Iz Beltagy, Doug Downey, and Daniel S Weld. 2020. Specter: Document-level representation learning using citation-informed transformers. *arXiv preprint arXiv:2004.07180.*

Filip Darmanovic. 2022. *SCI-3000: A novel dataset for the task of figure, table, and caption extraction from scientific PDFs.* Ph.D. thesis, Technische Universität Wien.

Sedigheh Eslami, Christoph Meinel, and Gerard De Melo. 2023. Pubmedclip: How much does clip benefit visual question answering in the medical domain? In *Findings of the Association for Computational Linguistics: EACL 2023*, pages 1151–1163.

William Falcon and Kyunghyun Cho. 2020. A framework for contrastive self-supervised learning and designing a new approach. *arXiv preprint arXiv:2009.00104.*

Sam Fletcher, Md Zahidul Islam, et al. 2018. Comparing sets of patterns with the jaccard index. *Australasian Journal of Information Systems*, 22.

Ross Girshick. 2015. Fast r-cnn. In *Proceedings of the IEEE International Conference on Computer Vision (ICCV).*

Ting-Yao Hsu, C Lee Giles, and Ting-Hao Huang. 2021. SciCap: Generating captions for scientific figures. In *Findings of the Association for Computational Linguistics: EMNLP 2021*, pages 3258–3264, Punta Cana, Dominican Republic. Association for Computational Linguistics.

Weiran Huang, Mingyang Yi, Xuyang Zhao, and Zihao Jiang. 2021. Towards the generalization of contrastive self-supervised learning. *arXiv preprint arXiv:2111.00743*.

Ashish Jaiswal, Ashwin Ramesh Babu, Mohammad Zaki Zadeh, Debapriya Banerjee, and Fillia Makedon. 2020. A survey on contrastive self-supervised learning. *Technologies*, 9(1):2.

Taranjit Kaur and Tapan Kumar Gandhi. 2019. Automated brain image classification based on vgg-16 and transfer learning. In *2019 international conference on information technology (ICIT)*, pages 94–98. IEEE.

Alex Krizhevsky. 2009. Learning multiple layers of features from tiny images. In *Learning Multiple Layers of Features from Tiny Images*.

Pengyuan Li, Xiangying Jiang, and Hagit Shatkay. 2018. Extracting figures and captions from scientific publications. In *Proceedings of the 27th ACM International Conference on Information and Knowledge Management*, pages 1595–1598.

Zihang Lin, Yian Yin, Lu Liu, and Dashun Wang. 2023. Sciscinet: A large-scale open data lake for the science of science research. *Scientific Data*, 10(1):315.

Xiaoqiang Lu, Binqiang Wang, Xiangtao Zheng, and Xuelong Li. 2017. Exploring models and data for remote sensing image caption generation. *IEEE Transactions on Geoscience and Remote Sensing*, 56(4):2183–2195.

National Library of Medicine. 2003. Pmc open access subset. `https://www.ncbi.nlm.nih.gov/pmc/tools/openftlist/`. May 15, 2024.

Jason Priem, Heather Piwowar, and Richard Orr. 2022. Openalex: A fully-open index of scholarly works, authors, venues, institutions, and concepts. *arXiv preprint arXiv:2205.01833*.

Alec Radford, Jong Wook Kim, Chris Hallacy, Aditya Ramesh, Gabriel Goh, Sandhini Agarwal, Girish Sastry, Amanda Askell, Pamela Mishkin, Jack Clark, et al. 2021. Learning transferable visual models from natural language supervision. In *International conference on machine learning*, pages 8748–8763. PMLR.

Anastasia Razdaibiedina and Alexander Brechalov. 2023. Miread: Simple method for learning high-quality representations from scientific documents.

Aneeshan Sain, Ayan Kumar Bhunia, Yongxin Yang, Tao Xiang, and Yi-Zhe Song. 2021. Stylemeup: Towards style-agnostic sketch-based image retrieval. In *Proceedings of the IEEE/CVF Conference on Computer Vision and Pattern Recognition (CVPR)*, pages 8504–8513.

Sachin Mehta Ben Bogin Madeleine van Zuylen Sravanthi Parasa Sameer Singh Matt Gardner Sanjay Subramanian, Lucy Lu Wang and Hannaneh Hajishirzi. 2020. MedICaT: A Dataset of Medical Images, Captions, and Textual References. In *Findings of EMNLP*.

Sasha Targ, Diogo Almeida, and Kevin Lyman. 2016. Resnet in resnet: Generalizing residual architectures.

Jian Wang, Zhiguo Cao, Yang Xiao, and Xinyuan Qi. 2018. Supervised guiding long-short term memory for image caption generation based on object classes. In *MIPPR 2017: Pattern Recognition and Computer Vision*, volume 10609, pages 148–155. SPIE.

Kuansan Wang, Zhihong Shen, Chiyuan Huang, Chieh-Han Wu, Yuxiao Dong, and Anshul Kanakia. 2020. Microsoft academic graph: When experts are not enough. *Quantitative Science Studies*, 1(1):396–413.

Xinlong Wang, Rufeng Zhang, Chunhua Shen, Tao Kong, and Lei Li. 2021. Dense contrastive learning for self-supervised visual pre-training. In *Proceedings of the IEEE/CVF Conference on Computer Vision and Pattern Recognition*, pages 3024–3033.

Yixuan Wei, Yue Cao, Zheng Zhang, Houwen Peng, Zhuliang Yao, Zhenda Xie, Han Hu, and Baining Guo. 2023. iclip: Bridging image classification and contrastive language-image pre-training for visual recognition. In *Proceedings of the IEEE/CVF Conference on Computer Vision and Pattern Recognition*, pages 2776–2786.

Siwei Wu, Yizhi Li, Kang Zhu, Ge Zhang, Yiming Liang, Kaijing Ma, Chenghao Xiao, Haoran Zhang, Bohao Yang, Wenhu Chen, Wenhao Huang, Noura Al Moubayed, Jie Fu, and Chenghua Lin. 2024. Scimmir: Benchmarking scientific multi-modal information retrieval.

Shukang Yin, Chaoyou Fu, Sirui Zhao, Ke Li, Xing Sun, Tong Xu, and Enhong Chen. 2023. A survey on multimodal large language models. *arXiv preprint arXiv:2306.13549*.

Liangzhe Yuan, Rui Qian, Yin Cui, Boqing Gong, Florian Schroff, Ming-Hsuan Yang, Hartwig Adam, and Ting Liu. 2022. Contextualized spatio-temporal contrastive learning with self-supervision. In *Proceedings of the IEEE/CVF Conference on Computer Vision and Pattern Recognition*, pages 13977–13986.

Roland S. Zimmermann, Yash Sharma, Steffen Schneider, Matthias Bethge, and Wieland Brendel. 2021. Contrastive learning inverts the data generating process. In *Proceedings of the 38th International Conference on Machine Learning*, volume 139 of *Proceedings of Machine Learning Research*, pages 12979–12990. PMLR.

First Steps in Building a Knowledge Base of Mathematical Results

Shrey Mishra
DI ENS, ENS,
PSL University, CNRS, Inria
Paris, France
shrey.mishra@ens.psl.eu

Yacine Brihmouche
Criteo
Paris, France
y.brihmouche@criteo.com

Théo Delemazure
LAMSADE, U. Paris-Dauphine,
PSL University, CNRS
Paris, France
theo@delemazure.fr

Antoine Gauquier
DI ENS, ENS,
PSL University, CNRS, Inria
Paris, France
antoine.gauquier@ens.psl.eu

Pierre Senellart
DI ENS, ENS,
PSL University, CNRS, Inria & IUF
Paris, France
pierre@senellart.com

Abstract

This paper explores first steps towards extracting information about theorems and proofs from scholarly documents to build a knowledge base of interlinked results. Specifically, we consider two main tasks: extractions of results and their proofs from the PDF of scientific articles; and establishing which results is used in the proof of which, across the scientific literature. We discuss the problem statement, methodologies, as well as preliminary findings employed in both phases of our approach, highlighting the challenges faced.

1 Introduction

The proliferation of academic publications, particularly in theoretical fields, presents a significant challenge in information retrieval and knowledge extraction. As of *May 2020* (which is the cut-off date we used to build our dataset), the arXiv[1] preprint repository alone hosted approximately *1.7 million academic papers* (see Figure 1), a substantial portion of which include theoretical results such as theorems, lemmas, and propositions (roughly one-third based on cursory search using keyword filtering). And arXiv constitutes a fraction of the entire collection of scientific publications (e.g., the pirate Sci-Hub Web site include 88 million academic papers, and the Crossref[2] publication database contains metadata about 158 million articles as of May 2024).

Researchers typically rely on academic search engines like Google Scholar[3] or AMiner[4] to find relevant literature. While effective for general searches, this method often falls short in mathematical fields such as mathematics or theoretical computer science, where the essence of the work is encapsulated in mathematical results (theorems, lemmas, etc.) rather than at the textual level. We discuss in this paper first steps in a project whose goal is to build a knowledge base of interlinked mathematical results, directly from the scientific literature in PDF format.

The goal of such project would be to enable researchers to perform queries at the level of individual mathematical results, such as:

- ***IR at the Theorem Level:*** For example, asking *Which variants of the vertex cover problem are solvable in polynomial time?* Traditional search engines lack the context-specific understanding to address such specialized inquiries directly.
- ***Visualization of Theoretical Dependencies:*** What does the graph of results used to prove other results look like within a given research article? A knowledge base could help visualize these connections, showing how individual results contribute to broader scientific advancements.
- ***Impact Analysis of Theoretical Foundations:*** How many published results depend on a particular theorem, and what would be the impact if this theorem were proven incorrect? Understanding the dependency network of a theorem could be crucial for assessing the robustness of a field's knowledge base.

Our methodology for constructing the knowledge graph involves a two-step process, as illustrated in Figure 2:

1. *Result Extraction:* The first step focuses on identifying and extracting theoretical results

[1] https://arxiv.org/
[2] https://www.crossref.org/
[3] https://scholar.google.com/
[4] https://www.aminer.org/

Proceedings of the Fourth Workshop on Scholarly Document Processing (SDP 2024), pages 165–174
August 16, 2024

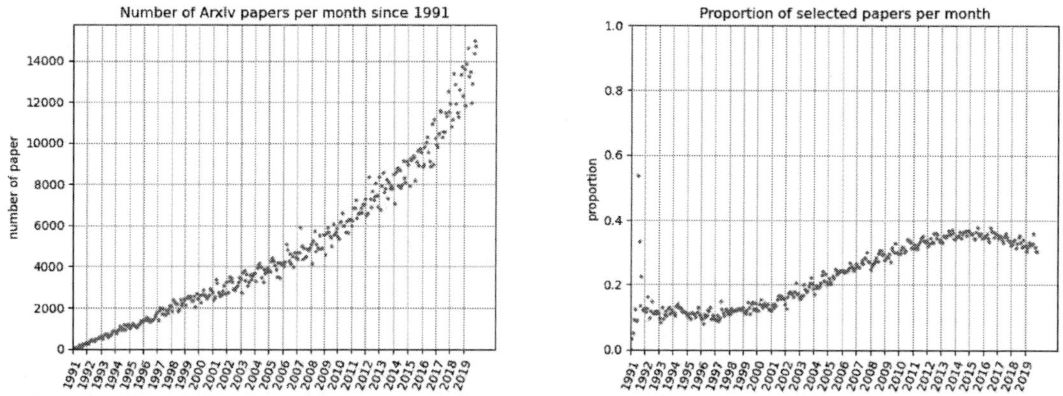

Figure 1: Evolution of the number of papers on arXiv **published** each month from its inception to May 2020 *(left panel)* and the proportion of them **containing mathematical results** *(right panel).*

from academic papers, along with their proofs. This involves sophisticated text and data mining techniques to discern and isolate relevant mathematical expressions and their accompanying discussions within a dense and complex document layout.

2. *Result Connection:* The second step is about pinpointing the exact papers and specific results that are referenced within the proof of a given result. This step is crucial for mapping out the dependencies and relationships between different results, enhancing our understanding of how concepts in theoretical fields are interconnected. Note that there are actually two subtasks of increasing complexity: identifying which paper of a given corpus is cited in the proof of a given result; and identifying which result within that paper is used in the proof of a given result.

In this paper, we report on preliminary work on each task (and subtask), considered individually (though in reality they could benefit from a unified approach). This strategy was employed to mitigate the risk of one task's methodology negatively impacting the others, particularly given the sequential dependencies inherent in this work.

We briefly discuss related work in Section 2 then explain how we built the (partly labeled) dataset on which we operate in Section 3, along with tools used to build it. We then discuss the methodology employed for the three subtasks in Section 4 before presenting preliminary experimental results in Section 5. Code, additional details, as well as instructions to rebuild the same datasets are provided in two online repositories: `https://github.com/PierreSenellart/theoremkb` for the overall project and `https://github.com/mv96/mm_extraction` specifically for the unimodal and multimodal extraction models.

2 Related Work

Result extraction. For the extraction task, two main related works are noteworthy. Ginev et al. (Ginev and Miller, 2020) addressed the classification of mathematical statements as a 13-class problem (where classes are, e.g., proposition, example, remark). However, their evaluation was limited to the first logical paragraph, which is easier to classify, relied solely on the text modality without capturing sequential dependencies among paragraphs, and, crucially, required the availability of an HTML-ized version of the LaTeX source.

In previous work (Mishra et al., 2021) we explored deep learning-based methods, including object detection and text classification, to extract proofs and theorems. We proposed several unimodal approaches across different modalities; however, there was no clear method for comparing and evaluating these modalities. For instance, our text-based approach used fine-tuned transformers on text lines extracted by the pdfalto tool, while the vision approach utilized bitmap renderings of entire PDF pages. In Section 5, we include the line-based approach as a baseline.

In contrast, this work proposes a modular multimodal classifier that operates at the paragraph level, incorporating text, vision, and font modalities simultaneously, while also capturing sequential information to predict paragraph labels.

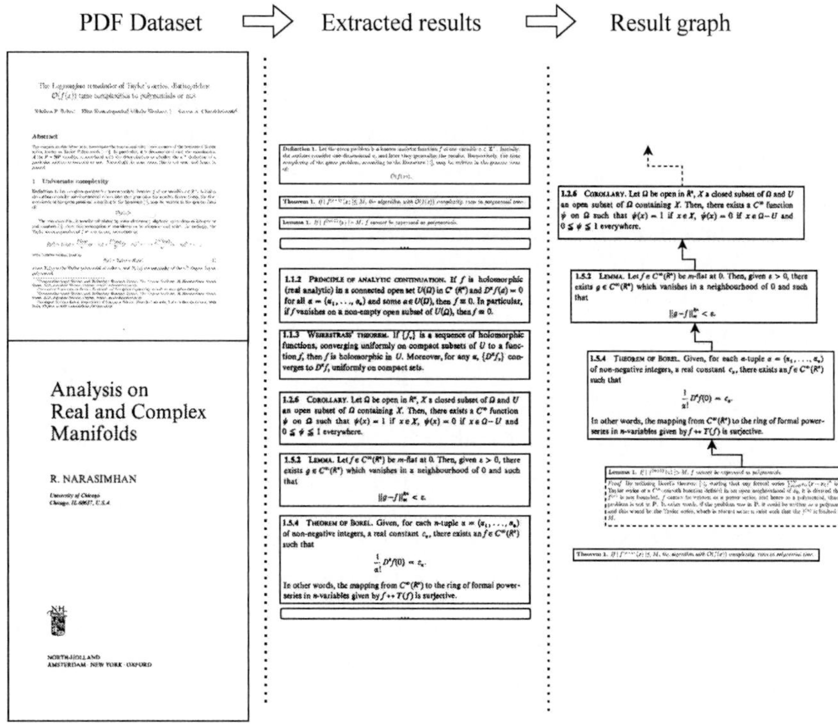

Figure 2: Two-step process for building a knowledge graph of papers: (i) result extraction; (ii) result connection

Result connection. A notable task is citation extraction and disambiguation. Cohan et al. (Cohan et al., 2019) proposed a classifier to detect citation intent based on the sentence context. It identifies three primary intents: Background, Result, and Method. They used a bidirectional LSTM with an attention layer and three independent MLPs for training. The main task was identifying citation intent, while auxiliary tasks included guessing the section title.

There are other projects whose goal is to create a structured knowledge base of mathematical results, though not by exploiting the content of PDF articles, including:

- MBASE (Kohlhase and Franke, 2001): Proposed in 2001 for formal representations of mathematical results, but development stopped in 2003.
- Logipedia[5]: A comprehensive library of formal mathematical statements for theorem provers.
- Ganesalingam and Gowers (Ganesalingam and Gowers, 2013): An automated model that writes proofs in a human style by mimicking researchers' reasoning.

[5]http://logipedia.inria.fr/

3 Dataset Construction

Our approach relies on training machine learning models, which requires constructing a (sizable) labeled dataset. We explain in this section which tools we use for basic parsing of PDF documents, how we built a labeled dataset using these tools and newly developed ones, and present the characteristics of our dataset.

3.1 Information Extraction Tools

One pivotal tool in our toolkit is Grobid[6] (Lopez, 2009), a robust application also used by platforms such as Semantic Scholar[7]. Grobid is precisely engineered to extract text from scientific documents and convert raw PDFs into XML files. These files contain structured information, including segmented texts at the level of sentences and paragraphs, and further annotate critical sections such as abstracts, introductions, author names, titles, and references, along with their precise page numbers and coordinates – Grobid does not extract mathematical statements and proofs, though, which is our focus here.

Unlike many document AI models (Xu et al., 2020, 2021; Huang et al., 2022) designed for ex-

[6]https://github.com/kermitt2/grobid
[7]https://www.semanticscholar.org

tracting information from single-page documents such as receipts or bills, Grobid leverages domain-specific knowledge to handle scientific content. It manages the layout complexities typical of multi-page scientific articles, such as page breaks and possible two-column layouts. It achieves this with remarkable efficiency, processing documents at ≈ 10 PDFs per second on a standard computer. We also rely on pdfalto[8], a lower-level tool by the same author as Grobid, that takes a PDF input and produce between other things a sequence of text lines with comprehensive font information for each character, such as typeface and size, along with their exact location on the page.

3.2 Automatic Labeling from LaTeX Sources

In order to construct a labeled dataset for the result extraction script, we have developed a custom tool that extracts the coordinates of mathematical statement and sources for document from which their LaTeX source is available. We insist on the fact that the availability of LaTeX source is only necessary to build a labeled dataset for training and evaluating our result extraction approach – they are not required at extraction time.

Even when LaTeX sources are available, extracting the coordinates of theorems and proofs in the resulting PDF is not trivial: indeed, there are many ways authors of a LaTeX document can use to create this form of environment, including by defining their own macros – and as TeX is a Turing-complete programming language, it is impossible to build a robust extractor just based on analyzing the source code. Instead of doing that, we developed a LaTeX package that performs the extraction, injected it in the prologue of the LaTeX document, and recompiled the entire document. The LaTeX package modifies the code of the `\newtheorem` macro (which is either the standard LaTeX one or the one provided by the `amsthm` or `ntheorem` package), of the `\declaretheorem` command (of the `thmtools` package), of the `\spnewtheorem` command (of Springer's document classes such as `llncs`) and of the `proof` environment, in order to add, whenever a LaTeX theorem or proof environment is used in the paper, a PDF hyperlink around the environment. This PDF hyperlink points to a URI that uniquely identifies the result within the document. After compilation, we extract the coordinates of these hyperlinks from the PDF document (we use pdfalto for this). Note that this does not cover all possible cases (documents written in an obsolete version of LaTeX; documents with a fully custom way of writing theorems and proofs; etc.) but this is fine: the goal is to build a labeled dataset large enough to be representative, not to have a foolproof labeling method.

Once the coordinates of every result and proof is obtained, we use a merging script to merge the output of Grobid and of pdfalto to match the paragraphs extracted by Grobid with the coordinates of text lines and the hyperlink-labeled results given by pdfalto. We also retrieve font information from pdfalto and we construct bitmap renderings of every PDF page using PyMuPDF's `fitz` module[9].

3.3 Dataset

We now report on the dataset used in experiments.

Extraction. We retrieved all papers (1.7 million) published on arXiv till May 2020 using arXiv's Bulk Data Access through Amazon S3[10]. This includes both PDF papers and, for documents that were written in LaTeX, their source as well. After filtering this massive corpus to isolate papers containing mathematical statements such as theorems or proofs, we reduced the count to *460 thousand papers*. Further refinement was necessary to exclude non-English papers, and papers that failed to compile using a contemporary PDF compiler (pdflatex from TeXlive 2019), or papers that experienced failures with any of the tools in our pipeline – Grobid, pdfalto, or bitmap rendering. This resulted in a final dataset of 197 thousand papers. Running our merging script on this dataset, we categorized each paragraph into distinct classes: ***Proof, Theorem*** (which includes other theorem-like environments such as definitions, lemmas, corollaries, remarks), ***Basic*** (neither proof nor theorem), and a marginal ***Overlap*** reject class for instances where multiple categories were erroneously grouped due to paragraph splitting bugs in Grobid. To construct our validation dataset, we randomly selected *3,682 papers* comprising approximately *0.5 million paragraphs* with their label, each enriched with font information, bitmap images, and the textual content present.

Connecting Papers and Results. For this task, no automatic labeling is possible so we need to create a smaller scale dataset. We decided to select

[8] https://github.com/kermitt2/grobid

[9] https://pymupdf.readthedocs.io/

[10] https://info.arxiv.org/help/bulk_data_s3.html

a topically consistent subset of papers, focusing on the domain of computational complexity, from 2010 to 2020, obtaining roughly *6 000 scientific articles* under the "Computer Science - Computational Complexity" (cs.CC) category of arXiv. This category was chosen due to the high likelihood of inter-citations among papers within this specific domain. After applying our extraction script we obtained *4 705 papers* that were compilable and did not trigger errors with the deployed tools. Of these, *3 711 papers* contained results that referenced another paper within the same dataset, which we manually labeled.

4 Methodology

In this section, we delve into the specific methodologies adopted for each of the three subtasks outlined in our study: the extraction task and the two connecting tasks – results to paper and results to results.

4.1 Extraction of Results

Intuitively, the following features can be used to isolate results and proofs in PDF papers. *Visual Features:* We identify vital visual indicators such as bold or italic text and the presence of a QED symbol, which typically denotes the end of a proof. *Font-Level Features:* Recognizing specific fonts used at the beginning of paragraphs, as seen in papers formatted in certain styles which consistently uses distinctive fonts for theorem declarations. *Language Information:* Analyzing the textual content within the spatial bounds of a paragraph to discern its nature based on linguistic patterns. *Structural Information:* Utilizing page numbers, relative positions, and the context of neighbouring paragraphs to improve prediction accuracy.

To effectively process these diverse data modalities, we deploy three different classifiers:

Font Model: This model uses an **LSTM** (Hochreiter and Schmidhuber, 1997) to process sequences of font data extracted by pdfalto, capturing dependencies in font usage throughout the document.

Vision-Based Model: We implement a CNN, specifically an **EfficientNetV2** (Tan and Le, 2021), to analyze visual clues. This model processes bitmap images of paragraphs, focusing on initial word formatting and the presence of end-of-proof symbols.

Language Model: A pretrained RoBERTa (Liu et al., 2019) language model is used, where the CLS token from the last layer helps identify significant text sections. The model operates on text extracted and structured by Grobid at the paragraph level.

To synthesize insights from these distinctive models trained on different modalities, we employ a **GMU-based mechanism**. This approach, inspired by Gated Multimodal Units (Arevalo et al., 2020), facilitates the integration of features from different modalities. Each model's output is frozen to prevent updates during this phase, ensuring stability in the embeddings they produce.

The features extracted from the Multimodal GMU are then used as input for a **CRF model** that captures sequential dependencies between blocks. Numerous studies (Patel and Caragea, 2019), (Al-Zaidy et al., 2019), (Wei et al., 2022) have demonstrated the efficiency of employing a CRF-based model on top of features extracted by a deep learning approach to model and extract important keyphrases, particularly within scholarly documents. CRF models have also been used to model sequential dependencies and clustering information over features extracted from CNN models on scientific document pages (Li et al., 2018). This model uses sequential information from the previous paragraphs to determine the paragraph's label across the entire document. It incorporates contextual features such as page numbers and coordinate information along with information about page breaks. This approach allows the model to understand and classify each paragraph's role within the broader structure of the document.

This methodology leverages the strengths of each modality and ensures that the extracted information aligns with how a human would typically look at the problem. By combining different techniques across different modalities, we aim to classify and link mathematical results robustly across various scientific literature.

4.2 Linking Results to Papers

We employed Grobid, a machine-learning tool designed to convert PDFs of scientific papers into structured XML files. This conversion crucially extracts bibliographic data (including titles, authors' names, and publication years of cited articles) from the article, with references to each bibliographic entry. We also integrated data from the S2ORC

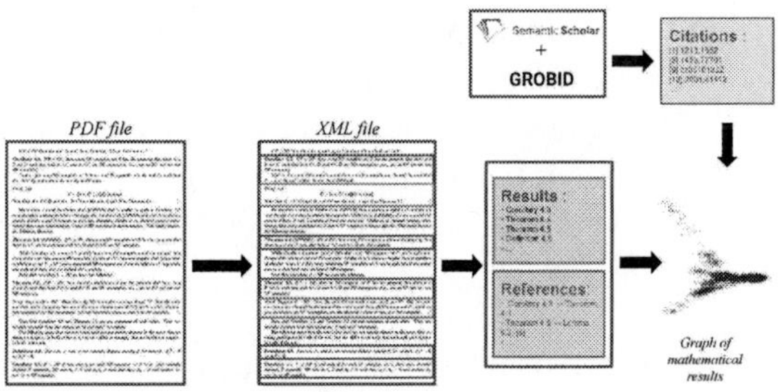

Figure 3: **Flow of the algorithm**. We convert a PDF file into an XML file with identified theorems and proofs following our extraction methodology. Finally, we associate references with papers in the corpus to build a graph of mathematical results

dataset (Lo et al., 2020) of Semantic Scholar, which maps paper references to arXiv IDs.

To systematically map connections from papers to papers within our dataset, we developed a high-level graph extraction algorithm summarized in Figure 3. This algorithm efficiently identifies and represents the relationships between papers based on their citations, creating a navigable and interactive graph.

Our graph extraction algorithm is designed to map the citations within and across papers, creating a network that can be navigated and analyzed. We proceed as follows. First, we extract theorems and proofs from PDF articles as previously described.[11] Second, within every identified proof, we search for explicit references to formal results (potentially from other papers), with simple regular expression patterns capturing strings such as "Theorem 1", "Lemma 2.54.2", "Problem A.1", "Proposition E.7.1.3.1". We also determine whether such a referenced link is internal (within the same paper) or external (pointing to another document), looking for references to bibliographic entries in the immediate context (such as "Theorem 1 of [2]" or "[27], Proposition 26,"). We primarily focus on these external references for building our citation graph, ignoring internal citations (i.e., references within the same paper), and retrieving the corresponding bibliographic entry. In cases where multiple results are referenced together, such as "Theorems 1, 5 from [2]", we split these into separate citations for clarity. Additionally, we filter out false bibliographic links by checking for specific keywords that indicate non-referential usage. We

[11]To evaluate independently both phases of our extract–connect approach, we can also start from the dataset with ground truth labels for the position of theorems and proofs.

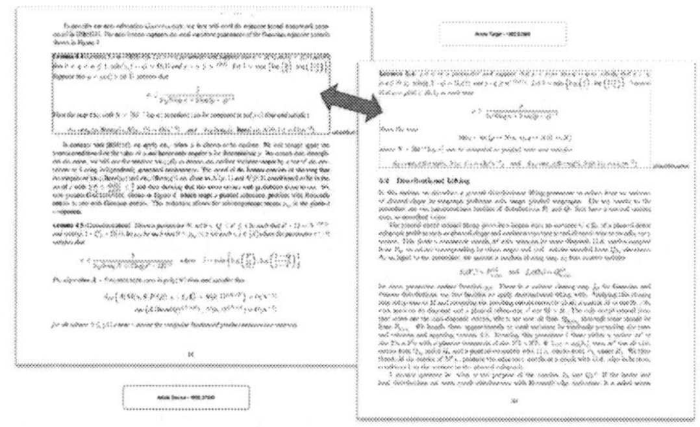

Figure 4: A clear, obvious link where the author did specify the connecting result.

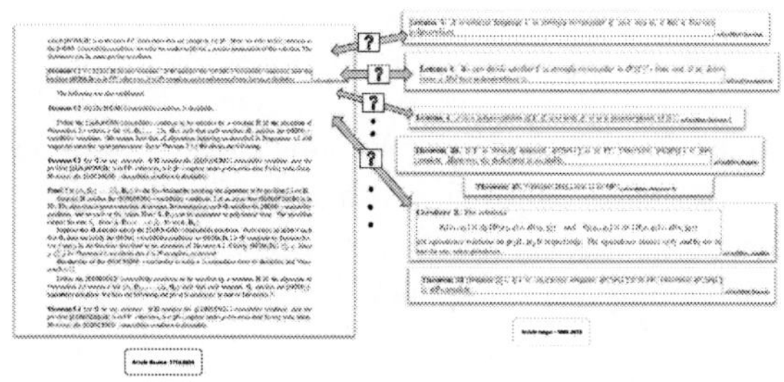

Figure 5: An ambiguous link where the author did not specify the connecting result

finally merged the Grobid-produced bibliographic entries with the S2ORC ones, allowing us to retrieve the arXiv ID of each bibliographic reference if it exists. Note that we encountered some occasional mismatches between our arXiv dataset and the S2ORC one, coming from the fact that an arXiv paper may have multiple versions, only the most recent of which is available in the bulk data dump. This means the tag used for the bibliographic entry may not match across these two datasets but we resolved inconsistencies by looking for a match in the whole bibliographic entry itself.

4.3 Linking Results to Results

A crucial step in constructing a knowledge graph of mathematical results is accurately linking specific results between papers. Thus, when citing Theorem 42 of reference [X] in the proof of a result, when restating Theorem 42 of reference [X] with another name in another paper (see Figure 4 for an example), or, simply, when using reference [X] in the proof of a result or when restating it without an explicit reference to a specific result, it is important to determine which result from the paper referenced by [X] is actually mentioned (see Figure 5 for an example of this case).

To address this linking challenge (determining

which result from the paper referenced by [X] is cited in the current paper), we employ a dual-representation strategy to establish the most likely matches between cited results in the source paper and possible references in the target paper. This involves the following steps:

1. **Structural Representation via TF-IDF Vectorization:** We vectorize paragraph content using a TF-IDF word vectorizer (Jones, 2004). This technique transforms the textual content into a high-dimensional vector space where each dimension corresponds to a term's frequency-inverse document frequency score. The resulting vectors capture the structural aspects of the text, such as the usage of specific terms and syntactic patterns often indicative of mathematical content.

2. **Semantic Representation with DistilBERT:** Parallel to the structural approach, we process the text using a ***pre-trained DistilBERT model*** (Sanh et al., 2019). This smaller, more efficient version of *BERT* is fine-tuned on a generic classification task to categorize text as proof, theorem, or introductory text. We use the **[CLS]** token embedding from the last layer of DistilBERT as the comprehensive vector representation of each paragraph. This semantic vector captures deeper linguistic and contextual nuances, identifying conceptual similarities between paragraphs that the TF-IDF approach might miss.

Both vectorization methods are applied in a zero-shot learning context, meaning no additional fine-tuning is done for this specific task. There is no training on specialized losses such as contrastive loss, which could otherwise enhance the model's ability to distinguish connected text segments. We compute the cosine similarity between the source paragraph vector from the source paper and all paragraph vectors from the target paper. The pair of paragraphs (one from the source and one from the target) with the highest cosine similarity is considered the likely match.

5 Experimental results

This section presents experimental results derived from implementing our methodologies across three specific subtasks: extraction, connecting papers, and linking specific results. We stress that results from the latter two tasks are preliminary at this stage.

5.1 Extraction

The extraction task involved training multiple machine learning classifiers on different modalities to recognize and categorize paragraph-level information content from academic papers. Table 1 summarizes the accuracy achieved by each classifier with or without sequential paragraph information, compared to two baselines: a dummy classifier that always predicts the most frequent *Basic* class, and the textual model, line-based, approach from (Mishra et al., 2021), reevaluated on the same dataset. We report standard accuracy, as well as mean-F_1 over the three classes *Basic*, *Theorem*, *Proof*.

The best-performing approach is the multimodal approach, which captures sequential information using the CRF model. However, the gains are modest with respect to the pure text-only approach augmented with the CRF model. Extra experiments are described in (Mishra et al., 2023).

5.2 Connecting results to papers

For connecting papers, we visualized the graph of linked results across the **entire arXiv corpus**. Figure 6 illustrates the interconnectedness of various papers through citations of famous theorems and lemmas. The visualization underscores the dense network of academic work, reinforcing the importance of effective result linking to navigate scholarly literature efficiently. For more details, see (Delemazure, 2020).

Figure 6: Largest connected component of the aggregated ArXiv graph generated with the networkx Python library, using a spectral layout.

Modality	Model chosen	Seq. approach	#Batches	#Params (M)	Accuracy (%)	Mean F_1 (%)
Dummy	always predict *Basic*	—	—	—	59.41	24.85
Line-based (Mishra et al., 2021)	Bert (fine-tuned)	—	—	110	57.31	55.71
Font	LSTM 128 cells	—	11	2	64.93	45.48
		CRF	11+1	2	71.50	64.51
Vision	EfficientNetV2M_avg	—	9	53	69.44	60.33
		CRF	9+1	53	74.63	70.82
Text	Pretrained RoBERTa-like	—	20	124	76.45	72.33
		CRF	20+1	124	83.10	80.99
Multimodal	GMU	—	10	185	76.86	73.87
		CRF	10+1	185	**84.19**	**82.91**

Table 1: Overall performance comparison (accuracy and mean F_1 over the three classes *Basic*, *Theorem*, and *Proof*) of individual modality models and multimodal model, with and without the sequential approach, for each model, the number of batches (1 000 PDF documents, roughly 200k samples) it was trained on is indicated (here "+" indicates additional batches on which further training of sequential paragraph model).

5.3 Linking results

In the final subtask of linking specific results between papers, we evaluated the effectiveness of two vectorization-based approaches: TF-IDF and DistilBERT embeddings on a small dataset of 45 theorems with manually labeled matches in other papers. The outcomes of these approaches are summarized below:

TF-IDF Vectors: This approach successfully matched **17/45 (38%)** results across different papers. TF-IDF vectors, which emphasize term frequency within the document context, proved particularly effective in matching results that use similar terminologies.

DistilBERT: The DistilBERT model achieved **7/45 (15%)** perfect matches. Despite its lower performance than TF-IDF in this zero-shot setting, DistilBERT captured deeper semantic relationships that were not as transparent through lexical similarity alone.

For more details, see (Brihmouche, 2022).

6 Conclusions

This paper presents a comprehensive framework for constructing a knowledge base of mathematical results. It aims to transcend the limitations of traditional search engines through an enhanced, result-oriented navigation system within academic literature. **Through preliminary experiments on distinct subtasks, we have demonstrated the feasibility of our proposed solution, establishing a proof of concept for a robust and scalable knowledge management system.**

In data extraction, our experiments have highlighted the efficacy of a multimodal approach, leveraging a GMU architecture followed by Sequential CRF modelling. This approach proved adept at capturing sequential and contextual nuances in text, offering a slight advantage over simpler, text-only methods. The ability of this architecture to integrate various data modalities into a cohesive model illustrates its potential for comprehensive information extraction from complex scientific texts, setting a high standard for subsequent refinement and application.

The construction of a citation graph detailing the connections between papers through cited results has unveiled a rich tapestry of scholarly communication. Notably, the longest path in this citation graph extends to 13 links, underscoring the depth and complexity of academic discourse. However, the aggregated nature of this graph means we must be cautious in interpreting these paths, as they do not guarantee a direct continuation of the topic from one paper to another.

Our examination of methodologies for linking specific results across papers has underscored the importance of precise terminology in the academic discourse of mathematics. The TF-IDF vectorization approach outperformed the semantic capabilities of the DistilBERT model, suggesting that the reuse of exact terms and phrases is crucial for accurately connecting related results, though our experiments are still preliminary.

Moving forward, we consider several avenues for exploration and development. Enhanced machine learning models, specifically tailored to the nuances of mathematical language and structured problem-solving in academia, could drastically reduce the dependency on manual labelling. Additionally, expanding the knowledge base to include more diverse fields of study and integrating more advanced semantic understanding tools will enhance the breadth and depth of the knowledge graph, providing unparalleled access to interconnected scientific knowledge.

Acknowledgments

This work was funded in part by the French government under management of Agence Nationale de la Recherche as part of the "Investissements d'avenir" program, reference ANR-19-P3IA-0001 (PRAIRIE 3IA Institute). This work was also made possible through HPC resources of IDRIS granted under the allocation 2020-AD011012097 made by GENCI (Jean Zay supercomputer).

References

Rabah A. Al-Zaidy, Cornelia Caragea, and C. Lee Giles. 2019. Bi-lstm-crf sequence labeling for keyphrase extraction from scholarly documents. In *The World Wide Web Conference, WWW 2019, San Francisco, CA, USA, May 13-17, 2019*, pages 2551–2557. ACM.

John Arevalo, Thamar Solorio, Manuel Montes-y Gómez, and Fabio A González. 2020. Gated multimodal networks. *Neural Computing and Applications*, 32.

Yacine Brihmouche. 2022. TheoremKB : une base de connaissance des résultats mathématiques. Master's thesis, Paris IX Dauphine, September.

Arman Cohan, Waleed Ammar, Madeleine van Zuylen, and Field Cady. 2019. Structural scaffolds for citation intent classification in scientific publications. In *Proceedings of the 2019 Conference of the North American Chapter of the Association for Computational Linguistics: Human Language Technologies, NAACL-HLT 2019, Minneapolis, MN, USA, June 2-7, 2019, Volume 1 (Long and Short Papers)*, pages 3586–3596. Association for Computational Linguistics.

Theo Delemazure. 2020. A Knowledge Base of Mathematical Results. Master's thesis, Ecole Normale Supérieure (ENS), September.

M. Ganesalingam and W. T. Gowers. 2013. A fully automatic problem solver with human-style output. *CoRR*, abs/1309.4501.

Deyan Ginev and Bruce R. Miller. 2020. Scientific statement classification over arxiv.org. In *Proceedings of The 12th Language Resources and Evaluation Conference, LREC 2020, Marseille, France, May 11-16, 2020*, pages 1219–1226. European Language Resources Association.

Sepp Hochreiter and Jürgen Schmidhuber. 1997. Long short-term memory. *Neural computation*, 9(8).

Yupan Huang, Tengchao Lv, Lei Cui, Yutong Lu, and Furu Wei. 2022. LayoutLMv3: Pre-training for document ai with unified text and image masking. In *ACM MM*.

Karen Spärck Jones. 2004. A statistical interpretation of term specificity and its application in retrieval. *J. Documentation*, 60(5):493–502.

Michael Kohlhase and Andreas Franke. 2001. Mbase: Representing knowledge and context for the integration of mathematical software systems. *J. Symb. Comput.*, 32(4):365–402.

Xiao-Hui Li, Fei Yin, and Cheng-Lin Liu. 2018. Page object detection from pdf document images by deep structured prediction and supervised clustering. In *2018 24th International Conference on Pattern Recognition (ICPR)*, pages 3627–3632.

Yinhan Liu, Myle Ott, Naman Goyal, Jingfei Du, Mandar Joshi, Danqi Chen, Omer Levy, Mike Lewis, Luke Zettlemoyer, and Veselin Stoyanov. 2019. Roberta: A robustly optimized BERT pretraining approach. *CoRR*, abs/1907.11692.

Kyle Lo, Lucy Lu Wang, Mark Neumann, Rodney Kinney, and Daniel Weld. 2020. S2ORC: The semantic scholar open research corpus. In *Proceedings of the 58th Annual Meeting of the Association for Computational Linguistics*, pages 4969–4983, Online. Association for Computational Linguistics.

Patrice Lopez. 2009. Grobid: Combining automatic bibliographic data recognition and term extraction for scholarship publications. In *ECDL*, volume 5714, pages 473–474.

Shrey Mishra, Antoine Gauquier, and Pierre Senellart. 2023. Multimodal machine learning for extraction of theorems and proofs in the scientific literature. *CoRR*, abs/2307.09047.

Shrey Mishra, Lucas Pluvinage, and Pierre Senellart. 2021. Towards extraction of theorems and proofs in scholarly articles. In *DocEng '21: ACM Symposium on Document Engineering 2021, Limerick, Ireland, August 24-27, 2021*, pages 25:1–25:4. ACM.

Krutarth Patel and Cornelia Caragea. 2019. Exploring word embeddings in crf-based keyphrase extraction from research papers. In *Proceedings of the 10th International Conference on Knowledge Capture, K-CAP 2019, Marina Del Rey, CA, USA, November 19-21, 2019*, pages 37–44. ACM.

Victor Sanh, Lysandre Debut, Julien Chaumond, and Thomas Wolf. 2019. Distilbert, a distilled version of bert: smaller, faster, cheaper and lighter. *arXiv:1910.01108*.

Mingxing Tan and Quoc Le. 2021. EfficientNetv2: Smaller models and faster training. In *ICML*.

Xin Wei, Lamia Salsabil, and Jian Wu. 2022. Theory entity extraction for social and behavioral sciences papers using distant supervision. In *Proceedings of the 22nd ACM Symposium on Document Engineering, DocEng 2022, San Jose, California, USA, September 20-23, 2022*, pages 7:1–7:4. ACM.

Yang Xu, Yiheng Xu, Tengchao Lv, Lei Cui, Furu Wei, Guoxin Wang, Yijuan Lu, Dinei Florencio, Cha Zhang, Wanxiang Che, et al. 2021. LayoutLMv2: Multi-modal pre-training for visually-rich document understanding. In *ACL/IJCNLP*.

Yiheng Xu, Minghao Li, Lei Cui, Shaohan Huang, Furu Wei, and Ming Zhou. 2020. LayoutLM: Pre-training of text and layout for document image understanding. In *SIGKDD*.

AutoRef : Generating Refinements of Reviews Given Guidelines

Soham Chitnis[1], **Manasi Patwardhan**[2], **Ashwin Srinivasan**[1],
Tanmay Tulsidas Verlekar[1], **Lovekesh Vig**[2], **Gautam Shroff**[2]

[1]Department of Computer Science & Information Systems, BITS Pilani, India
[2]TCS Research, India

Correspondence: manasi.patwardhan@tcs.com

Abstract

When examining reviews of research papers, we can distinguish between two hypothetical referees: the maximally lenient referee who accepts any paper with a vacuous review and the maximally strict one who rejects any paper with an overly pedantic review. Clearly, both are of no practical value. Our interest is in a referee who makes a balanced judgement and provides a review abiding by the guidelines. In this paper, we present a case study of automatic correction of an existing machine-generated or human review. The AutoRef system implements an iterative approach that progressively "refines" a review by attempting to make it more compliant with pre-defined requirements of a "good" review. It implements the following steps: (1) Translate the review requirements into a specification in natural language, of "yes/no" questions; (2) Given a $(paper, review)$ pair, extract answers to the questions ; (3) Use the results in (2) to generate a new review ; and (4) Return to Step (2) with the paper and the new review. Here, (2) and (3) are implemented by large language model (LLM) based agents. We present a case study using papers and reviews made available for the International Conference on Learning Representations (ICLR). Our initial empirical results suggest that AutoRef progressively improves the compliance of the generated reviews to the specification. Currently designed specification makes AutoRef progressively generate reviews which are stricter, making the decisions more inclined towards "rejections". This demonstrates the applicability of AutoRef for: (1) The progressive correction of overly lenient reviews, being useful for referees and meta-reviewers; and (2) The generation of progressively stricter reviews for a paper, starting from a vacuous review ("Great paper. Accept."), facilitating authors when trying to assess weaknesses in their papers.

1 Introduction

The modern practice of peer-review of scholarly articles is attributed to William Whewell's proposal in 1831 that manuscripts submitted to the Transactions of the Royal Society be subject to a review by two other members of the Royal Society. The referees–as they were called–would submit a written report on the claims of the paper. The process immediately ran into trouble, as the very first paper reviewed in this manner resulted in a strong disagreement between the two referees (Whewell was one of them). While conflicting opinions about a paper are not new, the number of such occurrences is greatly increased in the modern day, where 100s of 1000s of manuscripts are received for peer-review.[1] This high demand for refereeing effort inevitably results in researchers being unable to write the kind of comprehensive review that they would have liked and authors expect. It is in this context that we investigate the possibility of machine– assistant capable of refining reviews–by way of correction or completion–given some pre- defined notion of the ingredients of a "good" review. A natural extension of the machine- assisted correction of a review is machine-assisted generation of a review (viewed as a refinement of some default trivial review). In this paper, we demonstrate the working of the AutoRef system that is capable of both aspects.

The rest of the paper is organized as follows. In Section 2 we describe the AutoRef system. Related work is in Section 3. A case study of using AutoRef using conference submissions and reviews for the International Conference on Learning Representations (ICLR) is presented in

[1]The AI Index Report (Maslej et al., 2024) estimates the number of AI publications in journals to be around 230,000 in 2022 and the number of conference publications to be around 40,000. Obviously, the number of submissions reviewed would be much higher.

Proceedings of the Fourth Workshop on Scholarly Document Processing (SDP 2024), pages 175–190
August 16, 2024 ©2024 Association for Computational Linguistics

Section 4. Section 5 highlights some limitations of the current AutoRef implementation and concludes the paper.

2 The AutoRef System

We first present AutoRef conceptually, referring to the main computations that are performed.

2.1 Specification

We assume the following sets: P: the set of papers; D: the set of text-based reviews; G: the set of guidelines for review; T: the set of task-orderings that specify the guidelines; R: the set of "structured-reviews"; Q: the set of "structured-questionnaires" about any review in R; and F: the set of structured-feedbacks for elements of R (the elements of T, Q R, and F will be described shortly). Then AutoRef can be seen as an implementation of the following relations and functions[2]:

$\tau : G \hookrightarrow T$ τ non-deterministically returns a task-ordering t given a guideline g;

$\kappa : T \hookrightarrow Q$ κ returns a structured-questionnaire q, given a task-ordering t;

$\alpha : P \times D \times T \hookrightarrow R$ α returns a structured-review r, given a paper p, a (possibly empty) textual review d and a task-ordering t;

$\beta : R \hookrightarrow D$ β returns a textual review d from a structured-review r;

$\phi : P \times Q \times R \hookrightarrow F$ ϕ returns feedback f about a review r, given a paper p and a questionnaire q;

$\rho : P \times T \times R \times F \hookrightarrow R$, ρ returns a (new) review r' given a paper p, a partially-ordered set of tasks t, an review r for p, and feedback f about r;

Suppose we are given a paper p; and the ICLR review guidelines g. The following is a hypothetical description of the computations performed by AutoRef : (1) Given the review guideline g, obtain a task-ordering $t = \tau(g)$ (2) Given a task-ordering t, obtain a structured-questionnaire $q = \kappa(t)$ (3) Since no initial text-based review is provided, AutoRef calls $\alpha(p, t, \emptyset)$ to generate an initial structured-review r_0 (4) $\phi(p, q, r_0)$ provides feedback f_0 in the form of a pair consisting of a score and justification (s_0, e_0); (5) $\rho(p, t, r_0, f_0)$ results in review r_1 provided the score in s_0 satisfies some checks; and the process returns to Step (4) and iterates for some k steps. Finally, AutoRef returns the textual review $\beta(r_k)$.

Figure 1 shows a diagrammatic representation of the various components of AutoRef . D is simply the set of text-based reviews. We now specify T, Q, R, and F. For this, we assume we are given reviewer-guidelines that act as requirements, in a natural language, of a review (an example, used in experiments here, is available at [3]).

Task Orderings (the set T)

We assume we are given guidelines that consist of a set of requirements, in a natural language, of a review. We formalize these requirements in the form of a (partially-ordered) set of tasks. Example tasks are: 'Goal Determination', 'Methodology Extraction', 'Experiment Extraction', 'Clarity & Ambiguity Resolution', 'Questions for Authors', 'Decision', etc. Let Γ denote the set of all possible tasks. We will represent any partially-ordered set of tasks t by a labeled directed acyclic graph (DAG). Each vertex v_i in t is labelled with some task $t_i \in \Gamma$; and an edge from v_i to v_j in t denotes that task t_j depends directly on task t_i. For example, there may be an arc from 'Experiment Extraction' to 'Experiment Claim Support'. The set T is the set of all such labeled DAGs.

Structured Questionnaires, Reviews and Feedbacks (the sets Q, R and F)

Given a DAG $t \in T$, a structured questionnaire is a DAG with the same vertices and edges as t. However for every vertex v_k in t the vertex-label is (t_k, q_k), where q_k is a text-string denoting a "yes/no" question pertaining to task t_k.[4] The set Q is the set of all possible structured-questionnaires.

A structured review is a DAG with the same vertices and edges as t, with the vertex-label for v_k being (t_k, r_k), where r_k is a text-string denoting the part of a review pertaining to task t_k. The set

[2]We use $\hookrightarrow$ to denote nondeterministic function. That is, the function may return a different answer each time it is invoked, even with the same input.

[3]https://iclr.cc/Conferences/2023/ReviewerGuide

[4]Each question is intended to verify some aspect of the review, such as 'sufficiency of literature review', 'identification of claims', *etc.*

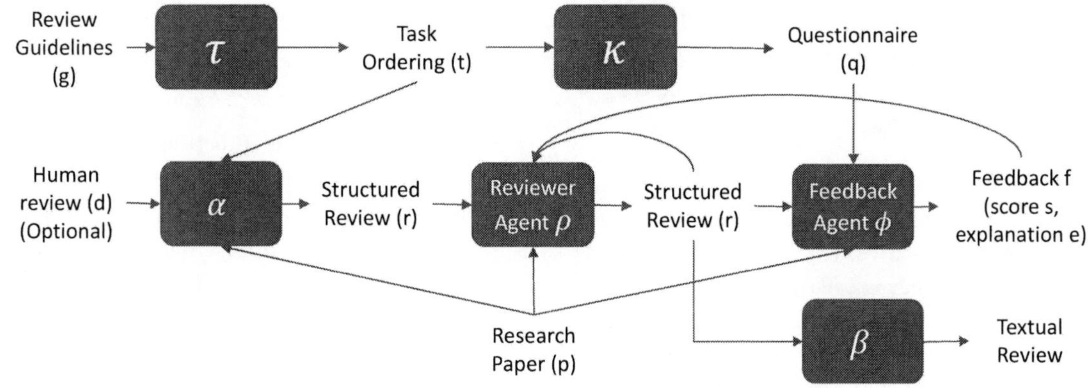

Figure 1: AutoRef System Components

R is the set of all possible structured-reviews.

Structured feedback is a DAG with the same vertices and edges as t, with the vertex-label for v_k being (s_k, e_k), where s_k is the score and e_k is the explanation for the score s_k pertaining to the question q_k. The set F is the set of all possible structured-feedbacks. Appendix A, B, C show examples of tasks and its partial ordering, structured-questionnaires and reviews from the experiments in this paper.

2.2 Implementation

In the implementation used in this paper, the relation τ between guideline(s) and task-ordering(s); and κ between task-ordering(s) and structured-quesionnaire(s) are manually done. The function α, β are translators from text-based reviews to structured reviews and *vice versa*. For reasons of space, we do not present procedures for these.[5] We focus here instead on implementing the ρ and ϕ functions. We call the former the 'Reviewer Agent' and the latter the 'Feedback Agent'.

The Reviewer Agent

The Reviewer Agent is an implementation of ρ, which is shown in Procedure 1.

ρ employs several auxiliary functions. We only provide brief descriptions of the main ones here:

- $Parents(\cdot)$: Given a vertex node v_k of a DAG r this function returns a sequence of parent vertices of v_k;

[5]The α function is slightly more involved, requiring identification of portions of the text-based review that correspond to specific tasks identified from the guidelines. β simply concatenates the review-fragments associated with each task, using an ancestral ordering of the DAG representing the structured review.

Algorithm 1 The function ρ

Input: p: a paper from P;
r: a structured-review from R;
f: feedback from F
Output: a structured-review from R
Let r' be a DAG with the same vertices and edges as r
Let $\langle v_1, v_2, \ldots, v_n \rangle$ be an ancestral vertices of r
for k= 1 to n **do**
    Let (s_k, e_k) be the vertex-label for v_k in f
    Let (t_k, r_k) be the vertex label for v_k in r
    Let (t_k, r'_k) be the vertex label for v_k in r'
    Let h be a sequence of (t_i, r_i) pairs s.t. $v_i \in Parents(v_k)$ and $(t_i, r_i) \in r$
    if $(s_k = 1)$ **then**
        if $ParentsUpdated(v_k)$ **then**
            $r'_k := UpdateReview(v_k, p, h, \emptyset)$
        else
            $r'_k := r_k$
        end if
    else
        $r'_k := UpdateReview(v_k, p, h, e_k)$
    end if
end for
return r'

- $ParentsUpdated(\cdot)$: Given a vertex node v_k of a DAG r, this function returns if the reviews of the patent vertices of v_k are updated after the last call to this function;

- $UpdateReview(\cdot)$: It refines the review r_k for task t_k, in the context of reviews of the parent tasks provided as the history h, the paper p and an optional explanation e_k in the feedback f. This function is implemented using an LLM with a higher value of the temperature parameter. The use of the LLM makes $UpdateReview$, and hence ρ, non-deterministic.

The reviewer agent refines the review for each task t_k. The refinement happens under any of the following two scenarios: (1) Reviews of any of the parent tasks are updated, (2) The score s_k assigned to the review r_k as a part of the feedback f is zero, indicating the need for improvement in the quality of the review. For (2), the refinement occurs in the context of explanation e_k provided as the part of the feedback f.

The Feedback Agent

The Feedback Agent is an implementation of ϕ, which is shown in Procedure 2.

Algorithm 2 The function ϕ

Input: p: a paper from P;
q: a structured-questionnaire from Q;
r: a structured-review from R
Output: a structured-feedback from F
Let f be a DAG with the same vertices and edges as r
Let $\langle v_1, v_2, \ldots, v_n \rangle$ be an ancestral ordering of vertices of r
for k = 1 to n **do**
    Let (s_k, e_k) be the vertex-label for v_k in f
    Let (t_k, r_k) be the vertex label for v_k in r
    Let (t_k, q_k) be the vertex label for v_k in q
    ans := $Answer$(q_k,r_k,"yes")
    rel := $Relevant$(p,r_k)
    if ans and rel **then**
        $s_k := 1$
    else
        $s_k := 0$
    end if
    $e_k := Explain(q_k, r_k, p, ans, rel)$
end for
return f

The main functions employed by ϕ are:

- $Answer(\cdot)$: The function returns a value "True" if the answer to the question q_k for review r_k is "Yes", otherwise "False".
- $Relevant(\cdot)$: The function returns a value "True" if the review r_k is relevant to paper p. If the cosine similarity of the vector representations[6] of the paper p and the review r_k is greater than a threshold[7] they are considered to be relevant.
- $Explain(\cdot)$: The function generates an explanation e_k for scoring a review r_k as either 0 ot 1 for the question q_k, in context of paper p. This function is implemented using an LLM with a higher value of temperature parameter. The use of the LLM makes $Explain$, and hence ϕ, non-deterministic.

The feedback agent assesses the review r_k for task t_k for (1) the question q_k and (2) the relevancy to the paper p. It provides a score s_k for the review as 1 if both the assessments are positive, otherwise 0. It provides an explanation e_k for the same.

Computation in `AutoRef` proceeds by repeatedly calling the Reviewer and Feedback agents in the simple iterative manner shown in Procedure 3.

Algorithm 3 `AutoRef`

Input: p: a paper from P;
g: a set of guidelines from G;
d: a textual review from D; N: Number of iterations
Output: a textual review from D
Let t be a task-ordering in $\tau(g, t)$
Let q be a structured-questionnaire in $\kappa(t, q)$
$r_0 := \alpha(p, d, t)$
$f_0 := \phi(p, q, r_0)$
$S_0 := AggregateScore(f_0)$
for $i = 1, \ldots, N$ **do**
    $r_i := \rho(p, r_{i-1}, f_{i-1})$
    $f_i := \phi(p, q, r_i)$
    $S_i := AggregateScore(f_i)$
    if $S_i < S_{i-1}$ **then**
        $r_i := r_{i-1}$
    end if
end for
return $\beta(r_N)$

Procedure 3 is a simple greedy procedure that stops after a fixed number of iterations N.The main function employed by `AutoRef` is $AggregateScore(\cdot)$. It adds the scores s_k provided for each task t_k, as the part of the feedback f_i for an iteration i. Thus, it provides an aggregated score for the complete review r_i for the

[6]OpenAI's $text-embedding-3-small$ is used for generating embeddings (OpenAI, 2024)

[7]By default the threshold is 0.5 except for "Significance & Value Assessment" has a threshold of 0.3.

iteration i. If the aggregated score for an iteration i is inferior to the prior iteration $i-1$, `AutoRef` ignores the review r_i and keeps the review of the prior iteration r_{i-1}. At the end of the iteration N, `AutoRef` generates a textual review for the final structured review r_N.

3 Related Work

The recent work on the peer-reviewing system is through introducing new datasets, novel tasks, and analysis. DISAPERE is a labeled dataset with fine-grained annotation of reviews and rebuttal sentence-wise that showcases the understanding of argumentative strategies used by the reviewers and authors (Kennard et al., 2022). ArgSciChat is a dataset of argumentative dialogues between researchers addressing both exploratory and argumentative interactions on the scientific paper (Ruggeri et al., 2023). NLPeer is a multidomain corpus of 5k papers and 11k review reports from five venues with unified data representations (Dycke et al., 2023). QASA is a question-answering dataset on scientific articles in AI and ML. The questions require full-stack reasoning through a 3-step process: associative selection of paragraphs followed by evidential rational generation, which is utilized to compose the answer systematically (Lee et al., 2023). ARIES (Aligned, Review-Informed Edits of Scientific Papers) is a dataset of Computer Science papers (drafts & revised versions, reviewer feedback, and authors' responses to the review (D'Arcy et al., 2023). ARIES introduced the novel task of editing scientific papers using peer reviews. PeerSum introduces a dataset for generating meta-reviews of scientific papers with RAMMER (Relationship-aware Multi-task Meta-review Generator) to generate meta-reviews (Li et al., 2023). Similarly, (Wu et al., 2022) attempts to generate meta-reviews through the reviews and rebuttal. All these datasets have been designed for fine-grained analysis of review data, generation of meta-reviews, or updating the paper based on the review. Our task is a review generation task and none of these datasets can be directly used for this task. Moreover, all of these datasets contain information sourced from the open web, which is dated earlier than the data employed to train the LLM utilized in our experimentation. There is a possibility that this data has been memorized by the LLM, making it unsuitable to showcase the effectiveness of our approach. Hence, we synthesized our own dataset elaborated in Section 4.2.

ReviewerGPT provided an exploratory study on reviewing papers using LLM, showing that LLM can identify errors and verify checklists, but LLMs struggled to discern a good paper against a relatively bad paper, with a naive prompt-based approach (Liu and Shah, 2023). (Liang et al., 2023) empirically analyze if large language models can provide useful feedback on research papers. A monolithic prompt is fed to the GPT-4 (Achiam et al., 2023) to generate reviews for a scientific paper. This monolithic prompt only focuses on these four aspects: significance, novelty, potential reasons for acceptance or rejection, and suggestions for improvement. MARG (Multi-agent Review Generation) (D'Arcy et al., 2024) proposes a multi-agent system to generate reviews for a scientific paper. The system has three multi-agent groups, each one of them focusing on different aspects: Experiments & evaluation, Clarity & reproducibility, and Novelty & Impact. Additionally, a multi-agent group is defined for refinement. Every multi-agent group has several worker agents, a leader agent, and an expert. The leader agent communicates with the rest of these agents, and when the task is complete, the final answer is returned. These approaches do not render the final decision of acceptance or rejection. On the other hand, our work renders the final decision for the paper following a task-ontology-based workflow. It focuses on several aspects, much more than the prior approaches, encompassing all the dimensions of the review generation process, leading to a comprehensive review. Furthermore, unlike previous approaches, `AutoRef` prioritizes the refinement process, aiming specifically to enhance the robustness and rigor of the review.

4 A Case Study

4.1 Goal(s)

The goal of `AutoRef` is to generate good reviews. We note that it does not immediately follow that the outcome of a good review will be necessary match the true outcome of the paper, although a case can perhaps be made for the converse (a bad review is likely *not* to match the true outcome). To this end, we focus our experiments on investigating the question: "How does the iterative refinement process in AutoRef manifest itself in changes to reviews?". We will also provide some preliminary observations on the question: "Can AutoRef be used to improve the reviews generated by human reviewers?".

4.2 Materials

Guidelines and Data

We focus information available for a single conference, namely: The International Conference on Learning Representations (ICLR). We have the following information available: (a) Guidelines for reviewers (from 2023:)[8]; (b) Papers submitted along with their outcomes; (c) Reviews from (human)-referees. From this corpus, we performed a stratified selection of 300 papers (we call this the dataset D). The papers have the following distribution of outcomes: 140 Accept, and 160 Reject.

Algorithms and Machines

We use Gemini Pro-1.0 for all our experiments (Team et al., 2023). We use the temperature value of 0.7 for the reviewer agent ρ to have diverse reviews as part of our iterative process. To ensure the feedback agent ϕ is deterministic, we set the temperature value to 0 and top-p to 0. For parsing the PDF version of the paper, we utilize the ScienceBeam parser (Ecer and Maciocci, 2017), which is the same as the baseline (Liang et al., 2023).

4.3 Method

We want to examine the progressive performance of AutoRef starting without any prior review (human- or machine-generated). For this, we follow these steps:

1. Generate a task-ordering t given the ICLR guidelines.
2. Generate a structured-questionnaire q using the task- ordering t.
3. For each paper p in the dataset D
    (a) Generate a text-version of the paper p.
    (b) Generate an initial structured-review r_0 assuming no prior review (that is, an empty text-file is used as a prior review).
    (c) Repeatedly refine the review using the AutoRef procedure, and on each iteration, record the change (if any) in the review score S.
4. Summarise the number of reviews on each iteration with a positive change in Review Score (review is improved according to AutoRef)

The following details are relevant:

- t and q are obtained manually. That is, the functions τ and κ are performed by a human.
- The number of iterations performed by AutoRef is specified by the value N in Algorithm 3. We obtain results for $N = 0, 1, 2, 3, 4$ ($N = 0$ results in no refinement being done, and the algorithm returns r_0 for paper p). The value of N denotes the maximum number of attempts to generate a review for paper p with a higher review score than that of r_0.

Additionally, we seek to gain some preliminary insights into performance of AutoRef when given an existing review. It is evident that with the benefit of knowing the final outcome of the paper, we can categorise human-reviews as follows: (A) Reviews where the review-outcome is *Accept* and the true outcome is *Accept*; (B) Reviews where the review-outcome is *Accept* and the true outcome is $Reject$; (C) Reviews where the review-outcome is $Reject$ and the true outcome is *Accept*; (D) Reviews where the review-outcome is $Reject$ and the true outcome if $Reject$.

The method we adopt is largely the same as above, with some differences:

- We restrict ourselves to 5 reviews each in categories (B). The reason this is simply logistic issues arising from a step that is currently not automated (converting a human-review to a structured-review). In this event, we have assumed that the reviews in categories (B) and (C) are probably likely to require refinement. We call this dataset E. (for "erroneous")
- Initial structured reviews are obtained for each review in E. This is currently done manually. (that is, the function α is performed by a human)

[8]https://iclr.cc/Conferences/2023/ReviewerGuide

- The refined reviews are obtained as before.
- The summary statistics are now tabulations of the number of reviews whose review score improves across iterations as before.

Clearly, with small numbers, we do not expect results of statistical significance. Instead, our purpose is to understand if AutoRef can be used as an assistant to reducing false-positive errors made by a human reviewer.

4.4 Results and Discussions

Iteration Old	Iteration New	# Samples with Increase in Score	Average of % Increase in score S
0	1	131	4.89%
1	2	125	4.53%
2	3	92	2.95%
3	4	79	1.89%
0	4	252	15.03%

Table 1: Progressive performance of AutoRef without any prior review. At 0th iteration the structured review is generated by the LLM. The results are on dataset D.

Iteration Old	Iteration New	# Samples with Increase in Score	Average of % Increase in score S
0	1	5	172.67%
1	2	4	10.68%
2	3	3	4.03%
3	4	2	1.26%
0	4	5	217.67%

Table 2: Progressive performance of AutoRef given an existing review. At 0th iteration the review is generated by a human is converted to a structured review using α. The results are on dataset E.

AutoRef starts with an automatically generated review), Table 1 tabulates the numbers of reviews whose score increases for for $N = 0, \ldots, 4$. The sample distribution over scores is shown diagrammatically in Fig. 2. Table 2 and Fig. 3 show the same results for the second experiment (that is, AutoRef starts with a human review). We observe that at every i^{th} iteration, there exist samples with an increase in the score. The mean and the mode of the scores shift towards the right. This indicates that the reviews are becoming better as AutoRef progresses, complying more with the natural language specifications of the conference review guidelines (feedback questionnaire). We can see that for auto-generated reviews, the number of reviews being refined to better ones progressively decreases. The average % increase in scores also decreases over the iterations. This trend can also be tentatively observed when AutoRef starts with a human-review. This indicates that reviews for some papers are converging, with no or less increment in the scores as AutoRef progresses.

Iteration	TP	FP	FN	TN
0	107	124	33	36
1	97	115	43	45
2	98	118	42	42
3	87	118	53	42
4	92	117	48	43

Table 3: Comparing the decisions of AutoRef generated Reviews with the Meta- Reviewer's decisions for the papers in the dataset D.

We are also able to examine the outcome of reviews purely generated by AutoRef in the usual 4 cases of: TP (Actual = *Accept*, AutoRef = *Accept*); FP (Actual = *Reject*, AutoRef = *Accept*); FN (Actual = *Accept*; AutoRef = *Reject*), and TN (Actual = *Reject*, AutoRef = *Reject*). This is shown in Table 3. Here, the 'Actual' outcome is the decision provided by the meta-reviewer for the papers in D. We observe a decrease in the overall 'Accepts' ('FP's and 'TP's) and an increase in 'Rejects' ('FN's and 'TN's) over the AutoRef iterations. This indicates AutoRef is generating stricter reviews over the iterations, which are more inclined towards rejection. However, in the attempt to generate stricter reviews along with converting falsely detected 'Accepts' to 'Rejects' (reducing FPs), AutoRef is also converting correctly detected 'Accepts' (reducing TPs).

Reviews	Precision	Recall
Human-reviews	0.70	0.81
AutoRef generated (0th iteration)	0.46	0.76
AutoRef generated (4th iteration)	0.44	0.66

Table 4: Comparing the review-outcome with the true (meta-review) outcome for human-reviews and AutoRef for iterations 0 & 4. Precision and Recall are computed for the "Accept" class.

We compare against human-generated reviews for the same set of papers (Table 4). The Precision of AutoRef is substantially lower than a human-reviewer, but Recall is roughly comparable. The Task-ordering t synthesized for AutoRef

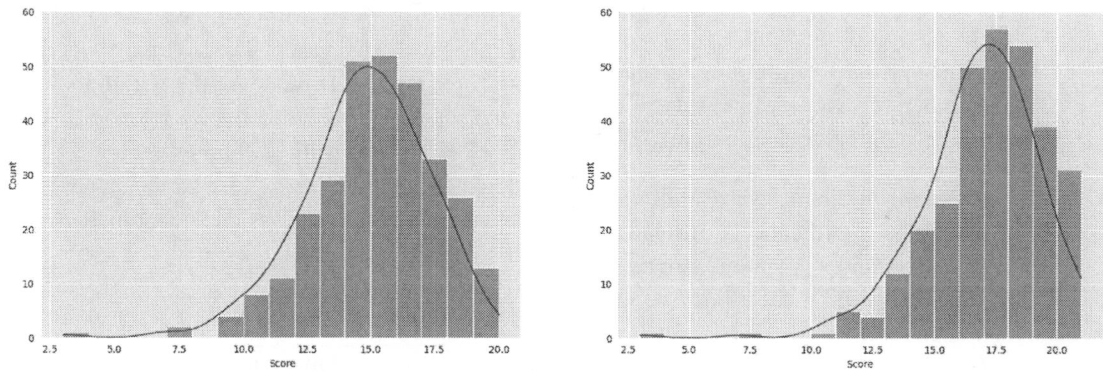

Figure 2: Progressive performance of AutoRef without any prior review. The histogram shows the distribution of scores of the papers in Dataset D at iteration 0 (left) and iteration 4 (right) of AutoRef

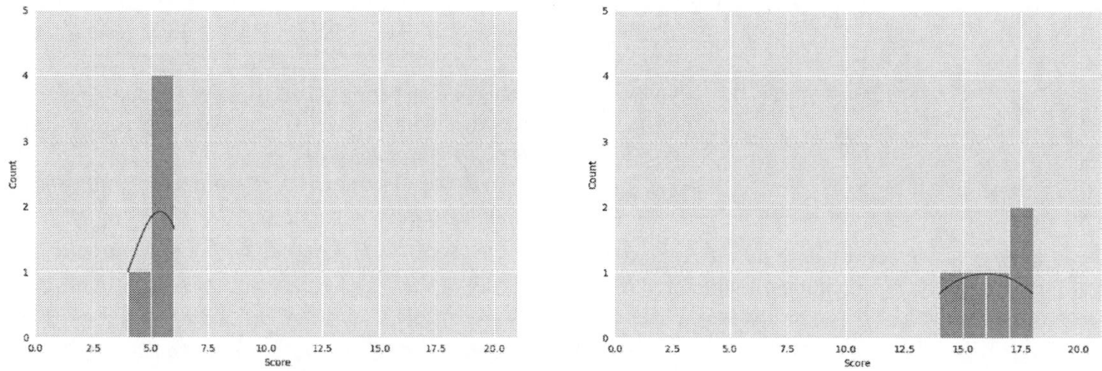

Figure 3: Progressive performance of AutoRef starting with a human-generated review. The histogram shows the distribution of scores of the papers in Dataset E at iteration 0 (left) and iteration 4 (right) of AutoRef

from guidelines g using τ can vary from the set of implicit task-orderings of distinct human reviewers. This leads to variations in reviews r by AutoRef and humans, leading to distinct decisions. Meta-reviewer refers to the human reviews while taking the final decision. Hence, having higher precision and recall for human-reviewers is obvious. Lower precision for the "Accept" class by AutoRef again points at AutoRef flipping the TPs into FNs in an attempt to reduce the FPs.

5 Concluding Remarks

We present AutoRef system, which implements an iterative approach that progressively "refines" a machine-generated or human provided review of a research paper. Our case study with ICLR papers demonstrates the capability of AutoRef to make the reviews more compliant with a review requirement specification, pre-defined in terms of "yes/no" questions. We observe a decrease in the 'Accepts' over the reviews generated over iterations of AutoRef , leading to the fact that AutoRef is generating stricter reviews. This demonstrates the applicability of AutoRef towards progressive correction of overly lenient review or vacuous reviews, being useful for referees, meta-reviewers, as well as authors to detect the weaknesses of the paper.

Further comparison of the outcomes of AutoRef generated reviews with meta-reviewers decisions yields lower precision as compared to outcomes of human reviews with comparable recall. In the attempt to generate stricter reviews along with converting falsely detected 'Accepts' to 'Rejects' (reducing FPs), AutoRef is also converting correctly detected 'Accepts' (reducing TPs), further reducing the precision as well as recall. This hints at the need for improvement in AutoRef to ensure better precision. Currently, the review decision is taken at the final leaf node of the task orderings based on the outcomes of the parent tasks. Reviewer agent being an LLM, this decision can be hallucinated. Instead, a more deterministic algorithm can be designed to make this decision based on LLM-generated outcomes of the parent tasks. Moreover, the current scoring system is very crude (+1 for each "yes" and 0 for each "no"). Clearly, several alterations could be made like increasing the weightage of more important questions and "negative marks" for incorrect answers. The questions themselves are fairly shallow and only examine superficial aspects of the review. Instead of just checking the relevancy of the review to the paper with respective vector representations, there is a need for having the paper in context for questionnaire-based evaluation of the review. More in-depth questions are possible, but it will need the language model to be able to detect those subtleties in the paper. We have also not utilized several features of language models, like using "few-shot" instances of good and bad reviews or the ability to generate multiple reviews when called repeatedly. Consequently, the current implementation should be seen as a first step in an automated review generation system. However, we do expect that the system's specification has been sufficiently abstracted to allow scope for significant improvements.

References

Josh Achiam, Steven Adler, Sandhini Agarwal, Lama Ahmad, Ilge Akkaya, Florencia Leoni Aleman, Diogo Almeida, Janko Altenschmidt, Sam Altman, Shyamal Anadkat, et al. 2023. Gpt-4 technical report. *arXiv preprint arXiv:2303.08774*.

Mike D'Arcy, Tom Hope, Larry Birnbaum, and Doug Downey. 2024. Marg: Multi-agent review generation for scientific papers. *Preprint*, arXiv:2401.04259.

Mike D'Arcy, Alexis Ross, Erin Bransom, Bailey Kuehl, Jonathan Bragg, Tom Hope, and Doug Downey. 2023. Aries: A corpus of scientific paper edits made in response to peer reviews. *Preprint*, arXiv:2306.12587.

Nils Dycke, Ilia Kuznetsov, and Iryna Gurevych. 2023. NLPeer: A unified resource for the computational study of peer review. In *Proceedings of the 61st Annual Meeting of the Association for Computational Linguistics (Volume 1: Long Papers)*, pages 5049–5073, Toronto, Canada. Association for Computational Linguistics.

Daniel Ecer and Giuliano Maciocci. 2017. Sciencebeam - using computer vision to extract pdf data.

Neha Nayak Kennard, Tim O'Gorman, Rajarshi Das, Akshay Sharma, Chhandak Bagchi, Matthew Clinton, Pranay Kumar Yelugam, Hamed Zamani, and Andrew McCallum. 2022. DISAPERE: A dataset for discourse structure in peer review discussions. In *Proceedings of the 2022 Conference of the North American Chapter of the Association for Computational Linguistics: Human Language Technologies*, pages 1234–1249, Seattle, United States. Association for Computational Linguistics.

Yoonjoo Lee, Kyungjae Lee, Sunghyun Park, Dasol Hwang, Jaehyeon Kim, Hong-in Lee, and Moontae Lee. 2023. Qasa: advanced question answering on scientific articles. In *Proceedings of the 40th International Conference on Machine Learning*, ICML'23. JMLR.org.

Miao Li, Eduard Hovy, and Jey Lau. 2023. Summarizing multiple documents with conversational structure for meta-review generation. In *Findings of the Association for Computational Linguistics: EMNLP 2023*, pages 7089–7112, Singapore. Association for Computational Linguistics.

Weixin Liang, Yuhui Zhang, Hancheng Cao, Binglu Wang, Daisy Ding, Xinyu Yang, Kailas Vodrahalli, Siyu He, Daniel Smith, Yian Yin, Daniel McFarland, and James Zou. 2023. Can large language models provide useful feedback on research papers? A large-scale empirical analysis. In *arXiv preprint arXiv:2310.01783*.

Ryan Liu and Nihar B. Shah. 2023. Reviewergpt? an exploratory study on using large language models for paper reviewing. *Preprint*, arXiv:2306.00622.

Nestor Maslej, Loredana Fattorini, Erik Brynjolfsson, John Etchemendy, Katrina Ligett, Terah Lyons, James Manyika, Helen Ngo, Juan Carlos Niebles, Vanessa Parli, et al. 2024. The ai index 2024 annual report. *AI Index Steering Committee, Institute for Human-Centered AI, Stanford University, Stanford, CA*.

OpenAI. 2024. New embedding and api updates.

Federico Ruggeri, Mohsen Mesgar, and Iryna Gurevych. 2023. A dataset of argumentative dialogues on scientific papers. In *Proceedings of the 61st Annual Meeting of the Association for Computational Linguistics (Volume 1: Long Papers)*, pages 7684–7699, Toronto, Canada. Association for Computational Linguistics.

Gemini Team, Rohan Anil, Sebastian Borgeaud, Yonghui Wu, Jean-Baptiste Alayrac, Jiahui Yu, Radu Soricut, Johan Schalkwyk, Andrew M Dai, Anja Hauth, et al. 2023. Gemini: a family of highly capable multimodal models. *arXiv preprint arXiv:2312.11805*.

Po-Cheng Wu, An-Zi Yen, Hen-Hsen Huang, and Hsin-Hsi Chen. 2022. Incorporating peer reviews and rebuttal counter-arguments for meta-review generation. In *Proceedings of the 31st ACM International Conference on Information & Knowledge Management*, CIKM '22, page 2189–2198, New York, NY, USA. Association for Computing Machinery.

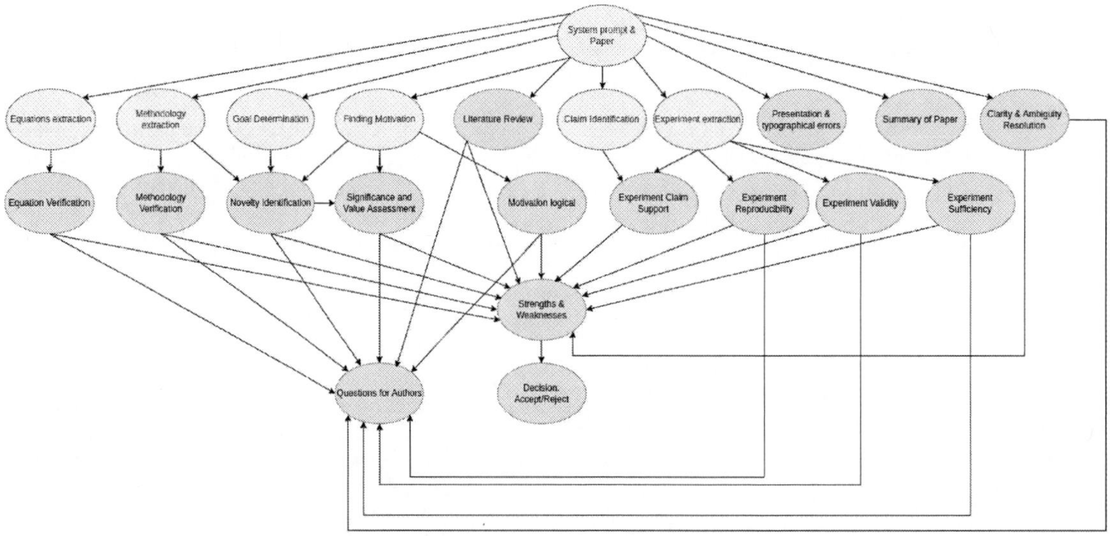

Figure 4: Directed acyclic graph representing the partially-order tasks

A Tasks

1. **Goal Determination:** What is the aim or objective of the paper? (Improvement, novel application, new findings)

2. **Finding Motivation:** What factors drove the authors to pursue the proposed approach, basically the motivation behind the work?

3. **Motivation Logical:** Is the motivation behind the paper logical?

4. **Literature Review:** Has the paper done sufficient literature review? In other words, has the paper cited all work related to it?

5. **Methodology Extraction:** What is the methodology or the approach of the paper?

6. **Equation Extraction:** What are the equations involved in the paper?

7. **Claim Identification:** Identify the specific claim(s) made by the paper. Ensure the claims are well-defined.

8. **Experiment Extraction:** What are the experiments conducted by the paper?

9. **Clarity & Ambiguity Resolution:** Assess the clarity and organization of the paper's writing. Identify any sections that require further clarification or explanation.

10. **Presentation & Typographical Error Detection:** Check for typographical errors and suggest improvements to the presentation. Evaluate the overall quality of the paper's presentation.

11. **Summary of the Paper:** Briefly summarize the paper.

12. **Methodology Verification:** Thoroughly examine the technical details of the proposed methodology and check for logical correctness. In case of mistakes, highlight them.

13. **Equation Verification:** Verify the accuracy and soundness of the mathematical equations.

14. **Novelty Identification:** Based on the previous conversation, identify any novel findings or contributions presented in the paper. Evaluate the significance and originality of these findings.

15. **Experiment Claim Support:** Based on the previous conversation, check if the experiments conducted support the claims.

16. **Experiment Reproducibility:** Determine if the experiments are reproducible.

17. **Experiment Validity:** Check the experiments for technical mistakes from a machine learning point of view.

18. **Experimental Sufficiency:** Determine if the experiments are sufficient. You should strictly assess the experiments. You may suggest any

additional experiments, including ablation experiments or experiments with more datasets, to strengthen the claims made by the paper.

19. **Significance and Value Assessment:** Determine the significance and value of the work presented in the paper. Consider its potential impact on the Machine Learning community.

20. **Strengths & Weaknesses Identification:** Based on the previous conversation, any positively identified points are the strengths, and any negatively identified points are the weaknesses. Consider the correctness of the methodology and equations, novelty, significance, claims, experimental analysis, and clarity of the work.

21. **Questions for Authors:** Based on the previous conversation, formulate questions for the authors to clarify any ambiguities or address concerns raised during the review process. While asking questions you must provide supporting evidence to what you are asking. **Do not ask trivial or shallow questions**. Ask only in-depth and specific questions that will help the community and the authors. Example: explanation of a certain part.

22. **Acceptance/Rejection Decision:** Compare the strengths and weaknesses of the paper. The following are labeled as major weaknesses: 1. Lack of motivation behind the proposed approach 2. Insufficient literature review 3. Proposed Methodology is unsound or logically incorrect. 4. Paper has limited novelty 5. Paper adds limited value to the Machine Learning community (Limited significance from a machine learning point of view) 6. Claim's made by the paper are factually incorrect. 7. Conducted experiments are insufficient to support the paper's claim. 8. Too many unclear and ambiguous parts in the paper. Minor weaknesses are: 1. Small mistakes like typographical errors in equations. 2. One or two sections need elaboration. If there are more than or equal to 1 major weakness, the paper must be rejected. When the weaknesses numerically outweigh the strengths, the paper must be rejected.

B Structured Questionnaire

1. **Goal**: Does the review identify the aim of the paper?

2. **Motivation 1**: Does the review find the motivation behind the paper?

3. **Motivation 2**:Does the review clearly state whether the motivation is logical or not?

4. **Literature Review**: Does the review assess the sufficiency of the literature review?

5. **Methodology Extraction**: Does the review extract the methodology of the paper?

6. **Equation Extraction**: Does the review extract the mathematical equations in the paper?

7. **Methodology Correctness**: Does the review assess soundness and logical correctness of the proposed methodology in the paper?

8. **Equation Correctness**: Does the review assess the correctness of the mathematical equations in the paper?

9. **Claims**: Does the review identify the claims made by the paper?

10. **Experiment Extraction**: Does the review extract the experiments from the paper?

11. **Experiment Claim Support**: Does the review check if the claims are supported by the experiments?

12. **Experiment Validity**: Does the review evaluate the validity and reliability of the experiments, highlighting any potential limitations or biases?

13. **Experimental Sufficiency**: Does the review clearly determine the sufficiency of the experiments and if the experiments are not sufficient then does it suggest any additional specific experiments to strengthen the claims?

14. **Experiment reproducibility**: Does the review assess whether the results presented in the paper can be reproduced by other researchers?

15. **Novelty Identification**: Does the review acknowledge and discuss any novel findings or significant contributions presented in the paper?

16. **Presentation Errors**: Does the review assess presentation of the paper and suggests any typographical errors or grammatical mistakes in the paper?

17. **Clarity**: Does the review assess the clarity and organization of the paper's writing?

18. Significance: Does the review evaluate the significance and contribution of the work to Machine Learning?

19. **Questions**: Are the questions posed to the authors non-trivial from machine Learning point of view?

20. **Strengths & Weaknesses**: Does the review provide a detailed analysis of both the strengths and weaknesses of the paper?

21. **Decision**: Does the review provide a clear and justified recommendation regarding the acceptance or rejection of the paper?

C Examples of Refinement of a Human Review

Table 5 and 8 showcase examples of human textual review from ICLR 2023. These reviews are converted into a structured-review using the function α, which in this case is manual. For $N = 4$, we refine the initial structured review. The initial structured reviews are shown in Table 6 and 9 and the structure review after 4 iterations of refinement are shown in Table 7 and 10. In the structured review, only some parts are shown. We follow the task-ordering as shown in Figure 4.

Summary of the paper: This paper aims to solve the exploration-exploitation tradeoff problem in the context of multi-agent reinforcement learning. While there have been a myriad of works on exploration-exploitation tradeoff on single age reinforcement learning, there are not many on the multi agent RL. This work proposes an adaptive entropy-regularization framework that learns adequate amount of exploration for each agent. To this end, this work proposes to decompose the joint soft value function into pure return and entropy sum. This disentanglements enable a more stable while updating the temperature parameters. This work focuses entropy-based MARL. **Strengths and Weaknesses:** - The strength of the paper comes from the idea that, while previous works encourage same level of exploration across agents, this work proposes to differentiate the level of exploration across agents in multi-agent RL setting. - Another strength comes from the core idea of this work: joint soft value function decomposition / separated factorization. - The motivation part 3.1 sounds convincing to me; one agent's exploration can hinder other agent's exploitation, resulting that simultaneous exploration of multiple agents can make learning unstable. Need a framework that can adaptively learn proper levels of exploration for each agent. - Experiments are well done, not extensive though. Questions. Q1. Question about ADER performance shown in Figure 2a. It seems that ADER outperforms other methods like SER-DCE, SER-MARL, but there is a point where ADER's performance suddenly jumps up in the middle. Is there any explanation on why this happens? Q2. In Appendix B, could you give me more justification on setting the coefficient beta_i? Especially, line B.7, beta_i are defined as softmax of expectation of \\partial V^R_{JT}(s,\\tau) / \\partial H (pi (I))) ? Could you give us more detailed explanations on it? And can you explain why it is difficult to directly obtain the partial derivative in discrete-action case, and using chain rule is justified? **Clarity, Quality, Novelty and Reproducibility:** This paper is well-written with high clarity. Somewhat novel, but not groundbreakingly novel. I think the authors showed good amount of experiments and evaluations on various benchmarks, and ablation studies, which seem to be reproducible. **Summary of the review:** I would give marginally above the acceptance threshold. It would be good if the authors could answer my questions. There might be some issues that I didn't catch, and if other reviewers have raised issues, I'm happy to discuss. **Correctness:** 4: All of the claims and statements are well-supported and correct. **Technical, Novelty, and Significance:** 3: The contributions are significant and somewhat new. Aspects of the contributions exist in prior work. **Empirical, Novelty and Significance:** 2: The contributions are only marginally significant or novel. **Flag for Ethics:** No **Recommendation:** 6: marginally above the acceptance threshold

Table 5: Example of Human Textual Review

Goal Determination: This paper aims to solve the exploration-exploitation tradeoff problem in the context of multi-agent reinforcement learning. **Motivation Logical:** The motivation part 3.1 sounds convincing to me; one agent's exploration can hinder other agent's exploitation, resulting that simultaneous exploration of multiple agents can make learning unstable. Need a framework that can adaptively learn proper levels of exploration for each agent. **Literature Review:** None **Clarity & Ambiguity Resolution:** None **Summary of the paper:** This paper aims to solve the exploration-exploitation trade-off problem in the context of multi-agent reinforcement learning. While there have been a myriad of works on exploration-exploitation tradeoff on single age reinforcement learning, there are not many on the multi agent RL. This work proposes an adaptive entropy-regularization framework that learns adequate amount of exploration for each agent. To this end, this work proposes to decompose the joint soft value function into pure return and entropy sum. This disentanglements enable a more stable while updating the temperature parameters. This work focuses entropy-based MARL **Novelty Identification:** The contributions are significant and somewhat new. **Experiment Claim Support:** All of the claims and statements are well-supported and correct. **Experimental Sufficiency:** Experiments are well done, not extensive though. **Decision:** Accept

Table 6: Initial Structured Review converted from the human textual review using α

Goal Determination: This paper aims to solve the exploration-exploitation tradeoff problem in the context of multi-agent reinforcement learning.

Motivation Logical: The motivation of the paper is to handle the multi-agent exploration-exploitation trade-off. The motivation is logical because in multi-agent reinforcement learning, the degree of necessity and benefit of exploration can be different across multiple agents and one agent's exploration can hinder other agents' exploitation. Thus, the balance of exploration and exploitation across multiple agents should also be considered for MARL in addition to that across the time dimension. The motivation is logical.

Literature Review: The paper cites a number of related works, including MAVEN (Mahajan et al., 2019) Coordinated exploration (Wang et al., 2019) Restricted space selection (Liu et al., 2021b), Intrinsic motivation-based exploration (Zheng et al., 2021) Joint exploration (Gupta et al., 2021). These works all address the problem of exploration in multi-agent reinforcement learning, and the paper discusses how its approach differs from and improves upon these methods. I have checked the paper, and it seems to have cited all related work. Yes, the paper has done sufficient literature review and has cited all related work.

Clarity & Ambiguity Resolution: The paper is well-written and organized. It is easy to follow the authors' arguments and the flow of the paper. However, there are a few sections that could be improved for clarity. The introduction could be more concise. The authors could remove some of the background information and focus on the main points of their paper. For example, they could remove the discussion of the history of reinforcement learning and focus on the specific problem that they are addressing in their paper. The methods section could be more detailed. The authors could provide more information about the algorithms they used and the experiments they conducted. For example, they could provide more information about the hyperparameters that they used and the specific tasks that they evaluated their algorithms on. The results section could be more visually appealing. The authors could use graphs and tables to illustrate their findings. For example, they could use a graph to show the performance of their algorithms on different tasks. By making these changes, the authors could improve the clarity and organization of their paper and make it easier for readers to understand their work.

Summary of the paper: This paper aims to solve the exploration-exploitation tradeoff problem in the context of multi-agent reinforcement learning. While there have been a myriad of works on exploration-exploitation tradeoff on single age reinforcement learning, there are not many on the multi agent RL. This work proposes an adaptive entropy-regularization framework that learns adequate amount of exploration for each agent. To this end, this work proposes to decompose the joint soft value function into pure return and entropy sum. This disentanglements enable a more stable while updating the temperature parameters. This work focuses entropy-based MARL

Novelty Identification: The novel findings or significant contributions presented in the paper are:\- The paper proposes a new framework, ADER, for adaptive exploration in MARL. ADER is able to handle the multi-agent exploration-exploitation trade-off. ADER is able to learn the adequate amount of exploration for each agent based on the degree of required exploration.

Experiment Claim Support: Claim 1:** The paper proposes an adaptive entropy-regularization framework (ADER) for multi-agent reinforcement learning (MARL) to handle the multi-agent exploration-exploitation trade-off. **Supporting Evidence:** The paper presents the ADER framework, which is designed to tackle the multi-agent exploration-exploitation trade-off in MARL. The framework incorporates entropy regularization with adaptive target entropy learning for each agent, enabling it to balance exploration and exploitation effectively. ......

Experimental Sufficiency: The experiments are sufficient because they cover a variety of tasks, including continuous action tasks, StarCraft II, and an ablation study. They show that ADER outperforms other state-of-the-art baselines in terms of both training speed and final performance. The experiments are sufficient to demonstrate the effectiveness of the proposed ADER framework for multi-agent reinforcement learning

Decision: **Major Weaknesses:** None **Minor Weaknesses:** The paper could be improved for clarity and organization. The paper does not provide enough implementation details to check for technical mistakes from a machine learning point of view. The paper does not provide enough information to determine if the experiments are reproducible. **Overall:** The strengths of the paper outweigh the weaknesses. The paper presents a novel and significant framework for adaptive exploration in thatMARL. The experiments show that ADER outperforms state-of-the-art baselines on various tasks. Therefore, the paper should be accepted.

Table 7: Structured Review after 4 iterations of refinement

Summary of the paper: The paper proposes an architecture and a training methodology (termed RoCourseNet) to generate a robust counterfactual (cf) along with the prediction for a given factual point. RoCourseNet builds on earlier work CounterNet [1] by modifying its objective to generate robust cfs i.e cfs which stay valid even when the underlying model shifts. As part of the RoCourseNet objective, the inner 'adversary' itself is proposed as a bilevel problem (called VDS in the paper). The paper proposes to learn a 'worst-case' classifier by looking at how the training dataset can change such that a classifier learnt on this new dataset maximally invalidates the old cfs. Experiments are performed on 3 real-world datasets and they compare against 4 baselines.

Strengths and Weaknesses of the paper: + The paper deals with a practical problem; generating robust recourses is necessary for models which are to be deployed in the real world
+ RoCourseNet outperforms the baselines convincingly in generating robust recourses for the 3 datasets considered
+ RoCourseNet works with the full model and not its locally linear approximation (via LIME etc.) which allows it to model larger number of model shifts via the VDS algorithm

- RoCourseNet involves a tri-level optimization problem. How much additional computational effort does ReCourseNet require? A comparison of the training time taken vs CounterNet seems necessary.
- The method lacks some flexibility of post-hoc counterfactual generation methods. Ex, different people have different notions of cost (proximity) or actionability. Can RoCourseNet solve this without retraining?

Other points:
In Algorithm1 VDS line (8) how is this gradient w.r.t \\delta computed? Is the only dependence of \\delta through \\theta(\\delta)?
Although not completely fair, a comparison of the training time w.r.t ROAR [2] may also be instructive.
Cite the published version of ROAR
[1] Hangzhi Guo, Thanh Nguyen, and Amulya Yadav. Counternet: End-to-end training of counterfactual aware predictions. In ICML 2021 Workshop on Algorithmic Recourse, 2021.
[2] Upadhyay, Sohini, Shalmali Joshi and Himabindu Lakkaraju. "Towards Robust and Reliable Algorithmic Recourse." NeurIPS (2021).

Clarity, Quality, Novelty, and Reproducibility: The paper is written clearly and is easy to follow. Code and implementation details are provided for reproducibility. The paper builds on existing work (CounterNet [1]), and novelty is in learning the 'adversarial model' for which they propose the VDS algorithm.

Summary of the review: The paper solves an important problem. The experimental protocol and results are convincing. The main issue I have is I feel the method is computationally expensive, and it lacks some flexibility that post-hoc cf-generation methods have. I propose acceptance, conditional on some time-complexity analysis.

Correctness: 4: All of the claims and statements are well-supported and correct.

Technical Novelty and Significance: 2: The contributions are only marginally significant or novel.

Empirical Novelty and Significance: 2: The contributions are only marginally significant or novel.

Flag for Ethics: No

Recommendation: 6: marginally above the acceptance threshold

Table 8: Example of Human Textual Review

Goal Determination: The paper proposes an architecture and a training methodology (termed RoCourseNet) to generate a robust counterfactual (cf) along with the prediction for a given factual point.

Motivation Logical: None

Literature Review: None

Clarity & Ambiguity Resolution: None

Summary of the paper: The paper proposes an architecture and a training methodology (termed RoCourseNet) to generate a robust counterfactual (cf) along with the prediction for a given factual point. RoCourseNet builds on earlier work CounterNet [1] by modifying its objective to generate robust cfs i.e cfs which stay valid even when the underlying model shifts. As part of the RoCourseNet objective, the inner 'adversary' itself is proposed as a bilevel problem (called VDS in the paper). The paper proposes to learn a 'worst-case' classifier by looking at how the training dataset can change such that a classifier learnt on this new dataset maximally invalidates the old cfs. Experiments are performed on 3 real-world datasets and they compare against 4 baselines.

Novelty Identification: The paper builds on existing work (CounterNet [1]), and novelty is in learning the 'adversarial model' for which they propose the VDS algorithm.

Experiment Claim Support: The experimental protocol and results are convincing.

Experiment Sufficiency: The authors should compare the training time of RoCourseNet to CounterNet and ROAR. the authors should explore the flexibility of RoCourseNet to solve different notions of cost or actionability without retraining.

Decision: Accept

Table 9: Initial Structured Review converted from the human textual review using α

Goal Determination: The paper proposes an architecture and a training methodology (termed RoCourseNet) to generate a robust counterfactual (cf) along with the prediction for a given factual point.

Motivation Logical: Yes, the motivation behind the paper is logical. The authors observe that existing approaches to recourse generation assume that the underlying model remains stationary over time. However, in practice, models are often updated regularly when new data is available to improve predictive accuracy on the new shifted data distribution. This shifted model might render previously recommended recourses ineffective (Rawal et al., 2020), and in turn, diminish end users' trust towards our system. The authors propose RoCourseNet, a training framework that jointly optimizes for predictions and recourses that are robust to future data shifts, to address this problem.

Literature Review: The paper has not cited all relevant work. It does not cite Pawelczyk et al. (2020a) who analyze the model multiplicity problem, which studies the validity of recourses under different ML models trained on the same data, and Black et al. (2022) who propose methods to ensure consistency under the model multiplicity setting.

Clarity & Ambiguity Resolution: The paper is well-written and organized. However, there are a few sections that could benefit from further clarification. These sections are the section on the proposed method and the section on the experimental results.

Summary of the paper: The paper proposes an architecture and a training methodology (termed RoCourseNet) to generate a robust counterfactual (cf) along with the prediction for a given factual point. RoCourseNet builds on earlier work CounterNet [1] by modifying its objective to generate robust cfs i.e cfs which stay valid even when the underlying model shifts. As part of the RoCourseNet objective, the inner 'adversary' itself is proposed as a \bilevel problem (called VDS in the paper). The paper proposes to learn a 'worst-case' classifier by looking at how the training dataset can change such that a classifier learnt on this new dataset maximally invalidates the old cfs. Experiments are performed on 3 real-world datasets and they compare against 4 baselines.

Novelty Identification: The paper builds on existing work (CounterNet [1]), and the novelty is in learning the 'adversarial model' for which they propose the VDS algorithm. RoCourseNet makes the following three novel contributions:

1. (Formulation-wise) We formulate the robust recourse generation problem as a tri-level (min-max-min) optimization problem, which consists of two sub-problems: (i) a bi-level (max-min) problem which simulates a worst-case attacker to find an adversarially shifted model by explicitly simulating the worst-case data shift in the training dataset; and (ii) an outer minimization problem which simulates an ML model designer who wants to generate robust recourses against this worst-case bi-level attacker. Unlike prior approaches, our bi-level attacker formulation explicitly connects shifts in the underlying data distribution to corresponding shifts in the ML model parameters.
2. (Methodology-wise) We propose RoCourseNet for solving our tri-level optimization problem for generating robust recourses. RoCourseNet relies on two key ideas: (i) we propose a novel Virtual Data Shift (VDS) algorithm to optimize for the inner bi-level (max-min) attacker problem, which results in an adversarially shifted model; and (ii) inspired by Guo et al. (2021), RoCourseNet leverages a block-wise coordinate descent training procedure to optimize the robustness of generated recourses against these adversarially shifted models. Unlike prior methods (Upadhyay et al., 2021), we require no intermediate steps in approximating the underlying model or data distribution.
3. (Experiment-wise) We conduct rigorous experiments on three real-world datasets to evaluate the robustness of several popular recourse generation methods under data shifts. Our results show that RoCourseNet generates highly robust CF explanations against data shifts, as it consistently achieves >96% robust validity, outperforming state-of-the-art baselines by $\sim$10%.

Experiment Claim Support: The experiments conducted by the authors support the claim that RoCourseNet outperforms state-of-the-art baselines in generating robust counterfactual explanations. This is evident from the fact that RoCourseNet consistently achieves >96% robust validity, which is $\sim$10% higher than the best performing baseline.

Experiment Sufficiency: The experiments conducted by the paper are sufficient to support the claims made in the paper. However, the following additional experiments could be conducted to further strengthen the claims:
Ablation experiments to study the impact of individual components of RoCourseNet on its performance.
Experiments with more datasets to demonstrate the generalizability of RoCourseNet's approach.
A human study to evaluate the quality of the explanations generated by RoCourseNet.

Decision: "**Major Weaknesses:** * Insufficient literature review **Strengths:** * The paper presents a novel approach to generating robust counterfactual explanations. * The proposed method is able to generate explanations that are robust to data shifts, which is a significant improvement over existing methods. * The paper provides a comprehensive experimental evaluation of the proposed method, which demonstrates its effectiveness on a variety of datasets. * The paper is well-written and organized, and the writing is clear and concise. **Decision:** The paper should be **rejected**. The paper has more weaknesses than strengths, and the major weaknesses are significant.

Table 10: Structured Review after 4 iterations of refinement

Artificial Intuition: Efficient Classification of Scientific Abstracts

Harsh Sakhrani, Naseela Pervez, Anirudh Ravi Kumar, Fred Morstatter
Information Sciences Institute, Viterbi School of Engineering, University of Southern California
Alexandra Graddy Reed
Sol Price School of Public Policy, University of Southern California
Andrea Belz
Information Sciences Institute, Viterbi School of Engineering, University of Southern California

Abstract

It is desirable to coarsely classify short scientific texts, such as grant or publication abstracts, for strategic insight or research portfolio management. These texts efficiently transmit dense information to experts possessing a rich body of knowledge to aid interpretation. Yet this task is remarkably difficult to automate because of brevity and the absence of context. To address this gap, we have developed a novel approach to generate and appropriately assign coarse domain-specific labels. We show that a Large Language Model (LLM) can provide metadata essential to the task, in a process akin to the augmentation of supplemental knowledge representing human intuition, and propose a workflow. As a pilot study, we use a corpus of award abstracts from the National Aeronautics and Space Administration (NASA). We develop new assessment tools in concert with established performance metrics.

1 Introduction

Analyzing technical documents is a crucial strategic task, enabling the management of research portfolios, tracking investment trends, and exploring scientific advancement. On a more tactical level, it can aid the preliminary screening of scientific abstracts in systematic reviews (Buchlak et al., 2020; Rios and Kavuluru, 2015; Ambalavanan and Devarakonda, 2020).

Several approaches are possible. First, authors can label their own work, but this presents several challenges: (1) authors that self-label their own texts may make idiosyncratic decisions, (2) authors in close disciplines may use different terms for related concepts, such as "robotics" and "autonomy", and (3) multidisciplinary projects may require novel or multiple labels.

A second method is to impose an external ontology. However, these schemes often have both fine- and coarse-granularities (e.g., "networks" versus "ad-hoc networks"). Another concern is that the scheme simply lacks appropriate labels, especially for emerging fields.

Automated processes do exist. Those with a large number of parameters are now customizable at lower computational cost (Hu et al., 2021; Ben Zaken et al., 2022). Although dedicated pretrained models can yield robust results, they incur significant expenses in manual annotation due to reliance on supervised learning (Beltagy et al., 2019; Chang et al., 2008; Cohan et al., 2020).

In summary, we face two distinct needs in the analysis of scientific documents: (1) a unified, coarse-grained, non-overlapping taxonomy, tailored to uniquely classify a set of documents; and (2) an unsupervised methodology that circumvents the reliance on manual annotation while effectively managing the peculiarities of scientific text. These challenges are exacerbated for abstracts.

In manual labeling, an expert's rapid progress often hinges on integrating prior knowledge, crucial for effective comprehension (Reid Smith and Hammond, 2021). In so doing, the expert rapidly identifies the phrases conveying the most information and uses those for classification. Importantly, this process is not a simple frequency or statistical analysis; indeed, the most important phrase may appear only once. Moreover, multigrams carrying high semantic value may not appear systematically in the same place in a sentence or paragraph.

Here we describe "artificial intuition," a method mimicking the expert's process to execute two objectives: generating an optimal label space and producing accurate predictions within this new space. We integrate tools into a novel workflow to identify important terms, augment them with relevant background information, then aggregate these enhanced documents into clusters for classification purposes.

As a pilot case to evaluate our methodology, we analyze award abstracts of federally funded projects from the National Aeronautics and Space Administration (NASA) Small Business Innova-

Proceedings of the Fourth Workshop on Scholarly Document Processing (SDP 2024), pages 191–201
August 16, 2024

tion Research (SBIR) Program. We obtain domain knowledge by extracting and ranking the abstract's keywords / keyphrases (which we will collectively refer to as "keywords"). We generate metadata for these keywords in a zero-shot setting and derive embeddings for the keyword-metadata concatenations using a pre-trained Sentence Transformer.

For label space generation, we implement a clustering process that represents the task of organizing awards into funding themes. This method not only clarifies the thematic organization of the documents but also reveals the hierarchical relationships between different topics. We introduce a novel evaluation scheme to assess whether the label set comprehensively spans the document space and can serve as a set of basis vectors.

To predict labels, we reinterpret the multilabel-classification problem as a semantic matching challenge wherein the document space is characterized by the keyword-metadata concatenation and the label space is described by the element closest to the centroid for each cluster. This retrieval-based perspective allows for flexibility in adapting to new label spaces without the need for retraining.

This framework accommodates various levels of parsimony, which we explore extensively in our experiments. Finally, using our test sample, we demonstrate the efficacy of our prediction methodology and quantify the performance.

2 Related Work

Various methodologies have been proposed for text classification. Bayesian approaches (Tang et al., 2016) classify the text by extracting features. One method is to first select document features with discriminative power, then compute the semantic similarity between features and documents (Zong et al., 2015), but this becomes more difficult as the number of features grows. Support Vector Machines (SVMs) can be used for document classification (Cai and Hofmann, 2004). However, these approaches are constrained by the requirement for manual feature engineering, limiting their ability to capture the complexity of natural language.

New deep learning techniques have advanced scientific document classification. Neural network-based architectures (Lee and Dernoncourt, 2016), particularly Convolutional Neural Networks (CNNs) (Sun et al., 2019) and Recurrent Neural Networks (RNNs) (Xun et al., 2019; Liu et al., 2016), outperform some traditional machine learning methods. These models automatically learn feature representations from data, capturing both the semantic and syntactic nuances of text.

These methods presume that documents are related to only one label. Newer approaches (e.g., (Liu et al., 2017; Song et al., 2022; Xiao et al., 2019; Blanco et al., 2019; Chang et al., 2020)) classify documents with multiple labels, and one alternative attempts to map 10,000 fine-grained labels for scientific documents (Zhang et al., 2022a) although most methods consider 10-50 coarse labels. These models are incompletely validated because many real-world datasets will have limited or poorly labeled data.

Weakly supervised learning and zero-shot learning (ZSL) models do not use annotated data. Some pre-trained language models demonstrate impressive performance in zero-shot document classification (Devlin et al., 2019; Beltagy et al., 2019; Liu et al., 2019) and can be used to assign multiple labels to a given document (Yin et al., 2019). On the other hand, hierarchical multi-class methods can use just class names - without training examples - as supervision (Shen et al., 2021; Zhang et al., 2022b). Large language models trained on scientific data, such as Galactica (Taylor et al., 2022) and SciNCL (Ostendorff et al., 2022), can be used to assign labels to a scientific document. Many approaches use metadata, such as generic descriptions, as supervision for further classification (Zhang et al., 2023). However, these methods are still potentially subject to noise. Here we describe a method to identify keywords and derive context-specific metadata to improve classification accuracy, particularly for short abstracts.

3 Approach

3.1 Problem Formulation

The scientific literature tagging task can be conceptualized as a multi-label classification (each paper can be relevant to more than one label) problem, where all candidate tags (e.g., "Aerodynamics," "Superconductance/Magnetics") constitute a label space Y of arbitrary size. We seek to:

- Construct a new label space Y comprising coarse-grained labels and aggregating correlated labels (e.g., merging "Optics" and "Photonics" into "Optical technologies").
- Develop an unsupervised multi-label classifier that can effectively map an abstract to the new

label space Y.

A simplistic approach would utilize a pre-trained language model to encode each document and label, generate their embeddings, and then conduct a nearest neighbor search in the embedding space. However, this method encounters two primary challenges: (1) the existing language models are largely trained on general English text that does not discern technical terms, and (2) analogous labels (e.g., "networking" and "ad-hoc networks") confound the results. One might augment the label embedding process with generic metadata, such as a brief description from Wikipedia or using solutions like Positive Instance Feature Aggregation (PIFA) (Yu et al., 2022).

Instead, we seek to generate a context-specific glossary. This has the added advantage that the labels can be fine-tuned, converting a multi-label problem into a simpler system. For instance, a thermal protection system (TPS) consists of materials suited to handle extremely high temperatures. In a conventional classification scheme, this might require two labels, such as "materials" and "temperature." In contrast, we create a system such that "thermal protection system" is itself sufficient to serve as the only label. This is possible only with a label space customized to the knowledge domain.

3.2 Implementation Components

- Yet Another Keyword Extractor (YAKE) (Campos et al., 2020) is a lightweight, unsupervised keyword extraction algorithm that uses statistical properties and contextual information.

- Mistral 7B is a Large Language Model (LLM) with strong performance of Llama-2 13B on key benchmarks (Jiang et al., 2023).

- Maximal Marginal Relevance (MMR) (Carbonell and Goldstein, 1998) iteratively selects candidate items that simultaneously maximize their relevance to the query and their novelty compared to previously selected items.

- Sentence Transformer (S-Transformer)[1] (Reimers and Gurevych, 2019) constructs dense vector representations of sentences to enable efficient comparison of text semantics.

[1]https://huggingface.co/sentence-transformers/all-mpnet-base-v2

3.3 Document Corpus

The NASA SBIR program publishes abstracts of funded projects. We used 1,230 abstracts from 2010 to 2015 extracted online from the publicly available archive[2]. The average abstract length is about 450 words. All abstracts were pre-processed by removing stop words, which were variations and combinations of: "NASA", "space", "mission(s)", "research", "SBIR", "spacecraft", "future", and "science". These words and multigrams comprising these words appeared in a large number of the abstracts, and therefore they provided little information to assist in classification. We randomly drew 100 abstracts (roughly 10%) for manual classification, described below.

3.4 Label Space Generation

We generate the label space as illustrated in Figure 1. Initially, pre-processed abstracts are submitted to YAKE to extract keywords. One hyperparameter of our workflow is the number of keywords $\hat{c}$. We estimated that $\hat{c}$ should be approximately 5 as it represents 1-2% of the abstract length. We confirmed that the F1 results, described in more detail below, showed a general lack of sensitivity to this parameter (Figure 2), and therefore we set $\hat{c} = 5$ in our main analyses.

We sought to supplement these keywords with contextual definitions to form metadata. We used Mistral-7B Instruct v0.2 with hyperparameters set at default values and submitted the following prompt:

> *Given the scientific abstract and the keywords that have been extracted for the document, provide a concise meta data/prior information for every keyword in context of the document. Incorporate any extra knowledge that can help classify the document to relevant topics.*

This combined data-keyword concatenation is processed using the S-Transformer model to produce embeddings. A critical aspect of this process is that the metadata generated for each keyword is tailored specifically to the context of the related document, ensuring that the embeddings are context-specific rather than generic. We use k-means clustering (Habibi and Popescu-Belis, 2015) to partition these embeddings into clusters, represented by the keyword closest to their centroids and

[2]sbir.gov

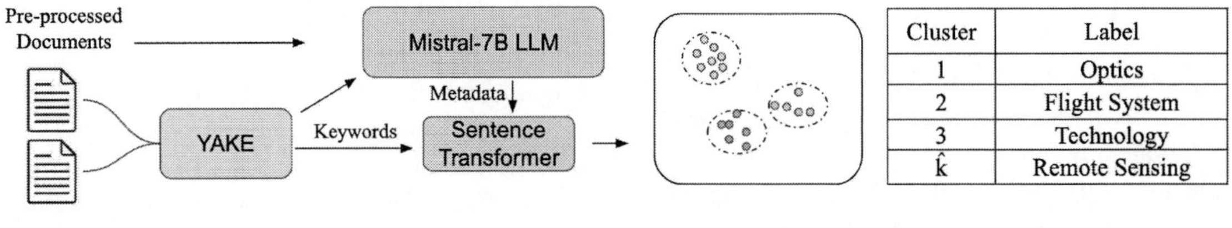

Figure 1: Label Space Generation flowchart. The clusters are named with the keyword closest to the cluster centroid.

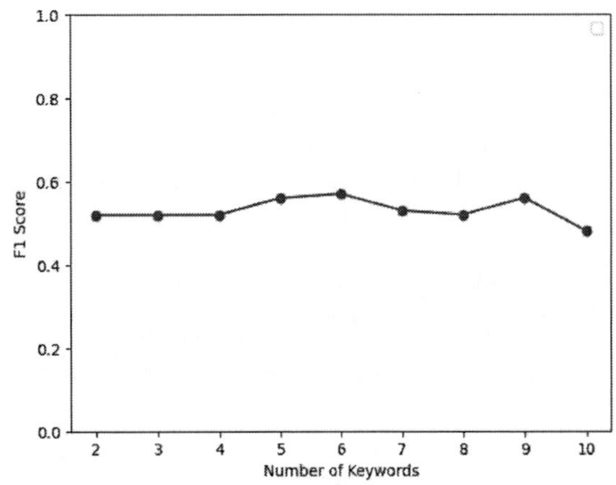

Figure 2: Variation of F1 score with the number of keywords at the threshold of top 1%.

effectively summarizing each cluster's thematic focus. This method approximates the scheme by which such abstracts would be sorted in a funding portfolio.

Unlike $\hat{c}$, the number of clusters $\hat{k}$ requires closer examination. We seek a parsimonious model that minimizes the number of labels per document. In practice, we seek to organize approximately 1,000 documents into approximately 10-20 classes. In addition to making this a tractable problem, it adequately represents the portfolio management process.

3.5 Annotation Task Design

We conducted a manual annotation task to label the test set of the NASA SBIR abstracts. We presented the annotator, a NASA expert, with a scientific abstract and the generated label set. The annotator was instructed to assign a label to the scientific abstract only if one of the presented labels was appropriate, and to leave it unlabeled otherwise. The same documents were labeled for each configuration for consistency.

4 Results

4.1 Label Space Orthogonality: Redundancy

Our first task is estimate the degree of overlap within the label space. To do so, we define the redundancy, $\mathcal{R}$, as a measure of the orthogonality between labels. This figure of merit (FOM) is intrinsic to the label space and assessed independently of individual document projections.

The labels are transformed into normalized embeddings using the S-Transformer model, resulting in a label matrix $\mathcal{L}$ of dimensions $\hat{k} \times v$ (in our case, $v = 768$). Each element $\mathcal{L}_{ij}$ represents the j-th dimension of the i-th label embedding.

To measure the orthogonality, we calculate the cosine similarity between each pair of distinct label embeddings. If the labels are orthogonal and distinct, the cosine similarity should approach 0; on the other hand, two labels capturing closely related ideas will give a cosine similarity that approaches 1. Formally, for normalized label vectors $\mathcal{T}_i$ and $\mathcal{T}_j$ in $\mathcal{L}$, we define redundancy $\mathcal{R}$ as the maximum cosine similarity among all pairs:

$$\mathcal{R} = \max_{i \neq j}(\text{cosine similarity}(\mathcal{T}_i, \mathcal{T}_j)) \quad (1)$$

where

$$\text{cosine similarity}(\mathcal{T}_i, \mathcal{T}_j) = \frac{\mathcal{T}_i \cdot \mathcal{T}_j}{\|\mathcal{T}_i\| \|\mathcal{T}_j\|}$$

A value of $\mathcal{R}$ close to 0 is desirable because orthogonal label embeddings suggest that each label contributes unique information without redundancy. Conversely, a value of $\mathcal{R}$ approaching 1 shows that at least one pair of labels shares a high degree of overlap. Overlap implies that multiple labels may be describing similar features within the documents, thus complicating the interpretability and utility of the label space. Our goal is to represent each key concept with a unique label.

To understand the redundancy in our basis vector set, we executed the label space generation process

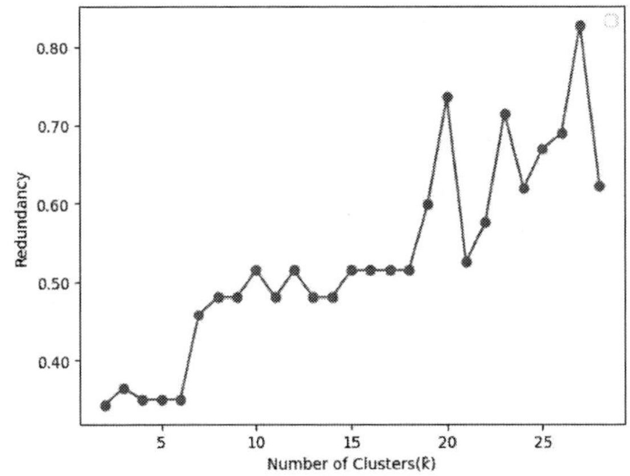

Figure 3: Variation of redundancy $\mathcal{R}$ with the number of clusters $\hat{k}$.

but systematically varied $\hat{k}$. We then evaluated $\mathcal{R}$ for each label space. $\mathcal{R}$ increased with $\hat{k}$ (Figure 3), as expected. Notably, we identified three general regimes: At low $\hat{k}$, $\mathcal{R}$ was fairly flat and low. The labels do not overlap. At approximately $\hat{k} = 8$, the redundancy increased to a new plateau. At much higher values of $\hat{k}$ (18 and higher), this FOM entered a regime in which the value dramatically oscillated.

We therefore conclude that at very low cluster numbers ($\hat{k} < 6$), the severely reduced $\mathcal{R}$ indicates that the labels are probably insufficient to describe the document set. At higher values of $\hat{k} > 18$, the risk of overlapping labels increases substantially, but the likelihood that each document is at least minimally described also increases.

4.2 Spanning the Document Space: Coverage

We defined the redundancy $\mathcal{R}$ to characterize the orthogonality of our proposed label space basis vectors. Next, we study how comprehensively these labels describe the documents, essentially determining if our labels can span the document space.

We architected a second workflow (Figure 4). Again we begin with YAKE usage for a single document. We submit these keywords to Mistral-7B for document-specific contextual definitions as supplementary metadata. Both the document itself and the keyword-metadata concatenations are subsequently processed through the S-Transformer model to generate their individual embeddings, refined using MMR. This forms a new keyword embedding matrix $\mathcal{C}$ of dimensions $v \times \hat{c}$, where v (768 in our case) represents the embedding dimension, and the extracted keywords are still parameterized by $\hat{c}$.

Likewise, we still have the label embedding $\mathcal{L}$ of dimensions $\hat{k} \times v$. As our goal is to understand the overlap between the labels and the corpus embeddings, we define a new matrix, termed "coverage", $\mathcal{W}$ with elements w_{ij}:

$$w_{ij} = \sum_{v} L_{iv} C_{vj}, \tag{2}$$

The coverage matrix $\mathcal{W}$ has the resulting dimension $\hat{k}$ x $\hat{c}$, where $\hat{k}$ represents the number of labels and $\hat{c}$ represents the number of keywords. In other words, $\mathcal{W}$ is the projection of the keywords onto the label space. (Strictly speaking, the S-Transformer embeddings of length v can be understood as creating a coordinate system to facilitate projections.) Each w_{ij} element ranges from -1 to 1.

A high value of any element w_{ij} indicates that a label and keyword are highly aligned. Therefore, finding the maximum value that appears in this matrix $\mathcal{W}$ will signify how well the label space describes the keywords of an individual document in the best case. Consequently, we define the coverage $\mathcal{S}$ for a given document d (where d is a member of the document corpus $\mathcal{D}$):

$$\mathcal{S}^d = \max(w_{ij}^d) \tag{3}$$

The coverage for the corpus D is simply the average of the individual documents' coverage:

$$\mathcal{S}^D = \frac{\sum_D S^d}{D} \tag{4}$$

This proposed figure of metric, coverage, provides critical validation that the new label space is pertinent to the knowledge domain encompassed by the documents. One would expect for coverage to be small if the label space is not large enough - namely, for small values of $\hat{k}$. An intermediate regime would appear if each new label adds significant new information. Eventually, a final regime would be reached wherein the new information provided by an additional label is marginal as the segmentation becomes finer, such as comparing 'Chemical Propulsion Technologies' and 'Electronic Propulsion Technologies'. In other words, a general analytical form for coverage should start near 0, then experience rapid growth until the space is largely covered and it tapers off. The corpus coverage is bounded by 1 because the individual documents' coverage is given by a cosine similarity of two normalized vectors, thus limited to 1.

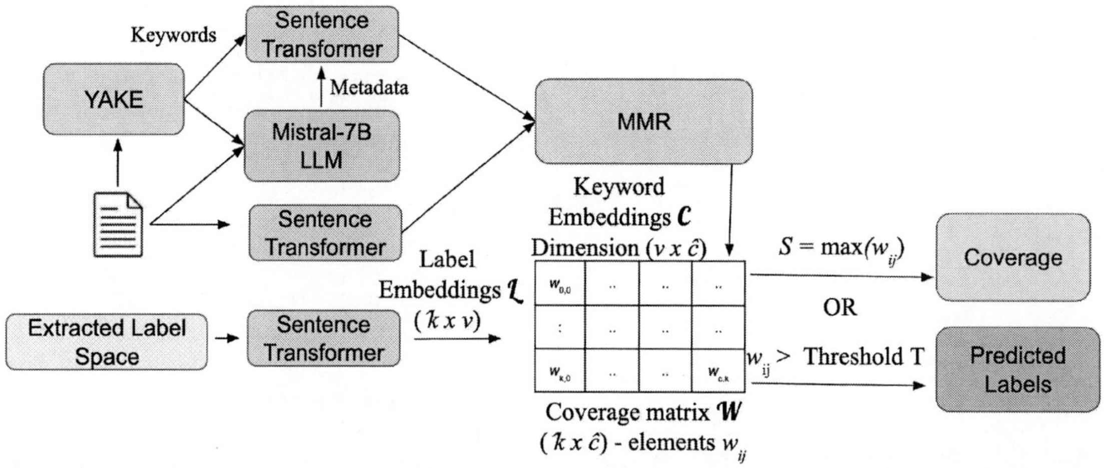

Figure 4: Analysis workflow and use of the coverage matrix $\mathcal{W}$. In one application (final step in green), the element with the maximum value is used to generate the Coverage. The second usage (blue final step) is to extract those values exceeding a specific threshold T for the label prediction task.

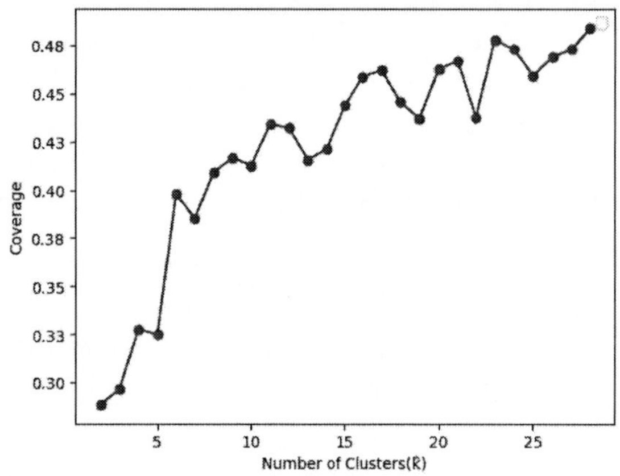

Figure 5: Variation of coverage S with $\hat{k}$.

Table 1: Labels at $\hat{k} = 15$

Advanced Optical Systems
Advanced Photovoltaic Systems
Aeroservoelastic Analysis and Aircraft Systems Analysis
Aeroservoelastic Analysis Tools
Electric Propulsion Systems
Electrolyzers
High Energy Density Electronics
LIDAR Remote Sensing
Multifunctional Composite Materials
Optical Communications Technology
Radiation-Hardened Electronics
Robotic Science Missions
Technologies Fault Management
Thermal Protection Systems
Unmanned Aircraft Systems

We tested this concept by varying the number of clusters $\hat{k}$ from 2 to 28 and evaluating coverage S for each newly developed label space. As $\hat{k}$ increased, the labels did indeed relate well to the documents, as represented by keywords (Figure 5). In addition, the variation revealed a generally asymptotic form, as expected.

4.3 Label Assignment: Precision and Recall

We seek to create a label space with high coverage, indicating relevance; and low redundancy or overlap. However, these measures act in opposition as higher coverage naturally can lead to greater redundancy. That is, these two measures form a trade space in which we strive to optimize $\hat{k}$.

We revisited the workflow generating the coverage matrix (Figure 4) and developed a prediction pipeline, mirroring the initial process through the creation of the coverage matrix $\mathcal{W}$.

In the coverage study, we took the maximum w_{ij} value to characterize the space. Here, we seek to find *all* relevant values of w_{ij}. To operationalize this, we analyze the distribution of all w_{ij} values and establish a threshold T, which defines the minimum percentile to be used as a filter for the w_{ij} values, effectively distinguishing between significant and negligible overlaps. For instance, setting $T = 1\%$ means we retain only the top 1% of the w_{ij} values, which is more restrictive than setting $T = 10\%$. In practical terms, for a system of 5 keywords and 15 labels, a 1% threshold would retain just one label (top 1% of 5x15 = 75 matrix elements results in one). On the other hand, a 10% threshold retains seven elements that could be distributed in

Table 2: Labels at $k = 25$

Advanced Aeroservoelastic Analysis and Rotorcraft Aeromechanics
Advanced Composite and Ceramic Matrix Materials
Advanced ESR Technologies for Space Exploration
Advanced Energy Storage and Power Systems
Advanced Fluid and Thermal Management Technologies
Advanced Laser and Optical Communication Technologies
Advanced Manufacturing Technologies for Aerospace
Advanced Microwave and Remote Sensing Technologies
Advanced Optical Systems for Scientific Missions
Advanced Structural Sensors and NDE Technologies
Advanced Thermal Protection Systems
Airborne Measurement and Sensing Systems
Automation and Control in Robotic Science Missions
Fault Management Technologies
High-End Computing and Data Handling
Highly Capable Propulsion Systems
Innovative Aerospace Structural Design
Innovative Fiber-Optic and Navigational Technologies
International Space Station
LIDAR Remote Sensing Technologies
Mars Sample Return Missions
Radiation-Hardened Electronics and Sensors
Regenerative Life Support Systems
Solar Power Technologies for Advanced Energy Solutions
Unmanned Aircraft Systems Operations

various ways. For instance, all five keywords might describe label 1, with two of those keywords linked to label 2; or only one keyword could be associated with each of seven labels. As the threshold T gets larger, the variability in possible outcomes increases.

For each document, we select labels associated with the values of w_{ij} that exceed the threshold T. However, to accurately evaluate the classification, a set of 'true' labels is required. While NASA maintains its own taxonomy of approximately 200 labels that could theoretically serve this purpose, the inconsistency in this taxonomy year-to-year and the excessive number of labels compared to our needs complicate its use. Instead, as noted in Section 3.5, we manually aligned the abstracts with our new labels.

Using the three regimes of Figure 3 as a guide, we considered three values for $\hat{k}$ - 4, 15, and 25 - and estimated the usual classification measures of precision, recall, and F1. Moreover, we varied the threshold T, hypothesizing that at low restrictive values of T, these measures should improve as only the most significant overlaps in the coverage matrix would be retained.

At $\hat{k} = 4$, the labels were: Propulsion Technologies, Remote Sensing Technologies, Thermal Protection Systems, and Unmanned Aircraft Systems. However, the manual classification task failed because the labels simply did not describe the abstracts.

At $\hat{k} = 15$, the labels consisted of words generally associated with space technologies (Table 1). Similarly, the $\hat{k} = 25$ generated labels related to space (Table 2); however, in this case the word "Advanced" preceded nearly half the technical topics, suggesting that the semantic content of that word decreases in this context. (Notably, the word "advanced" has been linked to other technical contexts where its semantic content is diluted (Belz et al., 2023)).

To evaluate our method's quality, we set aside $\hat{k} = 4$ and considered differences between $\hat{k} = 15$ and $\hat{k} = 25$. We focused on the F1 score and found that $\hat{k} = 15$ consistently yielded higher scores than the overdetermined space represented by $\hat{k} = 25$ (Figure 6). As a result, we concluded that $\hat{k} = 15$ represented a better set of labels to describe this space.

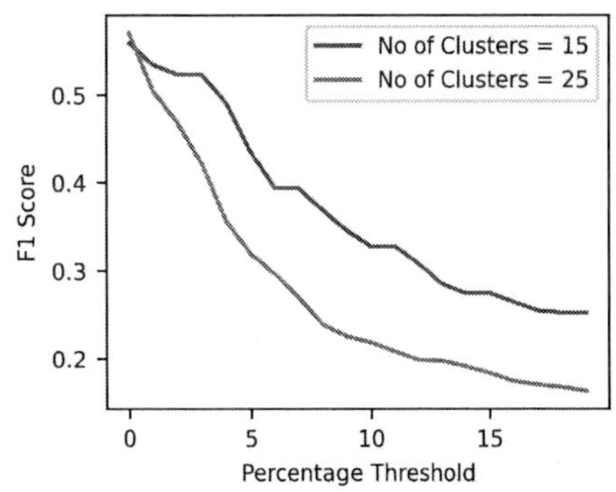

Figure 6: Variation of F1 scores for assigned labels with weights w exceeding the percentile threshold T, as defined in the text.

Our final task was to demonstrate the advantage of augmenting the abstract with the metadata extracted from the additional analysis of the keywords. Using the $\hat{k} = 15$ label space described above, we evaluated the performance of our model with and without the metadata generated by the LLM. We found that the LLM consistently improved the F1 score (Figure 7) for all tested values of the threshold T. This was due to improvement primarily in the precision (Table 3).

5 Discussion and Future Research

Scientific communication is designed to efficiently carry rich information between experts. The abstract of a grant or publication is perhaps the most striking example, wherein sophisticated concepts

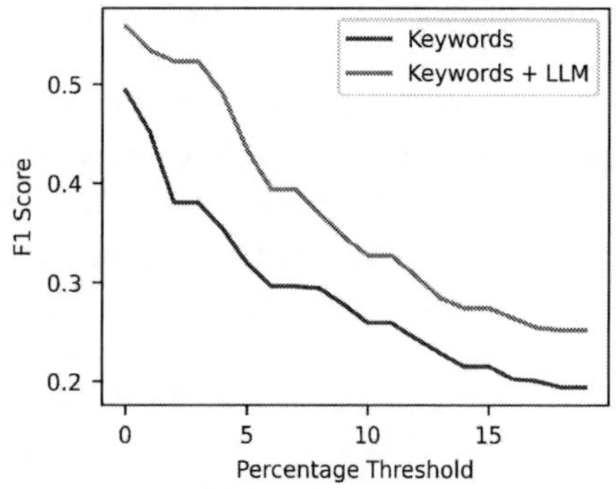

Figure 7: Variation of F1 scores for assigned labels with weights w exceeding the percentile threshold T, as defined in the text, for $\hat{k} = 15$.

Table 3: Precision, recall and F1 scores for $k = 15$ at varying thresholds (T).

T (%)	Precision	Recall	F1
1	0.56	0.56	0.56
5	0.35	0.79	0.49
10	0.22	0.81	0.35
15	0.16	0.86	0.27
20	0.15	0.91	0.25

are conveyed in a relatively dense, short vehicle. Years of study generate a large body of knowledge to guide the expert in a classification process. Indeed, this additional material and the associated judgments underpin the rapid decision-making characteristic of human intuition.

We have sought to replicate that process in an automated methodology. Our unsupervised approach is robust and flexible, enabling its use in various domains. Its independence from specific label sets underscores its adaptability and broad applicability. Our contributions range from applied text processing tasks to economics and public policy, with several interesting directions ahead.

First, we have tested this approach on a relatively narrow set of abstracts by selecting a NASA corpus of documents as the first test case. This exercise should be conducted on benchmark datasets such as Maple (Metadata-Aware Paper colLEction) [3]. This would demonstrate the generalizability of our approach.

Second, a different validation would be to compare these results with those of longer documents. For instance, one could analyze both publication abstracts and the full text. It is not clear if the publications would contain more noise; or perhaps the complete text would carry the metadata such that the LLM task would be less necessary.

In addition, here the manual classification exercise assigned only one label to each abstract as a rigorous test. We have not explored the opportunity to generate multiple labels for a single abstract. Indeed, the $\hat{k} = 25$ data set points to this, as some of the labels (such as "Advanced Thermal Protection Systems") addressed the technology itself, while others described the intended application (e.g., "Mars Sample Return missions"). In the future, we can develop a new weighting scheme addressing this complex classification.

Finally, our method opens lines of inquiry in business or public policy, as we could use this labeling method to generate metadata for the abstracts themselves. In this fashion, the labels could form a variable to be used in further assessment, such as patterns in funding, research direction, patents, or other corpora where scientific documents are condensed in short summaries. Using this method with public company reports could create entirely new industry categories, updating existing schemes (Shweta and Belz, 2021; Hoberg and Phillips, 2010, 2016). Moreover, these data could be combined with other tags, such as principal investigator, institution, or other bibliometric characteristics to create a complex profile. Such a data set could be used to track a number of interesting trends.

6 Conclusion

For labeling short scientific documents, such as abstracts, pre-existing domain-specific taxonomies are ambiguous. Defining a label space spanning the set of documents is an important task that humans execute easily. In this paper, we demonstrate that the text of the documents is insufficient to either define the label space or predict the labels. We present evidence that an LLM can provide critical metadata to address this gap, forming the basis for artificial intuition. Additionally, we propose both an architecture to address this and two novel measures to evaluate the constructed label spaces. Testing our model with a corpus of NASA award abstracts, we demonstrate a workflow that integrates the LLM's supplemental data successfully.

[3]https://github.com/yuzhimanhua/MAPLE/tree/master/

References

Ashwin Karthik Ambalavanan and Murthy V. Devarakonda. 2020. Using the contextual language model bert for multi-criteria classification of scientific articles. *Journal of Biomedical Informatics*, 112:103578.

Soumya Banerjee, Debarshi Kumar Sanyal, Samiran Chattopadhyay, Plaban Kumar Bhowmick, and Partha Pratim Das. 2020. Segmenting scientific abstracts into discourse categories: a deep learning-based approach for sparse labeled data. In *Proceedings of the ACM/IEEE Joint Conference on Digital Libraries in 2020*, pages 429–432.

Iz Beltagy, Kyle Lo, and Arman Cohan. 2019. SciBERT: A pretrained language model for scientific text. In *Proceedings of the 2019 Conference on Empirical Methods in Natural Language Processing and the 9th International Joint Conference on Natural Language Processing (EMNLP-IJCNLP)*, pages 3615–3620, Hong Kong, China. Association for Computational Linguistics.

Andrea Belz, Alexandra Graddy-Reed, FNU Shweta, Aleksandar Giga, and Shivesh Meenakshi Murali. 2023. Deterministic bibliometric disambiguation challenges in company names. In *2023 IEEE 17th International Conference on Semantic Computing (ICSC)*. IEEE.

Elad Ben Zaken, Yoav Goldberg, and Shauli Ravfogel. 2022. BitFit: Simple parameter-efficient fine-tuning for transformer-based masked language-models. In *Proceedings of the 60th Annual Meeting of the Association for Computational Linguistics (Volume 2: Short Papers)*, pages 1–9, Dublin, Ireland. Association for Computational Linguistics.

Alberto Blanco, Arantza Casillas, Alicia Pérez, and Arantza Diaz de Ilarraza. 2019. Multi-label clinical document classification: Impact of label-density. *Expert Systems with Applications*, 138:112835.

Buchlak, Quinlan, and Leveque JC. 2020. Machine learning applications to clinical decision support in neurosurgery. *an artificial intelligence augmented systematic review.*

Lijuan Cai and Thomas Hofmann. 2004. Hierarchical document categorization with support vector machines. In *Proceedings of the Thirteenth ACM International Conference on Information and Knowledge Management*, CIKM '04, page 78–87, New York, NY, USA. Association for Computing Machinery.

Ricardo Campos, Vítor Mangaravite, Arian Pasquali, Alípio Jorge, Célia Nunes, and Adam Jatowt. 2020. Yake! keyword extraction from single documents using multiple local features. *Information Sciences*, 509:257–289.

Jaime Carbonell and Jade Goldstein. 1998. The use of mmr, diversity-based reranking for reordering documents and producing summaries. In *Proceedings of the 21st Annual International ACM SIGIR Conference on Research and Development in Information Retrieval*, SIGIR '98, page 335–336, New York, NY, USA. Association for Computing Machinery.

Ming-Wei Chang, Lev-Arie Ratinov, Dan Roth, and Vivek Srikumar. 2008. Importance of semantic representation: Dataless classification. In *Aaai*, volume 2, pages 830–835.

Wei-Cheng Chang, Hsiang-Fu Yu, Kai Zhong, Yiming Yang, and Inderjit Dhillon. 2020. Taming pretrained transformers for extreme multi-label text classification.

Arman Cohan, Sergey Feldman, Iz Beltagy, Doug Downey, and Daniel Weld. 2020. SPECTER: Document-level representation learning using citation-informed transformers. In *Proceedings of the 58th Annual Meeting of the Association for Computational Linguistics*, pages 2270–2282, Online. Association for Computational Linguistics.

Jacob Devlin, Ming-Wei Chang, Kenton Lee, and Kristina Toutanova. 2019. Bert: Pre-training of deep bidirectional transformers for language understanding.

Santo Fortunato, Carl T. Bergstrom, Katy Börner, James A. Evans, Dirk Helbing, Staša Milojević, Alexander M. Petersen, Filippo Radicchi, Roberta Sinatra, Brian Uzzi, Alessandro Vespignani, Ludo Waltman, Dashun Wang, and Albert-László Barabási. 2018. Science of science. *Science*, 359(6379):eaao0185.

Maryam Habibi and Andrei Popescu-Belis. 2015. Keyword extraction and clustering for document recommendation in conversations. *IEEE/ACM Transactions on Audio, Speech, and Language Processing*, 23(4):746–759.

Gerard Hoberg and Gordon Phillips. 2010. Product market synergies and competition in mergers and acquisitions: A text-based analysis. *Review of Financial Studies*, 23(10):3773–3811.

Gerard Hoberg and Gordon Phillips. 2016. Text-based network industries and endogenous product differentiation. *Journal of Political Economy*, 124(5):1423–1465.

Edward J Hu, Yelong Shen, Phillip Wallis, Zeyuan Allen-Zhu, Yuanzhi Li, Shean Wang, Lu Wang, and Weizhu Chen. 2021. LoRA: Low-Rank adaptation of large language models.

Albert Q. Jiang, Alexandre Sablayrolles, Arthur Mensch, Chris Bamford, Devendra Singh Chaplot, Diego de las Casas, Florian Bressand, Gianna Lengyel, Guillaume Lample, Lucile Saulnier, Lélio Renard Lavaud, Marie-Anne Lachaux, Pierre Stock, Teven Le Scao, Thibaut Lavril, Thomas Wang, Timothée Lacroix, and William El Sayed. 2023. Mistral 7b.

Ji Young Lee and Franck Dernoncourt. 2016. Sequential short-text classification with recurrent and convolutional neural networks. In *Proceedings of the 2016 Conference of the North American Chapter of the Association for Computational Linguistics: Human Language Technologies*, pages 515–520, San Diego, California. Association for Computational Linguistics.

Jingzhou Liu, Wei-Cheng Chang, Yuexin Wu, and Yiming Yang. 2017. Deep learning for extreme multi-label text classification. In *Proceedings of the 40th International ACM SIGIR Conference on Research and Development in Information Retrieval*, SIGIR '17, page 115–124, New York, NY, USA. Association for Computing Machinery.

Pengfei Liu, Xipeng Qiu, and Xuanjing Huang. 2016. Recurrent neural network for text classification with multi-task learning.

Yinhan Liu, Myle Ott, Naman Goyal, Jingfei Du, Mandar Joshi, Danqi Chen, Omer Levy, Mike Lewis, Luke Zettlemoyer, and Veselin Stoyanov. 2019. Roberta: A robustly optimized bert pretraining approach.

Malte Ostendorff, Nils Rethmeier, Isabelle Augenstein, Bela Gipp, and Georg Rehm. 2022. Neighborhood contrastive learning for scientific document representations with citation embeddings.

Tanya Serry Reid Smith, Pamela Snow and Lorraine Hammond. 2021. The role of background knowledge in reading comprehension: A critical review. *Reading Psychology*, 42(3):214–240.

Nils Reimers and Iryna Gurevych. 2019. Sentence-bert: Sentence embeddings using siamese bert-networks.

Anthony Rios and Ramakanth Kavuluru. 2015. Convolutional neural networks for biomedical text classification: application in indexing biomedical articles. In *Proceedings of the 6th ACM Conference on Bioinformatics, Computational Biology and Health Informatics*, BCB '15, page 258–267, New York, NY, USA. Association for Computing Machinery.

Jiaming Shen, Wenda Qiu, Yu Meng, Jingbo Shang, Xiang Ren, and Jiawei Han. 2021. TaxoClass: Hierarchical multi-label text classification using only class names. In *Proceedings of the 2021 Conference of the North American Chapter of the Association for Computational Linguistics: Human Language Technologies*, pages 4239–4249, Online. Association for Computational Linguistics.

FNU Shweta and Andrea Belz. 2021. Computational linguistic analysis of submitted sec information (classi). In *2021 IEEE 33rd International Conference on Tools with Artificial Intelligence (ICTAI)*. IEEE.

Dezhao Song, Andrew Vold, Kanika Madan, and Frank Schilder. 2022. Multi-label legal document classification: A deep learning-based approach with label-attention and domain-specific pre-training. *Information Systems*, 106:101718.

Xingping Sun, Yibing Li, Hongwei Kang, and Yong Shen. 2019. Automatic document classification using convolutional neural network. *Journal of Physics: Conference Series*, 1176(3):032029.

B. Tang, H. He, P. M. Baggenstoss, and S. Kay. 2016. A bayesian classification approach using class-specific features for text categorization. *IEEE Transactions on Knowledge & Data Engineering*, 28(06):1602–1606.

Ross Taylor, Marcin Kardas, Guillem Cucurull, Thomas Scialom, Anthony Hartshorn, Elvis Saravia, Andrew Poulton, Viktor Kerkez, and Robert Stojnic. 2022. Galactica: A large language model for science.

Lin Xiao, Xin Huang, Boli Chen, and Liping Jing. 2019. Label-specific document representation for multi-label text classification. In *Proceedings of the 2019 Conference on Empirical Methods in Natural Language Processing and the 9th International Joint Conference on Natural Language Processing (EMNLP-IJCNLP)*, pages 466–475, Hong Kong, China. Association for Computational Linguistics.

Ran Xu, Yue Yu, Joyce Ho, and Carl Yang. 2023. Weakly-supervised scientific document classification via retrieval-augmented multi-stage training. In *Proceedings of the 46th International ACM SIGIR Conference on Research and Development in Information Retrieval*. ACM.

Guangxu Xun, Kishlay Jha, Ye Yuan, Yaqing Wang, and Aidong Zhang. 2019. MeSHProbeNet: a self-attentive probe net for MeSH indexing. *Bioinformatics*, 35(19):3794–3802.

Wenpeng Yin, Jamaal Hay, and Dan Roth. 2019. Benchmarking zero-shot text classification: Datasets, evaluation and entailment approach. *CoRR*, abs/1909.00161.

Hsiang-Fu Yu, Kai Zhong, Jiong Zhang, Wei-Cheng Chang, and Inderjit S Dhillon. 2022. Pecos: Prediction for enormous and correlated output spaces. *Journal of Machine Learning Research*, 23(98):1–32.

Yu Zhang, Bowen Jin, Xiusi Chen, Yanzhen Shen, Yunyi Zhang, Yu Meng, and Jiawei Han. 2023. Weakly supervised multi-label classification of full-text scientific papers.

Yu Zhang, Zhihong Shen, Chieh-Han Wu, Boya Xie, Junheng Hao, Ye-Yi Wang, Kuansan Wang, and Jiawei Han. 2022a. Metadata-induced contrastive learning for zero-shot multi-label text classification. In *Proceedings of the ACM Web Conference 2022*, WWW '22, page 3162–3173, New York, NY, USA. Association for Computing Machinery.

Yu Zhang, Zhihong Shen, Chieh-Han Wu, Boya Xie, Junheng Hao, Ye-Yi Wang, Kuansan Wang, and Jiawei Han. 2022b. Metadata-induced contrastive learning for zero-shot multi-label text classification.

Wei Zong, Feng Wu, Lap-Keung Chu, and Domenic Sculli. 2015. A discriminative and semantic feature selection method for text categorization. *International Journal of Production Economics*, 165:215–222.

Synthetic Context with LLM for Entity Linking from Scientific Tables

Yuji Oshima[1,2] **Hiroyuki Shindo**[1] **Hiroki Teranishi**[3,1]
Hiroki Ouchi[1,3] **Taro Watanabe**[1]
[1]Nara Institute of Science and Technology [2]Mercari inc. [3]RIKEN
{oshima.yuji.ov6, shindo, hiroki.ouchi, taro}@is.naist.jp
hiroki.teranishi@riken.jp

Abstract

Tables in scientific papers contain crucial information, such as experimental results. Entity Linking (EL) is a promising task that analyses tables and associates them with a knowledge base. EL for table cells requires identifying the referent concept of each cell while understanding the context relevant to each cell in the paper. However, extracting the relevant context from the paper is challenging because the relevant parts are scattered in the main text and captions. This study defines a rule-based method for extracting broad context from the main text, including table captions and sentences that mention the table. Furthermore, we propose synthetic context as a more refined context generated by large language models (LLMs). In a synthetic context, contexts from the entire paper are refined by summarizing, injecting supplemental knowledge, and clarifying the referent concept. We observe this approach improves accuracy for EL by more than 10 points on the S2abEL dataset, and our qualitative analysis suggests potential future works.

1 Introduction

Information analysis of scientific papers has numerous applications in accelerating science, such as paper retrieval, reading assistance, and automatic knowledge base construction. In particular in information science, crucial information, such as experimental results, evaluation datasets, tasks, and evaluation metrics, is often recorded in tables within the papers. Thus, the analysis of table information is an important research field.

For table analysis, entity linking (EL) that associates table cells in scientific papers with a knowledge base (KB) is an important task, and various methods and datasets have been proposed for this purpose (Kardas et al., 2020; Yang et al., 2022; Lou et al., 2023). S2abEL (Lou et al., 2023) is a large-scale evaluation dataset for EL targeting tables in papers for the machine learning field. In

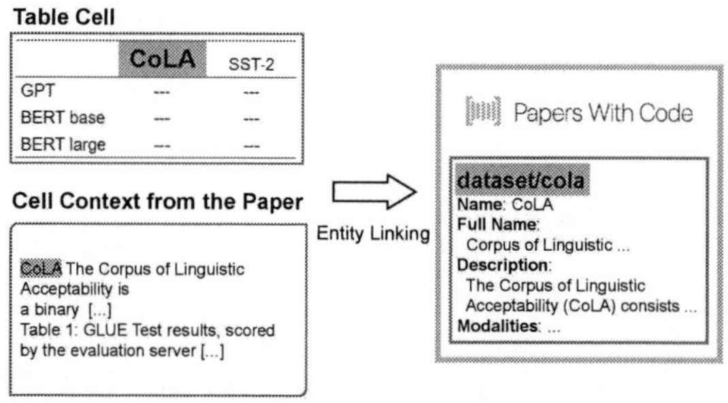

Figure 1: Example of entity linking for table cells in Devlin et al. (2019). Given a target table cell (e.g., "CoLA"), a model seeks to link it to the corresponding entity (e.g., "/dataset/cola") in *Papers with Code* by considering the contexts in the paper related to the cell.

the dataset, each table cell is linked to an entity defined in Papers With Code (PwC)[1], a free and open KB in the scientific domain, as illustrated in Figure 1. To correctly link the target table cell "CoLA" to the corresponding entity "/dataset/cola" in PwC, a model needs to understand the concept of CoLA from the contexts scattered in the main text, captions, and references.

However, extracting such contexts relevant to each cell from a paper has three technical challenges. (i) Relevant contexts for a cell text are scattered in an entire paper, and mentions are often abbreviated or paraphrased, (ii) The context or explanation for a referent concept of a cell can be insufficient, and (iii) General words such as "Ours," "Baseline," and "All" are often used in cell texts, and the referent is ambiguous. An example for the first, in the paper of *The Evolved Transformer* (So et al., 2019), a cell text "ET PERP" is interpreted as "the perplexity achieved by the Evolved Transformer", although the term "ET PERP" does not appear in the main text of the paper. Second, explanations for well-known methods such as LSTM are often omitted, and thus, sufficient contexts are

[1]https://paperswithcode.com/

Proceedings of the Fourth Workshop on Scholarly Document Processing (SDP 2024), pages 202–214
August 16, 2024

unavailable in the paper itself. Third, the cell text "All" stands for the entire dataset. Identifying the dataset requires understanding the context of the main text. However, the word "All" is general and frequently used in irrelevant contexts in the paper.

To address these challenges, we propose a data synthesis method for providing an EL model with supplemental contexts for table cells by using large language models (LLMs) such as ChatGPT (OpenAI, 2023) and LLaMa2 (Touvron et al., 2023). LLMs, acquiring specialized knowledge through pre-training, can be utilized as knowledge bases (Taylor et al., 2022). They also demonstrate high performance in a zero-shot setting for abbreviation expansion (Gorman et al., 2021) and coreference resolution (Wei et al., 2022). Therefore, we expect that they can generate additional information for table cells, which was not mined by previous methods.

In experiments, we use context data for EL obtained by our refined rule-based method and LLM-based method and confirm consistent improvements by both methods over the baseline proposed in S2abEL, including a 10-point improvement in accuracy for EL. Furthermore, by utilizing synthetic context, we improved the accuracy of a subtask that extracts relevant papers for a given table cell by more than 12 points in terms of top-5 accuracy. This result demonstrates the effectiveness of our approach in linking table cells to entities without relying on existing knowledge bases. Our qualitative analysis also reveals that synthetic context data captures better supplemental information through context completion and knowledge completion by LLMs[2].

2 Related Work

2.1 Entity Linking in Scientific Table

Table analysis is crucial for extracting experimental information and results in information extraction from scientific papers. For instance, Axcell (Kardas et al., 2020) extracts tables from the LaTeXsource of papers and performs linking of table cells to entities in a knowledge base. Similarly, S2abEL (Lou et al., 2023) constructs a dataset annotated with entities linked to cells, along with the type of information and the source references for that information, for comparable tasks. Axcell and S2abEL use features representing table cells, such as the cell's positional information and text from the main body that matches the cell's text. SciREX (Jain et al., 2020) and CitationIE (Viswanathan et al., 2021) aim to extract information from the entire paper, not only tables. Kostić et al. (2021) and Zhuang et al. (2022) perform entity extraction and relation extraction from both the text and tables. In these works, the entire document is converted into a feature. However, relevant descriptions of specific table cells are scattered throughout the document. Therefore, it is necessary to efficiently extract the contexts of the cells from the document.

2.2 Data Augmentation/Synthetic Data

Data augmentation and synthesis using LLMs are employed in various tasks. Lai et al. (2022) demonstrate the effectiveness of information completion using generative models, while Chen et al. (2023) show that information summarization is beneficial for entity linking. This study aims to generate sufficient and necessary information for linking by simultaneously performing information completion and summarization within the full context of papers. On the other hand, some studies leverage the asymmetry in task difficulty, where inverse problems are easier to solve than forward problems, to generate training data by solving inverse problems using LLMs. Wang et al. (2021) employ few-shot learning to create training data from labels, and Josifoski et al. (2023) generate synthetic training data for the general information extraction task. Although these are effective methods for problems that are difficult to solve directly with LLM's zero-shot or few-shot capabilities, synthesizing tables or papers from entities to be linked is challenging. Therefore, this study aims to enhance the learning efficiency of existing human-annotated data using synthetic data generated with LLMs.

3 Entity Linking in Scientific Tables

EL for scientific tables aims to map each table cell within a paper to an entity in a KB (PwC in our experiments) or "OutKB" if no corresponding entity is found in the KB. The baseline method *S2abEL* is proposed by Lou et al. (2023). They divide this task into the following subtasks:

1. **Attributed Source Matching (ASM)**: Identifying the *attributed source(s)* for a table cell within a paper. The attributed source(s) is the reference paper that originally proposed or introduced the concept that a target cell refers

[2] We will release our code and data to reproduce the experiments.

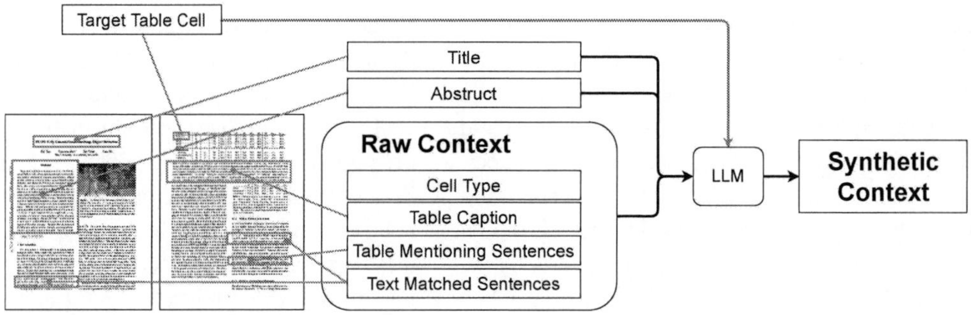

Figure 2: Generation of synthetic context: Sentences related to a particular cell (raw context) are provided to a Large Language Model (LLM). By having the LLM explain the content of the target cell, contextual information related to the target cell is extracted from the raw context.

to. This step aims to distinguish similar surface forms to find the correct referent entities in the subsequent subtasks. e.g., the paper by Warstadt et al. (2019) is identified as the attributed source of "CoLA".

2. **Entity Disambiguation (ED)**: Retrieving candidate entities from the KB that are likely to be linked to a target cell. Then, selecting the referent entity from the candidates for a given cell (or assign *OutKB* if none of them is appropriate). e.g., The entities associated with the paper by Warstadt et al. (2019) in PwC are added to the candidates for "CoLA" and "/dataset/cola" is selected from among them.

Note that Lou et al. (2023) perform cell type classification before the pipeline[3]. However, the classification of cell types has already exceeded the accuracy 90% in previous research, and replacing it with the correct types contributes less than a 1% improvement in the final EL accuracy. Therefore, we use the correct cell types to proceed to the subsequent subtasks.

4 Method

In this study, we aim to improve the overall accuracy of EL by enhancing the context of cells, which is the most important feature for both ASM and ED tasks in the baseline method. To this end, we first improve the rule-based context extraction method and then generate synthetic data to refine the context.

4.1 Supplementing Context Information

Meticulous cell context extraction: For EL, a model needs to interpret the concept that a cell text represents and extract appropriate contexts for it from the paper. As context information of a target cell, the prior research has utilized various features, including sentences retrieved by BM25 (Robertson and Zaragoza, 2009), the cell's position in the table, and the surrounding cells. However, the retrieval method can miss relevant sentences or extract irrelevant sentences due to text fluctuation (e.g., abbreviation, paraphrasing) or the use of general words, resulting in insufficient and erroneous information sourced from the main text. To alleviate this, we first collect text fragments covering broader contexts. Specifically, we use the following features as the contexts for a target cell: (i) The cell's text. (ii) The cell type. (iii) The table caption. (iv) Sentences referring to the table: Sentences that explicitly contain references to the table, such as "Table 1." (v) Sentences containing the cell's text. We refer to a set of the features as the *raw context* for a target cell.

For example, the raw context of a cell in the paper by Devlin et al. (2019) illustrated in Figure 1 is as follows: (i) *CoLA*. (ii) *dataset*. (iii) *"Table 1: GLUE Test results, scored by the evaluation server [...]"*. (iv) *"Results are presented in Table 1"*. (v) *"CoLA The Corpus of Linguistic Acceptability is a binary single-sentence [...]"*.

Synthetic context generation: To focus on essential information in a raw context and supplement it by injecting external knowledge, we employ an LLM to generate a description for a cell based on the corresponding raw context. We refer to a description generated by an LLM as a *synthetic context*. The process of synthetic context generation in this study is illustrated in Figure 2. In this research, we employ OpenAI's GPT-4 Turbo (1106) as the LLM.

[3]The cell types are *Method*, *Dataset*, *Metrics*, *Dataset&Metrics*, and *Other.*

For example, the synthetic context generated by the LLM for the example shown in Figure 1 is *"CoLA stands for Corpus of Linguistic Acceptability. It is a dataset used for a binary single-sentence classification task in natural language processing. [...]"*. This exhibits the LLM's capabilities of providing a synthetic context that summarizes adequate information for EL.

4.2 Subtasks of Entity Linking

We integrate the improved context extraction/generation methods into each subtask in the baseline pipeline as follows.

Attributed Source Matching: We follow the approach of S2abEL (Lou et al., 2023) for ASM. The potential attributed sources for a cell are all cited papers and the current document itself. Including the document itself is necessary for the case where the cell's referent concept is newly proposed in the document. To find the attributed source from the potential source, we calculate the relevance scores between the cell and each potential source. As features for a scoring model, we concatenate the title and abstract of a potential source and the cell's context. As the scoring model, S2abEL adopts SciBERT (Reimers and Gurevych, 2019). In this research, we employ SciBERT with raw context and GPT-2 (Radford et al., 2019) with synthetic context[4]. A scoring model is trained with binary cross-entropy loss.

Entity Disambiguation: To collect candidate entities for a target cell, we sort the attributed sources by the ASM score and then retrieve entities from the KB for each attributed source until we obtain k candidates for the cell. To select the most promising entity from the candidates, following the prior work, we employ a model to calculate a score for each entity candidate by feeding the concatenation of the entity name, its description, and the cell context into the model. We adopt SciBERT for the scoring model and train it with binary cross-entropy loss. The highest-scoring entity is linked to the cell when the score is greater than a predefined threshold. Otherwise, OutKB is assigned to the cell, representing being out of KB. We set the threshold to 0.5, the same as prior research.

[4]As the token length of synthetic contexts often exceeds the input token limit of SciBERT (512), we did not employ SciBERT with synthetic context.

5 Experiments

The experiments follow the setup of S2abEL, where training, validation, and test data are created from different topics. The results below represent the cross-validation average on the topics in S2abEL. This allows us to compare the generalization performance of the models without overfitting to specific topics.

5.1 End-to-end Entity Linking

In EL experiments, as explained in §3, the cell types are determined using the ground truth data.

5.1.1 Experimental Settings

In end-to-end entity linking experiments, we compare raw context and synthetic context against S2abEL (Lou et al., 2023) as the baseline. The baseline additionally leverages dense retrieval (DR) for ED to retrieve entity candidates from the KB directly, but we do not use it to see the sole effect when using raw context and synthetic context[5]. We apply the same context to both ASM and ED. We report three metrics: InKB accuracy, OutKB F1, and overall accuracy. InKB hit@1 accuracy shows the hit rate at the top when an entity to be linked is present. For OutKB entities, we report F1 score. The overall accuracy is determined as follows[6]:

1. For OutKB mentions: A cell is considered correct if predicted as an OutKB mention.
2. For InKB mentions: A cell is considered correct if ranked as the top prediction (@top1 hit).

The number of entity candidates k retrieved is set to $k = 50$ (the same as prior work) and $k = 20$. Training details are displayed in Appendix D.

5.1.2 Result

Table 1 shows that the raw context and synthetic context conditions have improved overall accuracy by over 10 points compared to the S2abEL baseline when $k = 50$. This indicates that the necessary context information for the EL task has been successfully extracted from the main text in the raw context. When comparing synthetic context to raw context, there is a slight improvement in overall

[5]The experimental results in S2abEL reported that the ASM-based retrieval method without using DR achieves over 90% recall when $k \geq 30$.

[6]In the S2abEL dataset, 42.8% cells are marked as OutKB mentions.

Method	Overall acc.	OutKB F1	InKB hit@1
$k = 50$			
S2abEL (Lou et al., 2023)	58.2	71.4	33.4
S2abEL w/o DR	60.8	71.7	27.1
Raw Context	69.9	**76.5**	47.1
Synthetic Context	**70.5**	76.4	**53.1**
$k = 20$			
S2abEL w/o DR	60.2	70.3	25.3
Raw Context	68.9	75.5	44.7
Synthetic Context	**70.8**	**76.6**	**52.2**

Table 1: Result of End-to-end Entity Linking

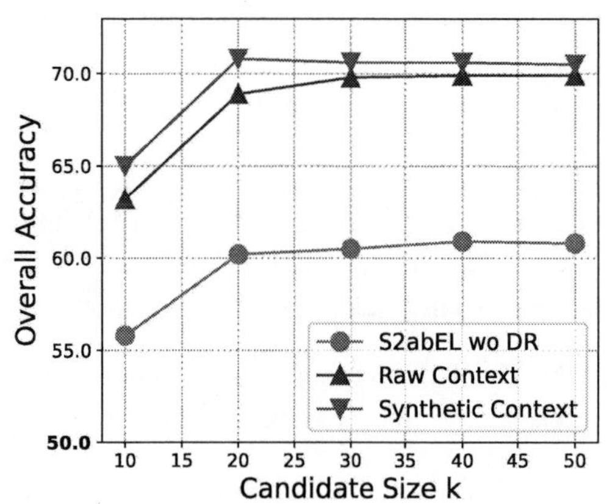

Figure 3: Evaluation of different Contexts on variation number of candidate entity.

accuracy and a 6-point increase in the InKB hit@1. This demonstrates that synthetic context effectively captures the appropriate information from raw context and is supplemented by the LLM.

In the results with smaller entity candidates $k = 20$, the difference between raw context and synthetic context has become more pronounced. This suggests that in the case of $k = 50$, there is almost no difference in the entity candidates extracted by raw context and synthetic context. We observe that the overall accuracy for synthetic context does not much degrade for smaller $k < 30$, compared with other conditions in Figure 3. In the synthetic context setting, the proposed EL pipeline achieves better accuracy with 20 candidates than with 50 candidates. This might be because, when the correct entity is successfully retrieved within the top 20 candidates ($k = 20$), increasing the number to 50 ($k = 50$) introduces noise, which leads to a decrease in accuracy.

5.2 Evaluating Method Combinations for ASM and ED in Entity Linking Tasks

5.2.1 Experimental Settings

To observe the effects of the proposed raw/synthetic contexts in ASM and ED subtasks, we compare the accuracy of EL with exhaustive combinations of contexts and subtasks[7]. The number of entity candidates is $k = 20$ since the difference of entity candidates is small in larger k.

5.2.2 Result

Table 2 shows that using either raw or synthetic context for only ASM or ED improves accuracy compared to using the context defined in S2abEL. When used only for ASM, the improvement in accuracy is about 1 or 2 points, while for ED, the improvement is around 6 to 7 points. When comparing the two proposed methods applied to ASM, it is observed that synthetic context improves the overall accuracy by 1 point, indicating that synthetic context is capable of enhancing ASM. When raw or synthetic context is applied only to ED, the improvements in InKB hit@1 are larger than when applied only to ASM. In any conditions, synthetic context consistently achieves higher accuracy than raw and S2abEL contexts. These results suggest that both raw context and synthetic context are effective for both ASM and ED tasks and that synthetic context is capable of representing more effective contexts than raw context.

5.3 Evaluating the Impact of Context in ASM

To directly observe the effect of the improved context, we evaluate using the precision of the ASM. This experiment is evaluated only on cells with attributed source papers. In the S2abEL dataset, some cells do not have an attributed source, and we filtered out these cells in this experiment. Furthermore, unlike when used as a subtask of EL, it is evaluated based on the accuracy of selecting the attributed source paper rather than the entity. The results are evaluated based on the accuracy of the top 1 and top 5 ranked by the score.

[7]To investigate the effects of context refinement solely, we do not use dense retrieval for collecting candidates in the pipeline.

ASM Method	ED Method	Overall acc.	OutKB F1	InKB hit@1
S2abEL	S2abEL	60.2	70.3	25.3
Raw Context	S2abEL	61.0	70.8	27.2
Synthetic Context	S2abEL	62.2	72.0	28.8
S2abEL	Raw Context	66.8	73.8	41.4
S2abEL	Synthetic Context	67.4	73.3	46.7
Raw Context	Raw Context	68.9	75.5	44.7
Synthetic Context	Synthetic Context	**70.8**	**76.6**	**52.2**

Table 2: Performance Comparison of ASM and ED Method Combinations in Entity Linking Tasks

5.3.1 Variation of Context and Scoring model

In the ASM task, we calculate scores for all cited references and the target paper to select the attributed source for the cell. The scoring model is given the cell's context and the title and abstract of each attributed source candidate. We compare variations of this scoring model and the cell context.

GPT4 Zeroshot We leverage GPT4-Turbo (1106) to ASM in a zero-shot setting. The raw contexts, along with the titles and abstracts of all cited references, are given to GPT4-Turbo, and it infers the attributed source paper directly. For GPT4 Zeroshot, the evaluation is based solely on the top 1 accuracy since it directly selects the cited reference without scoring.

Cell Context Three types of context are to be compared. S2abEL is the context defined in S2abEL paper (Lou et al., 2023), raw context, and synthetic context.

Scoring Model SciBERT and GPT2 are trained with each context. The cell context can be longer than the maximum input token length of BERT (512). Hence, GPT2, which allows more input tokens (1024), is used to capture all context. The detailed statistics of the token number of contexts are provided in Appendix C.

5.3.2 Result

Table 3 shows that the model fine-tuned with synthetic context demonstrates the highest performance in both @top1 and @top5 metrics compared to other conditions. The performance of GPT4 Turbo in zero-shot learning is lower than those of other fine-tuned models. When using the raw context with SciBERT, the @top1 accuracy is lower than the S2abEL, but the @top5 accuracy outperforms it. To compare SciBERT and GPT2 with raw context, GPT2 performs worse than SciBERT despite having larger parameters.

5.3.3 Error Analysis and Discussion

GPT4 zero-shot A drastic tendency was observed when GPT4 Turbo was prompted in a zero-shot manner to simultaneously choose attributed sources from both the cited references and the target papers. Depending on the prompt text, the GPT4 Turbo chooses them only from the target papers or only from cited references. To mitigate this issue, the prompt text was adjusted to choose the attributed source from the cited references first and then determine whether the concept was newly proposed. If the model determines it as a new concept, the attributed source from cited references is discarded, and the target paper is selected. Concrete examples of each are provided in Appendix B.

SciBERT vs GPT2 The raw context aims to extract sufficient information from the main text, which may include sentences with little relevance to the cell. This may explain why GPT2, which can use all the context, did not contribute to accuracy.

Synthetic Context Analysis The comparison of synthetic and raw context revealed that employing synthetic context improved accuracy in two ways: context completion and knowledge completion.

Context Completion Only the abbreviated name of a method or dataset is mentioned in the cell, but the full name and description are provided in the main text. For instance, a cell in a table is "ET Perp," and it refers to the "Perplexity achieved by the Evolved Transformer." However, the expression does not appear in the main text. Thus,

Cell Context	Scoring Model	accuracy@top1			accuracy@top5		
		all	method	dataset	all	method	dataset
GPT4 Turbo zero-shot	None	22.3	30.0	1.0	-	-	-
S2abEL (Lou et al., 2023)	SciBERT	49.3	55.3	29.8	63.2	64.9	53.7
Raw Context	SciBERT	45.0	45.3	44.7	67.3	65.6	69.1
Raw Context	GPT2	41.1	43.8	35.4	62.8	63.3	60.7
Synthetic Context	GPT2	**55.6**	**56.5**	**51.8**	**75.7**	**75.7**	**70.8**

Table 3: ASM Result of varying Cell Contexts and Scoring Model

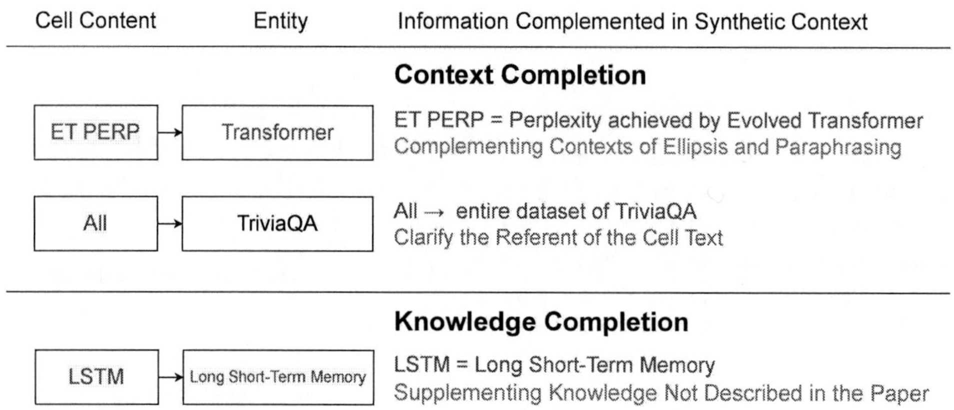

Figure 4: Completions in the synthetic contexts: There are two types of completions in synthetic contexts. **Context Completion**: LLM understands that the cell context is the abbreviated name and explains it in the synthetic context. Clarify the referent of the cell when the referent is ambiguous. **Knowledge Completion**: If the cell's content is not explained in the paper, LLM adds supplemental information.

baseline methods failed to link the cell to the Transformer correctly. In the synthetic context, the abbreviation context is explained by the LLM, and the cell is successfully linked to the correct entity.

We found that when the referent of a cell is ambiguous on its own, such as "baseline" and "All", the context supplements this by clarifying the referent in the synthetic context. Table 3 in the paper of Clark and Gardner (2018) contains a cell named "All." The synthetic context for this cell is *"[...]the term 'All' likely refers to the entire dataset of TriviaQA, which [...]"*, making the referent of the word "All" clear.

Knowledge Completion There may not be sufficient descriptions for well-known methods or datasets in the main text. For example, the concept of cell content "LSTM" might not be adequately explained despite many mentions of LSTM in the main text. Hence, previous methods misinterpret LSTM as a new concept. In the synthetic context data, LLM complemented the fact that LSTM stands for Long Short-Term Memory. And it allows the cell to successfully associate with the correct entity.

Errors in Synthetic Context On the other hand, errors were observed due to the misunderstanding injected in synthetic contexts. Specifically, in the paper of Bauer et al. (2018), the cell labeled *"Dev"* in Table 3 refers to a development set for evaluation. However, it is identified as a person name *"Devi Parikh,"* by LLM. The name is the author of a reference and included in the raw context but unrelated to the experiments in Table 3. This implies the raw context is not sufficient to identify essential information accurately.

5.4 Experimental Investigation of LLM for Synthetic Context

In this experiment, we measure the impact on task scores by various LLMs that generate synthetic contexts.

5.4.1 Experimental Settings

In previous experiments, GPT4 Turbo was used as the LLM. The quality of the synthetic context is believed to be influenced by the language com-

Generation Model	accuracy@top1 all	accuracy@top1 method	accuracy@top1 dataset	accuracy@top5 all	accuracy@top5 method	accuracy@top5 dataset
GPT4 Turbo	**55.6**	**56.5**	**51.8**	**75.7**	**75.7**	70.8
GPT3.5-16k	51.4	54.3	44.8	71.3	73.4	66.7
TULU v2 70B+DPO	54.0	55.8	49.2	74.5	74.6	**72.9**

Table 4: ASM Result of varying LLM models for synthetic context generation

prehension ability and specialized knowledge of relevant the domain of the LLMs. Therefore, in this experiment, we evaluate synthetic contexts generated by the following two models in addition to GPT4 Turbo. **GPT3.5 Turbo**: The training data of GPT3.5 Turbo is assumed to be similar to GPT4 Turbo. However, as the parameter size of it is smaller than GPT4-turbo, it has lower language comprehension and language refinement abilities. **TULU2 70B+DPO** (Ivison et al., 2023): An open-sourced model that continues learning from LLAMA2 70B using the instruction dataset and the direct preference optimization (DPO) algorithm (Rafailov et al., 2023). It demonstrates performance equivalent to GPT3.5-turbo in MT-Bench and AlpacaEval. Scientific documents in the machine learning field are included in the training dataset, such as SciERC (Luan et al., 2018) and Qasper (Dasigi et al., 2021). As a result, we expect it to have enough knowledge to perform knowledge completion.

5.4.2 Result

Table 4 shows that TULU v2 70B+DPO demonstrates higher accuracy than GPT3.5-16k and exhibits competitive performance with GPT4-Turbo. Regardless of the type of LLM, there is a consistent trend that method type cells have higher accuracy than dataset type cells. However, this trend is more pronounced in GPT3.5-16k.

5.4.3 Error Analysis and Discussion

We confirmed that TULU2 70B+DPO has knowledge about famous methods, datasets, and evaluation metrics and performs appropriate knowledge completion. This indicates that when the pretraining dataset for an LLM includes data related to the domain, knowledge completion can be expected to be effective in supplementing concepts, which are often abbreviated or omitted in a paper. Although an LLM used in our pipeline needs to be updated to learn newly introduced methods and concepts, frequent updates would not be necessarily required, as it takes some time for such concepts to become prevalent. We expect the knowledge update for LLMs can be partly resolved with retrieval-augmented generation.

Although we confirmed the knowledge of LLMs is effective for entity linking, we observed the outputs that are not based on facts, known as hallucinations (Ji et al., 2023). For example, a table cell in the paper of Zhong et al. (2019) is "CFC (ours)", and its attributed source is the paper itself. However, a part of the synthetic context generated by TULU2 70B+DPO is
"The term "CFC (ours)" in the context of the scientific paper titled "modelname for Multi-evidence Question Answering" refers to a new question answering model[...]", which refers to a non-existent paper title. Suppressing such hallucinations while leveraging the knowledge of LLMs is a challenge for future work.

6 Conclusion

In this study, we proposed new context extraction methods from the main text for entity linking of table cells of scientific papers. First, we propose a rule-based context extraction method (raw context) to collect broad context from a paper. Then, we introduce the synthesized data using an LLM to refine the raw context (synthetic context). By employing raw context and synthetic context, we improved the accuracy of entity linking by more than 10 points. In the qualitative analysis, we observe the LLM refines raw context by supplementing context and completing information.

7 Limitations

Application scope. Our entity linking method in this work depends on an existing KB. Thus, it cannot be applied to fields where KB does not exist. However, the @top1 accuracy for ASM tasks in section 5.3 can be considered linking table cells to papers, which allows linking to unknown concepts without depending on an existing KB. Therefore, there is potential for application as the automatic construction of knowledge bases in domains where organized KB does not exist yet.

Practicality. Our proposed method outperforms the existing method and achieves 53.1% @top1 accuracy in EL, 55.6% for @top1, and 75.7% for @top5 in ASM. These results suggest that fully automating the linking of table cells in papers is still challenging; however, it could potentially be used to assist manual annotation for table cells.

Model bias. Synthetic context depends on LLMs' generative capabilities and knowledge, making it susceptible to the model's bias. This study targets only English-language papers in the machine learning domain, which may limit generalization to other languages and fields.

Model availability. The experiments in this study were conducted using OpenAI's GPT4 Turbo 1106, GPT3.5 16k, and TULU2 70B+DPO. GPT4 Turbo and GPT3.5 are accessible via the OpenAI API, but access may be lost in the future due to model version updates. Currently, these models are supported by the Azure OpenAI API.

Acknowledgements

This work was supported by JST Moonshot R&D Grant Number JPMJMS2236. This research is also supported by the Mercari R4D PhD Support Program.

References

Lisa Bauer, Yicheng Wang, and Mohit Bansal. 2018. Commonsense for generative multi-hop question answering tasks. *arXiv preprint arXiv:1809.06309*.

Yulin Chen, Zhenran Xu, Baotian Hu, and Min Zhang. 2023. Revisiting sparse retrieval for few-shot entity linking. In *Proceedings of the 2023 Conference on Empirical Methods in Natural Language Processing*, pages 12801–12806, Singapore. Association for Computational Linguistics.

Christopher Clark and Matt Gardner. 2018. Simple and effective multi-paragraph reading comprehension. In *Proceedings of the 56th Annual Meeting of the Association for Computational Linguistics (Volume 1: Long Papers)*, pages 845–855, Melbourne, Australia. Association for Computational Linguistics.

Pradeep Dasigi, Kyle Lo, Iz Beltagy, Arman Cohan, Noah A. Smith, and Matt Gardner. 2021. A dataset of information-seeking questions and answers anchored in research papers. *ArXiv*, abs/2105.03011.

Jacob Devlin, Ming-Wei Chang, Kenton Lee, and Kristina Toutanova. 2019. Bert: Pre-training of deep bidirectional transformers for language understanding. In *North American Chapter of the Association for Computational Linguistics*.

Kyle Gorman, Christo Kirov, Brian Roark, and Richard Sproat. 2021. Structured abbreviation expansion in context. In *Findings of the Association for Computational Linguistics: EMNLP 2021*, pages 995–1005, Punta Cana, Dominican Republic. Association for Computational Linguistics.

Hamish Ivison, Yizhong Wang, Valentina Pyatkin, Nathan Lambert, Matthew Peters, Pradeep Dasigi, Joel Jang, David Wadden, Noah A Smith, Iz Beltagy, et al. 2023. Camels in a changing climate: Enhancing lm adaptation with tulu 2. *arXiv preprint arXiv:2311.10702*.

Sarthak Jain, Madeleine van Zuylen, Hannaneh Hajishirzi, and Iz Beltagy. 2020. SciREX: A challenge dataset for document-level information extraction. In *Proceedings of the 58th Annual Meeting of the Association for Computational Linguistics*, pages 7506–7516, Online. Association for Computational Linguistics.

Ziwei Ji, Nayeon Lee, Rita Frieske, Tiezheng Yu, Dan Su, Yan Xu, Etsuko Ishii, Ye Jin Bang, Andrea Madotto, and Pascale Fung. 2023. Survey of hallucination in natural language generation. *ACM Comput. Surv.*, 55(12).

Martin Josifoski, Marija Sakota, Maxime Peyrard, and Robert West. 2023. Exploiting asymmetry for synthetic training data generation: SynthIE and the case of information extraction. In *Proceedings of the 2023 Conference on Empirical Methods in Natural Language Processing*, pages 1555–1574, Singapore. Association for Computational Linguistics.

Marcin Kardas, Piotr Czapla, Pontus Stenetorp, Sebastian Ruder, Sebastian Riedel, Ross Taylor, and Robert Stojnic. 2020. AxCell: Automatic extraction of results from machine learning papers. In *Proceedings of the 2020 Conference on Empirical Methods in Natural Language Processing (EMNLP)*, pages 8580–8594, Online. Association for Computational Linguistics.

Bogdan Kostić, Julian Risch, and Timo Möller. 2021. Multi-modal retrieval of tables and texts using tri-encoder models. In *Proceedings of the 3rd Workshop on Machine Reading for Question Answering*, pages 82–91, Punta Cana, Dominican Republic. Association for Computational Linguistics.

Tuan Lai, Heng Ji, and ChengXiang Zhai. 2022. Improving candidate retrieval with entity profile generation for Wikidata entity linking. In *Findings of the Association for Computational Linguistics: ACL 2022*, pages 3696–3711, Dublin, Ireland. Association for Computational Linguistics.

Ilya Loshchilov and Frank Hutter. 2019. Decoupled weight decay regularization.

Yuze Lou, Bailey Kuehl, Erin Bransom, Sergey Feldman, Aakanksha Naik, and Doug Downey. 2023. S2abEL: A dataset for entity linking from scientific tables. In *Proceedings of the 2023 Conference on Empirical Methods in Natural Language Processing*, pages 3089–3101, Singapore. Association for Computational Linguistics.

Yi Luan, Luheng He, Mari Ostendorf, and Hannaneh Hajishirzi. 2018. Multi-task identification of entities, relations, and coreference for scientific knowledge graph construction. In *Proceedings of the 2018 Conference on Empirical Methods in Natural Language Processing*, pages 3219–3232, Brussels, Belgium. Association for Computational Linguistics.

OpenAI. 2023. Chatgpt. `https://chat.openai.com`.

Alec Radford, Jeffrey Wu, Rewon Child, David Luan, Dario Amodei, Ilya Sutskever, et al. 2019. Language models are unsupervised multitask learners. *OpenAI blog*, 1(8):9.

Rafael Rafailov, Archit Sharma, Eric Mitchell, Christopher D Manning, Stefano Ermon, and Chelsea Finn. 2023. Direct preference optimization: Your language model is secretly a reward model. In *Thirty-seventh Conference on Neural Information Processing Systems*.

Nils Reimers and Iryna Gurevych. 2019. Sentence-BERT: Sentence embeddings using Siamese BERT-networks. In *Proceedings of the 2019 Conference on Empirical Methods in Natural Language Processing and the 9th International Joint Conference on Natural Language Processing (EMNLP-IJCNLP)*, pages 3982–3992, Hong Kong, China. Association for Computational Linguistics.

Stephen Robertson and Hugo Zaragoza. 2009. The probabilistic relevance framework: Bm25 and beyond. *Foundations and Trends® in Information Retrieval*, 3(4):333–389.

David So, Quoc Le, and Chen Liang. 2019. The evolved transformer. In *International conference on machine learning*, pages 5877–5886. PMLR.

Ross Taylor, Marcin Kardas, Guillem Cucurull, Thomas Scialom, Anthony Hartshorn, Elvis Saravia, Andrew Poulton, Viktor Kerkez, and Robert Stojnic. 2022. Galactica: A large language model for science.

Hugo Touvron, Louis Martin, Kevin Stone, Peter Albert, Amjad Almahairi, Yasmine Babaei, Nikolay Bashlykov, Soumya Batra, Prajjwal Bhargava, Shruti Bhosale, et al. 2023. Llama 2: Open foundation and fine-tuned chat models. *arXiv preprint arXiv:2307.09288*.

Vijay Viswanathan, Graham Neubig, and Pengfei Liu. 2021. CitationIE: Leveraging the citation graph for scientific information extraction. In *Proceedings of the 59th Annual Meeting of the Association for Computational Linguistics and the 11th International Joint Conference on Natural Language Processing (Volume 1: Long Papers)*, pages 719–731, Online. Association for Computational Linguistics.

Zirui Wang, Adams Wei Yu, Orhan Firat, and Yuan Cao. 2021. Towards zero-label language learning. *arXiv preprint arXiv:2109.09193*.

Alex Warstadt, Amanpreet Singh, and Samuel R. Bowman. 2019. Neural network acceptability judgments. *Transactions of the Association for Computational Linguistics*, 7:625–641.

Jason Wei, Maarten Bosma, Vincent Y. Zhao, Kelvin Guu, Adams Wei Yu, Brian Lester, Nan Du, Andrew M. Dai, and Quoc V. Le. 2022. Finetuned language models are zero-shot learners.

Sean Yang, Chris Tensmeyer, and Curtis Wigington. 2022. TELIN: Table entity LINker for extracting leaderboards from machine learning publications. In *Proceedings of the first Workshop on Information Extraction from Scientific Publications*, pages 20–25, Online. Association for Computational Linguistics.

Victor Zhong, Caiming Xiong, Nitish Shirish Keskar, and Richard Socher. 2019. Coarse-grain fine-grain coattention network for multi-evidence question answering. *ArXiv*, abs/1901.00603.

Yuchen Zhuang, Yinghao Li, Junyang Zhang, Yue Yu, Yingjun Mou, Xiang Chen, Le Song, and Chao Zhang. 2022. ReSel: N-ary relation extraction from scientific text and tables by learning to retrieve and select. In *Proceedings of the 2022 Conference on Empirical Methods in Natural Language Processing*, pages 730–744, Abu Dhabi, United Arab Emirates. Association for Computational Linguistics.

A Prompt for Synthetic Context generation

Generate Synthetic Context as a summarization task in a zero-shot setting with an LLM. Synthetic context data generation was performed using GPT4-Turbo-1106-preview, GPT3.5-turbo-16k, and TULU2-70B DPO. The parameters during generation, temperature, and top-k were set to 0 to stabilize the generation. The input to the GPT4-Turbo-1106-preview and GPT3.5-turbo-16k models follows a format that embeds the text of the cell (CELL_CONTENT), the paper title (PAPER_TITLE), the abstract (PAPER_ABSTRACT), and the paper context information (PAPER_CONTEXT). The total number of prompt tokens to generate all synthetic context is 1182k, and for completion tokens, it is 1695k. Hence, generating all synthetic context with GPT4-Turbo 1106 costs about $170.

prompts

system_prompt : *You are a researcher in the field of machine learning. You are provided with a word that appears in a certain paper and information in the paper related to that word. Please explain the word based on the information provided.*
user_prompt : *Please explain the word {CELL_CONTENT}. The title of the paper in which this word appears is "{PAPER_TITLE}", and the abstract is "{PAPER_ABSTRUCT}". The category of this word is {CELL_TYPE}. The relevant descriptions in the text are written below. {PAPER_CONTEXT} Please provide your answer as concisely as possible.*

B GPT4 Turbo zero shot-learning prompt

In §5.3.1 of the experiment, GPT4 Turbo was evaluated directly in a zero-shot setting for Attributed Source Matching. Specifically, the main text information of the paper and the titles and abstracts of all cited references were embedded into the following template as input. As output, the ID of the cited reference that serves as the source and a flag indicating whether it represents a novel concept proposed in the paper were obtained. If it is determined that the flag represents a concept proposed in the paper, the source is cited as SourcePaper without using the cited reference ID.

prompts

system prompt : *You are tasked with identifying the source reference of the concept indicated by the cell text in a table within a machine learning academic paper. This paper is referred to as the "Source Paper" and its cited literature as "Reference Papers". The concept indicated by the cell text in the table is either a dataset or a method, which was proposed either in the cited literature. Your task is to estimate the paper in which this concept was proposed. For making your estimation, you will be provided with the cell text of the table, the type of concept that the cell text of the table is indicating, the caption of the respective table, and descriptions in the "SourcePaper" that are relevant to the respective table. You will also be presented with potential choices which include the title and abstract each of the cited literature. Please make a selection from these options. Your response should be in the following JSON format: { "estimate_result": "ID of a ReferencePaper", "is_source": "True or False" } Please input that ReferencePaper's ID into the estimate_result field. Also, if you believe that the content indicated by the cell text in the table is something newly proposed in the SourcePaper, please enter True in the is_source field.*

C Cell Contexts Statistics

We compare the statistics of the number of tokens for the input to the model used in S2abEL and the raw context and synthetic context used in this study. Table 5 shows the mean, standard deviation, maximum, and minimum number of tokens for the entire data and the mean and standard deviation of the number of tokens when the Cell type is method or dataset. Comparing the features of S2abEL and raw context, the raw context tends to have a smaller average number of tokens and a larger standard deviation. This is because, in S2abEL, information about the position of the table and surrounding cells was used as input. In contrast, in the raw context of this study, sentences that mention the table or cells in the captions or main text are added. As a result, the number of tokens varies significantly depending on the mention in the main text, leading to a larger standard deviation. The synthetic context summarizes and complements the raw context and

Name	all average	all std	all max	all min	method average	method std	dataset average	dataset std
S2abEL	522.6	221.1	1292	49	569.2	220.9	434.1	192.6
Raw Context	510.2	282.7	5044	29	499.4	268.8	530.9	306.5
Synthetic Context	385.6	98.6	2121	65	394.1	98.2	369.3	97.2

Table 5: Cell Contexts Token number Statistics

consistently has fewer tokens. Furthermore, when there are many mentions in the main text, only necessary information is extracted, and when there are no mentions, information is supplemented, leading to a significantly smaller standard deviation.

D Training Details

We trained all models using the AdamW optimizer (Loshchilov and Hutter, 2019) with linear decay warm-up. All models were trained using a single 48Gb NVIDIA A6000 GPU. To train GPT-2 for ASM, We added a short prompt before cell contexts. The prompt is "Given a table cell text from an academic paper in the field of Machine Learning, classify whether the information in the cell originates from provided cited literature or other. The reference information is". For evaluation, cross-validation is conducted on 10 paper categories within the S2abEL dataset. From S2abEL dataset, a category is selected for testing, another category is randomly selected for validation, and other categories are used for training.

parameter	GPT-2	SciBERT
learning rate	2e-5	2e-5
batch size	16	32
max token length	1024	512
epoch size	2	2
warm-up ratio	10%	10%

Table 6: Training Hyperparameters

E Detailed Entity Linking Result

Cross-validation is conducted on 10 categories of paper within the S2abEL dataset in the Entity Linking experiments. The results across all folds are presented.

Test fold	Overall acc.	OutKB F1	InKB hit@1	Overall acc.	OutKB F1	InKB hit@1	Overall acc.	OutKB F1	InKB hit@1
img_gen	48.3	55.6	26.7	53.8	57.1	37.4	48.6	46.9	43.1
misc	71.3	83.2	1.2	80.1	87.8	37.8	86.5	92.0	74.4
mt	49.2	60.6	22.5	50.0	59.9	21.2	62.2	68.8	39.4
nli	61.4	73.4	26.6	66.4	76.9	36.6	64.8	72.7	52.3
object_det	31.2	36.8	15.8	64.7	60.5	58.7	65.1	73.6	59.5
pose_estim	65.8	77.3	29.6	84.2	95.8	67.6	70.7	82.7	41.7
qa	73.7	84.4	22.6	82.3	90.2	52.2	82.5	89.6	51.7
sem_seg	63.2	73.3	49.5	67.7	66.3	55.0	76.7	73.7	68.8
speech_rec	69.0	79.3	28.1	67.2	78.0	35.7	76.9	83.0	50.2
text_class	68.8	79.0	30.6	73.0	82.6	45.1	73.8	83.0	41.4
average	60.2	70.3	25.3	68.9	75.5	44.7	70.8	76.6	52.2

Papilusion at DAGPap24: Paper or Illusion? Detecting AI-generated Scientific Papers

Nikita Andreev, Alexander Shirnin
Vladislav Mikhailov, Ekaterina Artemova
CAIT and Applied AI Institute, HSE University
University of Oslo, Toloka AI
Correspondence: `ashirnin@hse.ru`

Abstract

This paper presents Papilusion, an AI-generated scientific text detector developed within the DAGPap24 shared task on detecting automatically generated scientific papers. We propose an ensemble-based approach and conduct ablation studies to analyze the effect of the detector configurations on the performance. Papilusion is ranked 6th on the leaderboard, and we improve our performance after the competition ended, achieving 99.46 (+9.63) of the F1-score on the official test set.

1 Introduction

A series of the DAGPap shared tasks addresses mitigation of the risks associated with misusing language technologies in the scientific domain, such as fabricating research publications (Else and Van Noorden, 2021; Van Noorden, 2021) and affecting the peer review ecosystem at the leading AI conferences (Liang et al., 2024). DAGPap22 (Kashnitsky et al., 2022) focuses on a well-established task formulation in the artificial text detection field (Uchendu, 2023), which requires to determine if a given text is human-written or AI-generated. DAGPap24[1] offers a less explored task formulation, which is framed as a token-level classification problem. Developing robust and reliable AI-generated scientific text detectors promotes analyzing scientific text collections at scale and assisting non-expert and expert users in identifying the fabricated content (Cabanac et al., 2021; Else, 2023).

This paper proposes Papilusion[2], an AI-generated text detection system for tagging text segments, which are produced by a generative language model (LM) or modified through synonym replacement and summarization. The token-level AI-generated text detection accounts for a more practical scenario, where a generative LM is used as a writing assistant. Papilusion is an ensemble of encoder-only sequence taggers that leverages the strengths of multiple independently finetuned LMs to enhance the accuracy of detecting AI-generated text. We conduct ablation studies to analyze the impact of various hyperparameter and LM configurations on the target performance.

Papilusion is ranked 6th among 30 participating teams at DAGPap24, with 89.83 of the F1-score on the leaderboard. After the competition ends, we improve our solution achieving 99.46 (+9.63) of the F1-score on the official evaluation set.

2 Background

The DAGPap24 dataset is a collection of human-machine mixed scientific texts, where the text segments can be (i) human-written, (ii) modified through an NLTK-based synonym replacement (Bird and Loper, 2004), (iii) produced by ChatGPT, and (iv) summarized. The organizers provide 5000, 5000, and 20000 training, development, and test examples, respectively. The average number of tokens[3] is 5591.

Task Formulation The task is to assign one of the four corresponding labels to each token in a given text, as it was described above. The example for a text with a synonym replacement is shown below. Here, "`1`" stands for a synonym replacement, and "`0`" refers to the human-written segment:

- `text:` "this was continued until successful intravascular positioning. An observer, blinded to the lens allocation, <...>"
- `tokens:` `["this", "was", "continued", "until", "successful", "intravascular", "positioning.",`

[1] `github.com/ChamezopoulosSavvas/DAGPap24`

[2] Papilusion is named after a pokémon *Papilusion*, which is the French name for *Butterfree*.

[3] The tokens are provided by the organizers and are obtained by splitting a text based on whitespace characters.

Proceedings of the Fourth Workshop on Scholarly Document Processing (SDP 2024), pages 215–219
August 16, 2024 ©2024 Association for Computational Linguistics

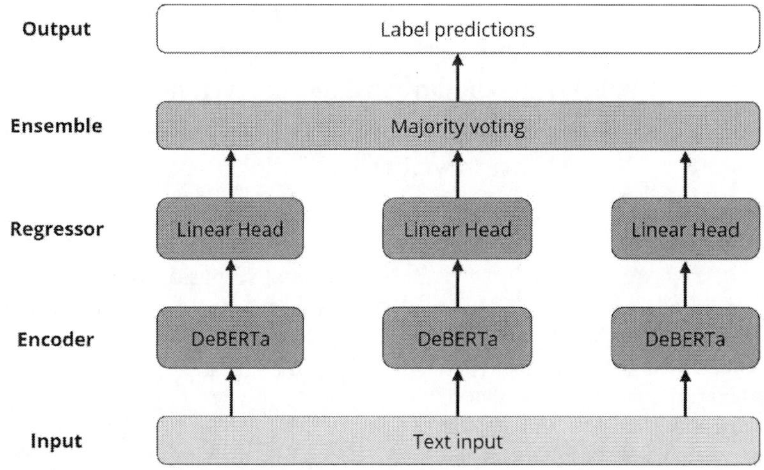

Figure 1: The Papilusion pipeline involves fine-tuning three distinct encoder models, which are based on the same architecture but trained independently with different hyperparameters. These models use linear heads to predict labels that differentiate between human-written and machine-generated text. Finally, a majority vote is applied to aggregate the predicted labels.

"An", "observer,", "blinded", "to", "the", "lens", "allocation," <...>]

- labels: [1, 1, 1, 1, 1, 1, 1, 0, 0, 0, 0, 0, 0, 0 <...>]

Performance Metric The performance is evaluated using the macro-averaged F1-score.

3 Papilusion

The Papilusion pipeline involves several key steps (see Figure 1):

1. **Model Fine-Tuning:** We fine-tuned encoder models to predict the corresponding labels. Although based on the same architecture, the models were fine-tuned with different hyperparameters to create a more diverse ensemble. Each model was trained on a sequence labeling task, predicting labels for every token in the input sequence.

2. **Majority Voting:** After fine-tuning multiple models, we used a majority voting strategy to aggregate their predictions. This approach involved combining the predictions from each model and selecting for each token the label that received the most votes across the ensemble of models. It is a popular ensembling method, which helps to gain better performance by using several models (Wani et al., 2018; K. et al., 2020). For the ensemble we chose three best models, based on the performance metric on the development dataset.

By using encoder models fine-tuned for text classification and applying a majority voting mechanism, we aimed to improve the accuracy and robustness of our classification system.

4 Experiments

Overview We conducted a wide series of experiments with a family of DeBERTaV3 models (He et al., 2023). We investigate experiments with bottom layers freezing (Ingle et al., 2022) and the size of the input sequence as the most important hyperparameters for the efficient model selection. We used longer sequences to fit in more context for a model. Additionally, we believe that there are some dependencies between the size of the model and effectiveness of a layer freezing and using various input sequences lengths. In our experiments we conducted a detailed research and comparison of various setups.

Model	Params	Hidden size	Layers
Xsmall	22M	384	12
Small	44M	768	6
Base	86M	768	12
Large	304M	1024	24
DistillBERT	66M	768	6

Table 1: Model architectures comparison. The DistillBERT model was used as a baseline by the competition organizers.

Model size	Xsmall			Small		Base			Large			
Frozen layers	0	6	12	0	6	0	6	12	0	6	12	18
256 input	97.32	97.00	**79.20**	95.88	82.74	96.99	96.22	89.68	-	-	98.12	98.17
512 input	**98.33**	**97.71**	78.49	**98.81**	**83.31**	**98.55**	**98.72**	**90.66**	-	**98.83**	98.82	99.07
1024 input	86.38	85.82	55.65	88.13	63.14	88.12	80.97	71.24	**96.29**	-	**98.84**	**99.21**
2048 input	67.87	62.95	28.99	65.30	45.47	66.21	56.40	50.25	92.87	92.87	-	-

Table 2: Test results obtained after the end of competition. The symbol '-' is used to denote experiment results where with the given configuration it was not possible to achieve satisfactory or adequate outcomes.

Competition-included experiments During the competition we utilized competition organizers' baseline code and did several approaches of fine-tuning DeBERTa models. During the competition timeline we tried several variations of different hyperparameters such as input sequence length, model size, freezing several bottom layers of the model, learning rate scheduler. Our final submission brought us to 6th place with **89.83** F1 metric which was obtained with the ensemble of 3 DeBERTa-base models with different number of frozen layers and the default input sequence length (512 tokens).

Post-competition study After the end of competition we identified a tokenization issue in the code: the chunk function truncated sequence by the number of words, not tokens which resulted in information loss. We fixed our training scripts with proper tokenization in chunk function, along with some minor adjustments in the prediction function. These modifications significantly improved the models' performance, resulting in a score increase of +9.63, and enabled us to conduct a detailed study of various models and hyperparameter variations. The results are shown in the Table 2

We used the following hyperparameters for our experiments:

- Model size - {Xsmall, Small, Base, Large}
- Input sequence length - {256, 512, 1024, 2048}
- Frozen layers - {0, 6, 12, 18}

We fixed other hyperparameters (learning rate, scheduler, seed, validation dataset size) to perform fair comparison. In this case, we can see how changing previously mentioned hyperparameters affects the result. Additionally, we did a series of ensemble mixtures based on majority voting technique for our best models to improve our final score.

Hardware specification We run experiments on a single GPU TESLA V100 32GB. Model fine-tuning is conducted using the transformers library (Wolf et al., 2020). The fine-tuning for DeBERTa requires approximately 4-12 hours to complete depending on the size of the model and the length of the sequence. The inference on the official test set runs within 1 hour. For DeBERTa-large model we lower the batch size down to 4, for other model versions we set the batch size to 16.

5 Results

Competition phase During the competition we fine-tuned base DeBERTa models with different number of frozen bottom layers and then applied majority voting for 3 models. This brought us to the 6th place (see Table 3) and the best score among the teams below 90.0 F1 score.

Place	Test score
1st place	99.54
...	
4th place	99.24
5th place	95.54
6th place (**Our system**)	89.83
7th place	89.82
8th place	89.67
Baseline	86.36

Table 3: Competition results.

Post-competition phase Table 4 provides results of our best setups, ensembles based on those setups and comparison to the test scores on the leaderboard. More detailed results in various setups provided in the table 2, and our main outcomes are:

- 1024-token sequence inputs are typically better for DeBERTa-large model; however, we found that using a 512-token sequence results in comparable quality across almost all model types.

Setup	Model	Frozen layers	input length	Test score
a)	Xsmall	0	512	98.33
b)	Small	0	512	98.81
c)	Base	6	512	98.72
d)	Large	18	256	98.17
e)	Large	18	512	99.07
f)	Large	12	1024	98.84
g)	Large	18	1024	**99.21**
b) & c) & g)				99.28
d) & e) & g)				99.45
e) & f) & g)				**99.46**
1st place solution				**99.54**
2nd place solution				99.44
Baseline*	DistilBERT	0	512	93.64

Table 4: Comparison of best results across various experimental configurations, denoted by letters (a, b, c, etc.). Our ensemble achieves the 2nd place compared to competition scores. '&' sign stands for ensembling via majority voting. With '*' we mark improved baseline results obtained by ourselves after the competition.

- Freezing more of the bottom layers generally leads to better results for the DeBERTa-large model, while for other models it is better to not freeze the layers.
- Despite freezing all 12 encoder layers, we achieve a 90.66 F1 score with the Base DeBERTa. This result indicates that the task is relatively simple for these models.
- Ensembling the best single models leads to the score improvement.

The usage of DeBERTa models with corrected input sequence chunking allowed us to achieve significant improvements over the baseline. We got **98.33** F1 score with only Xsmall model version. It is **3 times smaller** than DistillBERT, that was used as the baseline model by competition organizers. Also we figured out that freezing of some layers could be helpful, especially for bigger models when model is already trained and have sufficient knowledge, thus we achieve our best single-model score of **99.21** with DeBERTa-large and 18/24 layers frozen. With the majority voting ensemble of our best Large models we achieve **99.46** F1 score which is compared to the second place based on the competition results.

As it was mentioned, the smallest DeBERTa model already gets F1 score above 98, while larger ones improve just moderately depending on their settings. This suggests that the problem we are addressing might be not particularly complex, reducing the need for large models. Upon a close examination of the dataset's origin, we hypothesize that the construction process may have relied heavily on basic generation rules and may not have included sufficient filtering of simple samples. This could have resulted in notable differences among various classes within the dataset. Additionally, we believe that synonym replacement is a simple and difficult-to-control process, likely causing a significant shift in the data distribution and making the task easier. Furthermore, the task of designing and creating text that combines inputs from both humans and LMs presents a separate significant and unique challenge.

6 Conclusion

In this paper, we proposed Papilusion, an AI-generated text detection system designed for the DAGPap24 shared task. Our system ranked 6th in the competition, achieving an F1 score of 89.83. Post-competition enhancements, including fixing tokenization errors and optimizing model parameters, increased F1 score to 99.46.

Through comprehensive ablation studies, we identified the most impactful hyperparameters and model configurations, leading to substantial performance improvements.

While our experiments demonstrate that larger models achieve the best results when resources are not limited, we also found that even the small models (DeBERTa-Xsmall) exhibit promising performance metrics with minimal computational resources.

Acknowledgements

AS's work results from a research project implemented in the Basic Research Program at the National Research University Higher School of Economics (HSE University). We acknowledge the computational resources of HSE University's HPC facilities.

References

Steven Bird and Edward Loper. 2004. NLTK: The natural language toolkit. In *Proceedings of the ACL Interactive Poster and Demonstration Sessions*, pages 214–217, Barcelona, Spain. Association for Computational Linguistics.

Guillaume Cabanac, Cyril Labbé, and Alexander Magazinov. 2021. Tortured phrases: A dubious writing style emerging in science. evidence of critical issues affecting established journals. *arXiv preprint arXiv:2107.06751*.

Holly Else. 2023. Abstracts written by chatgpt fool scientists. *Nature*, 613(7944):423.

Holly Else and Richard Van Noorden. 2021. The fight against fake-paper factories that churn out sham science. *Nature*, 591(7851):516–520.

Pengcheng He, Jianfeng Gao, and Weizhu Chen. 2023. DeBERTav3: Improving deBERTa using ELECTRA-style pre-training with gradient-disentangled embedding sharing. In *The Eleventh International Conference on Learning Representations*.

Digvijay Ingle, Rishabh Tripathi, Ayush Kumar, Kevin Patel, and Jithendra Vepa. 2022. Investigating the characteristics of a transformer in a few-shot setup: Does freezing layers in RoBERTa help? In *Proceedings of the Fifth BlackboxNLP Workshop on Analyzing and Interpreting Neural Networks for NLP*, pages 238–248, Abu Dhabi, United Arab Emirates (Hybrid). Association for Computational Linguistics.

Rishivardhan K., Kayalvizhi S, Thenmozhi D., Raghav R., and Kshitij Sharma. 2020. SSN-NLP at SemEval-2020 task 4: Text classification and generation on common sense context using neural networks. In *Proceedings of the Fourteenth Workshop on Semantic Evaluation*, pages 580–584, Barcelona (online). International Committee for Computational Linguistics.

Yury Kashnitsky, Drahomira Herrmannova, Anita de Waard, George Tsatsaronis, Catriona Catriona Fennell, and Cyril Labbe. 2022. Overview of the DAGPap22 shared task on detecting automatically generated scientific papers. In *Proceedings of the Third Workshop on Scholarly Document Processing*, pages 210–213, Gyeongju, Republic of Korea. Association for Computational Linguistics.

Weixin Liang, Zachary Izzo, Yaohui Zhang, Haley Lepp, Hancheng Cao, Xuandong Zhao, Lingjiao Chen, Haotian Ye, Sheng Liu, Zhi Huang, et al. 2024. Monitoring ai-modified content at scale: A case study on the impact of chatgpt on ai conference peer reviews. *arXiv preprint arXiv:2403.07183*.

Adaku Uchendu. 2023. *Reverse Turing Test in the Age of Deepfake Texts*. Ph.D. thesis, The Pennsylvania State University.

Richard Van Noorden. 2021. Hundreds of gibberish papers still lurk in the scientific literature. *Nature*, 594(7862):160–161.

Nikhil Wani, Sandeep Mathias, Jayashree Aanand Gajjam, and Pushpak Bhattacharyya. 2018. The whole is greater than the sum of its parts: Towards the effectiveness of voting ensemble classifiers for complex word identification. In *Proceedings of the Thirteenth Workshop on Innovative Use of NLP for Building Educational Applications*, pages 200–205, New Orleans, Louisiana. Association for Computational Linguistics.

Thomas Wolf, Lysandre Debut, Victor Sanh, Julien Chaumond, Clement Delangue, Anthony Moi, Pierric Cistac, Tim Rault, Remi Louf, Morgan Funtowicz, Joe Davison, Sam Shleifer, Patrick von Platen, Clara Ma, Yacine Jernite, Julien Plu, Canwen Xu, Teven Le Scao, Sylvain Gugger, Mariama Drame, Quentin Lhoest, and Alexander Rush. 2020. Transformers: State-of-the-art natural language processing. In *Proceedings of the 2020 Conference on Empirical Methods in Natural Language Processing: System Demonstrations*, pages 38–45, Online. Association for Computational Linguistics.

Multi-head Span-based Detector for AI-generated Fragments in Scientific Papers

German Gritsai[1,2] Ildar Khabutdinov[1,2] Andrey Grabovoy[1]
Advacheck OÜ, Estonia[1]
Université Grenoble Alpes, France[2]
{gritsai, khabutdinov, grabovoy}@advacheck.com

Abstract

This paper describes a system designed to distinguish between AI-generated and human-written scientific excerpts in the DAGPap24 competition hosted within the Fourth Workshop on Scientific Document Processing. In this competition the task is to find artificially generated token-level text fragments in documents of a scientific domain. Our work focuses on the use of a multi-task learning architecture with two heads. The application of this approach is justified by the specificity of the task, where class spans are continuous over several hundred characters. We considered different encoder variations to obtain a state vector for each token in the sequence, as well as a variation in splitting fragments into tokens to further feed into the input of a transform-based encoder. This approach allows us to achieve a 9% quality improvement relative to the baseline solution score on the development set (from 0.86 to 0.95) using the average macro F_1-score, as well as a score of 0.96 on a closed test part of the dataset from the competition.

1 Introduction

Modern advances in the field of text generation models provide high quality artificial texts that are hardly distinguishable from human-written texts at fluent reading. Text generation systems such as Llama (Touvron et al., 2023), ChatGPT (Ray, 2023), Mistral (Jiang et al., 2023) are increasing the list of successfully solved problems in updated benchmarks (Li et al., 2023) with the release of each newer version of the product. Although the progress of such models is impressive, it poses new challenges for scientists, as the development of these systems implies the emergence and spread of generated fragments in texts of the scientific domain. In the field of Natural Language Processing there are already a large number of methodologies for detecting texts generated by machine learning models (Jawahar et al., 2020), including approaches for the scientific domain (Liyanage and Buscaldi, 2023; Gritsay and Chekhovich, 2023). Therefore, the improvement of artificial text detection techniques occurs simultaneously with the improvement of text generation methods. In order to prevent the gap between quality generation and precision of detection from growing, it is necessary to periodically update and modernise existing detection approaches with newly generated fragments. Indeed, increasing the appearance of generated fragments in scientific papers carries with it a potential increase in plagiarism (Bakhteev et al., 2022), fake studies (Bakhteev et al., 2020) and missinformation.

The DAGPap24 competition allowed us to perform a further cycle of updates and make a reliable AI-generated scientific text detection system. The challenge is to build a detection system that is robust to generated fragments from fundamentally different frameworks and diverse scientific domains.

In this paper, we present a solution that was developed for the DAGPap24 competition by our team. We propose a method to find artificially generated fragments at the token level using a multi-task architecture. Our model has two classifiers for each token, that are trained jointly and allow the model to have a higher generalisation capability and to process the text sequences arriving at the input faster. We introduce the aforementioned architecture in this paper and conduct experiments to tune its components to obtain the best result.

2 Data and task description

The DAGPap24 competition has been formulated as one classification task for the English language. Participants had to identify intervals in the scientific text that were human-written or machine-generated accordingly. The intervals are not fixed in advance and have to be labelled automatically by

Proceedings of the Fourth Workshop on Scholarly Document Processing (SDP 2024), pages 220–225
August 16, 2024

the detection algorithm based on the context. The problem has been proposed to be solved by token classification approaches from the competition organisers. A large number of works on artificial text detection is dealing with the classification problem at sequence level (Ippolito et al., 2020). However, the approach of token classification and their subsequent grouping into intervals of the same class is also able to show a competitive performance in this task, in some cases producing better results than the established approach (Jafari, 2022). According to the organisers the task contains scientific texts whose tokens should be classified into one of four classes: human, generated by ChatGPT, generated using synonyms from NLTK (Loper and Bird, 2002), generated using an unnamed summarisation model.

2.1 Task Definition

In this competition, it is expected that the problem of detecting machine-generated fragments will be solved as a token classification task. There is a given dataset $\mathcal{D} = \{(x_i, y_i)\}_{i=1}^{N}$, where each document x_i is represented by a finite combination of tokens:

$$x_i = \{x_i^1, \ldots, x_i^m\}, \quad x_i^j \in \mathcal{W}, \quad j \in \{1, \ldots, m\},$$

$$y_i = \{y_i^1, \ldots, y_i^m\}, \qquad y_i^j \in \{0, 1, 2, 3\},$$

where $\mathcal{W}$ corresponds to chosen tokens vocabulary. The labels $y_i^j \in \{1, 2, 3\}$ correspond to tokens that are likely machine-generated with synonym-replacement, ChatGPT-generated or summarized respectively and $y_i^j = 0$ corresponds to human-written ones.

Formally, the task is to find a multiclass classifier that minimizes the empirical risk on the dataset $\mathcal{D}$:

$$\hat{g} = \operatorname*{argmin}_{g \in F} \sum_{i=1}^{N} \sum_{j}^{M_i} [g(x_i^j) \neq y_i^j], \qquad (1)$$

where M_i is a number of tokens in i-th document, F is a set of all considered classification models.

2.2 Data

The organisers of the competition provided a training dataset that contained 5000 samples. Each sample was represented by text, annotations, tokens of the corresponding text and labels for each token. Example rows from the dataset can be seen in Table 1.

All texts in the rows of the dataset are documents from the scientific domain in which some parts have been replaced by machine-generated sequences. Fake text can even start in the middle of a sentence, so it is important to take the context into account when doing classification.

Before starting to build a model solution to the problem, we analysed the provided dataset. Some of its statistics can be seen in Table 2. The texts written by humans are equalled by the remaining three classes in terms of quantity, so to balance the classes all the artificially generated samples could be combined into one group. The human-written texts remain, understandably, longer in terms of average length for both tokens and characters. What is also notable is the length and quality of the generated texts under the summarised label. The excerpts of this class are shorter than the others and when analysed visually they immediately catch the eye due to the lack of postprocessing of the summarization model, the texts are contaminated with unnecessary symbols.

3 Approach

3.1 Model

There are several ways to solve the given problem, we have chosen the token classification approach. One of its subfields is Grammatical Error Correction (GEC) (Bryant et al., 2023), which aims to correct as many errors as possible in a given passage. It correlates with our task, where, for example, the junction from one class to another can be in an uncommon place and of any length, so we need to identify the boundaries very precisely. One state-of-the-art solution is the approach described by (Omelianchuk et al., 2020). Their GECToR model has a custom multi-head transformer-based architecture with and solves the GEC problem with sequence tagging. We decided to use a similar architecture with our extension in the machine-generated fragments detection domain where we need to solve the problem at the token level. The architecture we use is shown in Figure 1.

3.2 Training and inference stages

The token sequence that comes to the input of the algorithm is vectorised using a BERT-like encoder (Devlin et al., 2018), further the vector for each token is fed in parallel to the input of two linear layers with dropout. The major difference from the standard BERT-like approach for this task is the

Text	Annotations	Tokens	Token Label Ids
The number of osteoporotic fractures ...	[[0, 3264, 'chatgpt'], ...]	['The', 'number', 'of', 'osteoporotic', 'fractures', ...]	[2, 2, 2, 2, 2, 2, ...]
Blade surface roughness ranks amongst ...	[[0, 34694, 'human'], ...]	['Blade', 'surface', 'roughness', 'ranks', 'amongst', 'the', ...]	[0, 0, 0, 0, 0, 0, ...]

Table 1: A pair of examples of string representations in the provided dataset. Each sample is represented by a text string, its markup, partitioning into tokens and labels to each token.

Label	Count	Mean length symbols	Mean length tokens
Human	13346	10054.69	4370.62
NLTK-replace	4245	3773.91	518.54
ChatGPT	4447	2599.63	353.37
Summarized	4376	1597.54	333.13

Table 2: Statistics collected for each class of the provided dataset to train the models. It can be seen that half of the texts are human-written.

presence of two classification heads and multi-task learning. In our approach, one head (Linear A) is responsible for binary classification - human or machine-generated, while the second head (Linear B) solves the multi-class classification for the 4 classes that have been posed in the current competition. Thus, when training such a network, the loss function aggregates the error values from both heads and sums them up.

Previous studies have captured that the multi-task learning approach reduces the probability of overfitting and increases the generalisability of the trained system (Crawshaw, 2020). As for inference, we calculate the probability for each token of a given sequence to contain machine-generated data using *Linear A* and softmax. If the maximum probability among all tokens of the sequence has a value that is higher than a predefined threshold, then classification of each token of the given sequence is performed by multiclass layer - *Linear B*, otherwise we produce a label of human class. This approach on inference reflects the specificity of the current task, where, based on the statistics obtained in the previous section, it can be seen that texts are not interrupted by single insertions of a token from another class, and most often spans have long continuity intervals. Among the classes present, the length of human texts is most often higher than the others. Due to the limited number of characters that can be included in one sequence and fed to the BERT-like encoder input, sequences in this paradigm will most often contain only tokens of the same class.

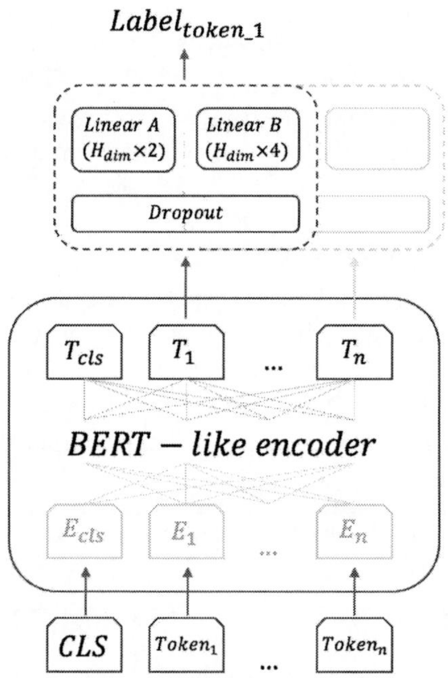

Figure 1: A multi-task architecture to solve the token classification problem. Each token, after receiving a vector for text representation via encoder, is classified in two heads: Linear A - binary and Linear B - multiclass.

4 Experiments

The organisers of the competition presented a basic solution: DistilBERT (Sanh et al., 2019) and SciBERT (Beltagy et al., 2019). Both models were fine-tuned with the classical architecture and pipeline of the token classification task. Considering the limited time of the competition, we planned experiments with the architecture described in the previous section: varying the input sequence length, changing BERT-like encoders and selecting hyperparameters.

4.1 Varying the input sequence length

BERT-like models have a constraint on the length of the input sequence. In earlier studies in the machine-generated fragment detection task, we analysed the effect of input length on detection quality (Gritsay et al., 2022). In the current task, each example was accompanied by a sentence partitioning into word tokens. However, depending on the choice of tokeniser, these token-words can be broken down into different numbers of smaller tokens to feed into the model input. For example, the dictionaries of the tokeniser adapted for this domain - SciBERT - have a large number of complete token-words, which means that splitting the original ones into smaller units will be minimal. Given this fact, we need to make sure that after tokenisation by the chosen tokeniser, the sequence that comes to the input of the model is not clipped and does not lose information that is useful for training algorithms. For different models we tried different ways of partitioning.

4.2 Changing BERT-like encoders

The baseline result that was shown with the SciBERT model displayed high score. Currently, there are a large number of pre-trained encoders that are able to show good basic quality solution to the problem. However, further pre-training under the specific domain performs differently for all models. This is the motivation behind the encoder variation approach. Looking back at the experience of (Omelianchuk et al., 2020), who proposed the GECToR architecture, we also examined XLNet (Yang et al., 2019). In addition, we tried the approach with the QLoRa adapter (Dettmers et al., 2023) pre-training for the token classification task with the large language model (LLM) Mistral. This language model, according to benchmark results, is capable of solving an impressive number of tasks at a high level. Domain-specific LLM adaptor training may sometimes circumvent the quality of problem solving with established encoder models, such as RoBERTa (Liu et al., 2019), DeBERTa (He et al., 2020), etc.

5 Results

The results of the experiments can be seen in Table 3. The specificity of the task, scientific domain, allowed us to keep the SciBERT model as the main encoder for our architecture after the experiments. However, as shown in the table, the best quality is achieved when the texts are divided into intervals of 350 token-words. Given the limited input context of transformed-based models, it is the case that the least amount of information is lost after tokenisation, thus achieving the highest quality. In addition, the dropout value was selected, and after varying it was set to 0.7. Also it was observed that with the threshold value set to 0.55, a quality improvement is obtained to drop human-written sequences during inference. The previously described architecture with two linear layers together with these settings helped our team to achieve the quality of 0.96 average macro F_1-score on the development set. As for the test set, the results were similar and we took 5th place in the competition with an average of 0.96.

6 Conclusion

In this paper we present a descriptive overview of the solution approach that was used by our team to solve the DAGPap24 competition for detecting AI-generated fragments in scientific documents. A token classification approach was chosen to map each token to one of four pre-defined classes. In our solution, we used a BERT-based encoder and two linear layers to process the output vectors of the encoder for each token in sequence. One of the layers is responsible for binary classification and the other for the predefined 4 classes. Exploring shared training, the classification quality becomes better for identical model settings, and on the provided development dataset, this method helped to improve the quality by 9% on the macro F_1-score metric.

In the future work we would be interested in analysing the distribution of the metric across classes and based on this we would like to add weights to the loss function during pre-training for class balancing. In addition, it would be interesting to observe this approach on a larger dataset, where classes can be defined by more common text generation methods.

References

Oleg Bakhteev, Yury Chekhovich, Georgy Gorbachev, Tatyana Gorlenko, Andrey Grabovoy, Kirill Grashchenkov, Alexander Kildyakov, Andrey Khazov, Vladislav Komarnitsky, and Artemiy et al. Nikitov. 2022. Cross-language plagiarism detection: a case study of european universities academic works.

BERT-like encoder + tokens partition length	Development Set		
	P	R	F_1
DistilBERT + 512 (baseline)	0.86	0.83	0.84
SciBERT + 512 (baseline)	0.89	0.86	0.87
Mistral w. QLoRA + 512	0.93	0.89	0.91
XLNet + 512	0.91	0.92	0.91
XLNet + 350	0.96	0.95	0.95
SciBERT + 185	0.92	0.89	0.91
SciBERT + 300	0.94	0.93	0.93
SciBERT + 350	**0.97**	**0.96**	**0.96**
SciBERT + 400	0.93	**0.96**	0.94
SciBERT + 512	0.89	0.93	0.9

Table 3: Results on a development dataset with different settings for the proposed multi-task architecture.

In *Academic Integrity: Broadening Practices, Technologies, and the Role of Students*, pages 143–161. Springer.

Oleg Bakhteev, Aleksandr Ogaltsov, and Petr Ostroukhov. 2020. Fake News Spreader Detection Using Neural Tweet Aggregation—Notebook for PAN at CLEF 2020. In *CLEF 2020 Labs and Workshops, Notebook Papers*. CEUR-WS.org.

Iz Beltagy, Kyle Lo, and Arman Cohan. 2019. Scibert: A pretrained language model for scientific text. In *EMNLP/IJCNLP (1)*, pages 3613–3618. Association for Computational Linguistics.

Christopher Bryant, Zheng Yuan, Muhammad Reza Qorib, Hannan Cao, Hwee Tou Ng, and Ted Briscoe. 2023. Grammatical Error Correction: A Survey of the State of the Art. *Computational Linguistics*, 49(3):643–701.

Michael Crawshaw. 2020. Multi-task learning with deep neural networks: A survey. *ArXiv*, abs/2009.09796.

Tim Dettmers, Artidoro Pagnoni, Ari Holtzman, and Luke Zettlemoyer. 2023. Qlora: Efficient finetuning of quantized llms. Cite arxiv:2305.14314Comment: Extended NeurIPS submission.

Jacob Devlin, Ming-Wei Chang, Kenton Lee, and Kristina Toutanova. 2018. Bert: Pre-training of deep bidirectional transformers for language understanding. Cite arxiv:1810.04805Comment: 13 pages.

German Gritsay, Andrey Grabovoy, and Yury Chekhovich. 2022. Automatic detection of machine generated texts: Need more tokens. In *2022 Ivannikov Memorial Workshop (IVMEM)*, pages 20–26.

GM Gritsay and Yu V Chekhovich. 2023. Artificially generated text fragments search in academic documents. In *Doklady Mathematics*, volume 108, pages S434–S442. Springer.

Pengcheng He, Xiaodong Liu, Jianfeng Gao, and Weizhu Chen. 2020. Deberta: Decoding-enhanced bert with disentangled attention. *CoRR*, abs/2006.03654.

Daphne Ippolito, Daniel Duckworth, Chris Callison-Burch, and Douglas Eck. 2020. Automatic detection of generated text is easiest when humans are fooled. In *Proceedings of the 58th Annual Meeting of the Association for Computational Linguistics, ACL 2020, Online, July 5-10, 2020*, pages 1808–1822. Association for Computational Linguistics.

Amir Jafari. 2022. Comparison study between token classification and sequence classification in text classification. *ArXiv*, abs/2211.13899.

Ganesh Jawahar, Muhammad Abdul-Mageed, and Laks Lakshmanan, V.S. 2020. Automatic detection of machine generated text: A critical survey. In *Proceedings of the 28th International Conference on Computational Linguistics*, pages 2296–2309, Barcelona, Spain (Online). International Committee on Computational Linguistics.

Albert Q. Jiang, Alexandre Sablayrolles, Arthur Mensch, Chris Bamford, Devendra Singh Chaplot, Diego de Las Casas, Florian Bressand, Gianna Lengyel, Guillaume Lample, Lucile Saulnier, Lélio Renard Lavaud, Marie-Anne Lachaux, Pierre Stock, Teven Le Scao, Thibaut Lavril, Thomas Wang, Timothée Lacroix, and William El Sayed. 2023. Mistral 7b. *CoRR*, abs/2310.06825.

Junyi Li, Xiaoxue Cheng, Xin Zhao, Jian-Yun Nie, and Ji-Rong Wen. 2023. HaluEval: A large-scale hallucination evaluation benchmark for large language models. In *Proceedings of the 2023 Conference on Empirical Methods in Natural Language Processing*, pages 6449–6464, Singapore. Association for Computational Linguistics.

Yinhan Liu, Myle Ott, Naman Goyal, Jingfei Du, Mandar Joshi, Danqi Chen, Omer Levy, Mike Lewis, Luke Zettlemoyer, and Veselin Stoyanov. 2019. Roberta: A robustly optimized bert pretraining approach. Cite arxiv:1907.11692.

Vijini Liyanage and Davide Buscaldi. 2023. Detecting artificially generated academic text: The importance of mimicking human utilization of large language models. In *Natural Language Processing and Information Systems*, pages 558–565, Cham. Springer Nature Switzerland.

Edward Loper and Steven Bird. 2002. Nltk: The natural language toolkit. *arXiv preprint*.

Kostiantyn Omelianchuk, Vitaliy Atrasevych, Artem Chernodub, and Oleksandr Skurzhanskyi. 2020. GECToR – grammatical error correction: Tag, not rewrite. In *Proceedings of the Fifteenth Workshop on Innovative Use of NLP for Building Educational Applications*, pages 163–170, Seattle, WA, USA → Online. Association for Computational Linguistics.

Partha Pratim Ray. 2023. Chatgpt: A comprehensive review on background, applications, key challenges, bias, ethics, limitations and future scope. *Internet of Things and Cyber-Physical Systems*, 3:121–154.

Victor Sanh, Lysandre Debut, Julien Chaumond, and Thomas Wolf. 2019. Distilbert, a distilled version of bert: smaller, faster, cheaper and lighter.

Hugo Touvron, Thibaut Lavril, Gautier Izacard, Xavier Martinet, Marie-Anne Lachaux, Timothée Lacroix, Baptiste Rozière, Naman Goyal, Eric Hambro, Faisal Azhar, Aurelien Rodriguez, Armand Joulin, Edouard Grave, and Guillaume Lample. 2023. Llama: Open and efficient foundation language models. *Preprint*, arXiv:2302.13971.

Zhilin Yang, Zihang Dai, Yiming Yang, Jaime Carbonell, Russ R Salakhutdinov, and Quoc V Le. 2019. Xlnet: Generalized autoregressive pretraining for language understanding. In *Advances in Neural Information Processing Systems*, volume 32. Curran Associates, Inc.

Guiding Large Language Models via External Attention Prompting for Scientific Extreme Summarization

Yuan Chang, Ziyue Li, Xiaoqiu Le*
National Science Library, Chinese Academy of Sciences
Department of Information Resources Management, School of Economics and Management,
University of Chinese Academy of Sciences
{changyuan, liziyue, lexq}@mail.las.ac.cn

Abstract

Scientific extreme summarization, the task of generating concise one-sentence summaries (TLDRs) for scientific papers, presents significant challenges due to the need for deep domain-specific understanding and the ability to distill salient information. This study identifies the critical role of titles and keywords in enhancing TLDR generation through quantitative analysis. We propose a novel method, External Attention Prompting (EAP), which leverages LLMs by guiding them to focus on the most critical parts of the source text through varying degrees of attention signals. Our method employs Markdown emphasis syntax to annotate attention levels, enabling LLMs to prioritize salient information effectively. Extensive experiments demonstrate that EAP significantly outperforms baseline methods across various LLMs and metrics in both zero-shot and few-shot settings. Further evaluations by GPT-4 demonstrate that EAP can enable LLMs to generate TLDRs of higher human-aligned quality.

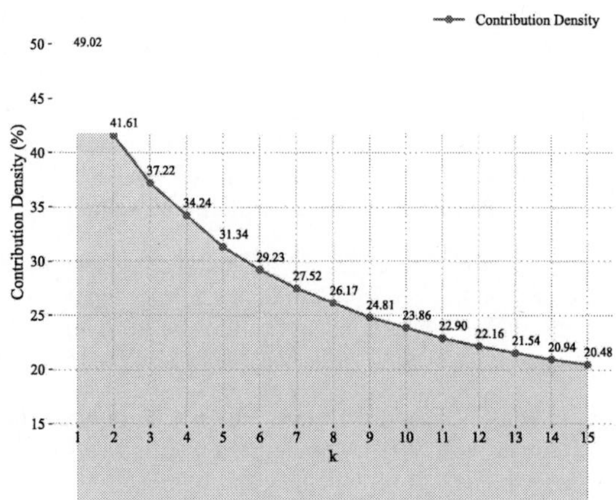

Figure 1: Contribution density of top-k TextRank keywords from abstracts on the SciTLDR training set, showing diminishing returns as k increases.

1 Introduction

The rapid growth of scientific literature has made it increasingly difficult for researchers to keep up with the research frontiers and quickly identify the most relevant and impactful information. In this context, recent work (Cachola et al., 2020; Lu et al., 2020; Mao et al., 2022; Takeshita et al., 2022; Atri et al., 2023; Stiglic et al., 2023; Syed et al., 2024) has studied the problem of scientific extreme summarization, which involves generating a concise one-sentence summary (TLDR: Too Long; Didn't Read) that captures the key aspects of a scientific paper. Scientific extreme summarization is a challenging task that requires a deep understanding of domain-specific content to accurately identify and distill the most salient points (Cachola et al., 2020). This task demands advanced methods capable of leveraging domain knowledge and prioritizing the most important content.

Previous studies have found that key content such as the titles and keywords of source documents are helpful to improve performance in summarization task, as they often contain key information (Chen et al., 2019; Çano and Bojar, 2019; Lee et al., 2020; Cachola et al., 2020; Koto et al., 2022; Mao et al., 2022). Our analysis on the SciTLDR dataset (Cachola et al., 2020) further indicates that their contributions to generating highly compressed summaries differ as they contain diverse density of key information (see Section 2), suggesting that they should be given unequal levels of importance.

In this work, we leverage large language models (LLMs) to tackle the scientific extreme summarization task, as they have demonstrated emergent abilities such as in-context learning and made remarkable advances in solving various NLP problems (Wei et al., 2022; Zhao et al., 2023). We propose a novel method called External Attention Prompting (EAP) that enhances the performance of LLMs by guiding them to pay varying degrees of attention to

*Corresponding Author

Proceedings of the Fourth Workshop on Scholarly Document Processing (SDP 2024), pages 226–242
August 16, 2024 ©2024 Association for Computational Linguistics

different segments of the source text. Our method involves constructing prompts that assign different levels of attention signals to the n-grams in the source text based on their importance, using Markdown emphasis syntax to annotate the attention strength. This approach enables the LLMs to prioritize the salient information and generate more accurate and informative TLDRs. Experimental results demonstrate that our proposed prompting method significantly enhances the performance of LLMs in this task, outperforming baseline methods.

The main contributions of this work are as follows:

- We provide insights into the importance of different source input components (title, abstract, and keywords) for scientific extreme summarization, highlighting the role of the title and keywords in capturing key information.
- We propose a novel prompting method, External Attention Prompting, that enhances the performance of LLMs in scientific extreme summarization by guiding them to focus on the most critical parts of the source text.
- We conduct extensive experiments on the SciTLDR dataset, demonstrating the effectiveness of our approach in improving the quality of generated TLDRs.

2 Source Contribution Analysis

Generating high-quality TLDRs requires capturing precisely the salient aspects of the document. In this section, we conduct a preliminary experiment to investigate whether components such as the title, abstract and keywords contribute differently to the formation of a TLDR. By identifying the most influential parts, we aim to enhance the summarization process by directing the model's attention to the most critical information.

To do this, we firstly introduce the concept of contribution density, which measures the averaged contribution of tokens from a specific source input components (e.g., title, abstract, and keywords) to the gold TLDR. We first tokenize the input components and remove stopwords. Then, the contribution density $CD(c)$ for an input component c is calculated as:

$$CD(c) = \frac{\sum_{t \in c} TF(t, TLDR)}{|c|} \tag{1}$$

where t is a token in the input component c, $TF(t, TLDR)$ is the term frequency of token t in the gold TLDR, and $|c|$ is the total number of tokens in the input component c.

The calculation of contribution density draws inspiration from methods used in previous works (See et al., 2017; Narayan et al., 2018; Cachola et al., 2020) to assess abstractiveness and extractiveness of generated summaries. However, in this context, it serves as an analytical tool rather than a direct evaluation metric for summary quality assessment. The term "contribution" represents how frequently the words from source input appear in the gold TLDR. We use contribution density as a proxy to quantify the relative importance of different source input components in contributing to extreme summarization.

We take the training set of SciTLDR (Cachola et al., 2020) for analysis, and calculate the contribution density for title and abstract, which are 49.2 and 11.9, respectively. The results align with our intuition that the title often captures the most core idea of a paper. While titles may contain less overall information than abstracts, the information they do contain is more densely packed with content relevant to the TLDR. In other words, any given n-gram from the title is more likely to contribute to the TLDR than a random n-gram from the abstract. Abstracts may contain more information that is either less important or not sufficiently crucial to be included in the TLDR.

Additionally, we calculate the contribution densities for the top-k keywords from abstract using TextRank algorithm (Mihalcea and Tarau, 2004), the results are shown in Figure 1. The contribution density decreases as k increases, indicating diminishing returns with more keywords. This highlights the importance of selecting a concise set of highly relevant keywords.

The above findings from our source contribution analysis underscore the necessity of focusing on the most important parts of the input text when generating a TLDR.

3 External Attention Prompting

Based on the insight from section 2, we propose a novel method called **External Attention Prompting (EAP)**. The core idea of our method is to guide LLMs to focus on the most critical parts of the source text when generating TLDRs. As illustrated in Figure 2, our method leverages external signals

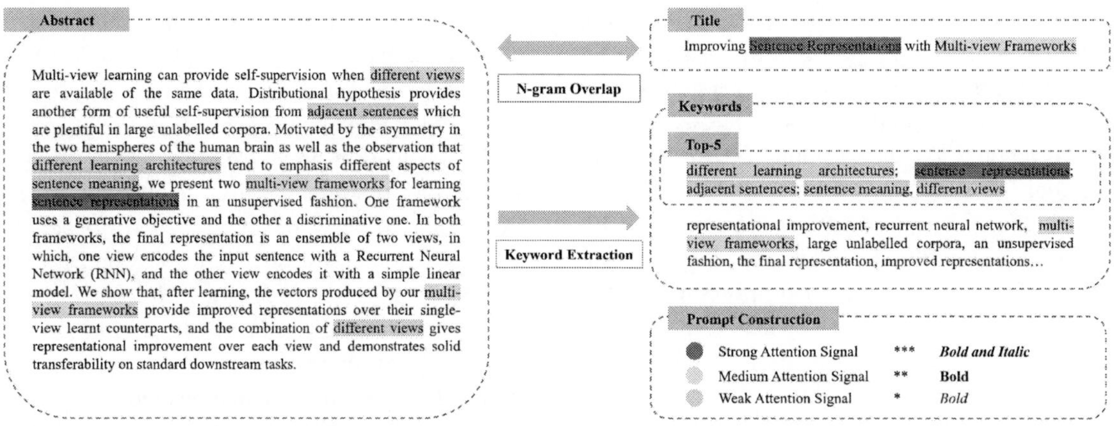

Figure 2: Overview of the proposed External Attention Prompting (EAP) method.

derived from the paper's title and keywords to modulate the attention of the LLM. By emphasizing different segments of the source text with varying degrees of importance, we aim to enhance LLMs' ability to distill the essence of the scientific paper into a concise and informative TLDR.

3.1 Attention Signal Acquisition

To effectively guide the model's attention, this method first acquires attention signals. We hypothesize that certain n-grams within the text, particularly those overlapping with the title and keywords, are more indicative of the core content. To identify these n-grams, we perform the following steps:

Title Overlap Extraction We extract n-grams from the title and identify their occurrences in the source text. To ensure relevance, we remove stop words and retain only the longest overlapping n-grams.

Keyword Extraction Using the TextRank algorithm (Mihalcea and Tarau, 2004), we extract keywords from the source text, removing stop words to focus on meaningful terms.

Attention Signal Levels Definition We define attention signals of different levels as follows:

- **Strong Attention Signal**: N-grams present in both the title and the top-5 keywords.
- **Medium Attention Signal**: N-grams present in both the title and any keyword.
- **Weak Attention Signal**: N-grams present in either the title or the top-5 keywords.

3.2 Prompt Construction

To operationalize these attention signals, we employ Markdown emphasis syntax to "visually" highlight the importance of different n-grams within the source text. Markdown is chosen for its inherent three-level emphasis system (italic, bold, and bold-italic) and because there is a large amount of Markdown-formatted text in the training corpus of LLMs, enabling them to understand the emphasis cues implied by such annotations. Specifically, we mark n-grams of strong attention signal with *** (***bold and italic***), n-grams of medium attention signal with ** (**bold**) and n-grams of weak attention signal with * (*italic*).

By using Markdown's built-in emphasis features, we avoid the need for custom formatting, allowing the model to leverage its pre-existing understanding of these conventions. This approach ensures that the model can efficiently recognize and prioritize the marked text without additional fine-tuning or instruction.

The marked source text, along with necessary instructions, is then used to construct the prompt, which is fed into the LLMs to generate the TLDR. Furthermore, we explicitly instruct the model to pay special attention to the emphasized parts of the text. The prompt template used for this method can be seen in Appendix B.

The term "External" in this method reflects two key aspects:

External attention signals. The attention signals are derived from external information such as the title and keywords, rather than being internally recognized by the model. This external guidance directs the model to follow specific cues.

External implementation. The attention mechanism is implemented through external input (i.e., the prompt) without fine-tuning LLMs. This makes the method applicable even when model parameters are inaccessible.

The proposed method is highly generalizable and can be applied to various tasks requiring controlled text generation or tasks where the importance of different parts of the input is known a priori. The attention signals can be provided by domain experts, making the approach adaptable to different contexts. This method is particularly suitable for tasks with long input texts, such as summarization and reading comprehension, where the model needs to focus on key content.

The external attention mechanism makes use of the LLMs' capabilities in in-context learning and instruction following. By providing clear, externally defined attention signals, LLMs can better understand and prioritize the critical content, leading to improved performance in specific tasks.

4 Experiments

4.1 Experimental Setup

Dataset. We evaluate our method on SciTLDR (Cachola et al., 2020), a widely used benchmark for scientific extreme summarization, featuring high-quality, human-generated gold TLDRs. Our experiments focus on the abstract-only subset (including title), rather than the AIC (abstract+introduction+conclusion) and full text subsets, to reduce API usage costs and to accommodate the limited context length of most LLMs. Additionally, abstracts are generally more accessible than full texts , making this setting more applicable to real-world scenarios.

Baselines. We compare the proposed EAP method with two baselines:

- **Standard Prompting (SP)**: This baseline only provide necessary instructions and the abstracts to LLMs to generate the TLDRs. No additional guidance or emphasis is included.

- **Explicit Guidance Prompting (EGP)**: In this baseline, the abstract is supplemented with the paper's title and the top-5 keywords extracted using the TextRank algorithm. The LLMs are explicitly instructed to "pay attention to" the title and keywords, thereby directing its focus towards these critical components. This method provides explicit guidance to the model without altering the abstract.

- **Random Attention Prompting (RAP)**: This baseline is a variant of our proposed EAP method. It randomly applies different levels of emphasis to n-grams in the source text, maintaining the same number of emphasized n-grams and n-gram lengths as the corresponding EAP method. This baseline is designed to investigate whether the performance changes in EAP are due to the specific attention signals or simply the presence of Markdown emphasis, regardless of the content being emphasized.

All methods are evaluated under both zero-shot and few-shot settings. In the few-shot setting, we use the same two demonstration examples in prompt for all methods, with the input processed according to each respective method. The specific prompts utilized for all methods are detailed in Appendix B.

Large language models. To evaluate the effectiveness and generalizability of our proposed approach, we conduct experiments leveraging a diverse set of LLMs, including GPT-3.5, Llama-3, GLM-4, and DeepSeek-V2, encompassing both open-source and black-box models. The detailed information on the versions of LLMs used in our experiments is summarized in Table 2.

Evaluation metrics. In our evaluation, we use Rouge-1, Rouge-2, and Rouge-L metrics (Lin, 2004), consistent with previous work in summarization (Narayan et al., 2018; Lewis et al., 2020; Cachola et al., 2020). Considering SciTLDR provides multiple target summaries for a given paper, we follow Cachola et al. (2020) to taking the maximum Rouge score calculated over multiple gold TLDRs as the final Rouge score. This can effectively handles the variability in gold TLDRs.

Additionally, we use the Rouge-K metric (Takeshita et al., 2024), a keyword-oriented evaluation metric which specifically assesses the inclusion of essential keywords in the generated summaries, as it aligns with our goal of ensuring that the generated TLDRs capture the most critical content from the source documents.

Implementation details. All LLMs utilized in this work are accessed via API calls and configured with the same generation parameters: temperature of 0.1 and a maximum tokens limit of 128. Evaluation results for each LLM are averaged over three independent inferences for each input to mitigate the impact of sampling randomness of LLMs.

	Method	GPT-3.5			Llama-3			GLM-4			DeepSeek-V2		
		R-1	R-2	R-L	R-1	R-2	R-L	R-1	R-2	R-L	R-1	R-2	R-L
Zero-shot	SP	32.04	12.04	26.04	32.54	12.36	**26.92**	31.46	10.73	**26.00**	30.49	10.48	25.09
	EGP	32.56	12.40	**26.48**	32.31	11.96	26.50	31.13	10.20	25.39	30.41	10.61	24.98
	RAP	31.26	11.19	25.36	32.15	11.95	26.22	31.12	10.40	25.61	29.42	9.72	23.72
	EAP*	**32.64**†	**12.50**†	26.43	**32.74**	**12.37**	26.78	**31.54**	**10.92**	**26.00**	**30.97**	**10.91**	**25.42**
Few-shot	SP	33.76	13.22	27.91	34.29	13.24	28.33	31.76	10.90	26.27	33.73	13.03	28.06
	EGP	33.32	12.90	27.40	33.76	12.90	27.75	31.79	11.03	26.05	33.62	12.76	28.17
	RAP	33.01	12.77	27.23	34.26	13.28	28.25	31.86	10.94	26.27	32.34	11.82	26.88
	EAP*	**34.39**†	**13.69**†	**28.49**†	**34.78**†	**13.80**†	**28.82**†	**32.34**†	**11.39**†	**26.84**†	**34.23**†	**13.34**	**28.58**

Table 1: Rouge scores for different prompting methods across various LLMs in zero-shot and few-shot settings. Best results per metric are **bolded**. The method marked with * is the proposed method in this paper. Scores marked with † indicate that the EAP method significantly ($\alpha = 0.05$) outperforms the Standard Prompting (SP) method, determined using the Wilcoxon signed-rank test (Dror et al., 2018).

LLM	Version
GPT-3.5	gpt-3.5-turbo-0125
Llama-3	llama-3-70b-instruct
GLM-4	glm-4 (2024-01-16)
DeepSeek-V2	deepseek-chat (2024-05-17)

Table 2: Specifications of large language models used in the experiments.

4.2 Main Results and Analysis

The experimental results, as presented in Table 1, demonstrate the effectiveness of the proposed EAP method across various LLMs and metrics in both zero-shot and few-shot settings. This indicates that the external attention signals effectively guide the LLMs to generate more accurate and informative TLDRs.

Zero-shot results. In the zero-shot setting, EAP outperforms all baseline methods (SP, EGP and RAP) across all LLMs on Rouge-1/2, suggesting that the external attention signals provided by EAP are effective even without prior examples. However, in the case of the Rouge-L metric, the EAP method underperforms compared to the baseline methods for GPT-3.5 and Llama-3, possibly due to the additional complexity and noise introduced by this attention mechanism.

Few-shot results. In the few-shot setting, EAP consistently outperforms all baseline methods across all metrics and LLMs. The majority of these improvements are statistically significant, as evidenced by the Wilcoxon signed-rank test ($\alpha = 0.05$). This indicates that providing demonstration examples helps LLMs learn how to effectively distill the core content by focusing on segments of varying importance, leading to the generation of more precise and comprehensive TLDRs. This enhanced performance can be attributed to the strong in-context learning capabilities of LLMs.

Explicit vs. implicit guidance. The EGP method, which explicitly provides titles and keywords as additional input, shows mixed results. In some cases, it performs worse than the SP method, which does not include any additional guidance. This suggests that merely adding extra information without fine-grained control can confuse the model, leading to inconsistent results. In contrast, the EAP method implicitly emphasizes different parts of the source text, allowing the model to better understand and prioritize the critical content. This implicit approach appears to be more effective in guiding the model's attention, resulting in more stable and improved performance.

Random Attention Prompting results. The RAP baseline generally underperforms compared to SP and EAP methods across all LLMs and metrics in both zero-shot and few-shot settings. In the zero-shot setting, RAP often performs worse than SP, suggesting that random emphasis can be detrimental to the LLMs' understanding of the source text. In the few-shot setting, while RAP shows some improvement over SP in certain cases (e.g., for GLM-4), it still consistently underperforms compared to EAP. These results indicate that the performance gains of EAP are not merely due to the presence of Markdown emphasis, but rather the strategic placement of attention signals on important content. The effectiveness of EAP over RAP underscores the importance of deriving attention signals from key content such as titles and keywords, rather than applying emphasis randomly.

Results across LLMs. The results indicate that the EAP method consistently enhances performance across different models, demonstrating its generalizability and effectiveness. However, the degree of improvement varies among models, which may be related to the inherent capabilities of each model. For instance, models with stronger in-context learning abilities might benefit more from the EAP method, as they can better utilize the implicit attention signals to generate high-quality summaries.

Rouge-K results. The Rouge-K metric (Takeshita et al., 2024), which assesses the inclusion of essential keywords in the generated summaries, provides additional insights into the performance of the EAP method. As shown in Figure 3, in the zero-shot setting, EAP achieves higher Rouge-K scores compared to the baseline methods on Llama-3 and DeepSeek-V2. However, the EGP method surpasses EAP on GPT-3.5 and GLM-4, suggesting that explicitly providing keywords may be more effective for certain models in the absence of demonstration examples. In the few-shot setting, EAP consistently outperforms all the baseline methods across all models in terms of Rouge-K. This indicates that the combination of implicit attention signals and demonstration examples enables the models to better capture and include the most critical points in the generated TLDRs. The RAP method shows inconsistent performance on Rouge-K across different settings and models. In some cases, RAP outperforms SP or EGP methods, while in others, it underperforms. This variability can be attributed to the random nature of the attention signals in RAP, which may occasionally emphasize important content by chance. It is worth noting that the Rouge-K scores for all models and most methods are significantly lower in the few-shot setting compared to the zero-shot setting. This unexpected result may be attributed to the demonstration examples potentially biasing the models towards generating summaries that prioritize overall content coverage rather than focusing on specific keywords. Further investigation is needed to fully understand this phenomenon and its implications for keyword-oriented summarization tasks.

4.3 LLM as Evaluator

Setup. In addition to using traditional automatic metrics, we explore the use of LLMs as evaluators to assess the quality of generated TLDRs. This approach aims to address the limitations of automatic metrics, which may not fully capture the nuances of human preferences and the overall quality of the summaries (Zheng et al., 2023). By leveraging LLMs, we seek to provide a more comprehensive and human-aligned evaluation of the generated TLDRs.

To this end, we employ GPT-4 (version gpt-4-0613), which is currently recognized as one of the most advanced LLMs, to assess the quality of TLDRs generated by our method compared to a baseline method.

We randomly sample 100 data points and collect TLDRs generated by GPT-3.5 using both the baseline SP method and our EAP method under a few-shot setting. The evaluation criteria focus on the TLDR's ability to concisely capture the key aspects of a scientific paper while maintaining faithfulness to the source. To mitigate position bias (Zheng et al., 2023), each pair is evaluated twice with the positions of the two TLDRs swapped. A method is considered the winner for a sample only if both evaluations favored the same TLDR. In cases of conflicting results or ties, the sample is marked as a tie. The above process is repeated with three different random seeds, resulting in three rounds of evaluation.

Results. The results of GPT-4 evaluation are summarized in Table 3, showing that the proposed EAP method consistently outperforms the baseline SP method, achieving an average win rate of 37.33 % compared to the baseline's 26.00 %. The average tie rate is 36.67 %, with an average conflict rate of 23.67 %. These results indicate that the EAP method significantly enhances the performance of LLMs in generating TLDRs, as judged by GPT-4.

4.4 Ablation Study

To investigate the effects of different components in EAP method, we conduct an ablation study to address two key research questions: (1) Does the multi-level attention signal mechanism contribute to the performance improvement compared to using a uniform attention signal? (2) Are attention signals derived from the title essential for enhancing the

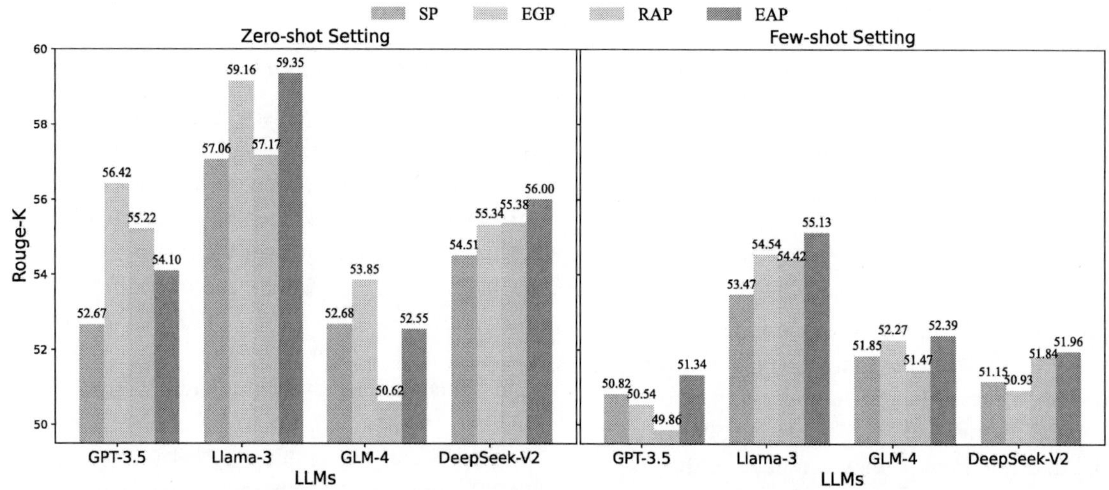

Figure 3: Rouge-K scores of SP, EGP, RAP and EAP methods across the tested LLMs.

Rounds	SP Win Rate	EAP Win Rate	Tie (Conflict)
Round1	26%	35%	39% (27%)
Round2	23%	40%	37% (23%)
Round3	29%	37%	34% (21%)
Avg.	26%	**37.33%**	36.67% (23.67%)

Table 3: GPT-4 evaluation results comparing EAP and SP methods for TLDR generation.

summarization quality?

To investigate the role of multi-level attention signals, we design an ablation variant of our method, in which we remove the differentiation between strong, medium, and weak attention signals. Instead, we uniformly apply a single level of attention signal by marking all relevant n-grams from the title and keywords with bold Markdown syntax.

To assess the importance of attention signals derived from the title, we create another ablation variant in which we exclude attention signals derived from the title and only mark the top-5 keywords extracted using the TextRank algorithm in the source text.

We conduct experiments using the same setup as described in Section 4.1, maintaining consistency in dataset, baselines, and evaluation metrics. The results are summarized in Table 4.

Multi-Level Attention Signals The variant without multi-level attention signals exhibit a slight decline in performance across vast majority metrics and LLMs compared to the original EAP method. This suggests that the differentiation between strong, medium, and weak attention signals plays a crucial role in guiding the LLMs to prioritize the most salient information effectively.

Title-Derived Attention Signals: The variant without title attention shows a noticeable reduction in performance, indicating that while the multi-level attention mechanism is advantageous, the title-derived signals play a more crucial role in capturing the core idea of scientific papers, thereby contributing significantly to the overall performance improvement.

5 Related Work

Scientific Extreme Summarization Scientific extreme summarization, the task of generating extreme one-sentence summaries (TLDRs) for scientific papers, has gained increasing attention in recent years. Several datasets have been proposed to facilitate research in this area, including SciTLDR (Cachola et al., 2020), a high-quality dataset with human-written summaries, and CiteSum (Mao et al., 2022), which contains automatically generated summaries based on citations. Additionally, multi-document(Lu et al., 2020), multilingual (Takeshita et al., 2022) and multimodal (Atri et al., 2023) datasets have been introduced to explore the task in diverse settings. Existing ap-

	Method	GPT-3.5			Llama-3			GLM-4			DeepSeek-V2		
		R-1	R-2	R-L	R-1	R-2	R-L	R-1	R-2	R-L	R-1	R-2	R-L
Zero-shot	EAP	32.64	12.50	26.43	32.74	12.37	26.78	31.54	10.92	26.00	30.97	10.91	25.42
Zero-shot	w/o MLA	32.41	12.19	26.20	32.67	12.41	26.68	31.49	10.81	25.82	30.97	10.91	25.39
Zero-shot	Δ	-0.23	-0.31	-0.23	-0.07	+0.04	-0.10	-0.05	-0.11	-0.18	0.00	0.00	-0.03
Zero-shot	w/o TA	31.61	11.50	25.65	32.30	12.06	26.34	31.22	10.60	25.70	30.89	10.62	25.19
Zero-shot	Δ	-1.03	-1.00	-0.78	-0.44	-0.31	-0.44	-0.32	-0.32	-0.30	-0.08	-0.29	-0.23
Few-shot	EAP	34.39	13.69	28.49	34.78	13.80	28.82	32.34	11.39	26.84	34.23	13.34	28.58
Few-shot	w/o MLA	34.02	13.35	28.04	34.58	13.63	28.66	32.45	11.38	26.71	34.15	13.19	28.48
Few-shot	Δ	-0.37	-0.34	-0.45	-0.20	-0.17	-0.16	+0.11	-0.01	-0.13	-0.08	-0.15	-0.10
Few-shot	w/o TA	33.26	12.75	27.45	34.11	13.20	28.14	31.91	11.10	26.34	33.94	12.98	28.19
Few-shot	Δ	-1.13	-0.94	-1.04	-0.67	-0.60	-0.68	-0.43	-0.29	-0.50	-0.29	-0.36	-0.39

Table 4: Ablation study results. "w/o MLA" denotes the variant without multi-level attention signals, and "w/o TA" represents the variant without title-derived attention signals. Δ indicates the performance difference between each variant and the full EAP method. The results demonstrate that both multi-level attention and title-derived signals contribute to the effectiveness of EAP, with title-derived signals playing a more crucial role.

proaches to scientific extreme summarization primarily rely on fine-tuned Transformer-based models, such as BART (Lewis et al., 2020) and T5 (Raffel et al., 2023), which have achieved promising results. However, the potential of LLMs for this task remains largely unexplored. While LLMs are trained for general-purpose tasks and may not match the performance of task-specific fine-tuned models (Takeshita et al., 2024), their extensive domain knowledge and strong in-context learning abilities make them a promising avenue for investigation in scientific extreme summarization.

Key Content Utilization for Summarization Previous studies have explored various key content, such as titles, keywords, topics, and key segments, to enhance summarization performance (Chen et al., 2019; Koto et al., 2022; Srivastava et al., 2023; Tang et al., 2023). These methods typically focus on incorporating key content as additional input features or using the prediction of key content as an auxiliary task. For instance, Koto et al. (2022) investigated the impact of incorporating titles and keyphrases as structured input and target outputs in news summarization. Cachola et al. (2020) leveraging titles as auxiliary training signals to improve model performance in the scientific extreme summarization task. In this work, we use key content to compute attention signals, rather than as additional input or target, to guide LLMs to focus on the important parts of the source text.

Prompt Optimization and Engineering Prompt engineering has emerged as a crucial area of research to enhance the capabilities of LLMs on complex tasks. Early approaches focused on tuning soft prompts, which are continuous embedding vectors optimized using gradient descent methods (Li and Liang, 2021; Vu et al., 2022; An et al., 2022; Tam et al., 2023). However, these approaches require access to the Internal parameters of LLMs, limiting their applicability to black-box models. Another direction involves designing task-specific natural language instructions and selecting appropriate in-context demonstrations (Shin et al., 2020; Brown et al., 2020; Deng et al., 2022; Zhou et al., 2023; Sun et al., 2023). Despite the promising results, these methods may struggle to capture fine-grained, instance-specific (Li et al., 2023). proposes a method that generates instance-specific prompts tailored to each input using a small, tunable policy model optimized through supervised fine-tuning and reinforcement learning. In this work, we aim to provide LLMs with instance-specific attention signals derived from key content to enhance their performance in the task of scientific extreme summarization.

6 Conclusion

In this work, we have presented External Attention Prompting (EAP), a novel method for improving the performance of large language models (LLMs) in the task of scientific extreme summarization. By utilizing external attention signals derived from the title and keywords of scientific papers, EAP effectively guides LLMs to focus on the most salient information, resulting in more accurate and informative TLDRs. Our extensive experiments on the SciTLDR dataset demonstrate the superiority of EAP over standard prompting and explicit guidance methods, particularly in few-shot settings. The results underscore the importance of multi-level attention and the significant role of title emphasis in enhancing summarization quality. Future work could explore the application of EAP to other domains and tasks, further validating its versatility and effectiveness in various text generation scenarios.

7 Limitations

This work has the following limitations: (1) The heuristic-based design and computation of attention signals in EAP may not fully capture salient information in diverse contexts. Future work could explore automated methods. (2) The keyword extraction algorithm used in this work for computing attention signals only considers TextRank. Future research should explore and compare the effectiveness of various keyword extraction methods. (3) Our experiments focus on the abstract-only subset of SciTLDR, which may not fully represent the challenges of summarizing entire scientific papers. Furthermore, SciTLDR is focused on the computer science domain, which may limit the generalizability of our findings.

Acknowledgments

The authors thank all the anonymous reviewers for their valuable comments and constructive feedback. The authors acknowledge financial support from the National Social Science Fund of China (No. 23BTQ102). Xiaoqiu Le is the corresponding author.

References

Shengnan An, Yifei Li, Zeqi Lin, Qian Liu, Bei Chen, Qiang Fu, Weizhu Chen, Nanning Zheng, and Jian-Guang Lou. 2022. Input-tuning: Adapting unfamiliar inputs to frozen pretrained models. *Preprint*, arXiv:2203.03131.

Yash Kumar Atri, Vikram Goyal, and Tanmoy Chakraborty. 2023. Fusing multimodal signals on hyper-complex space for extreme abstractive text summarization (tl;dr) of scientific contents. In *Proceedings of the 29th ACM SIGKDD Conference on Knowledge Discovery and Data Mining*, KDD '23, page 3724–3736, New York, NY, USA. Association for Computing Machinery.

Tom B. Brown, Benjamin Mann, Nick Ryder, Melanie Subbiah, Jared Kaplan, Prafulla Dhariwal, Arvind Neelakantan, Pranav Shyam, Girish Sastry, Amanda Askell, Sandhini Agarwal, Ariel Herbert-Voss, Gretchen Krueger, Tom Henighan, Rewon Child, Aditya Ramesh, Daniel M. Ziegler, Jeffrey Wu, Clemens Winter, Christopher Hesse, Mark Chen, Eric Sigler, Mateusz Litwin, Scott Gray, Benjamin Chess, Jack Clark, Christopher Berner, Sam McCandlish, Alec Radford, Ilya Sutskever, and Dario Amodei. 2020. Language models are few-shot learners. In *Proceedings of the 34th International Conference on Neural Information Processing Systems*, NIPS '20, Red Hook, NY, USA. Curran Associates Inc.

Isabel Cachola, Kyle Lo, Arman Cohan, and Daniel Weld. 2020. TLDR: Extreme summarization of scientific documents. In *Findings of the Association for Computational Linguistics: EMNLP 2020*, pages 4766–4777, Online. Association for Computational Linguistics.

Erion Çano and Ondřej Bojar. 2019. Keyphrase generation: A text summarization struggle. In *Proceedings of the 2019 Conference of the North American Chapter of the Association for Computational Linguistics: Human Language Technologies, Volume 1 (Long and Short Papers)*, pages 666–672, Minneapolis, Minnesota. Association for Computational Linguistics.

Wang Chen, Yifan Gao, Jiani Zhang, Irwin King, and Michael R. Lyu. 2019. Title-guided encoding for keyphrase generation. In *Proceedings of the Thirty-Third AAAI Conference on Artificial Intelligence and Thirty-First Innovative Applications of Artificial Intelligence Conference and Ninth AAAI Symposium on Educational Advances in Artificial Intelligence*, AAAI'19/IAAI'19/EAAI'19. AAAI Press.

Mingkai Deng, Jianyu Wang, Cheng-Ping Hsieh, Yihan Wang, Han Guo, Tianmin Shu, Meng Song, Eric Xing, and Zhiting Hu. 2022. RLPrompt: Optimizing discrete text prompts with reinforcement learning. In *Proceedings of the 2022 Conference on Empirical Methods in Natural Language Processing*, pages 3369–3391, Abu Dhabi, United Arab Emirates. Association for Computational Linguistics.

Rotem Dror, Gili Baumer, Segev Shlomov, and Roi Reichart. 2018. The hitchhiker's guide to testing statistical significance in natural language processing. In *Proceedings of the 56th Annual Meeting of the Association for Computational Linguistics (Volume 1: Long Papers)*, pages 1383–1392, Melbourne, Australia. Association for Computational Linguistics.

Fajri Koto, Timothy Baldwin, and Jey Han Lau. 2022. LipKey: A large-scale news dataset for absent keyphrases generation and abstractive summarization. In *Proceedings of the 29th International Conference on Computational Linguistics*, pages 3427–3437, Gyeongju, Republic of Korea. International Committee on Computational Linguistics.

Daniel Lee, Rakesh M. Verma, Avisha Das, and Arjun Mukherjee. 2020. Experiments in extractive summarization: Integer linear programming, term/sentence scoring, and title-driven models. *CoRR*, abs/2008.00140.

Mike Lewis, Yinhan Liu, Naman Goyal, Marjan Ghazvininejad, Abdelrahman Mohamed, Omer Levy, Veselin Stoyanov, and Luke Zettlemoyer. 2020. BART: Denoising sequence-to-sequence pre-training for natural language generation, translation, and comprehension. In *Proceedings of the 58th Annual Meeting of the Association for Computational Linguistics*, pages 7871–7880, Online. Association for Computational Linguistics.

Xiang Lisa Li and Percy Liang. 2021. Prefix-tuning: Optimizing continuous prompts for generation. In *Proceedings of the 59th Annual Meeting of the Association for Computational Linguistics and the 11th International Joint Conference on Natural Language Processing (Volume 1: Long Papers)*, pages 4582–4597, Online. Association for Computational Linguistics.

Zekun Li, Baolin Peng, Pengcheng He, Michel Galley, Jianfeng Gao, and Xifeng Yan. 2023. Guiding large language models via directional stimulus prompting. *Preprint*, arXiv:2302.11520.

Yao Lu, Yue Dong, and Laurent Charlin. 2020. Multi-XScience: A large-scale dataset for extreme multi-document summarization of scientific articles. In *Proceedings of the 2020 Conference on Empirical Methods in Natural Language Processing (EMNLP)*, pages 8068–8074, Online. Association for Computational Linguistics.

Yuning Mao, Ming Zhong, and Jiawei Han. 2022. CiteSum: Citation text-guided scientific extreme summarization and domain adaptation with limited supervision. In *Proceedings of the 2022 Conference on Empirical Methods in Natural Language Processing*, pages 10922–10935, Abu Dhabi, United Arab Emirates. Association for Computational Linguistics.

Rada Mihalcea and Paul Tarau. 2004. TextRank: Bringing order into text. In *Proceedings of the 2004 Conference on Empirical Methods in Natural Language Processing*, pages 404–411, Barcelona, Spain. Association for Computational Linguistics.

Shashi Narayan, Shay B. Cohen, and Mirella Lapata. 2018. Don't give me the details, just the summary! topic-aware convolutional neural networks for extreme summarization. In *Proceedings of the 2018 Conference on Empirical Methods in Natural Language Processing*, pages 1797–1807, Brussels, Belgium. Association for Computational Linguistics.

Colin Raffel, Noam Shazeer, Adam Roberts, Katherine Lee, Sharan Narang, Michael Matena, Yanqi Zhou, Wei Li, and Peter J. Liu. 2023. Exploring the limits of transfer learning with a unified text-to-text transformer. *Preprint*, arXiv:1910.10683.

Abigail See, Peter J. Liu, and Christopher D. Manning. 2017. Get to the point: Summarization with pointer-generator networks. In *Proceedings of the 55th Annual Meeting of the Association for Computational Linguistics (Volume 1: Long Papers)*, pages 1073–1083, Vancouver, Canada. Association for Computational Linguistics.

Taylor Shin, Yasaman Razeghi, Robert L. Logan IV, Eric Wallace, and Sameer Singh. 2020. AutoPrompt: Eliciting Knowledge from Language Models with Automatically Generated Prompts. In *Proceedings of the 2020 Conference on Empirical Methods in Natural Language Processing (EMNLP)*, pages 4222–4235, Online. Association for Computational Linguistics.

Vivek Srivastava, Savita Bhat, and Niranjan Pedanekar. 2023. A few good sentences: Content selection for abstractive text summarization. In *Machine Learning and Knowledge Discovery in Databases: Research Track*, pages 124–141, Cham. Springer Nature Switzerland.

Gregor Stiglic, Leon Kopitar, Lucija Gosak, Primoz Kocbek, Zhe He, Prithwish Chakraborty, Pablo Meyer, and Jiang Bian. 2023. Improving primary healthcare workflow using extreme summarization of scientific literature based on generative ai. *Preprint*, arXiv:2307.15715.

Hong Sun, Xue Li, Yinchuan Xu, Youkow Homma, Qi Cao, Min Wu, Jian Jiao, and Denis Charles. 2023. Autohint: Automatic prompt optimization with hint generation. *Preprint*, arXiv:2307.07415.

Shahbaz Syed, Khalid Al Khatib, and Martin Potthast. 2024. TL;DR progress: Multi-faceted literature exploration in text summarization. In *Proceedings of the 18th Conference of the European Chapter of the Association for Computational Linguistics: System Demonstrations*, pages 195–206, St. Julians, Malta. Association for Computational Linguistics.

Sotaro Takeshita, Tommaso Green, Niklas Friedrich, Kai Eckert, and Simone Paolo Ponzetto. 2022. X-scitldr: cross-lingual extreme summarization of scholarly documents. In *Proceedings of the 22nd ACM/IEEE Joint Conference on Digital Libraries*, JCDL '22. ACM.

Sotaro Takeshita, Simone Paolo Ponzetto, and Kai Eckert. 2024. Rouge-k: Do your summaries have keywords? *Preprint*, arXiv:2403.05186.

Weng Tam, Xiao Liu, Kaixuan Ji, Lilong Xue, Jiahua Liu, Tao Li, Yuxiao Dong, and Jie Tang. 2023. Parameter-efficient prompt tuning makes generalized and calibrated neural text retrievers. In *Findings of the Association for Computational Linguistics: EMNLP 2023*, pages 13117–13130, Singapore. Association for Computational Linguistics.

Peggy Tang, Kun Hu, Lei Zhang, Junbin Gao, Jiebo Luo, and Zhiyong Wang. 2023. Topiccat: Unsupervised topic-guided co-attention transformer for extreme multimodal summarisation. In *Proceedings of the 31st ACM International Conference on Multimedia*, MM '23, page 6643–6652, New York, NY, USA. Association for Computing Machinery.

Tu Vu, Brian Lester, Noah Constant, Rami Al-Rfou', and Daniel Cer. 2022. SPoT: Better frozen model adaptation through soft prompt transfer. In *Proceedings of the 60th Annual Meeting of the Association for Computational Linguistics (Volume 1: Long Papers)*, pages 5039–5059, Dublin, Ireland. Association for Computational Linguistics.

Jason Wei, Yi Tay, Rishi Bommasani, Colin Raffel, Barret Zoph, Sebastian Borgeaud, Dani Yogatama, Maarten Bosma, Denny Zhou, Donald Metzler, Ed H. Chi, Tatsunori Hashimoto, Oriol Vinyals, Percy Liang, Jeff Dean, and William Fedus. 2022. Emergent abilities of large language models. *Preprint*, arXiv:2206.07682.

Wayne Xin Zhao, Kun Zhou, Junyi Li, Tianyi Tang, Xiaolei Wang, Yupeng Hou, Yingqian Min, Beichen Zhang, Junjie Zhang, Zican Dong, Yifan Du, Chen Yang, Yushuo Chen, Zhipeng Chen, Jinhao Jiang, Ruiyang Ren, Yifan Li, Xinyu Tang, Zikang Liu, Peiyu Liu, Jian-Yun Nie, and Ji-Rong Wen. 2023. A survey of large language models. *Preprint*, arXiv:2303.18223.

Lianmin Zheng, Wei-Lin Chiang, Ying Sheng, Siyuan Zhuang, Zhanghao Wu, Yonghao Zhuang, Zi Lin, Zhuohan Li, Dacheng Li, Eric P. Xing, Hao Zhang, Joseph E. Gonzalez, and Ion Stoica. 2023. Judging llm-as-a-judge with mt-bench and chatbot arena. *Preprint*, arXiv:2306.05685.

Yongchao Zhou, Andrei Ioan Muresanu, Ziwen Han, Keiran Paster, Silviu Pitis, Harris Chan, and Jimmy Ba. 2023. Large language models are human-level prompt engineers. *Preprint*, arXiv:2211.01910.

A Case Study

To further illustrate the effectiveness of our proposed EAP method, we present a case study comparing the generated TLDRs from EAP and the baseline SP method in zero-shot setting using GPT-3.5.

Table 5 showcases an example from the SciTLDR dataset, where the source paper is about combining differentiable decision trees (DDTs) with supervised variational autoencoders (SVAEs) to enhance the interpretability of classification tasks.

The TLDR generated by the SP method fails to capture the core idea of the paper, instead focusing on individual components such as DDTs and SVAEs without highlighting their synergistic combination. In contrast, the EAP method, guided by the attention signals derived from the title and keywords, successfully identifies the key aspects of the work, even in the absence of demonstration examples. The generated TLDR concisely conveys the main contribution: the integration of DDTs and SVAEs to create an interpretable and competitive classifier+VAE for high-dimensional data.

Moreover, the EAP-generated TLDR achieves a significantly higher Rouge-1 score (46.51) compared to the SP-generated TLDR (27.03), indicating its superior quality and relevance to the gold TLDRs. This case study demonstrates how the EAP method effectively guides the LLM to focus on the most critical information, resulting in more accurate and informative summaries.

B Prompts

The prompts employed in this work for the standard prompting, explicit guidance prompting, and external attention prompting methods in the zero-shot and few-shot settings are illustrated in Figures 4, 5, 6, 7 and Figures 8, 9, 10, 11, respectively.

Title	Interpretable Classification via Supervised Variational Autoencoders and Differentiable Decision Trees
Source abstract	As deep learning-based classifiers are increasingly adopted in real-world applications, the importance of understanding how a particular label is chosen grows. Single decision trees are an example of a simple, interpretable classifier, but are unsuitable for use with complex, high-dimensional data. On the other hand, the variational autoencoder (VAE) is designed to learn a factored, low-dimensional representation of data, but typically encodes high-likelihood data in an intrinsically non-separable way. We introduce the differentiable decision tree (DDT) as a modular component of deep networks and a simple, differentiable loss function that allows for end-to-end optimization of a deep network to compress high-dimensional data for classification by a single decision tree. We also explore the power of labeled data in a supervised VAE (SVAE) with a Gaussian mixture prior, which leverages label information to produce a high-quality generative model with improved bounds on log-likelihood. We combine the SVAE with the DDT to get our classifier+VAE (C+VAE), which is competitive in both classification error and log-likelihood, despite optimizing both simultaneously and using a very simple encoder/decoder architecture.
TLDR-AU	We combine differentiable decision trees with supervised variational autoencoders to enhance interpretability of classification.
TLDR-PR1	This paper proposes a hybrid model of a variational autoencoder composed with a differentiable decision tree, and an accompanying training scheme, with experiments demonstrating tree classification performance, neg. log likelihood performance, and latent space interpretability.
TLDR-PR2	The paper tries to build an interpretable and accurate classifier via stacking a supervised VAE and a differentiable decision tree
	Standard Prompting (SP)
Generated TLDR	The paper introduces the differentiable decision tree (DDT) as a modular component of deep networks and a simple, differentiable loss function that allows for end-to-end optimization of a deep network to compress high-dimensional data for classification by a single decision tree, and explores the power of labeled data in a supervised VAE (SVAE) with a Gaussian mixture prior, which leverages label information to produce a high-quality generative model with improved bounds on log-likelihood.
Rouge-1	27.03
	External Attention Prompting (EAP)
Attention Signals	**Strong:** the differentiable decision tree **Medium:** a simple, interpretable classifier; the variational autoencoder; single decision trees; a supervised VAE; classification error **Weak:** deep learning-based classifiers; high-dimensional data; high-likelihood data; labeled data
Generated TLDR	The differentiable decision tree (DDT) and supervised VAE (SVAE) are combined to create an interpretable and competitive classifier+VAE for high-dimensional data with improved bounds on log-likelihood.
Rouge-1	46.51

Table 5: A case study comparing the TLDRs generated by GPT-3.5 using the standard prompting method and external attention prompting method in the zero-shot setting. TLDR-AU refers to the gold TLDR written by author and TLDR-PR1 and TLDR-PR2 are gold TLDRs derived from the perspective of peer reviewers, according to the representation in SciTLDR. The attention signals that are mentioned in EAP generated TLDR are highlighted in red. The EAP method, guided by attention signals derived from the title and keywords, generates a more accurate and informative TLDR that captures the core idea of the paper, even without demonstration examples.

```
# Task: Extreme summarization of scientific documents

## Task Definition
Given the abstract of a scientific paper, generate a short one-sentence summary that captures the key aspects of the paper.

## Input

### Abstract
[source abstract]

### One-sentence summary
```

Figure 4: The prompt for standard prompting in the zero-shot setting.

```
# Task: Extreme summarization of scientific documents

## Task Definition
Given the title and abstract of a scientific paper, as well as a list of keywords, generate a short one-sentence summary that captures the key aspects of the paper. You should pay attention to the given title and keywords when summarizing.

## Input

### Title
[source title]

### Abstract
source abstract

### Keywords
[source keywords]

### One-sentence summary
```

Figure 5: The prompt for explicit guidance prompting in the zero-shot setting.

```
# Task: Extreme summarization of scientific documents

## Task Definition
Given the abstract of a scientific paper, generate a short one-sentence summary that captures the key aspects of the paper. You should pay attention to the emphasized content in the input abstract when summarizing.

## Input

### Abstract
[source abstract]

### One-sentence summary
```

Figure 6: The prompt for random attention prompting in the zero-shot setting.

Task: Extreme summarization of scientific documents

Task Definition
Given the abstract of a scientific paper, generate a short one-sentence summary that captures the key aspects of the paper. You should pay attention to the emphasized content in the input abstract when summarizing.

Input

Abstract
[source abstract]

One-sentence summary

Figure 7: The prompt for external attention prompting in the zero-shot setting.

Task: Extreme summarization of scientific documents

Task Definition
Given the abstract of a scientific paper, generate a short one-sentence summary that captures the key aspects of the paper.

EXAMPLE 1

Abstract
Due to the success of deep learning to solving a variety of challenging machine learning tasks, there is a rising interest in understanding loss functions for training neural networks from a theoretical aspect. Particularly, the properties of critical points and the landscape around them are of importance to determine the convergence performance of optimization algorithms. In this paper, we provide a necessary and sufficient characterization of the analytical forms for the critical points (as well as global minimizers) of the square loss functions for linear neural networks. We show that the analytical forms of the critical points characterize the values of the corresponding loss functions as well as the necessary and sufficient conditions to achieve global minimum. Furthermore, we exploit the analytical forms of the critical points to characterize the landscape properties for the loss functions of linear neural networks and shallow ReLU networks. One particular conclusion is that: While the loss function of linear networks has no spurious local minimum, the loss function of one-hidden-layer nonlinear networks with ReLU activation function does have local minimum that is not global minimum.

One-sentence summary
We provide necessary and sufficient analytical forms for the critical points of the square loss functions for various neural networks, and exploit the analytical forms to characterize the landscape properties for the loss functions of these neural networks.

EXAMPLE 2

Abstract
Reinforcement learning in an actor-critic setting relies on accurate value estimates of the critic. However, the combination of function approximation, temporal difference (TD) learning and off-policy training can lead to an overestimating value function. A solution is to use Clipped Double Q-learning (CDQ), which is used in the TD3 algorithm and computes the minimum of two critics in the TD-target. We show that CDQ induces an underestimation bias and propose a new algorithm that accounts for this by using a weighted average of the target from CDQ and the target coming from a single critic. The weighting parameter is adjusted during training such that the value estimates match the actual discounted return on the most recent episodes and by that it balances over- and underestimation. Empirically, we obtain more accurate value estimates and demonstrate state of the art results on several OpenAI gym tasks.

One-sentence summary
A method for more accurate critic estimates in reinforcement learning.

Input

Abstract
[source abstract]

One-sentence summary

Figure 8: The prompt for standard prompting in the few-shot setting.

Task: Extreme summarization of scientific documents

Task Definition
Given the abstract of a scientific paper, generate a short one-sentence summary that captures the key aspects of the paper. You should pay attention to the given title and keywords when summarizing.

EXAMPLE 1

Title
Critical Points of Linear Neural Networks: Analytical Forms and Landscape Properties

Abstract
Due to the success of deep learning to solving a variety of challenging machine learning tasks, there is a rising interest in understanding loss functions for training neural networks from a theoretical aspect. Particularly, the properties of critical points and the landscape around them are of importance to determine the convergence performance of optimization algorithms. In this paper, we provide a necessary and sufficient characterization of the analytical forms for the critical points (as well as global minimizers) of the square loss functions for linear neural networks. We show that the analytical forms of the critical points characterize the values of the corresponding loss functions as well as the necessary and sufficient conditions to achieve global minimum. Furthermore, we exploit the analytical forms of the critical points to characterize the landscape properties for the loss functions of linear neural networks and shallow ReLU networks. One particular conclusion is that: While the loss function of linear networks has no spurious local minimum, the loss function of one-hidden-layer nonlinear networks with ReLU activation function does have local minimum that is not global minimum.

Keywords
ReLU activation function; linear neural networks; critical points; loss functions

One-sentence summary
We provide necessary and sufficient analytical forms for the critical points of the square loss functions for various neural networks, and exploit the analytical forms to characterize the landscape properties for the loss functions of these neural networks.

EXAMPLE 2

Title
Dynamically Balanced Value Estimates for Actor-Critic Methods

Abstract
Reinforcement learning in an actor-critic setting relies on accurate value estimates of the critic. However, the combination of function approximation, temporal difference (TD) learning and off-policy training can lead to an overestimating value function. A solution is to use Clipped Double Q-learning (CDQ), which is used in the TD3 algorithm and computes the minimum of two critics in the TD-target. We show that CDQ induces an underestimation bias and propose a new algorithm that accounts for this by using a weighted average of the target from CDQ and the target coming from a single critic. The weighting parameter is adjusted during training such that the value estimates match the actual discounted return on the most recent episodes and by that it balances over- and underestimation. Empirically, we obtain more accurate value estimates and demonstrate state of the art results on several OpenAI gym tasks.

Keywords
more accurate value estimates; Reinforcement learning; off-policy training; several OpenAI gym

One-sentence summary
A method for more accurate critic estimates in reinforcement learning.

Input

Abstract
[source abstract]

One-sentence summary

Figure 9: The prompt for explicit guidance prompting in the few-shot setting.

```
# Task: Extreme summarization of scientific documents

## Task Definition
Given the abstract of a scientific paper, generate a short one-sentence summary that captures the key aspects of the paper. You should pay attention to the emphasized content in the input abstract when summarizing.

## EXAMPLE 1

### Abstract
Due to the success of deep ***learning to solving*** a variety of challenging machine learning tasks, there is a rising interest in understanding ***loss function***s for training neural networks from a theoretical aspect. Particularly, the properties of critical points and the landscape around them are of importance to determine the convergence performance of optimization algorithms. In this paper, we provide a necessary and sufficient characterization of the analytical forms for the critical points (as well as global minimizers) of the square ***loss function***s for *linear neural networks*. We show that the analytical forms of the critical points characterize the values of the corresponding ***loss function***s as well as the necessary and sufficient conditions to achieve global minimum. Furthermore, we exploit the analytical forms of the critical points to characterize the landscape properties for the ***loss function***s of *linear neural networks* and **shallow ReLU networks**. One particular conclusion is that: While the ***loss function*** of linear networks has no spurious local minimum, the ***loss function*** of **one-hidden-layer nonlinear networks** with ReLU **activation function** does have local minimum that is not global minimum.

### One-sentence summary
We provide necessary and sufficient analytical forms for the critical points of the square loss functions for various neural networks, and exploit the analytical forms to characterize the landscape properties for the loss functions of these neural networks.

## EXAMPLE 2

### Abstract
Reinforcement learning in an actor-critic setting relies on accurate value estimates of the critic. However, the combination of *function approximation*, temporal difference (TD) learning and off-policy **training can lead** to an overestimating value function. A solution is to use Clipped Double Q-learning (CDQ), which is used in the TD3 *algorithm and computes* the minimum of two critics in the TD-target. We show that CDQ induces an underestimation bias and propose a new algorithm that accounts for this by ***using a weighted average*** of the target from CDQ and the target coming from a single critic. The weighting parameter is adjusted during training such that the value estimates match the actual discounted return on the most recent episodes and by that it balances over- and underestimation. Empirically, we obtain more accurate value estimates and demonstrate state of the art results on several ***OpenAI gym*** tasks.

### One-sentence summary
A method for more accurate critic estimates in reinforcement learning.

## Input

### Abstract
[source abstract]

### One-sentence summary
```

Figure 10: The prompt for random attention prompting in the few-shot setting.

Task: Extreme summarization of scientific documents

Task Definition
Given the abstract of a scientific paper, generate a short one-sentence summary that captures the key aspects of the paper. You should pay attention to the emphasized content in the input abstract when summarizing.

EXAMPLE 1

Abstract
Due to the success of deep learning to solving a variety of challenging machine learning tasks, there is a rising interest in understanding *loss functions* for training neural networks from a theoretical aspect. Particularly, the properties of ***critical points*** and the landscape around them are of importance to determine the convergence performance of optimization algorithms. In this paper, we provide a necessary and sufficient characterization of **the analytical forms** for the ***critical points*** (as well as global minimizers) of the square *loss functions* for ***linear neural networks***. We show that **the analytical forms** of the ***critical points*** characterize the values of the corresponding *loss functions* as well as the necessary and sufficient conditions to achieve global minimum. Furthermore, we exploit **the analytical forms** of the ***critical points*** to characterize **the landscape properties** for the *loss functions* of ***linear neural networks*** and shallow ReLU networks. One particular conclusion is that: While the loss function of linear networks has no spurious local minimum, the loss function of one-hidden-layer nonlinear networks with *ReLU activation function* does have local minimum that is not global minimum.

One-sentence summary
We provide necessary and sufficient analytical forms for the critical points of the square loss functions for various neural networks, and exploit the analytical forms to characterize the landscape properties for the loss functions of these neural networks.

EXAMPLE 2

Abstract
Reinforcement learning in **an actor-critic setting** relies on accurate ***value estimates*** of the critic. However, the combination of function approximation, temporal difference (TD) learning and *off-policy training* can lead to an overestimating value function. A solution is to use Clipped Double Q-learning (CDQ), which is used in the TD3 algorithm and computes the minimum of two critics in the TD-target. We show that CDQ induces an underestimation bias and propose a new algorithm that accounts for this by using a weighted average of the target from CDQ and the target coming from a single critic. The weighting parameter is adjusted during training such that the ***value estimates*** match the actual discounted return on the most recent episodes and by that it balances over- and underestimation. Empirically, we obtain ***more accurate value estimates*** and demonstrate state of the art results on *several OpenAI gym* tasks.

One-sentence summary
A method for more accurate critic estimates in reinforcement learning.

Input

Abstract
[source abstract]

One-sentence summary

Figure 11: The prompt for external attention prompting in the few-shot setting.

Simulating Expert Discussions with Multi-agent for Enhanced Scientific Problem Solving

Ziyue Li, Yuan Chang, Xiaoqiu Le*
National Science Library, Chinese Academy of Sciences
Department of Information Resources Management, School of Economics and Management, University of Chinese Academy of Sciences
{liziyue, changyuan, lexq}@mail.las.ac.cn

Abstract

Large Language Models (LLMs) have shown remarkable potential across various domains, yet their application in addressing complex scientific problems remains a formidable challenge. This paper presents a novel methodology to augment the problem-solving capabilities of LLMs by assigning them roles as domain-specific experts. By simulating a panel of experts, each LLM is tasked with delivering professional and cautious responses to scientific inquiries. Our approach involves querying multiple LLMs and assessing the consistency of their responses. High agreement among the LLMs suggests greater confidence in the proposed solution, whereas discrepancies prompt a collaborative discussion among the LLMs to reach a consensus. This method emulates real-world scientific problem-solving processes, fostering a more reliable and robust mechanism for LLMs to tackle scientific questions. Our experimental results show that assigning roles to multiple LLMs as domain-specific experts significantly improves their accuracy and reliability in solving scientific problems. This framework has the potential to advance the application of AI in scientific research, enhancing its effectiveness and trustworthiness.

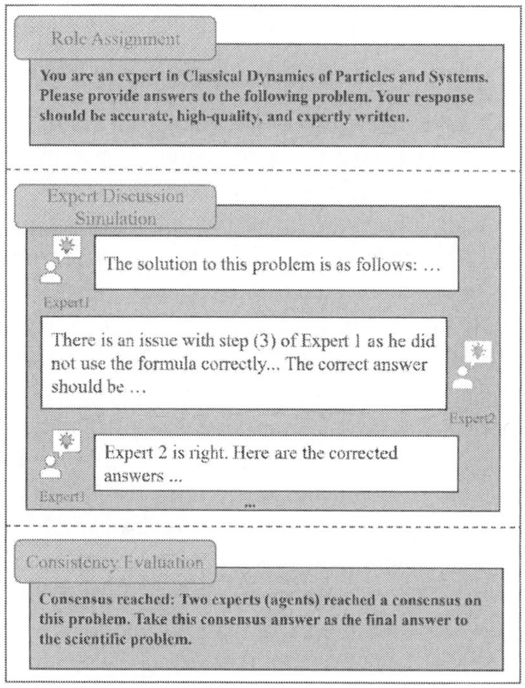

Figure 1: Simulating Expert Discussions with Multi-agent (SEDM).

1 Introduction

Large Language Models (LLMs) have achieved remarkable success in a wide range of natural language processing tasks, including text generation (Swanson et al., 2021; Yang et al., 2023), machine translation (Burda-Lassen, 2023; Alves et al., 2023), and text summarization (Laban et al., 2023). Despite their versatility and strong performance across various domains, the application of LLMs to solving complex scientific problems has remained a significant challenge. The primary obstacle lies not in the absence of domain-specific knowledge within these models, but rather in their limited ability to effectively harness this knowledge when confronted with intricate scientific problems that demand expert-level understanding and reasoning (Addlesee, 2024).

The application of LLMs to scientific problem-solving presents a unique challenge due to the stringent requirements for precision and reliability in research. Minor inaccuracies can have far-reaching consequences, undermining the validity and trustworthiness of results. While LLMs possess extensive knowledge, their current architectures often struggle to consistently apply this knowledge to meet the rigorous demands of scientific inquiry. This limitation underscores the need for innovative approaches to enhance the problem-solving capabilities of LLMs in specialized domains. Improving the performance of LLMs in accurately and reliably

*Corresponding Author

Proceedings of the Fourth Workshop on Scholarly Document Processing (SDP 2024), pages 243–256
August 16, 2024

solving complex scientific problems could significantly advance their utility in research settings and unlock new potentials for artificial intelligence in science.

In this study, we introduce a novel methodology called **Simulating Expert Discussions with Multi-agent (SEDM)** that enhances the problem-solving capabilities of LLMs by assigning them roles as domain-specific experts, as illustrated in Figure 1. This approach involves simulating a panel of experts, where each LLM is tasked with providing professional and cautious responses to scientific inquiries. By querying multiple LLMs and evaluating the consistency of their responses, we can gauge the confidence in the proposed solutions. High agreement among the LLMs indicates greater reliability, while discrepancies trigger a collaborative discussion among the models to reach a consensus. This method mirrors real-world scientific problem-solving processes, fostering a more dependable mechanism for LLMs to address scientific questions. We evaluate the performance of SEDM on a range of problems across various scientific domains, including physics, chemistry, and mathematics. We use accuracy as the evaluation metric and compare SEDM with baseline methods such as direct LLM usage and few-shot learning.

In summary, our contributions are:

- We propose a novel multi-agent framework that assigns specific expert roles to LLMs, enabling them to collaboratively address scientific problems.
- We develop a discussion architecture for multi-agent systems, and experiments have shown that this architecture can effectively enable multiple agents to reach the correct consensus.
- We demonstrate through extensive experiments that our approach significantly improves the accuracy LLMs in scientific problem-solving. For instance, when using the GPT-4 model, SEDM achieves an average accuracy of 57.18% across all subjects, representing an improvement of 32 percentage points compared to direct query and 36 percentage points compared to few-shot learning. These results advance the application of AI in scientific research.

2 Related Work

Large Language Model Reasoning Large language models (LLMs) have demonstrated significant reasoning capabilities, especially when scaled to hundreds of billions of parameters (Ouyang et al., 2022; OpenAI et al., 2024). Various techniques, such as chain-of-thought prompting (Wei et al., 2022; Kojima et al., 2022; Shi et al., 2022) and rationale engineering (Fu et al., 2023; Zhou et al., 2022), have been proposed to further elicit and enhance the reasoning abilities of LLMs. However, despite these advancements, LLMs still struggle with complex reasoning tasks, particularly in the domain of scientific problem-solving (Chen et al., 2023; Wang et al., 2024; Ma et al., 2024). LLMs often struggle to provide reliable and consistent answers to intricate scientific questions (Wang et al., 2024), necessitating the development of novel approaches to improve their reasoning capabilities in this context.

Multi-Model Collaboration and Role-Playing Previous studies have explored the benefits of role-playing in LLMs, demonstrating that assigning distinct roles can lead to more specialized and accurate outputs (Lu et al., 2024; Guan et al., 2024; Tao et al., 2024; Bhattacharyya et al., 2024). Additionally, collaborative frameworks where multiple models interact and discuss to reach a consensus have shown promise in improving the robustness of the generated solutions (Du et al., 2024; Lu et al., 2024; Sadler et al., 2024; Mehta et al., 2024; Figueras et al., 2023; Xiong et al., 2023). Considering the complexity and rigor of scientific research, more effective methods are needed to stimulate the optimal intelligence of multi-agent systems.

Large Language Models in Solving Scientific Problems Recent studies have explored the potential of LLMs in scientific problem-solving, including theorem proof (Dong et al., 2023; Song et al., 2024), hypothesis generation (Qi et al., 2023; Yang et al., 2024) and scientific discovery (Boiko et al., 2023; AI4Science and Quantum, 2023). However, the understanding and reasoning capabilities of LLMs in fundamental STEM(Science, Technology, Engineering, and Mathematics) domains remain underexplored (Wang et al., 2024; Ma et al., 2024). While LLMs exhibit impressive performance on high-level scientific tasks, their ability to grasp complex scientific concepts, engage in rigorous logical reasoning, and provide reliable solutions to domain-specific problems is still uncertain. These challenges necessitate a more nuanced approach to harnessing the full potential of LLMs.

3 Method: Simulating Expert Discussions with Multi-agent

We propose a novel approach called Simulating Expert Discussions with Multi-agent (SEDM) to enhance the scientific problem-solving capabilities of large language models (LLMs) by simulating expert discussions. The overall framework of our methodology is illustrated in Figure 2. We assign multiple LLMs with domain-specific expert roles and simulate a panel discussion among these experts on a given scientific problem. By analyzing and evaluating the consistency of the LLM experts' responses, we derive reliable solutions.

3.1 Role Assignment

In our proposed approach, we assign domain-specific expert roles to multiple LLMs to address a given scientific problem within a particular domain. This assignment of expert roles is motivated by the following rationale:

- **Fostering Collaboration and Consensus** Scientific progress often relies on collaboration and consensus-building among experts within the same domain. By assigning identical roles, we encourage LLMs to engage in simulated collaborative discussions, challenging each other's assumptions, reconciling differences, and ultimately converging towards a consensus solution.

- **Enhancing Reliability through Ensemble Methods** Despite being instances of the same LLM architecture, each individual model may exhibit variations in its outputs due to factors such as random initialization, stochastic sampling, or sensitivity to input perturbations. By employing an ensemble of multiple LLMs with identical roles, we can leverage the collective wisdom of the group, mitigating the impact of individual model instabilities and enhancing the overall reliability of the proposed solutions.

- **Exploring Diverse Reasoning Paths** While sharing the same domain knowledge and expertise, each LLM may explore different reasoning paths and problem-solving strategies when presented with the same scientific problem. Assigning identical roles allows us to capture and analyze these diverse reasoning paths, potentially uncovering novel insights or alternative approaches that a single LLM might overlook.

Through this approach, we create a simulated panel of domain-specific experts with shared expertise but diverse reasoning perspectives. This setup emulates the real-world dynamics of scientific discourse, where experts from the same field evaluate and build upon each other's work, ultimately advancing our understanding of complex scientific problems.

3.2 Expert Discussion Simulation

At the heart of our proposed methodology lies the simulation of a panel discussion among multiple LLMs, each assuming the role of a domain-specific expert within the same scientific field. The overall overview of expert discussion simulation phase is shown in Figure 3. This approach aims to leverage the collective knowledge and diverse perspectives of the LLMs to tackle complex scientific problems effectively. The simulation process encompasses the following key steps:

Problem Presentation The initial step involves presenting a well-defined scientific problem or inquiry to the panel of LLMs.

Individual Responses Upon receiving the problem, each LLM, operating within its assigned expert role, generates an independent response. This response is based on the LLM's knowledge and understanding of the specific sub-discipline or area of specialization it represents. By providing individual responses, the LLMs contribute their unique perspectives and insights to the problem-solving process, mimicking the diversity of opinions often encountered in real-world scientific discussions.

Response Analysis and Comparison Once all the LLMs have provided their individual responses, the next step involves collecting and analyzing these responses for consistency and complementarity. The analysis focuses on identifying areas of agreement and divergence among the LLMs' perspectives. High levels of agreement among the responses suggest a strong consensus and increased confidence in the proposed solution. Conversely, divergent viewpoints highlight areas that require further exploration, clarification, or synthesis, open-

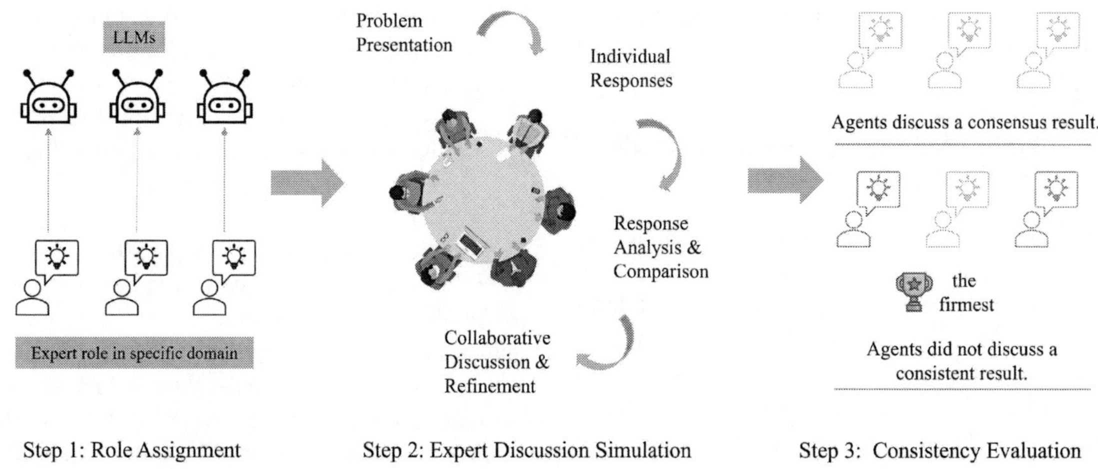

Figure 2: Framework of the SEDM (Simulated Expert Discussion with Multi-agent) approach to enhance LLM scientific problem-solving. Key steps: (1) Role Assignment of domain-specific experts to multiple LLMs; (2) Expert Discussion Simulation involving problem presentation, individual responses, response analysis, and collaborative discussion; (3) Consistency Evaluation - if consensus is reached, the agreed solution is adopted; otherwise, the solution of the most persistent expert (agent) is selected.

ing up opportunities for a more comprehensive understanding of the problem.

Collaborative Discussion and Refinement In cases where the initial responses reveal discrepancies or complementary insights, a collaborative discussion phase is initiated. During this phase, the LLMs engage in a simulated dialogue, exchanging their perspectives, challenging assumptions, and working towards reconciling any differences. This discussion process closely resembles the way experts within the same scientific domain would interact and collaborate in real-world settings, fostering a rigorous and iterative refinement of ideas. Through this iterative process of discussion, the LLMs aim to converge towards a more comprehensive and well-supported solution to the scientific problem at hand.

The simulated expert discussion within a specific domain, as outlined above, harnesses the collective knowledge and diverse perspectives of the LLMs to tackle complex scientific problems. By emulating the rigorous process of scientific inquiry, where ideas are scrutinized, refined, and synthesized through critical discourse among experts, our methodology aims to enhance the problem-solving capabilities of LLMs in scientific domains. This approach not only leverages the strengths of individual LLMs but also promotes a collaborative and iterative problem-solving process, ultimately leading to more reliable and comprehensive solutions to scientific challenges.

3.3 Consistency Evaluation

Upon completion of the expert discussion simulation, we conduct a consistency evaluation of the solutions proposed by the multiple LLMs assuming expert roles. This evaluation process is crucial for ensuring the reliability and robustness of the proposed solutions. Specifically, we employ the following strategies:

Consensus Determination When all experts reach a unanimous agreement during the discussion process, we consider that they have achieved consensus on the given problem. In such cases, we directly adopt the solution unanimously agreed upon by the experts as the final result. The attainment of consensus often indicates that the solution has undergone thorough discussion and argumentation, lending it higher credibility and reliability.

Maximum Discussion Round Limit Recognizing that expert discussions in the real world cannot continue indefinitely, we set a maximum number of discussion rounds for the expert deliberations. This limit serves to prevent the discussion process from entering an endless loop while also encouraging the experts to reach consensus or make decisions within a reasonable timeframe.

If the experts fail to reach complete agreement within the maximum number of discussion rounds, we resort to the following strategy: we select the solution proposed by the expert (agent) who most persistently defended their viewpoint throughout the discussion. The rationale behind this strategy is that

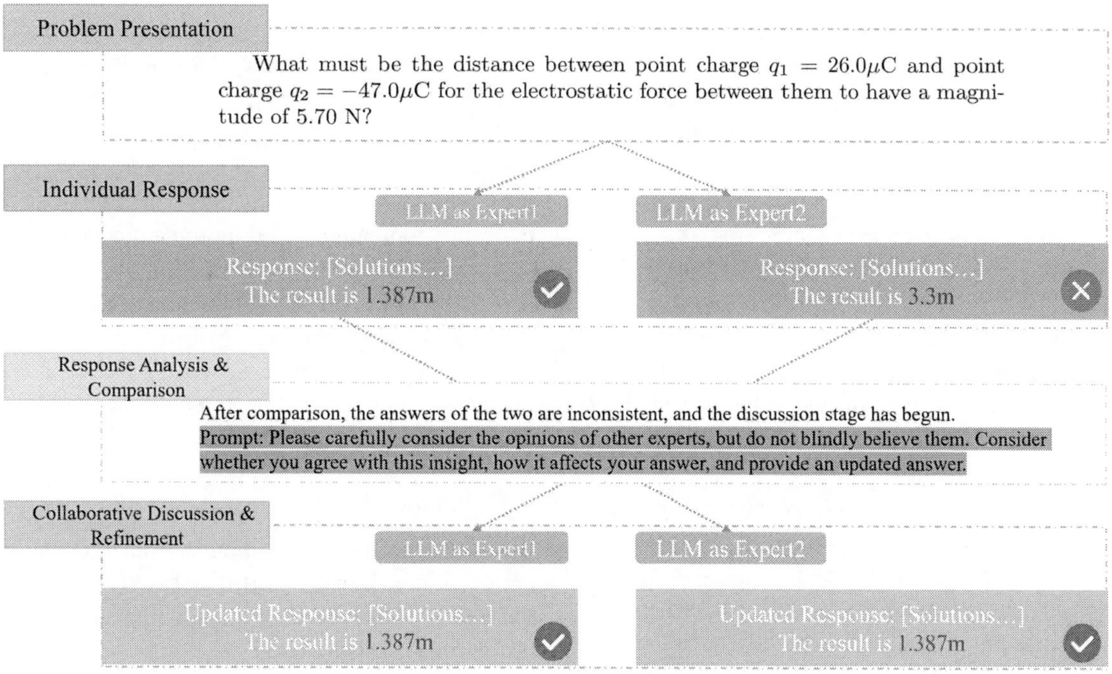

Figure 3: Overview of expert discussion simulation phase.

the expert who firmly maintains their stance likely possesses a deeper understanding of the problem and has provided more comprehensive arguments, rendering their proposed solution more convincing and reliable.

Discussion Convergence Analysis Although we establish a maximum number of discussion rounds, empirical evidence suggests that expert discussions often converge to consensus or a few primary viewpoints within a relatively small number of rounds. We conduct a convergence analysis of the discussion process, quantifying the frequency of achieving consensus or converging to main viewpoints at different round thresholds. Through extensive case studies, we observe that expert discussions typically reach consensus or converge to primary viewpoints within 2-3 rounds. This finding aligns with real-world expert discussion scenarios, demonstrating the effectiveness and practicality of our approach.

By employing these consistency evaluation strategies, we effectively synthesize the opinions of multiple experts to derive reliable and robust problem solutions. Moreover, by analyzing the convergence properties of the discussion process, we validate the efficacy of our method.

4 Experiment

4.1 Experimental Setup

Dataset In our experiment, we used the SciBench dataset (Wang et al., 2024), which is a comprehensive benchmark specifically designed to evaluate the scientific problem-solving ability of Large Language Models (LLMs). SciBench covers university level problems in various scientific disciplines, including mathematics, physics, and chemistry. This dataset includes open-ended questions from textbooks and open-ended questions from undergraduate exams, ensuring a rigorous evaluation of LLM's reasoning and computational skills. In this experiment, we use open-ended questions as testing. This dataset provides a solid foundation for testing and improving LLM's ability to solve problems in complex scientific environments.

Baseline To establish a baseline for our proposed multi-expert framework, we conducted experiments using two state-of-the-art LLMs: GPT-3.5 and GPT-4. Specifically, we utilized the gpt-3.5-turbo-0125 version for GPT-3.5 and the gpt-4-turbo version for GPT-4. For each model, we employed two query methods:

- Direct Querying: The scientific problem was directly presented to the LLM without any additional context or examples.

- Few-Shot Learning (Brown et al., 2020): We provided the LLM with a small set of representative examples of scientific problems and their solutions before presenting the target problem. This approach aims to prime the model with relevant context and improve its performance on the specific task.

4.2 Main Results

We evaluate the performance of our proposed Simulating Expert Discussions with Multi-agent (SEDM) approach against two baselines: direct querying of the LLM and few-shot learning. The experiments are conducted across three scientific domains: physics, chemistry, and mathematics. Each domain is further divided into subdomains, such as thermodynamics and classical mechanics for physics, to assess the model's performance on a diverse range of scientific problems. In the main experiment, we used the setting of 2 experts and 2 discussion rounds.

Table 1 presents the accuracy scores of the models on the test set. The results demonstrate that SEDM significantly outperforms the baselines across most domains and subdomains. For GPT-3.5, SEDM achieves an average accuracy of 33.25%, markedly higher than the 9.59% for Direct response and 9.60% for few-shot learning. Similarly, for GPT-4, SEDM attains an average accuracy of 57.18%, compared to 25.09% for Direct and 21.46% for few-shot.

However, it is important to note that SEDM does not always achieve the highest scores in every subdomain. For instance, in GPT-4's performance in statistics domain, the direct querying approach slightly outperforms SEDM. This may be attributed to the nature of statistical problems, which are often more standardized and formulaic compared to other subdomains. Many statistical problems can be solved by applying specific formulas or algorithms, which aligns well with the strengths of language models. Consequently, direct querying may be sufficient to handle these relatively standard problems.

Despite these few exceptions, SEDM consistently demonstrates robust performance improvements across the majority of subdomains, highlighting its effectiveness and adaptability in enhancing the problem-solving capabilities of LLMs. It is worth noting that the performance of few-shot learning is comparable to or slightly worse than direct querying. This may be due to the limited ability of the selected prompt examples to fully capture the diversity of the domain, leading to a decrease in the performance of few-shot learning.

The results also reveal some variation in performance across subdomains. For instance, in physics, the models achieve higher accuracy in fundamental concepts compared to thermodynamics and classical mechanics. This suggests that the complexity and specificity of the subdomain can influence the model's performance. Nevertheless, SEDM consistently outperforms the baselines in almost all subdomains, demonstrating its robustness and adaptability.

4.3 Further Analysis

Solution Quality In addition to evaluating the accuracy of the models, we also assess the quality of the generated solutions. We randomly sample 100 problems and evaluate the solutions using LLMs and human evaluation based on three criteria: (1) the correctness of the reasoning steps, (2) the clarity of the explanations, and (3) the appropriateness of the mathematical notations and symbols used. Each criterion was rated on a scale of 1 to 5, with 5 being the highest quality.

For the human evaluation, we employed three expert annotators. To ensure reliability, we calculated the inter-annotator agreement using Fleiss' kappa (Fleiss, 1971) for each of the three criteria:

- Correctness of reasoning steps: $\kappa = 0.71$
- Clarity of explanations: $\kappa = 0.62$
- Appropriateness of mathematical notations and symbols: $\kappa = 0.55$

The overall average kappa value was 0.63, indicating substantial agreement among the annotators.

The detailed prompts for LLM evaluation and the specific guidelines for human evaluation are provided in Appendix B. Table 2 presents the average quality scores for solutions from GPT-4. Compared to baseline, SEDM consistently achieves higher quality scores in both LLM and human evaluations. The solutions generated by SEDM demonstrate clearer reasoning steps, more coherent explanations, and more precise use of mathematical notations. This suggests that the multi-expert discussion framework not only improves the accuracy of the solutions but also enhances their overall quality and readability.

Subject		Physics			Chemistry				Math			Avg
		fund	thermo	class	quan	chemmc	atkins	matter	calc	stat	diff	
GPT-3.5	Direct	10.96	2.94	2.13	8.82	20.51	4.67	2.04	9.30	28.00	6.00	9.59
	Few Shot	8.22	1.49	0.00	11.76	15.38	5.61	4.08	13.95	26.67	**10.00**	9.60
	SEDM *	**40.85**	**36.36**	**25.00**	**30.30**	**55.26**	**37.14**	**17.02**	**38.10**	**44.44**	8.00	**33.25**
GPT-4	Direct	15.07	11.94	8.51	14.71	23.08	27.10	22.45	42.86	**56.00**	18.00	25.09
	Few Shot	26.03	5.97	12.77	17.65	30.77	15.87	12.24	33.33	49.33	8.00	21.46
	SEDM *	**81.69**	**27.27**	**37.50**	**57.58**	**81.58**	**59.05**	**53.19**	**78.57**	51.39	**44.00**	**57.18**

Table 1: The accuracy scores (%) of different baseline methods and our proposed SEDM approach across various scientific domains using GPT-3.5 and GPT-4 models under the setting of 2 experts and 2 discussion rounds. The best results for each subject are in **bold**.

Eval. Method	LLM Evaluation			Human Evaluation		
	(1)	(2)	(3)	(1)	(2)	(3)
Direct	3.20	3.40	3.80	4.00	4.25	4.25
SEDM *	4.20	3.60	4.60	4.75	4.25	4.50

Table 2: The average quality score of solutions from GPT-4 evaluated by LLMs and humans.

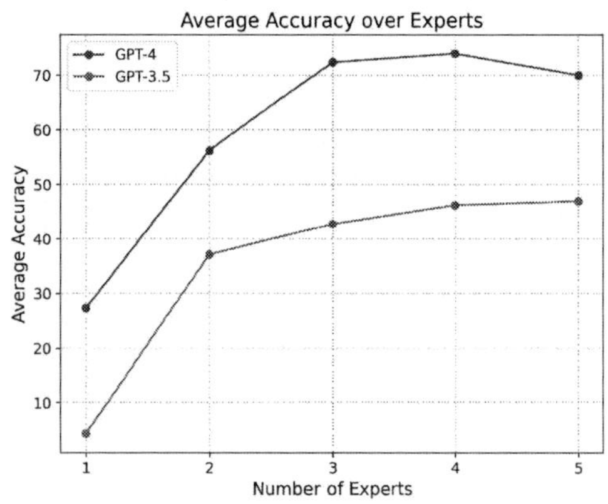

Figure 4: The relationship between the number of experts and the average accuracy of GPT-3.5 and GPT-4.

Number of Experts We investigate the impact of the number of experts in the panel on the performance of SEDM. We vary the number of experts from 2 to 5 and evaluate the accuracy of the generated solutions.Figure 4 shows the relationship between the number of experts and the average accuracy of GPT-3.5 and GPT-4. The results reveal that increasing the number of experts generally leads to higher accuracy. However, the performance gains diminish as the number of experts exceeds 4. This suggests that a panel of 2-4 experts strikes a balance between performance improvement and computational efficiency. Having too many experts may introduce redundancy and increase the computational overhead without significant performance benefits.

Number of Discussion Rounds We also investigate the impact of the number of discussion rounds on the performance of SEDM. We conducte experiments with varying numbers of discussion rounds, ranging from 1 to 5, and measure the accuracy of the generated solutions, as illustrated in Figure 5. The results indicate that increasing the number of discussion rounds generally improves the accuracy, but the performance gains plateau after 3 rounds. This suggests that 2-4 discussion rounds provide a good trade-off between performance and efficiency.

Ablation Study The ablation study results presented in Table 3 demonstrate the effectiveness of each component in our proposed SEDM framework. By comparing the performance of the full SEDM framework with its variants, we can gain insights into the contributions of the expert role assignment and the expert discussion components.

When the expert role assignment is removed, the performance of both GPT-3.5 and GPT-4 drops sig-

	GPT-3.5	GPT-4
w/o Expert role	11 / 100	42 / 100
w/o Expert discussion	17 / 100	55 / 100
Full SEDM*	**45** / 100	**87** / 100

Table 3: Ablation study results showing the effectiveness of each component in our proposed SEDM framework. We report the number of correctly answered questions out of 100 test samples. "w/o" denotes the removal of the corresponding component from the full SEDM framework.

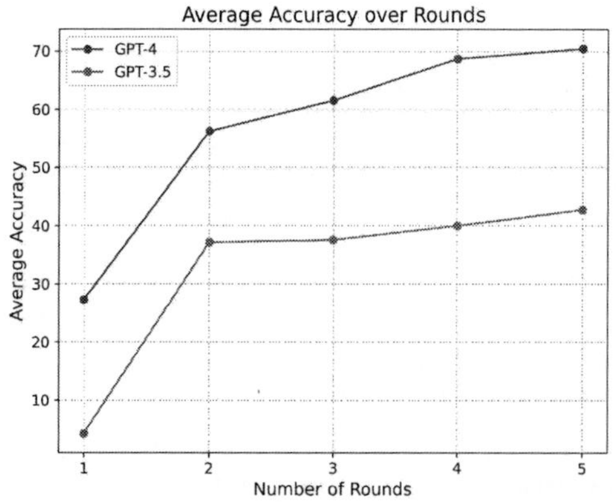

Figure 5: The relationship between the number of discussion rounds and the average accuracy of GPT-3.5 and GPT-4.

nificantly. GPT-3.5 achieves only 11 out of 100 correctly answered questions, while GPT-4 manages to answer 42 out of 100 questions correctly. This substantial decrease in performance highlights the importance of assigning domain-specific expert roles to the LLMs, as it enables them to provide more accurate and reliable responses to scientific inquiries.

Similarly, the removal of the expert discussion component also leads to a notable decline in performance. GPT-3.5 correctly answers 17 out of 100 questions, and GPT-4 achieves 55 out of 100 correct answers. This finding suggests that the collaborative discussion among the LLMs plays a crucial role in reaching a consensus and improving the overall accuracy of the system.

The ablation study provides strong evidence for the effectiveness of our proposed SEDM framework. By assigning domain-specific expert roles to LLMs and facilitating collaborative discussions among them, we can significantly enhance their performance in addressing complex scientific questions. This finding underscores the potential of our approach to advance the application of AI in scientific research, offering a more reliable and trustworthy solution for tackling scientific problems.

5 Conclusion

In this paper, we have introduced a novel approach called Simulating Expert Discussions with Multi-agent (SEDM) to enhance the scientific problem-solving capabilities of LLMs. By assigning domain-specific expert roles to multiple LLMs and simulating a panel discussion, our method leverages the collective knowledge and diverse perspectives of these models to tackle complex scientific problems effectively.

The proposed SEDM framework represents a significant step forward in harnessing the potential of LLMs for scientific problem-solving. By simulating expert discussions and leveraging the collective intelligence of multiple models, we can enhance the accuracy, reliability, and robustness of LLM-generated solutions. This approach opens up new avenues for applying artificial intelligence in scientific research, enabling more effective and trustworthy problem-solving.

6 Limitations

While the Simulating Expert Discussions with Multi-agent (SEDM) approach has shown promise in enhancing the scientific problem-solving capabilities of LLMs, several limitations warrant further investigation.

Firstly, the current study is limited to a subset of scientific domains, namely physics, chemistry, and mathematics. Future research should explore the generalizability of SEDM to a broader range of disciplines to assess its adaptability and effectiveness across diverse problem types and domain-specific challenges.

Secondly, the current implementation of SEDM employs fixed LLMs assuming expert roles within a specific domain. Although effective, this approach may not fully capture the complexity of real-world scientific collaborations. Future work could investigate more dynamic role assignment strategies, allowing for the inclusion of interdisciplinary experts to enrich discussions.

Acknowledgments

The authors thank all the anonymous reviewers for their valuable comments and constructive feedback. The authors acknowledge financial support from the National Social Science Fund of China (No. 23BTQ102). Xiaoqiu Le is the corresponding author.

References

Angus Addlesee. 2024. Grounding LLMs to in-prompt instructions: Reducing hallucinations caused by static pre-training knowledge. In *Proceedings of Safety4ConvAI: The Third Workshop on Safety for Conversational AI @ LREC-COLING 2024*, pages 1–7, Torino, Italia. ELRA and ICCL.

Microsoft Research AI4Science and Microsoft Azure Quantum. 2023. The impact of large language models on scientific discovery: a preliminary study using gpt-4. *Preprint*, arXiv:2311.07361.

Duarte Alves, Nuno Guerreiro, João Alves, José Pombal, Ricardo Rei, José de Souza, Pierre Colombo, and Andre Martins. 2023. Steering large language models for machine translation with finetuning and in-context learning. In *Findings of the Association for Computational Linguistics: EMNLP 2023*, pages 11127–11148, Singapore. Association for Computational Linguistics.

Abhidip Bhattacharyya, Martha Palmer, and Christoffer Heckman. 2024. ReCAP: Semantic role enhanced caption generation. In *Proceedings of the 2024 Joint International Conference on Computational Linguistics, Language Resources and Evaluation (LREC-COLING 2024)*, pages 13633–13649, Torino, Italia. ELRA and ICCL.

Daniil Boiko, Robert MacKnight, Ben Kline, and Gabe Gomes. 2023. Autonomous chemical research with large language models. *Nature*, 624:570–578.

Tom B. Brown, Benjamin Mann, Nick Ryder, Melanie Subbiah, Jared Kaplan, Prafulla Dhariwal, Arvind Neelakantan, Pranav Shyam, Girish Sastry, Amanda Askell, Sandhini Agarwal, Ariel Herbert-Voss, Gretchen Krueger, Tom Henighan, Rewon Child, Aditya Ramesh, Daniel M. Ziegler, Jeffrey Wu, Clemens Winter, Christopher Hesse, Mark Chen, Eric Sigler, Mateusz Litwin, Scott Gray, Benjamin Chess, Jack Clark, Christopher Berner, Sam McCandlish, Alec Radford, Ilya Sutskever, and Dario Amodei. 2020. Language models are few-shot learners. *Preprint*, arXiv:2005.14165.

Olena Burda-Lassen. 2023. Machine translation of folktales: small-data-driven and LLM-based approaches. In *Proceedings of the 2023 CLASP Conference on Learning with Small Data (LSD)*, pages 68–71, Gothenburg, Sweden. Association for Computational Linguistics.

Wenhu Chen, Ming Yin, Max Ku, Pan Lu, Yixin Wan, Xueguang Ma, Jianyu Xu, Xinyi Wang, and Tony Xia. 2023. TheoremQA: A theorem-driven question answering dataset. In *Proceedings of the 2023 Conference on Empirical Methods in Natural Language Processing*, pages 7889–7901, Singapore. Association for Computational Linguistics.

Qingxiu Dong, Li Dong, Ke Xu, Guangyan Zhou, Yaru Hao, Zhifang Sui, and Furu Wei. 2023. Large language model for science: A study on p vs. np. *Preprint*, arXiv:2309.05689.

Yilun Du, Shuang Li, Antonio Torralba, Joshua B. Tenenbaum, and Igor Mordatch. 2024. Improving factuality and reasoning in language models through multiagent debate.

Blanca Figueras, Irene Baucells, and Tommaso Caselli. 2023. Dynamic stance: Modeling discussions by labeling the interactions. In *Findings of the Association for Computational Linguistics: EMNLP 2023*, pages 6503–6515, Singapore. Association for Computational Linguistics.

Joseph L Fleiss. 1971. Measuring nominal scale agreement among many raters. *Psychological bulletin*, 76(5):378.

Yao Fu, Hao Peng, Ashish Sabharwal, Peter Clark, and Tushar Khot. 2023. Complexity-based prompting for multi-step reasoning. *Preprint*, arXiv:2210.00720.

Weihong Guan, Shi Feng, Daling Wang, Faliang Huang, Yifei Zhang, and Yuan Cui. 2024. Improving role-oriented dialogue summarization with interaction-aware contrastive learning. In *Proceedings of the 2024 Joint International Conference on Computational Linguistics, Language Resources and Evaluation (LREC-COLING 2024)*, pages 8913–8924, Torino, Italia. ELRA and ICCL.

Takeshi Kojima, Shixiang (Shane) Gu, Machel Reid, Yutaka Matsuo, and Yusuke Iwasawa. 2022. Large language models are zero-shot reasoners. In *Advances in Neural Information Processing Systems*, volume 35, pages 22199–22213. Curran Associates, Inc.

Philippe Laban, Wojciech Kryscinski, Divyansh Agarwal, Alexander Fabbri, Caiming Xiong, Shafiq Joty, and Chien-Sheng Wu. 2023. SummEdits: Measuring LLM ability at factual reasoning through the lens of summarization. In *Proceedings of the 2023 Conference on Empirical Methods in Natural Language Processing*, pages 9662–9676, Singapore. Association for Computational Linguistics.

Li-Chun Lu, Shou-Jen Chen, Tsung-Min Pai, Chan-Hung Yu, Hung-yi Lee, and Shao-Hua Sun. 2024. Llm discussion: Enhancing the creativity of large language models via discussion framework and role-play. *arXiv preprint arXiv:2405.06373*.

Yubo Ma, Zhibin Gou, Junheng Hao, Ruochen Xu, Shuohang Wang, Liangming Pan, Yujiu Yang, Yixin Cao, Aixin Sun, Hany Awadalla, and Weizhu Chen. 2024. Sciagent: Tool-augmented language models for scientific reasoning. *Preprint*, arXiv:2402.11451.

Nikhil Mehta, Milagro Teruel, Xin Deng, Sergio Figueroa Sanz, Ahmed Awadallah, and Julia Kiseleva. 2024. Improving grounded language understanding in a collaborative environment by interacting with agents through help feedback. In *Findings of the Association for Computational Linguistics: EACL 2024*, pages 1306–1321, St. Julian's, Malta. Association for Computational Linguistics.

OpenAI, Josh Achiam, Steven Adler, Sandhini Agarwal, Lama Ahmad, Ilge Akkaya, Florencia Leoni Aleman, Diogo Almeida, Janko Altenschmidt, Sam Altman, Shyamal Anadkat, Red Avila, Igor Babuschkin, Suchir Balaji, Valerie Balcom, Paul Baltescu, Haiming Bao, Mohammad Bavarian, Jeff Belgum, Irwan Bello, Jake Berdine, Gabriel Bernadett-Shapiro, Christopher Berner, Lenny Bogdonoff, Oleg Boiko,

Madelaine Boyd, Anna-Luisa Brakman, Greg Brockman, Tim Brooks, Miles Brundage, Kevin Button, Trevor Cai, Rosie Campbell, Andrew Cann, Brittany Carey, Chelsea Carlson, Rory Carmichael, Brooke Chan, Che Chang, Fotis Chantzis, Derek Chen, Sully Chen, Ruby Chen, Jason Chen, Mark Chen, Ben Chess, Chester Cho, Casey Chu, Hyung Won Chung, Dave Cummings, Jeremiah Currier, Yunxing Dai, Cory Decareaux, Thomas Degry, Noah Deutsch, Damien Deville, Arka Dhar, David Dohan, Steve Dowling, Sheila Dunning, Adrien Ecoffet, Atty Eleti, Tyna Eloundou, David Farhi, Liam Fedus, Niko Felix, Simón Posada Fishman, Juston Forte, Isabella Fulford, Leo Gao, Elie Georges, Christian Gibson, Vik Goel, Tarun Gogineni, Gabriel Goh, Rapha Gontijo-Lopes, Jonathan Gordon, Morgan Grafstein, Scott Gray, Ryan Greene, Joshua Gross, Shixiang Shane Gu, Yufei Guo, Chris Hallacy, Jesse Han, Jeff Harris, Yuchen He, Mike Heaton, Johannes Heidecke, Chris Hesse, Alan Hickey, Wade Hickey, Peter Hoeschele, Brandon Houghton, Kenny Hsu, Shengli Hu, Xin Hu, Joost Huizinga, Shantanu Jain, Shawn Jain, Joanne Jang, Angela Jiang, Roger Jiang, Haozhun Jin, Denny Jin, Shino Jomoto, Billie Jonn, Heewoo Jun, Tomer Kaftan, Łukasz Kaiser, Ali Kamali, Ingmar Kanitscheider, Nitish Shirish Keskar, Tabarak Khan, Logan Kilpatrick, Jong Wook Kim, Christina Kim, Yongjik Kim, Jan Hendrik Kirchner, Jamie Kiros, Matt Knight, Daniel Kokotajlo, Łukasz Kondraciuk, Andrew Kondrich, Aris Konstantinidis, Kyle Kosic, Gretchen Krueger, Vishal Kuo, Michael Lampe, Ikai Lan, Teddy Lee, Jan Leike, Jade Leung, Daniel Levy, Chak Ming Li, Rachel Lim, Molly Lin, Stephanie Lin, Mateusz Litwin, Theresa Lopez, Ryan Lowe, Patricia Lue, Anna Makanju, Kim Malfacini, Sam Manning, Todor Markov, Yaniv Markovski, Bianca Martin, Katie Mayer, Andrew Mayne, Bob McGrew, Scott Mayer McKinney, Christine McLeavey, Paul McMillan, Jake McNeil, David Medina, Aalok Mehta, Jacob Menick, Luke Metz, Andrey Mishchenko, Pamela Mishkin, Vinnie Monaco, Evan Morikawa, Daniel Mossing, Tong Mu, Mira Murati, Oleg Murk, David Mély, Ashvin Nair, Reiichiro Nakano, Rajeev Nayak, Arvind Neelakantan, Richard Ngo, Hyeonwoo Noh, Long Ouyang, Cullen O'Keefe, Jakub Pachocki, Alex Paino, Joe Palermo, Ashley Pantuliano, Giambattista Parascandolo, Joel Parish, Emy Parparita, Alex Passos, Mikhail Pavlov, Andrew Peng, Adam Perelman, Filipe de Avila Belbute Peres, Michael Petrov, Henrique Ponde de Oliveira Pinto, Michael, Pokorny, Michelle Pokrass, Vitchyr H. Pong, Tolly Powell, Alethea Power, Boris Power, Elizabeth Proehl, Raul Puri, Alec Radford, Jack Rae, Aditya Ramesh, Cameron Raymond, Francis Real, Kendra Rimbach, Carl Ross, Bob Rotsted, Henri Roussez, Nick Ryder, Mario Saltarelli, Ted Sanders, Shibani Santurkar, Girish Sastry, Heather Schmidt, David Schnurr, John Schulman, Daniel Selsam, Kyla Sheppard, Toki Sherbakov, Jessica Shieh, Sarah Shoker, Pranav Shyam, Szymon Sidor, Eric Sigler, Maddie Simens, Jordan Sitkin, Katarina Slama, Ian Sohl, Benjamin Sokolowsky, Yang Song, Natalie Staudacher, Felipe Petroski Such, Natalie Summers, Ilya Sutskever, Jie Tang, Nikolas Tezak, Madeleine B. Thompson, Phil Tillet, Amin Tootoonchian, Elizabeth Tseng, Preston Tuggle, Nick Turley, Jerry Tworek, Juan Felipe Cerón Uribe, Andrea Vallone, Arun Vijayvergiya, Chelsea Voss, Carroll Wainwright, Justin Jay Wang, Alvin Wang, Ben Wang, Jonathan Ward, Jason Wei, CJ Weinmann, Akila Welihinda, Peter Welinder, Jiayi Weng, Lilian Weng, Matt Wiethoff, Dave Willner, Clemens Winter, Samuel Wolrich, Hannah Wong, Lauren Workman, Sherwin Wu, Jeff Wu, Michael Wu, Kai Xiao, Tao Xu, Sarah Yoo, Kevin Yu, Qiming Yuan, Wojciech Zaremba, Rowan Zellers, Chong Zhang, Marvin Zhang, Shengjia Zhao, Tianhao Zheng, Juntang Zhuang, William Zhuk, and Barret Zoph. 2024. Gpt-4 technical report. *Preprint*, arXiv:2303.08774.

Long Ouyang, Jeff Wu, Xu Jiang, Diogo Almeida, Carroll L. Wainwright, Pamela Mishkin, Chong Zhang, Sandhini Agarwal, Katarina Slama, Alex Ray, John Schulman, Jacob Hilton, Fraser Kelton, Luke Miller, Maddie Simens, Amanda Askell, Peter Welinder, Paul Christiano, Jan Leike, and Ryan Lowe. 2022. Training language models to follow instructions with human feedback. *Preprint*, arXiv:2203.02155.

Biqing Qi, Kaiyan Zhang, Haoxiang Li, Kai Tian, Sihang Zeng, Zhang-Ren Chen, and Bowen Zhou. 2023. Large language models are zero shot hypothesis proposers. *Preprint*, arXiv:2311.05965.

Philipp Sadler, Sherzod Hakimov, and David Schlangen. 2024. Sharing the cost of success: A game for evaluating and learning collaborative multi-agent instruction giving and following policies. In *Proceedings of the 2024 Joint International Conference on Computational Linguistics, Language Resources and Evaluation (LREC-COLING 2024)*, pages 14770–14783, Torino, Italia. ELRA and ICCL.

Freda Shi, Mirac Suzgun, Markus Freitag, Xuezhi Wang, Suraj Srivats, Soroush Vosoughi, Hyung Won Chung, Yi Tay, Sebastian Ruder, Denny Zhou, Dipanjan Das, and Jason Wei. 2022. Language models are multilingual chain-of-thought reasoners. *Preprint*, arXiv:2210.03057.

Peiyang Song, Kaiyu Yang, and Anima Anandkumar. 2024. Towards large language models as copilots for theorem proving in lean. *Preprint*, arXiv:2404.12534.

Ben Swanson, Kory Mathewson, Ben Pietrzak, Sherol Chen, and Monica Dinalescu. 2021. Story centaur: Large language model few shot learning as a creative writing tool. In *Proceedings of the 16th Conference of the European Chapter of the Association for Computational Linguistics: System Demonstrations*, pages 244–256, Online. Association for Computational Linguistics.

Yufei Tao, Ameeta Agrawal, Judit Dombi, Tetyana Sydorenko, and Jung In Lee. 2024. ChatGPT roleplay dataset: Analysis of user motives and model naturalness. In *Proceedings of the 2024 Joint International Conference on Computational Linguistics, Language Resources and Evaluation (LREC-COLING 2024)*, pages 3133–3145, Torino, Italia. ELRA and ICCL.

Xiaoxuan Wang, Ziniu Hu, Pan Lu, Yanqiao Zhu, Jieyu Zhang, Satyen Subramaniam, Arjun R Loomba, Shichang Zhang, Yizhou Sun, and Wei Wang. 2024. Scibench: Evaluating college-level scientific problem-solving abilities of large language models.

Jason Wei, Xuezhi Wang, Dale Schuurmans, Maarten Bosma, brian ichter, Fei Xia, Ed Chi, Quoc V Le, and Denny Zhou. 2022. Chain-of-thought prompting elicits reasoning in large language models. In *Advances in Neural Information Processing Systems*, volume 35, pages 24824–24837. Curran Associates, Inc.

Kai Xiong, Xiao Ding, Yixin Cao, Ting Liu, and Bing Qin. 2023. Examining inter-consistency of large language models collaboration: An in-depth analysis via debate. In *Findings of the Association for Computational Linguistics: EMNLP 2023*, pages 7572–7590, Singapore. Association for Computational Linguistics.

Fangkai Yang, Pu Zhao, Zezhong Wang, Lu Wang, Bo Qiao, Jue Zhang, Mohit Garg, Qingwei Lin, Saravan Rajmohan, and Dongmei Zhang. 2023. Empower large language model to perform better on industrial domain-specific question answering. In *Proceedings of the 2023 Conference on Empirical Methods in Natural Language Processing: Industry Track*, pages 294–312, Singapore. Association for Computational Linguistics.

Zonglin Yang, Xinya Du, Junxian Li, Jie Zheng, Soujanya Poria, and Erik Cambria. 2024. Large language models for automated open-domain scientific hypotheses discovery. *Preprint*, arXiv:2309.02726.

Hattie Zhou, Azade Nova, Hugo Larochelle, Aaron Courville, Behnam Neyshabur, and Hanie Sedghi. 2022. Teaching algorithmic reasoning via in-context learning. *Preprint*, arXiv:2211.09066.

A Experiment Prompts

The prompts employed in this work for the Direct querying, few-shot learning, and Simulating Expert Discussions with Multi-agent (SEDM) are illustrated in Figures 6, 7, and 8.

B Evaluation Criteria and Prompts for Solution Quality Assessment

The prompts used for LLM evaluation and the guidelines provided for human evaluation of solution quality are presented in Figure 9 and Table 4 respectively. These criteria focus on assessing the correctness of reasoning steps, clarity of explanations, and appropriate use of mathematical notations.

Please provide answers to the following problem.

Question: [scientific problem]

Please reiterate the pure numerical answer at the end of the answer.

Figure 6: The prompt for Direct querying.

Criterion	1 (Poor)	2 (Fair)	3 (Good)	4 (Very Good)	5 (Excellent)
Correctness of Reasoning Steps	Most steps are incorrect or missing	Several major errors in reasoning	Minor errors in reasoning, but overall approach is correct	Reasoning is correct with very minor oversights	All reasoning steps are perfectly correct and complete
Clarity of Explanations	Explanations are confusing or absent	Explanations are unclear and difficult to follow	Explanations are mostly clear but some points are ambiguous	Explanations are clear with minor areas for improvement	Explanations are exceptionally clear, concise, and easy to understand
Appropriateness of Mathematical Notations and Symbols	Incorrect or missing notations and symbols throughout	Several major errors in notation and symbol usage	Minor errors in notation and symbol usage, but generally appropriate	Notations and symbols are correct with very minor inconsistencies	All mathematical notations and symbols are perfectly appropriate and consistently used

Table 4: Human Evaluation Guidelines for Scientific Problem Solutions.

Please provide answers to the following problem.

Question: [scientific problem]

Please reiterate the pure numerical answer at the end of the answer.

Task Example 1:
Question: The logistic model has been applied to the natural growth of the halibut population in certain areas of the Pacific Ocean. [12] Let y, measured in kilograms, be the total mass, or biomass, of the halibut population at time t. The parameters in the logistic equation are estimated to have the values $r = 0.71/$ year and $K = 80.5 \times 10^6$ kg. If the initial biomass is $y_0 = 0.25K$, find the biomass 2 years later.

Solution: It is convenient to scale the solution (11)

$$y = \frac{y_0 K}{y_0 + (K - y_0)\, e^{-rt}}$$

to the carrying capacity K; thus we write Eq. (11) in the form

$$\frac{y}{K} = \frac{y_0/K}{(y_0/K) + [1 - (y_0/K)]\, e^{-rt}}$$

Using the data given in the problem, we find that

$$\frac{y(2)}{K} = \frac{0.25}{0.25 + 0.75e^{-1.42}} \cong 0.5797.$$

Consequently, $y(2) \cong 46.7 \times 10^6$ kg.

Task Example 2:
Question: Find the bonding and antibonding Hückel molecular orbitals for ethene.

Solution: The equations for c_1 and c_2 associated with Equation

$$\begin{vmatrix} H_{11} - ES_{11} & H_{12} - ES_{12} \\ H_{12} - ES_{12} & H_{22} - ES_{22} \end{vmatrix} = 0$$

are

$$c_1(\alpha - E) + c_2\beta = 0 \quad \text{and} \quad c_1\beta + c_2(\alpha - E) = 0$$

For $E = \alpha + \beta$, either equation yields $c_1 = c_2$. Thus,

$$\psi_{\mathrm{b}} = c_1\,(2p_{z1} + 2p_{z2})$$

The value of c_1 can be found by requiring that the wave function be normalized. The normalization condition on ψ_π gives $c_1^2(1 + 2S + 1) = 1$. Using the Hückel assumption that $S = 0$, we find that $c_1 = 1/\sqrt{2}$.
Substituting $E = \alpha - \beta$ into either of the equations for c_1 and c_2 yields $c_1 = -c_2$, or

$$\psi_{\mathrm{a}} = c_1\,(2p_{z1} - 2p_{z2})$$

The normalization condition gives $c^2(1 - 2S + 1) = 1$, or $c_1 = 1/\sqrt{2}$.

Figure 7: The prompt for few-shot learning.

You are an expert in Physical Chemistry. Please provide answers to the following problem. Your response should be accurate, high-quality, and expertly written.

Question: [scientific problem]

Please reiterate the pure numerical answer at the end of the answer.

These are the opinions from other experts:
One expert response:[One expert response]
One expert response:[One expert response]
...

Please carefully consider the opinions of other experts, but do not blindly believe them. Consider whether you agree with this insight, how it affects your answer, and provide an updated answer.

Figure 8: The prompt for Simulating Expert Discussions with Multi-agent.

Please evaluate the quality of the following solution to the given scientific problem, on a scale of 1-5 (with 5 being the highest) for each of these criteria:
1. Correctness of the reasoning steps
2. Clarity of the explanations
3. Appropriateness of the mathematical notation and symbols used
Provide a score from 1-5 for each criterion, along with a brief justification for each score.

Scientific problem: [scientific problem]

Solution: [solution]

Figure 9: The prompt for LLM evaluation of solution quality.

An Analysis of Tasks and Datasets in Peer Reviewing

Moritz Staudinger[1] **Wojciech Kusa**[1,2] **Florina Piroi**[1] **Allan Hanbury**[1]
[1]TU Wien, Vienna, Austria
[2]Allegro, Warsaw, Poland
{moritz.staudinger,wojciech.kusa,florina.piroi,allan.hanbury}@tuwien.ac.at

Abstract

Taking note of the current challenges of the peer review system, this paper inventories the research tasks for analysing and possibly automating parts of the reviewing process, like matching submissions with a reviewer's domain of expertise. For each of these tasks we list their associated datasets, analysing their quality in terms of available documentation of creation and use. Building up on this, we give a set of recommendations to take into account when collecting and releasing data.

1 Introduction

Peer Reviewing is a vital part of academic integrity since as early as 1665, when Henry Oldenburg founded the Philosophical Transactions of the Royal Society and established the concept of reviewing the work of others (Kachooei and Ebrahimzadeh, 2022). Since then, the concept of peer review has remained largely unchanged, and nearly every journal has adopted it to select the best publications to publish. In recent decades, peer reviewing has become more of a burden for various reasons, like the overwhelming number of article submissions to review, their often less than optimal quality of content, lack of time to keep up with the majority of published research, or the fact that reviewing is voluntary and researchers find they have less time to review other work.

Technological advances that allow to share research and cooperate worldwide combined with the increasing number of researchers have caused a dramatic increase in the research published daily. The availability of Large Language Models (LLMs) has in fact simplified some tasks of the scientific writing process, like proof reading or text reformulation. This means that the time from idea to written research is significantly shorter. In the Computer Science domain, the number of publications over the last 10 years (2014–2023) has increased dramatically, submissions to ACL have increased sevenfold, and submissions to NeurIPS eight-fold[1].

Accounting for these factors, it is harder to find sufficient numbers of reviewers for such conferences. In 2016, about 33% of the NeurIPS reviewers were PhD students (Shah et al., 2018), a percentage that is most likely higher today. The outcome is that there are more inexperienced researchers that have to review larger numbers of submissions, eventually leading to reviews of lower quality.

In recent years, there are efforts to automate and optimize the different peer review steps to lighten the load of the reviewers, area chairs, and programme committees[2]. Researchers interested in this domain have defined research tasks and collected data to address them.

In this work, we make an inventory of tasks and datasets associated with Peer Review Automation and Optimization, and give recommendations on how to collect and publish such datasets. Without claiming that our work is exhaustive, we see it as a necessary contribution to this field. We examine the available datasets, the tasks they have been used or created for, discussing use cases and automation tasks.This work complements the very recently published Dagstuhl Proceedings (Kuznetsov et al., 2024), and the analyses in Drori and Te'eni (2024) or Lin et al. (2023a).

The paper is structured as follows: Section 2 gives an account of the tasks and their datasets in the Peer Review Analysis domain. Section 3 shows the overlaps between various datasets. Section 4 discusses some recommendations on the creation of datasets in the Peer Review domain. Section 5 comments on the current advances in this domain, concluding with Section 6.

[1]`https://github.com/lixin4ever/Conference-Acceptance-Rate`, (Access: May 2024)

[2]A description of these roles is available at `https://aclrollingreview.org/reviewing`

Proceedings of the Fourth Workshop on Scholarly Document Processing (SDP 2024), pages 257–268
August 16, 2024 ©2024 Association for Computational Linguistics

2 Datasets and Tasks

In our effort to understand the research challenges in the scientific peer reviewing domain we analyzed 53 datasets that contain peer reviews. For each of them, mostly created in the last 5 years, we looked at the research tasks for which these sets were used.

Datasets: Of these datasets, 37 cover publications that are in the ML and NLP scientific domains, obtained from the OpenReview portal[3], 6 are in the NLP domain and obtained from ACL Rolling Review[4], 5 datasets cover multiple domains and journals, 3 obtained from F1000[5] and 2 from PeerJ[6]. In Tables 1 to 8 we use the following abbreviations to indicate the source of the collected reviews: OR (OpenReview), ACL (ACL Rolling Review), CO (CoNLL and COLING), F (F1000 Journal), PJ (PeerJ), RS (ShitMyReviewerSays), and SG for self gathered data.

Though most of the datasets can be used for more than one task, in our work we choose to assign them to the task they were used for at their creation time. What we observed is that most of the researchers in this domain opt to create their own datasets from scratch using the OpenReview API, instead of using one of the many available datasets. This affects the reproducibility and comparability of research results, as not all datasets are publicly available or well documented to foster their reuse.

Tasks: Reviews can be looked at with different research aims in mind. Earlier work (Cho, 2008), for example, analyzed the helpfulness of student reviews, while more recent work looks at various aspects of peer reviewing, like Discourse Analysis (Kennard et al., 2022; Ruggeri et al., 2023), Peer Review Quality (Verma et al., 2023; Ghosal et al., 2022b; Bharti et al., 2023) or meta review generation (Chen et al., 2023; Ridenour et al., 2022).

In the following we will discuss the most common tasks and datasets for peer reviewing.

2.1 Review Analysis

Tasks grouped under this title aim to understand how reviews impact the submissions they were written for, aiming to detect biases in scoring, for example. For this area we identified three datasets (Table 1). The first one listed is used to look at how review scores for submissions to ICLR 2017-2022 affect their acceptance rate and their future citations (Wang et al., 2023). The second listed dataset was used in research that looked at peer reviews for journal submissions in the medical domain (BMC, BMJ, PLOS Medicine), examining their length and quality (Geldsetzer et al., 2023). The "ICLR Database" (Zhang et al., 2022) has been used in research that analysed fairness disparities in the review process and the geographical and institutional distribution of submissions.

Dataset	Year	Public	Origin
Wang et al. (2023)	2023	Yes	OR
Geldsetzer et al. (2023)	2023	Partly	
ICLR Database (Zhang et al., 2022)	2022	Yes	OR

Table 1: Datasets used in Review Analysis tasks.

2.2 Reviewer Assignment

In content preparatory phases of a conference, submissions are assigned to reviewers, ideally, based on their experience and interests. Most often, this is done via a bidding process, after which reviewers get assigned papers to review, according to their bids. This bidding process is, nevertheless, prone to manipulation, such as reviewers either voting to review submissions from their friends and close colleagues (choosing to grade them highly) or, when having sent in submissions, bidding to review similar submissions to their own, then negatively scoring them to improve their own submission acceptance chances, as the dataset (Jecmen et al., 2023) and research in Jecmen et al. (2024) demonstrate. To avoid this kind of malicious bidding, one possibility is to automatically match submissions to reviewers. Two further datasets created to investigate the effectiveness of such matching and, at the same time, to analyse the impact of malicious bidding are listed in Table 2.

The dataset and the method introduced by Stelmakh et al. (2020) detect malicious behavior at the meta-review level. To evaluate different methods of fair assignment of reviewers, Stelmakh et al. (2023) created a gold-level dataset on the self-reported expertise of reviewers for given publications.

Dataset	Year	Public	Origin
Malicious Bidding (Jecmen et al., 2023)	2023	Yes	SG
Reviewer-Paper-Match (Stelmakh et al., 2023)	2023	Yes	SG
Stelmakh et al. (2020)	2020	Yes	SG

Table 2: Datasets used in Reviewer Assignment tasks.

[3]https://openreview.net/
[4]https://aclrollingreview.org
[5]https://f1000research.com/
[6]https://peerj.com/

2.3 Score and Acceptance Prediction

To ease decision making, reviewers are asked to numerically score the different aspects of a submission, such as *Soundness, Presentation, Contribution*, and give an *Overall Score*. These scores are then used by area chairs to decide on the acceptance of a submission, and to formulate their meta-review. Fernandes and Vaz-de Melo (2023, 2022) analyzed the *Review Score Prediction (RSP)* and the *Paper Decision Prediction (PDP)* tasks, by evaluating models on two self-mined datasets of ICLR conference submissions (Table 3). The two datasets mainly introduced in their research differ in the number of reviews (14,459 vs 18,170) in them. In their work, they trained models on reviews, to predict RSP and PDP values on Submission-Review tuples. This was similar to the dataset and prediction task, proposed by Kang et al. (2018), who created one of the first Peer Review datasets, to allow score prediction as well as review generation.

Liu et al. (2023b) conducted a study on the willingness of reviewers to change their scores after the author rebuttal and revision phases. Specifically, they conducted a randomized controlled trial on 108 participants to find under which conditions reviewers tend to change their original scores. With PEERAssist, Bharti et al. (2021) explored score prediction with a deep neural architecture, and outperformed a similar architecture using sentiment analysis (Ghosal et al., 2019). Ribeiro et al. (2021) used a private dataset of two non-disclosed conferences to perform RSP, PDP, and sentiment analysis to extract review polarities. Datasets that tackle these tasks are listed in Table 3.

Dataset	Year	Public	Origin
Fernandes and Vaz-de Melo (2023)	2023	Yes	OR
ReviewerAnchoring (Liu et al., 2023b)	2023	Yes	OR
Fernandes and Vaz-de Melo (2022)	2022	Yes	OR
PEERAssist (Bharti et al., 2021)	2021	Yes	OR
Ribeiro et al. (2021)	2021	No	
PeerRead (Kang et al., 2018)	2018	Yes	OR,ACL,CO

Table 3: Score and Acceptance Prediction datasets.

2.4 Revision, Dialogue, Rebuttal Analysis

Some peer review processes include a dialogue between the authors and the reviewers, a dialogue with visible effects on the final version of a publication. Analyzing differences between consequent submission versions as well as the dialogue among reviewers or between reviewers and authors is, therefore, of interest. Having access to such information allow experiments on predicting changes over time or finding disagreements between different parties. Table 4 lists the peer review datasets used for approaching any of these tasks.

Among the datasets that investigate the differences between submission versions we mention CASIMIR (Jourdan et al., 2024), ARIES (D'Arcy et al., 2023), and arXivEdits (Jiang et al., 2022). The CASIMIR collection contains 3.7 million sentence pairs, from different submission revisions. A possible use case is the analysis of differences between revisions and prediction necessary revisions. The ARIES dataset has been created for the task where revised submissions are annotated to trace the edits back to the reviewer comments. arXivEdits does not contain reviews, but a set of 751 arXiv publications with revision history and sentence alignment across multiple paper revisions.

Datasets were created with the aim to understand and classify the arguments and disagreements made in the reviews, like APE (Argument Pair Extraction) (Cheng et al., 2020) and the AMPERE dataset (Hua et al., 2019). The APE dataset contains 4,764 argument pairs from the review-rebuttal phases, while the AMPERE dataset contains proposition and argument type annotations, aiming to answer research questions on argument classification. In the same direction, Singh et al. (2021) analyzed peer reviews looking at discussion comparisons, to better understand the factors that affect the acceptance decisions. Another dataset that explores disagreements between reviewer comments is ContraSciView (Kumar et al., 2023), a dataset of around 28,000 annotated review pairs, if they agree or contradict each other. They further proposed a model to detect contradictory statements in Peer Reviews. Finally, here, we note the ArgSciChat dataset (Ruggeri et al., 2023) containing argumentative dialogues, argumentative and exploratory questions and answers for 20 papers in the NLP domain.

Rebuttal strategies are of interest to researchers, with data collected for and work looking into rebuttal generation based on reviewers' comments and evaluations (the Jiu-Jitsu dataset (Purkayastha et al., 2023)). Huang et al. (2023) conducted an empirical study on ICLR papers, to detect the most common rebuttal strategies and predict the changes in review scores before and after the rebuttal phase. Similarly, DISAPERE (DIscourse Structure in Academic PEer REview) (Kennard et al., 2022) is a dataset of 20,000 labeled review-rebuttal sentences combinations, to analyze the interpretation of reviews and response strategies. ReAct (Choudhary et al., 2021) is a dataset that falls into this group (rebuttal and revision strategy support). The authors annotated review sentences such that, on one side, review recommendation can be quickly classified into actionable (possible to answer in a revision), and on the other side the revision action can be classified by finer-grained types, like *Suggestion, Question,* or *Disagreement.*

Dataset	Year	Public	Origin
CASIMIR (Jourdan et al., 2024)	2024	Yes	OR
Huang et al. (2023)	2023	No	OR
Jiu-Jitsu (Purkayastha et al., 2023)	2023	Yes	OR
ARIES (D'Arcy et al., 2023)	2023	Yes	OR
ArgSciChat (Ruggeri et al., 2023)	2023	Yes	SG
ContraSciView (Kumar et al., 2023)	2023	Yes	OR
arXivEdits (Jiang et al., 2022)	2022	Yes	
DISAPERE (Kennard et al., 2022)	2022	Yes	OR
COMPARE (Singh et al., 2021)	2021	Yes	OR
ReAct (Choudhary et al., 2021)	2021	Yes	OR
APE (Cheng et al., 2020)	2020	Yes	OR
AMPERE (Hua et al., 2019)	2019	Yes	OR, ACL

Table 4: Datasets for Revision, Dialogue and Rebuttal analysis and prediction.

2.5 Review Generation

While review generation may solve some of the reviewing issues, such as speeding up the academic review process or generating high quality reviews, it may also introduce new threats into the academic review process. For example, authors could tune their submissions so that automated review models would accept them.

Table 5 shows a list of datasets suitable for review generation tasks. The first model for automatic review generation is ReviewRobot (Wang et al., 2020), trained on data from OpenReview combined with multiple knowledge graphs to obtain domain knowledge to conduct reviews. In 2022 Yuan et al. (2022) published their ASAP-Review dataset and a model for review generation, but found that their model is less constructive and less factual then human-written reviews. Another dataset published for researchers to work on the generation of reviews and the prediction of scoring results is the ORB dataset (Szumega et al., 2023). The dataset is, though, not well documented.

With every new LLM release, researchers make use of them to generate reviews. One dataset to enable their use is, for example, the Review-Revision Multiple-Choice Questions (RR-MCQ) dataset, that allows to have a quick assessment on LLM performance in the scientific review domain (Zhou et al., 2024). Similarly, Liu and Shah (2023) created a dataset to identify errors in computer science publications, where they manually modified the publications to contain factual inaccuracies.

Kuznetsov et al. (2022) looked into assisting the peer review process providing several datasets for tasks like review generation, pragmatic tagging, or score prediction. The Yes-Yes-Yes dataset (Dycke et al., 2022) contains review from the ACL Rolling Review, 2021, and, later, the same authors created F1000RD (Kuznetsov et al., 2022), the first multidomain corpus of peer reviews of the F1000Research platform. These datasets were combined and released later (Dycke et al., 2023a). Based on the F1000RD dataset, a Pragmatic Tagging dataset was released for the PragTag Shared-Task (Dycke et al., 2023b).

Dataset	Year	Public	Origin
RR-MCQ (Zhou et al., 2024)	2024	Yes	OR
NLPEER (Dycke et al., 2023a)	2023	Yes	ACL,CO,F
PragTag (Dycke et al., 2023b)	2023	Yes	F
ORB (Szumega et al., 2023)	2023	Yes	OR
ReviewerGPT (Liu and Shah, 2023)	2023	Partly	OR
Yes-Yes-Yes (Dycke et al., 2023a)	2022	Yes	ACL
F1000RD (Kuznetsov et al., 2022)	2022	Yes	F
ASAP-Review (Yuan et al., 2022)	2022	Yes	OR
ReviewRobot (Wang et al., 2020)	2020	Yes	OR

Table 5: Datasets for Review Generation.

2.6 Metareview Generation

Writing metareviews is a task performed by Area Chairs, who read through all the reviews for a submission, check on disagreements between them, and provide a summary of the reviews with a final decision. Table 6 lists the datasets used in research on metareview analysis and generation.

Sun et al. (2024b) created an own peer review dataset, covering five years of review data from OpenReview, and trained a model on it to generate metareview texts. PeerSum (Li et al., 2023) is a different dataset for metareview generation, which features explicit conflicting information in source documents that the meta-reviewers have to handle. ORSUM (Zeng et al., 2023) is a corpus for scientific opinion summarization, which uses a undisclosed dataset from 39 conferences and workshops that published their peer reviews on OpenReview. The MOPRD (Multidsciplinary Open Peer Review Dataset) (Lin et al., 2023b) dataset was created to enable metareview generation, editorial decision prediction, author rebuttal generation, and scientometric analysis of papers from multiple disciplines.

It is composed of paper metadata, manuscripts of the initial submission and multiple revisions, review comments, meta-reviews, author rebuttal letters, and editorial decisions of papers from Biology, Chemistry, Computer Science, Environment and Medicine published on PeerJ. Wu et al. (2022) constructed a Peer Review and Rebuttal Counter-Arguments (PRRCA) dataset, which contains both the reviews, and the authors responses to model the peer review evaluation process.

The Meta-Review Dataset (MReD) (Shen et al., 2022) is a sentence-level annotated dataset of 23,675 reviews and their corresponding 7,089 meta-reviews. Each sentence is categorized into one of nine categories (abstract, strength, weakness, rating summary, area chair disagreement, rebuttal process, suggestion, decision, and miscellaneous) to then generate the meta-reviews based on these sentences.

Dataset	Year	Public	Origin
MetaWriter (Sun et al., 2024b)	2024	No	OR
PeerSum (Li et al., 2023)	2023	Yes	OR
ORSUM (Zeng et al., 2023)	2023	Yes	OR
MOPRD (Lin et al., 2023b)	2023	No	PJ
PRRCA (Wu et al., 2022)	2022	Yes	OR
MReD (Shen et al., 2022)	2022	Yes	OR

Table 6: Overview of Metareview Datasets.

2.7 Quality Analysis

Analyzing reviews in scientific papers can help to measure the helpfulness of the conducted peer review, the politeness or harshness of the peer reviewer, the reviewer confidence on a given topic, or the reviewer disagreement. Research in this area aims to detect and measure quality issues in conducted reviews. Table 7 presents a list of datasets for quality analysis of peer reviews.

The datasets in this subsection are used in, roughly seen, two types of tasks. One is classifying the reviews by detecting politeness levels and harshness (e.g., PolitePEER in Bharti et al. (2023) or Verma et al. (2022)), and detecting review polarities (Wang and Wan, 2018). The other task is exploring the content of the reviews from different argumentative points of view, in order to detect disagreement between reviewers and scoring differences between reviewers and submission versions (Chakraborty et al., 2020; Gao et al., 2019), or to estimate the review helpfulness by checking its thoroughness (Severin et al., 2023) and detecting suggestions for improvement to the submission authors (Pfütze et al., 2022), finding arguments in peer reviews as in AMSR (Argument Mining in Scientific Reviews) (Fromm et al., 2021).

A combination of the two types of tasks is seen in ReviVal (Verma et al., 2023), in which the authors use the dataset to grade reviews based on *Exhaustiveness* and *Strength* of the review texts, or in SubstanReview (Guo et al., 2023), in which the authors look at substantiation levels of reviews by verifying that subjective statements (claims) are backed up by justifications (evidence). HedgePeer (Ghosal et al., 2022b) provides a dataset for uncertainty detection in peer reviews by annotating the review comments in terms of hedge cues and spans. Finally, the dataset introduced in by Ghosal et al. (2022a) aims to facilitate the analysis of the reviewers' confidence on certain sections and aspects of the paper and then use those insights to investigate further the quality of peer reviews.

Dataset	Year	Public	Origin
PolitePEER (Bharti et al., 2023)	2023	Yes	OR,RS
ReviVal (Verma et al., 2023)	2023	No	OR
SubstanReview (Guo et al., 2023)	2023	Yes	ACL,CO
Severin et al. (2023)	2023	Yes	
HedgePeer (Ghosal et al., 2022b)	2022	Yes	OR
Ghosal et al. (2022a)	2022	Yes	OR
Pfütze et al. (2022)	2022	No	SG
Verma et al. (2022)	2022	Yes	OR,RS
AMSR(Fromm et al., 2021)	2021	Yes	OR
Chakraborty et al. (2020)	2020	No	OR
ACL-2018(Gao et al., 2019)	2019	Yes	ACL
Wang and Wan (2018)	2018	No	OR

Table 7: Review Quality Analysis datasets.

2.8 Citation Prediction

An interesting task, which is not directly associated with the Peer Review domain, is to predict the popularity and citations of accepted publications based on their reviews. To our knowledge, there currently are two datasets on this topic (see Table 8). The CiteTracked (Plank and Dalen, 2019) dataset links reviews from the NeurIPS conference with their citations to predict the impact of the submissions. Li et al. (2019) performed a similar study on ICLR reviews, but provided further data and metadata to their models, such as information about the authors.

Dataset	Year	Public	Origin
CiteTracked (Plank and Dalen, 2019)	2019	No	OR
Citation-Count-Pred (Li et al., 2019)	2019	Yes	OR

Table 8: Citation Prediction Datasets.

3 Dataset Similarities and Discrepancies

In the last years, OpenReview has become the primary data source for review-related tasks, and, therefore, many of the published datasets overlap. We look more closely into the datasets which, among others, contain the ICLR conference review data (35 sets, see Table 9).

We detected several inconsistencies across these datasets coming from the same primary source (here, OpenReview). One of them is in the number of reviews for one year of the conference (2017). Namely, Kang et al. (2018); Verma et al. (2023) report 427 submissions, while Wang and Wan (2018); Zhang et al. (2022) and Chakraborty et al. (2020) reported 490 and 491 submissions (the latter difference possibly being a reporting error on the workshop track). Later, Bharti et al. (2021) cleaned this dataset by removing duplicates or empty reviews and reports 354 qualitative reviews for ICLR 2017. These differences can be due to authors agreeing to publish their submissions later than the dataset creation time, not filtering out duplicates, including workshop submissions[7], or, more likely, are due to reporting inaccuracies. We found, for example, that Zhang et al. (2022) reported 47 workshop papers. Some studies excluded data due to poor quality or availability issues (Fernandes and Vaz-de Melo, 2023; Cheng et al., 2020; Chakraborty et al., 2020), while other studies avoid any kind of reporting on data quality and filtering.

Most of the datasets were extended with annotations to allow the evaluation of the conducted experiments. However, the number of annotations is rather small (in the hundreds), and do not follow a common structure, to allow the integration of multiple datasets and the interchangeability of datasets. While many of the datasets contain several hundred annotated sentences or reviews, such as D'Arcy et al. (2023) and Zhou et al. (2024); others, like Kumar et al. (2023) and Jourdan et al. (2024) annotated larger amounts of data. The ASAP-Review dataset was extended by manually annotating 8,582 publications with sentence level labels on sentiment and aspect categories (Kumar et al., 2023; Yuan et al., 2022). Jourdan et al. (2024) automatically aligned more than 3.7 million sentence pairs for revision analysis and labeled the most likely intention behind each edit.

[7]Workshop submissions are different from the main conference submissions as they are often reviewed more leniently than conference submissions.

Furthermore, different conferences use different review guidelines and numerical scoring scales, which can lead to biases if these conferences are combined. For example, ICTIR allows reviewers to score papers on a scale from -3 to 3, while NeurIPS uses a scale from 1 to 10.

4 Guidelines for Dataset Publication

As is obvious from the previous sections, the number of datasets recently published in the area of scientific peer review analysis is already considerable, although their re-use is impeded by the non-transparent way in which the data was collected. Therefore, we advocate for the adherence to data creation and publication guidelines such that their reuse is facilitated. Making sure that such datasets are findable, that they are well documented, and additionally, that machine-readable meta-data about them is available are ways to contribute towards their reuse. The current list of available datasets published following the above-mentioned Dagstuhl seminar[8] is a first step toward achieving this, however incomplete or lacking machine-interpretable data and meta-data. Some of the recommendations we make in the following subsections are, in fact, aligning with the FAIR principles for data sharing[9].

Furthermore, whenever possible, we recommend researchers to describe their datasets through appropriate metadata schema[10].

4.1 Dataset Reuse

As discussed in the previous section, there are many overlaps between existing datasets. Although existing datasets may not fit all research questions, there are several datasets targeting the same task that overlap significantly (Shen et al., 2022; Zeng et al., 2023; Sun et al., 2024b). Therefore, an obvious recommendation is to investigate existing datasets for their appropriateness to the task at hand. Ideally, such datasets are visible to search portals like DataCite[11] or OpenAire[12]. Overview studies like our work or Kuznetsov et al. (2024) are for now an alternative. If necessary these datasets should be extended instead of creating a new dataset from similar underlying sources.

[8]https://github.com/OAfzal/nlp-for-peer-review

[9]FAIR: Findable, Accessible, Interoperable, Re-usable https://www.gofair.foundation/interpretation

[10]E.g. schema.org/docs/data-and-datasets.html

[11]https://datacite.org/

[12]https://www.openaire.eu/

	ICLR								
Dataset	**2013-2016**	**2017**	**2018**	**2019**	**2020**	**2021**	**2022**	**2023**	**Ann.**
Kang et al. (2018)		✓							
Wang and Wan (2018)		✓	✓						✓
Hua et al. (2019)		✓	✓						✓
Li et al. (2019)	✓	✓							
Cheng et al. (2020)	✓(-2015)	✓	✓	✓	✓				✓
Chakraborty et al. (2020)		✓	✓	✓					✓
Wang et al. (2020)		✓	✓	✓	✓				✓
Singh et al. (2021)		✓	✓	✓	✓				✓
Choudhary et al. (2021)			✓						✓
Bharti et al. (2021)		✓	✓	✓	✓				
Fromm et al. (2021)				✓	✓				✓
Ghosal et al. (2022a)			✓						✓
Kennard et al. (2022)				✓	✓				✓
Shen et al. (2022)			✓	✓	✓	✓			✓
Yuan et al. (2022)		✓	✓	✓	✓				✓
Fernandes and Vaz-de Melo (2022)				✓	✓	✓			
Wu et al. (2022)		✓	✓	✓	✓	✓			✓
Verma et al. (2022)			✓						✓
Zhang et al. (2022)		✓	✓	✓	✓	✓	✓		
Ghosal et al. (2022b)			✓						✓
Bharti et al. (2023)	?	?	?	?	?	?			✓
Kumar et al. (2023)		✓	✓	✓	✓				✓
Szumega et al. (2023)	?	?	✓	✓	✓	✓			
Wang et al. (2023)		✓	✓	✓	✓	✓	✓		
Fernandes and Vaz-de Melo (2023)			✓	✓		✓			
Li et al. (2023)			✓	✓	✓	✓	✓		✓
Zeng et al. (2023)	?	?	?	?	?	?	?		✓
Huang et al. (2023)							✓		
Purkayastha et al. (2023)			✓	✓	✓				✓
Verma et al. (2023)		✓	✓	✓					✓
D'Arcy et al. (2023)	?	?	?	?	?	?	?		✓
Liu et al. (2023a)							✓		
Jourdan et al. (2024)	✓	✓	✓	✓	✓	✓	✓	?	✓
Sun et al. (2024b)			✓	✓	✓	✓	✓		✓
Zhou et al. (2024)								✓	✓
Sum	3	16	24	21	18	10	7	1	25

Table 9: ICLR data used as source for Peer Reviewing Tasks, per year, marking which datasets were annotated. A question mark indicates that the data was not disclosed.

4.2 Preprocessing and Annotation

When data collected from the open review portals is processed or annotated, details about the processing should be made available. This includes annotation guidelines, inclusion or exclusion criteria for the data points in the final dataset, software. This type of documentation is relevant to researchers who need to understand how data was obtained in order to decide its appropriateness to their task. We found little evidence of preprocessing and annotation documentation. This issue was confirmed, for example by Bharti et al. (2021), who mentioned the lack of documented preprocessing on the datasets when reporting on duplicates and empty reviews in the ICLR 2017 data.

4.3 Availability and Documentation

A key factor for dataset reuse is that it is actually available and the data is provided in an easy to process form, such that integrating it into other processing pipelines needs little overhead.

Many of the datasets that we refer to are available for download, for the remaining, however, either only data acquisition scripts (Geldsetzer et al., 2023) or insufficient selection criteria and indication of review platform source are provided (Matsui et al., 2021; Lin et al., 2023b; Liu and Shah, 2023; Sun et al., 2024b). In some cases we have found outdated links (Li et al., 2023).

Besides data availability, another issue is the missing documentation of the datasets contents. Several of the published datasets state that they investigated publications from the OpenReview platform, but do not elaborate on which conference and years they use (Bharti et al., 2023; Zeng et al., 2023; D'Arcy et al., 2023; Szumega et al., 2023; Jourdan et al., 2024), making that research difficult to reproduce, if at all possible.

Therefore, we recommend clearly stating the selection criteria for the data (e.g. conferences, years, platforms), whether the data is built on previous datasets (e.g., Guo et al. (2023)), and report descriptive statistics on the released collection, not only for the full dataset, but also for slices of the data (see Sun et al. (2024b)).

4.4 Canonical Splits

The datasets we reported on can be, and are, used both for analysis and for training machine learning models. To make the results of classification or generation tasks comparable, in the classical ML tradition, such datasets should have predefined canonical splits for training, validation, and testing. PeerRead (Kang et al., 2018), ORSUM (Zeng et al., 2023), PolitePeer (Bharti et al., 2023), SubstanReview (Yuan et al., 2022) do contain such predefined splits, but others do not (e.g. Bharti et al. (2021); Kumar et al. (2023); Purkayastha et al. (2023)).

Thus, we recommend to define canonical data splits to make model performance comparable.

4.5 Licensing

As already stated in, for example, (Kuznetsov et al., 2022; Dycke et al., 2022, 2023a) many of the datasets here are not licensed and ethically questionable, as reviewers may not have the option to opt-out of their reviews being published. Furthermore, many of the datasets are published without a clear license, although the original data is licensed. An example of this is the OpenReview platform, which is licensed as CC-BY 4.0[13], but the datasets built on it rarely mention or re-apply this license.

Thus, we advise using clear licenses for published data, and pro-active data collection whenever possible, as proposed by (Dycke et al., 2022).

[13]https://openreview.net/legal/terms

5 Discussion

The recent Dagstuhl Proceedings, *What Can Natural Language Processing Do for Peer Review*, suggest that it is mostly up to researchers in the NLP domain to solve many tasks until AI-assisted Peer Reviewing or Automated (Peer) Reviewing becomes possible. While this is true for most of the tasks in Section 2, there are challenges that, we believe, will profit from solutions that don't rely solely on Large Language Models or Text Analysis.

In our work on this paper, we note that research in peer review (Liu and Shah, 2023; D'Arcy et al., 2024; Ghosal et al., 2019; Fytas et al., 2021; Sun et al., 2024a) aim to automatically generate or predict peer reviews, leaving out the use of domain knowledge to measure the impact, novelty or compare the results to previous research results that use same datasets. One can argue that the knowledge is already encoded in LLMs, we comment that its use is not tractable. To our knowledge, ReviewRobot (Wang et al., 2020) is the only tool that uses Controlled Knowledge-Driven-Generation, to generate reviews using domain knowledge by accessing multiple knowledge graphs.The quality of the results is, however, heavily dependent on the quality of the information extraction processes that provide the content of the knowledge graphs.

In the IR community, information extraction is a long-standing research task, the latest efforts for fine-grained entity extraction being visible in the organization of the RUFEERS task at TREC[14], and the State-of-the-Art task at CLEF[15]. We hope that research in information extraction may contribute to automated population of knowledge graphs, noting that the most extensive knowledge graph (Open Research Knowledge Graph) (Kabongo et al., 2024), which supports comparing scientific publications by various parameters (including datasets), is currently curated by hand.

In conclusion, we believe connecting the research on LLMs with Information Extraction as pursued by the IR community or the Semantic Web community, can help extract the contributions of papers and compare their results to previous ones and effectively support reviewers in their work.

6 Conclusion

In this work, we gave an overview of 53 different datasets for scientific peer reviewing and the tasks

[14]https://tac.nist.gov/2024/RUFEERS/

[15]https://simpletext-project.com/2024/en/

these datasets have been created for. We found several issues with these datasets, such as poor documentation, overlapping data, unclear licensing, and a lack of canonical splits. For this reasons we propose several guidelines for publishing new datasets in this domain, guidelines that, in fact, apply to publishing datasets in general. We also see a need for the creation of a taxonomy of tasks in AI-assisted or automated peer reviewing, and the need for a well-documented dataset that consists of peer reviews from various domains, which can be used for different subtasks.

Currently, the analysis of peer review texts and tool or model development has been done by researchers in the NLP domain. We hope that researchers in other Computer Science fields will assist with their expertise. The Semantic Web community or the Information Retrieval community, are currently only slightly involved in this process. Therefore, we believe that it is necessary to get these communities more involved in this research. This can be done via future shared-tasks, and, although we see the irony, new datasets and tasks that are tailored to make use of the expertise in these domains.

Acknowledgments

While this paper critiques the numerous datasets available, we recognize that creating a dataset is an extremely challenging task. Therefore, as a community, we should be thankful and acknowledge the efforts of everyone who creates and shares datasets with the community.

References

Prabhat Kumar Bharti, Meith Navlakha, Mayank Agarwal, and Asif Ekbal. 2023. PolitePEER: does peer review hurt? a dataset to gauge politeness intensity in the peer reviews. *Language Resources and Evaluation*.

Prabhat Kumar Bharti, Shashi Ranjan, Tirthankar Ghosal, Mayank Agrawal, and Asif Ekbal. 2021. PEERAssist: Leveraging on paper-review interactions to predict peer review decisions. In *Towards Open and Trustworthy Digital Societies*, pages 421–435. Springer International Publishing.

Souvic Chakraborty, Pawan Goyal, and Animesh Mukherjee. 2020. Aspect-based sentiment analysis of scientific reviews. In *Proceedings of the ACM/IEEE Joint Conference on Digital Libraries in 2020*, JCDL '20, pages 207–216. Association for Computing Machinery.

Haotian Chen, Han Zhang, Houjing Guo, Shuchang Yi, Bingsheng Chen, and Xiangdong Zhou. 2023. SALAS: Supervised aspect learning improves abstractive multi-document summarization through aspect information loss. In *Machine Learning and Knowledge Discovery in Databases: Research Track*, pages 55–70. Springer Nature Switzerland.

Liying Cheng, Lidong Bing, Qian Yu, Wei Lu, and Luo Si. 2020. APE: Argument pair extraction from peer review and rebuttal via multi-task learning. In *Proceedings of the 2020 Conference on Empirical Methods in Natural Language Processing (EMNLP)*, pages 7000–7011. Association for Computational Linguistics.

Kwangsu Cho. 2008. Machine classification of peer comments in physics: 1st international conference on educational data mining, EDM 2008. *Educational Data Mining 2008 - 1st International Conference on Educational Data Mining, Proceedings*, pages 192–196.

Gautam Choudhary, Natwar Modani, and Nitish Maurya. 2021. ReAct: A review comment dataset for actionability (and more). In *Web Information Systems Engineering – WISE 2021*, pages 336–343. Springer International Publishing.

Mike D'Arcy, Tom Hope, Larry Birnbaum, and Doug Downey. 2024. Marg: Multi-agent review generation for scientific papers.

Mike D'Arcy, Alexis Ross, Erin Bransom, Bailey Kuehl, Jonathan Bragg, Tom Hope, and Doug Downey. 2023. ARIES: A corpus of scientific paper edits made in response to peer reviews.

Iddo Drori and Dov Te'eni. 2024. Human-in-the-loop AI reviewing: Feasibility, opportunities, and risks. *Journal of the Association for Information Systems*, 25(1):98–109.

Nils Dycke, Ilia Kuznetsov, and Iryna Gurevych. 2022. Yes-yes-yes: Proactive data collection for ACL rolling review and beyond. In *Findings of the Association for Computational Linguistics: EMNLP 2022*, pages 300–318. Association for Computational Linguistics.

Nils Dycke, Ilia Kuznetsov, and Iryna Gurevych. 2023a. NLPeer: A unified resource for the computational study of peer review. In *Proceedings of the 61st Annual Meeting of the Association for Computational Linguistics (Volume 1: Long Papers)*, pages 5049–5073. Association for Computational Linguistics.

Nils Dycke, Ilia Kuznetsov, and Iryna Gurevych. 2023b. Overview of PragTag-2023: Low-resource multi-domain pragmatic tagging of peer reviews. In *Proceedings of the 10th Workshop on Argument Mining*, pages 187–196. Association for Computational Linguistics.

Gustavo Lúcius Fernandes and Pedro O. S. Vaz-de Melo. 2022. Between acceptance and rejection: challenges for an automatic peer review process. In *Proceedings of the 22nd ACM/IEEE Joint Conference on Digital Libraries*, JCDL '22, pages 1–12. Association for Computing Machinery.

Gustavo Lúcius Fernandes and Pedro O. S. Vaz-de Melo. 2023. Enhancing the examination of obstacles in an automated peer review system. *International Journal on Digital Libraries*.

Michael Fromm, Evgeniy Faerman, Max Berrendorf, Siddharth Bhargava, Ruoxia Qi, Yao Zhang, Lukas Dennert, Sophia Selle, Yang Mao, and Thomas Seidl. 2021. Argument mining driven analysis of peer-reviews. *Proceedings of the AAAI Conference on Artificial Intelligence*, 35(6):4758–4766. Number: 6.

Panagiotis Fytas, Georgios Rizos, and Lucia Specia. 2021. What makes a scientific paper be accepted for publication?

Yang Gao, Steffen Eger, Ilia Kuznetsov, Iryna Gurevych, and Yusuke Miyao. 2019. Does my rebuttal matter? insights from a major NLP conference. In *Proceedings of the 2019 Conference of the North American Chapter of the Association for Computational Linguistics: Human Language Technologies, Volume 1 (Long and Short Papers)*, pages 1274–1290. Association for Computational Linguistics.

Pascal Geldsetzer, Markus Heemann, Pauli Tikka, Grace Wang, Marika Mae Cusick, Ali Lenjani, and Nandita Krishnan. 2023. Prevalence of short peer reviews in 3 leading general medical journals. *JAMA Network Open*, 6(12):e2347607.

Tirthankar Ghosal, Sandeep Kumar, Prabhat Kumar Bharti, and Asif Ekbal. 2022a. Peer review analyze: A novel benchmark resource for computational analysis of peer reviews. *PLOS ONE*, 17(1):e0259238. Publisher: Public Library of Science.

Tirthankar Ghosal, Kamal Kaushik Varanasi, and Valia Kordoni. 2022b. HedgePeer: a dataset for uncertainty detection in peer reviews. In *Proceedings of the 22nd ACM/IEEE Joint Conference on Digital Libraries*, JCDL '22, pages 1–5. Association for Computing Machinery.

Tirthankar Ghosal, Rajeev Verma, Asif Ekbal, and Pushpak Bhattacharyya. 2019. DeepSentiPeer: Harnessing sentiment in review texts to recommend peer review decisions. In *Proceedings of the 57th Annual Meeting of the Association for Computational Linguistics*, pages 1120–1130. Association for Computational Linguistics.

Yanzhu Guo, Guokan Shang, Virgile Rennard, Michalis Vazirgiannis, and Chloé Clavel. 2023. Automatic analysis of substantiation in scientific peer reviews. In *Findings of the Association for Computational Linguistics: EMNLP 2023*, pages 10198–10216. Association for Computational Linguistics.

Xinyu Hua, Mitko Nikolov, Nikhil Badugu, and Lu Wang. 2019. Argument mining for understanding peer reviews. In *Proceedings of the 2019 Conference of the North American Chapter of the Association for Computational Linguistics: Human Language Technologies, Volume 1 (Long and Short Papers)*, pages 2131–2137. Association for Computational Linguistics.

Junjie Huang, Win-bin Huang, Yi Bu, Qi Cao, Huawei Shen, and Xueqi Cheng. 2023. What makes a successful rebuttal in computer science conferences?: A perspective on social interaction. *Journal of Informetrics*, 17(3):101427.

Steven Jecmen, Nihar B. Shah, Fei Fang, and Leman Akoglu. 2024. On the detection of reviewer-author collusion rings from paper bidding.

Steven Jecmen, Minji Yoon, Vincent Conitzer, Nihar B. Shah, and Fei Fang. 2023. A dataset on malicious paper bidding in peer review.

Chao Jiang, Wei Xu, and Samuel Stevens. 2022. arxivedits: Understanding the human revision process in scientific writing.

Leane Jourdan, Florian Boudin, Nicolas Hernandez, and Richard Dufour. 2024. CASIMIR: A corpus of scientific articles enhanced with multiple author-integrated revisions.

Salomon Kabongo, Jennifer D'Souza, and Sören Auer. 2024. ORKG-leaderboards: a systematic workflow for mining leaderboards as a knowledge graph. *International Journal on Digital Libraries*, 25(1):41–54.

Amir R. Kachooei and Mohammad H. Ebrahimzadeh. 2022. Editorial: What is peer review? *Archives of Bone and Joint Surgery*, 10(1):1–2.

Dongyeop Kang, Waleed Ammar, Bhavana Dalvi, Madeleine van Zuylen, Sebastian Kohlmeier, Eduard Hovy, and Roy Schwartz. 2018. A dataset of peer reviews (PeerRead): Collection, insights and NLP applications. In *Proceedings of the 2018 Conference of the North American Chapter of the Association for Computational Linguistics: Human Language Technologies, Volume 1 (Long Papers)*, pages 1647–1661. Association for Computational Linguistics.

Neha Nayak Kennard, Tim O'Gorman, Rajarshi Das, Akshay Sharma, Chhandak Bagchi, Matthew Clinton, Pranay Kumar Yelugam, Hamed Zamani, and Andrew McCallum. 2022. DISAPERE: A dataset for discourse structure in peer review discussions. In *Proceedings of the 2022 Conference of the North American Chapter of the Association for Computational Linguistics: Human Language Technologies*, pages 1234–1249. Association for Computational Linguistics.

Sandeep Kumar, Tirthankar Ghosal, and Asif Ekbal. 2023. When reviewers lock horns: Finding disagreements in scientific peer reviews. In *Proceedings of the 2023 Conference on Empirical Methods in Natural Language Processing*, pages 16693–16704. Association for Computational Linguistics.

Ilia Kuznetsov, Osama Mohammed Afzal, Koen Dercksen, Nils Dycke, Alexander Goldberg, Tom Hope, Dirk Hovy, Jonathan K. Kummerfeld, Anne Lauscher, Kevin Leyton-Brown, Sheng Lu, Mausam, Margot Mieskes, Aurélie Névéol, Danish Pruthi, Lizhen Qu, Roy Schwartz, Noah A. Smith, Thamar Solorio, Jingyan Wang, Xiaodan Zhu, Anna Rogers, Nihar B. Shah, and Iryna Gurevych. 2024. What can natural language processing do for peer review?

Ilia Kuznetsov, Jan Buchmann, Max Eichler, and Iryna Gurevych. 2022. Revise and resubmit: An intertextual model of text-based collaboration in peer review. *Computational Linguistics*, 48(4):949–986.

Miao Li, Eduard Hovy, and Jey Lau. 2023. Summarizing multiple documents with conversational structure for meta-review generation. In *Findings of the Association for Computational Linguistics: EMNLP 2023*, pages 7089–7112. Association for Computational Linguistics.

Siqing Li, Wayne Xin Zhao, Eddy Jing Yin, and Ji-Rong Wen. 2019. A neural citation count prediction model based on peer review text. In *Proceedings of the 2019 Conference on Empirical Methods in Natural Language Processing and the 9th International Joint Conference on Natural Language Processing (EMNLP-IJCNLP)*, pages 4914–4924. Association for Computational Linguistics.

Jialiang Lin, Jiaxin Song, Zhangping Zhou, Yidong Chen, and Xiaodong Shi. 2023a. Automated scholarly paper review: Concepts, technologies, and challenges. *Information Fusion*, 98:101830.

Jialiang Lin, Jiaxin Song, Zhangping Zhou, Yidong Chen, and Xiaodong Shi. 2023b. MOPRD: A multidisciplinary open peer review dataset. *Neural Computing and Applications*, 35(34):24191–24206.

Meng-Huan Liu, An-Zi Yen, Hen-Hsen Huang, and Hsin-Hsi Chen. 2023a. ContributionSum: Generating disentangled contributions for scientific papers. In *Proceedings of the 32nd ACM International Conference on Information and Knowledge Management*, pages 5351–5355. ACM.

Ryan Liu, Steven Jecmen, Vincent Conitzer, Fei Fang, and Nihar B. Shah. 2023b. Testing for reviewer anchoring in peer review: A randomized controlled trial.

Ryan Liu and Nihar B. Shah. 2023. ReviewerGPT? an exploratory study on using large language models for paper reviewing.

Akira Matsui, Emily Chen, Yunwen Wang, and Emilio Ferrara. 2021. The impact of peer review on the contribution potential of scientific papers. *PeerJ*, 9:e11999.

Dominik Pfütze, Eva Ritz, Julius Janda, and Roman Rietsche. 2022. A corpus for suggestion mining of german peer feedback. In *Proceedings of the Thirteenth Language Resources and Evaluation Conference*, pages 5539–5547. European Language Resources Association.

Barbara Plank and Reinard van Dalen. 2019. CiteTracked: A Longitudinal Dataset of Peer Reviews and Citations. In *BIRNDL@SIGIR*.

Sukannya Purkayastha, Anne Lauscher, and Iryna Gurevych. 2023. Exploring jiu-jitsu argumentation for writing peer review rebuttals. In *Proceedings of the 2023 Conference on Empirical Methods in Natural Language Processing*, pages 14479–14495. Association for Computational Linguistics.

Ana Carolina Ribeiro, Amanda Sizo, Henrique Lopes Cardoso, and Luís Paulo Reis. 2021. Acceptance decision prediction in peer-review through sentiment analysis. In *Progress in Artificial Intelligence*, pages 766–777. Springer International Publishing.

Michael Ridenour, Ameeta Agrawal, and Olubusayo Olabisi. 2022. Assessing inter-metric correlation for multi-document summarization evaluation. In *Proceedings of the 2nd Workshop on Natural Language Generation, Evaluation, and Metrics (GEM)*, pages 428–438. Association for Computational Linguistics.

Federico Ruggeri, Mohsen Mesgar, and Iryna Gurevych. 2023. A dataset of argumentative dialogues on scientific papers. In *Proceedings of the 61st Annual Meeting of the Association for Computational Linguistics (Volume 1: Long Papers)*, pages 7684–7699. Association for Computational Linguistics.

Anna Severin, Michaela Strinzel, Matthias Egger, Tiago Barros, Alexander Sokolov, Julia Vilstrup Mouatt, and Stefan Müller. 2023. Relationship between journal impact factor and the thoroughness and helpfulness of peer reviews. *PLoS biology*, 21(8):e3002238.

Nihar B. Shah, Behzad Tabibian, Krikamol Muandet, Isabelle Guyon, and Ulrike von Luxburg. 2018. Design and analysis of the nips 2016 review process.

Chenhui Shen, Liying Cheng, Ran Zhou, Lidong Bing, Yang You, and Luo Si. 2022. MReD: A meta-review dataset for structure-controllable text generation. In *Findings of the Association for Computational Linguistics: ACL 2022*, pages 2521–2535. Association for Computational Linguistics.

Shruti Singh, Mayank Singh, and Pawan Goyal. 2021. COMPARE: A taxonomy and dataset of comparison discussions in peer reviews.

Ivan Stelmakh, Nihar B. Shah, and Aarti Singh. 2020. Catch me if i can: Detecting strategic behaviour in peer assessment.

Ivan Stelmakh, John Wieting, Graham Neubig, and Nihar B. Shah. 2023. A gold standard dataset for the reviewer assignment problem.

Lu Sun, Aaron Chan, Yun Seo Chang, and Steven P. Dow. 2024a. ReviewFlow: Intelligent scaffolding to support academic peer reviewing. In *Proceedings of the 29th International Conference on Intelligent User Interfaces*, IUI '24, pages 120–137. Association for Computing Machinery.

Lu Sun, Stone Tao, Junjie Hu, and Steven P. Dow. 2024b. MetaWriter: Exploring the potential and perils of AI writing support in scientific peer review. *Proceedings of the ACM on Human-Computer Interaction*, 8:94:1–94:32.

Jaroslaw Szumega, Lamine Bougueroua, Blerina Gkotse, Pierre Jouvelot, and Federico Ravotti. 2023. The open review-based (ORB) dataset: Towards automatic assessment of scientific papers and experiment proposals in high-energy physics.

Rajeev Verma, Tirthankar Ghosal, Saprativa Bhattacharjee, Asif Ekbal, and Pushpak Bhattacharyya. 2023. ReviVal: Towards automatically evaluating the informativeness of peer reviews. In *Proceedings of the Annual International ACM SIGIR Conference on Research and Development in Information Retrieval in the Asia Pacific Region*, SIGIR-AP '23, pages 95–103. Association for Computing Machinery.

Rajeev Verma, Rajarshi Roychoudhury, and Tirthankar Ghosal. 2022. The lack of theory is painful: Modeling harshness in peer review comments. In *Proceedings of the 2nd Conference of the Asia-Pacific Chapter of the Association for Computational Linguistics and the 12th International Joint Conference on Natural Language Processing (Volume 1: Long Papers)*, pages 925–935. Association for Computational Linguistics.

Gang Wang, Qi Peng, Yanfeng Zhang, and Mingyang Zhang. 2023. What have we learned from OpenReview? *World Wide Web*, 26(2):683–708.

Ke Wang and Xiaojun Wan. 2018. Sentiment analysis of peer review texts for scholarly papers. In *The 41st International ACM SIGIR Conference on Research & Development in Information Retrieval*, SIGIR '18, pages 175–184. Association for Computing Machinery.

Qingyun Wang, Qi Zeng, Lifu Huang, Kevin Knight, Heng Ji, and Nazneen Fatema Rajani. 2020. ReviewRobot: Explainable paper review generation based on knowledge synthesis. In *Proceedings of the 13th International Conference on Natural Language Generation*, pages 384–397. Association for Computational Linguistics.

Po-Cheng Wu, An-Zi Yen, Hen-Hsen Huang, and Hsin-Hsi Chen. 2022. Incorporating peer reviews and rebuttal counter-arguments for meta-review generation. In *Proceedings of the 31st ACM International Conference on Information & Knowledge Management*, CIKM '22, pages 2189–2198. Association for Computing Machinery.

Weizhe Yuan, Pengfei Liu, and Graham Neubig. 2022. Can we automate scientific reviewing? *Journal of Artificial Intelligence Research*, 75:171–212.

Qi Zeng, Mankeerat Sidhu, Hou Pong Chan, Lu Wang, and Heng Ji. 2023. Scientific opinion summarization: Meta-review generation with checklist-guided iterative introspection.

Jiayao Zhang, Hongming Zhang, Zhun Deng, and Dan Roth. 2022. Investigating fairness disparities in peer review: A language model enhanced approach.

Ruiyang Zhou, Lu Chen, and Kai Yu. 2024. Is LLM a reliable reviewer? a comprehensive evaluation of LLM on automatic paper reviewing tasks. In *Proceedings of the 2024 Joint International Conference on Computational Linguistics, Language Resources and Evaluation (LREC-COLING 2024)*, pages 9340–9351. ELRA and ICCL.

Zero-shot Scientific Claim Verification Using LLMs and Citation Text

Carlos Alvarez* **Maxwell Bennett*** **Lucy Lu Wang**
University of Washington
{calvar, maxmiles, lucylw}@uw.edu

Abstract

Due to rapidly changing and advancing science, it is important to check the veracity of scientific claims and whether they are supported by research evidence. Previous versions of this task depended on supervised training, where labeled datasets were constructed through manual claim writing and evidence identification, sometimes coupled with mining citation relationships in papers. In this work, we investigate whether zero-shot scientific claim verification could be enabled using large language models (LLMs) and distant supervision examples taken directly from citation texts. We derive an in-context learning (ICL) dataset, SCitance, consisting of citation sentences ("citances"), LLM-generated negations, evidence documents, and veracity labels, and find that prompting GPT-4 with ICL examples from this dataset yields comparable performance (within 1 point F1) to previous finetuned models trained on manually curated claim-evidence pairs. Our results suggest that prompting LLMs with citance-evidence pairs directly poses a viable alternative to finetuning scientific claim verification models with manually-curated data.[1]

1 Introduction

Verifying scientific claims is important for assessing the rigor of the research enterprise and for addressing concerns such as misinformation or misinterpretation of scientific output. Prior work in scientific claim verification relies on manually annotated supervision data (expert-written claims verified against documents) (Wadden et al., 2020; Sarrouti et al., 2021; Saakyan et al., 2021), which can be expensive to curate and difficult to scale. This has inspired work in zero- or few-shot settings, which have demonstrated success by extracting claims using supervised models, then training claim verification models on the extracted claims (Pan et al., 2021; Wright et al., 2022). Here, we investigate two questions: (i) whether expert-written claims are needed at all, and (ii) whether large language models (LLMs) can verify scientific claims in zero- or few-shot settings with no need for supervision labels or model finetuning.

Towards (i), we investigate whether citation sentences ("citances") and citing relationships from the scientific literature could be used directly as noisy labeled data, without converting citances to claims. We construct a dataset of citance-evidence pairs, SCitance, based on the claim-evidence pairs from SciFact (Wadden et al., 2020), and use these as in-context learning (ICL) examples for prompting. To derive contradictory examples, we use GPT-3.5 to generate negations of citances. Towards (ii), we design zero- and few-shot prompts for claim verification using GPT-3.5 and GPT-4, and find that GPT-4 with ICL performs comparably at abstract-level verification compared to supervised models trained on expert-annotated claim-evidence pairs (within 1 point F1). This result indicates that contemporary LLMs could be adapted to perform scientific claim verification with few supervision labels, which could dramatically lower the costs associated with domain transfer of these models.

2 Related Work

Scientific Claim Verification Since the introduction of large-scale fact verification datasets such as FEVER (Thorne et al., 2018) and UKP Snopes (Hanselowski et al., 2019), notable datasets supporting claim verification in the scientific domain have followed (Wadden et al., 2020; Saakyan et al., 2021; Sarrouti et al., 2021; Kotonya and Toni, 2020). We base our work on SciFact (Wadden et al., 2020), a dataset of 1,400 expert-written biomedical claims paired with evidence abstracts, which using citances as a source of claims and their corresponding evidence relationships. In this work, our focus is exploring LLMs for verifying scien-

*denotes equal contribution

[1]Code and data at https://github.com/larchlab/scitance

Proceedings of the Fourth Workshop on Scholarly Document Processing (SDP 2024), pages 269–276
August 16, 2024 ©2024 Association for Computational Linguistics

tific claims using citation contexts from existing literature directly.

Since the emergence of LLMs, many works have explored prompting for fact/claim verification. Zhang and Gao (2023) experimented with ICL for news claim verification, finding that prompting with a few examples achieves performance comparable to that of supervised models. They and others (Wang and Shu, 2023) also demonstrated the ability of LLMs to support explainable claim verification, where rationales are provided alongside veracity judgements or grounded to knowledgebases. LLMs have also been used to coordinate fact-checking of complex claims (Pan et al., 2023), which are similar to citances in scientific text.

Negation generation Prior work has investigated how to automatically generate negations to train claim verification systems. Pan et al. (2021) introduce QACG, which automatically generates QA pairs from Wikipedia and converts these into supporting, contradicting, or unrelated claims. Wright et al. (2022) use an knowledge-based entity substitution approach, KBIN, which substitutes biomedical entities with related entities from the UMLS knowledgebase. In their analysis, they find that KBIN most often produces claim variations, rather than true negations.

Alternatively, Saakyan et al. (2021) introduce a novel approach to negation generation that uses masked language model infilling. After generating several negations of salient words, the method selects negations with the highest contradiction score using a RoBERTa model (Liu et al., 2019) trained on Multi-NLI (Williams et al., 2018). However, this method requires some human supervision to optimize contradiction score thresholds, and can only modify a claim by changing a single word or multi-word expression. In our work, we investigate whether LLMs can generate negations; LLMs do not rely on specific knowledgebases and can produce multiple modifications to the same sentence, which is necessary for negating citances with complex syntax and multiple clauses.

3 Dataset

We derive our dataset, SCitance, from SciFact (Wadden et al., 2020), a dataset of 1.4K manually-written scientific claims from citances in biomedical papers verified against over 5000 evidence documents. For each claim-evidence pair, trained annotators provided labels for whether the evidence supports, refutes, or offers insufficient information (NEI) towards the claim. To validate whether citance-evidence relationships can be used to train scientific fact checking models directly, without the need to extract and rewrite claims, we make use of the original citances in SciFact (mapping provided by the authors) rather than the rewritten claims to train our models.

Fold	Support	Refute	NEI	All
Train	178	155	134	467
Dev	38	31	29	98
Test	35	39	17	91
All	251	225	180	656

Table 1: Distribution of labels in SCitance

We keep all citance-evidence pairs from the train and dev set with SUPPORT and NEI labels, yielding 251 supporting and 180 NEI entries. These numbers are notably lower than SciFact's due to: (i) in SciFact, multiple claims could be written based on a single citance; and (ii) each claim from the same citance with the same supporting evidence document translates to only one instance in our dataset. This also carries over to NEI examples.

Generating citance negations Mapping claims to citances only yields SUPPORT and NEI-labeled training instances, yet contradictory claim-evidence relationships are necessary to train a claim verification model. While claim negations were written manually for SciFact to produce contradictory training samples, subsequent analysis has shown that this process may introduce lexical biases into negations that could be used by models to shortcut predictions (Wadden et al., 2020; Wright et al., 2022). To offset the cost of producing manual negations and mitigate lexical biases, we use GPT-3.5[2] to automatically negate citances. Negating citances remains a non-trivial task. Citances from scientific papers have complex syntactic structure, offering multiple correct ways to negate the content, where some negations need to be reflected as multiple changes across the entire sentence.

To identify effective prompt instructions for generating negations, we examine prompt variants for both GPT-3.5 and GPT-4 and compare results on 20 citances sampled from SCitance. We evaluate the resulting negations on several criteria: (i) the negation should maintain all clauses in the origi-

[2]The model we used to generate negations in SCitance, `text-davinci-003`, has since been deprecated.

Includes NEI	Input	Model setting	Micro-F1	Macro-F1
Yes	Citance-abstract pairs	MultiVerS*	73.8	73.6
Yes	Citance-abstract pairs	Zero-shot GPT-3.5	44.2	34.5
Yes	Citance-abstract pairs	Few-shot GPT-3.5	43.7	36.5
Yes	Citance-abstract pairs	Zero-shot GPT-4	80.1	79.1
Yes	Citance-abstract pairs	Few-shot GPT-4	75.4	73.3
No	Citance-abstract pairs	Zero-shot GPT-4	88.1	88.1
No	Citance-abstract pairs	Few-shot GPT-4	86.8	86.7
No	Citance-only	Zero-shot GPT-4	69.7	68.4
No	Citance-only	Few-shot GPT-4	71.6	70.9

Table 2: SCitance test set performance. All experiments are conducted in the abstract-provided setting (where the gold abstract is provided as input), except for citance-only (in which no evidence abstracts are provided). *MultiVerS was trained on claim-abstract pairs.

nal citance, (ii) the negation should be active, not passive (i.e., simply inserting a negation word like "not"), and (iii) only the main claims made in the citance should be negated. Our evaluation found that the instruction "Please negate this sentence by changing as few words as possible in the original sentence" yielded the best results.

Upon comparing model outputs, we find that GPT-4 tends to negate by inserting negation words like "not" rather than flipping the meaning of words in the sentence. For example, with the citance "Approximately 90% of SIDS deaths occur in infants aged less than 6 months old," GPT-4 changed "...[do not] occur..." whereas GPT-3.5 changed "90%" to "10%." Based on these findings, we elect to use GPT-3.5 to generate negations. We implement two additional checks to improve the quality of negations. First, we only keep negations within $\pm 10\%$ of the original citance token length.[3] Second, we verify successful negation by feeding the original and negated citance into GPT-4 and asking the model to determine whether they are proper negations of one another.

Full prompts and additional evaluation examples are provided in Appendix B. The final 251 SUPPORT, 225 REFUTE, and 180 NEI instances in SCitance are split into train, dev, and test sets. Label distributions are provided in Table 1.

4 Experiments

We adopt the abstract-level scientific claim verification task definition from Wadden et al. (2020). Given a claim and retrieved evidence abstract, the goal is to determine whether the evidence supports, refutes, or offers insufficient information towards the claim. Here, instead of only claims, we provide either citances or claims as our verification objection. We report performance on SCitance and SciFact (via the public leaderboard[4]).

Models We compare prompting methods against pretrained language models on this task. MultiVerS (Wadden et al., 2022) is a supervised model that uses the Longformer encoder (Beltagy et al., 2020) to create a shared encoding for claims and abstracts, with multiple classification heads to simultaneously predict the claim veracity label and extract evidence sentences. We report results from the version of MultiVerS trained on FEVER and weak supervision datasets, then fine-tuned on SciFact (Wadden et al., 2020).

All prompting experiments are conducted with two models using the OpenAI API: GPT-3.5 (`gpt-3.5-turbo-0125`) and GPT-4 (`gpt-4-0613`) (OpenAI, 2023). Temperature was set to 0.2 and no limit was placed on maximum tokens.

Prompt settings We prompt models in zero- and few-shot ICL settings (prompts in Appendix A). For few-shot experiments, we use similar instructions as in the zero-shot setting, but include examples from the train split of SCitance or SciFact depending on the experiment. We randomly select an example corresponding to each label (SUPPORT, REFUTE, NEI) to include before providing the test sample. We report model performance on abstract-level classification for SCitance and SciFact.

Retrieval setting When evaluating on SCitance, we report performance in the abstract-provided setting, without incorporating a retrieval

[3] In rare cases, entire clauses are removed in the negation.

[4] `https://leaderboard.allenai.org/scifact/`

step. When evaluating on SciFact via the leaderboard, we employ dense retrieval using Sentence-BERT (Reimers and Gurevych, 2019) with the `S-PubMedBert-MS-MARCO-SCIFACT` checkpoint as implemented by Deka et al. (2022). We retrieve the top 3 documents per claim and use these as evidence abstracts in prompting.

5 Results

Performance on SCitance Model performance on SCitance is provided in Table 2. Surprisingly, zero-shot prompting with GPT-4 yields the best results on SCitance (80.1 micro-F1), markedly higher than MultiVerS trained on claim-abstract pairs and several points better than the few-shot setting with in-context examples (75.4 micro-F1). This indicates that GPT-4 is able to reason about citation-evidence relationships out-of-the-box and without modifying citances into atomic claims. By contrast, we observe significantly worse performance from zero- and few-shot GPT-3.5, with micro-F1 scores of 44.2. and 43.7. For MultiVerS, this task variant represents a domain shift, and the model, having been trained on claim-abstract pairs, performs less well when given citances.

Performance on SciFact On the SciFact test set, we see comparable performance between few-shot prompting with GPT-4 and MultiVerS (Table 3). Using SciFact's own training data as in-context learning examples provided a marginal boost to performance over using citances. In contrast to performance on SCitance, zero-shot prompting with GPT-4 performed less well—by a difference of 3 points. GPT-3.5, however, performs far worse in both zero- and few-shot settings, similar to its performance on SCitance. Nonetheless, these results suggest that citance-abstract relationships may provide comparable in-context supervision to claim-abstract relationships (as shown in GPT-4 results), and claim rewriting may be unnecessary when generalizing these methods to other domains.

Ablations We conduct citance-only experiments to assess biases introduced by our negation generation procedure. We retain only citances with support or refute labels and prompt GPT-4 for the veracity of each citance. Table 2 shows zero- and few-shot results comparing using only citances as input against using citance-abstract pairs. Low F1-scores associated with citance-only settings indicate that negation generation did not introduce significant biases into the data that can be exploited by LLMs for claim verification.

Model	Setting	F1
MultiVerS	Trained on claims	72.5
GPT-3.5	Zero-shot	35.0
	Few-shot (ICL w/ citances)	39.0
	Few-shot (ICL w/ claims)	39.9
GPT-4	Zero-shot	68.6
	Few-shot (ICL w/ citances)	71.7
	Few-shot (ICL w/ claims)	72.2

Table 3: Performance on SciFact test set

6 Discussion & Conclusion

This study explores zero-shot scientific claim verification using LLMs and citation texts directly, demonstrating effective transfer to verifying scientific claims. GPT-4, when prompted with ICL examples from SCitance, performs within 1-pt F1 of finetuned models that rely on manually curated claim-evidence pairs. Thus, using citation sentences directly as noisy labeled data and prompting LLMs to produce small numbers of negations and counter-examples can serve as a potential alternative to manual data curation. Such datasets would be much easier to create in a novel scientific domain due to the common occurrence of citation relationships in scientific literature that could be used to bootstrap annotations.

However, there are limitations to our approach. Negating or generating variants of complex sentences while preserving logical internal relationships remains a challenge. Our work also does not contend with explainability, an important facet of claim verification that has received ample attention in recent years. While we did not conduct experiments to this effect, prior efforts in news and general domain claim verification (Zhang and Gao, 2023; Wang and Shu, 2023) suggest that LLMs excel at rationalizing verification decisions, which could also be tested in the scientific domain.

SCitance was based on claim-evidence relationships validated by annotators for SciFact, so they are not truly devoid of any manual curation. Follow-up work should investigate whether a dataset like SCitance could be constructed directly from citation relationships from independent sets of scientific documents. This would demonstrate the feasibility of citation-based dataset construction to support task transfer to other scientific disciplines.

Limitations

As discussed, our approach faces several limitations. Prompt engineering was crucial for performance, yet minor changes in prompt instruction can lead to signficant changes in performance. Even with our best-performing prompts, the model would still fail in some cases to contend with the complex structure of naturally occurring citances. Our study also does not address the important explainability aspect of claim verification. Finally, the demonstrated effectiveness of LLMs is limited to one dataset in a single scientific subdomain, and the dataset used was not entirely free from manual curation since it is based on SciFact. The involvement of other datasets and domains, as well as constructing other such datasets automatically from scratch would be opportunities for future work.

References

Iz Beltagy, Matthew E. Peters, and Arman Cohan. 2020. Longformer: The long-document transformer.

Pritam Deka, Anna Jurek-Loughrey, and P Deepak. 2022. Improved methods to aid unsupervised evidence-based fact checking for online health news. *Journal of Data Intelligence*, 3(4):474–504.

Andreas Hanselowski, Christian Stab, Claudia Schulz, Zile Li, and Iryna Gurevych. 2019. A richly annotated corpus for different tasks in automated fact-checking. In *Proceedings of the 23rd Conference on Computational Natural Language Learning (CoNLL)*, pages 493–503, Hong Kong, China. Association for Computational Linguistics.

Neema Kotonya and Francesca Toni. 2020. Explainable automated fact-checking for public health claims. In *Proceedings of the 2020 Conference on Empirical Methods in Natural Language Processing (EMNLP)*, pages 7740–7754, Online. Association for Computational Linguistics.

Yinhan Liu, Myle Ott, Naman Goyal, Jingfei Du, Mandar Joshi, Danqi Chen, Omer Levy, Mike Lewis, Luke Zettlemoyer, and Veselin Stoyanov. 2019. Roberta: A robustly optimized bert pretraining approach. *ArXiv*, abs/1907.11692.

OpenAI. 2023. GPT-4 Technical Report.

Liangming Pan, Wenhu Chen, Wenhan Xiong, Min-Yen Kan, and William Yang Wang. 2021. Zero-shot fact verification by claim generation. In *Proceedings of the 59th Annual Meeting of the Association for Computational Linguistics and the 11th International Joint Conference on Natural Language Processing (Volume 2: Short Papers)*, pages 476–483, Online. Association for Computational Linguistics.

Liangming Pan, Xiaobao Wu, Xinyuan Lu, Anh Tuan Luu, William Yang Wang, Min-Yen Kan, and Preslav Nakov. 2023. Fact-checking complex claims with program-guided reasoning. In *Proceedings of the 61st Annual Meeting of the Association for Computational Linguistics (Volume 1: Long Papers)*, pages 6981–7004, Toronto, Canada. Association for Computational Linguistics.

Alec Radford, Jeff Wu, Rewon Child, David Luan, Dario Amodei, and Ilya Sutskever. 2019. Language models are unsupervised multitask learners.

Nils Reimers and Iryna Gurevych. 2019. Sentence-BERT: Sentence embeddings using Siamese BERT-networks. In *Proceedings of the 2019 Conference on Empirical Methods in Natural Language Processing and the 9th International Joint Conference on Natural Language Processing (EMNLP-IJCNLP)*, pages 3982–3992, Hong Kong, China. Association for Computational Linguistics.

Arkadiy Saakyan, Tuhin Chakrabarty, and Smaranda Muresan. 2021. COVID-fact: Fact extraction and verification of real-world claims on COVID-19 pandemic. In *Proceedings of the 59th Annual Meeting of the Association for Computational Linguistics and the 11th International Joint Conference on Natural Language Processing (Volume 1: Long Papers)*, pages 2116–2129, Online. Association for Computational Linguistics.

Mourad Sarrouti, Asma Ben Abacha, Yassine Mrabet, and Dina Demner-Fushman. 2021. Evidence-based fact-checking of health-related claims. In *Findings of the Association for Computational Linguistics: EMNLP 2021*, pages 3499–3512, Punta Cana, Dominican Republic. Association for Computational Linguistics.

James Thorne, Andreas Vlachos, Christos Christodoulopoulos, and Arpit Mittal. 2018. FEVER: a large-scale dataset for fact extraction and VERification. In *Proceedings of the 2018 Conference of the North American Chapter of the Association for Computational Linguistics: Human Language Technologies, Volume 1 (Long Papers)*, pages 809–819, New Orleans, Louisiana. Association for Computational Linguistics.

David Wadden, Shanchuan Lin, Kyle Lo, Lucy Lu Wang, Madeleine van Zuylen, Arman Cohan, and Hannaneh Hajishirzi. 2020. Fact or fiction: Verifying scientific claims.

David Wadden, Kyle Lo, Lucy Lu Wang, Arman Cohan, Iz Beltagy, and Hannaneh Hajishirzi. 2022. Multivers: Improving scientific claim verification with weak supervision and full-document context.

Haoran Wang and Kai Shu. 2023. Explainable claim verification via knowledge-grounded reasoning with large language models. In *Findings of the Association for Computational Linguistics: EMNLP 2023*, pages 6288–6304, Singapore. Association for Computational Linguistics.

Adina Williams, Nikita Nangia, and Samuel Bowman. 2018. A broad-coverage challenge corpus for sentence understanding through inference. In *Proceedings of the 2018 Conference of the North American Chapter of the Association for Computational Linguistics: Human Language Technologies, Volume 1 (Long Papers)*, pages 1112–1122, New Orleans, Louisiana. Association for Computational Linguistics.

Dustin Wright, David Wadden, Kyle Lo, Bailey Kuehl, Arman Cohan, Isabelle Augenstein, and Lucy Lu Wang. 2022. Generating scientific claims for zero-shot scientific fact checking. In *Proceedings of the 60th Annual Meeting of the Association for Computational Linguistics (Volume 1: Long Papers)*, pages 2448–2460, Dublin, Ireland. Association for Computational Linguistics.

Xuan Zhang and Wei Gao. 2023. Towards LLM-based fact verification on news claims with a hierarchical step-by-step prompting method. In *Proceedings of the 13th International Joint Conference on Natural Language Processing and the 3rd Conference of the Asia-Pacific Chapter of the Association for Computational Linguistics (Volume 1: Long Papers)*, pages 996–1011, Nusa Dua, Bali. Association for Computational Linguistics.

A Prompts

Prompts used for all experiments are reproduced in full in Table 4. Experiments on SciFact use the same prompts as the associated settings for SCitance, with test claims instead of citances.

B Negation Prompts

We test six prompts on twenty citances using both GPT-3.5 and GPT-4, and compare the resulting negations to determine the optimal setting for negation generation. Through qualitative evaluation, we find that "Please negate this sentence by changing as few words as possible in the original sentence" yields the best results.

We evaluate negations on the following criteria: (i) the negation should maintain all clauses in the citance, (ii) the negation should be active, not passive (e.g., inserting a negation word like "not"), and (iii) only the main claim made in the citance should be negated. For (iii) for example, with a more complex citance such as "Such sequence variation is likely to consist of rare variants, present in less than 1% of the population, with potentially larger penetrance effects than previously identified common variants", it is essential that the inner dependent clause is not changed to "...present in more than..." because that clause provides context but is not the main claim in the citance.

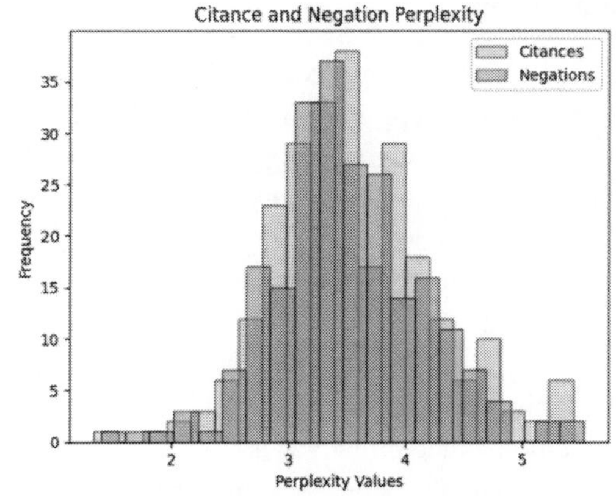

Figure 1: Distribution of GPT-2 perplexity scores associated with citances and automatically generated negations. The distributions overlap.

C Assessing lexical bias in negations

We assess lexical bias among generate negations. When predicting the verification label, certain trigger words (e.g., "not") may correlate with the contradiction label, and may be exploited by the classification model as a shortcut.

To determine if negations contain different lexical distributions to the original citances, we calculate and compare perplexity score distributions generated using GPT-2 for citances and negations (Radford et al., 2019). We conduct an independent two-tailed T-test and find that any difference between the two perplexity distributions (Figure 1) is not statistically significant ($t = 0.727$; $p = 0.468$).

NEI	Task	Setting	Prompt
No	Citance-only	Zero-shot	"Given a claim, please determine whether the existing academic literature SUPPORTS or CONTRADICTS the claim (even if you cannot reference specific abstracts). Please return your answer as only the capitalized token, as well as an explanation or rationale for the answer. Claim: {}"
No	Citance-only	Few-shot	"The following are examples of claims from a research paper and the corresponding abstract from the paper they are citing. This is an example of an abstract that SUPPORTS the claim: Supporting abstract: {} Claim: {} This is an example of an abstract that CONTRADICTS the claim: Contradicting abstract: {} Claim: {} Please obey the following: With no specific abstracts, please make an estimation whether the existing academic literature (and not the abstracts above) SUPPORTS or CONTRADICTS the claim. You must choose SUPPORTS or CONTRADICTS. Please return your answer as only the capitalized token, as well as an explanation or rationale for the answer. Claim: {}"
No	Citance-abstract pairs	Zero-shot	"Please obey the following: With a specific abstract, please make an estimation whether the abstract SUPPORTS or CONTRADICTS the claim. You must choose SUPPORTS or CONTRADICTS. Please return your answer as only the capitalized token, as well as an explanation or rationale for the answer. Abstract: {} Claim: {}"
No	Citance-abstract pairs	Few-shot	"The following are examples of claims from a research paper and the corresponding abstract from the paper they are citing. This is an example of an abstract that SUPPORTS the claim: Supporting abstract: {} Claim: {} This is an example of an abstract that CONTRADICTS the claim: Contradicting abstract: {} Claim: {} Please obey the following: given a new abstract and claim pair, please make an estimation whether the abstract SUPPORTS or CONTRADICTS the claim. You must choose SUPPORTS or CONTRADICTS. Please return your answer as the capitalized token, as well as an explanation or rationale for the answer. New abstract: {} Claim: {}"
Yes	Citance-abstract pairs	Zero-shot	"Please obey the following: With a specific abstract, please make an estimation whether the abstract SUPPORTS, CONTRADICTS, or if there is NOT_ENOUGH_INFO to determine. You must choose SUPPORTS or CONTRADICTS or NOT_ENOUGH_INFO. Please return your answer as only the capitalized token, as well as an explanation or rationale for the answer. Abstract: {} Claim: {}"
Yes	Citance-abstract pairs	Few-shot	"The following are examples of claims from a research paper and the corresponding abstract from the paper they are citing. This is an example of an abstract that SUPPORTS the claim: Supporting abstract: {} Claim: {} This is an example of an abstract that CONTRADICTS the claim:Contradicting abstract: {} Claim: {} This is an example of an abstract with NOT_ENOUGH_INFO about the claim: Missing info abstract: {} Claim: {} Please obey the following: given a new abstract and claim pair, please make an estimation whether the abstract SUPPORTS, CONTRADICTS, or if there is NOT_ENOUGH_INFO to determine. You must choose SUPPORTS or CONTRADICTS or NOT_ENOUGH_INFO. Please return your answer as the capitalized token, as well as an explanation or rationale for the answer. New abstract: {} Claim: {}"

Table 4: Model Prompts

Negation prompt
"Please provide two different examples of a negated version of the following sentence, by changing as few words as possible in the original sentence: "
"A negated sentence is a sentence that has had one or more words added, removed, or changed so that the resulting sentence has the opposite meaning from the original. Here are two examples: Original sentence: Biodegradable and biocompatible 0DBMs seem to be promising candidates to solve the problem, since they show great abilities to deliver the biomolecules in to cells, and some 0DBMs even show inductive properties themselves. Negated sentence: Biodegradable and biocompatible 0DBMs do not seem to be promising candidates to solve the problem, since they show limited abilities to deliver the biomolecules in to cells, and some 0DBMs even lack inductive properties themselves. Original sentence: Approximately 90% of SIDS deaths occur in infants aged less than 6 months. Negated sentence: Approximately 10% of SIDS deaths occur in infants aged less than 6 months. Please provide a negated version of the following sentence: "
"Please provide a new sentence with the opposite meaning as the following, by changing as few words as possible in the original: "
"Please provide a new sentence with the opposite meaning as the following, by changing a small number of words: "
"Please provide a new sentence with the opposite meaning as the following: "
"Please negate this sentence by changing as few words as possible in the original sentence: "

Table 5: Prompt variants tested for negation generation

Researcher Representations Based on Aggregating Embeddings of Publication Titles: A Case Study in a Japanese Academic Database

Hiroyoshi Nagao
Doshisha University
nagao21@mm.doshisha.ac.jp

Marie Katsurai
Doshisha University
katsurai@mm.doshisha.ac.jp

Abstract

Constructing researcher representations is crucial for search and recommendation in academic databases. While recent studies presented methods based on knowledge graph embeddings, obtaining a complete graph of academic entities might be sometimes challenging due to the lack of linked data. By contrast, the textual list of publications of each researcher, which represents their research interests and expertise, is usually easy to obtain. Therefore, this study focuses on creating researcher representations based on textual embeddings of their publication titles and assesses their practicality. We aggregate embeddings of each researcher's multiple publications into a single vector and apply it to research field classification and similar researcher search tasks. We experimented with multiple language models and embedding aggregation methods to compare their performance. From the model perspective, we confirmed the effectiveness of using sentence embedding models and a simple averaging approach.

1 Introduction

Academic databases equipped with search and recommendation functions have supported researchers' activities. Traditional search approaches primarily involve users inputting specific keywords and then retrieving corresponding papers and authors (Wu et al., 2019; Fricke, 2018). However, in actual research scenarios, researchers often need to efficiently find papers to read based on their previous interests or discover individuals in other fields with similar research interests. To address these requirements, methods for constructing researcher representations in a feature space have been actively studied in recent years (Chaiwanarom and Lursinsap, 2015; Katsurai et al., 2016; Ganesh et al., 2016; Färber et al., 2023). In particular, with the development of academic graphs such as Microsoft Academic Graph (MAG)[1], there have been presented several methods based on knowledge graph embeddings to construct researchers' vector representations (Priem et al., 2022; Färber et al., 2023). However, these studies assume well-organized graph databases as input resources, making it difficult to apply these methods to databases lacking sufficient linked data. For example, Grant-in-Aid for Scientific Research database (KAKEN), one of typical academic databases in Japan, comprises records of research accomplishments of grant projects but does not link them to their authors and presentation venues. Using such databases would first require data linking to construct a graph structure before applying graph embedding methods.

Compared with obtaining a complete graph structure, the textual list of publications of each researcher is more accessible. Recent development of language models pre-trained using large-scale text data (Devlin et al., 2019; Feng et al., 2022; Wang et al., 2022) has significantly improved several retrieval and recommendation tasks, and academic-specific language models were released for certain languages (Beltagy et al., 2019; Labrak et al., 2023; Yamauchi et al., 2022). Under such background, this study attempts to construct researcher representations solely from the textual publication information using pre-trained language models. The usefulness of these representations is then examined through experiments on two practical application tasks: research field classification and similar researcher search.

2 Related Work

Researcher representations have been studied using a variety of methods, such as topic models (Chaiwanarom and Lursinsap, 2015; Katsurai et al., 2016)

[1] https://www.microsoft.com/en-us/research/project/microsoft-academic-graph/

Proceedings of the Fourth Workshop on Scholarly Document Processing (SDP 2024), pages 277–282
August 16, 2024

and document embeddings (Ganesh et al., 2016). Recent methods focused on the graph structure of academic entities and calculated the node features using graph embedding methods. MAG was a typical example of a large-scale academic graph, and its successor project, OpenAlex (Priem et al., 2022), has recently been used. Färber et al. (2023) constructed an RDF-based knowledge graph platform called SemOpenAlex and experimentally evaluated the embedding methods for various nodes such as researchers and papers on the graph. Such knowledge graph-derived researcher representations are used to solve academic tasks such as author name disambiguation (Santini et al., 2022).

On the other hand, the newly emerging pre-trained language models have substantially promoted the development of text processing for information retrieval and recommendation, and we can expect their effectiveness on researcher embeddings. It is known that a certain domain task often benefits from a language model pre-trained using text in the target domain. However, in scientific domains, we observed cases where general domain models are sufficient (Zheng et al., 2022; Brokman and Kavuluru, 2024). Taking into account the above matters, this paper includes an experiment that compares the performance between general language models and domain-specific models in a single language embedding setting.

3 Methodology

Our method aims to construct a researcher's representation using a comprehensive list of publication titles related to their research grant project. Since most researchers in Japan use both English and Japanese languages to present their research, we investigate in experiments whether we should embed both the two languages' text to calculate the researchers' representations.

3.1 Text Embedding Based on Pre-trained Language Models

To acquire semantic information from the text of each publication title, we exploit the BERT architecture (Devlin et al., 2019) as a pre-trained text encoder. First, the given text is divided into subwords by the tokenizer associated with the model. These subwords are then input into the model to obtain embedding representations at the subword level. Next, pooling operations are applied to the obtained token representations to derive the publication text embeddings. There are two choices for pooling: CLS pooling, which uses the representation of the special initial token, and mean pooling, which averages the representations of all tokens. Based on a conventional study (Reimers and Gurevych, 2019), we use mean pooling.[2]

Language	Count
Japanese	3,122,244
English	3,283,871
Others	779

Table 1: Statistics of languages used in KAKEN projects.

3.2 Aggregating Publication Text Embeddings

The interests of researchers are diverse, and it is not clear how to best aggregate publication titles' embeddings. The first method is arithmetic averaging (hereafter referred to simply as **averaging**), commonly used for pooling word representations into sentence representations. However, researchers do not necessarily contribute equally to all their publications. For example, contributions are generally more distributed in co-authored papers compared to single-authored papers. Therefore, as the second method, we consider **weighted averaging** using the inverse of the number of authors as weights. This assumes that the fewer the authors, the greater the individual contribution to the publication. This method is inspired by author evaluation metrics like the h-index, which takes into account the influence of the number of authors (Abramo et al., 2013). In subsequent experiments, we compare the performance of these two methods.

4 Experiments

We used the KAKEN API[3] to collect KAKEN projects as of October 2023 and the publication titles linked to the projects' members. We explain details about the KAKEN API in Appendix A. Table 1 shows the distribution of languages in the publication titles. As shown in Table 1, Japanese researchers usually publish papers in Japanese and English. "Other" category included languages such as Russian and Mongolian. We exploited multilingual models to embed Japanese and English

[2]Actually, in downstream tasks mentioned later, mean pooling outperformed CLS pooling in all tasks.

[3]https://support.nii.ac.jp/en/kaken/api/api_outline

Category	Research field name	Count
A	arts	26,170
B	algebra	5,812
C	strength of materials	7,451
D	materials engineering	4,477
E	organic/inorganic chemistry	3,295
F	agriculture	5,372
G	biology	3,177
H	pharmacy	3,876
I	internal/social medicine	27,165
J	information science	3,591
K	environmental analysis	1,675

Table 2: Large categories of research fields in KAKEN.

Model	Large F1	Medium F1	Small F1
mE5 (avg)	0.606	**0.514**	**0.396**
mE5 (weighted)	0.604	0.510	0.361
mBERT	0.582	0.455	0.311
LaBSE	**0.607**	0.504	0.367

Table 3: Results of research field classification.

publication titles into the same space. Specifically, we adopted the following three models: Multilingual BERT (mBERT)[4] (Devlin et al., 2019), Multilingual E5 (mE5)[5] (Wang et al., 2022), and LaBSE[6] (Feng et al., 2022); each model had 110 million parameters. Among these, mE5 and LaBSE are so called sentence embedding models. We aim to find out whether such models are suitable for embedding publication titles.

To verify the effectiveness of the constructed researcher representations, we conducted two practical application tasks: research field classification (see Section 4.1) and similar researcher search (see Section 4.2). Since there is no multilingual pretrained model in the scientific domain, we also investigate the performance of domain-specific models in single language embedding setting (see Section 4.3).

[4]https://huggingface.co/bert-base-multilingual-cased

[5]https://huggingface.co/intfloat/multilingual-e5-base

[6]https://huggingface.co/sentence-transformers/LaBSE

4.1 Research Field Classification

Research field classification is a task to identify the main research fields of a researcher based on their representation. The ground-truth labels were determined based on area categories[7] of the research projects associated with each researcher. Each research project was manually classified by its representative researcher in terms of three levels: large, medium, and small categories. These levels have 11, 65, and 305 categories, respectively. Table 2 shows area category names and number of researchers for only large categories due to space constraints. We provided three-level labels for each researcher using their project labels. Appendix B describes the labeling procedure. We obtained a dataset of 92,061 researchers who have at least three publication titles. All data was split into training, validation, and test sets in an 8:1:1 ratio, keeping the original label distribution. At the training stage, we added a linear layer as a classifier. Specifically, we froze the weights of the text encoder and trained only the linear layer. We used a scheduler that increases the learning rate until a certain point and then fixes it. We set the period of time until the learning rate was fixed to one epoch.

Table 3 shows the F1 scores of classification results. In Appendix B, we also evaluate the accuracy. The model "avg" denotes aggregation using the averaging, while "weighted" represents aggregation using the weighted averaging. Notably, aggregation using the averaging exhibited superior performance, indicating that weighting by the inverse of the number of authors did not enhance performance. Hereafter, references to each model refer to the case where aggregation using the averaging was employed. Focusing on different models, mE5 and LaBSE demonstrated similar performance. Conversely, mBERT exhibited a significant performance gap compared to mE5, with 5% lower F1 scores in the middle sections and 8% lower in the small sections, although no significant performance difference was observed in the large category classification.

4.2 Similar Researcher Search

This experiment defined positive and negative examples for a query researcher. We ranked the com-

[7]Because category names are reviewed and updated at a few years intervals, we focused on the category hierarchy introduced in 2018 fiscal year. Details are available in https://www.jsps.go.jp/j-grantsinaid/02_koubo/shinsakubun.html.

Model	MAP	NDCG
mE5 (avg)	**0.783**	**0.856**
mE5 (weighted)	0.758	0.839
mBERT	0.711	0.805
LaBSE	0.765	0.843

Table 4: Results of researcher search based on research content similarity.

Language	Model	MAP	NDCG
Multi	mE5	**0.783**	**0.856**
English	mE5	0.740	0.815
	SciBERT	0.701	0.785
	BERT	0.650	0.747
Japanese	mE5	0.777	0.851
	AcRoBERTa	0.576	0.696
	RoBERTa	0.514	0.645

Table 5: Comparison among different language resources in the researcher search task.

bined set of researchers using the similarity between the researcher representations and evaluated whether the positive examples were ranked higher. For each query, we defined co-investigators of research projects as positive examples, and randomly selected other researchers as negative examples. From the 92,061 researchers, we extracted up to 10 queries per small research category, totaling 2,980 queries, where each query had at least 5 positive examples. We used cosine similarity as the measure of similarity between the researcher representations. We set the maximum number of positive examples to 10, and if there were more than 10 positive examples, we preferentially selected those associated with more research projects. We set the number of negative examples to 50.

Table 4 shows the MAP and NDCG of results obtained by each model's similarity measure. As shown, mE5 achieved the best performance, followed by LaBSE and mBERT. Similar to research field classification, there was no significant performance disparity between mE5 and LaBSE, while a noticeable 7% difference in MAP was noted compared to mBERT. Combined with the results in section 4.1, we observed that the sentence embedding models positively influenced the embedding of paper titles and their subsequent aggregation.

4.3 Influence of Input Language

In the researcher search task, we further investigated the influence of multilingualism and domain adaptation, which can be used as future guidelines for designing a multilingual model specialized in the academic domain. We considered the following three settings: (i) embedding only Japanese titles, (ii) embedding only English titles, and (iii) embedding both Japanese and English titles. All settings used mE5 as a multilingual model, which was the best performing model in the previous experiments. The first setting used Academic RoBERTa (Yamauchi et al., 2022) (hereafter, **AcRoBERTa**), a model specific to the Japanese academic domain, and normal RoBERTa[8]. The second setting used SciBERT (Beltagy et al., 2019), a model specific to the English academic domain, and normal BERT. The third setting used only mE5 and no additional models.

Table 5 shows the results of different models for each setting. Focusing on mE5, using multilingual inputs resulted in higher performance than using only Japanese or only English inputs. This suggests that better feature representations are obtained by aggregating embeddings of publications in both Japanese and English titles of researchers. On the other hand, comparing the results for only English inputs, mE5, which is not specialized, showed higher performance than the domain-specific SciBERT. This observation was also noted when the input was only Japanese. Since AcRoBERTa has a very small training corpus compared to other models, it is considered that models trained on large corpora are advantageous for obtaining researcher representations in all fields. In conclusion, at least for inputs such as publication titles that are relatively short texts, it is suggested that the influence of adaptation to sentence embeddings is more important than the effect of domain adaptation.

5 Conclusion

In this paper, we focused on the titles of researchers' publications in academic databases and constructed researcher representations by aggregating their text embeddings. We then evaluated the performance of these representations in two practical tasks. The results of the experiments showed that the performance of each task improved with sentence embedding models. Additionally, inputting publica-

[8]https://huggingface.co/nlp-waseda/roberta-base-japanese

tions in multiple languages was more effective than in a single language. However, there were practical challenges with domain-specific models, as general-domain models outperformed them. These results suggest the need for the development of new multilingual models that are robust in sentence representation and have domain knowledge.

Acknowledgments

This research was partly supported by JSPS KAKENHI Grant Number JP20H04484.

References

Giovanni Abramo, Ciriaco Andrea D'Angelo, and Fulvio Viel. 2013. Assessing the accuracy of the h-and g-indexes for measuring researchers' productivity. *Journal of the American Society for Information Science and Technology*, 64(6):1224–1234.

Iz Beltagy, Kyle Lo, and Arman Cohan. 2019. SciBERT: A pretrained language model for scientific text. In *Proceedings of the 2019 Conference on Empirical Methods in Natural Language Processing and the 9th International Joint Conference on Natural Language Processing (EMNLP-IJCNLP)*, pages 3615–3620, Hong Kong, China. Association for Computational Linguistics.

Aviv Brokman and Ramakanth Kavuluru. 2024. How important is domain specificity in language models and instruction finetuning for biomedical relation extraction? *arXiv preprint arXiv:2402.13470*.

Paweena Chaiwanarom and Chidchanok Lursinsap. 2015. Collaborator recommendation in interdisciplinary computer science using degrees of collaborative forces, temporal evolution of research interest, and comparative seniority status. *Knowledge-Based Systems*, 75:161–172.

Jacob Devlin, Ming-Wei Chang, Kenton Lee, and Kristina Toutanova. 2019. BERT: Pre-training of deep bidirectional transformers for language understanding. In *Proceedings of the 2019 Conference of the North American Chapter of the Association for Computational Linguistics: Human Language Technologies, Volume 1 (Long and Short Papers)*, pages 4171–4186, Minneapolis, Minnesota. Association for Computational Linguistics.

Michael Färber, David Lamprecht, Johan Krause, Linn Aung, and Peter Haase. 2023. Semopenalex: The scientific landscape in 26 billion rdf triples. In *The Semantic Web – ISWC 2023*, pages 94–112, Cham. Springer Nature Switzerland.

Fangxiaoyu Feng, Yinfei Yang, Daniel Cer, Naveen Arivazhagan, and Wei Wang. 2022. Language-agnostic BERT sentence embedding. In *Proceedings of the 60th Annual Meeting of the Association for Computational Linguistics (Volume 1: Long Papers)*, pages 878–891, Dublin, Ireland. Association for Computational Linguistics.

Suzanne Fricke. 2018. Semantic scholar. *Journal of the Medical Library Association: JMLA*, 106(1):145.

J Ganesh, Soumyajit Ganguly, Manish Gupta, Vasudeva Varma, and Vikram Pudi. 2016. Author2vec: Learning author representations by combining content and link information. In *WWW (Companion volume)*, pages 49–50.

Marie Katsurai, Ikki Ohmukai, and Hideaki Takeda. 2016. Topic representation of researchers' interests in a large-scale academic database and its application to author disambiguation. *IEICE Transactions on Information and Systems*, 99(4):1010–1018.

Yanis Labrak, Adrien Bazoge, Richard Dufour, Mickael Rouvier, Emmanuel Morin, Béatrice Daille, and Pierre-Antoine Gourraud. 2023. DrBERT: A robust pre-trained model in French for biomedical and clinical domains. In *Proceedings of the 61st Annual Meeting of the Association for Computational Linguistics (Volume 1: Long Papers)*, pages 16207–16221, Toronto, Canada. Association for Computational Linguistics.

Jason Priem, Heather Piwowar, and Richard Orr. 2022. Openalex: A fully-open index of scholarly works, authors, venues, institutions, and concepts. *arXiv preprint arXiv:2205.01833*.

Nils Reimers and Iryna Gurevych. 2019. Sentence-BERT: Sentence embeddings using Siamese BERT-networks. In *Proceedings of the 2019 Conference on Empirical Methods in Natural Language Processing and the 9th International Joint Conference on Natural Language Processing (EMNLP-IJCNLP)*, pages 3982–3992, Hong Kong, China. Association for Computational Linguistics.

Cristian Santini, Genet Asefa Gesese, Silvio Peroni, Aldo Gangemi, Harald Sack, and Mehwish Alam. 2022. A knowledge graph embeddings based approach for author name disambiguation using literals. *Scientometrics*, 127(8):4887–4912.

Liang Wang, Nan Yang, Xiaolong Huang, Binxing Jiao, Linjun Yang, Daxin Jiang, Rangan Majumder, and Furu Wei. 2022. Text embeddings by weakly-supervised contrastive pre-training. *arXiv preprint arXiv:2212.03533*.

Jian Wu, Kunho Kim, and C. Lee Giles. 2019. Citeseerx: 20 years of service to scholarly big data. In *Proceedings of the Conference on Artificial Intelligence for Data Discovery and Reuse*, AIDR '19, New York, NY, USA. Association for Computing Machinery.

Hiroki Yamauchi, Tomoyuki Kajiwara, Marie Katsurai, Ikki Ohmukai, and Takashi Ninomiya. 2022. A Japanese masked language model for academic domain. In *Proceedings of the Third Workshop on Scholarly Document Processing*, pages 152–157.

```
Researcher
├─ ID
├─ Name
├─ Affiliation
├─ Research projects
│  ├─ ID
│  ├─ Title
│  ├─ Research category
│  ├─ Members
│  └─ Keywords
└─ Publications
   ├─ ID
   ├─ Title
   ├─ Authors (unparsed)
   ├─ Organizer (unparsed)
   └─ Publication date
```

Figure 1: Researcher data that can be obtained using the KAKEN API.

Zhe Zheng, Xin-Zheng Lu, Ke-Yin Chen, Yu-Cheng Zhou, and Jia-Rui Lin. 2022. Pretrained domain-specific language model for general information retrieval tasks in the aec domain. *arXiv preprint arXiv:2203.04729*.

A Use of KAKEN API

KAKEN is a public database that includes information regarding projects supported by KAKENHI, a grant program provided by the Japan Society for the Promotion of Science. The program supports research projects in diverse research fields, including natural sciences, engineering, social sciences, and humanities, for researchers affiliated with Japanese institutions. KAKEN provides an API that allows a search of KAKENHI projects using several types of queries (e.g., research periods, researcher names). Figure 1 shows items that can be obtained for each researcher through the KAKEN API.

B Labeling Procedure for Research Field Classification

We determined a unique field in each category level for a researcher using the following method. We first extracted the research projects with explicitly defined small categories from the set of research projects held by the researcher, and assigned the most frequent small category as the ground-truth one. Next, we listed the large, medium pairs to which the small research category belongs in the category hierachy defined in KAKEN. If the pair was uniquely determined, the process was completed. Finally, for each listed pair, we calculated the sum of the frequencies of the large and medium sections from the set of research projects. The pair with the highest frequency was then determined.

Model	Large Acc	Medium Acc	Small Acc
mE5 (avg)	**0.759**	**0.588**	**0.475**
mE5 (weighted)	0.757	0.586	0.468
mBERT	0.744	0.530	0.398
LaBSE	0.756	0.580	0.473

Table 6: Results of research field classification.

C Accuracy of Research Field Classificaiton

At the training stage, we searched for the maximum learning rate in the range of 1e-5, 3e-5, 5e-5, 1e-4 and adopted the evaluation value of the trial with the highest performance on the validation set. Table 6 shows accuracy of research field classification. As described in Section 4.1, in terms of the aggregation method, the averaging was slightly higher than the weighting by the inverse of the number of authors. In the comparison between models, as with the F1 Score, a notable difference in performance was observed between mE5 and mBERT. In the comparison between the models, the difference in performance between mE5 and mBERT was 8% in the small section, which is as significant as in the F1 Score.

CoSAEmb: Contrastive Section-aware Aspect Embeddings for Scientific Articles

Shruti Singh and **Mayank Singh**
{singh_shruti, singh.mayank}@iitgn.ac.in
LINGO, Indian Institute of Technology Gandhinagar
India

Abstract

Research papers are long documents that contain information about various aspects such as background, prior work, methodology, and results. Existing works on scientific document representation learning only leverage the title and abstract of the paper. We present CoSAEmb, a model that learns representations from the full-text of 97402 scientific papers from the S2ORC dataset. We present a novel supervised contrastive training framework for long documents using triplet loss and margin gradation. Our framework can be used to learn representations of long documents with any existing encoder-only transformer model without retraining it from scratch. CoSAEmb shows improved performance on information retrieval from the paper's full-text in comparison to models trained only on paper titles and abstracts. We also evaluate CoSAEmb on SciRepEval and CSFCube benchmarks, showing comparable performance with existing state-of-the-art models.

1 Introduction

Scientific papers contain dense detailed information in the paper text. However, existing works on scientific document representation learning are restricted to either the title and abstract of the paper or encode sentence-level information. SciBERT (Beltagy et al., 2019) and BioBERT (Lee et al., 2020) are the earliest transformer-based representation learning models for scientific texts, both of which use the BERT model as base architecture. Both of these models operate at the sentence level. Models such as SPECTER (Cohan et al., 2020), OAG-BERT (Liu et al., 2022), Siamese-SciBERT (Ostendorff et al., 2022a), and SciNCL (Ostendorff et al., 2022b) encode the title and the abstract of the paper. Mysore et al. (2022) learn multiple aspect-specific vectors of research papers at the sentence level. We posit that the title and the abstract embeddings or sentence vectors fail to capture the intricate details of the paper. In contrast to existing methods, our training strategy (described in Section 3) takes into consideration the full-text of the paper in a contrastive learning setup. We propose to learn section embeddings for a paper, which are clustered together in the embedding space. The relative distance of dissimilar papers and similar papers with respect to a candidate is enforced to be larger than a margin. We leverage the positive pairs in contrastive learning to minimize the distance between the section embeddings of the same paper, ensuring that intra-paper similarity is preserved. Likewise, the negative instances in the contrastive loss ensure dissimilar papers are farther away. This setup ensures that section embeddings of the same paper are closer to each other in the embedding space than embeddings of other papers, preserving the local information context. Similarly, similar papers are closer in the embedding space in comparison to dissimilar papers, preserving interdocument relations. We present a schematic of the embedding space in Figure 1.

2 Related Works

SciBERT (Beltagy et al., 2019) and BioBERT (Lee et al., 2020) train a BERT architecture model on the Semantic Scholar corpus and biomedical corpora, respectively. Both models take sentences as input and learn sentence representations. These are not specifically trained to represent research papers.

SPECTER (Cohan et al., 2020) is initialized from SciBERT and uses a citation-based triplet loss for fine-tuning the model. It encodes the paper's title and abstract. It leverages citations to construct triplets for contrastive loss, i.e., w.r.t. to a query paper (q), a positive paper (k_+) is one of its cited papers. Similarly, a negative paper (k_-) for q is a paper that is not cited by q (but could be cited by k_+). SPECTER is evaluated on SciDocs (Co-

Proceedings of the Fourth Workshop on Scholarly Document Processing (SDP 2024), pages 283–292
August 16, 2024 ©2024 Association for Computational Linguistics

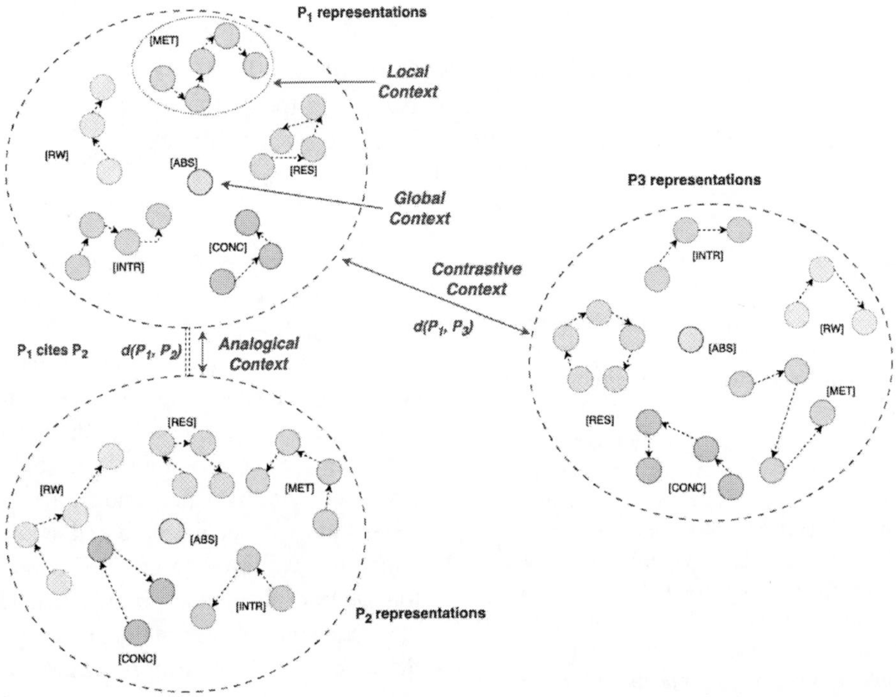

Figure 1: P_1, P_2, and P_3 represent three papers, and P_1 cites P_2. Aspect vectors are constructed from sections of research papers. Multiple vectors are learned for each section depending on model's context length. A hierarchy of distances is introduced between embeddings of different paper sections using contrastive loss with margin gradation.

han et al., 2020) benchmark consisting of seven tasks categorized into document classification, user activity prediction, citation prediction, and recommendation. Our proposed approach builds upon SPECTER by introducing a technique to utilize existing 512 context length limited transformers for large documents of any length. SciNCL (Ostendorff et al., 2022b) extends the SPECTER model with controlled nearest neighbor sampling over the citation graph that avoids collision between positive and negative samples.

OAG-BERT (Liu et al., 2022) encodes paper titles, abstracts, and heterogeneous entities such as authors, research fields, venues, and affiliations using a BERT model. They design strategies such as entity-type embeddings to denote heterogeneous entities and entity-aware 2D positional embeddings to demarcate inter and intra-entity token boundaries. The model also uses span-aware entity masking instead of BERT's random word masking to make the model learn entities.

FeRoSA (Chakraborty et al., 2016) is a faceted recommendation system for scientific articles. It recommends papers from the induced subnetwork of the candidate paper (built from cited papers and papers with highly similar content) for the facets: background (introduction), alternative approaches (related works), method, and comparison (results and conclusion). Edges in the network are assigned facets based on the section in which the paper is cited in the candidate paper. FeRoSA supports faceted recommendation, while our framework is focused on learning faceted representations for scientific articles that can be further used for downstream tasks such as faceted recommendation.

Aspect embeddings, i.e., embeddings for different facets of the paper, are learned in (Ostendorff et al., 2022a) and (Mysore et al., 2022). Embeddings for facets such as task, method, and dataset, are learned in Ostendorff et al. (2022a); however, these are again learned from the title and abstract of the paper. Ostendorff et al. (2022a) use the PWC dataset (Kardas et al., 2020), which contains task, method, and dataset labels for papers. The best-performing model Siamese-SciBERT is fine-tuned on the PWC dataset based on aspect labels. ASPIRE (Mysore et al., 2022), on the other hand, leverages co-citation sentences as a source of document similarity. However, unlike our proposed method, both these models use only the title and the abstract to learn aspect vectors. We also present a comparison of CoSAEmb with other models

Model	Input	Contrastive	Citation Information	Entity Information
SciBERT	Sentence			
SBERT	Sentence	✓		
SPECTER	Title & Abstract	✓	✓	
OAG-BERT	Title & Abstract			✓
Siamese-BERT	Title & Abstract	✓		
SciNCL	Title & Abstract	✓	✓	
ASPIRE	Sentence	✓	✓	
CoSAEmb *(ours)*	Full-text paragraphs	✓	✓	

Table 1: All existing models either encode title+abstract of the paper, or represent the full-text of the paper at sentence level.

in Table 1.

Singh et al. (2023) train multi-format scientific models for four types of tasks, specifically classification, proximity, search, and regression, in order to improve the generalization ability of models. They also introduce SciRepEval benchmark, which consists of twenty-five tasks to evaluate scientific document representations across diverse task formats. In this work, we limit our approach to learning embeddings for different facets of the paper and do not attempt to generalize them to diverse tasks.

As outlined in Tay et al. (2022), works on efficient transformers address the quadratic time complexity by using one of the techniques: (i) sparsify the attention matrix using fixed patterns, (ii) learnable patterns that learn the access pattern in a data-driven fashion (rephrase, arrange tokens based on similarity), (iii) introducing memory modules, (iv) low-rank approximation of the self-attention matrix, (v) kernels, (vi) recurrence, or a combination of these. Multiple variants of efficient transformers such as Linformer (Wang et al., 2020), Longformer (Beltagy et al., 2020), BigBird (Zaheer et al., 2020), Reformer (Kitaev et al., 2020), Performer (Choromanski et al., 2021) have been proposed. While multiple efficient long document transformers are proposed (e.g., Tay et al. (2022) discuss thirty-two efficient transformers), only Longformer has been adapted for scientific papers and evaluation on the QASPER benchmark (Dasigi et al., 2021) shows significant scope for adoption of these models for the scientific domain. The performance and effectiveness of other efficient transformer models on scientific documents are largely unexplored. Unlike works on efficient transformers, we focus on reusing the existing models such as SciBERT and SPECTER with contrastive fine-tuning to learn full-text document representations.

3 CoSAEmb

In this section, we present CoSAEmb (pronounced ko-saam-bee), COntrastive Section-aware Aspect Embeddings. CoSAEmb is a supervised contrastive training framework for long documents using margin gradation. Scientific articles are long documents containing information on multiple aspects. We learn aspect representations for long documents instead of relying on a single document vector to capture all the information from various aspects. We briefly discuss the intuition behind our document representation framework next.

3.1 Motivation

A document presents a sequence of ideas in a continuous flow. The information in a document can be categorized into topics or aspects. For example, a product review can discuss different aspects of the product, such as its price and the quality of specific components. In scientific documents, key aspects can be defined as problem motivation, limitations of previous works, methodology, results, and conclusions drawn. This aspect-specific information is typically addressed in the Introduction, Related Works, Methods, Results, and Conclusion sections of the paper, respectively. In our work, we assume aspect-specific information is present in specific sections; and hence learn aspect vectors from the corresponding paper sections.

When reading a research paper, three types of document context contribute to its understanding:

1. ***Local Information Context:*** Each paragraph or sentence in a research paper contains information which could be understood as an answer to a highly specific fine-grained question. E.g., '*What evaluation metric was used for comparison? Why was a specific parameter*

included in the algorithm? How are the limitations of a specific previous work addressed? The paragraphs of the paper establish the local context necessary for comprehending and interpreting individual sentences.

2. ***Global Information Context:*** Global information represents the paper's main objective, primary contributions, and key findings. It provides a concise summary of the paper, combining coarse-grained information across multiple aspects. Generally, an abstract of the paper is an apt representative of global information.
3. ***Analogical or Contrastive Context:*** Human learning frequently involves drawing analogies or making comparisons to familiar concepts (Hofstadter, 1995; Schwartz and Bransford, 1998; Gentner et al., 2003). This concept positions a document with respect to others, capturing the similarities, dissimilarities, and shared properties. It emphasizes understanding inter-document relations through analogy or contrast. E.g., Two papers may be similar due to their common field of study, shared authors, or connected by a citation. This information about various inter-document relations may not be explicitly present in the document and is often acquired by humans with time.

We base our document representation framework on the above-discussed information contexts. As depicted by a schematic in Figure 1, we capture local information context for a paper P_1 by creating paragraph vectors for different aspects (sections in our case). The paragraph length is determined by the encoder model's context length. The global information is captured by the abstract vector. Finally, to capture inter-document relations, we employ citation information. If P_1 cites P_2 but does not cite P_1, then representations of P_1 is closer to P_2 in comparison to P_3. The reorientation of these document representations (paragraph or aspect vectors which constitute the local context, title and abstract vector constituting the global context) in the embedding space to capture these similarities is discussed in Section 3.3.

CoSAEmb leverages contrastive learning to represent long documents using a transformer model. CoSAEmb learns multiple representations for different aspects of the research papers specified in sections by learning section embeddings. We use a transformer model to compute representations for different sections of the paper, including the abstract. The model is fine-tuned using contrastive loss to optimize the local section and global abstract representations of the document. As we learn multiple aspect embeddings for the same paper capturing different aspects, it should be ensured that embeddings of the same paper are close to each other in the embedding space. In addition, it is also desirable that embeddings of similar papers should be closer than dissimilar papers.

3.2 Architecture

We use an encoder-only transformers model, specifically SciBERT (Beltagy et al., 2019) for encoding document sections. Each section is split into chunks of length 512, which is the maximum length supported by most models. Hence, we construct multiple embeddings for a paper from the full-text of the paper, which are reoriented using a triplet loss. Let t denote a triplet consisting of a query/anchor (q), positive (k_+), and negative key (k_-).

$$t = (q, k_+, k_-) \tag{1}$$

Triplet loss enforces an order of distances, i.e., the difference between the distance between the anchor and the positive key and the anchor and negative key is at least a certain value, called margin in triplet loss. The detailed loss function is presented in Section 3.4. We discuss the formulation of three types of triplets that reorient the embeddings to encapsulate similarity between sections and papers.

3.3 Embedding Reorientation Triplets

We construct three types of triplets to reorient the embeddings to optimize the section and abstract representations by training on local context, global context, and analogical or contrastive context.

3.3.1 Section Representations (Local context)

For each candidate paper p_c (section text represented by p_c^{intr}, p_c^{rel}, p_c^{meth}, p_c^{res}, p_c^{conc} and title+abstract represented by p_c^{abs}), we train the model with the triplet loss function. The triplet loss contains an anchor p_c, a positive (p_+), and a negative (p_-) instance with respect to the anchor.

Section representations are obtained from SciBERT. However, a section text may exceed 512 tokens, so we further break it down into chunks. The first chunk is prepended with the title, and the rest chunks prepend the last sentence from the preceding chunk. For example, let the

'Introduction' section consists of lines $\mathcal{L} = [l_1, l_2, ... \ l_n]$. We split the sentences into sentence chunks such that total token size of the chunk is approximately 512. The chunk set $\mathcal{C} = [\mathcal{C}_1, \mathcal{C}_2, ..., \mathcal{C}_p]$; such that

$$\mathcal{C}_1 = [l_1, l_2, ..., l_i]$$
$$\mathcal{C}_2 = [l_{i+1}, l_{i+2}, ..., l_j]$$
$$\mathcal{C}_3 = [l_{j+1}, l_{j+2}, ..., l_k]$$
$$...$$
$$\mathcal{C}_p = [l_{m+1}, ..., l_n]$$

Special tokens are appended to the sentence chunks to indicate the section as follows:

$$p_c^{intr\_C_1} = \texttt{[TTL] title [INTR]} \ l_1, l_2, ..., l_i$$
$$p_c^{intr\_C_2} = \texttt{[INTR]} \ l_i \ \texttt{[INTR]} \ l_{i+1}, l_{i+2}, ..., l_j$$
$$p_c^{intr\_C_3} = \texttt{[INTR]} \ l_j \ \texttt{[INTR]} \ l_{j+1}, l_{j+2}, ..., l_k$$
$$...$$
$$p_c^{intr\_C_p} = \texttt{[INTR]} \ l_m \ \texttt{[INTR]} \ l_{m+1}, l_{m+2}, ..., l_n$$

Chunks from the same section *sec*, are used to construct triplets of the form:

$$(p_c^{sec\_C_{i+1}}, \ p_c^{sec\_C_i}, \ p_-^{abs}); i \geq 1 \quad (2)$$
$$\text{sec} \in \{\texttt{intr, rel, met, res, conc}\}$$

Similarly, we introduce other special tokens [INTR], [RW], [MET], [RES], and [CONC] for the introduction, related works, method, results, and conclusion sections, respectively.

3.3.2 Abstract Representations (Global context)

An abstract contains a summary of the paper and discusses multiple aspects such as method and results. So we consider an abstract to create document representations. But we also fine-tune the model using contrastive setup to influence the abstract embeddings by section embeddings. The triplets are formulated to ensure that local and global context is efficiently captured. The global context triplets for a candidate paper p_c are formulated as follows:

$$(p_c^{sec\_C_1}, \ p_c^{abs}, \ p_-^{abs}); \quad (3)$$
$$\text{sec} \in \{\texttt{intr, rel, met, res, conc}\}$$

p_-^{abs} is the concatenated title and abstract (i.e. p_-^{abs} = [TTL] title [SEP] [ABS] abstract, where [TTL] and [ABS] are special tokens) of a paper that p_c cites. $p_c^{\text{sec}\_C_1}$ is formulated in a similar way, e.g., the 'Introduction' section p_c^{intr} = [TTL] title [SEP] [INTR] introduction, and denotes that only the first chunk is used.

As the abstract is a concise summary of the paper, we consider the abstract embedding a representative of the paper summary encoding high-level details. The paper triplets formulated in Equations (2) and (3) ensure that section embeddings representing information from various sections of the paper are similar to the abstract embedding, while preserving specific details from the section text. We posit that section information embeddings (or aspect embeddings) influence abstract embeddings and vice-versa, robustifying the embeddings to noise during the training using intra-document triplets. We also posit that the placement of abstract embedding in the vicinity of section embeddings allows orientation of the document vectors in a cluster-like structure, leading to a better-defined subspace. While initially the aspect vectors could be randomly distributed in the representation space, contrastive training reorganizes the vectors together into a cohesive document vector cluster. Section embeddings encode the specific low-level details from different sections of the paper. These embeddings capture the intra-document relations.

3.3.3 Inter-document Relation Representations (Analogical or Contrastive Context)

Multiple inter-document relations between scientific papers, such as papers belonging to the same field of study, cited papers, papers with the same authors, and co-cited papers, represent highly similar papers. In our work, similar to the SPECTER (Cohan et al., 2020), we use the citation information to capture inter-document information. We formulate inter-doc triplets based on citations as follows:

$$(p_c^{abs}, p_+^{abs}, p_-^{abs}) \quad (4)$$

With respect to the anchor paper p_c, the positive paper p_+ is cited by p_c. On the contrary, the negative paper p_- is not cited by p_c, but it could be cited by another paper that is cited by p_c. The triplets formulated using Equation (4) ensure that semantically similar papers are closer to each other in the embedding space than dissimilar papers. Positive papers p_+ can be sampled from the citations of the candidate paper p_c. Negative papers p_- can be sampled (i) randomly (easy negatives) or (ii) from the two-hop neighbor papers which weren't cited originally by p_c (hard negatives). Similar to p_c^{abs} in previous paper triplets, the format of each component is as: [TTL] title [SEP] [ABS] abstract.

3.4 Contrastive Learning Setup and Margin Gradation

Similar to SPECTER, we start with a SciBERT (Beltagy et al., 2019) initialized model, and train the Transformer model with the triplet loss $\mathcal{L}(t)$ defined in Equation (5). However, we use margin gradation for the triplet loss. We incrementally increase the margin value as we go from inter-document to global to local context.

$$\mathcal{L}(t) = \max(0, d(q, k_+)^2 - d(q, k_-)^2 + m_t) \quad (5)$$

where, triplets t are sampled from the triplet set $\mathcal{T}$ defined below. $\mathcal{S}$ denotes the set of local context triplets constructed from sections, $\mathcal{G}$ denotes the set of global context triplets and $\mathcal{I}$ denotes inter-document (or cross-document) triplets. $\mathcal{P}$ denotes the set of candidate anchor papers and $\mathcal{F} = \{\texttt{intr}, \texttt{rel}, \texttt{met}, \texttt{res}, \texttt{conc}\}$.

$$\mathcal{T} = \{t_i : t_i \in \mathcal{I}\} \cup \{t_g : t_g \in \mathcal{G}\} \cup \{t_s : t_s \in \mathcal{S}\} \quad (6)$$

$$\mathcal{I} = \{t_c = (p_c^{abs}, p_+^{abs}, p_-^{abs}) : p_c \in \mathcal{P}\} \quad (7)$$

$$\mathcal{G} = \{(p_c^{abs}, p_c^{sec\_C_1}, p_-^{abs}) : p_c \in \mathcal{P}, sec \in \mathcal{F}\} \quad (8)$$

$$\mathcal{S} = \{(p_c^{sec\_C_i}, p_c^{sec\_C_{i+1}}, p_-^{abs}) : \text{ i} \geq 1, sec \in \mathcal{F}\} \quad (9)$$

The margin parameter in triplet loss for a triplet (q, k_+, k_-) enforces that the relative distance between positive pairs (q and k_+) and negative pairs (q and k_-) is greater than the margin value. A small distance in the embedding space translates to high similarity. The positive pairs in local context triplets consist of consecutive section chunks and hence are the most similar positive pair across the three triplet types. So we set the highest margin value for local context triplets. In contrast, the inter-document triplets contain abstracts from two papers as positives, so we set the margin to be the least there. To summarize, we set $m_{t_i} < m_{t_g} < m_{t_s}$, to ensure that intra-document embedding similarity is higher than inter-document similarity. This enforces an order of distances, i.e., with respect to a candidate paper q's abstract representation, a dissimilar paper (which is not cited by q) is at the maximum distance, followed by a similar paper (which is cited by q), followed by the section representation of the same paper which would be at the least distance.

Section	Frequency	Section Triplets
Introduction	81768	136417
Related Works	28663	28814
Method	97104	954025
Results	62400	115419
Conclusion	73218	21039

Table 2: Section headings identified for the 97402 papers in the dataset. Section triplets denote the number of local context triplets constructed from each section.

Triplet type	Frequency
Local Context (Eq. 2)	1255714
Global Context (Eq. 3)	343153
Inter-document (Eq. 4)	684100

Table 3: Distribution of different types of triplets in the dataset. The inter-document triplets are taken from the SPECTER training set to ensure a fair comparison. The Local context and Global context capturing triplets are created from paper full-text, only for the papers that are originally present in the SPECTER training set.

4 Experiment Details

Training Dataset CoSAEmb requires full-text of research papers and citation information to construct the section, abstract, and inter-document triplets for training the model. For a fair comparison of our methodology with SPECTER, we use the training dataset of SPECTER, which consists of 684100 triplets in the train set. Based on the citation information, these triplets are constructed from around 146000 query papers sampled from the Semantic Scholar corpus (Ammar et al., 2018). However, these triplets are constructed only from the title and abstracts of the papers (format similar to our inter-document triplets). We use the Semantic Scholar corpus to construct section triplets by extracting the full-text of the papers present in SPECTER's training set. We extract full-text of 97402 papers from the Semantic Scholar corpus.

We use keyword matching to categorize section

	background				method			
	RP	P@20	R@20	$NDCG_{\%20}$	RP	P@20	R@20	$NDCG_{\%20}$
SciBERT (2019)	17.32	23.75	38.33	45.53	9.92	8.85	29.87	30.13
SPECTER (2020)	26.48	32.19	50.77	68.07	9.21	12.58	36.36	36.66
OAG-BERT (2022)	13.85	18.12	23.63	37.32	13.62	7.47	26.81	23.73
ASPIRE (2022)	26.53	35.00	55.25	69.53	10.65	15.66	49.02	43.00
CoSAEmb *(ours)*	27.76	33.75	52.79	67.27	12.73	15.00	43.04	41.14
	result				*Aggregated*			
	RP	P@20	R@20	$NDCG_{\%20}$	RP	P@20	R@20	$NDCG_{\%20}$
SciBERT (2019)	9.92	16.53	34.33	38.51	12.32	16.17	34.06	38.00
SPECTER (2020)	17.72	25.9	59.95	56.11	17.69	23.38	48.96	53.31
OAG-BERT (2022)	9.87	13.16	30.42	34.00	12.40	12.84	26.92	31.58
ASPIRE (2022)	19.64	26.46	55.69	59.78	18.84	25.52	53.15	57.20
CoSAEmb *(ours)*	20.54	24.06	51.25	54.50	20.32	24.11	49.98	54.06

Table 4: CSFCube Benchmark: Results for the set of baselines methods. Metrics are R-Precision (RP), Precision@20 (P@20), Recall@20 (R@20), and $NDCG_{\%20}$ are computed.

headings into five classes: Introduction, Related Works, Method, Results, and Conclusion. We use the dataset of 25,482 section headings organized manually into previously mentioned five categories by Chakraborty et al. (2016) to collect seed keywords. To facilitate the categorization of new section headings in full texts, we developed a straightforward algorithm that assigns one of the following labels to each heading: Introduction, Related Works, Results, Conclusion, or Methods based on the dataset curated by Chakraborty et al. (2016). Section headings that do not match any of category headings in the dataset are automatically assigned to the Methods category. We present the distribution of different section headings in the dataset in Table 2. The statistics of total triplets in the dataset are presented in Table 3. As each section from the paper contributes to one global context triplet (as defined in Equation (3)), the total count of sections listed in Table 2 matches the number of Global Context triplets in Table 3. Likewise, the sum of section triplets presented in Table 2 equals the total number of Local Context triplets, which is 1255714.

Training Details We implement our model in PyTorch and train our model on three NVIDIA V100 GPUs. The model is trained for two epochs with a slanted triangular learning rate of 2e-5 with warmup steps equal to 0.1 fractions of the total steps. We use a batch size of 32, which fits on our three GPUs. We run ablations for margin values m_{t_i}, m_{t_g}, and m_{t_s}: (0.5, 1, 1.5), (1, 2, 3), and (2, 4, 6). The best results are obtained with m_{t_i} = 1, m_{t_g} = 2, and m_{t_s}=3.

5 Evaluation and Results

The description of datasets used for evaluating the capability of the CoSAEmb model are as follows:

CSFCube (Mysore et al., 2021) CSFCube is an annotated corpus of 50 query abstract-facet pairs from the ACL Anthology. The candidate set for each query is constructed from the S2ORC corpus using six methods, including TF-IDF and averaged word2vec. The three facets in the dataset are background, method, and result. As this dataset supports query by aspect, it is a relevant database to evaluate the model in an aspect-based retrieval scenario.

SciRepEval (Singh et al., 2023) SciRepEval is a benchmark for evaluating scientific document representations, which consists of twenty-five tasks across four formats: classification (e.g., field of study, MeSH Descriptors classification, etc.), regression (e.g., predict tweet mentions, peer-review rating, and maximum h-index of authors), proximity (e.g., same author detection, highly influential citations, etc.), and ad-hoc search (e.g., rank a candidate set for a query on TREC-COVID, CORD-19 datasets).

Full-text Paragraph Retrieval We curate a dataset of 1500 papers from arXiv (cs.CL and cs.AI categories, submitted to arXiv in 2022 so as to avoid overlap with the training dataset) and use it to evaluate if CoSAEmb model is able to generalize

	SCIREPEVAL (SciNCL + Adapters + MTL CTRL)	COSAEMB + Adapters + MTL CTRL
Out of Task Avg	62.5	58.2
In Task Avg	59.1	58.3
SciDocs Avg	90.6	89.0
All Avg	71.2	67.9

Table 5: As per evaluations in SCIREPEVAL, we present the results of COSAEMB with Adapters and MTL CTRL (control codes). While the results don't outperform SCIREPEVAL, they are comparable.

Model	Recall@1	Recall@3
SciBERT	40.10	53.50
SPECTER	74.70	82.83
COSAEMB (w/o margin gradation) ($m_{t_i} = m_{t_g} = m_{t_s} = 1$)	75.96	82.87
COSAEMB (with margin gradation) ($m_{t_i} = 1, m_{t_g} = 2\ m_{t_s} = 3$)	76.71	83.44

Table 6: Full-text paragraph retrieval performance. COSAEMB (with margin gradation, i.e. $m_{t_i} = 1, m_{t_g} = 2, m_{t_s} = 3$) shows improved performance over SciBERT and SPECTER in retrieving the paragraphs of a paper. COSAEMB model variant trained without margin gradation (COSAEMB ($m_{t_i} = m_{t_g} = m_{t_s} = 1$)) benefits from more data but the gain is not as significant as observed with margin gradation.

the order of distances among different paper section embeddings, on papers unseen during training. We set up a simple retrieval setup, where section embedding is used as a query and embeddings from a candidate set are retrieved based on Euclidean distance. The candidate set is composed of other section texts from the same paper as well as other papers. We evaluate if COSAEMB embeddings retrieve other section texts from the same paper. We also evaluate a model trained with $m_{t_i} = m_{t_g} = m_{t_l}$ to evaluate if margin gradation contributes to performance gain, or if the gain is observed because of increased training data.

While the COSAEMB models perform comparable to existing state-of-the-art models on CSFCube and SCIREPEVAL benchmark, it shows an improved performance in retrieving the full-text paragraphs. On the CSFCube dataset, COSAEMB performs slightly better on R-Precision metric, for most aspects. Unlike ASPIRE, COSAEMB is not trained on any aspect-specific data and is just trained on full-text sections data only. For the CSFCube dataset, similar to other models we use the title and abstract text for query. However, for each of the specific facets, we separate the title and abstract with our special tokens in addition to the `[SEP]` token (for facet background, we use `[INTR]` and `[RW]`; for method facet we use token `[MET]`, and for result facet we use `[RES]`). In comparison to SPECTER, which is the fairest baseline to COSAEMB, improved performance can be observed for the 'method' aspect. This could be attributed to the full-text information available to COSAEMB during training. On the SCIREPEVAL dataset, we observe slightly worse performance of COSAEMB. It could denote that it is not always required to utilize full-text information for the tasks present in SCIREPEVAL benchmark. Singh et al. (2023) pretrain a new model similar to SPECTER to increase the domain coverage with data from 23 fields, which leads to a 15-point increase for In Task performance, which also indicates that training the model on diverse domain data would be helpful.

6 Conclusion

We present COSAEMB, a technique to learn section-aware embeddings with any existing encoder-only transformer model without retraining it from scratch. It can be adapted to several domains that deal with long documents such as legal and research papers. We use contrastive loss to represent multiple section embeddings of papers in a compact cluster, and maximize the distance to dissimilar and minimize the distance to similar papers. Margin gradation introduces a hierarchy of distances. The representations can be used for various downstream applications, such as the generation of related works for manuscripts, predicting appropriate submission venues for manuscripts, and predicting missing citations or comparisons.

Acknowledgments

This work is supported by Prime Minister's Research Fellowship (PMRF), awarded to Shruti (PMRF-1701251) by the Government of India. We extend our heartfelt gratitude to Prof. Nipun Batra for his generous support in providing access to GPU computing facilities. Additionally, we are thankful for the use of the PARAM Ananta supercomputing facility at IIT Gandhinagar, launched under the National Supercomputing Mission by the Government of India.

References

Waleed Ammar, Dirk Groeneveld, Chandra Bhagavatula, Iz Beltagy, Miles Crawford, Doug Downey, Jason Dunkelberger, Ahmed Elgohary, Sergey Feldman, Vu Ha, Rodney Kinney, Sebastian Kohlmeier, Kyle Lo, Tyler Murray, Hsu-Han Ooi, Matthew Peters, Joanna Power, Sam Skjonsberg, Lucy Lu Wang, Chris Wilhelm, Zheng Yuan, Madeleine van Zuylen, and Oren Etzioni. 2018. Construction of the literature graph in semantic scholar. In *Proceedings of the 2018 Conference of the North American Chapter of the Association for Computational Linguistics: Human Language Technologies, Volume 3 (Industry Papers)*, pages 84–91, New Orleans - Louisiana. Association for Computational Linguistics.

Iz Beltagy, Kyle Lo, and Arman Cohan. 2019. SciBERT: A pretrained language model for scientific text. In *Proceedings of the 2019 Conference on Empirical Methods in Natural Language Processing and the 9th International Joint Conference on Natural Language Processing (EMNLP-IJCNLP)*, pages 3615–3620, Hong Kong, China. Association for Computational Linguistics.

Iz Beltagy, Matthew E Peters, and Arman Cohan. 2020. Longformer: The long-document transformer. *arXiv preprint arXiv:2004.05150*.

Tanmoy Chakraborty, Amrith Krishna, Mayank Singh, Niloy Ganguly, Pawan Goyal, and Animesh Mukherjee. 2016. Ferosa: A faceted recommendation system for scientific articles. In *Advances in Knowledge Discovery and Data Mining*, pages 528–541, Cham. Springer International Publishing.

Krzysztof Marcin Choromanski, Valerii Likhosherstov, David Dohan, Xingyou Song, Andreea Gane, Tamás Sarlós, Peter Hawkins, Jared Quincy Davis, Afroz Mohiuddin, Lukasz Kaiser, David Benjamin Belanger, Lucy J. Colwell, and Adrian Weller. 2021. Rethinking attention with performers. In *9th International Conference on Learning Representations, ICLR 2021, Virtual Event, Austria, May 3-7, 2021*. OpenReview.net.

Arman Cohan, Sergey Feldman, Iz Beltagy, Doug Downey, and Daniel Weld. 2020. SPECTER: Document-level representation learning using citation-informed transformers. In *Proceedings of the 58th Annual Meeting of the Association for Computational Linguistics*, pages 2270–2282, Online. Association for Computational Linguistics.

Pradeep Dasigi, Kyle Lo, Iz Beltagy, Arman Cohan, Noah A. Smith, and Matt Gardner. 2021. A dataset of information-seeking questions and answers anchored in research papers. In *Proceedings of the 2021 Conference of the North American Chapter of the Association for Computational Linguistics: Human Language Technologies*, pages 4599–4610, Online. Association for Computational Linguistics.

Dedre Gentner, Jeffrey Loewenstein, and Leigh Thompson. 2003. Learning and transfer: A general role for analogical encoding. *Journal of Educational Psychology*, 95:393–408.

Douglas R Hofstadter. 1995. *Fluid concepts and creative analogies: Computer models of the fundamental mechanisms of thought.* Basic books.

Marcin Kardas, Piotr Czapla, Pontus Stenetorp, Sebastian Ruder, Sebastian Riedel, Ross Taylor, and Robert Stojnic. 2020. AxCell: Automatic extraction of results from machine learning papers. In *Proceedings of the 2020 Conference on Empirical Methods in Natural Language Processing (EMNLP)*, pages 8580–8594, Online. Association for Computational Linguistics.

Nikita Kitaev, Lukasz Kaiser, and Anselm Levskaya. 2020. Reformer: The efficient transformer. In *8th International Conference on Learning Representations, ICLR 2020, Addis Ababa, Ethiopia, April 26-30, 2020*. OpenReview.net.

Jinhyuk Lee, Wonjin Yoon, Sungdong Kim, Donghyeon Kim, Sunkyu Kim, Chan Ho So, and Jaewoo Kang. 2020. Biobert: a pre-trained biomedical language representation model for biomedical text mining. *Bioinformatics*, 36(4):1234–1240.

Xiao Liu, Da Yin, Jingnan Zheng, Xingjian Zhang, Peng Zhang, Hongxia Yang, Yuxiao Dong, and Jie Tang. 2022. OAG-BERT: Towards a unified backbone language model for academic knowledge services. In *Proceedings of the 28th ACM SIGKDD Conference on Knowledge Discovery and Data Mining*, pages 3418–3428.

Sheshera Mysore, Arman Cohan, and Tom Hope. 2022. Multi-vector models with textual guidance for fine-grained scientific document similarity. In *Proceed-*

ings of the 2022 Conference of the North American Chapter of the Association for Computational Linguistics: Human Language Technologies, pages 4453–4470, Seattle, United States. Association for Computational Linguistics.

Sheshera Mysore, Tim O' Gorman, Andrew McCallum, and Hamed Zamani. 2021. Csfcube - a test collection of computer science research articles for faceted query by example. In *Proceedings of the Neural Information Processing Systems Track on Datasets and Benchmarks*, volume 1.

Malte Ostendorff, Till Blume, Terry Ruas, Bela Gipp, and Georg Rehm. 2022a. Specialized document embeddings for aspect-based similarity of research papers. In *Proceedings of the 22nd ACM/IEEE Joint Conference on Digital Libraries*, JCDL '22, New York, NY, USA. Association for Computing Machinery.

Malte Ostendorff, Nils Rethmeier, Isabelle Augenstein, Bela Gipp, and Georg Rehm. 2022b. Neighborhood contrastive learning for scientific document representations with citation embeddings. In *Proceedings of the 2022 Conference on Empirical Methods in Natural Language Processing*, pages 11670–11688, Abu Dhabi, United Arab Emirates. Association for Computational Linguistics.

Daniel L. Schwartz and John D. Bransford. 1998. A time for telling. *Cognition and Instruction*, 16:475–522.

Amanpreet Singh, Mike D'Arcy, Arman Cohan, Doug Downey, and Sergey Feldman. 2023. SciRepEval: A multi-format benchmark for scientific document representations. In *Proceedings of the 2023 Conference on Empirical Methods in Natural Language Processing*, pages 5548–5566, Singapore. Association for Computational Linguistics.

Yi Tay, Mostafa Dehghani, Dara Bahri, and Donald Metzler. 2022. Efficient transformers: A survey. *ACM Comput. Surv.*, 55(6).

Sinong Wang, Belinda Z Li, Madian Khabsa, Han Fang, and Hao Ma. 2020. Linformer: Self-attention with linear complexity. *arXiv preprint arXiv:2006.04768*.

Manzil Zaheer, Guru Guruganesh, Kumar Avinava Dubey, Joshua Ainslie, Chris Alberti, Santiago Ontanon, Philip Pham, Anirudh Ravula, Qifan Wang, Li Yang, et al. 2020. Big bird: Transformers for longer sequences. *Advances in Neural Information Processing Systems*, 33:17283–17297.

Integrating Table Representations into Large Language Models for Improved Scholarly Document Comprehension

Buse Sibel Korkmaz
Imperial College London
London, UK
buse.korkmaz18@imperial.ac.uk

Antonio del Rio Chanona
Imperial College London
London, UK
a.del-rio-chanona@imperial.ac.uk

Abstract

We address the challenge of interpreting and reasoning over scientific tables with Large Language Models (LLMs), a crucial aspect of scholarly documents. Despite significant progress in natural language processing, the integration of tabular data into scientific LLMs remains limited. We propose an innovative approach leveraging intermediate task pre-training on table question-answering datasets, followed by model adaptation to comprehend tables in computer science literature. Our findings reveal that incorporating table understanding substantially improves the performance of LLMs on scientific literature understanding tasks, which we showcase in peer-review score prediction. This improvement underscores the importance of utilizing tabular data in the training of scientific language models. The code and models are publicly available.[1]

1 Introduction

Large Language Models (LLMs) have experienced significant advancements in recent years and have been adapted to numerous natural language understanding and generation tasks (Zhao et al., 2023). Particularly in the scientific community, they have received increasing attention with their applications to scientific literature understanding tasks such as citation prediction (Cohan et al., 2020), paper classification (Zhang et al., 2023d), scientific literature search (Faggioli et al., 2023; Lála et al., 2023) and paper recommendation (Kanakia et al., 2019) to accelerate scientific discovery. In addition, domain-specialized research assistant language models have been developed (Beltagy et al., 2019; Luo et al., 2022; Taylor et al., 2022; Azerbayev et al., 2024).

Although these specialized models on scientific texts demonstrate success in the scientific literature understanding benchmarks such as MAPLE (Zhang et al., 2023d) and SciRepEval (Singh et al., 2023), the benchmarks and the corpora used in the training of these scientific language models predominantly focus on textual data. A critical component - and the focus of this study - often remains overlooked, which is *tables*. Tables encapsulate key findings, offering a condensed view of the research outcomes. In this work, contrary to the existing approaches, we hypothesize that understanding tables can significantly enhance the performance of LLMs on scientific literature tasks by providing a more holistic understanding of research papers.

We first tackle the challenge of interpreting tables and reasoning over them to answer questions requiring arithmetic operations and choosing information from specific cells through intermediate task pre-training. Then, we adapt our trained model to comprehend scientific tables in published computer science papers. This training process is designed to enable the models to reason with scientific table data. The scientific tables dataset we use is fundamentally different from the datasets used in intermediate task pre-training for table question-answering, incorporating more extensive summaries of scientific tables. Finally, we demonstrate that utilizing table representations extracted from fine-tuned LLMs with our approach improves the prediction of peer-review scores.

Overall, we develop a pipeline that allows LLMs to incorporate scientific knowledge from tables. The main contributions of this work are: (i) we apply an intermediate task pre-training approach that allows LLMs to understand tables, (ii) we do a detailed comparison of scientific table understanding by different models with different sizes, architectures, and under various settings, and (iii) we show how learning to represent scientific tables improves the understanding of scholarly documents, using the peer-review score prediction as a case study.

[1] https://github.com/buseskorkmaz/Integrating-Table-Representations-into-LLMs

Proceedings of the Fourth Workshop on Scholarly Document Processing (SDP 2024), pages 293–306
August 16, 2024 ©2024 Association for Computational Linguistics

2 Related Work

2.1 Scientific language models

The majority of pre-training datasets for scientific LLMs consist primarily of textual data, with a notable absence of tables. Widely used datasets in pre-training such as MAPLE (Zhang et al., 2023d), SciFact (Wadden et al., 2020), SciERC (Luan et al., 2018), ACL-ARC (Bird et al., 2008), SciCite (Cohan et al., 2019), GENIA (Kim et al., 2003), and BC5CDR (Li et al., 2016) include only titles, abstracts, references, or citations. The S2ORC (Lo et al., 2020) dataset includes full texts with parsed tables, yet its potential for enhancing table understanding in LLMs remains largely under-explored.

Models such as SciBERT (Beltagy et al., 2019) have been trained exclusively on words and sentences from scientific texts. Similarly, SPECTER (Cohan et al., 2020) focuses on titles, abstracts, and citations, without incorporating table data into its training process. BioMedGPT (Zhang et al., 2023a) acknowledges the significance of tabular data understanding but leaves it as a future task. Even recently developed models such as SciMult (Zhang et al., 2023c) and SciNCL (Ostendorff et al., 2022), which includes the S2ORC (Lo et al., 2020) dataset in its training mix, fail to leverage table data effectively. SciMult is trained on datasets of MAPLE, SciFact, and SciRepEval (Singh et al., 2023), which do not include tabular data, and SciNCL, despite its access to a dataset with parsed scientific tables (S2ORC) does not utilize table data in the training.

2.2 Table understanding

Recent advancements in table understanding have seen significant contributions. Pasupat and Liang (2015) introduced a compositional semantic parsing approach, which established the WikiTQ dataset for benchmarking. TAPAS by Herzig et al. (2020), leveraged the BERT architecture (Devlin et al., 2019), and advanced table parsing by identifying operations through a classification layer for answer generation. Eisenschlos et al. (2020) focused on enhancing table entailment through pre-training on open-source tables, aligning closely with our approach in Section 3.2. Hegselmann et al. (2023) explored the application of LLMs for few-shot classification of tabular data. Li et al. (2023) recognized the value of information in tables and developed a scientific information extraction pipeline to improve data availability for tabular content within scientific papers.

Moreover, improvements in table understanding have enhanced adjacent tasks such as table-based fact verification, as seen with the TabFact dataset (Chen et al., 2020), and extended to specialized fields such as finance, demonstrated by the TAT-QA benchmark (Zhu et al., 2021). Zhang et al. (2023b) developed a generalist table understanding model, TableLlama based on LLaMA-2 (7B) (Touvron et al., 2023) using fine-tuned 1.24M tables for 8 different table-based tasks such as table interpretation, augmentation and QA. We evaluate their model for the scientific table understanding task to investigate the capabilities of a generalist model in a scientific domain.

2.3 Peer-review prediction

The utilization of language models in predicting peer review outcomes, as highlighted by Rogers and Augenstein (2020), reflects their potential to understand the scientific literature. Accurately predicting the quality of scientific research through models could address the subjectivity, biases, and inefficiencies identified in the peer review process (Shah, 2022).

The PeerRead dataset (Kang et al., 2018) serves as a foundational dataset for peer-review prediction research, covering acceptance outcomes and review helpfulness. The availability of public peer-review datasets has accelerated the expansion of peer-review research, including studies on review content and decision outcomes (Gao et al., 2019), the introduction of innovative approaches to publication representation (Muangkammuen et al., 2023) and the development of predictive models for review scores.

In peer-review prediction, the accurate construction of scholarly document representations is important to learn the correct relationship between the documents and their peer reviews. The PeerRead dataset (Kang et al., 2018) includes comprehensive details of document bodies and associated peer reviews along with outcomes. Despite the dataset's richness, the predominant methodology focuses on utilizing only the textual components of documents for representation. For example, peer-review prediction models DeepSentiPeer (Ghosal et al., 2019) and PeerAssist (Bharti et al., 2021) rely on the Science Parse library by AllenAI for extracting information from scholarly documents in PeerRead. Unfortunately, this library does not parse tables. This is a limitation if we are to capture the full scope of a scholarly document for peer review pre-

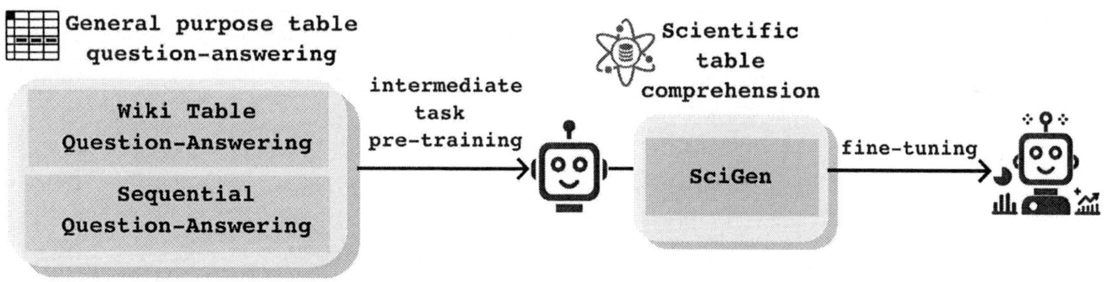

Figure 1: Overview of the training methodology for enhancing large language models with scientific table understanding. The training process begins with intermediate task pre-training using the WikiTQ and SQA datasets to build foundational table reasoning skills. This is followed by fine-tuning on the SciGen dataset to adapt the model specifically for scientific tables. The final model effectively integrates structured table data into text, improving performance on scientific literature tasks such as peer-review score prediction.

diction, as findings in result tables can substantially influence review outcomes.

3 Methodology

3.1 Datasets

WikiTableQuestions (WikiTQ) (Pasupat and Liang, 2015) WikiTQ is a benchmark dataset designed for evaluating the ability of models to perform question-answering (QA) over complex tables sourced from Wikipedia. This dataset challenges models to understand and interpret tabular data in context, requiring both a semantic understanding of questions and the ability to extract and reason relevant information from structured data. The inclusion of WikiTQ in our intermediate task pre-training regimen aims to enhance the model's proficiency in handling structured data and improve its capability to reason over tables, an essential skill for understanding scientific tables.

SQA (Iyyer et al., 2017) The SQA dataset extends the complexity of QA by introducing a sequential aspect, where answers to follow-up questions depend on the context established by previous interactions. However, our end use case is to describe scientific tables that do not have a conversational nature. Hence, we use a portion of the SQA dataset including the first questions in the sequence of questions over a given table. This dataset enables our model to further improve fundamental table understanding by adding diversity to the set of questions.

SciGen (Moosavi et al., 2021) SciGen stands out for its focus on generating coherent and contextually accurate textual descriptions from scientific tables, primarily containing numerical data. The ability of arithmetic reasoning to interpret tables in scientific papers and generate appropriate textual

	ALCHEMY		TANGRAMS		SCENE	
system	3utts	5utts	3utts	5utts	3utts	5utts
LONG+16	56.8	52.3	64.9	27.6	23.2	14.7
REINFORCE	58.3	44.6	**68.5**	**37.3**	47.8	33.9
BS-MML	58.7	47.3	62.6	32.2	53.5	32.5
RANDOMER	**66.9**	**52.9**	65.8	37.1	**64.8**	**46.2**

Parse columns, rows and values in the table

<R> <C> system <C> Alchemy 3utts <C> Alchemy 5utts <C> Tangrams 3utts <C> Tangrams 5utts <C> Scene 3utts <C> Scene 5utts <R> <C> Long+16 <C> 56.8 <C> 52.3 <C> 64.9 <C> 27.6 <C> 23.2 <C> 14.7 <R> <C> REINFORCE <C> 58.3 <C> 44.6 <C> [BOLD] 68.5 <C> [BOLD] 37.3 <C> 47.8 <C> 33.9 <R> <C> BS-MML <C> 58.7 <C> 47.3 <C> 62.6 <C> 32.2 <C> 53.5 <C> 32.5 <R> <C> RandoMer <C> [BOLD] 66.9 <C> [BOLD] 52.9 <C> 65.8 <C> 37.1 <C> [BOLD] 64.8 <C> [BOLD] 46.2

Figure 2: An example of parsing tables for use with large language models. The table (Guu et al., 2017) structure is encoded using special tokens, with rows represented by <R>, columns by <C>, and associated captions by <CAP> as in (Moosavi et al., 2021).

narratives presents the main challenge we aim to address. Thus, we subsequently fine-tune our model to adapt scientific tables on the SciGen dataset following pre-training on WikiTQ and SQA datasets.

3.2 Experimental Setup

Pre-trained LLMs We use FlanT5 (Chung et al., 2022) and LLaMA-2 (Touvron et al., 2023) as pre-trained language models. Our task requires learning representations from structured tables. To compare how different architectures adapt to tabular data representation in our problem, we choose T5 (Roberts et al., 2019) and FlanT5 (Chung et al., 2022) to represent encoder-decoder architecture, and LLaMA-2 as a representative of decoder-only architectures.

Data pre-processing Following Moosavi et al. (2021), we denote rows with <R>, columns <C> and

Test Dataset	Setting	Model	Parameters	METEOR	ROUGE-1	BertS
Test (C&L)	Zero	T5-base*	0.22B	0.04	n/a	0.76
		T5-large*	0.77B	0.06	n/a	0.76
		FlanT5-small	0.08B	0.06	0.09	0.79
		FlanT5-base	0.25B	0.04	0.06	0.74
		FlanT5-large	0.78B	0.10	0.12	0.79
		FlanT5-xl	3B	0.08	0.10	0.78
		LLaMA2-7B-chat-hf	7B	0.08	0.07	0.70
		TableLlama	7B	0.13	0.14	0.77
Test (Other)	Zero	T5-base*	0.22B	0.04	n/a	0.76
		T5-large*	0.77B	0.06	n/a	0.76
		FlanT5-small	0.08B	0.06	0.08	0.79
		FlanT5-base	0.25B	0.05	0.07	0.74
		FlanT5-large	0.78B	0.11	0.12	0.79
		FlanT5-xl	3B	0.08	0.09	0.78
		LLaMA2-7B-chat-hf	7B	0.08	0.07	0.70
		TableLlama	7B	0.13	0.13	0.77

Table 1: The evaluation of pre-trained models (zero-shot referring to not fine-tuned) on the test datasets. The scores of the models with * are taken from the SciGen (Moosavi et al., 2021), except ROUGE-1 since it is not reported.

associated caption from scientific tables as <CAP>. Figure 2 demonstrates an example of this parsing operation. For LLaMA-2, we also see the benefit of using a special token for instructions [INST]. We also share the results reported in (Moosavi et al., 2021) over the SciGen dataset for T5 models (Roberts et al., 2019) in our result tables denoted with an asterisk (*) to benchmark our approach.

Intermediate task pre-training Our main goal is interpreting scientific tables to incorporate the learned representations into scientific language models and achieve better results over scientific literature tasks through a more comprehensive understanding of scholarly articles. As an initial experiment, we analyze the capabilities of the chosen LLMs on the SciGen test dataset and report results in Table 1 as a baseline to improve upon during intermediate task pre-training and fine-tuning. This test dataset includes further two subsets focusing on publications from Computational and Linguistics (Test C&L in Table 2) fields and a wide range of subfields of computer science (Test Other). The qualitative examination of generated texts from pre-trained language models (red-coloured zero-shot example in Figure 3) concludes that the models are not capable of understanding table structure represented with tokens <R> and <C>.

To address this first challenge, we employ an intermediate task pre-training approach, similarly (Eisenschlos et al., 2020). We use WikiTQ and SQA datasets to pre-train language models before fine-tuning them on scientific articles in the SciGen dataset. This intermediate step helps the language models to (1) capture the semantic relationships in the tables via our special tokens to represent them, (2) reason over tables to be able to answer questions requires arithmetic operations such as finding the maximum, and minimum values or selecting an answer from a specific cell.

Fine-tuning on scientific tables After the models gain the capability of understanding tables, we move to the next step to obtain specialized language models for scientific tables. At this stage, we utilize the large training dataset under SciGen. We use the provided "text" for each table as a reference and we expect the fine-tuned language model to produce similar text for a given table for the prompt of "Explain the given table". Further implementation details are given in Appendix A. Figure 1 depicts the end-to-end training methodology explained in this section.

Evaluation metrics Following the evaluations in previous work on SciGen (Moosavi et al., 2021), we use a subset of their metrics in our evaluation such as METEOR (Denkowski and Lavie, 2014), and BertScore (BertS) (Zhang et al., 2019). Considering our generations for scientific tables are expected to be similar to the reference text, we

Setting	Model	METEOR	ROUGE-1	BertS
		Test (C&L)		
SciGen-Large	T5-base*	0.13(+0.11)	n/a	0.79(+0.06)
	T5-large*	0.16(+0.12)	n/a	0.81(+0.07)
	FlanT5-small	0.04(-0.02)	0.05(-0.04)	0.82(+0.03)
	FlanT5-base	0.03(-0.01)	0.07(+0.01)	0.82(+0.08)
	FlanT5-large	0.08(-0.02)	0.14(+0.02)	0.79
	FlanT5-xl	0.14(+0.06)	0.23(+0.13)	0.85(+0.07)
	LLaMA2-7B-chat-hf	0.15(+0.07)	0.17(+0.10)	0.78(+0.08)
WikiTQ	FlanT5-xl	0.08	0.12(+0.02)	0.81(+0.03)
WikiTQ + SQA	FlanT5-xl	0.08	0.10	0.79(+0.01)
WikiTQ + SciGen	FlanT5-xl	0.14(+0.06)	0.23(+0.13)	0.85(+0.07)
WikiTQ + SQA + SciGen	FlanT5-xl	0.15(+0.07)	0.24(+0.14)	0.85(+0.07)
		Test (Other)		
SciGen-Large	T5-base*	0.13(+0.10)	n/a	0.79(+0.05)
	T5-large*	0.16(+0.11)	n/a	0.81(+0.06)
	FlanT5-small	0.03(-0.03)	0.04(-0.02)	0.82(+0.03)
	FlanT5-base	0.03(-0.02)	0.07	0.82(+0.08)
	FlanT5-large	0.07(-0.04)	0.12	0.77(-0.02)
	FlanT5-xl	0.13(+0.05)	0.23(+0.14)	0.85(+0.07)
	LLaMA2-7B-chat-hf	0.15(+0.07)	0.17(+0.10)	0.78(+0.08)
WikiTQ	FlanT5-xl	0.07(-0.01)	0.10(+0.01)	0.81(+0.03)
WikiTQ + SQA	FlanT5-xl	0.08	0.09	0.79(+0.01)
WikiTQ + SciGen	FlanT5-xl	0.13(+0.05)	0.23(+0.14)	0.85(+0.07)
WikiTQ + SQA + SciGen	FlanT5-xl	0.14(+0.06)	0.23(+0.14)	0.85(+0.07)

Table 2: The change in the scores compared to before applying the corresponding settings for each model is given in the parenthesis. We obtain the best results after applying intermediate task pre-training on WikiTQ and SQA to improve the reasoning capability of the model and subsequent fine-tuning on SciGen to adapt scientific table understanding.

also add the ROUGE (Lin, 2004) score into our evaluation metrics set.

4 Understanding Scientific Tables

4.1 Zero-shot Evaluation

We share the evaluation of models in zero-shot task (without fine-tuning or intermediate task pre-training) results in Table 1. These results serve as a baseline for the comparison in Table 2. We can see that while LLaMA-2 is the largest model (with 7B parameters) in the table, the ROUGE and BERTScore of this model are lower than the FlanT5-large (0.78B) and FlanT5-xl (3B). Considering the increasing computational demand in training associated with larger model sizes, we chose to use FlanT5-xl in our detailed experiments under different settings. It is worth noting that, the fine-tuning of SciGen dataset results in Table 2 demonstrates substantial improvement for LLaMA-2. This indicates that LLaMA-2 could also be adapted to scientific tables, although not with the same capacity as encoder-decoder architecture-based models.

The zero-shot evaluation results for TableLlama Zhang et al. (2023b) further validate the importance of adaptation to the scientific domain since being trained on a large training dataset and a variety of tasks, its performance on SciGen is still close to other language models which are not trained on table specific tasks.

4.2 Quantitative results

In Table 2, we report the scores obtained in each setting and model. When we compare the scores by model size, we can see that the largest model of FlanT5 family (Chung et al., 2022), FlanT5-xl (3B parameters) achieves the best scores on both test datasets introduced in (Moosavi et al., 2021). The scores of METEOR, ROUGE-1 and BertS also

Model	FNR	Precision	f1-score	Accuracy	FPR
SVM	08.00% (±0.48%)	94.77% (±0.25%)	93.34% (±0.18%)	93.44% (±0.16%)	05.07%
XGBoost	10.12% (±0.55%)	90.74% (±0.39%)	90.30% (±0.36%)	90.35% (±0.35%)	09.17%
DNN	24.40% (±3.53%)	90.40% (±1.73%)	82.23% (±1.45%)	83.72% (±0.89%)	08.13%
RF	13.07% (±0.35%)	92.73% (±0.32%)	89.73% (±0.22%)	90.05% (±0.21%)	06.82%
K-NN	7.45% (±0.48%)	93.36% (±0.70%)	91.38% (±0.55%)	91.28% (±0.57%)	10.00%
ELM	16.50% (±0.29%)	92.25% (±0.67%)	87.66% (±0.30%)	88.24% (±0.36%)	07.00%
Malytics	**05.53%** (±0.46%)	**95.88%** (±0.40%)	**95.17%** (±0.20%)	**95.20%** (±0.20%)	**04.06%**
[15]	11.60% (±2.76%)	88.16% (±1.8%)	– –	88.26% (±1.73%)	–

Reference:
Table IV provides more inside into Malytics. Table IV shows the average FNR, precision, f1-score, accuracy and FPR of Malytics with our proposed feature representation. The main important index of the test is FNR as a measure that shows how well Malytics detected new families.

Zero:
R> C> [EMPTY] C> (0. 18%) C> (0. 16%) C> (0. 15%) C> [EMPTY] C> (0. 55%) C> (0. 39%) C> (0. 36%) C> (0. 35%) C> [EMPTY] C> C> [EMPTY] C> (0. 35%) C> [EMPTY] C> C> DNN C> 24. 40% C> 90. 40% C> 82. 23% C> 83. 72% C> 08. 13% R> C> [EMPTY] C> (3. 53%) C> (1. 73%) C> (0. 89%) C> [EMPTY] C> C> RF C> 13. 07% C> 92. 73% C> 89. 73% C> 90. 05% C> 06. ... C> [EMPTY].

SciGen:
We also compare the performance of the proposed method with the state-of-the-art methods. We observe that the proposed method outperforms the state-of-the-art methods in all the metrics. The performance of the proposed method is comparable to the state-of-the-art methods.

WikiTQ+SciGen:
We can see that the K-NN model outperforms the other models in all the metrics. The performance of the K-NN model is comparable to the performance of the SVM model. The performance of the XGBoost model is comparable to the performance of the DNN model. The performance of the RF model is comparable to the performance of the RF model. The performance of the K-NN model is comparable to the performance of the RF model.

WikiTQ+SQA+SciGen:
We can see that the proposed model outperforms all the baselines in terms of FNR, precision, f1-score, accuracy, and FPR. The performance of the proposed model is comparable to the baselines, which shows that the proposed model is able to learn a good representation of the data.

Figure 3: Generations from different models for the sample table. The original caption of the table is "The Mean and Std of Malytics and the baselines for Dex Share Dataset". We find the green-coloured generation of our proposed approach (WikiTQ+SQA+SciGen) is a more descriptive and helpful summary for literature understanding.

show an increasing trend by model size.

Considering the FlanT5-xl is the most prominent model in our benchmarking set, we conduct the intermediate task pre-training step using different datasets with this model. During the intermediate task pre-training, we use WikiTQ and SQA datasets introduced in Section 3.1. The largest increase in the scores happens when we use the SciGen dataset. It is an expected result since this dataset focuses on scientific tables and has a structure similar to the test datasets. We also see the benefit of WikiTQ in intermediate task pre-training with the increase in scores. Interestingly, when we move to the intermediate task pre-training on SQA after WikiTQ, the scores do not improve. We hypothesize that the difference between the structure of scientific tables and table QA tasks becomes more pronounced after two subsequent pre-training on table QA datasets without fine-tuning on scientific tables. As a final step of our training, we fine-tune the model, which is trained on both WikiTQ and SQA previously, on scientific tables which achieves the highest scores in our comparison of different settings. Consequently, our experiments demonstrate the essential advantage of leveraging intermediate task pre-training on table QA datasets, substantially improving LLMs' understanding and analysis of scientific tables.

4.3 Qualitative results

We share examples generated under different settings in Figure 3 for a sample table in the Test (Other) dataset, taken from (Yousefi-Azar et al., 2018). The table structure is encoded in the model input by using the tokens mentioned in Section 3.2. The dataset includes a reference text that assists us in quantifying the quality of our generations. The colourful texts in Figure 3 are the generations of the models. The red-coloured text is generated by FlanT5-xl without applying any intermediate task pre-training or fine-tuning. The generated text is non-sensible and indicates the model needs to adapt our table structure to understand the given information and produce a coherent text.

The generation of SciGen further demonstrates our motivation for intermediate task pre-training. Even though the generation is relatively high quality compared to the zero setting and factually correct for the given table sample, it is too generic and it is hard to extract tangible information using this generation. Thus, we find this kind of generation is not helpful for scientific literature understanding tasks. Comparing the SciGen generation, WikiTQ+SciGen output seems to contain more concrete information, however, some of the generated information is not factually correct when checking the table. Finally, the green-coloured generation is produced by the model pre-trained on WikiTQ and SQA, and fine-tuned on SciGen. We see the improvement in the generation quality as the output

Setting	Data	MSE	F1-score
Zero	Title + Abstract + Introduction + Table captions	6.54	0.14
	Title + Abstract + Introduction + Table representations	5.60	0.17
SciGen	Title + Abstract + Introduction + Table captions	3.02	0.24
	Title + Abstract + Introduction + Table representations	2.63	0.30
WikiTQ	Title + Abstract + Introduction + Table captions	5.49	0.23
	Title + Abstract + Introduction + Table representations	5.21	0.23
WikiTQ+SciGen	Title + Abstract + Introduction + Table captions	3.11	0.16
	Title + Abstract + Introduction + Table representations	6.05	0.24
WikiTQ+SQA+SciGen	Title + Abstract + Introduction + Table captions	2.61	0.28
	Title + Abstract + Introduction + Table representations	**2.30**	**0.38**

Table 3: Peer-review score prediction results using FlanT5-xl under different training settings. The model is evaluated on a subset of the PeerRead dataset, with embeddings generated from the title, abstract, introduction, and table captions or representations. The best results are obtained when the model is pre-trained on the WikiTQ and SQA datasets, followed by fine-tuning on the SciGen dataset (WikiTQ+SQA+SciGen setting). This demonstrates the promising potential of improved table understanding for scholarly document-based tasks.

is more concise, factually correct, and closer to the given reference. This conclusion aligns with our quantitative analysis findings in Section 4.2.

5 Peer Review Score Prediction

5.1 Experiments

To demonstrate the potential benefit of learning representations from tabular data in scientific articles, we incorporate tables into the peer-review score prediction task. We use the intersection of PeerRead (Kang et al., 2018) and SciGen (Moosavi et al., 2021) datasets, 55 publications across ICLR 2017, ACL 2017, and CoNLL 2016 as source data. Utilizing the entire content of the publications for peer-review prediction is impractical due to the context window length limitation of language models. Thus, previous approaches develop peer review predictive models using metadata, abstract and introduction sections of the paper (Singh et al., 2023).

In this section, we conduct experiments with table captions or representations generated by the models in addition to the title, abstract, and introduction to evaluate how table comprehension influences the accuracy of peer review score predictions, aligning them more closely with human reviewers' evaluations. We employ FlanT5-xl, identified in Section 4 as the most effective model, to create summaries of the tables. The summaries' embeddings serve as input for the prediction model, and we use XGBoost (Chen and Guestrin, 2016) for regression and classification. We then predict recommendation scores using embeddings from the FlanT5-xl model, which is fine-tuned under different settings. We evaluate our predictions using Mean Squared Error (MSE) and F1-score, defined as follows:

$$\text{MSE} = \frac{1}{n}\sum_{i=1}^{n}(y_i - \hat{y}_i)^2 \quad (1)$$

where n is the number of samples, y_i is the true peer-review score, and $\hat{y}_i$ is the predicted value.

$$\text{F1-score} = 2 \cdot \frac{\text{precision} \cdot \text{recall}}{\text{precision} + \text{recall}} \quad (2)$$

where $precision = \frac{\text{TP}}{\text{TP+FP}}$ and $recall = \frac{\text{TP}}{\text{TP+FN}}$, with TP being true positives, FP being false positives, and FN being false negatives. We share our findings in Table 3.

5.2 Results

The MSE and F1-scores in Table 3 show improvements in all settings when the table representations are used in peer-review prediction, except WikiTQ+SciGen. This finding validates our hypothesis that scientific language models could benefit from learning tabular data to fully interpret scientific literature. We only see a drop in the MSE score of WikiTQ+SciGen generations. We suspect the model in this setting hallucinates more as in the given sample Figure 3 and it misleads the XGBoost algorithm in peer review score prediction. Lastly, we obtain the lowest MSE and highest F1-score using the embeddings from the WikiTQ+SQA+SciGen setting. This conclusion reinforces the findings in Section 4 and shows the effectiveness of our proposed approach.

6 Conclusions

Scientific language model development and document comprehension have accelerated progress in recent years parallel to advancements in large language models. However, their ability to effectively understand and reason over tabular data in scientific literature has remained under-explored. In this work, we addressed this issue by proposing an approach that combines intermediate task pre-training on table question-answering datasets with model adaptation to comprehend tables in computer science literature.

Our experiments demonstrated that by understanding tables better, LLMs can achieve higher performance in scientific literature understanding tasks. We validated this claim through a case study on peer-review score prediction, where our best-performing model, pre-trained on WikiTQ and SQA datasets and fine-tuned on the SciGen dataset, outperformed other settings in terms of mean squared error and F1-score. These results emphasize the importance of integrating tabular data into the training process of scientific language models.

Moreover, our qualitative analysis showed that the proposed approach generates more informative and contextually relevant summaries of scientific tables compared to generalist table models and models without intermediate task pre-training or fine-tuning. This finding suggests that our method can enhance the comprehension of scientific literature by providing more accurate and descriptive table representations. Future research directions could include extending our approach to other scientific domains, exploring the integration of table representations with other elements of scientific papers (e.g., figures and equations), and developing more sophisticated table encoding techniques. Additionally, incorporating larger and more diverse datasets for pre-training and fine-tuning could further improve the performance of LLMs on scientific literature tasks.

References

Zhangir Azerbayev, Hailey Schoelkopf, Keiran Paster, Marco Dos Santos, Stephen Marcus McAleer, Albert Q. Jiang, Jia Deng, Stella Biderman, and Sean Welleck. 2024. Llemma: An open language model for mathematics. In *The Twelfth International Conference on Learning Representations*.

Iz Beltagy, Kyle Lo, and Arman Cohan. 2019. SciBERT: A pretrained language model for scientific text. In *Proceedings of the 2019 Conference on Empirical Methods in Natural Language Processing and the 9th International Joint Conference on Natural Language Processing (EMNLP-IJCNLP)*, pages 3615–3620.

Prabhat Kumar Bharti, Shashi Ranjan, Tirthankar Ghosal, Mayank Agrawal, and Asif Ekbal. 2021. Peerassist: leveraging on paper-review interactions to predict peer review decisions. In *Towards Open and Trustworthy Digital Societies: 23rd International Conference on Asia-Pacific Digital Libraries, ICADL 2021, Virtual Event, December 1–3, 2021, Proceedings 23*, pages 421–435. Springer.

Steven Bird, Robert Dale, Bonnie Dorr, Bryan Gibson, Mark Joseph, Min-Yen Kan, Dongwon Lee, Brett Powley, Dragomir Radev, and Yee Fan Tan. 2008. The ACL Anthology reference corpus: A reference dataset for bibliographic research in computational linguistics. In *Proceedings of the Sixth International Conference on Language Resources and Evaluation (LREC'08)*, Marrakech, Morocco. European Language Resources Association (ELRA).

Tianqi Chen and Carlos Guestrin. 2016. Xgboost: A scalable tree boosting system. In *Proceedings of the 22nd acm sigkdd international conference on knowledge discovery and data mining*, pages 785–794.

Wenhu Chen, Hongmin Wang, Jianshu Chen, Yunkai Zhang, Hong Wang, Shiyang Li, Xiyou Zhou, and William Yang Wang. 2020. TabFact: A large-scale dataset for table-based fact verification. In *International Conference on Learning Representations*.

Hyung Won Chung, Le Hou, Shayne Longpre, Barret Zoph, Yi Tay, William Fedus, Yunxuan Li, Xuezhi Wang, Mostafa Dehghani, Siddhartha Brahma, et al. 2022. Scaling instruction-finetuned language models. *arXiv preprint arXiv:2210.11416*.

Arman Cohan, Waleed Ammar, Madeleine van Zuylen, and Field Cady. 2019. Structural scaffolds for citation intent classification in scientific publications. In *Proceedings of the 2019 Conference of the North American Chapter of the Association for Computational Linguistics: Human Language Technologies, Volume 1 (Long and Short Papers)*, pages 3586–3596, Minneapolis, Minnesota. Association for Computational Linguistics.

Arman Cohan, Sergey Feldman, Iz Beltagy, Doug Downey, and Daniel Weld. 2020. SPECTER: Document-level representation learning using citation-informed transformers. In *Proceedings of the 58th Annual Meeting of the Association for Computational Linguistics*, pages 2270–2282, Online. Association for Computational Linguistics.

Michael Denkowski and Alon Lavie. 2014. Meteor Universal: Language specific translation evaluation for any target language. In *Proceedings of the Ninth Workshop on Statistical Machine Translation*, pages 376–380, Baltimore, Maryland, USA. Association for Computational Linguistics.

Jacob Devlin, Ming-Wei Chang, Kenton Lee, and Kristina Toutanova. 2019. BERT: Pre-training of deep bidirectional transformers for language understanding. In *Proceedings of the 2019 Conference of the North American Chapter of the Association for Computational Linguistics: Human Language Technologies, Volume 1 (Long and Short Papers)*, pages 4171–4186, Minneapolis, Minnesota. Association for Computational Linguistics.

Julian Eisenschlos, Syrine Krichene, and Thomas Müller. 2020. Understanding tables with intermediate pre-training. In *Findings of the Association for Computational Linguistics: EMNLP 2020*, pages 281–296, Online. Association for Computational Linguistics.

Guglielmo Faggioli, Thibault Formal, Simon Lupart, Stefano Marchesin, Stephane Clinchant, Nicola Ferro, and Benjamin Piwowarski. 2023. Towards query performance prediction for neural information retrieval: Challenges and opportunities. In *Proceedings of the 2023 ACM SIGIR International Conference on Theory of Information Retrieval*, ICTIR '23, page 51–63, New York, NY, USA. Association for Computing Machinery.

Yang Gao, Steffen Eger, Ilia Kuznetsov, Iryna Gurevych, and Yusuke Miyao. 2019. Does my rebuttal matter? insights from a major NLP conference. In *Proceedings of the 2019 Conference of the North American Chapter of the Association for Computational Linguistics: Human Language Technologies, Volume 1 (Long and Short Papers)*, pages 1274–1290, Minneapolis, Minnesota. Association for Computational Linguistics.

Tirthankar Ghosal, Rajeev Verma, Asif Ekbal, and Pushpak Bhattacharyya. 2019. DeepSentiPeer: Harnessing sentiment in review texts to recommend peer review decisions. In *Proceedings of the 57th Annual Meeting of the Association for Computational Linguistics*, pages 1120–1130, Florence, Italy. Association for Computational Linguistics.

Kelvin Guu, Panupong Pasupat, Evan Liu, and Percy Liang. 2017. From language to programs: Bridging reinforcement learning and maximum marginal likelihood. In *Proceedings of the 55th Annual Meeting of the Association for Computational Linguistics (Volume 1: Long Papers)*, pages 1051–1062, Vancouver, Canada. Association for Computational Linguistics.

Stefan Hegselmann, Alejandro Buendia, Hunter Lang, Monica Agrawal, Xiaoyi Jiang, and David Sontag. 2023. Tabllm: Few-shot classification of tabular data with large language models. In *International Conference on Artificial Intelligence and Statistics*, pages 5549–5581. PMLR.

Jonathan Herzig, Pawel Krzysztof Nowak, Thomas Müller, Francesco Piccinno, and Julian Eisenschlos. 2020. TaPas: Weakly supervised table parsing via pre-training. In *Proceedings of the 58th Annual Meeting of the Association for Computational Linguistics*, pages 4320–4333, Online. Association for Computational Linguistics.

Mohit Iyyer, Wen-tau Yih, and Ming-Wei Chang. 2017. Search-based neural structured learning for sequential question answering. In *Proceedings of the 55th Annual Meeting of the Association for Computational Linguistics (Volume 1: Long Papers)*, pages 1821–1831, Vancouver, Canada. Association for Computational Linguistics.

Anshul Kanakia, Zhihong Shen, Darrin Eide, and Kuansan Wang. 2019. A scalable hybrid research paper recommender system for Microsoft Academic. In *The world wide web conference*, pages 2893–2899.

Dongyeop Kang, Waleed Ammar, Bhavana Dalvi, Madeleine van Zuylen, Sebastian Kohlmeier, Eduard Hovy, and Roy Schwartz. 2018. A dataset of peer reviews (PeerRead): Collection, insights and NLP applications. In *Proceedings of the 2018 Conference of the North American Chapter of the Association for Computational Linguistics: Human Language Technologies, Volume 1 (Long Papers)*, pages 1647–1661, New Orleans, Louisiana. Association for Computational Linguistics.

J-D Kim, Tomoko Ohta, Yuka Tateisi, and Jun'ichi Tsujii. 2003. Genia corpus—a semantically annotated corpus for bio-textmining. *Bioinformatics*, 19(suppl_1):i180–i182.

Diederik P. Kingma and Jimmy Ba. 2015. Adam: A method for stochastic optimization. In *3rd International Conference on Learning Representations, ICLR 2015, San Diego, CA, USA, May 7-9, 2015, Conference Track Proceedings*.

Jakub Lála, Odhran O'Donoghue, Aleksandar Shtedritski, Sam Cox, Samuel G Rodriques, and Andrew D White. 2023. PaperQA: Retrieval-augmented generative agent for scientific research. *arXiv preprint arXiv:2312.07559*.

Jiao Li, Yueping Sun, Robin J Johnson, Daniela Sciaky, Chih-Hsuan Wei, Robert Leaman, Allan Peter Davis, Carolyn J Mattingly, Thomas C Wiegers, and Zhiyong Lu. 2016. Biocreative v cdr task corpus: a resource for chemical disease relation extraction. *Database*, 2016.

Yuhan Li, Jian Wu, Zhiwei Yu, Börje F. Karlsson, Wei Shen, Manabu Okumura, and Chin-Yew Lin. 2023. All data on the table: Novel dataset and benchmark for cross-modality scientific information extraction.

Chin-Yew Lin. 2004. ROUGE: A package for automatic evaluation of summaries. In *Text Summarization Branches Out*, pages 74–81, Barcelona, Spain. Association for Computational Linguistics.

Kyle Lo, Lucy Lu Wang, Mark Neumann, Rodney Kinney, and Daniel Weld. 2020. S2ORC: The semantic scholar open research corpus. In *Proceedings of the 58th Annual Meeting of the Association for Computational Linguistics*, pages 4969–4983, Online. Association for Computational Linguistics.

Yi Luan, Luheng He, Mari Ostendorf, and Hannaneh Hajishirzi. 2018. Multi-task identification of entities, relations, and coreference for scientific knowledge graph construction. In *Proceedings of the 2018 Conference on Empirical Methods in Natural Language Processing*, pages 3219–3232, Brussels, Belgium. Association for Computational Linguistics.

Renqian Luo, Liai Sun, Yingce Xia, Tao Qin, Sheng Zhang, Hoifung Poon, and Tie-Yan Liu. 2022. BioGPT: generative pre-trained transformer for biomedical text generation and mining. *Briefings in Bioinformatics*, 23(6):bbac409.

Nafise Sadat Moosavi, Andreas Rücklé, Dan Roth, and Iryna Gurevych. 2021. SciGen: a dataset for reasoning-aware text generation from scientific tables. In *Thirty-fifth Conference on Neural Information Processing Systems Datasets and Benchmarks Track (Round 2)*.

Panitan Muangkammuen, Fumiyo Fukumoto, Jiyi Li, and Yoshimi Suzuki. 2023. Intermediate-task transfer learning for peer review score prediction. In *Proceedings of the 13th International Joint Conference on Natural Language Processing and the 3rd Conference of the Asia-Pacific Chapter of the Association for Computational Linguistics: Student Research Workshop*, pages 40–47, Nusa Dua, Bali. Association for Computational Linguistics.

Malte Ostendorff, Nils Rethmeier, Isabelle Augenstein, Bela Gipp, and Georg Rehm. 2022. Neighborhood contrastive learning for scientific document representations with citation embeddings. In *Proceedings of the 2022 Conference on Empirical Methods in Natural Language Processing*, pages 11670–11688, Abu Dhabi, United Arab Emirates. Association for Computational Linguistics.

Panupong Pasupat and Percy Liang. 2015. Compositional semantic parsing on semi-structured tables. In *Proceedings of the 53rd Annual Meeting of the Association for Computational Linguistics and the 7th International Joint Conference on Natural Language Processing (Volume 1: Long Papers)*, pages 1470–1480, Beijing, China. Association for Computational Linguistics.

Adam Roberts, Colin Raffel, Katherine Lee, Michael Matena, Noam Shazeer, Peter J. Liu, Sharan Narang, Wei Li, and Yanqi Zhou. 2019. Exploring the limits of transfer learning with a unified text-to-text transformer. Technical report, Google.

Anna Rogers and Isabelle Augenstein. 2020. What can we do to improve peer review in NLP? In *Findings of the Association for Computational Linguistics: EMNLP 2020*, pages 1256–1262, Online. Association for Computational Linguistics.

Nihar B Shah. 2022. Challenges, experiments, and computational solutions in peer review. *Communications of the ACM*, 65(6):76–87.

Shinichi Shirakawa, Yasushi Iwata, and Youhei Akimoto. 2018. Dynamic optimization of neural network structures using probabilistic modeling. In *Proceedings of the AAAI Conference on Artificial Intelligence*, volume 32.

Amanpreet Singh, Mike D'Arcy, Arman Cohan, Doug Downey, and Sergey Feldman. 2023. SciRepEval: A multi-format benchmark for scientific document representations. In *Proceedings of the 2023 Conference on Empirical Methods in Natural Language Processing*, pages 5548–5566, Singapore. Association for Computational Linguistics.

Ross Taylor, Marcin Kardas, Guillem Cucurull, Thomas Scialom, Anthony Hartshorn, Elvis Saravia, Andrew Poulton, Viktor Kerkez, and Robert Stojnic. 2022. Galactica: A large language model for science. *arXiv preprint arXiv:2211.09085*.

Hugo Touvron, Louis Martin, Kevin Stone, Peter Albert, Amjad Almahairi, Yasmine Babaei, Nikolay Bashlykov, Soumya Batra, Prajjwal Bhargava, Shruti Bhosale, et al. 2023. Llama 2: Open foundation and fine-tuned chat models. *arXiv preprint arXiv:2307.09288*.

David Wadden, Shanchuan Lin, Kyle Lo, Lucy Lu Wang, Madeleine van Zuylen, Arman Cohan, and Hannaneh Hajishirzi. 2020. Fact or fiction: Verifying scientific claims. In *Proceedings of the 2020 Conference on Empirical Methods in Natural Language Processing (EMNLP)*, pages 7534–7550, Online. Association for Computational Linguistics.

Yu-Siang Wang, Yen-Ling Kuo, and Boris Katz. 2020. Investigating the decoders of maximum likelihood sequence models: A look-ahead approach. *arXiv preprint arXiv:2003.03716*.

Mahmood Yousefi-Azar, Leonard G. C. Hamey, Vijay Varadharajan, and Shiping Chen. 2018. Malytics: A malware detection scheme. *IEEE Access*, 6:49418–49431.

Kai Zhang, Jun Yu, Zhiling Yan, Yixin Liu, Eashan Adhikarla, Sunyang Fu, Xun Chen, Chen Chen, Yuyin Zhou, Xiang Li, et al. 2023a. Biomedgpt: A unified and generalist biomedical generative pre-trained transformer for vision, language, and multimodal tasks. *arXiv preprint arXiv:2305.17100*.

Tianshu Zhang, Xiang Yue, Yifei Li, and Huan Sun. 2023b. Tablellama: Towards open large generalist models for tables. *arXiv preprint arXiv:2311.09206*.

Tianyi Zhang, Varsha Kishore, Felix Wu, Kilian Q Weinberger, and Yoav Artzi. 2019. Bertscore: Evaluating text generation with bert. In *International Conference on Learning Representations*.

Yu Zhang, Hao Cheng, Zhihong Shen, Xiaodong Liu, Ye-Yi Wang, and Jianfeng Gao. 2023c. Pre-training multi-task contrastive learning models for scientific literature understanding. In *Findings of the Association for Computational Linguistics: EMNLP 2023*, pages 12259–12275, Singapore. Association for Computational Linguistics.

Yu Zhang, Bowen Jin, Qi Zhu, Yu Meng, and Jiawei Han. 2023d. The effect of metadata on scientific literature tagging: A cross-field cross-model study. In *Proceedings of the ACM Web Conference 2023*, pages 1626–1637.

Wayne Xin Zhao, Kun Zhou, Junyi Li, Tianyi Tang, Xiaolei Wang, Yupeng Hou, Yingqian Min, Beichen Zhang, Junjie Zhang, Zican Dong, et al. 2023. A survey of large language models. *arXiv preprint arXiv:2303.18223*.

Fengbin Zhu, Wenqiang Lei, Youcheng Huang, Chao Wang, Shuo Zhang, Jiancheng Lv, Fuli Feng, and Tat-Seng Chua. 2021. TAT-QA: A question answering benchmark on a hybrid of tabular and textual content in finance. In *Proceedings of the 59th Annual Meeting of the Association for Computational Linguistics and the 11th International Joint Conference on Natural Language Processing (Volume 1: Long Papers)*, pages 3277–3287, Online. Association for Computational Linguistics.

A Implementation Details

We use cross-entropy as a loss function, Adam (Kingma and Ba, 2015) as an optimizer with a fixed learning rate of 1e-6 in all iterations of intermediate task pre-training and fine-tuning. We experiment with larger learning rates but the best results are obtained with 1e-6. We train our models with an early-stopping approach with a maximum of 5 epochs using an A100 GPU for FlanT5 variants and 3 A100 GPUs for LLaMA-2-chat-hf. While tokenizing the tables, the maximum length is chosen as 512. The batch size for FlanT5-xl is 2 and LLaMA-2 is 1. Our longest training takes 30 hours for the full pipeline with the WikiTQ+SQA+SciGen setting for FlanT5-xl.

B Additional Examples

We share more examples of different samples from the test dataset in this section.

random	beam	ALCHEMY 3utts	ALCHEMY 5utts	TANGRAMS 3utts	TANGRAMS 5utts	SCENE 3utts	SCENE 5utts
		classic beam search					
None	32	30.3	23.2	0.0	0.0	33.4	20.1
None	128	59.0	46.4	60.9	28.6	24.5	13.9
		randomized beam search					
$\epsilon = 0.05$	32	58.7	45.5	61.1	32.5	33.4	23.0
$\epsilon = 0.15$	32	**61.3**	48.3	**65.2**	**34.3**	50.8	33.5
$\epsilon = 0.25$	32	60.5	**48.6**	60.0	27.3	**54.1**	**35.7**

Reference:
Table 3 shows that (cid:15)-greedy randomized beam search consistently outperforms classic beam search. Even when we increase the beam size of classic beam search to 128, it still does not surpass randomized beam search with a beam of 32, and further increases yield no additional improvement.

Zero:
R> C> None C> 32 C> 30. 3 C> 23. 2 C> 0. 0 C> 0. 0 C> 33. 4 C> 20. 1 R> C> None C> 128 C> 59. 0 C> 46. 4 C> 60. 9 C> 28. 6 C> 24. 5 C> 13. 9 R> C> [BOLD] randomized beam search C> [BOLD] randomized beam search C> [BOLD] randomized beam search C> [BOLD] randomized beam search C> [BOLD] randomized beam search C> [B C> ...

SciGen:
We also compare the performance of randomized beam search with classic beam search. We observe that randomized beam search outperforms classic beam search on all the datasets. This is because the randomized beam search is more flexible and can be used to search for more than one beam.

WikiTQ+SciGen:
We also compare the performance of our randomized beam search with classic beam search. We observe that the randomized beam search outperforms the classic beam search in all cases. This is because the randomized beam search is able to learn a more diverse set of features.

WikiTQ+SQA+SciGen:
We also compare the performance of randomized beam search with classic beam search. We observe that randomized beam search outperforms classic beam search on all datasets. This is expected since the randomized beam search is based on a random search of the beams.

Figure 4: The original caption of the table is “Randomized beam search. All listed models use gradient weight qMML and Tokens to represent execution history.”. Taken from (Guu et al., 2017).

	Test error (%)	Time (hour)
AdaptiveNet	1.645 (0.072)	1.01
BO (budget=10)	1.780	9.59
BO (budget=20)	1.490	18.29

Reference:
Table 3 shows that the test errors of the stochastic networks obtained by the proposed method and the Bayesian optimization with different budgets, where budget indicates the number of hyper-parameters to be evaluated. we observe that the computational time of the Bayesian optimization proportionally increases for the number of budgets while our method is more computationally efficient. The proposed method can find a competitive stochastic network with reasonable computational time. The Bayesian optimization could find a better configuration in this case within several ten budgets.

Zero:
R> C> [EMPTY] C> Test error (%) C> Time (hour) R> C> AdaptiveNet C> 1. 645 (0. 072) C> 1. 01 R> C> BO (budget=10) C> 1. 780 C> 9. 59 R> C> BO (budget=20) C> 1. 490 C> 18. 29.

SciGen:
The proposed method is able to achieve the best performance in terms of test error and computational time. The results show that the proposed method is able to achieve the best performance in terms of test error and computational time.

WikiTQ+SciGen:
The proposed method is able to achieve better performance than the Bayesian optimization with different budgets.

WikiTQ+SQA+SciGen:
The proposed method is able to achieve a better performance than the Bayesian optimization with different budgets. The results show that the proposed method is able to adapt the stochastic network with a lower computational time.

Figure 5: The original caption of the table is “Test errors (%) and computational time of the proposed method (AdaptiveNet) and the Bayesian optimization (BO) with different budgets in the experiment of adaptation of stochastic network. The mean values over 30 trials are reported in the proposed method, and the value in parentheses denotes the standard deviation. For the Bayesian optimization, the result of a single run is reported.”. Taken from (Shirakawa et al., 2018).

Search Strategy	BLEU
Greedy Search	86.24
2-LA	86.65
3-LA	86.71
4-LA	86.77
5-LA	**86.79**
Beam Search (B=10)	86.28

Reference:
Table 1: The performances of the IM2LATEX-100K Bi-LSTM model. We discover that the look-ahead improves the model from the greedy search method – noted that LA is more directly comparable to the greedy search because of their same beam size. We also show the scores of the beam search for the reference.

Zero:
R> C> Search Strategy C> BLEU R> C> Greedy Search C> 86. 24 R> C> 2-LA C> 86. 65 R> C> 3-LA C> 86. 71 R> C> 4-LA C> 86. 77 R> C> 5-LA C> [BOLD] 86. 79 R> C> Beam Search (B=10) C> 86. 28 CAP>.

SciGen:
We also compare the performance of the beam search with the greedy search. The results show that the look-ahead improves the model from the greedy search.

WikiTQ+SciGen:
We also compare the performance of the beam search with the greedy search. The results show that the look-ahead improves the model from the greedy search.

WikiTQ+SQA+SciGen:
We also compare the performance of the beam search with the greedy search. The results show that the look-ahead improves the model from the greedy search method. The 4-LA and 5-LA are more directly comparable to the greedy search because of their same beam size.

Figure 6: The original caption of the table is "The performances of the IM2LATEX-100K Bi-LSTM model. We discover that the look-ahead improves the model from the greedy search method—noted that LA is more directly comparable to the greedy search because of their same beam size. We also show the scores of the beam search for the reference". Taken from (Wang et al., 2020).

Harnessing CLIP for Evidence Identification in Scientific Literature: A Multimodal Approach to the Context24 Shared Task

Anukriti Kumar **Lucy Lu Wang**
University of Washington
{anukumar, lucylw}@uw.edu

Abstract

Knowing whether scientific claims are supported by evidence is fundamental to scholarly communication and evidence-based decision-making. We present our approach to Task 1 of the Context24 Shared Task—Contextualizing Scientific Figures and Tables (SDP@ACL2024), which focuses on identifying multimodal evidence from scientific publications that support claims. We finetune CLIP, a state-of-the-art model for image-text similarity tasks, to identify and rank figures and tables in papers that substantiate specific claims. Our methods focus on text and image preprocessing techniques and augmenting the organizer-provided training data with labeled examples from the SciMMIR and MedICaT datasets. Our best-performing model achieved NDCG@5 and NDCG@10 values of 0.26 and 0.30, respectively, on the Context24 test split. Our findings underscore the effectiveness of data augmentation and preprocessing in improving the model's ability in evidence matching.

1 Introduction

Scientific claims, essential for communicating findings in literature reviews, research problem formulation, and interpreting conflicting data, require careful contextualization and verification with supporting empirical evidence and methodological details. Figures and tables in papers presenting key results, measures, and sample characteristics are critical for understanding and validating claims. However, retrieving such contextual information from scientific papers is challenging and time-consuming, particularly when researchers and practitioners encounter claims without direct access to the source materials.

Recent advancements in multimodal AI models, which excel at image-text similarity tasks, present an opportunity to automate the retrieval and contextualization of evidence. However, their application for evidence identification in scientific literature remains underexplored. Existing research primarily focuses on text summarization (Zhu et al., 2021; Li et al., 2020; Rafi and Das, 2023), entity recognition (Liu et al., 2023; Chen and Feng, 2023), and information retrieval (Jin et al., 2023; Imhof and Braschler, 2018), with limited attention to integrating visual evidence from figures and tables.

This paper presents our approach to Task 1 of the Context24 Shared Task,[1] focusing on evidence identification for scientific claims. The task involves predicting a ranked list of figures or tables from a relevant research paper that provides supporting evidence for a given scientific claim. We leverage the Contrastive Language–Image Pretraining (CLIP) model's image-text similarity capabilities, augment training data with diverse datasets and augmentation techniques, and employ text-image pre-processing methods to retrieve and rank relevant figures and tables from scientific papers.

The contributions of our work are as follows:

- We introduce a comprehensive dataset that combines augmented training data from the shared task with additional data from SciMMIR (Wu et al., 2024) and MedICaT (Subramanian et al., 2020), significantly expanding the scope and diversity of the training samples (§3).
- We finetune the CLIP model on this combined dataset and demonstrate the impact of more training data, as well as text and image pre-processing techniques on enhancing the model's relevancy matching capabilities (§4; §5).

2 Related Work

Scientific Evidence Identification Early work on scientific evidence identification focused on text analysis and argument mining techniques, like those of Guo et al. (2011), who investigated weakly-supervised approaches for detecting argu-

[1] https://sdproc.org/2024/sharedtasks.html#context24

Proceedings of the Fourth Workshop on Scholarly Document Processing (SDP 2024), pages 307–313
August 16, 2024 ©2024 Association for Computational Linguistics

ment zones in scientific abstracts using features such as location, word bi-grams, and verb cues. Building on this, Houngbo and Mercer (2014) further explored the identification of rhetorical structures in biomedical articles; their analysis of the IMRaD structure (Introduction, Methods, Results, and Discussion) clarifies how different sections of a scientific paper contribute to the overall argumentative flow. Later, Faiz and Mercer (2014) developed techniques to extract "higher order relations" between biomedical entities, useful in the identification of causal links essential for evidence-based conclusions.

Neural models and machine learning further transformed capabilities in this domain. Techniques such as Bi-LSTM (Lauscher et al., 2018a,b) and BiLSTM-CRF (Li et al., 2021b; Achakulvisut et al., 2019) were adapted to parse and analyze argumentative structures in scientific texts for sentence-level classification and multi-task learning. These works enhanced the ability to distinguish between different types of evidence based on linguistic cues and discourse patterns. Further, Pinto et al. (2019) introduced learning-to-rank techniques combined with metadata features, such as journal impact factor and citation metrics, to optimize the retrieval process. Wadden et al. (2020) introduced the task of scientific claim verification, to select abstracts from research literature that either support or refute a given scientific claim; the authors introduced the SciFact dataset and baseline models, demonstrating that domain adaptation techniques significantly improve performance compared to models trained on Wikipedia or political news. The authors later extended the SciFact dataset into the open domain by integrating retrieval in the data curation process (Wadden et al., 2022).

Image-Text Matching Recent advancements in vision-language pretraining (VLP) have significantly reshaped the landscape of evidence identification. VLP aims to learn universal and transferable features from images and text, applicable across image-text retrieval tasks (Tan and Bansal, 2019; Zhang et al., 2020; Chen et al., 2019; Zhang et al., 2021; Kim et al., 2021; Jia et al., 2021; Li et al., 2021a; Wang et al., 2021; Li et al., 2022). Multimodal models like CLIP (Radford et al., 2021), BLIP-2 (Li et al., 2023), and Stable Diffusion (Rombach et al., 2021) that have undergone significant multimodal pretraining, have the potential to improve the alignment of text-based claims with image-based evidence.

Our work builds on these advancements by fine-tuning a model based on the CLIP architecture (Huang et al., 2023) on large-scale scientific datasets with an image-text matching objective. Extending beyond the typical focus on biomedical or computer science domains in prior works (Wang et al., 2022; Lin et al., 2023; Eslami et al., 2023), our approach covers a broader range of scientific disciplines. We leverage these image-text embeddings to retrieve and match scientific claims with their supporting evidence.

3 Datasets

This section describes the Context24 dataset (§3.1) and outlines our strategies for data enrichment (§3.2) and external data augmentation (§3.3).

3.1 Context24 Dataset

The Context24 dataset[2] comprises 474 scientific claims used in lab notes and discussions for synthesis and research planning, across domains of biology, computer science, and the social sciences. These claims are accompanied by "gold" annotations identifying figures and tables in the full text of research papers that provide key supporting evidence. We randomly sample 156 claims as the validation set, representing 34% of the dataset.

3.2 Data Enrichment

We enrich the training dataset with additional context. We leverage GPT-4 (OpenAI, 2023) to extract sub-captions and references for each of the associated figures and tables to provide a deeper contextual understanding for each claim.

Data cleaning Before enrichment, we perform the following steps:

- We eliminate unnecessary spaces, punctuation, and non-standard characters that could interfere with text processing;
- We convert all claims to lowercase to maintain consistency across the dataset, and correct formatting inconsistencies that could affect subsequent text parsing;
- We address common textual errors, such as excessive repetition of characters or patterns, non-standard characters (e.g., control characters or invalid Unicode), and executable commands,

[2]Training dataset: https://github.com/oasisresearchlab/context24/blob/main/task1-train-dev-2024-04-25-update.json

which throw errors when input into the GPT-4 API, by removing or heuristically fixing them.

Sub-caption Extraction Using GPT-4, we parse figure captions to extract descriptions for each sub-figure. This extraction is guided by the prompt: "This is a caption for a figure consisting of multiple sub-figures. Extract image descriptions for all sub-figures." Each extracted sub-caption is aligned with its corresponding sub-figure.

Reference Extraction Similarly, we extract textual references to figures and tables from the full texts of papers using the prompt: "This is the full text of a scientific paper. Extract only the relevant details mentioned regarding the figures and tables." These references were mapped to the corresponding claims and captions to strengthen the linkage between textual claims and the paper contexts.

Verification of GPT-4 Responses We manually review a random sample of extracted sub-captions and references (N=20) by comparing them with the original text (captions and full texts) to identify hallucinations or inaccuracies.

We found that GPT-4 accurately extracted sub-captions and references in 75% of cases (N=15). However, hallucinations occurred in 10% of cases (N=2), where GPT-4 fabricated content not present in the original text. The remaining 15% (N=3) contained minor inaccuracies such as incorrect sub-figure associations or slight misinterpretations of the text. As a result, we implement a series of post-processing steps:

- We filter out responses containing phrases like "Sorry..." or similar, as these often indicate GPT-4's inability to provide meaningful content;
- We discard responses with less than three words to ensure sufficient descriptive content;
- We compare extracted sub-captions and references against standard mention formats in scientific papers, e.g., "In Figure X, we...", to flag potential extraction errors. By cross-referencing GPT-4's outputs with these patterns, we discard text that deviates from our expectations.

This hybrid approach of automated extraction followed by heuristic curation ensures a higher degree of accuracy and reliability in the enrichment data. We refer to the resulting data with sub-captions and references as the augmented training data (ATD).

Dataset	Size
`Context24 Training Data`	456
`Context24 References Data`	609
`Context24 Captions Data`	438
`Context24 Augmented Cleaned Data`	1466
`SciMMIR`	530975
`MedICaT`	2118
Total (Combined)	534559

Table 1: Dataset Statistics

3.3 External Data Augmentation

To further augment and diversify our training data, we integrate two external datasets: SciMMIR (Wu et al., 2024) and MedICAT (Subramanian et al., 2020). Statistics for the augmented dataset are provided in Table 1.

SciMMIR Dataset SciMMIR (Wu et al., 2024) is a large-scale collection of scientific image-text pairs extracted from papers published on arXiv between May-October 2023. This dataset comprises approximately 530K image-text pairs, categorized into training (N=498K), validation (N=16.4K), and test splits (N=16.3K).

MedICaT Dataset MedICaT (Subramanian et al., 2020) is a collection of 217K medical images and their captions and references extracted from 131K open-access biomedical articles in PubMed Central. The dataset includes inline references for 74% of figures, and manually annotated subfigures and subcaptions for a subset of 2118 figures. For this study, we use only the subfigure-subcaption pairs in MedICaT for training.

4 Experiments

We detail the model selection and training process, and experiments to assess the impact of training data variation and preprocessing techniques.

4.1 Baseline Model

We select OpenAI's CLIP model, specifically the `clip-vit-base-patch32` variant from Hugging Face,[3] as our base image and text encoder. CLIP utilizes a vision transformer architecture (ViT-B/32) as an image encoder and a masked self-attention transformer as a text encoder. These encoders are trained to maximize the similarity of (image, text) pairs via contrastive loss, making them a suitable choice for this multimodal retrieval task.

[3]HuggingFace CLIP base model: https://huggingface.co/openai/clip-vit-base-patch32

4.2 Training Details

We train the CLIP model by minimizing the contrastive loss between the embeddings for images and corresponding text (claims, captions, and references) on the Context24 and augmented datasets. We finetune all models on Nvidia A100 GPUs, with 100 epochs and early stopping. We conduct hyperparameter tuning to select learning rates (0.00001 to 0.001), batch sizes (16, 32, and 64), and the margin parameter in the contrastive loss function. The final training was over 10 epochs, with a batch size of 32, a learning rate of 0.0001, and a decay rate of 0.01. We chose the Adam optimizer for its adaptive learning rate capabilities. Additionally, we employed 5-fold cross-validation for better model robustness and generalizability.

4.3 Variation in Training Data

We assess the impact of different dataset configurations on the performance of the CLIP model. Initially, we train the model using only the Context24 training dataset (TD) to establish baseline performance. To evaluate the effects of data augmentation, we compare three augmented datasets, one enriched with additional text snippets such as sub-captions and references (ATD), adding the SciMMIR dataset, and adding the SciMMIR and MedICaT datasets.

4.4 Variation in Preprocessing Techniques

We additionally explore how preprocessing techniques affect the CLIP model's performance. We apply text transformation techniques such as Named Entity Recognition (NER) and semantic role labeling (SRL) to enhance the model's understanding of grammatical structures and relationships between entities within the text. Specifically, we tag named entities and include SRL labels alongside the original tokens in the input, providing richer context and improving the text representation for the model. Additionally, we implement various image data augmentation techniques—including random cropping, rotation, resizing, and color jittering—during training to improve the model's robustness to visual variations.

5 Results

Following the Context24 shared task, we report Normalized Discounted Cumulative Gain (NDCG) at 5 and 10 to assess the ranking of the retrieved figures and tables. Additionally, we report precision and recall for the top 5 and 10 retrieved images (i.e., P@5, R@5, P@10, and R@10).

5.1 Results on Validation Split

Table 2 presents the performance differences achieved through augmenting the training dataset. No preprocessing is conducted on any of these model variants. Notably, the addition of data shows steady improvements in NDCG@5 (0.19 to 0.27), NDCG@10 (0.21 to 0.29), and P/R@k. P@5 increased from 0.49 with initial training data to 0.76 with the combined dataset (ATD + SciMMIR + MedICaT). Similarly, R@5 showed substantial improvement, from 0.46 to 0.75.

Table 3 highlights the impact of preprocessing on model performance. Using the model finetuned on the combined dataset without any preprocessing techniques as a baseline, the addition of image-text preprocessing, while leading to minimal gains in NDCG, led to substantial gains in P/R@k: P@5 increased to 0.86 and R@5 to 0.82.

The results from our experiments on the validation dataset underscore the significance of dataset enhancement and image-text preprocessing on the performance of image-text similarity models like CLIP in identifying scientific evidence.

5.2 Results on Test Split

We apply our finetuned CLIP model, trained with the combined dataset and enhanced with image-text pre-processing techniques, to a test set comprising 111 scientific claims. Before inference, we perform data cleaning and context enrichment, as detailed in Section 3.2. The model computes similarity scores between the textual claims and the associated visual evidence (figures or tables). These scores were used to rank the evidence, and final rankings were submitted to the eval.ai platform.[4] Our team secured third place on the leaderboard, with NDCG@5 of 0.26 and NDCG@10 of 0.30 on the test split.

6 Future Work

Our current approach leverages the entire MedICaT subcaption subset and SciMMIR datasets for training the CLIP model. However, we can potentially improve performance by selecting subsets of these datasets that more closely align with the scientific domains or types of claims in the Context24 dataset. This approach might enhance the

[4]Evaluation platform for Context24: https://eval.ai/web/challenges/challenge-page/2306/overview

Training Data Used	NDCG@5	NDCG@10	P@5	P@10	R@5	R@10
Training Data (TD)	0.19	0.21	0.49	0.48	0.46	0.46
Augmented TD (ATD)	0.23	0.26	0.56	0.67	0.54	0.61
ATD + MedICAT	0.24	0.27	0.58	0.67	0.55	0.61
ATD + SciMMIR	0.26	0.28	0.75	0.73	0.74	0.65
ATD + SciMMIR + MedICaT	0.27	0.29	0.76	0.73	0.75	0.65

Table 2: Performance metrics for CLIP model finetuned with different datasets (without pre-processing)

Preprocessing Techniques	NDCG@5	NDCG@10	P@5	P@10	R@5	R@10
No pre-processing	0.27	0.29	0.76	0.73	0.75	0.65
Image pre-processing	0.27	0.31	0.77	0.75	0.76	0.71
Text-Image pre-processing	0.28	0.32	0.86	0.81	0.82	0.77

Table 3: Performance metrics for CLIP model finetuned on the combined dataset (ATD + SciMMIR + MedICaT) with different pre-processing techniques

relevance and quality of the training data to the task. In future work, we will explore using text and image embedding similarity methods to filter the augmentation data by domain relevance.

We also acknowledge the challenge presented by complex figures with multiple sub-figures, which are not fully described in the captions. While our method of using GPT-4 to extract corresponding subcaptions was somewhat effective, the observed hallucinations and inaccuracies highlight the need for continuous refinement and validation of automated methods. To address this, future work might explore alternative models or techniques for subcaption-subfigure alignment.

Currently, we use references and captions from figures and tables as additional image-text pairs to train the CLIP model. Another potential enhancement involves augmenting the claims with this contextual information *before* computing similarity scores with the images. This method could provide a more holistic understanding of the claim and its context by incorporating essential details directly alongside the claim text in claim verification.

7 Conclusion

In this paper, we presented our approach to Task 1 of the Context24 Shared Task, which focuses on identifying multimodal evidence for scientific claims. We enhanced our training data by integrating sub-captions and inline references as well as additional data from SciMMIR and MedICaT. We finetuned the CLIP model on this enriched dataset, applying image-text preprocessing and augmentation techniques to effectively align scientific claims with their corresponding figures and tables. We secured third place on the leaderboard, with NDCG@5 and NDCG@10 scores of 0.26 and 0.30, respectively on the test dataset. Our findings underscore the significance of expanding training data and employing preprocessing techniques on the model's performance.

Acknowledgments

This work is supported in part by the University of Washington eScience Insitute's Azure Cloud Credits for Research and Teaching.

References

Titipat Achakulvisut, Chandra Bhagavatula, Daniel Ernesto Acuna, and Konrad Paul Kording. 2019. Claim extraction in biomedical publications using deep discourse model and transfer learning. *ArXiv*, abs/1907.00962.

F. Chen and Yujian Feng. 2023. Chain-of-thought prompt distillation for multimodal named entity recognition and multimodal relation extraction.

Yen-Chun Chen, Linjie Li, Licheng Yu, Ahmed El Kholy, Faisal Ahmed, Zhe Gan, Yu Cheng, and Jingjing Liu. 2019. Uniter: Universal image-text representation learning. In *European Conference on Computer Vision*.

Sedigheh Eslami, Christoph Meinel, and Gerard De Melo. 2023. Pubmedclip: How much does clip benefit visual question answering in the medical domain? In *Findings*.

Syeed Ibn Faiz and Robert E. Mercer. 2014. Extracting higher order relations from biomedical text. In *ArgMining@ACL*.

Yufan Guo, Anna Korhonen, and T. Poibeau. 2011. A weakly-supervised approach to argumentative zoning of scientific documents. In *Conference on Empirical Methods in Natural Language Processing*.

Hospice Houngbo and Robert E. Mercer. 2014. An automated method to build a corpus of rhetorically-classified sentences in biomedical texts. In *ArgMining@ACL*.

Zhi Huang, Federico Bianchi, Mert Yuksekgonul, Thomas J. Montine, and James Y Zou. 2023. Leveraging medical twitter to build a visual–language foundation model for pathology ai. *bioRxiv*.

Melanie Imhof and Martin Braschler. 2018. A study of untrained models for multimodal information retrieval. *Information Retrieval Journal*, 21:81–106.

Chao Jia, Yinfei Yang, Ye Xia, Yi-Ting Chen, Zarana Parekh, Hieu Pham, Quoc V. Le, Yun-Hsuan Sung, Zhen Li, and Tom Duerig. 2021. Scaling up visual and vision-language representation learning with noisy text supervision. *ArXiv*, abs/2102.05918.

Zhenkun Jin, Xingshi Wan, Xin Nie, Xinlei Zhou, Yuanyuan Yi, and Gefei Zhou. 2023. Ranking on heterogeneous manifold for multimodal information retrieval. *2023 IEEE Intl Conf on Parallel & Distributed Processing with Applications, Big Data & Cloud Computing, Sustainable Computing & Communications, Social Computing & Networking (ISPA/BDCloud/SocialCom/SustainCom)*, pages 989–996.

Wonjae Kim, Bokyung Son, and Ildoo Kim. 2021. Vilt: Vision-and-language transformer without convolution or region supervision. In *International Conference on Machine Learning*.

Anne Lauscher, Goran Glavas, and K. Eckert. 2018a. Arguminsci: A tool for analyzing argumentation and rhetorical aspects in scientific writing. In *ArgMining@EMNLP*.

Anne Lauscher, Goran Glavas, Simone Paolo Ponzetto, and K. Eckert. 2018b. Investigating the role of argumentation in the rhetorical analysis of scientific publications with neural multi-task learning models. In *Conference on Empirical Methods in Natural Language Processing*.

Haoran Li, Junnan Zhu, Jiajun Zhang, Xiaodong He, and Chengqing Zong. 2020. Multimodal sentence summarization via multimodal selective encoding. In *International Conference on Computational Linguistics*.

Junnan Li, Dongxu Li, Silvio Savarese, and Steven C. H. Hoi. 2023. Blip-2: Bootstrapping language-image pre-training with frozen image encoders and large language models. In *International Conference on Machine Learning*.

Junnan Li, Dongxu Li, Caiming Xiong, and Steven C. H. Hoi. 2022. Blip: Bootstrapping language-image pre-training for unified vision-language understanding and generation. In *International Conference on Machine Learning*.

Junnan Li, Ramprasaath R. Selvaraju, Akhilesh Deepak Gotmare, Shafiq R. Joty, Caiming Xiong, and Steven C. H. Hoi. 2021a. Align before fuse: Vision and language representation learning with momentum distillation. In *Neural Information Processing Systems*.

Xiangci Li, Gully A. Burns, and Nanyun Peng. 2021b. Scientific discourse tagging for evidence extraction. In *Conference of the European Chapter of the Association for Computational Linguistics*.

Weixiong Lin, Ziheng Zhao, Xiaoman Zhang, Chaoyi Wu, Ya Zhang, Yanfeng Wang, and Weidi Xie. 2023. Pmc-clip: Contrastive language-image pre-training using biomedical documents. In *International Conference on Medical Image Computing and Computer-Assisted Intervention*.

Weide Liu, Xiaoyang Zhong, Jingwen Hou, Shaohua Li, Haozhe Huang, and Yuming Fang. 2023. Integrating large pre-trained models into multimodal named entity recognition with evidential fusion. *ArXiv*, abs/2306.16991.

OpenAI. 2023. Gpt-4 technical report.

José María González Pinto, Serkan Çelik, and Wolf-Tilo Balke. 2019. Learning to rank claim-evidence pairs to assist scientific-based argumentation. In *International Conference on Theory and Practice of Digital Libraries*.

Alec Radford, Jong Wook Kim, Chris Hallacy, Aditya Ramesh, Gabriel Goh, Sandhini Agarwal, Girish Sastry, Amanda Askell, Pamela Mishkin, Jack Clark, Gretchen Krueger, and Ilya Sutskever. 2021. Learning transferable visual models from natural language supervision. In *International Conference on Machine Learning*.

Shaik Rafi and Ranjita Das. 2023. Abstractive text summarization using multimodal information. *2023 10th International Conference on Soft Computing & Machine Intelligence (ISCMI)*, pages 141–145.

Robin Rombach, A. Blattmann, Dominik Lorenz, Patrick Esser, and Björn Ommer. 2021. High-resolution image synthesis with latent diffusion models. *2022 IEEE/CVF Conference on Computer Vision and Pattern Recognition (CVPR)*, pages 10674–10685.

Sanjay Subramanian, Lucy Lu Wang, Sachin Mehta, Ben Bogin, Madeleine van Zuylen, Sravanthi Parasa, Sameer Singh, Matt Gardner, and Hannaneh Hajishirzi. 2020. Medicat: A dataset of medical images, captions, and textual references. *ArXiv*, abs/2010.06000.

Hao Hao Tan and Mohit Bansal. 2019. Lxmert: Learning cross-modality encoder representations from transformers. In *Conference on Empirical Methods in Natural Language Processing*.

David Wadden, Shanchuan Lin, Kyle Lo, Lucy Lu Wang, Madeleine van Zuylen, Arman Cohan, and Hannaneh Hajishirzi. 2020. Fact or fiction: Verifying scientific claims. In *Proceedings of the 2020 Conference on Empirical Methods in Natural Language Processing (EMNLP)*, pages 7534–7550, Online. Association for Computational Linguistics.

David Wadden, Kyle Lo, Bailey Kuehl, Arman Cohan, Iz Beltagy, Lucy Lu Wang, and Hannaneh Hajishirzi. 2022. SciFact-open: Towards open-domain scientific claim verification. In *Findings of the Association for Computational Linguistics: EMNLP 2022*, pages 4719–4734, Abu Dhabi, United Arab Emirates. Association for Computational Linguistics.

Wenhui Wang, Hangbo Bao, Li Dong, and Furu Wei. 2021. Vlmo: Unified vision-language pretraining with mixture-of-modality-experts. *ArXiv*, abs/2111.02358.

Zifeng Wang, Zhenbang Wu, Dinesh Agarwal, and Jimeng Sun. 2022. Medclip: Contrastive learning from unpaired medical images and text. In *Conference on Empirical Methods in Natural Language Processing*.

Siwei Wu, Yizhi Li, Kang Zhu, Ge Zhang, Yiming Liang, Kaijing Ma, Chenghao Xiao, Haoran Zhang, Bohao Yang, Wenhu Chen, Wenhao Huang, N. A. Moubayed, Jie Fu, and Chenghua Lin. 2024. Scimmir: Benchmarking scientific multi-modal information retrieval. *ArXiv*, abs/2401.13478.

Pengchuan Zhang, Xiujun Li, Xiaowei Hu, Jianwei Yang, Lei Zhang, Lijuan Wang, Yejin Choi, and Jianfeng Gao. 2021. Vinvl: Revisiting visual representations in vision-language models. *2021 IEEE/CVF Conference on Computer Vision and Pattern Recognition (CVPR)*, pages 5575–5584.

Yuhao Zhang, Hang Jiang, Yasuhide Miura, Christopher D. Manning, and C. Langlotz. 2020. Contrastive learning of medical visual representations from paired images and text. In *Machine Learning in Health Care*.

Junnan Zhu, Lu Xiang, Yu Zhou, Jiajun Zhang, and Chengqing Zong. 2021. Graph-based multimodal ranking models for multimodal summarization. *Transactions on Asian and Low-Resource Language Information Processing*, 20:1 – 21.

CSIRO-LT at Context24: Contextualising Scientific Figures and Tables in Scientific Literature

Necva Bölücü, Vincent Nguyen, Roelien C. Timmer, Huichen Yang
Maciej Rybinski, Stephen Wan, Sarvnaz Karimi
[1]CSIRO Data61, Australia
firstname.lastname@csiro.au

Abstract

Finding evidence for claims from content presented in experimental results of scientific articles is difficult. The evidence is often presented in the form of tables and figures, and correctly matching it to scientific claims presents automation challenges. The Context24 shared task is launched to support the development of systems able to verify claims by extracting supporting evidence from articles. We explore different facets of this shared task modelled as a search problem and as an information extraction task. We experiment with a range of methods in each of these categories for the two subtasks of evidence identification and grounding context identification in the Context24 shared task.

1 Introduction

Finding evidence relating to scientific claims in research articles is a time-consuming task. These claims can be supported by the article's text, figures or tables. The *Context24* international shared task[1], organised as part of the *Scholarly Document Processing* workshop at the ACL 2024 Conference, set a challenge for developing methods for two tasks: (1) *Evidence Identification,* where given a scientific claim and a relevant research paper, participating systems should identify key figures or tables from the article that provide supporting evidence for the claim; and, (2) *Grounding Context Identification* where given a scientific claim and a relevant research article, participating systems should identify all grounding contexts that discuss the experiment that led to the claim. The *grounding context* can be found in different research article sections, such as in the results sections, including figures and tables.

Our team participated in both tasks with methods drawing from information retrieval and natural language processing (NLP) research, including statistical ranking models, dense retrieval and the use of large language models (LLMs), including multimodal LLMs.

[1]https://sdproc.org/2024/sharedtasks.html#context24

2 Background and Related Work

Searching for Evidence In 2020, when the COVID-19 pandemic hit the world, the information retrieval community through TREC, established an international shared task called TREC-COVID (Roberts et al., 2021) in response to the overwhelming amount of publications on COVID-19 emerging. This task was designed to research search algorithms to find scientific evidence on what COVID-19 is, what are the symptoms of the disease, and what preventive methods are approved by the public health authorities (e.g., mask-wearing, what type of mask). Due to the public interest in this, there was a need to access reputable information and sift through misleading information (i.e., information without any scientific basis). While this task was largely tackled as an information retrieval problem known as *pandemic information retrieval* (Nguyen et al., 2020), it paved the way for further research in the NLP community. Some data have been proposed in the scientific domain as well, such as SciFact-Open (Wadden et al., 2022a).

Fact Checking and Fake News Detection News is the most common way to disseminate information rapidly. However, fake news— characterised by low-quality, intentionally misleading information— poses significant threats by distorting public perception and causing negative impacts on both individuals and society at large (Shu et al., 2017). Addressing the problem has become imperative, prompting researchers to focus on the automatic verification of facts and detection of fake news.

Numerous studies and public datasets have been developed for the task, covering various domains

Proceedings of the Fourth Workshop on Scholarly Document Processing (SDP 2024), pages 314–323
August 16, 2024 ©2024 Association for Computational Linguistics

Dataset	Domain	Task 1		Task 2	
		Training	Test	Training	Test
akamatsulab	Cell biology	213	51	28	49
BIOL403	Cell biology	60	—	—	—
dg-social-media-polarization	Social sciences (political science, economics, HCI)	78	—	—	—
megacoglab	Various (HCI, psychology, economics, CS, public health)	123	60	14	60
Total		474	111	42	109

Table 1: Dataset specifications. Sizes in the last four columns represent the number of claims in each dataset.

and applications. AVERITEC (Schlichtkrull et al., 2024) and MultiFC (Augenstein et al., 2019) are examples of such datasets. To increase the popularity of the task and the development of effective systems, shared tasks such as Fact Extraction and VERification (FEVER) (Thorne et al., 2018) have been organised. FEVER focuses on verifying factoid claims using evidence from Wikipedia and also introduced new methods, including machine learning algorithms for fact verification (Ahmad et al., 2020; Barnabò et al., 2023; Nie et al., 2019; Sahoo and Gupta, 2021), the application of LLMs for detecting fake news (Hu et al., 2024), and fact-checking using multi-modality sources such as images (Fung et al., 2021; Jindal et al., 2020) and videos (Micallef et al., 2022).

Scientific Claim Verification Evaluating the validity of claims in scientific texts is a specialised area of research essential due to the rapid increase in scientific publications. This task aims to determine whether proposed scientific claims are supported or refuted by retrieving relevant evidence from scientific documents, which may include sentences, figures, or tables. Wadden et al. (2020) introduce the task with the SciFACT dataset, consisting of scientific claims with corresponding abstracts that either support or refute the claim, with a baseline method for the task. The success of retrieval-based approaches has led to the development of document-level (Pang et al., 2020) and sentence-level (Soleimani et al., 2020) methods for the task. With advancements in LLMs, new systems on this task employ LLMs for document retrieval (Pradeep et al., 2021a,b), multi-task label prediction for scientific fact verification (Li et al., 2021; Wadden et al., 2022b), and automatically generating verifiable scientific claims and fact-checking (Wright et al., 2022; Singh et al., 2024).

3 Dataset

The claims and papers used in the Context24 shared task come from four separate datasets, each of which comes from a different set of research domains. Table 1 shows a breakdown of the claims per dataset for both sub-tasks. For Task 1, the number of claims is 474 for training and 111 for testing, and for Task 2, it is 42 for training and 109 for testing. Task 1 involves 193 articles in the training set and 46 in the testing set, while Task 2 includes 31 training articles and 44 testing articles, demonstrating that an article may contain one or more claims.

Silver Dataset annotation In addition to the annotated data, we constructed a silver-annotated dataset utilising a silver data corpus containing 17,007 (unannotated) articles provided by the shared task organisers. We used the GPT3.5 model fine-tuned with the training set of Task 2 (see Section 4.2) to automatically generate claims and corresponding evidence for each of the articles (as opposed to generating evidence, given an article and a claim, which was the objective of task 2). Similar to the main dataset, the silver-annotated dataset includes multiple claims per article.

4 Methods

4.1 Task 1: Evidence Identification

As mentioned above, this task requires a ranked list of relevant key figures and tables based on a given scientific claim and a research paper. All images of figures and tables alongside the article's full text are provided.

We tackle evidence identification as an information retrieval task. As described below, we experiment with multiple methods of document preprocessing, representation, indexing, and ranking.

Article Chunking We experiment with three approaches to splitting full-text articles into fragments. We use sentence splitting, fixed-size chunking, and semantic splitting using `semantic_splitter` Python library. The intention is to capture the articles' text content at different granularity levels.

Indexing Logic Our experiments cover two separate base approaches to creating indices. In the first one (henceforth referred to as 'element-guided'), we directly index representations of tables and figures aggregated from article chunks (see previous paragraph) that cite them. We detect table and figure citations using a simple rule-based approach that searches the chunks for specific expressions, such as: 'Table NUM', 'Figure NUM', 'Tab. NUM', etc. For example, to represent FIG 1 in a specific article, we concatenate all citing chunks (i.e., those containing mentions of 'Figure 1', 'Fig. 1', 'FIG 1', etc.) found in this article. This concatenated text becomes a *document* in our index. We then rank the evidence (so, tables and figures) using the claim's text as a query and calculating the relevance of the *documents* (so, representations of tables and figures) to the query using a specific method (as discussed further in this section). We create a single index for all the evidence across the entire article corpus, which is important for indexing methods that use corpus statistics for relevance calculations (in particular, inverted indices with BM25 relevance).

In our second approach (henceforth referred to as 'chunk-guided'), articles are first chunked at specific levels of granularity (sentences, paragraphs, and chunks of 128, 256, 512, and 1024 tokens). These chunks are indexed in separate indices using Elasticsearch, that is, sentences and paragraphs, and each window-size chunk results in a separate index of chunks. In this setup, the claims are used as queries to rank the snippets of the corresponding document. This produces a ranked list of snippets. We then extract table and figure mentions from the ranked elements of this list. We contemplate three evidence-ranking methods for the chunk-guided approach:

1. Since each snippet may reference more than one figure or table, we score the tables and figures using reciprocal rank fusion – we sum the inverse rank score of all citing snippets for every table and figure. We refer to this approach as 'rank fusion scoring'.
2. One could reasonably assume that relevant evidence should be mentioned in one of the most relevant paragraphs. We, therefore, concatenate the snippets from the relevance-ranked list and rank the tables and figures by the order of mentions in this concatenated text.
3. We delegate the task of producing the ranked list of evidence to an LLM (Llama 3 70B); the ranked list of snippets is included in the LLM prompt together with the claim text.

Indexing and retrieval methods For the element-guided approach, we evaluate two indexing and relevance scoring models. Our baseline experiments use a traditional inverted index with *BM25* relevance scoring. We also evaluate an embedding-based approach, where the evidence representations and the claim are vectorised using a *Mistral E5* embedding model, and relevance is then calculated as a cosine similarity of the embedding vectors.

For the experiments with the chunk-guided approach, we have used a *hybrid index* combining BM25 relevance and embeddings, implemented using DeBIR (Nguyen et al., 2023).[2] In this setup, we evaluate two universal embedding models: Mistral E5 and BGE v1.5 Large.

Image Retrieval Experiment We use a multimodal embedding model CLIP (Radford et al., 2021)– which is OpenAI Contrastive Learning In Pretraining—to generate embedding from images and claim texts. The evidence in this experiment is ranked directly by relevance, i.e., the cosine similarity between the text (claim) embedding and image (figure or table) embedding.

Use of Captions We also carry out some experiments that leverage text extracted with OCR from caption images. In the element-guided approach, we would append the corresponding caption to the (concatenated) textual representation of a specific figure or table. In the chunk-guided approach, each caption is considered a separate document for retrieval.

Use of a LLM to Rewrite the Evidence Representations We also present experiments with the reformulation of the table and figure textual

[2]Preliminary testing on the training set showed that BM25 significantly outperforms embedding-only approaches. We, therefore, only compared against BM25 as we are limited by the number of runs during the shared task.

Run Name (as submitted)	Description
Top-k merge	Round-robin ranking fusion of all our runs except near identical and other round-robin mergers
RS Merge w/ Rank s=2	Reciprocal ranking fusion of all runs, except other round-robin mergers, where the ranking of the run is also considered for fusion.
top-k merge all-runs	Round-robin ranking fusion of all our runs except other round-robin mergers
E5 on LLM-rephrased descriptions	Element-guided Mistral E5 indexing with LLM-rephrased descriptions (original chunk size of 1500 characters with semantic chunking)
E5	Element-guided Mistral E5 indexing with a chunk size of 100 tokens
Hier-Caption+E5+DeBEIR	Hierarchical retrieval approach over all granularities using the DeBEIR scorer with E5 embeddings and rank-score fusion. Captions are excluded from retrieval.
e5+HierAll+DeBEIR+RS	Same as above, except captions, are also considered.
e5+HierCapSent512+DeBeIR	Similar to the above, however, only the captions, sentences and chunk size of 512 are considered for retrieval.
E5 w. semantic chunking	Element-guided Mistral E5 indexing with semantic chunking with a chunk size of 1000 characters
Plain BM25 100 word chunks	Element-guided inverted index with BM25 ranking and 100-token chunking
BM25 (Articles as Document) + UM	Chunk-guided retrieval of documents (chunk size of 512) using unique merging.
BM25 (Articles as Document) + RS	Chunk-guided retrieval of documents (chunk size of 512) using reciprocal rank-score fusion and BM25 relevance scoring.
BGE + DeBEIR + 512 + RS	Chunk-guided retrieval of documents (chunk size of 512) using reciprocal rank-score fusion and BGE embedding model and cosine similarity.
BM25 'element-as-document'	Element-guided inverted index with BM25 ranking and semantic chunking with chunk size of 1000 characters
BM25 with citing contexts and captions	Element-guided inverted index with BM25 ranking and 100-token chunking, with captions
BM25 on LLM-rephrased descriptions	Element-guided inverted index with BM25 with LLM-rephrased descriptions
Llama3-70b+figures merging	Using the articles retrieved with E5 embeddings, DeBEIR and a chunk size of 512. Llama3 was used to extract and order elements.
Image_embedding (BaselLine)	Text-to-image retrieval with CLIP

Table 2: Summary of submitted runs for Task 1 (evidence identification).

representations in our element-guided approach. We used a Mistral-7B-instruct-v0.2 model with a prompt asking what is presented in a specific figure given its text representation. That is, it cites chunks from the scientific article. The index would then be created using LLM-generated texts (i.e., the reformulations).

Hierarchical approach and ranking fusion experiments Finally, our submissions also include approaches that combine different ranking methods. In particular, we experiment with a *hierarchical* approach where the claim is used to query chunk-guided indices at all levels of granularity and the final result is aggregated using reciprocal rank fusion from the resulting rankings (of different granularities).

We further explore the idea of fusing signals from different ranking systems with a simple *round-robin* approach that merges runs by appending unique results from a specific top portion of each individual ranking, with the top portion growing each of the round-robin passes.

Although the hierarchical and round-robin merged runs employ a similar principle, the intuition behind them is slightly different. With the hierarchical runs, we investigate merging results at different granularities, but we still use a single retrieval approach across the merged runs. With the round-robin merge, the intention is to combine high-confidence results from a reasonably diverse set of techniques.

Submitted Runs In Table 2, we summarise the runs we submitted for evaluation, with a short description of each run. Each description conveys how the run relates to the methods presented above.

4.2 Task 2: Grounding Context Identification

This task requires systems to generate a list of text fragments, based on a specific research article, that provides information on a given scientific claim. The approaches we experiment with for this task are described below.

Retrieval-based Approach In our approach, we employ *BM25* as a retrieval model in various configurations. The documents are segmented into sentences, and the query is the provided claim. For a given article, we retrieve n sentences that are most relevant to the given claim. Different systems

Run Name (as submitted)	Description
rule_based_claude_postprocess	Retrieval with rule-based filtering with Claude LLM to generate evidence with post-processing
gpt_clean_postprocess	LLM (GPT4) zero-shot setting with post-processing
rule-based	Retrieval with rule-based filtering approach
bm25_5_llama3	Retrieval-based approach using retrieval+LLM using a combination of BM25 and Llama3 LLM
claude_zero_shot	LLM (Claude) zero-shot setting
llama3_full_article	LLM (Claude) zero-shot setting
bm25_clean_page	Retrieval-based approach with collected documents
claude_clean	LLM (Claude)zero-shot setting with collected documents
gpt_finetuned_clause	LLM (GPT3.5) fine-tuned setting at clause level
bm25_5+claude	Retrieval-based approach using a combination of BM25 and Claude LLM
debier_256	Retrieval-based approach with a chunk size of 256 using Debier as the retrieval method
gpt_sentence	LLM (GPT4) zero-shot setting at clause level instead of sentence level
bm25_5_left_neighbor	Retrieval-based approach using retrieval+heuristic combination left sentences are selected as neighbour
claude_prompt (who, how, what)	LLM (Claude) zeros-hot setting with prompt using the definition of the shared task for Task 2
llama3-8b ft 5epoch lre-6	LLM (Llama3-8B) fine-tuned setting on the training set of the shared task
sft llama3-8b silver data	LLM (Llama3-8B) fine-tuned setting on silver dataset

Table 3: Summary of submitted runs for Task 2 (Grounding Context Identification).

that leverage the retrieval model are listed below:

- **Simple retrieval:** We apply BM25 directly to the article, which has been split into sentences, to retrieve n sentences as evidence. This method serves as a straightforward way to identify evidence as the most relevant sentences (based on the BM25 scoring).

- **Retrieval + LLM:** In this approach, BM25 is used to retrieve the most promising candidate sentences from the article, narrowing down the content before it is processed by an LLM. Instead of using the entire article in the prompt for the LLM, we only provide the sentences retrieved by the BM25 method. This can improve the efficiency and focus of the LLM's processing by concentrating on the most relevant sentences.

- **Heuristic:** Here, we augment the retrieval results by concatenating adjacent (neighbour) sentences to those retrieved by BM25, thus using them as additional evidence. This method enhances comprehension and topic continuity by using neighbour sentences to provide additional context.

- **Retrieval with rule-based filtering:** Upon inspecting the training set we observe that evidence fragments often share a common writing style and, consequently, contain similar patterns. In this approach, we build a list of *common expressions*—such as 'assigned to', 'of all prior', and 'in the absence of'—using the ground truth grounding contexts. For each ground truth context, we include the longest sub-sequence of tokens (which includes at least one verb, adjective, noun, or noun phrase) shared by at least one other ground truth context. At inference, we filter BM25 results obtained with a *simple retrieval* using the list of common expressions. That is, we discard candidate sentences that do not contain any of the common expressions.

LLM In addition to the approaches utilising the retrieval method, we also investigate the use of LLMs in zero-shot, few-shot and fine-tuning scenarios.

Zero- and few-shot learning leverages the LLM's pre-trained knowledge to perform tasks without additional task-specific training (Brown et al., 2020; Radford et al., 2019). For this task, we provide the article and claim in the prompt to extract evidence in zero-shot learning and we select k in-context samples from the train set in few-shot learning. Fine-tuning involves adapting a pre-trained LLM to the task using the provided annotated dataset. We finetune two different language models: Llama3 8B (AI@Meta, 2024)[3] and GPT-3.5.

Submitted Runs Table 3 summarises the runs we submitted for evaluation, with a short description

[3] https://github.com/meta-llama/llama3

of each run. Each description conveys how the run relates to the methods presented above.

5 Experimental Setup

We use the default b and $k1$ parameter values in BM25 implementation, utilising rank_bm25 library for the element-guided approach in Task 1 and the retrieval-based approach in Task 2, and Elasticsearch for the chunk-guided approach in Task 1.

In Task 2, we use two different tools to identify sentences in the full-text articles: NLTK (Bird and Loper, 2004) and SpaCy (Honnibal and Montani, 2017), with the best results reported. We use the PoS tagger of the NLTK library for the retrieval with the rule-based filtering approach proposed for Task 2. We retrieved the original pdf files from the publishers using DOIs in the original articles. This led to a cleaner version of the document collection. It also provided us with information missing from the articles, such as the page numbers.

In Task 1, we use the following instructions (prompts) to create E5 query embeddings for element-, and chunk-guided approaches, respectively:

- Given a claim, retrieve descriptions of figures and tables that support the claim
- Given a claim, retrieve documents that contain references to figures and tables that support the claim

In Task 2, we use the following prompt for zero-shot experiments of LLMs:

- Please extract evidence clauses from the given article for the given claim CLAIM [Given Article Start] FULL TEXT [Given Article End]

For fine-tuning the OpenAI GPT model in Task 2, we use the provided API (OpenAI, 2023). The steps applied before fine-tuning are the preparation of the training data and its upload to the OpenAI servers. The format of the training data is JSONL. One sample template of the training data is given below:

```
"messages": [
{"role": "system",
 "content":
    FULL TEXT},
{"role": "user", "content":
 "What are evidences for the
  given claim:" CLAIM},
{"role": "assistant",
"content": EVIDENCE}
]
```

We use the default hyperparameters of the API for fine-tuning. After fine-tuning the GPT3.5 model, we use the following prompts for inference:

- What are evidences for the given claim: CLAIM
- What are evidence clauses for the given claim: CLAIM

For our experiments with LLaMA-3 8B[4], we fine-tune the model on the training data and silver dataset separately for Task 2. Given the relatively small size of the training dataset.

We eliminate the introductory sentences from LLM outputs (e.g., 'Here are two relevant evidence sentences from the given article:') using pattern-based matching with `colon` (:) as postprocessing in Task 2.

Metrics For both sub-tasks, we follow the evaluation procedure put in place by the shared task organisers. For Sub-task 1 a typical ranking metric of NDCG (Järvelin and Kekäläinen, 2002) at 5 and 10 is used. For the grounding sub-task, BERT score (Zhang et al., 2020) and ROUGE (Lin, 2004) variants are reported to measure the overlap between the identified context and the ground truth.

6 Experimental Results

6.1 Task 1: Evidence Identification

The test set results of our evidence identification experiments are shown in Table 4.

Our best single-model runs are element-guided E5 ('E5', nDCG@5 of .55) and element-guided E5 with LLM-reformulated texts ('E5 on LLM-rephrased descriptions', nDCG@10 of 0.60). Both runs used fixed-sized chunking with a window size of 100 tokens. While the method outperforms other single model runs, our experiments indicate that it is sensitive to prompt used for query embedding (approximately -10% on development set) and to chunking strategy (see 'E5 w. semantic chunking' run, we also observed similar trend on development set).

[4]We use the code of llama-recipes https://github.com/meta-llama/llama-recipes and models hosted on Hugginface https://huggingface.co/meta-llama/Meta-Llama-3-8B.

Run Name	nDCG@5	nDCG@10
Top-k merge	0.5542	0.6160
RS Merge w/ Rank s=2	0.5598	0.5942
top-k merge all-runs	0.5464	0.6005
E5 on LLM-rephrased descriptions	0.5464	0.6005
E5	0.5542	0.5894
Hier-Caption+E5+DeBEIR	0.5309	0.5654
e5+HierAll+DeBEIR+RS	0.5251	0.5653
e5+HierCapSent512+DeBeIR	0.5116	0.5560
E5 w. semantic chunking	0.4809	0.5304
Plain BM25 100 word chunks	0.4665	0.5195
BM25 (Articles as Document) + UM	0.4636	0.5199
BM25 (Articles as Document) + RS	0.4681	0.5129
BGE + DeBEIR + 512 + RS	0.4639	0.5145
BM25 'element-as-document'	0.4597	0.5183
BM25 with citing contexts and captions	0.4622	0.5098
BM25 on LLM-rephrased descriptions	0.4552	0.5092
Llama3-70b+figures merging	0.4625	0.4954
Image_embedding(BaselLine)	0.2954	0.3681

Table 4: Evidence identification task results based on NDCG.

Run Name	BERT Score	ROUGE-1	ROUGE-2	ROUGE-L
rule_based_claude_postprocess	0.8577	0.3773	0.1955	0.2716
gpt_clean_postprocess	0.8525	0.3663	0.1968	0.2544
rule-based	0.8651	0.3485	0.1782	0.2731
bm25_5_llama3	0.8499	0.3431	0.1950	0.2718
claude_zero_shot	0.8530	0.3686	0.1812	0.2552
llama3_full_article	0.8569	0.3420	0.1781	0.2492
bm25_clean_page	0.8486	0.3462	0.1800	0.2284
claude_clean	0.8492	0.3551	0.1622	0.2367
gpt_finetuned_clause	0.8510	0.3301	0.1865	0.2330
bm25_5+claude	0.8471	0.3443	0.1768	0.2257
debier_256	0.8531	0.3426	0.1589	0.2385
gpt_sentence	0.8477	0.3122	0.1668	0.2114
bm25_5_left_neighbor	0.8411	0.2977	0.1617	0.1920
claude_prompt (who, how, what)	0.7877	0.2941	0.0877	0.1650
sft llama3-8b silver data	0.7751	0.2093	0.0394	0.1325
llama3-8b ft 5epoch lre-6	0.7743	0.2077	0.0398	0.1296

Table 5: Grounding Context Identification task results based on BERT Score.

We have observed some improvement over single system runs with our fused runs. More specifically hierarchical runs outperform single-granularity counterparts. Also, our best overall scores are attained by the round-robin merged runs (although, admittedly, the improvements over the best single model E5 runs used in this scenario are relatively small).

All of our BM25 runs scored close to 0.46 and 0.51 for nDCG@5 and nDCG@10, respectively. This is a somewhat surprising result, as we have observed much more pronounced differences in the effectiveness of different BM25 flavours on the training set.

Ranking evidence directly using an LLM yielded scores lower than most of the BM25 baselines (slightly). Our experiment with image and text embeddings resulted in significantly lower scores.

6.2 Task 2: Grounding Context Identification

Table 5 demonstrates the performance of our methods on the test set of Task 2.

We achieve the highest BERT Score with the retrieval with the rule-based filtering approach ('rule_based', BERTScore of 0.87) among all methods. Most methods yield BERT scores ranging between 0.84 and 0.87, except for the fine-tuning LLM (Llama3-8B). Our best runs are based on retrieval-based approach which are retrieval with rule-based filtering ('rule_based', ROUGE-L of 0.27), retrieval with a combination of rule-based filtering and LLM ('rule_based_claude_postprocess', ROUGE-L of 0.27) and retrieval + LLM ('bm25_5_llama3', ROUGE-L of 0.27) in terms of ROUGE-L score. This indicates that selecting evidence from the article enhances semantic similarity and coherence across longer text sequences.

An important observation is that the retrieval-based approach results achieve comparable or better BERT scores to LLMs (e.g., claude_clean and gpt_sentence). This suggests that the extractive approach (BM25) remains superior for the task due to its simplicity, despite LLMs' remarkable performance in other NLP tasks.

Combining the retrieval method with LLMs, named Retrieval + LLM (e.g., bm25_5+claude and bm25_5_llama3) improves ROUGE scores by focusing the grounding context on relevant fragments only. However, in terms of ROUGE scores, LLM methods with zero-shot settings (gpt_clean_postprocess and claude_zero_shot), as well as the Retrieval + LLM approach (rule_based_claude_postprocess) outperform other methods.

LLMs are sensitive to provided prompts in zero-shot settings (e.g., claude_clean and claude_prompt (who, how, what)). Additionally, post-processing significantly influences ROUGE scores by removing irrelevant parts of generated evidence, as ROUGE evaluates the overlap of n-grams between generated evidence and human-annotated references.

7 Conclusions

We participated in the Context24 Shared Task for multimodal evidence and grounding context identification for scientific claims. There were two subtasks for evidence identification and grounding evidence identification. For the former, we treated it as an information retrieval task where both statistical and dense retrieval methods were investigated. We obtained promising results with the Mistral E5 dense retrieval model and with our ranking fusion experiments. For the second subtask, our best method used a filtering mechanism where frequent expressions were identified from the training data. This method yielded higher results than those we obtained using generative models.

References

Iftikhar Ahmad, Muhammad Yousaf, Suhail Yousaf, and Muhammad Ovais Ahmad. 2020. Fake news detection using machine learning ensemble methods. *Complexity*, 2020(1):8885861.

AI@Meta. 2024. Llama 3 model card.

Isabelle Augenstein, Christina Lioma, Dongsheng Wang, Lucas Chaves Lima, Casper Hansen, Christian Hansen, and Jakob Grue Simonsen. 2019. MultiFC: A real-world multi-domain dataset for evidence-based fact checking of claims. In *Proceedings of the 2019 Conference on Empirical Methods in Natural Language Processing and the 9th International Joint Conference on Natural Language Processing (EMNLP-IJCNLP)*, pages 4685–4697, Hong Kong, China. Association for Computational Linguistics.

Giorgio Barnabò, Federico Siciliano, Carlos Castillo, Stefano Leonardi, Preslav Nakov, Giovanni Da San Martino, and Fabrizio Silvestri. 2023. Deep active learning for misinformation detection using geometric deep learning. *Online Social Networks and Media*, 33:100244.

Steven Bird and Edward Loper. 2004. NLTK: The natural language toolkit. In *Proceedings of the ACL Interactive Poster and Demonstration Sessions*, pages

214–217, Barcelona, Spain. Association for Computational Linguistics.

Tom Brown, Benjamin Mann, Nick Ryder, Melanie Subbiah, Jared D Kaplan, Prafulla Dhariwal, Arvind Neelakantan, Pranav Shyam, Girish Sastry, Amanda Askell, et al. 2020. Language models are few-shot learners. *Advances in neural information processing systems*, 33:1877–1901.

Yi Fung, Christopher Thomas, Revanth Gangi Reddy, Sandeep Polisetty, Heng Ji, Shih-Fu Chang, Kathleen McKeown, Mohit Bansal, and Avirup Sil. 2021. Infosurgeon: Cross-media fine-grained information consistency checking for fake news detection. In *Proceedings of the 59th Annual Meeting of the Association for Computational Linguistics and the 11th International Joint Conference on Natural Language Processing (Volume 1: Long Papers)*, pages 1683–1698.

Matthew Honnibal and Ines Montani. 2017. spaCy 2: Natural language understanding with Bloom embeddings, convolutional neural networks and incremental parsing. *To appear*, 7(1):411–420.

Beizhe Hu, Qiang Sheng, Juan Cao, Yuhui Shi, Yang Li, Danding Wang, and Peng Qi. 2024. Bad actor, good advisor: Exploring the role of large language models in fake news detection. In *Proceedings of the AAAI Conference on Artificial Intelligence*, volume 38, pages 22105–22113.

Kalervo Järvelin and Jaana Kekäläinen. 2002. Cumulated gain-based evaluation of ir techniques. *ACM Trans. Inf. Syst.*, 20(4):422–446.

Sarthak Jindal, Raghav Sood, Richa Singh, Mayank Vatsa, and Tanmoy Chakraborty. 2020. Newsbag: A multimodal benchmark dataset for fake news detection. In *CEUR Workshop Proc*, volume 2560, pages 138–145.

Xiangci Li, Gully A Burns, and Nanyun Peng. 2021. A paragraph-level multi-task learning model for scientific fact-verification. In *SDU@ AAAI*.

Chin-Yew Lin. 2004. Rouge: A package for automatic evaluation of summaries. In *Text summarization branches out*, pages 74–81.

Nicholas Micallef, Marcelo Sandoval-Castañeda, Adi Cohen, Mustaque Ahamad, Srijan Kumar, and Nasir Memon. 2022. Cross-platform multimodal misinformation: Taxonomy, characteristics and detection for textual posts and videos. In *Proceedings of the International AAAI Conference on Web and Social Media*, volume 16, pages 651–662.

Vincent Nguyen, Sarvnaz Karimi, and Zhenchang Xing. 2023. DeBEIR: A python package for dense bi-encoder information retrieval. *Journal of Open Source Software*, 8(87):5017.

Vincent Nguyen, Maciek Rybinski, Sarvnaz Karimi, and Zhenchang Xing. 2020. Pandemic literature search: Finding information on COVID-19. In *Proceedings of the 18th Annual Workshop of the Australasian Language Technology Association*, pages 92–97.

Yixin Nie, Haonan Chen, and Mohit Bansal. 2019. Combining fact extraction and verification with neural semantic matching networks. In *Proceedings of the AAAI conference on artificial intelligence*, volume 33, pages 6859–6866.

OpenAI. 2023. Fine-tuning. `https://platform.openai.com/docs/guides/fine-tuning/fine-tuning`. OpenAI Platform.

Liang Pang, Jun Xu, Qingyao Ai, Yanyan Lan, Xueqi Cheng, and Jirong Wen. 2020. Setrank: Learning a permutation-invariant ranking model for information retrieval. In *Proceedings of the 43rd international ACM SIGIR conference on research and development in information retrieval*, pages 499–508.

Ronak Pradeep, Xueguang Ma, Rodrigo Nogueira, and Jimmy Lin. 2021a. Scientific claim verification with VerT5erini. In *Proceedings of the 12th International Workshop on Health Text Mining and Information Analysis*, pages 94–103, online. Association for Computational Linguistics.

Ronak Pradeep, Xueguang Ma, Rodrigo Nogueira, and Jimmy Lin. 2021b. Scientific Claim Verification with VerT5erini. In *Proceedings of the 12th International Workshop on Health Text Mining and Information Analysis*, pages 94–103.

Alec Radford, Jong Wook Kim, Chris Hallacy, Aditya Ramesh, Gabriel Goh, Sandhini Agarwal, Girish Sastry, Amanda Askell, Pamela Mishkin, Jack Clark, et al. 2021. Learning transferable visual models from natural language supervision. In *International conference on machine learning*, pages 8748–8763. PMLR.

Alec Radford, Jeffrey Wu, Rewon Child, David Luan, Dario Amodei, Ilya Sutskever, et al. 2019. Language models are unsupervised multitask learners. *OpenAI blog*, 1(8):9.

Kirk Roberts, Tasmeer Alam, Steven Bedrick, Dina Demner-Fushman, Kyle Lo, Ian Soboroff, Ellen Voorhees, Lucy Lu Wang, and William R. Hersh. 2021. Searching for scientific evidence in a pandemic: An overview of TREC-COVID. *Journal of Biomedical Informatics*, 121(C).

Somya Ranjan Sahoo and Brij B Gupta. 2021. Multiple features based approach for automatic fake news detection on social networks using deep learning. *Applied Soft Computing*, 100:106983.

Michael Schlichtkrull, Zhijiang Guo, and Andreas Vlachos. 2024. Averitec: A dataset for real-world claim verification with evidence from the web. *Advances in Neural Information Processing Systems*, 36.

Kai Shu, Amy Sliva, Suhang Wang, Jiliang Tang, and Huan Liu. 2017. Fake news detection on social media: A data mining perspective. *ACM SIGKDD explorations newsletter*, 19(1):22–36.

Nikhil Singh, Lucy Lu Wang, and Jonathan Bragg. 2024. Figural1y: Ai assistance for writing scientific alt text. In *Proceedings of the 29th International Conference on Intelligent User Interfaces*, pages 886–906.

Amir Soleimani, Christof Monz, and Marcel Worring. 2020. Bert for evidence retrieval and claim verification. In *Advances in Information Retrieval: 42nd European Conference on IR Research, ECIR 2020, Lisbon, Portugal, April 14–17, 2020, Proceedings, Part II 42*, pages 359–366. Springer.

James Thorne, Andreas Vlachos, Christos Christodoulopoulos, and Arpit Mittal. 2018. FEVER: a large-scale dataset for fact extraction and VERification. In *Proceedings of the 2018 Conference of the North American Chapter of the Association for Computational Linguistics: Human Language Technologies, Volume 1 (Long Papers)*, pages 809–819, New Orleans, Louisiana. Association for Computational Linguistics.

David Wadden, Shanchuan Lin, Kyle Lo, Lucy Lu Wang, Madeleine van Zuylen, Arman Cohan, and Hannaneh Hajishirzi. 2020. Fact or fiction: Verifying scientific claims. In *PEMNLP*, pages 7534–7550.

David Wadden, Kyle Lo, Bailey Kuehl, Arman Cohan, Iz Beltagy, Lucy Lu Wang, and Hannaneh Hajishirzi. 2022a. SciFact-open: Towards open-domain scientific claim verification. In *Findings of the Association for Computational Linguistics: EMNLP 2022*, pages 4719–4734, Abu Dhabi, United Arab Emirates. Association for Computational Linguistics.

David Wadden, Kyle Lo, Lucy Lu Wang, Arman Cohan, Iz Beltagy, and Hannaneh Hajishirzi. 2022b. MultiVerS: Improving scientific claim verification with weak supervision and full-document context. In *Findings of the Association for Computational Linguistics: NAACL 2022*, pages 61–76.

Dustin Wright, David Wadden, Kyle Lo, Bailey Kuehl, Arman Cohan, Isabelle Augenstein, and Lucy Lu Wang. 2022. Generating scientific claims for zero-shot scientific fact checking. In *Proceedings of the 60th Annual Meeting of the Association for Computational Linguistics (Volume 1: Long Papers)*, pages 2448–2460, Dublin, Ireland. Association for Computational Linguistics.

Tianyi Zhang, Varsha Kishore, Felix Wu, Kilian Q. Weinberger, and Yoav Artzi. 2020. Bertscore: Evaluating text generation with BERT. In *8th International Conference on Learning Representations, ICLR 2020, Addis Ababa, Ethiopia, April 26-30, 2020*. OpenReview.net.

OSX at Context24: How Well Can GPT Tackle Contextualizing Scientific Figures and Tables

Tosho Hirasawa
OMRON SINIC X Corp
tosho.hirasawa@sinicx.com

Abstract

Identifying the alignment between different parts of a scientific paper is fundamental to scholarly document processing. In the Context24 shared task, participants are given a scientific claim and asked to identify (1) key figures or tables that support the claim and (2) methodological details. While employing a supervised approach to train models on task-specific data is a prevailing strategy for both subtasks, such an approach is not feasible for low-resource domains. Therefore, this paper introduces data-free systems supported by Large Language Models. We propose systems based on GPT-4o and GPT-4-turbo for each task. The experimental results reveal the zero-shot capabilities of GPT-4* in both tasks. https://github.com/toshohirasawa/context24

1 Introduction

In scientific writing, the alignment between different sections of a paper and the consistency between textual claims and visual elements are paramount for effective communication (Gopen and Swan, 1990). A well-aligned paper presents a coherent narrative from introduction to conclusion, with each section building logically upon the last. This structural integrity is complemented by the harmonious integration of figures and tables with the text, where visual data reinforce and clarify written assertions (Franzblau and Chung, 2012). Such alignment serves multiple crucial functions: it enhances reader comprehension, strengthens the paper's argumentative force, and facilitates critical evaluation by peers. When research questions, methodologies, results, and interpretations are presented consistently across both prose and visual formats, it becomes easier for readers to grasp the study's significance and situate its findings within the broader scientific context. This holistic approach to alignment not only elevates the quality of individual papers but also contributes to the overall efficiency of knowledge dissemination in the scientific community.

Building upon the importance of alignment in scientific writing, the Context24 shared task at the 4th Workshop on Scholarly Document Processing (SDP 2024) addresses a critical challenge in scientific communication: the efficient interpretation and contextualization of scientific claims. This task aligns with the broader goal of enhancing the coherence between claims and supporting evidence in scientific papers. The two tracks of the shared task - **Evidence Identification** and **Grounding Context Identification** - aim to automate the process of linking claims with their supporting visual elements and methodological details, respectively. By facilitating the rapid identification of supporting evidence and grounding context, the Context24 task has the potential to significantly enhance the efficiency of scientific communication, enabling researchers to evaluate and build upon existing work more quickly.

Evidence Identification This track requires participants to identify key figures or tables from a given research paper that provide supporting evidence for a specific scientific claim. Participants must not only locate the relevant visual data but also ensure that it directly supports the stated claim.

Grounding Context Identification In this track, participants must identify all relevant methodological details associated with a scientific claim. These details are often scattered throughout the paper and include figures, tables, and textual descriptions that elucidate the experimental setup, measurement methods, sample characteristics, and other critical information necessary for understanding the basis of the claim.

This paper outlines our approach to the Context24 shared task. Our system was based on the GPT-4 family and exclusively utilized the trial

Proceedings of the Fourth Workshop on Scholarly Document Processing (SDP 2024), pages 324–331
August 16, 2024 ©2024 Association for Computational Linguistics

data provided by the organizers, without incorporating any supplementary datasets. Our system achieved the second-highest rank in both tracks. The findings indicate that GPT-4 models can identify grounding information in both cross-modal and unimodal ways without supervised tuning.

2 Related Work

Our zero-shot approach to multimodal scientific claim verification is motivated by two key factors in the current research landscape. First, there is a notable scarcity of large-scale annotated datasets specifically designed for multimodal scientific claim verification. As highlighted by Wadden et al. (2020), creating such datasets requires significant domain expertise and is highly resource-intensive. This lack of training data presents a substantial challenge for supervised learning approaches in this domain.

Secondly, recent advancements in large language models (LLMs) have demonstrated remarkable zero-shot and few-shot capabilities across various tasks. Brown et al. (2020) showed that GPT-3 can perform complex tasks without task-specific fine-tuning, while Wei et al. (2022) further demonstrated the effectiveness of instruction-tuning in enhancing zero-shot performance. These findings suggest that LLMs could potentially address complex tasks like scientific claim verification without extensive labeled data.

In the realm of multimodal models, several architectures have been developed to bridge the gap between vision and language. CLIP (Contrastive Language-Image Pre-training) (Radford et al., 2021b) demonstrated strong zero-shot performance on various vision tasks through natural language supervision. More recent models like LLaVA (Liu et al., 2023) have extended this approach to incorporate more general vision-language capabilities. In the scientific domain, models like ScienceQA (Lu et al., 2022) have been developed to handle scientific figures and text, showing promising results in tasks like answering questions about scientific figures and diagrams.

Our choice of CLIP for this task was motivated by its strong zero-shot performance and its ability to align visual and textual representations in a shared embedding space. This alignment is particularly crucial for our task, where we need to match textual claims with visual evidence from scientific figures and tables.

Recent work on effective instruction writing for LLMs informed the development of our prompting strategy. Kojima et al. (2022) demonstrated that carefully crafted prompts can induce step-by-step reasoning in LLMs, improving their performance on complex tasks. Similarly, Mishra et al. (2022) showed that prompts encouraging LLMs to explain their reasoning often lead to more accurate outputs. These insights guided our approach to designing prompts that encourage the model to articulate its reasoning process when evaluating the relevance of visual evidence to textual claims.

3 Evidence Identification

In the Evidence Identification task, we identified key figures and tables using a pipeline system supported by GPT-4o. Given a claim x and K candidate images (figures and tables) $Z = \{z_1, z_2, \cdots, z_K\}$, we first computed the supportiveness score s_i between the claim and the i-th image. Afterward, we sorted the candidate images based on their scores to determine the final ranking.

3.1 Pipeline

Supportiveness Score. We utilized GPT-4o to compute the supportiveness score for each claim-image pair. Specifically, given a claim x, a candidate image $z_i \in Z$, and the corresponding extracted caption t_i, we computed the supportiveness score $s_i = \text{GPT-4o}(x, z_i, t_i; P)$, where P is our prompt constructed following the OpenAI's instruction[1]. Since the extracted caption t_i is available only for a limited number of images, we asked GPT-4o to extract the text from the candidate image and use this output as an alternative to the extracted caption. The entire prompt is shown in Table 5. Note that 53 candidate images in the test data were rejected by GPT-4o because they "*may contain content that is not allowed by our safety system.*" We assigned a zero score to these images.

In addition to following the OpenAI's instructions, we also embedded task-specific knowledge into the prompt. One of our findings was that some images contain overwhelming amounts of data to support the given claim and were assigned unexpectedly high scores using a naive prompt. To mitigate this behavior, we added an evaluation instruction to penalize these images:

[1]https://platform.openai.com/docs/guides/prompt-engineering

Reduce the score by 3 if the image contains more information than necessary to support the statement.

, where the deduction value of 3 is determined based on the performance of the validation data.

The single supportiveness score was extracted from the output of GPT-4o using a regular expression:

```
^(?P<score>[0-9]{1,2})$
```

, and the match named "score" was then converted into an INT value. In our experiment, every output of GPT-4o contains a match.

We sampled the supportiveness scores five times for each claim-image pair and used the mean score as the final supportiveness score.

Ranking. Once we obtained the supportiveness scores for all candidate images, we sorted them based on their supportiveness scores, from high (supportive) to low (non-supportive).

3.2 Experiments

Experiment settings. We used the official dataset for our validation and testing. To reduce the evaluation cost, we randomly selected 10 instances from each dataset category (BIOL403, akamatsulab, dg-social-media-polarization, and megacoglab) to obtain a balanced validation dataset of 40 instances. We employed GPT-4o as our backbone, limiting the number of tokens in the GPT-4o output to 32 to reduce the computational cost. For evaluation metrics, we employed normalized documented cumulative gain (NDCG) (Järvelin and Kekäläinen, 2017) at 5 and 10.

As baselines, we examined two systems: (i) a system that outputs a list of randomly shuffled images (**Random**) and (ii) a CLIP-based system[2] that outputs the similarity of the claim-image pair as the supportiveness score (**CLIP**).

Experiment results. Table 1 shows the results for the validation and test data. Our first finding is that the CLIP-base system failed to determine the key images; its performance was even worse than random chance. Our in-depth analysis revealed that some images have the same style and differ only in minor details. Since CLIP learns to distinguish images in the same batch with larger differences than those of the candidate images, the nature of scientific images makes it more challenging for CLIP to identify the key images.

	Valid.		Test	
Model	@5	@10	@5	@10
Oracle	0.91	0.91	n/a	n/a
Random	0.29	0.33	0.22	0.29
CLIP	0.18	0.25	n/a	n/a
Ours	0.63	0.66	0.64	0.69

Table 1: NDCG scores at 5 ("@5") and 10 ("@10") on validation ("Valid.") and Test data. "Random" shows the performance of randomly shuffled candidate images; "Oracle" shows the performance of ground truth, which serves as the upper boundary of the models.

Prompt	Input	Valid.	Test
Naive	x,z	0.562	0.671
Naive	x,z,t	0.566	n/a
Instruction	x,z	0.590	0.654
Instruction	x,z,t	0.639	0.631

Table 2: NDCG@5 scores on the validation and test data for different prompts and input types.

Meanwhile, our GPT-backed system achieved more than double the performance of the random baseline. This finding indicates the GPT-4o's capability in identifying grounding information.

3.3 Discussion

Prompt ablation. Table 2 shows the performance of models with different prompt types and input sources. The Naive prompt systems use a simple prompt without instruction (see Appendix C for details). The Instruction prompt systems follow the OpenAI's instructions (as described in Section 3.1). While the instruction and additional input t improved the performance for the validation data, they reduced performance for the test data. The different tendencies in prompts and input sources may stem from the different distributions of the validation and test data. While the validation data is balanced across four datasets, the test data comprises two datasets. This indicates our proposed system performs well on two omitted datasets (BIOL403 and dg-social-media-polarization) but worse on the test datasets (akamatsulab and megacoglab). Table 3 shows the validation perfor-

[2]From the OpenCLIP (Ilharco et al., 2021; Cherti et al., 2023) project, we used the SOTA CLIP (Radford et al., 2021a) model (ViT-H-14-378-quickgelu model, pre-trained on the dfn5b dataset, with no fine-tuning.)

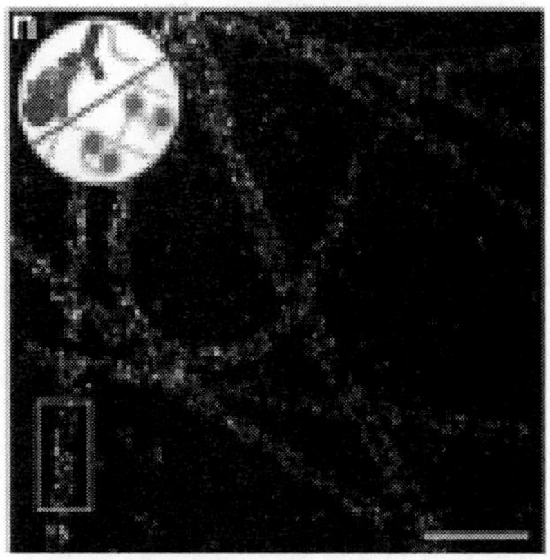

(a) Microscopic image

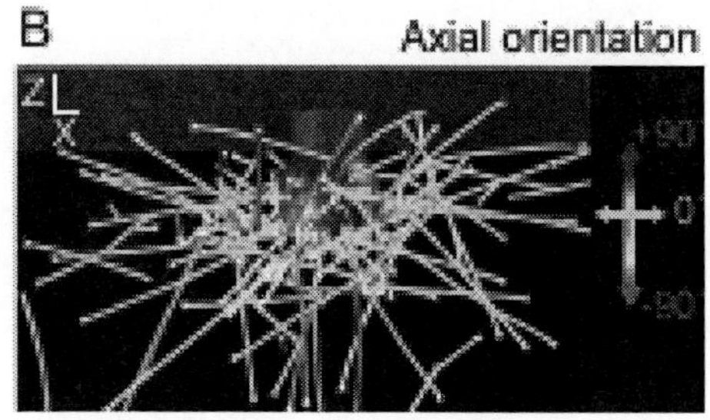

(b) 3D orientation or alignment of structures

(c) A tracing of a neural or cellular structure

Figure 1: Images that are prohibited for ChatGPT-4o.

Dataset	Naive	Instruction
BIOL403	0.452	0.635
akamatsulab	0.403	0.488
dg-social-media-polarization	0.594	0.701
megacoglab	0.798	0.732

Table 3: The validation NDCG@5 scores for four datasets under two different prompt methods.

mance for each dataset, indicating our system has been improved for three datasets (BIOL403, akamatsulab, and dg-social-media-polarization), but failed for the megacoglab dataset.

Prohibited Images. We found that 54 out of $3,714$ (1.45%) are prohibited for ChatGPT-4o with our latest prompt. Figure 1 shows some prohibited images of different types. However, as the system's rejection of these images might have been due to a misunderstanding about the type of required analysis or interpretation, we may avoid this behavior by rephrasing our prompts or declaring the clear purpose of our prompts.

Fine-tuning CLIP. Fine-tuning a general-purpose CLIP to fit a specific task requirement is a well-established way to utilize CLIP models (Ha et al., 2024). Following the latest manner, we also have tried to fine-tune a CLIP model for the Evidence Identification task. Technically, we fine-tuned a CLIP model[3] on the train data in two different ways: (a) continuous training with batch-level contrastive loss and (b) adopting the CLIP model for an NLI task. To transform the Evidence Identification task into an NLI task, we annotated findings images and other images in the same paper with a label of 0 (entailment) and 1 (neutral). The best checkpoints in both ways were selected w.r.t. the NDCG@5 score on the validation data. In our experiment, the NLI model outperformed the continuously trained model by around 0.1 NDCG@5 score but underperformed the ChatGPT-4o pipeline. This observation suggested the close images in the same article are preferable to the images from other articles.

4 Grounding Context Identification

In the Grounding Context Identification, we identified the methodological details in a zero-shot manner using GPT-4-turbo. Most part of the prompt P is cited from the official task definition[4]. We only appended a prompt to format the output.

Given a claim x and the full text of the corresponding article d, we first asked GPT-4-turbo to generate the output $r = \text{GPT-4-turbo}(x, d; P)$, where P is the prompt shown in Table 6. We then split the output by the new lines and trimmed the empty lines to obtain the final prediction.

4.1 Experiments

Experiment settings. We have not refined our prompt from the first version (as shown in Table 6). We employed GPT-4-turbo because it accepts a longer context than GPT-4o. The number of tokens in the output is limited to $1,024$. We sampled only one response for each claim. For evaluation metrics, we employed BERTScore (Zhang et al.,

[3] `openai/clip-vit-base-patch32`

[4] `https://github.com/oasisresearchlab/context24?tab=readme-ov-file#task-description-1`

Model	BS	R-1	R-2	R-L
Ours	0.86	0.32	0.17	0.26

Table 4: BERTScore ("B"), ROUGE-1 ("R-1"), ROUGE-2 ("R-2"), and ROUGE-L("R-L") scores on the test data.

2020) and ROUGE (Lin, 2004).

Experiment results. Table 4 shows the performance of our model for the test data. Compared to the first-placed model, our model achieved nearly comparable performance (-0.01 BERTScore and -0.01 ROUGE-L score). Considering the minimal effort required to tune the prompt, this observation demonstrates the capability of GPT-4-turbo to identify the alignments between a claim and the corresponding methodological details.

5 Conclusion

In this paper, we introduced GPT-4-based systems designed to identify key images and methodological details for a given claim. Our systems achieved considerable high performance in both subtasks within the Context24 Shared Task.

Acknowledgment

This work is supported by JST Moonshot R&D Program Grant Number JPMJMS2236. We used the computational resources of AI Bridging Cloud Infrastructure (ABCI) provided by National Institute of Advanced Industrial Science and Technology (AIST).

References

Tom Brown, Benjamin Mann, Nick Ryder, Melanie Subbiah, Jared D Kaplan, Prafulla Dhariwal, Arvind Neelakantan, Pranav Shyam, Girish Sastry, Amanda Askell, et al. 2020. Language models are few-shot learners. *Advances in neural information processing systems*, 33:1877–1901.

Mehdi Cherti, Romain Beaumont, Ross Wightman, Mitchell Wortsman, Gabriel Ilharco, Cade Gordon, Christoph Schuhmann, Ludwig Schmidt, and Jenia Jitsev. 2023. Reproducible scaling laws for contrastive language-image learning. In *Proceedings of the IEEE/CVF Conference on Computer Vision and Pattern Recognition*, pages 2818–2829.

Lauren E Franzblau and Kevin C Chung. 2012. Graphs, tables, and figures in scientific publications: the good, the bad, and how not to be the latter. *The Journal of hand surgery*, 37(3):591–596.

George D Gopen and Judith A Swan. 1990. The science of scientific writing. *American scientist*, 78(6):550–558.

Seokhyeon Ha, Sunbeom Jeong, and Jungwoo Lee. 2024. Domain-aware fine-tuning: Enhancing neural network adaptability. In *Thirty-Eighth AAAI Conference on Artificial Intelligence, AAAI 2024, Thirty-Sixth Conference on Innovative Applications of Artificial Intelligence, IAAI 2024, Fourteenth Symposium on Educational Advances in Artificial Intelligence, EAAI 2014, February 20-27, 2024, Vancouver, Canada*, pages 12261–12269. AAAI Press.

Gabriel Ilharco, Mitchell Wortsman, Ross Wightman, Cade Gordon, Nicholas Carlini, Rohan Taori, Achal Dave, Vaishaal Shankar, Hongseok Namkoong, John Miller, Hannaneh Hajishirzi, Ali Farhadi, and Ludwig Schmidt. 2021. Openclip. If you use this software, please cite it as below.

Kalervo Järvelin and Jaana Kekäläinen. 2017. Ir evaluation methods for retrieving highly relevant documents. *SIGIR Forum*, 51(2):243–250.

Takeshi Kojima, Shixiang Shane Gu, Machel Reid, Yutaka Matsuo, and Yusuke Iwasawa. 2022. Large language models are zero-shot reasoners. In *Advances in Neural Information Processing Systems 35: Annual Conference on Neural Information Processing Systems 2022, NeurIPS 2022, New Orleans, LA, USA, November 28 - December 9, 2022.*

Chin-Yew Lin. 2004. ROUGE: A package for automatic evaluation of summaries. In *Text Summarization Branches Out*, pages 74–81, Barcelona, Spain. Association for Computational Linguistics.

Haotian Liu, Chunyuan Li, Qingyang Wu, and Yong Jae Lee. 2023. Visual instruction tuning. In *Advances in Neural Information Processing Systems 36: Annual Conference on Neural Information Processing Systems 2023, NeurIPS 2023, New Orleans, LA, USA, December 10 - 16, 2023.*

Pan Lu, Swaroop Mishra, Tanglin Xia, Liang Qiu, Kai-Wei Chang, Song-Chun Zhu, Oyvind Tafjord, Peter Clark, and Ashwin Kalyan. 2022. Learn to explain: Multimodal reasoning via thought chains for science question answering. In *Advances in Neural Information Processing Systems 35: Annual Conference on Neural Information Processing Systems 2022, NeurIPS 2022, New Orleans, LA, USA, November 28 - December 9, 2022.*

Swaroop Mishra, Daniel Khashabi, Chitta Baral, and Hannaneh Hajishirzi. 2022. Cross-task generalization via natural language crowdsourcing instructions. In *Proceedings of the 60th Annual Meeting of the Association for Computational Linguistics (Volume 1: Long Papers), ACL 2022, Dublin, Ireland, May 22-27, 2022*, pages 3470–3487. Association for Computational Linguistics.

Alec Radford, Jong Wook Kim, Chris Hallacy, A. Ramesh, Gabriel Goh, Sandhini Agarwal, Girish

Sastry, Amanda Askell, Pamela Mishkin, Jack Clark, Gretchen Krueger, and Ilya Sutskever. 2021a. Learning transferable visual models from natural language supervision. In *ICML*.

Alec Radford, Jong Wook Kim, Chris Hallacy, Aditya Ramesh, Gabriel Goh, Sandhini Agarwal, Girish Sastry, Amanda Askell, Pamela Mishkin, Jack Clark, Gretchen Krueger, and Ilya Sutskever. 2021b. Learning transferable visual models from natural language supervision. In *Proceedings of the 38th International Conference on Machine Learning, ICML 2021, 18-24 July 2021, Virtual Event*, volume 139 of *Proceedings of Machine Learning Research*, pages 8748–8763. PMLR.

David Wadden, Shanchuan Lin, Kyle Lo, Lucy Lu Wang, Madeleine van Zuylen, Arman Cohan, and Hannaneh Hajishirzi. 2020. Fact or fiction: Verifying scientific claims. In *Proceedings of the 2020 Conference on Empirical Methods in Natural Language Processing (EMNLP)*, pages 7534–7550, Online. Association for Computational Linguistics.

Jason Wei, Maarten Bosma, Vincent Y. Zhao, Kelvin Guu, Adams Wei Yu, Brian Lester, Nan Du, Andrew M. Dai, and Quoc V. Le. 2022. Finetuned language models are zero-shot learners. In *The Tenth International Conference on Learning Representations, ICLR 2022, Virtual Event, April 25-29, 2022*. OpenReview.net.

Tianyi Zhang, Varsha Kishore, Felix Wu, Kilian Q. Weinberger, and Yoav Artzi. 2020. Bertscore: Evaluating text generation with bert. In *International Conference on Learning Representations*.

A Prompts for tasks

Table 5 and table 6 show our prompts for the Evidence Identification and the Grounding Context Identification tasks, respectively.

B Prompt for OCR

Table 7 shows our prompt for GPT-4o to extract text in candidate images that have no official extracted captions.

C Naive Prompt

Table 8 shows the `Naive` prompt for GPT-4o to determine the supportiveness score of a given claim-image pair.

Role	Prompt
System	Instruction: Evaluate the given image along with its caption and the provided sentence (delimited with XML tags) to determine how well the image supports the sentence. Follow the steps below to ensure a comprehensive analysis. Steps: 1. Description of the Image: Provide a brief description of the image, including key elements and details that stand out. 2. Sentence Analysis: Break down the sentence into its main components and key points. 3. Comparison: Compare the elements and details of the image with the key points of the sentence. 4. Evaluation: Rate the supportiveness of the image on a scale of 1 to 10, where 1 means the image does not support the sentence at all and 10 means the image perfectly supports the sentence. Reduce the score by 3 if the image contains more information than necessary to support the statement. 5. Explanation: Provide a detailed explanation for the rating, highlighting specific aspects of the image that either support or do not support the sentence. Format: Supportiveness Score: [Your rating here] Image Description: • [Your description here] Sentence Analysis: • [Your analysis here] 4. Comparison: • [Your comparison here] 5. Explanation: • [Your explanation here] Example: Supportiveness Score: 2 Image Description: • The image shows a bustling city street with tall skyscrapers, busy traffic, and pedestrians walking on the sidewalks. Sentence Analysis: • The sentence states, "The serene countryside is a perfect getaway from the city's hustle and bustle." Comparison: • The image depicts a busy city street, which is in direct contrast to the serene countryside mentioned in the sentence. Explanation: • The image does not support the sentence as it shows a bustling city street rather than a serene countryside. The elements of the image (skyscrapers, busy traffic, pedestrians) are the opposite of what is described in the sentence.
User	<image>ENCODED_IMAGE</image> <sentence>CLAIM</sentence> <caption>CAPTION</caption>

Table 5: Prompt to assess the supportativeness score of each image. "ENCODED_IMAGE", "CLAIM", and "CAPTION" are replaced by the base64-encoded image, the claim text, and the caption (or OCR text), respectively.

Role	Prompt
System	Given a scientific claim and a relevant research paper, identify all grounding context from the paper discussing methodological details of the experiment that resulted in this claim. For the purposes of this task, grounding context is restricted to quotesa from the paper. These grounding context quotes are typically dispersed throughout the full-text, often far from where the supporting evidence is presented. For maximal coverage for this task, search for text snippets that cover the following key aspects of the empirical methods of the claim: 1. What observable measures/data were collected 2. How (with what methods, analyses, etc.) from 3. Who(m) (which participants, what dataset, what population, etc.) You should output only the text snippets and must not contain any explanation.
User	<claim>CLAIM</claim> <full-text>FULLTEXT</full-text>

Table 6: Prompt to extract methodological details in a paper. "CLAIM" and "FULLTEXT" are replaced by the claim text and the full text of the paper, respectively.

Role	Prompt
System	You are an Optical Character Recognition (OCR) machine. You will extract all the characters from the image provided by the user, and you will only provide the extracted text in your response. As an OCR machine, You can only respond with the extracted text.
User	ENCODED_IMAGE

Table 7: Our prompt for GPT-4o to extract text from an image. "ENCODED_IMAGE" is replaced by the base64-encoded image.

Role	Prompt
System	You will receive a sentence and an image from a scientific paper. Determine how well the image supports the sentence and report the score on a scale from 0 to 10, where 0 means wholly irrelevant and 10 means highly supporting. Afterward, provide a detailed explanation for your relevance score, highlighting specific elements of the image and the sentence that influenced your decision.
User	<image>ENCODED_IMAGE</image> <sentence>CLAIM<sentence>

Table 8: `Naive` prompt. "ENCODED_IMAGE" and "CLAIM" are replaced by the base64-encoded image and the claim text, respectively.

Association for Computational Linguistics
209 N. Eighth Street
Stroudsburg, Pennsylvania 18360

ISBN 979-8-3313-0154-5

9 798331 301545

CURRAN ASSOCIATES INC.
proceedings.com

Association for Computational Linguistics
209 N. Eighth Street
Stroudsburg, Pennsylvania 18360

ISBN 979-8-3313-1923-6

CURRAN ASSOCIATES INC.
proceedings.com